THE ROUGH GUIDE TO

Laos

This fifth edition updated by

Edward Aves and Steve Vickers

ROUGH
GUIDES

roughguides.com

Contents

Introduction to
Laos

Often overlooked in favour of its better-known neighbours, landlocked Laos remains one of Southeast Asia's most beguiling destinations. Caught in the middle of the two Indochina wars and long isolated from the rest of the world, the country retains a slow, rustic charm, and its people – incredibly laidback and friendly, even by Asian standards – are undoubtedly one of the highlights of any visit.

Laos's lifeline is the Mekong river, which runs the length of the country, at times bisecting it and at others serving as a boundary with Thailand; the rugged Annamite Mountains historically have acted as a buffer against Vietnam, with which Laos shares its eastern border. Most people visit the country as part of a wider trip in the region, often entering from Thailand and following the Mekong further south. However, Laos alone rewards further exploration, and with a little more time it's not hard to feel like you're visiting places where few Westerners venture. From the forest-clad mountains of the north to the islands of the far south, there's enough here to keep you occupied for weeks, and still feel as though you'd barely scratched the surface.

For such a small country, Laos is surprisingly diverse in terms of its people. Colourfully dressed hill tribes populate the higher elevations, while in the lowland river valleys, coconut palms sway over the Buddhist monasteries of the ethnic Lao. The country also retains some of the French influence it absorbed during colonial days: the familiar smell of freshly baked bread and coffee mingles with exotic local aromas in morning markets, and many of the old shop houses of its larger towns now (appropriately) house French restaurants.

The effects of the wars, and of its communist government, are unmistakable – it remains completely inadvisable to strike out into the countryside without following paths for fear of UXO (unexploded ordnance) – and the country remains heavily dependent on its neighbours for all manner of products; indeed in some parts of the country, the local markets stock more Chinese and Vietnamese goods than Lao.

ABOVE BAGUETTES ON SALE IN A VIENTIANE MARKET; MOTORCYCLISTS, VANG VIENG

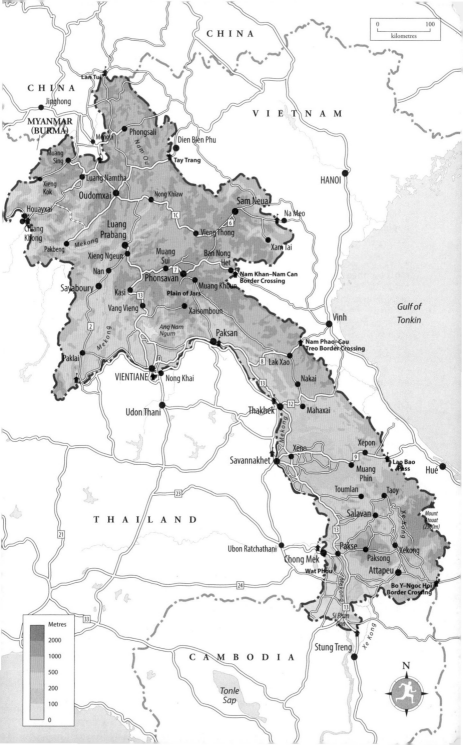

FACT FILE

• The **Lao People's Democratic Republic**, as it's officially known, is Southeast Asia's only landlocked country, and is bordered by Myanmar (Burma), Cambodia, China, Thailand and Vietnam.

• Covering more than 236,000 square kilometres, Laos is roughly the same size as the UK, yet has a **population** of just under seven million.

• Per capita, Laos is the **most bombed nation** in history. In 1964–73, the US dropped more than two million tonnes of ordnance on the country – more than the total amount that fell across Europe during World War II.

• A constitutional monarchy until 1976, Laos is now a one-party dictatorship and one of the world's last official **communist** states. Look out for Socialist Realist posters and the hammer and sickle flags that adorn buildings across the country.

• The official **language** is Lao, a tonal language closely related to Thai, although the written scripts differ. More than eighty languages are still spoken across Laos by ethnic tribes. Despite historic ties to France, English is now the most widely spoken European language.

• The country's top-selling brew, **Beerlao**, is made using local rice. Having won international awards, it's now exported to more than a dozen countries worldwide.

However, whether you're riding through the countryside on a rickety old bus crammed with sacks of rice and blaring Lao pop music, sailing down the Mekong past staggeringly beautiful scenery, or being dragged by a stranger to celebrate a birth over too much beer and *lào-láo*, it's hard not to be won over by this utterly fascinating country and its people.

Where to go

Set on a broad curve of the Mekong, **Vientiane** is Southeast Asia's most modest capital city. It lacks the frenetic buzz of Ho Chi Minh City and Bangkok, but has transformed itself since the 1990s, and is home to an increasingly cosmopolitan food scene. Robbed of its most splendid temples in battles with Siam long ago, Vientiane is better suited to long lunches and lazy walks by the Mekong than it is for breakneck tours of monuments and museums. Few tourists passing through the capital miss a chance for a half-day journey out to **Xieng Khuan**, its riverside meadow filled with mammoth religious statues, one of Laos's most bizarre sights.

From Vientiane, it makes sense to head north to **Vang Vieng**, a once-sleepy town set in a landscape of glimmering green paddies and sawtoothed karst hills. A great spot for caving, kayaking, rock climbing and long walks in the countryside, the town is also notorious for its wild tubing scene, and although things have quietened down a little in recent years, it still remains the country's party capital for young backpackers. From here the mountainous old Royal Road to Luang Prabang rollercoasters through some of Laos's most stunning scenery. The more intrepid can indulge in a muddy expedition through Laos's northwestern frontier, stopping off in the remote outpost of **Sayaboury**, home to a large portion of the country's diminishing elephant population.

The gilded temples and restored French–Indochinese shop houses of tiny, cultured **Luang Prabang** possess a spellbinding majesty that make this Laos's most enticing townscape. Though the city is filled with

MORNING MARKETS

Markets remain a mainstay of daily life in Laos, crammed full of stalls selling everything from pigs' heads, congealed blood and pungent *pa dàek* (fermented fish paste) to bamboo baskets for sticky rice and imported toiletries from Vietnam. They're also a great place for a quick meal – even in the smallest you'll be able to find someone selling *fŏe* – though you'll generally need to get there early to see the best of them.

tourists, the dusty side streets, Mekong views and quiet mornings still lend plenty of charm. Most visitors combine a stay here with a couple of day-trips, to the sacred **Pak Ou Caves**, two riverside grottoes brimming with thousands of Buddha images, and to beautiful **Kuang Si waterfall**, the perfect spot for a refreshing dip on a hot day.

A few hours north up the emerald Nam Ou river from Luang Prabang is the quiet town of **Nong Khiaw**, picturesquely surrounded by towering limestone peaks and a great base for trekking and kayaking in the region. Just a little further up the river, isolated **Muang Ngoi** is a popular travellers' spot, where it's hard to drag yourself away from the temptation of spending your days soaking up the views from a hammock. Following the river even further north is one of the greatest highlights of a trip to Laos, passing through stunning scenery on resolutely local boats to get to **Phongsali**, from which you can explore further into the isolated far north, or join an overnight trek to local hill-tribe villages.

Improved roads means that it's now a lot easier to explore the **far north**, which boasts more spectacular landscape and is home to a patchwork of upland tribal groups. The easy-going town of **Luang Namtha** is the main northern centre for treks and kayaking trips into the magnificent Nam Ha NBCA, visiting hill-tribe settlements en route. Just four hours by road from Luang Namtha is **Houayxai**, on the Thai border, from where you can join a slow boat down the Mekong for the picturesque trip south to Luang Prabang – one of Southeast Asia's great river journeys.

BUN BANG FAI

Also known as the rocket festival, this **rain-making ritual** predates Buddhism in Laos, and is a madcap combination of fireworks and firewater. In May, crude **rockets** are fashioned from stout bamboo poles stuffed with gunpowder and, after being blessed, are propped up on wooden launch platforms that resemble rickety ladders to heaven. As villagers dance and cheer, the rockets are shot skywards. The thundering noise and clouds of smoke reassuringly simulate rainy season conditions, which are in turn supposed to inspire the spirits to produce the real thing. Celebrations **in the south** can be wonderfully bawdy: men brandishing foot-long, **wooden phalluses** give the local girls something to giggle about. The rocket festival is also very popular with the ethnic Lao in northeastern Thailand, where it has evolved into more of a sporting event, with participants wagering on what heights the rockets will attain.

Lost in the misty mountains of the far northeast, **Hua Phan** province was the nerve centre of communist Laos during the Second Indochina War, and remains well removed from the Mekong Valley centres of lowland Lao life. The provincial capital, **Sam Neua**, has a resolutely Vietnamese feel (hardly surprising when you consider its proximity to the border), and though it has a rather limited tourist infrastructure, there's a certain charm about the place once you dig a little deeper. The main reason for a stay here is to visit **Vieng Xai**, where the communist Pathet Lao directed their resistance from deep within a vast cave complex, and where the last Lao king was exiled until his untimely demise. South along Route 6 from Hua Phan is **Xieng Khuang** province, the heartland of Laos's Hmong population. **Phonsavan**, a cool and dusty town, is the starting point for trips out to the mystical **Plain of Jars**.

To the **south**, the tail of Laos is squeezed between the formidable Annamite Mountains to the east and the Mekong river as it barrels towards Cambodia. **Thakhek** is a good base from which to visit the **Mahaxai Caves** and **Khammouane Limestone NBCA**, the highlight of which is **Kong Lo Cave**, a cave with a river that can be navigated by canoe. Genial **Savannakhet**, almost as culturally Vietnamese as it is Lao, makes a pleasant urban retreat, with an architectural charm second only to Luang Prabang. The cool and fertile **Bolaven Plateau**, where most of Laos's coffee is grown, is a refreshing stop during the hot season, not least to try a cup of the famous brew. To the southwest lies diminutive **Champasak**, with its red-dirt streets and princely villas. The ruins of **Wat Phou**, the greatest of the Khmer temples outside Cambodia, perch on a forested hilltop nearby.

ABOVE BUN BANG FAI, OUDOMXAI **OPPOSITE CLOCKWISE FROM TOP** BOATS ON THE MEKONG RIVER; SI PHAN DON; PAK OU CAVE

Anchoring the tail of Laos, the countless river islands of **Si Phan Don** lie scattered across the Mekong, swollen to 14km from bank to bank, all the way to the Cambodian border. One of the most significant wetlands in the country, Si Phan Don is the perfect spot to while away lazy days, and harbours scores of long-established fishing communities, as well as centuries-old lowland Lao traditions.

When to go

November to January are the most pleasant months to travel in lowland Laos, when daytime temperatures are agreeably warm, evenings are slightly chilly and the countryside is green and lush after the rains. However, at higher elevations temperatures are significantly cooler, sometimes dropping to freezing point. In **February**, temperatures begin to climb, reaching a peak in April, when the lowlands are baking hot and humid. During this time, the highlands are, for the most part, equally hot, if a bit less muggy than the lowlands, though there are places, such as Paksong on the Bolaven Plateau, that have a temperate climate year-round. Owing to slash-and-burn agriculture, much of the north, including Luang Prabang, becomes shrouded in smoke from **March** until the beginning of the monsoon, which can at times be quite uncomfortable, and of course doesn't do your photographs any favours. The rainy season (generally **May to September**) affects the condition of Laos's network of unpaved roads, some of which become impassable after the rains begin. On the other hand, rivers which may be too low to navigate during the dry season become important transport routes after the rains have caused water levels to rise. Note that the climate in some northern areas – notably Phongsali and Hua Phan (Sam Neua) – can be surprisingly temperamental, even in the hot season, so you could have one scorcher of a day, followed by a cold, wet day that's enough to convince you you're no longer in Southeast Asia.

AVERAGE DAILY MAXIMUM TEMPERATURES AND MONTHLY RAINFALL

	Jan	Feb	Mar	Apr	May	Jun	Jul	Aug	Sep	Oct	Nov	Dec
VIENTIANE												
°C	28	30	33	34	32	32	31	31	31	31	29	28
mm	5	15	38	99	267	302	267	292	302	109	15	3
LUANG PRABANG												
°C	28	32	34	36	35	34	32	32	33	32	29	27
mm	15	18	31	109	163	155	231	300	165	79	31	13

OPPOSITE FROM TOP RICE PADDY FIELD; KONG LO CAVE; TUBING IN VANG VIENG

Author picks

Our indefatigable authors have combed the length and breadth of Laos, enduring bone-jangling bus journeys and pounding sun-baked streets, to bring you the very best that the country has to offer; here are some of their personal highlights.

Bicycle rides Away from towns and cities, paved roads give way to dusty tracks and sandy riverside trails. Trundling along on two wheels is one of the best ways to explore small villages, like those found in Si Phan Don (see p.241) and Luang Namtha (see p.186).

Lao people The kindness and good humour of Lao people surprises plenty of first-time visitors. Almost everywhere foreigners go, they're greeted by warm smiles, waves, and – from kids, especially – cries of "Sabaidee!"

Caves From long, natural tunnels such as Kong Lo Cave (see p.214), which attracts kayakers, to the lofty underground hideaways of the Pathet Lao, subterranean Laos has plenty of tales to tell.

Markets Sultry and sometimes stinky, wet markets in Laos provide a colourful insight into local life, with all manner of creatures, roots and plants laid out for sale.

Exploring by river The original Lao highways are still the best, whether seen from a bamboo raft, kayak, old-fashioned slow boat or the inside of an inflated tractor inner tube (see p.88).

Local pop Maddening, deafening, and yet somehow strangely catchy: no public bus ride would be complete without the tinny blare of pop tunes from Laos and Thailand.

Courses Pick up some new skills as you explore the country: in Luang Prabang, excellent cookery schools are attached to some of the city's top restaurants (see p.129), or learn the art of traditional weaving at the wonderful Ock Pop Tok Living Crafts Centre (see p.118).

Our author recommendations don't end here. We've flagged up our favourite places – a perfectly sited hotel, an atmospheric café, a special restaurant – throughout the guide, highlighted with the ★ symbol.

18

things not to miss

It's not possible to see everything that Laos has to offer in one trip – and we don't suggest you try. What follows is a selective taste, in no particular order, of the country's highlights: stunning temples, amazing journeys and great activities. All highlights have a page reference to take you straight into the Guide, where you can find out more.

1 GIBBON EXPERIENCE
Page 196

This innovative ecotourism project near Houayxai offers the chance to zip-line through lush jungle, spending the night in treehouses high in the forest canopy – one of Laos's most exhilarating adventures.

2 PLAIN OF JARS
Page 148

Ancient funerary urns, the remnants of a lost civilization, lie scattered across the heart of the northeast.

3 WATERFALLS OF THE BOLAVEN PLATEAU
Page 250

Scale steep steps to waterfalls surrounded by lush tropical forest, then cool off with a hard-earned dip.

4 VIENG XAI
Page 158

A dusty village edged by monumental limestone karsts, which sheltered the Pathet Lao during the Second Indochina War.

5 LUANG PRABANG
Page 100

At the confluence of the Mekong and the Nam Khan, Laos's most enchanting city has atmospheric temples, fine dining and world-class hotels, such as the *Belle Rive*, pictured here.

 COLONIAL ARCHITECTURE
Page 214

Time and tropical sunlight have worked their magic on the French–Indochinese shop houses found in riverside towns such as Savannakhet.

7 **LAO FOOD**
Page 31

Fiery, herby and fragrant, Lao food is a delight to discover – and there's always excellent beer to wash it down with.

8 **TREKKING**
Page 41

Rugged mountain forests set the scene for hikers exploring the remote hill villages of the north.

 THE NAM OU
Page 169

This tropical waterway in the mountainous north passes through some of the country's most inspiring scenery.

10 **VANG VIENG**
Page 85

Best known for its parties, Vang Vieng is in a breathtakingly beautiful location – and is a superb spot for outdoor adventures.

 PHONGSALI
Page 175

Spend nights beneath the glowing Milky Way in this sleepy northern town, which serves as a gateway to the surrounding countryside.

 THAT LUANG
Page 67

The country's most important religious building is best seen at sunset when the golden stupa seems to glow in the fading light.

Itineraries

Laos isn't a huge country, but getting around it can take time – especially if you veer away from the usual tourist trail. The classic route, "Between Two Capitals", is deservedly popular with visitors wanting a quick introduction to Laos, with a good mix of cities and natural beauty, plus plenty of tourist comforts along the way. The other two itineraries suggested here require more time, but reward handsomely with sleepy temples, plunging waterfalls, hill-tribe treks and mysterious ruins.

BETWEEN TWO CAPITALS

This route is well trodden, with good road and river connections, and could easily be covered in ten days. Allow an extra week if you want to spend time exploring the countryside around Vang Vieng.

❶ **Houayxai** Once a staging post for Chinese merchants, this little border town is now best known as the launching point for slow boat rides to Luang Prabang. **See p.194**

❷ **Luang Prabang** A mountain kingdom for more than a millennium, Laos's former capital has blossomed into a world-class tourist destination, yet retains its exotic charm. **See p.100**

❸ **Vang Vieng** Set among epic karsts, the notorious backpacker capital is slowly shaking off its bad reputation and emerging as an outdoor playground for active travellers. **See p.85**

❹ **Ang Nam Ngum** Fresh fish and boat rides draw Lao families to this vast, island-speckled reservoir, created with the damming of the Nam Ngum river. **See p.84**

❺ **Vientiane** The engine room of modern Laos is a fast-growing Asian city, but traces of French rule are still seen everywhere, from wide boulevards to street-side baguette stands. **See p.58**

WATERFALLS AND RUINS

Easily covered in two or three relaxed weeks, this route takes in some of southern Laos's most picturesque spots, with plenty of hammock time built in.

❶ **Savannakhet** Start in the south's colonial gem, where sun-yellowed villas have been restored as restaurants, hotels and tour offices organizing treks into nearby jungles. **See p.214**

❷ **Pakse** This thriving Mekong city is a natural base for trips around the Bolaven Plateau, and is within easy day-tripping distance of sleepy silk-weaving villages. **See p.227**

❸ **Tad Lo** A chilled backpacker community is growing up near the base of these falls, which slosh splendidly over rounded rocks and swimming holes. **See p.252**

❹ **Tad Fan and Tad Yuang** After touring the Bolaven Plateau's coffee plantations, take a dip at Tad Yuang, a picture-perfect dual cascade. The much taller Tad Fan, surrounded by dense jungle, is just a kilometre away. **See p.250**

❺ **Champasak** Dusty orange light lends a magical feel to mornings and evenings in this town on the Mekong's west bank, once the capital of a bustling kingdom. **See p.233**

ABOVE LANE XANG AVENUE, VIENTIANE; NAM OU RIVER, MUANG NGOI

⑥ Wat Phou A Khmer ruin to rival many of the temples at Angkor, Wat Phou occupies a prime location beneath pristine forests. **See p.236**

⑦ Si Phan Don On its final push through Laos, the Mekong splits into a web of serene tropical islets, inviting island-hopping tourists to kick back with a glass or two of *lào-láo*. **See p.239**

NORTHERN ESCAPE

Travelling through the mountainous north can be tough, with cooler temperatures and cramped bus rides that make even the locals feel queasy. Allow yourself around two weeks for this route.

① Vieng Xai Monuments are all that remain of plans to make this chilly communist backwater the new Lao capital after the Pathet Lao successfully hid out in its caves. **See p.158**

② Sam Neua It's not big on sights, but Sam Neua is a good base for textile enthusiasts. The region's designs are some of the most sophisticated in all of Laos. **See p.153**

③ Phonsavan and the Plain of Jars Cluster munitions dropped during the Second Indochina War still litter the Plain of Jars, famed for its mysterious stone urns. **See p.148**

④ Nong Khiaw Surrounded by karst mountains, Nong Khiaw makes an ideal base for trekking, cycling and kayaking trips. **See p.167**

⑤ The Nam Ou Take a scenic boat ride along this lazy river, parts of which are still edged by impenetrable jungle. **See p.169**

⑥ Phongsali Let the crisp air of this small, high-altitude town soothe the soul before setting out on a trek to local hill-tribe villages. **See p.175**

⑦ Nam Ha NBCA Biking and hiking trips through this protected area are best organized in Luang Namtha, a relaxed centre that's home to the north's best-value accommodation. **See p.187**

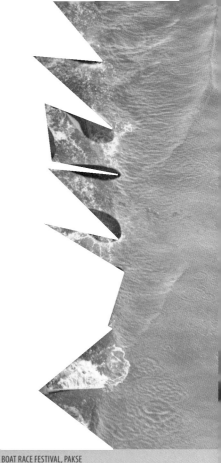

BOAT RACE FESTIVAL, PAKSE

Basics

Getting there

As Laos is often part of a wider trip to the region, many people choose to travel there overland, with the crossings from Thailand near Vientiane and at Houayxai the most popular options. There are currently no direct flights to Laos from outside Asia – most visitors fly via Bangkok, from where it takes just over an hour to reach Vientiane, and just under two hours to Luang Prabang. Direct flights to Laos are also possible from Chiang Mai (Thailand), Ho Chi Minh City and Hanoi (Vietnam), Siem Reap and Phnom Penh (Cambodia), Guangzhou and Kunming (China), Seoul (Korea), Singapore and Kuala Lumpur (Malaysia). Because of the lack of direct flights from outside Asia, it can be quite expensive to fly to Laos, though this is more than compensated for by the low cost of living and travelling once in the country.

The **high season** for flights to Southeast Asia is from the beginning of July through to the end of August and also includes most of December and early January, during which period fares can be significantly higher than at other times of the year. If Laos is only one stop on a longer journey, you might want to consider buying a **Round-the-World (RTW) ticket**, which can be tailored to the destinations you want to visit. Also worth considering if you live in Australia, New Zealand or the west coast of North America are **Circle Pacific** tickets, which feature Bangkok as a standard option.

Package tours to Laos, some of which take in the country as part of a wider Indochina trawl, are inevitably more expensive and less spontaneous than if you travel independently, but are worth investigating if you have limited time or a specialist interest. Booking through a tour company in Laos (see p.29) will undoubtedly save you money compared to booking in your home country.

Flights from the UK and Ireland

Most flights from the UK and Ireland to Laos will involve a change of plane at Bangkok; an alternative route is via Vietnam, though this requires a change of plane in France or Germany first. In total, flying to Laos from the UK will take at least fifteen hours, though this varies greatly according to connection times – flying on Thai Airways (⊕thaiair.com) to Vientiane is usually the quickest option.

Flying from Ireland will involve changing planes at least twice – once in London or another European hub, and again at Bangkok or Ho Chi Minh City – with a journey time of at least eighteen and a half hours.

Because of the lack of direct flights, prices are generally high throughout the year. Expect to pay at least £650 from London and €800 from Dublin, though prices often rise over £1000/€1500 respectively. With flights to Bangkok alone significantly cheaper (from £550/€600), it's worth considering travelling overland by train between the Thai capital and Vientiane (see p.71).

Flights from the US and Canada

Flying to Laos from North America usually involves one stop, in Bangkok, if you're travelling from the west coast, and two stops, often Hong Kong and Bangkok, from the east coast. Expect journey lengths of at least nineteen and twenty-three hours, respectively.

Fares from the west coast start at around $1200, while you should expect to pay upwards of $1500 from the east coast. From Canada, prices start at around Can$1500 for Vancouver departures, Can$1700 from Toronto.

Flights from Australia, New Zealand and South Africa

Flights from Perth to Vientiane are via Bangkok or Singapore, while those from elsewhere in Australia may go via Vietnam or Kuala Lumpur (the latter requiring an additional change at Bangkok); average journey time is around thirteen hours from Perth and sixteen hours from Sydney, depending on connections. Flights from Perth start at around

A BETTER KIND OF TRAVEL

At Rough Guides we are passionately committed to travel. We believe it helps us understand the world we live in and the people we share it with – and of course tourism is vital to many developing economies. But the scale of modern tourism has also damaged some places irreparably, and climate change is accelerated by most forms of transport, especially flying. All Rough Guides' flights are carbon-offset, and every year we donate money to a variety of environmental charities.

Aus$800, Aus$900 from Sydney; a cheaper alternative could be to fly with the budget airline Air Asia (W airasia.com) to Kuala Lumpur, from where you can connect to Vientiane. From New Zealand, flying to Laos involves at least two stops, usually in Australia, Hong Kong, Vietnam or Bangkok; the journey takes around nineteen hours and fares start at around NZ$2200.

Expect a journey upwards of eighteen hours if you're flying from South Africa, with at least two stops en route. Prices start at around R9500.

Getting there from neighbouring countries

Landlocked Laos is easily accessed from most of its neighbouring countries, either overland or by flying. Note that visa on arrival is not available at all overland entry points (see box, p.24), and check locally for the most up-to-date information.

From Thailand

Lao Airlines (W laoairlines.com) operates flights from Bangkok to Vientiane, Luang Prabang, Pakse and Savannakhet and from Chiang Mai to Luang Prabang. In addition, Bangkok Airways (W bangkokair .com) offers flights to Luang Prabang and Vientiane. Both Thai Airways and newcomer Lao Central Airlines (W flylaocentral.com) run direct flights from Bangkok to Vientiane (the latter also connects Bangkok with Luang Prabang). All of these flights take between one hour and one hour forty minutes.

At the time of writing, there are six main routes across the Thai border into Laos: Chiang Khong–Houayxai (see p.197); Nong Khai–Vientiane (see p.70); Nakhon Phanom–Thakhek (see p.210); Mukdahan–Savannakhet (see p.218); Chong Mek–Pakse (see p.232); and Beung Kan (see p.207). Visas on arrival are available to foreign tourists at all but the last crossing, but check locally before travelling as the situation can change. It's possible to get visas in advance from the Laos Embassy in Bangkok (see p.24). A quick and convenient way of crossing into Laos is to use direct international buses, such as those running from Chiang Rai to Houayxai and Loei to Luang Prabang.

From Vietnam

Vietnam Airlines (W vietnamairlines.com) flies from Hanoi to Vientiane and Luang Prabang (both 1hr), and from Ho Chi Minh City (Saigon) to Vientiane (3hr); Lao Airlines also connects Hanoi with Vientiane and Luang Prabang, and has additional routes from Da Nang to Savannakhet and Ho Chi Minh City to Pakse.

It's also possible to travel overland into Laos at six main border points: Tay Trang–Sop Houn (see p.174); Nam Xoi–Na Meo (see p.155); Cau Treo–Nam Phao (see p.208); Lao Bao–Dansavanh (see p.221); and Ngoc Hoi–Bo Y (see p.257). Lao visas on arrival are available at all of these crossings.

From Cambodia

Lao Airlines operates direct **flights** from **Siem Reap** to Luang Prabang (1hr 30min) and Pakse (1hr). Vietnam Airlines has a direct route from Phnom Penh to Vientiane (1hr 20min). The only way to cross overland into Laos is at the Dom Kralor–Veun Kham crossing (see p.249), where it's possible to get a visa on arrival.

From China

It's possible to travel by road or air into Laos from China's southwestern **Yunnan** province. Lao Airlines operates **flights** from Kunming to Vientiane (1hr 20min). There are also Lao Airlines flights from Guangzhou to Vientiane (2hr) and from Jinghong to Luang Prabang (1hr). The quickest and most straightforward border crossing is at Mo Han–Boten, with direct services running from Jinghong to Luang Namtha and Oudomxai (see p.186 & p.181), though a second international border point (Meng Kang–Lan Tui) opened in late 2013 at the northern tip of remote Phongsali province (see p.178), currently a two-day bus journey from Phongsali town.

AGENTS AND OPERATORS

Abercrombie & Kent Australia ☎ 1300 851800, New Zealand ☎ 0800 441638, UK ☎ 0845 485 1537, US ☎ 888 611 4711; W abercrombiekent.com. Luxury tour operator with a couple of Indochina offerings.

Adventure World Australia ☎ 1300 295049, W adventureworld .com.au; New Zealand ☎ 0800 238368, W adventureworld.co.nz. A good range of tours, ranging from three to fifteen days.

Adventures Abroad US ☎ 1800 665 3998, W adventures-abroad .com. Small-group tour specialists with several regional tours that include Laos on their itinerary, plus one trip out of Bangkok that concentrates exclusively on Laos.

Bamboo Travel UK ☎ 020 7720 9285, W bambootravel.co.uk. Highly recommended company piecing together private, tailor-made trips around Laos and its Southeast Asian neighbours.

Buffalo Tours Vietnam ☎ 020 8545 2830, W buffalotours.com. Vietnam-based tour operator with a range of options for Laos, including luxury hotels and culinary tours, plus offices in the UK and Australia.

Exodus UK ☎ 0845 287 7655, W exodus.co.uk. Various Indochina packages from this specialist in cultural and adventure tourism, including a cycling trip in Laos and northern Vietnam.

Exotissimo Vientiane ☎ 021 454 6403, Luang Prabang ☎ 071 252879; W exotissimo.com. A well-established tour operator with branches throughout Indochina, offering anything from honeymoons and family trips to hotel bookings and treks.

Explore Worldwide UK ☎ 0845 291 4541, ⓦ exploreworldwide .com. A number of Laos options, combining the country with Vietnam and Cambodia.

Inside Vietnam UK ☎ 01172 443370, ⓦ insidevietnamtours.com. As the name suggests, this UK tour operator specializes in Vietnam, but also has tours covering Laos and Cambodia.

Journeys International US ☎ 1800 255 8735, ⓦ journeys-intl .com. Specialists in small-group nature and culture explorations, offering a couple of week-long trips in Laos or an extended trip in the region.

North South Travel UK ☎ 01245 608291, ⓦ northsouthtravel .co.uk. A friendly, competitive travel agency, offering discounted fares worldwide. Profits are used to support projects in the developing world, especially the promotion of sustainable tourism.

Selective Asia UK ☎ 01273 670001, ⓦ selectiveasia.com. Helpful and knowledgeable staff and an excellent range of Laos trips, all of which can be tailor-made to suit a range of budgets.

STA Travel Australia ☎ 134 782, New Zealand ☎ 0800 474400, South Africa ☎ 0861 781781, UK ☎ 0333 321 0099, US ☎ 1800 781 4040; ⓦ statravel.co.uk. Worldwide specialists in independent travel; also student IDs, travel insurance, car rental, rail passes, and more. Good discounts for students and under-26s.

Stray ☎ 071 260584, ⓦ straytravel.asia. Cool, Kiwi-run company running flexible (and quite costly) bus tours through Southeast Asia.

Symbiosis UK ☎ 0845 123 2844, ⓦ symbiosis-travel.com. An environmentally aware operator that aims to reduce the negative impact of tourism. Tours include "Laos Ancient and Wild", which encompasses trekking, hill-tribe visits, kayaking and a stay in Luang Prabang.

Trailfinders Ireland ☎ 01 677 7888, UK ☎ 020 7368 1200; ⓦ trailfinders.com. One of the best-informed and most efficient agents for independent travellers.

Travel CUTS Canada ☎ 1800 592 2887, ⓦ travelcuts.com. Canadian youth and student travel firm.

Travel Indochina UK ☎ 01865 268940, ⓦ travelindochina.co.uk. An excellent range of tours that take in Laos – either on its own or in conjunction with Thailand, Vietnam or Cambodia.

USIT Ireland ☎ 016 021906, ⓦ usit.ie. Ireland's main student and youth travel specialists.

Wendy Wu Tours South Africa ☎ 011 394 1660, ⓦ wendywutours .co.za. Short tours just focusing on Laos or a 28-day "Grand tour of Indochina".

World Expeditions Australia ☎ 073216 0823, Canada ☎ 613 241 2700, New Zealand ☎ 09 368 4161, UK ☎ 020 8545 9030, US ☎ 1613 241 2700; ⓦ worldexpeditions.com. An interesting array of group trips, including a cycling expedition along the banks of the Mekong.

Entry requirements

Unless you hold a passport from Japan, Russia, Switzerland or one of the ASEAN member states, you'll need a visa to enter Laos. The good news is that you probably won't need to arrange it in advance; thirty-day visas are now available on arrival at most international borders. Note that all visitors must hold a passport that is valid for at least six months from the time of entry into Laos.

Visas on arrival take just a few minutes to process, cost around $35 (prices vary according to nationality), and are available to passengers flying into Luang Prabang Airport, Pakse Airport and Wattay Airport in Vientiane. Travellers to Laos from Thailand can pick up visas on arrival at any of the border crossings open to foreign tourists (except the border at Paksan), as can those entering from Vietnam (at Nam Khan, Na Meo, Bo Y, Tay Trang, Cau Treo and Lao Bao) and Cambodia (Dom Kralor). From China it's possible to pick up a visa at the Mo Han crossing, but not currently at Meng Kang. Only US dollars are accepted as payment and a passport-sized photo is required. If you forget the photo, border officials will usually turn a blind eye for an extra $1. Note that passport holders from a number of countries, including Pakistan, Turkey and Zambia, are not eligible for visas on arrival and must obtain one in advance – for a comprehensive list see ⓦ laos-guide-999.com. To cross into Laos from all other points, you'll need to arrange a visa before arriving at the border. Like visas on arrival, **pre-arranged tourist visas** allow for a stay of up to thirty days. Prices are generally a little higher though – especially if you pay a tour operator to help you out – so avoid buying one unless your border crossing demands it. If it does, visas can be obtained directly from Lao embassies and consulates. At the Lao embassy in Bangkok (see p.24), thirty-day visas cost 1400 baht for nationals of the UK, US and Ireland, 1200 baht for those from Australia, New Zealand and South Africa, and 1680 baht for Canadians. You'll need to take two passport-sized photos with you but, provided you apply before noon, processing can usually be done on the same day. **Advance visas** can also be obtained at the Lao consulate in Khon Kaen, in the northeast of Thailand, or through one of the many travel agents concentrated on or around Khao San Road. However, prices (and processing fees) can vary wildly. Wherever you choose to get your visa, bear in mind that Lao visa regulations and prices are subject to frequent change.

The Lao embassy in Hanoi, and consulates in Ho Chi Minh City and Da Nang, can also issue visas, but it's important to note that the prices charged vary from place to place. Lao visas issued in Vietnam are also slightly more expensive than those issued in Thailand.

LAO VISAS

Visa on arrival Thirty days. Available at Wattay International Airport (Vientiane), Pakse Airport, Luang Prabang International Airport, and all Thai–Lao border crossings open to foreigners except the border at Paksan. Also available at border crossings with Vietnam (Nam Khan, Na Meo, Bo Y, Tay Trang, Cau Treo and Lao Bao), Cambodia (Dom Kralor) and China (Mo Han).

Tourist visa (T) Thirty days. Required for all border crossings where visa on arrival is not available. Can be arranged in advance at Lao embassies and consulates, or through tour operators in Thailand, Vietnam and Cambodia.

Visitor visa (B3) One-month stay. Extendable for two further months. Lao guarantor required, and intended for those visiting relatives who work in Laos.

Transit visa (TR) Allows for a maximum of five days' stay and intended to help travellers who wish to make a short stopover in Laos. The visa is only valid for one province, and takes three working days to process. To qualify you must have proof of an onward journey within five days.

Business visa (B2) One-month stay, but can be extended until the end of your business term. Requires a Lao sponsor.

Multiple entry visa Only issued by the Ministry of Foreign Affairs, Consular Department.

Extending visas

Visa **extensions** are fairly easy to obtain, but you'll need to plan ahead if you want to avoid overstaying your visa (there's currently a $10 penalty for each extra day you spend in the country). The cheapest option is to visit the immigration office off Lane Xang Avenue in Vientiane before your visa expires. Here, visa extensions are issued at the cost of $2 per day, to a maximum of sixty days. Alternatively, you could leave the country and enter again (which might work out cheaper if you're planning to extend by twenty days or more) or pay a local travel agent to arrange the visa extension for you. Generally this is more expensive, with most vendors charging around $4 per extra day required. Thirty-day business visas that have the potential to be extended can also be arranged in advance at the Lao embassies and consulates listed below.

LAO EMBASSIES AND CONSULATES

Australia (and New Zealand) 1 Dalman Crescent, O'Malley, Canberra ☎ 02 6286 4595, ⓦ laosembassy.net.

Cambodia 15–17 Mao Tse Tung Blvd, Phnom Penh ☎ 23 997 931.

China 11 E 4th St, Sanlitun, Chaoyang, Beijing ☎ 010 532 1224, Camelia Hotel, Suite 3226, 154 E Dong Feng Rd, Kunming ☎ 087 1317 6624.

Hong Kong Room 1402 Arion Commercial Centre, 2–12 Queen's Rd West, Hong Kong ☎ 2544 1186.

India A 104/7, Parrmanand Estate, New Delhi ☎ 011 632 3048.

Indonesia 33 Jalan Kintamani Raya, Kuningan Timur, Jakarta ☎ 021 522 9602.

Japan 3-3-22, Nishi-Azabu, Minato-ku ☎ 03 5411 2291.

Malaysia 25 Jalan Damai, Kuala Lumpur ☎ 032 483 895.

Myanmar (Burma), Diplomatic Headquarters, Taw Win Road, Yangon (Rangoon) ☎ 012 2482.

New Zealand Contact embassy in Canberra.

Philippines 34 Lapu-Lapu St, Magallanes, Makati, Manila ☎ 028 525 759.

Singapore 479-B Gold Hill Centre, Thomson Rd ☎ 6250 6044.

Thailand 502/13 Ramkhamhaeng Soi 39, Bangkapi, Bangkok ☎ 025 393642; 19/1–3 Phothisan Rd, Khon Kaen ☎ 043 223698, ⓦ laoembassybkk.com.

US 2222 S St NW, Washington DC ☎ 202 332 6416, ⓦ laoembassy.com.

Vietnam 22 Rue Tran Bing Trong, Hanoi ☎ 049 424576; 93 Pasteur St, District 1, Ho Chi Minh City ☎ 088 297667.

Getting around

Getting around on Laos's transport system is an adventure in itself, what with its barely seaworthy boats, aged jalopies with hard seats and hot, crowded buses. Don't be fooled by maps and distance charts – seemingly short rides can take hours, as tired vehicles slow to a crawl in their uphill battle against muddy, mountainous roads. Take heart though in knowing that many visitors have their best encounters with the people of Laos amid the adversity of a bad bus ride.

Laos's road system has improved significantly over the past few years. Roads have been upgraded, new highways have been built, and getting around is easier than ever, though often still challenging. Keep in mind that a newly graded and paved road this year may get no maintenance, and after just two or even one rainy season the road will revert to being nothing but a potholed track. Some roads are only built to last a season, being washed away each year by the monsoon.

The country's main thoroughfare is **Route 13**, which stretches from Luang Prabang to the Cambodian border, passing through Vientiane, Savannakhet and Pakse. Route 13 sees a steady flow of bus traffic, and it's usually possible to flag down a vehicle during daylight hours provided it's not already full. Off main roads like Route 13, you'll encounter a wide-range of road conditions – from freshly paved carriageways to bone-rattling, potholed tracks. With the ever-improving road conditions, **buses** have largely supplanted **river travel**, the traditional means of getting around.

You only need to travel for a week or two in Laos before you realize that **timetables** are irrelevant: planes, buses and boats leave on a whim and estimated times of arrival are pointless. Wherever you go in Laos, the driver does not seem to be in any hurry to arrive.

For journeys mentioned throughout this guide we've tried to give an idea of how long they will take in hours and minutes. Given the poor condition of many roads and buses, as well as the many unscheduled stops en route, all travel times should be taken as best estimates.

Inter-town transport

Visitors hoping to see rural Laos can expect hours of arduous, bone-crunching travel on the country's motley fleet of lumbering jitter-boxes. Buses link only larger towns, and on many routes can be few and far between, a fact which makes a number of attractions, such as ruins and waterfalls, difficult to reach. Even when there is transport, you may find that the limited bus timetable will allow you to get to a particular site, but not make a same-day return trip – something of a problem given the dearth of accommodation in far-flung spots. In the rainy season, some unpaved roads dissolve into rivers of mud, slowing buses to a crawl or swallowing them whole. Even vehicles in reasonably good condition make painfully slow progress, as drivers combat **mountainous roads** and make frequent (and at times long) stops to pick up passengers, load goods and even haggle for bargains at roadside stalls.

Buses

Ordinary buses provide cheap transport between major towns and link provincial hubs with their surrounding districts. Cramped, overloaded and designed for the smaller Lao frame, these buses are profound tests of endurance and patience. Seats often have either torn cushions or are nothing more than a hard plank. Luggage – ranging from incontinent roosters to sloshing buckets of fish and the inevitable fifty-kilo sacks of rice – is piled in every conceivable space, filling up the aisle and soaring skywards from the roof. **Breakdowns** are commonplace and often require a lengthy roadside wait as the driver repairs the bus on a lonely stretch of road. Typical fares are in the order of 110,000K for Vientiane to Luang Prabang or Pakse, though fares could rise rapidly if fuel prices increase.

Operating out of Vientiane, a fleet of blue, **government-owned buses** caters mostly to the capital's outlying districts, although it does provide a service to towns as far north as Vang Vieng and as far south as Pakse. While newer than many vehicles in Laos, these Japanese- and Korean-built buses are not air-conditioned and have cramped seats, a situation that worsens as rural passengers pile in. Buses plying **remote routes** tend to be in worse shape: aged jalopies cast off from Thailand or left behind by the Russians, which reach new lows in terms of discomfort and are even more prone to breakdowns. These vehicles range in style from buses in the classic sense of the word to souped-up tourist vans. Converted Russian flat-bed trucks, once the mainstay of travel in Laos, still operate in remote areas.

In most instances, **tickets** should be bought from the town's bus station – it's best to arrive with plenty of time in order to buy your ticket and grab a seat, especially in towns that are busy transport hubs, such as Oudomxai. In larger towns with an established tourist infrastructure, you'll often be able to buy your tickets from a travel agent; this will usually be a little more expensive, but will include transport to the bus station. In more rural areas, you'll pay for your ticket once on board.

At the other end of the spectrum you'll find air-conditioned **VIP buses**, running popular routes such as Vientiane to Luang Prabang. These services usually leave from their own private "stations", and reservations, which can be made through guest-houses and travellers' cafés, are recommended.

Additionally, you'll find a number of **van** and **minibus** services in the more touristy towns, connecting to other popular tourist destinations, such as Vang Vieng and Si Phan Don. Prices for these services are higher than for the local bus alternative and the journey time will usually be a fair bit quicker, though you may find yourself just as crammed in as on a regular bus, and of course you miss out on the opportunity to meet local people. The situation changes rapidly at this end of the market, so check with travel agents for the latest information on routes and bookings. It's also worth shopping around if booking minibus tickets – regardless of how much you pay for your ticket, and where you buy it, you're likely to end up on the same minibus.

Reliable timetables only exist in regional hubs like Vientiane, Luang Prabang and Savannakhet; elsewhere it's best to go to the bus station the night before you plan to travel to find out the schedule for the next day. Most departures are usually around 8 or 9am, and very few buses leave after midday. Many drivers will sit in the bus station long after their stated departure time, revving their engines in an attempt to lure enough passengers to make the trip worthwhile.

Sawngthaews

In rural areas, away from the Mekong Valley, the bus network is often replaced by **sawngthaews** – converted pick-up trucks – into which drivers stuff as many passengers as they possibly can. Passengers are crammed onto two facing benches in the back ("sawngthaew" means "two rows"); latecomers are left to dangle off the back, with their feet on a running board, an experience that, on a bumpy road, is akin to inland windsurfing.

Sawngthaews also ply routes between larger towns and their satellite villages, a service for which they charge roughly the same amount as buses. They usually depart from the regular bus station, but will only leave when a driver feels he has enough passengers to make the trip worth his while. Some drivers try to sweat extra kip out of passengers by delaying departure. Your fellow passengers may agree to this, but most often they grudgingly wait. In some situations, you can save yourself a lot of trouble and waiting by getting a few fellow travellers together and flat-out **hiring the driver** to take you where you want to go, the fares being so ridiculously low as to make this quite affordable. To catch a sawngthaew in between stops, simply flag it down from the side of the road and tell the driver where you're headed so he knows when to let you off. The fare is usually paid when you get off. If the driver is working without a fare collector, he will tend to stop on the outskirts of his final destination to collect fares.

City transport

With even the capital too small to support a proper local bus system, transport within Lao towns and cities is left to squadrons of motorized **samlaw** (literally, "three wheels") vehicles, more commonly known as jumbos and tuk-tuks. Painted in primary

reds, blues and yellows, the two types of samlaw look alike and both function as shared taxis, with facing benches in the rear to accommodate four or five passengers. **Jumbos** are the original Lao vehicle, a home-made three-wheeler consisting of a two-wheeled carriage soldered to the front half of a motorcycle, a process best summed up by the name for the vehicle used in the southern town of Savannakhet – Skylab (pronounced "sakai-laeb"), after the doomed space station that fell to earth, piece by piece, in the late 1980s. The much more common **Tuk-tuks**, offspring of the three-wheeled taxis known for striking terror in Bangkok pedestrians, are really just bigger, sturdier jumbos, the unlikely product of some Thai factory, which take their name from their incessantly sputtering engines. Lao tend to refer to these vehicles interchangeably.

Although most northern towns are more than manageable on foot, the Mekong towns tend to sprawl, so you'll find tuk-tuks particularly useful for getting from a bus station into the centre of town. To flag down a tuk-tuk, wave your hand, palm face down and parallel to the ground. Tell the driver where you're going, bargain the price and pay at the end.

Tuk-tuks are also on hand for inner-city journeys. Payment is usually per person, according to the distance travelled and your bargaining skills. Rates vary from town to town and are prone to fluctuate in step with rising petrol prices, but figure on paying around 5000–10,000K per kilometre. In some towns, tuk-tuks run set routes to the surrounding villages and leave from a stand, usually near the market, once full. Chartering tuk-tuks is also a good way to get to sites within 10 to 15km of a city – often it suits both parties if you agree to pay the driver for the round trip, plus a little extra for the time they spend waiting.

Boats

With the country possessing roughly 4600km of navigable **waterways**, including stretches of the Mekong, Nam Ou, Nam Ngum, Xe Kong and seven other arteries, it's no surprise to learn that rivers are the ancient highways of mountainous Laos. Road improvements in recent years, however, have led to the decline of river travel between many towns, with buses and sawngthaews replacing the armada of boats that once plied regular routes.

The main **Mekong route** that remains links Houayxai to Luang Prabang. Boats very rarely ply the stretches of river between Luang Prabang, Pakse and Si Phan Don. Aside from the larger,

ADDRESSES AND STREET NAMES

Lao **addresses** can be terribly confusing, firstly because property is usually numbered twice – when numbered at all – to show which lot it stands in, and then to signify where it is on that lot. To add to the confusion, some cities have several conflicting address systems – Vientiane, for example, has three, although no one seems to use any of them. To avoid confusion, numbers are often omitted from addresses given in the Guide, and locations are described using landmarks instead.

Only a few cities in Laos actually have **street names** – and that's just the start of the problem. Signs are few and far between and many roads have several entirely different names, sometimes changing name from block to block. If you ask for directions, locals most likely won't know the name of a street with the exception of the three or four largest avenues in Vientiane. Use street names to find a hotel on a map in the Guide, but when asking directions or telling a tuk-tuk driver where to go you'll have better luck mentioning a landmark, monastery or prominent hotel. Fortunately, Lao cities, even Vientiane, are relatively small, making it more of a challenge to get lost than it is to figure out where you're going.

so-called "slow boats" on the Mekong routes, smaller passenger boats still cruise up the wide Nam Ou river (Luang Prabang–Hat Sa), and a few others, provided water levels are high enough, though note that boat transport on sections of the Nam Ou is likely to be interrupted by dam construction. Currently, there are no boat services from Luang Prabang to Nong Khiaw, though they may have resumed by the time you read this. Boats on the Nam Tha need to be chartered.

Slow boats

The dwindling number of diesel-chugging cargo boats that lumber up and down the **Mekong routes** are known as "**slow boats**" (*heua sa*). Riding aboard one of these boats, hammered together from ill-fitting pieces of wood and powered by a jury-rigged engine that needed to be coaxed along by an on-board mechanic, was one of Asia's last great travel adventures. Today, a small number of the boats have been adapted to cater almost solely to foreign tourists (with seating for up to eighty people), and now ply the part of the Mekong most popular with Western visitors, namely Houayxai to Luang Prabang.

On smaller waterways, travel is by long, narrow boats powered by a small outboard engine. Confusingly, these are also known as "slow boats", although, unlike the big Mekong cargo boats, they only hold eight people and never attempt major Mekong routes. They never have a fixed schedule and only leave if and when there are enough passengers – as with tuk-tuks, these boats can usually be hired outright, but you'll need a small group to keep costs down.

Owing to the casual nature of river travel in Laos, the best way to deal with uncertain departures is to simply **show up early** in the morning and head

down to the landing and ask around. Be prepared for contradictory answers to questions regarding price, departure and arrival time, and even destination. Given variations in currents and water levels and the possibility of breakdowns and lengthy stops to load passengers and cargo, no one really knows how long a trip will take. On occasion, boats don't make their final destination during the daytime. If you're counting on finding a guesthouse and a fruit shake at the end of the journey, such unannounced stopovers can take you out of your comfort zone, as passengers are occasionally forced to sleep in the nearest village or aboard the boat. It's also a good idea to bring extra water and food just in case.

The **northern Mekong and Nam Ou** services (Houayxai–Pakbeng–Luang Prabang, and Luang Prabang–Nong Khiaw–Muang Ngoi–Muang Khoua–Hat Sa) are somewhat better managed, with **tickets** sold from a wooden booth or office near the landing (buy tickets on the day of departure). Fares are generally posted, but foreigners tend to pay significantly more than locals. Always arrive early in the morning to get a seat. **Southern Mekong** services (Pakse–Champasak–Don Khong) have now all but stopped thanks to the improved state of Route 13, and most trips south now combine a bus journey along this road with a quick ferry ride across the water.

Travelling by river in Laos can be dangerous and reports of boats **sinking** are not uncommon. The Mekong has some particularly tricky stretches, with narrow channels threading through rapids and past churning whirlpools. The river can be especially rough late in the rainy season, when the Mekong swells and uprooted trees and other debris are swept into the river.

Speedboats

Speedboats (*heua wai*) are a faster but more expensive alternative to slow boats. Connecting towns along the Mekong from Vientiane to Houayxai, these five-metre-long terrors are usually powered by a 1200cc Toyota car engine and can accommodate up to eight passengers. There are no speedboats on the Nam Ou these days.

Donning a crash helmet and being catapulted up the Mekong river at 50km an hour may not sound like most people's idea of relaxed holiday travel, but if you're up for it, speedboats can shave hours or days off a river journey and give you a thrilling spin at the same time. It's by no means safe, of course, although captains swear by their navigational skills. The boats skim the surface of churning whirlpools and slalom through rapids sharp enough to turn the wooden hull into toothpicks.

Speedboats have their own landings in Luang Prabang and Houayxai and depart when full, which means you should arrive early – they can leave before their stipulated departure time – and, conversely, should be prepared for a wait. Seating is incredibly **cramped**, so you may want to consider paying for the price of two seats. **Crash helmets** are handed out before journeys – to spare your hearing from the overpowering screech of the engine. To avoid the worst of the noise, try sitting near the front. For safety's sake, insist on being given a life jacket to wear before paying.

Tickets generally cost a lot more than what you might pay to take a slow boat: the journey from Luang Prabang to Pakbeng, for example, is around $24. Speedboats can also be **chartered** for around $50 per hour – Luang Prabang to Houayxai, for example, costs $100.

Cross-river ferries

Clunky metal car **ferries** and **pirogues** – dug-out wooden skiffs propelled by poles, paddles or tiny engines – are both useful means of fording rivers in the absence of a bridge. Both leave when they have a sufficient number of passengers and usually charge around 5000K, unless you're taking a vehicle across, in which case you can expect to pay 10,000–20,000K. If you don't want to wait, you can always hire a pirogue. In the outback, fishermen can usually be persuaded to ferry you across to the opposite bank for a small sum.

Planes

Government-owned **Lao Airlines** (Ⓦ laoairlines .com) is the country's main domestic carrier. Its safety record, which had been steadily improving, has taken a knock again after an accident in October 2013, when a Lao Airlines turboprop travelling from Vientiane hit bad weather, plunging into the Mekong as it approached Pakse, killing all 49 people on board.

Since the accident, the airline has continued to operate as normal, and it still has the most comprehensive domestic schedule by far, with flights from Vientiane to Oudomxai, Luang Namtha, Luang Prabang, Pakse and Xieng Khuang (for the Plain of Jars).

Laos also has two private airlines. **Lao Central Airlines** (Ⓦ flylaocentral.com) has a small fleet flying between Vientiane, Luang Prabang and Bangkok. **Lao Skyway** (Ⓦ laoskyway.com) flies from Vientiane to Luang Prabang, Luang Namtha, Oudomxai, Sam Neua, Sayaboury and Boun Neua (for Phongsali).

If you're travelling on any of these routes during the peak season it's wise to **book ahead**. Sample one-way **fares** are Vientiane to Luang Prabang $60; Vientiane to Pakse $104; Vientiane to Oudomxai $230; Vientiane to Luang Namtha $235; Vientiane to Xieng Khuang $190.

Trains

At the time of writing, the only train line operating in Laos is the 3.5km section of track connecting Vientiane with Nong Khai, Thailand. In the race to develop Laos and extract its wealth of natural resources, controversial country-spanning tracks are being planned, however, and by the end of the decade both Vientiane and Savannakhet will be connected to China and Vietnam by high-speed lines.

Vehicle and bike rental

Renting a **private vehicle** is expensive, but is sometimes the only way you'll be able to get to certain spots. Self-drive is an option, and cars can be rented from a couple of agencies in Vientiane only. However, it's usually easier and cheaper to hire a **car and driver**. Tour agencies will rent out air-conditioned vans and 4WD pick-up trucks as well as provide drivers. Prices are inflated by the rates paid by UN organizations, and can be as high as $80–100 per day, sometimes more if you're hiring a car to head upcountry from Vientiane. When settling on a price, it's important to clarify who is responsible for what: check who pays for the driver's food and lodging, fuel and repairs, and be sure to ask what happens in case of a major breakdown or accident. If you're looking for a safe driver and English-speaking guide to help you get the most out of a trip upcountry, consider contacting Bangkok-based Backyard Travel (𝕎 backyardtravel.com), which can put together a bespoke itinerary that suits your preferred route.

Motorbikes

One of the best ways to explore the countryside is to rent a **motorbike**. This is easiest in tourist-friendly places like Vientiane, Vang Vieng, Luang Prabang, Thakhek and Pakse, but even then you're often limited to smaller bikes, usually 100cc step-throughs such as the Honda Dream. Rental prices for the day are generally $6–10, depending on the age and condition of the bike. More powerful 125cc **dirt bikes** suitable for cross-country driving are available in larger cities for around $20 per day.

A licence is not needed, but you'll be asked to leave your passport as a deposit and may be required to return the bike by dark. If possible, avoid leaving your passport (attempts to extort money for "damage" are not unheard of) and arrange to leave a cash deposit instead – $30 or so should do the job. Insurance is not available, so it's a good idea to make sure your travel insurance covers you for any potential accidents.

Before zooming off, be sure to **check the bike** thoroughly for any scratches and damaged parts and take it for a test run to make sure the vehicle is running properly. As far as **equipment** goes, a helmet offers essential protection, although few rental places will have one to offer you; bear in mind it's illegal (never mind dangerous) to ride without a helmet. **Sunglasses** are essential in order to fend off the glare of the tropical sun and keep dust and bugs out of your eyes. Proper shoes, long trousers and a long-sleeved shirt are all worthwhile additions to your biking outfit and will provide a thin layer of protection if you take a spill.

Bicycles

Bicycles are available in most major tourist centres; guesthouses, souvenir shops and a few tourist-oriented restaurants may keep a small stable of Thai- or Chinese-made bikes to rent out for around $2–3 per day. In some centres, such as Luang Prabang, Luang Namtha and Nong Khiaw, it's also possible to hire **mountain bikes** for around $6 a day.

Organized tours

Although less spontaneous and considerably more expensive than independent travel, **organized tours** are worth looking into if you have limited time or prefer to have someone smooth over the many logistical difficulties of travelling in Laos. Although the government encourages travellers to visit Laos through an authorized tour company, the tours aren't bogged down in political rhetoric and guides tend to be easy-going and informative.

About a dozen **tour companies** have sprung up in Vientiane, all offering similar tours in roughly the same price range, although it never hurts to shop around and bargain. A typical multi-day package might include a private cruise down the Mekong river on a slow boat operated by the tour company, with guided day-tours around Luang Prabang and other towns. While some tours include accommodation, meals and entry fees, others don't, so check what you're getting before paying.

Organized **adventure tours** are rapidly gaining popularity in Laos. These can be single- or multi-day programmes and usually involve hill-tribe trekking, cycling or river kayaking, or combinations of two of them or even all three. Rafting tours are also available, and organized rock climbing is just starting to take off. The main centres for adventure tours are Vientiane, Vang Vieng, Luang Prabang and Luang Namtha.

All Laos's tour companies are authorized by the Lao National Tourism Administration, which ensures that you won't be dealing with a fly-by-night organization.

Guides are generally flexible about adjusting the itinerary, but if you want more **freedom**, an alternative is to set up your own custom-made tour by gathering a group of people and renting your own vehicle plus driver.

LOCAL TOUR OPERATORS

Diethelm Travel Laos Nam Phou Place, PO Box 2657, Vientiane ☎ 021 215920, 𝕎 diethelmtravel.com.

Exotissimo 15 Kaysone Rd, Vientiane ☎ 021 454640, 𝕎 exotissimo.com.

Green Discovery 54 Setthathilat Rd, Vientiane ☎ 021 223022, 𝕎 greendiscoverylaos.com. Branches in Luang Prabang, Luang Namtha, Nong Khiaw, Thakhek, Pakse and Vang Vieng.

Lao National Tourism Administration 𝕎 ecotourismlaos.com.

Savannakhet Eco Guide Unit Latsaphanit Rd, Savannakhet ☎ 041 214203, 𝕎 savannakhet-trekking.com.

Tiger Trail Sisavangvong Rd, Luang Prabang ☎ 071 252655, 𝕎 laos-adventures.com. Also a branch in Nong Khiaw.

Accommodation

The influx of foreign visitors has meant a rapid increase in hotels and improved standards in tourist centres, although out in the boondocks change comes more slowly and comfort can be harder to

come by. Expect to find higher standards of accommodation, as well as the greatest variety, in larger towns. Provincial towns, with the exception of popular stopovers on backpacker routes, tend to lag far behind, with small towns on well-travelled highways offering at best one or two rather rustic guesthouses.

Outside Luang Prabang, Pakse, Vang Vieng and the capital, finding a place to stay is a far simpler process than in most Southeast Asian countries – often because there are only one or two places in town and they're just a short walk from one another. Few towns have touts or taxi drivers trying to influence your decision.

Once you've found a spot, ask to see a number of rooms before reaching a decision, as standards and room types can vary widely within the same establishment. En-suite showers and flush toilets are found in all but the most basic of accommodation.

Establishments that do not quote their prices in dollars or baht keep a close eye on the exchange rates and change their prices accordingly, keeping the room rate at roughly the same dollar value. Many establishments will allow you to pay in Lao kip, US dollars or Thai baht, regardless of which currency their rates are quoted in; exchange rates are generally fairly close to the official rate. Count on being able to use credit cards only at higher-end establishments in cities.

Prices for the most basic double rooms start at around 50,000K in the provinces and 60,000–70,000K in Vientiane and Luang Prabang. Dorm beds (only usually found in the main tourist areas) can be had for as little as 30,000K per night. At these prices rooms can be pretty shabby, although there are a few diamonds in the rough.

For 100,000–200,000K you can buy yourself considerably more comfort, whether it's the luxuries of a standard hotel or the cosiness and hospitality of a smart guesthouse with a garden, tucked away in a quiet side street. If you're willing and able to spend around $25, you can actually get something quite luxurious, with wi-fi and a flat-screen TV.

Further up the scale, a whole host of expensive hotels has appeared on the scene, and with many of them struggling to fill rooms, managers can be amenable to discounts, especially in low season. Before settling on a price at mid-range and high-end hotels, check whether service charge and tax are included in the quoted price.

Most places are open to **negotiation**, especially in the low season, so it's a good idea to try and bargain; your case will be helped if you are staying for several days.

Throughout the Guide, we've listed prices for the **cheapest double room in high season**, unless otherwise stated. Not all accommodation places have **phones**, which is why some listings in this Guide don't have numbers alongside. Online booking services include ⓦagoda.com, ⓦlaos-hotels.com, ⓦlaos-hotel-link.com and ⓦteam workz.asia.

Budget accommodation

The distinction between a **guesthouse** and a **budget hotel** is rather blurry in Laos. Either can denote anything ranging from a bamboo-and-thatch hut to a multi-storey concrete monstrosity. There's very little that's standard from place to place – even rooms within one establishment can vary widely – although in tourist centres the cheapest bet is generally a fan room with shared washing facilities. As you tack on extra dollars, you'll gain the luxury of a private bathroom with a hot-water shower and an air conditioner. In small towns in the most remote areas you'll find that the facilities are often rustic at best – squat toilets and a large jar of water with a plastic scoop with which to shower, though this is rapidly changing. The further off the beaten track you go the greater the chances are that you'll be pumping your own water from a well or bathing in a stream.

Mid-range accommodation

Mid-range hotels have been opening up in medium-sized towns all over Laos in the last few years, greatly improving the accommodation situation. Most of these hotels are compact, of up to five storeys, and offer spacious, air-conditioned rooms with tiled floors and en-suite bathrooms for between 100,000 and 200,000K. The mattresses are usually hard – but at least the sheets and quilts are consistently clean. The bathroom fittings in such hotels are usually brand new but a few don't have water heaters and often sinks and toilets aren't properly plumbed in. Because the standard of construction is poor and there is no concept of maintaining buildings, such hotels tend to age quickly.

Top-end hotels

Once you've crossed the $25 threshold, you enter a whole new level of comfort. In the former French

Food and drink

Fiery and fragrant, with a touch of sour, Lao food owes its distinctive taste to fermented fish sauce, lemongrass, coriander leaves, chillies and lime juice. Eaten with the hands along with the staple, sticky rice, much of Lao cuisine is roasted over an open fire and served with fresh herbs and vegetables. Pork, chicken, duck and water buffalo all end up in the kitchen, but freshwater fish is the main source of protein in the Lao diet. Many in rural Laos, especially in the more remote mountainous regions, prefer animals of a wilder sort – mouse deer, wild pigs, rats, birds or whatever else can be caught. Though you may not encounter them on menus, you're likely to see them being sold by the side of the road when travelling in these parts.

Closely related to Thai cuisine, Lao food is, in fact, more widely consumed than you might think: in addition to the more than two million ethnic Lao in Laos, Lao cuisine is the daily sustenance for roughly a third of the Thai population, while more than a few Lao dishes (see p.33) are commonplace on the menus of Thai restaurants in the West. Although Lao cuisine isn't strongly influenced by that of its other neighbours, Chinese and Vietnamese immigrants have made their mark on the culinary landscape by opening restaurants and noodle stalls throughout the country, while the French introduced bread, pâté and pastries.

Vientiane and **Luang Prabang** are the country's culinary centres, boasting excellent Lao food and international cuisine. Towns with a well-developed tourist infrastructure usually have a number of restaurants serving a mix of Lao, Thai, Chinese and Western dishes, usually of varying standards, but once you're off the well-beaten tourist trail it can be hard to find much variety beyond fried rice and noodle soup.

towns on the Mekong this level of expense translates into an atmospheric room in a restored colonial villa or accommodation in a recently built establishment where rooms boast some of the trappings of a high-end hotel, such as cable television, fridge, air conditioning and a hot-water shower.

Colonial-era hotels often have a limited number of rooms, so **book ahead** if you want to take advantage of them – well in advance if you plan to visit during the peak months (Dec & Jan). Many of these places are firmly ensconced on the tour-group circuit, so push for a discount if you're travelling independently.

Thanks to foreign investors, a raft of **top-end hotels** have opened their doors in Vientiane and Luang Prabang, charging upwards of $100 a night. The best hotels in the capital and Luang Prabang have international-class facilities, including business centres and gyms. At the moment, there's a glut of high-end hotel accommodation in the capital, so don't hesitate to ask for discounts, especially for longer-term stays.

Staying in villages

Should you find yourself stuck in a small town for the night, a victim of the tired machinery of Laos's infrastructure or the yawning distances between villages, villagers are usually kind enough to find space for you in the absence of a local guesthouse. Don't expect much in the way of luxuries: you'll most likely find yourself bathing at the local well or in the river and going to the bathroom under the stars. Many small towns don't have so much as a noodle shop, so you'll also need to prepare yourself for some very authentic cooking. Before leaving, you should offer to remunerate your host with a sum of cash equivalent to what you would have paid in a budget guesthouse.

If there's a local **police station**, you should make yourself known to them, otherwise ask for permission to stay from the **village headman**; the government doesn't encourage foreigners to spend the night at a villager's house.

Where to eat

Food is generally very inexpensive in Laos, with the cheapest options those sold by hawkers – usually fruit, small dishes like papaya salad, and grilled skewered meat – and the most expensive being the high-end tourist restaurants (usually French or European) in Luang Prabang and Vientiane.

Though hygiene standards have improved over recent years, basic food preparation knowledge in many places still falls behind other countries in the region. However, though a little caution is a good idea, especially when you first arrive in the country in order to allow your stomach time to adjust to the change of cuisine, it's best just to exercise common sense. Generally, noodle stalls and restaurants that do a brisk business are a safe bet, though you may find that this denies you the opportunity to seek out more interesting, less touristy food.

Markets, street stalls and noodle shops

Morning markets (*talat são*), found in most towns throughout Laos, remain open all day despite their name and provide a focal point for noodle shops, coffee vendors and fruit stands. In Luang Prabang, Vientiane and Luang Namtha, vendors hawking pre-made dishes gather towards late afternoon in **evening markets** known as *talat láeng*. Takeaways include grilled chicken (*pîng kai*), spicy papaya salad (*tam màk hung*) and in some instances a variety of dishes, displayed in trays and ranging from minced pork salad *(larp mu)* to stir-fried vegetables (*khùa phák*).

Most market vendors offer only takeaway food, with the exception of noodle stalls, where there is always a small table or bench on which to sit, season and eat your noodle soups. Outside the markets, **noodle shops** (*hân khài fõe*) feature a makeshift kitchen surrounded by a handful of tables and stools, inhabiting a permanent patch of pavement or even an open-air shop house. Most stalls specialize in one general food type, or, in some cases, only one dish; for example a stall with a mortar and pestle, unripe papayas and plastic bags full of pork rinds will only offer spicy papaya salad and variants on that theme. Similarly, a noodle shop will generally only prepare noodles with or without broth – they won't have meat or fish dishes that are usually eaten with rice.

Restaurants

Proper **restaurants** (*hân ahân*) aren't far ahead of noodle shops in terms of comfort; most are open-sided establishments tucked beneath a corrugated tin roof. Ethnic **Vietnamese** and **Chinese** dominate the restaurant scene in some parts of Laos; indeed it can be downright difficult to find a Lao restaurant in some northern towns. Most towns that have even the most basic of tourist infrastructure have at least one restaurant with an English-language menu – even if the translation can lead to some amusement. Away from the larger tourist centres, dishes usually encompass variations on fried rice and noodle dishes, often with a few Lao, Chinese or Thai options intended to be eaten with sticky or steamed rice.

Tourist restaurants in larger centres usually offer a hotchpotch of cuisine – often encompassing standard Lao dishes like *larp* and *mók pa* alongside sandwiches, pastas and steaks. The most expensive restaurants in Vientiane and Luang Prabang generally serve French cuisine, often in very sophisticated, un-Lao surroundings, but at very reasonable prices – a meal for two, including wine, is unlikely to stretch past $40.

When it comes to **paying**, the normal sign language will be readily understood in most restaurants, or simply say "*khãw sék dae*" ("the bill, please"). You'll generally only be able to use **credit cards** at upscale establishments in Vientiane and Luang Prabang. **Tipping** is only expected in top-end restaurants – ten percent should suffice.

What to eat

So that a variety of tastes can be enjoyed during the course of a meal, Lao **meals** are eaten communally, with each dish being served at once, rather than in courses. The dishes – typically a fish or meat dish and soup, with a plate of fresh vegetables such as string beans, lettuce, basil and mint served on the side – are placed in the centre of the table, and each person helps him- or herself to only a little at a time. When ordering a meal, if there are two of you it's common to order two or three dishes, plus your own individual servings of rice, while three diners would order three or four different dishes.

The staple of Lao meals is **rice**, with **noodles** a common choice for breakfast or as a snack. Most meals are enjoyed with **sticky rice** (*khào niaw*), which is served in a lidded wicker basket (*típ khào*) and eaten with the hands. Although it can be tricky at first, it's fairly easy to pick up the proper technique if you watch the Lao around you. Grab a small chunk of rice from the basket, press it into a firm wad with

---

VEGETARIAN FOOD

Although very few people in Laos are vegetarian, it's usually fairly easy to persuade cooks to put together a vegetable-only rice or vegetable dish. In many places that may be your only option unless you eat fish. If you don't eat fish, keep in mind that most Lao cooking calls for fish sauce so when ordering a veggie-only dish, you may want to add "*baw sai nâm pa*" ("without fish sauce").

your fingers and then dip the rice ball into one of the dishes. Replace the lid of the *típ khào* when you have finished eating or you will be offered more rice.

Plain steamed **white rice** (*khào jâo*) is eaten with a fork and spoon – the spoon and not the fork is used to deliver the food to your mouth. If you're eating a meal with steamed white rice, it's polite to only put a small helping of each dish onto your rice at a time. Chopsticks (*mâi thu*) are reserved for **noodles**, the main exception being Chinese-style rice served in bowls.

If you are **dining with a Lao family** as a guest, wait until you are invited to eat by your host before taking your first mouthful. While dipping a wad of sticky rice into the main dish, try not to let grains of rice fall into it, and dip with your right hand only. Resist the temptation to continue eating after the others at the table have finished. Custom dictates that a little food should be left on your plate at the end of the meal.

Flavours

In addition to chillies, coriander, lemongrass and lime juice, common ingredients in Lao food include ginger, coconut milk, galangal, shallots and tamarind. Another vital addition to a number of Lao dishes is *khào khùa*, raw rice roasted in a wok until thoroughly browned and then pounded into powder; it's used to add both a nutty flavour and an agreeably gritty texture to food.

The definitive accent, however, comes from the fermented fish mixtures that are used to salt Lao food. An ingredient in nearly every recipe, *nâm pa*, or **fish sauce**, is made by steeping large quantities of fish in salt in earthen containers for several months and then straining the resulting liquid, which is golden brown. Good fish sauce, it has been said, should attain the warm, salty smell of the air along a beach on a sunny day. Most Lao use *nâm pa* imported from Thailand.

While *nâm pa* is found in cooking across Southeast Asia, a related concoction, *pa dàek*, is specific to Laos and northeastern Thailand. Unlike the bottled and imported *nâm pa*, thicker *pa dàek* retains a home-made feel, much thicker than fish sauce, with chunks of fermented fish as well as rice

husks, and possessing a scent that the uninitiated usually find foul. However, as *pa dàek* is added to cooked food, it's unlikely that you'll really notice it in your food, and its saltiness is one of the pleasurable qualities of the cuisine.

Use of **monosodium glutamate** (MSG) is also common. The additive, which resembles salt in appearance, sometimes appears on tables in noodle shops alongside various other seasonings – it's generally coarser and shinier than salt.

Standard dishes

If Laos were to nominate a national dish, a strong contender would be *larp*, a "**salad**" of minced meat or fish mixed with garlic, chillies, shallots, galangal, ground sticky rice and fish sauce. Traditionally, *larp* is eaten raw (*díp*), though you're more likely to encounter it *súk* (cooked), and is often served with lettuce, which is good for cooling off your mouth after swallowing a chilli. The notion of a "meat salad" is a common concept in Lao food, although in Luang Prabang you'll find Lao salads closer to the Western salad, with many falling into the broad category of *yam*, or "mixture", such as *yam sìn ngúa*, a spicy beef salad.

Another quintessentially Lao dish is *tam màk hung*, a spicy **papaya salad** made with shredded green papaya, garlic, chillies, lime juice, *pa dàek* and, sometimes, dried shrimp and crab juice. One of the most common street-vendor foods, *tam màk hung*, is known as *tam sòm* in Vientiane; stalls producing this treat are identifiable by the vendor pounding away with a mortar and pestle. Each vendor also has their own particular recipe, but it's also completely acceptable to pick out which ingredients – and how many chillies – you'd like when you order. One of several variants on *tam màk hung* is *tam kûay tani*, which replaces shredded papaya with green banana and eggplant.

Usually not far away from any *tam màk hung* vendor, you'll find someone selling *pîng kai*, basted **grilled chicken**. Fish, *pîng pa*, is another grilled favourite, with whole fish skewered, stuffed with herbs and lemongrass, and thrown on the barbecue.

Soup is a common component of Lao meals and is served along with the other main courses during a meal. Fish soups, *kaeng pa* (or *tôm yám paw* when lemongrass and mushrooms are included), frequently appear on menus, as does *kaeng jèut*, a clear, mild soup with vegetables and pork, which can also be ordered with bean curd (*kaeng jèut tâo hû*).

A speciality of southern Laos and Luang Prabang, well worth ordering if you can find it, is *mók pa* or fish steamed in banana leaves. Other variations, including

mók kheuang nai kai (chicken giblets grilled in banana leaves) and *mók pa fa lai* (with freshwater stingray), are also worth sampling, though they appear less frequently on restaurant menus.

Restaurants catering to travellers can whip up a variety of **stir-fried dishes**, which tend to be a mix of Thai, Lao and Chinese food, and are usually eaten with steamed rice. **Fried rice** is a reliable standby throughout the country, as are Chinese and Thai dishes such as pork with basil over rice (*mū phát bai holapha*), chicken with ginger (*khùa khing kai*) and mixed vegetables (*khùa phák*).

Very popular with both locals and tourists are DIY **sin dad** ("Lao barbecue") restaurants, where you grill slithers of meat or fish on a Korean-style table-top wood or charcoal stove, which is covered over with a thin metal plate; vegetables and eggs are boiled in a broth poured into the channel around the rim of the plate. It's a fun and sociable way to eat in a group.

Noodles

When the Lao aren't filling up on glutinous rice, they're busy eating *fõe*, the ubiquitous **noodle soup** that takes its name from the Vietnamese soup *pho*. Although primarily eaten in the morning for breakfast, *fõe* can be enjoyed at any time of day, and in more remote towns you may find that it's your only option.

The basic bowl of *fõe* consists of a light broth to which is added thin rice noodles and slices of meat (usually beef, water buffalo or grilled chicken). It's served with a plate of fresh raw leaves and herbs, usually including lettuce, mint and coriander. Flavouring the broth is pretty much up to you: containers of chilli, sugar, vinegar and fish sauce (and sometimes lime wedges and MSG) are on the tables of every noodle shop, allowing you to find the perfect balance of spicy, sweet, sour and salty. Also on offer at many noodle shops is *mi*, a yellow wheat noodle served in broth with slices of meat and a few vegetables. It's also common to eat *fõe* and *mi* softened in broth but served without it (*hàeng*), and at times fried (*khùa*).

Many other types of noodle soup are dished up at street stalls. *Khào biak sèn* is another soup popular in the morning, consisting of soft, round rice noodles, slices of chicken and fresh ginger and served in a chicken broth, though it's hard to find outside bigger towns. More widely available, and a favourite at family gatherings during festivals, is *khào pûn*, a dish of round, white, translucent flour noodles, onto which is scooped one of any number of sweet, spicy coconut-milk based sauces. These noodles also find their way into several Vietnamese dishes, such as barbecued pork meatballs (*nâm néuang*) and spring rolls (*yáw*), in which they are served cold with several condiments and a sauce. There's also a Lao incarnation of *khào soi*, the spicy noodle curry eaten throughout northern Thailand and the Shan States of Myanmar (Burma); the version common in Laos (in Luang Prabang and certain northwestern towns) consists of rice noodles served in almost clear broth and topped with a spicy meat curry.

Fruits and desserts

The best way to round off a meal or fill your stomach on a long bus ride is with **fresh fruit** (*màk mâi*), as the country offers a wide variety, from the more commonly known bananas, papayas, mangoes, pineapples, watermelons and green apples imported from China to more exotic options: crisp green guavas; burgundy lychees, with tart, sweet white fruit hidden in a coat of thin leather; wild-haired, red rambutans, milder and cheaper than lychees; dark purple mangosteen, tough-skinned treasures with a velvety smooth inside divided into succulent sweet segments; airy, bell-shaped green rose apples; pomelos, gigantic citruses whose thick rinds yield a grapefruit without the tartness; fuzzy, brown sapodillas, oval in shape and almost honey-sweet; large, spiky durian, notoriously stinky yet divinely creamy; oblong jackfruit, with sweet, yellow flesh possessing the texture of soft leather; and rare Xieng Khuang avocados, three times the size of those available in the West, with a subtle perfumed flavour. Restaurants occasionally serve fruit to end a meal, and, throughout the country, handcart-pushing hawkers patrol the streets with ready-peeled segments.

Desserts don't really figure on many restaurant menus, although some tourist restaurants usually have a few featuring **coconut milk** or cream, notably banana in coconut milk (*nâm wăn màk kûay*). Markets often have a food stall specializing in inexpensive coconut-milk desserts, generally called *nâm wăn*. Look for a stall displaying a dozen bowls, containing everything from water chestnuts to corn to fluorescent green and pink jellies, from which one or two items are selected and then added to a sweet mixture of crushed ice, slabs of young coconut meat and coconut milk. Also popular are light Chinese **doughnuts**, fried in a skillet full of oil and known as *khào nõm khu* or *pá thawng ko*, and another fried delight, crispy bananas (*kûay khaek*).

Sticky rice, of course, also turns up in a few desserts. As **mangoes** begin to ripen in March, look for *khào niaw màk muang*, sliced mango splashed

with coconut cream served over sticky rice; those who don't mind the smell of durian can try the durian variant on this dessert. *Khào lām*, another treat, this one popular during the cool season, is cooked in sections of bamboo, which is gradually peeled back to reveal a tube of sticky rice and beans joined in coconut cream. Another thing to look out for at street stalls is *kanom krok* – delicious, soft little pancakes made with rice flour and coconut.

Soft drinks and juices

Brand-name **soft drinks**, such as 7-Up, Coca-Cola and Fanta, are widely available. Most vendors pour the drink into a small plastic pouch packet (which is then tied with a string or rubber band and inserted with a straw) for taking away.

A particularly refreshing alternative, available in most towns with tourist restaurants, are fruit shakes (*màk mài pan*), made from your choice of fruit, blended with ice, liquid sugar and condensed milk. Even more readily available are freshly squeezed **fruit juices**, such as lemon (*nâm màk nao*), plus coconut water (*nâm màk phao*) enjoyed directly from the fruit after it has been dehusked and cut open. Also popular is the exceptionally sweet sugar-cane juice, *nâm oi*.

Hot drinks

Laos's best **coffee** is grown on the Bolaven Plateau, outside Paksong in southern Laos, where it was introduced by the French in the early twentieth century. Most of the coffee produced is robusta, although some arabica is grown as well. Quality is generally very high, and the coffee has a rich, full-bodied flavour. Some establishments that are accustomed to foreigners may serve instant coffee (*kafeh net*, after the Lao word for Nescafé, the most common brand); if you want locally grown coffee ask for *kafeh Láo* or *kafeh thông*, literally "bag coffee", after the traditional technique of preparing the coffee.

Traditionally, hot coffee is served with a complimentary glass of weak Chinese tea or hot water, to be drunk in between sips of the very sweet coffee, though you're unlikely to experience this in many places. If you prefer your coffee black, and without sugar, order *kafeh dam baw sai nâm tan*. A perfect alternative for the hot weather is *kafeh yén*, in which the same concoction is mixed with crushed ice.

Black and Chinese-style **tea** are both served in Laos. Weak Chinese tea is often found, lukewarm, on tables in restaurants and can be enjoyed free of charge. Stronger Chinese tea (*sá jin*) you'll need to order. If you request *sá hâwn*, you usually get a brew based on local or imported black tea, mixed with sweetened condensed milk and sugar; it's available at most coffee vendors.

Alcoholic drinks

Beerlao, the locally produced lager, is regarded by many as one of Southeast Asia's best beers, and is the perfect companion to a Lao meal. Containing five percent alcohol, the beer owes its light, distinctive taste to the French investors who founded the company in 1971, although the company was later state-owned, with Czechoslovakian brewmasters training the Lao staff, until it was privatized in the

---

LÀO-LÁO AND OTHER RICE SPIRITS

Drunk with gusto by the Lao is **lào-láo**, a clear rice alcohol with the fire of a blinding Mississippi moonshine. Most people indulge in local brews, the taste varying from region to region and even town to town.

Drinking *lào-láo* often takes on the air of a sacred ritual, albeit a rather boisterous one. After (or sometimes during) a meal, the host will bring out a bottle of *lào-láo* to share with the guests. The host begins the proceedings by pouring a shot of *lào-láo* and tossing it onto the ground to appease the house spirit. He then pours himself a measure, raising the glass for all to see before throwing back the drink and emptying the remaining droplets onto the floor, in order to empty the glass for the next drinker. The host then pours a shot for each guest in turn. After the host has completed one circuit, the bottle and the glass are passed along to a guest, who serves him- or herself first, then the rest of the party, one by one. Guests are expected to drink at least one shot in order not to offend the house spirit and the host, although in such situations there's often pressure, however playful, to drink much more. One polite escape route is to take a sip of the shot and then dump out the rest on the floor during the "glass emptying" move.

Another rice alcohol, *lào hái*, also inspires a festive, communal drinking experience. Drunk from a large earthenware jar with thin bamboo straws, *lào hái* is fermented by households or villages in the countryside and is weaker than *lào-láo*, closer to a wine in taste than a backwoods whisky. Drinking *lào hái*, however, can be a bit risky as unboiled water is sometimes added to the jar during the fermentation process.

mid-1990s. Nearly all that goes into making Beerlao is imported, from hops to bottle caps, although locally grown rice is used in place of twenty percent of the malt. Also available is the stronger Beerlao Dark, which has a smooth, malty flavour and is generally more expensive than regular Beerlao.

Occasionally, **draught** Beerlao, known as *bia sót* and sometimes appearing on English signs as "Fresh Beer", is available at bargain prices by the litre. Often served warm from the keg, the beer is poured over ice, though some establishments serve it chilled. There are dozens of *bia sót* outlets in the capital, most of which are casual outdoor beer gardens with thatch roofs. You can usually get snacks here too, known as "**drinking food**" or *káp kâem* – typical dishes include spicy papaya salad, fresh spring rolls, omelette, fried peanuts (*thua jeun*), shrimp-flavoured chips (*khào kiap kûng*) and grilled chicken.

Other Asian beers, including Tiger and Singha, are often available (sometimes on tap in Luang Prabang), and closer to the Chinese border you'll find cheaper and less flavoursome Chinese lagers on many menus.

In Vientiane, Luang Prabang and other larger, more touristy, towns, you'll find a good range of Western spirits and liquors, and European-style restaurants usually have imported wine available by the glass or bottle.

Festivals

Lao festivals are an explosion of colour, where parades, games, music and dancing are all accompanied by copious amounts of *lào-láo*. If you happen to be in a town or village that is gearing up for a festival, consider altering your plans so that you can attend – unless you're a teetotaller, in which case you're advised to clear out immediately. In rural areas especially, a festival can transform an entire village into a wild, week-long party.

Because the Lao calendar is dictated by both solar and lunar rhythms, the **dates** of festivals change from year to year, and even just a few days prior to a parade or boat race, there is sometimes confusion over just when it will take place. For the Lao this is not really a problem, as the days leading up to and immediately following large festivals are equally packed with celebrations.

Visitors are most likely to encounter the festivals of the Buddhist **lowland Lao**. On certain Buddhist

BOAT RACES

Lao boat races are rooted in ancient beliefs that predate the arrival of Buddhism in the country. To this day, many lowland Lao believe the Mekong and other local waterways are home to naga, serpent-like creatures that leave the river during the rainy season and inhabit the flooded paddy fields (see box, p.242). The boat races, held between October and December, seek to lure the naga out of the fields and back into the rivers, so that ploughing may begin.

holy days, the faithful **make merit** by walking clockwise around a stupa or a *sim* three times while holding offerings of incense, lotus blossoms and candles in a prayer-like gesture. Visitors are free to take part in this picturesque ritual, called *wian thian* in Lao, and may even be encouraged to do so. Hill-tribe festivals are less open to outsider participation. If you do happen to come across one, watch from a distance and do not interfere unless it is clear that you are being invited to join in.

MAJOR FESTIVALS

February The Makkha Busa Buddhist holy day, observed under a full moon in February, commemorates a legendary sermon given by the Buddha after 1250 of his disciples spontaneously congregated around the enlightened one.

April Lao New Year, or *pi mai lao*, is celebrated all over Laos in mid-April, most stunningly in Luang Prabang, where the town's namesake Buddha image is ritually bathed (see box, p.103).

May During Bun Bang Fai, also known as the rocket festival, crude projectiles are made from stout bamboo poles stuffed with gunpowder and fired skywards. It's hoped the thunderous noise will encourage the spirits to make it rain after months of dry weather (see box, p.8).

October Lai Heau Fai, on the full moon in October, is a festival of lights most magically celebrated in Luang Prabang. In the days leading up to the festival residents build large floats and festoon them with lights (see box, p.103).

November In the days leading up to the full moon, the great That Luang stupa in Vientiane comes to resemble the centrepiece of a fairground, with street vendors setting up booths in the open spaces around it. The week-long That Luang Festival then kicks off with a mass alms-giving to hundreds of monks.

December–January Bun Pha Wet, which commemorates the Jataka tale of the Buddha's second-to-last incarnation as Pha Wet, or Prince Vessantara, takes place at local monasteries on various dates throughout December or January. In larger towns, expect live bands and dancing.

Health

Healthcare in Laos is so poor as to be virtually non-existent; the life expectancy is 66 for men and 69 for women. Malaria and other mosquito-borne diseases are rife, and you'll need to take a number of precautions to avoid contracting these, especially if you plan on spending long periods of time in rural regions. The nearest medical care of any competence is in neighbouring Thailand; if you find yourself afflicted by anything more serious than travellers' diarrhoea, it's best to head for the closest Thai border crossing and check into a hospital.

Plan on consulting a doctor at least two months before your travel date to discuss which diseases you should receive immunization against. Some antimalarials must be taken several days before arrival in a malarial area in order to be effective. If you are going to be on the road for some time, a dental check-up is also advisable.

Vaccinations

While there are no mandatory vaccinations for Laos (except yellow fever if you are coming from an infected area), a few are recommended. Hepatitis A, typhus, tetanus and polio are the most important ones, but you should also consider hepatitis B, rabies and Japanese encephalitis – your doctor or travel health specialist will consider your travel plans and advise you accordingly. All shots should be recorded on an International Certificate of Vaccination and carried with your passport when travelling abroad.

Hepatitis A is contracted via contaminated food and water and can be prevented by the Havrix vaccine which provides protection for up to ten years. Two injections two to four weeks apart are necessary, followed by a booster a year later. The older one-shot vaccine only provides protection for three months. **Hepatitis B** is spread via sexual contact, transfusions of tainted blood and dirty needles. Vaccination is recommended for travellers who plan on staying for long periods of time (six months or more). Note that the vaccine can take up to six months before it is fully effective.

Rabies can be prevented by a vaccine that consists of two injections over a two-month period with a third a year later and boosters every two to five years. If you haven't had shots and are bitten by a potentially rabid animal, you will need to get the jabs immediately.

Japanese encephalitis, a mosquito-borne disease, is quite rare, but doctors may recommend a vaccination against it. The course of injections consists of two shots at two-week intervals plus a booster.

MEDICAL RESOURCES

ⓦ istm.org Website of the International Society for Travel Medicine, with a full list of clinics specializing in international travel health.
ⓦ fitfortravel.nhs.uk UK NHS website carrying information about travel-related diseases and how to avoid them.

UK AND IRELAND

Hospital for Tropical Diseases Travel Clinic, 2nd floor, Mortimer Market Building, Capper St, London WC1E 6JB ☎ 020 3447 5999, ⓦ thehtd.org/Travelclinic.aspx (Wed 1–5pm, Fri 9am–1pm, by appointment only). A consultation costs £20.
MASTA (Medical Advisory Service for Travellers Abroad) ☎ 0330 100 4224, ⓦ masta-travel-health.com. Travel clinics around the UK.
Trailfinders Immunization clinic (no appointment necessary) at 194 Kensington High St, London (Mon–Wed & Fri 9am–5pm, Thurs 10am–6pm, Sat 10am–5.15pm (☎ 020 7938 3999, ⓦ trailfinders .com/travelessentials/travelclinic.htm).
Tropical Medical Bureau 54 Grafton St, Dublin 2 ☎ 01271 5272, ⓦ tmb.ie. Travel clinics in Dublin and elsewhere across the Republic of Ireland.
Well Travelled Clinics Pembroke Place, Liverpool L3 5QA ☎ 0151 705 3223, ⓦ welltravelledclinics.co.uk. An offshoot of the Liverpool School of Tropical Medicine, offering pre-travel advice and vaccinations.

US AND CANADA

ⓦ cdc.gov/travel The US government's official site for travel health, with country-by-country advice.
ⓦ csih.org The website of the Canadian Society for International Health contains an extensive list of travel health centres in Canada.
MEDJET Assistance ☎ 1800 527 7478, ⓦ medjetassistance.com. Annual membership programme for travellers which, in the event of illness or injury, will fly members home or to the hospital of their choice in a medically equipped jet.
Travel Medicine ☎ 1800 872 8633, ⓦ travmed.com. Sells first-aid kits, mosquito netting, water filters, reference books and other health-related travel products; the website includes a list of US travel clinics.

AUSTRALIA AND NEW ZEALAND

Travel Doctor Australia ☎ 1300 658844, ⓦ tmvc.com.au; New Zealand ☎ 09 373 3531, ⓦ traveldoctor.co.nz. Clinics in major Australian and New Zealand cities; travel health factsheets available online.

General precautions

The average traveller to Laos has little to worry about as long as they use common sense and exercise a few precautions. The changes in climate and diet experienced during travel collaborate to lower your resistance, so you need to take special care to maintain a healthy intake of food and water and to try to minimize the effects of heat and humidity on the body. Excessive alcohol consumption should be avoided, as the dehydrating effects of alcohol are amplified by the heat and humidity.

Good **personal hygiene** is essential; hands should be washed before eating, especially given that much of the Lao cuisine is traditionally eaten with the hands. Cuts or scratches, no matter how minor, can become infected very easily and should be thoroughly cleaned, disinfected and bandaged to keep dirt out.

Most health problems experienced by travellers are a direct result of something they've eaten. Avoid eating uncooked vegetables and fruits that cannot be peeled. Dishes containing raw meat or fish are considered a delicacy in Laos but people who eat them risk ingesting worms and other parasites. Cooked food that has been sitting out for an undetermined period should be treated with suspicion.

Stomach trouble and viruses

Most travellers experience some form of **stomach trouble** during their visit to Laos, simply because their digestive system needs time to adapt to the local germs. To deal with travellers' diarrhoea, it is usually enough to drink lots of liquids and eat lightly, avoiding spicy or greasy foods in favour of bland noodle soups until your system recovers. The use of Lomotil or Imodium should be avoided, as they just prevent your body clearing the cause of the diarrhoea, unless long-distance road travel makes it absolutely necessary. Diarrhoea accompanied by severe stomach cramps, nausea or vomiting is an indication of **food poisoning**. As with common diarrhoea, it usually ends after a couple of days. In either case, be sure to increase your liquid intake to make up for lost fluids. It's a very good idea to bring **oral rehydration salts** with you from home; the sachets are easily mixed with bottled water. If symptoms persist or become worse after a couple of days, consider seeking medical advice in Thailand.

Blood or mucus in the faeces is an indication of dysentery. There are two types of dysentery and they differ in their symptoms and treatment. **Bacillary dysentery** has an acute onset, with severe abdominal pain accompanied by the presence of blood in the diarrhoea. Fever and vomiting may also be symptoms. Bacillary dysentery requires immediate medical attention and antibiotics are usually prescribed. **Amoebic dysentery** is more serious: the onset is gradual with bloody faeces accompanied by abdominal pain. Symptoms may eventually disappear but the amoebas will still be in the body and will continue to feed on internal organs, causing serious health problems in time. If you contract either type of dysentery, seek immediate medical advice in Thailand.

Hepatitis A, a viral infection contracted by consuming contaminated food or water, is quite common in Laos. The infection causes the liver to become inflamed and resulting symptoms include nausea, abdominal pains, dark-brown urine and light-brown faeces that may be followed by jaundice (yellowing of the skin and whites of eyes). Vaccination is the best precaution; if you do come down with hepatitis A, get plenty of rest and eat light meals of non-fatty foods.

Another scatological horror is **giardia**, symptoms of which include a bloated stomach, evil-smelling burps and farts, and diarrhoea or floating stools. As with dysentery, treatment by a physician in Thailand should be sought immediately.

WHAT ABOUT THE WATER?

The simple rule while travelling in Laos is not to drink river or tap water. Contaminated water is a major cause of sickness owing to the presence of pathogenic organisms: bacteria, viruses and microscopic giardia cysts. These micro-organisms cause diseases such as diarrhoea, gastroenteritis, typhoid, cholera, dysentery, polio, hepatitis A, giardia and bilharzia, and can be present even when water looks clean.

Safe **bottled water** is available almost anywhere, though when buying, check that the seal is unbroken as bottles are occasionally refilled from the tap. More often than not, when checking into a private room, you'll be provided with a bottle of water free of charge. Water purifying tablets, carried with you from home, are an environmentally friendly alternative as they help to reduce the number of plastic bottles left behind after your travels.

Chinese **tea** made from boiled water is generally safe, but travellers should shun **ice** that doesn't look factory-made. Some of the fanciest hotels have filtration systems that make tap water safe enough to clean your teeth with, but as a general rule, you're best off using purified or bottled water.

Occasional outbreaks of **cholera** occur in Laos. The initial symptoms are a sudden onset of watery but painless diarrhoea. Later nausea, vomiting and muscle cramps set in. Cholera can be fatal if adequate fluid intake is not maintained. Copious amounts of liquids, including oral rehydration solution, should be consumed and urgent medical treatment in Thailand should be sought.

Like cholera, **typhoid** is also spread in small, localized epidemics. The disease is sometimes difficult to diagnose, as symptoms can vary widely. Generally, they include headaches, fever and constipation, followed by diarrhoea.

Mosquito-borne illnesses

Malaria, caused by the plasmodium parasite, is rife in much of Laos. **Symptoms** include chills, a high fever and then sweats, during which the fever falls; the cycle repeats every couple of days. These symptoms aren't so different from those of flu, making diagnosis difficult without a blood test; if you think you've contracted malaria, check into a Thai hospital immediately.

Vientiane is said to be malaria-free, but visitors to other parts of Laos should take all possible precautions to avoid contracting this sometimes fatal disease. Night-feeding mosquitoes are the carriers, so take extra care in the evening, particularly at dawn and dusk. High-strength mosquito **repellent** that contains the chemical compound DEET is a necessity, although bear in mind that prolonged use may be harmful. A natural alternative is citronella oil, found in some repellents. Wearing trousers, long-sleeved shirts and socks gives added protection.

If you plan on travelling in remote areas, bring a **mosquito net**. Most guesthouses provide nets but some of these have holes; gather up the offending section of net and twist a rubber band around it. Many hotels have replaced nets with screened-in windows, which is fine if the room door remains shut at all times, but doors are usually left wide open when maids are tidying up the rooms between guests. If you can't get hold of a mosquito net, try pyrethrum **coils** which can be found in most markets and general stores in Laos.

For added insurance against malaria, it's advisable to take **antimalarial tablets**. Though **doxycycline**, **atovaquone/proguanil** (commonly referred to by its trade name **Malarone**) and **mefloquine** are the most commonly prescribed antimalarials for Laos, the plasmodium parasites are showing resistance to the last drug. While none of the antimalarials guarantees that you will not contract malaria, the risks will be greatly reduced. Note that some antimalarials can have unpleasant side effects. Mefloquine in particular can sometimes cause dizziness, extreme fatigue, nausea and nightmares. Pregnant or lactating women are advised not to take mefloquine.

Day-feeding mosquitoes are the carriers of **dengue fever**. The disease is common in urban as well as rural areas, and outbreaks occur annually during the rainy season. The symptoms are similar to malaria and include fever, chills, aching joints and a red rash that spreads from the torso to the limbs and face. Dengue can be fatal in small children. There is no preventative vaccination or prophylactic. As with malaria, travellers should use insect repellent, keep skin covered with loose-fitting clothing and wear socks. There is no specific treatment for dengue other than rest, lots of liquids and paracetamol for pain and fever. Aspirin should be avoided as it can aggravate the proneness to internal bleeding which dengue sometimes produces.

Sun-related maladies

The Lao hot season, roughly March to May, can be brutal, especially in the lowlands. To prevent **sunburn**, fair-skinned people should wear sunblock and consider purchasing a wide-brimmed straw hat. UV protective sunglasses are useful for cutting the sun's glare, which can be especially harsh during river journeys. The threat of **dehydration** increases with physical exertion. Even if you don't feel thirsty, drink plenty of water. Not having to urinate or passing dark-coloured urine are sure signs that your system is not getting enough liquids.

Heat exhaustion, signified by headaches, dizziness and nausea, is treated by resting in a cool place and increasing your liquid intake until the symptoms disappear. **Heatstroke**, indicated by high body temperature, flushed skin and a lack of perspiration, can be life-threatening if not treated immediately. Reducing the body's temperature by immersion in tepid water is an initial treatment but no substitute for prompt medical attention. Heat and high humidity sometimes cause **prickly heat**, an itchy rash that is easily avoided by wearing loose-fitting cotton clothing.

Critters that bite and sting

In Laos the **bugs** are thick, especially during the rainy season when they swarm round light bulbs and pummel bare skin until you feel like a trampoline at a flea circus. Fortunately, most flying insects pose no threat and are simply looking for a place to land and rest up.

Visitors who spend the night in hill-tribe villages where hygiene is poor risk being infected by **scabies**. These microscopic creatures are just as loathsome as their name suggests, causing severe itching by burrowing under the skin and laying eggs. Scabies is most commonly contracted by sleeping on dirty bedclothes or being in prolonged physical contact with someone who is infected. More common are **head lice**, especially among children in rural areas. Like scabies, it takes physical contact, such as sleeping next to an infected person, to contract head lice, though it may also be possible to contract head lice by wearing a hat belonging to someone who is infected.

The **leeches** most commonly encountered in Laos are about the size and shape of an inchworm, and travellers are most likely to pick them up while trekking through wooded areas. Take extra care when relieving yourself during breaks on long-distance bus rides. The habit of pushing deep into a bush for privacy gives leeches just enough time to grab hold of your shoes or trousers. Later they will crawl their way beneath clothing and attach themselves to joint areas (ankles, knees, elbows) where veins are near the surface of the skin. An anaesthetic and anticoagulant in the leeches' saliva allows the little vampires to gorge themselves on blood without the host feeling any pain. Tucking your trouser-legs into your socks is an easy way to foil leeches. Wounds left by sucking leeches should be washed and bandaged as soon as possible to avoid infection.

Laos has several varieties of poisonous **snakes**, including the king cobra, but the Lao habit of killing every snake they come across, whether venomous or not, keeps areas of human habitation largely snake-free. Travelling in rural areas greatly increases the risk of snakebite, but visitors can lessen the chances of being bitten by not wearing sandals or flip-flops outside urban areas. While hiking between hill-tribe villages especially, take the precaution of wearing boots, socks and long trousers. If you are bitten, the number-one rule is not to panic; remain still to prevent the venom from being quickly absorbed into the bloodstream. Snakebites should be washed and disinfected and immediate medical attention sought – a challenge in most parts of Laos, making avoidance of the problem vital. Huge, black **scorpions** the size of large prawns lurk under the shade of fallen leaves and sting reflexively when stepped on, another solid reason to restrict flip-flop-wearing to urban areas. While the sting is very painful, it is not fatal and pain and swelling usually disappear after a few hours.

Animals that are infected with **rabies** can transmit the disease by biting or even by licking an open wound. Dogs are the most common carriers but the disease can also be contracted from the bites of gibbons, bats and other mammals. Travellers should stay clear of all wild animals and resist the urge to pet unfamiliar dogs or cats. If bitten by a suspect animal, wash and disinfect the wound with alcohol or iodine and seek urgent medical help; the disease is fatal if left untreated.

Sexually transmitted diseases

Prostitution is on the rise in Laos, and with it the inevitable scourge of **sexually transmitted diseases** (STDs). Gonorrhoea and syphilis are common but easily treated with antibiotics. Symptoms of the former include pain or a pus-like discharge when urinating. An open sore on or around the genitals is a symptom of syphilis. In women symptoms are internal and may not be noticed. The number of cases of **AIDS** is also rising in Laos, mostly the result of Lao prostitutes contracting HIV in Thailand.

Bring **condoms** from home; most sold in Laos are imported from Thailand, and may be defective.

The media

Tightly controlled by the communist party since the Pathet Lao came to power in 1975, Laos's minuscule media struggles to compete with flashy Thai TV gameshows and the multitude of channels offered by satellite dishes. With only one-tenth of the population of its neighbour, it's very hard for Laos to compete with Thailand.

Newspapers and magazines

Laos has only one **English-language newspaper**, the *Vientiane Times*, established in 1994. Despite being somewhat thin, self-censored and nearly impossible to find outside the capital, it is nonetheless a good window on Laos. Published by the Ministry of Information and Culture, the *Vientiane Times* focuses primarily on business and trade issues, although interesting cultural pieces do slip in from time to time, and the occasional column showcasing people's opinion on a selected social topic is a worthwhile read. You'll also find ads for restaurant specials and local teaching jobs.

There are two **Lao-language dailies** and five weeklies. Of the two dailies, *Wieng Mai* and *Pasason*, the latter is more widely read. Both get their international news from KPL, the government news agency, and, for the most part, have their own reporters who file domestic news. Neither is known for independent-minded reportage. In fact it's fair to say you'll find much more news about Laos online (a list of recommended websites appears below) than you can in the country.

Foreign publications are extremely difficult to find outside Vientiane, and even in the capital there are scant copies. *Newsweek, The Economist, Time* and the *Bangkok Post* are all sold at minimarkets in Vientiane.

ONLINE NEWS ABOUT LAOS

Ⓦ **vientianetimes.org.la** The official website of the *Vientiane Times* contains most of the stories from Laos's only English-language newspaper.

Ⓦ **laosguide.com/#/news** News gathered from around the world, with a strong bias towards issues affecting Laos.

Ⓦ **laosnews.net** Daily news updates from Laos, including links to stories about its economy and tourist industry.

Ⓦ **muonglao.com** An online magazine running articles that focus on the people and culture of Laos.

Ⓦ **bangkokpost.net** The website of Thailand's leading English-language daily, which often runs stories about Laos.

Television and radio

Lao television's two **government-run channels** broadcast a mix of news, cultural shows and Chinese soaps for several hours a day, with no English programming. Reception is poor in rural areas. One of the oddest sights in Laos is that of rickety bamboo and thatch huts and houses all over the country with huge, modern satellite dishes attached to the roofs. Many mid-range and top-end hotels provide **satellite TV** – though often these show only a handful of channels – as do a few coffee shops and bakeries in Luang Prabang, Vang Vieng and Vientiane.

Lao radio thrives, helped along by the fact that newspapers and TV stations are not available to many people in the countryside. The main radio station, **Lao National Radio**, can be picked up in the vicinity of Vientiane or on shortwave in roughly seventy percent of the country. LNR gets its international news from a number of sources, including CNN, BBC, Xinhua and KPL, and broadcasts news in English twice a day. Tuning into LNR will also give you a chance to hear traditional **Lao music**, which you otherwise may only get to hear at festivals.

Social media

Until recently, access to social media sites such as Facebook and Twitter was uncontrolled. But at the end of 2013, officials – having studied censorship models in Vietnam and China – announced plans to start punishing users for "inappropriate" posts.

Sports and outdoor activities

Laos is one of the better outdoor-adventure destinations in Southeast Asia: there are excellent trekking opportunities, vast cave systems to be explored and crashing whitewater rivers to be rafted. With the emergence of a number of specialized travel companies offering inexpensive, organized, adventure tours in previously remote reaches, it's now easier than ever to experience the wild side of Laos.

Over seventy percent of the country comprises high terrain, with chains of **mountains** reaching heights of over 2800m running its entire length. Covering many of these ranges are expanses of virgin **rainforest**. And from these highlands run steep, narrow valleys through which **rivers** rush down from the mountain heights to join the "Mother of Waters", the Mekong river, which flows the entire length of Laos.

Trekking

The easiest and most popular adventure sport in Laos is **trekking**, with new routes opening up across the country all the time. Trekking is rapidly becoming a major money-earner for Laos, with a range of one- to five-day treks (usually with an environmentally conscious ethos) attracting visitors from around the world.

The **far north** has mountain scenery, forest areas and colourful ethnic hill tribes living in traditional villages. There are excellent **tourist** facilities available in many northern towns, with government-run tourist offices and numerous private operators running programmes for tourists who want to take part in guided treks that are environmentally friendly and have a low impact on the local peoples. Responsible trekking agencies should always be transparent on where your fees go and how they benefit local communities.

LAO SPORTS

PETANG

One of the quirkiest legacies of French colonial rule is surely **petang** – a form of boules you'll see being played in dusty front yards and side streets right around the country.

Like boules, the aim is to throw a small wooden ball, or *cochonnet*, into the centre of a hard gravel court, and then take it in turns to toss larger metal balls towards it. Players are awarded a point for each time their ball lands nearer to the *cochonnet* than their opponent's, and the game ends when one of the players scores thirteen points.

Official rules state *petang* should be played in teams of two or three, but in practice it's usually a casual affair, giving people the chance to chat and while away an afternoon.

KATAW

Team sports aren't played too often in Laos, simply because equipment is prohibitively expensive. The honourable exception is **kataw**. Played with a grapefruit-sized woven wicker ball, it's thought to have originated in the Malay Archipelago, but is also quite popular in Thailand. *Kataw* is a hands-free hotchpotch of volleyball, football and tennis, played both with and without a net. Players have to use their feet, legs, chests and heads to keep the ball aloft, and the acrobatics involved are simply astounding. Games are played just about anywhere, but are commonly seen in schoolyards or monastery grounds.

MUAY LAO

Another sport you might encounter in Laos is **Muay Lao**, or Lao boxing, which sees fighters striking each other with their fists, knees, elbows and feet. The sport is essentially like *Muay Thai* kickboxing, Thailand's national sport, but in Laos professional bouts are held fairly infrequently.

COCKFIGHTING

As with the rest of Southeast Asia, **cockfighting** is a celebrated diversion in Laos – no surprise, as the blood sport originated in this region. Betting is, of course, the whole point. Cockfights take place on Sundays and the local cockpit can usually be found by wandering around and listening for the exuberant cheers of the spectators. Unlike in some Southeast Asian countries, knives are not attached to the rooster's legs in Laos, which means that cockfights last much longer and the birds don't usually die in the ring.

RHINOCEROS BEETLE FIGHTING

Another sport that relies on a wager to sharpen excitement is **rhinoceros beetle fighting**. Although it is difficult to say just how far back the tradition of beetle fighting goes, it is known to be popular among ethnic Tai peoples from the Shan States to northern Vietnam. The walnut-sized beetles hiss alarmingly when angered and it doesn't require much goading to get them to do battle. Pincer-like horns are used by the beetles to seize and lift an opponent, and the fight is considered finished when one of the two beetles breaks and runs. The fighting season is during the rains when the insects breed. They are sometimes peddled in markets tethered to pieces of sugar cane.

For visitors interested in exploring rural Laos on foot, the best towns to head for are Luang Namtha, Muang Sing, Luang Prabang and Vang Vieng, all of which have developed programmes for travellers wanting to make a series of day-trips based out of town or take part in multi-day treks involving camping and village stays.

In **South Central Laos**, guiding units have been set up to allow visitors to discover sacred lakes, ancient forests and interact with local tribes. The tours (see p.217 and p.212) have been built to foster development and improve the lives of local people without destroying the region's natural beauty.

NBCAs and eco-tours

A handful of Lao companies organize **eco-tours** to wilderness areas featuring rare and exotic flora and fauna. Here, nature lovers and birdwatchers will find some of the rarest species on the planet and vast forest canopies. Although Laos does not have any national parks in the Western sense, since 1993 the government has established twenty-one **National Biodiversity Conservation Areas (NBCAs)**, many still with villagers and hill tribes living within their boundaries. Unfortunately, though NBCA status means government recognition of their biodiversity, this status has not conferred any real protection (see p.296).

The NBCAs are scattered around the country, often in remote border areas without roads. While many of the parks are inaccessible short of mounting a professional expedition, several have been developed for eco-tourism and have **visitor centres** and **guided walks**. The best developed NBCAs for tourists are Phou Khao Khouay (see p.83), Nam Ha (see box, p.187) and Khammouane Limestone (see p.214), all of which can be reached by road.

Watersports

While most river-journey enthusiasts are satisfied with a slow boat down the Mekong between Houayxai and Luang Prabang, many opportunities exist for exploring Laos's faster waterways. Several companies offer **whitewater-rafting** trips out of Luang Prabang on a number of northern rivers, including the Nam Ou, the Nam Xuang and the Nam Ming.

Even more popular are **river-kayaking** adventures ranging from easy day-trips for beginners to multi-day adventures down rivers with grade 5 rapids. Professional guided kayaking tours are currently operated on a regular basis on eight northern rivers as well as the Ang Nam Ngum Reservoir (near the capital) and in Si Phan Don. The best bases for kayaking tours are Vientiane, Vang Vieng, Luang Prabang, Nong Khiaw and Luang Namtha. Another fantastic region for kayaking is the Khammouane Limestone NBCA (see p.214). Among other scenic wonders, this NBCA features a 7km-long natural river-tunnel through the heart of a mountain, and is becoming popular for organized tours out of Vientiane.

Caves and rock climbing

With its great forests of limestone karst scenery receding into the distance like an image in a Chinese scroll painting, Laos is a great destination for cave exploring, spelunking and rock-climbing. Prime areas for limestone karst scenery in Laos include Vang Vieng, Kasi, Thakhet and Vieng Xai. For most tourists, **cave exploring** is limited to climbing up to and wandering around in caves that are fairly touristy and have clearly defined pathways. Serious spelunkers can find vast cave and tunnel systems to explore in the Khammouane Limestone NBCA and the Hin Nam No NBCA, but should seek local permission before launching any major expeditions as many caves have yet to have archeological surveys done. With so many awesome unclimbed

and unnamed peaks, **rock climbing** is one sport that seems to have a huge future in Laos. At present the sport is still in its infancy, but new routes continue to open up around Vang Vieng.

Mountain biking

With some of the best untamed scenery in Southeast Asia, many unpaved roads, and little traffic, Laos is becoming a very hot destination for cross-country **mountain-bike touring**. A lot of independent travellers do self-organized mountain-bike touring in northern Laos, bringing their bikes with them from home. **Route 13** from Luang Prabang to Vientiane seems to be the most popular route, but be warned that despite the beautiful scenery, the route is also extremely mountainous, crossing several large ranges before reaching the Vientiane Plain. There are much better routes in **Hua Phan** and **Xieng Khuang** provinces where you'll find fantastic landscapes, plenty of remote villages and paved roads with very few vehicles on them.

It's a good idea to plan carefully. What appear to be very short distances on the map can often take many hours, even in a vehicle. One good thing about bicycle touring in Laos is that should things get too difficult, you can always flag down a passing sawngthaew and throw the bike on the roof. Another alternative is to join an **organized cycling tour**. There are plenty to choose from; London-based Red Spokes (℡ 020 7502 7252, Ⓦ redspokes .co.uk) runs a popular two-week tour that takes in Luang Prabang, Vang Vieng and Vientiane, as well as some rural stretches with spectacular scenery.

Alternative therapies

During their period of colonization, the French regarded traditional Lao therapies as quaint and amusing, and this attitude was passed on to the Lao elite who studied in France. In an essay about traditional Lao medicine written in the 1950s by a former Minister of Health, the traditional Lao doctor is repeatedly referred to as "the quack". But renewed interest, partially fuelled by a similar rekindling of enthusiasm in neighbouring China, has seen a resurgence of confidence in traditional techniques.

Tourism has been partially responsible for renewed interest in traditional massage and herbal sauna, though these alternative therapies are generally limited to larger towns and cities. Besides the obvious physical benefits the Lao massage and sauna afford the recipient, administering massage and sauna to others is believed to bring spiritual merit to those who perform the labour, making Lao massage and sauna a win-win proposition for all involved.

Lao massage

Traditional **Lao massage** owes more to **Chinese** than to Thai schools, utilizing medicated balms and salves which are rubbed into the skin. Muscles are kneaded and joints are flexed while a warm compress of steeped herbs is applied to the area being treated. In practice, though, the standard massage offered at Lao spas and massage joints is "dry", with balms and hot compresses available as optional extras. Besides massage, Lao doctors may utilize other "exotic" treatments that have been borrowed from neighbouring countries. One decidedly Chinese therapy that is sometimes employed in Laos is **acupuncture** (*fang khem*), in which long, thin needles are inserted into special points that correspond to specific organs or parts of the body. Another imported practice is the application of **suction cups** (*kaew dut*), a remedy popular in neighbouring Cambodia. Small glass jars are briefly heated with a flame and applied to bare skin; air within the cup contracts as it cools, drawing blood under the skin into the mouth of the cup. Theoretically, toxins within the bloodstream are in this way brought to the surface of the skin.

Lao herbal saunas

Before getting a massage, many Lao opt for some time in the **herbal sauna**. This usually consists of a rustic wooden shack divided into separate rooms for men and women; beneath the shack a drum of water sits on a wood fire. Medicinal herbs boiling in the drum release their juices into the water and the resulting steam is carried up into the rooms. The temperature inside is normally quite high and bathers should spend no more than fifteen minutes at a time in the sauna, taking frequent breaks to cool off by lounging outside and sipping herbal tea to replace water that the body so profusely sweats out. The **recipes** of both the saunas and teas are jealously guarded but are known to contain such herbal additives as carambola, tamarind, eucalyptus and citrus leaves.

Culture and etiquette

While history may have given them ample reason to distrust outsiders, the Lao are a genuinely friendly people and interacting with them is one of the greatest joys of travelling through the country. Always remember, though, that Laos is a Buddhist country and so it's important to dress and behave in a way that is respectful.

Because of the sheer diversity of **ethnic groups** in Laos, it is difficult to generalize when speaking of "Lao" attitudes and behaviour. The dominant group, the "Lao Loum", or **lowland Lao**, who make up the majority in the valleys of the Mekong and its tributaries, are Theravada Buddhists and this has a strong effect on their attitudes and behaviour. The focus here is on dos and don'ts within that culture; customs among the **hill-tribe peoples** are often different from those of the lowlanders.

Dress and appearance

Appearance is very important in Lao society. **Conservative dress** is always recommended, and visitors should keep in mind that the Lao dislike foreigners who come to their country and dress in what they deem a disrespectful manner. This includes men appearing shirtless in public, and women bearing their shoulders and thighs. Be aware also that dreadlocks, tattoos and body-piercing are viewed with disfavour by lowland Lao, although hill-tribe people are usually more accepting. Dressing too casually (or too outrageously) can also be counterproductive in dealings with Lao authorities, such as when applying for visa extensions at immigration.

When in urban areas or visiting Buddhist monasteries or holy sites, visitors should refrain from outfits that would be more suited to the beach. Women especially should avoid wearing anything that reveals too much skin or could be conceived of as provocative – this includes shorts and sleeveless shirts. Sandals or flip-flops can be worn for all but the most formal occasions; in fact, they are much more practical than shoes, since footwear must be **removed** upon entering private homes, certain Buddhist monastery buildings or any living space. The habit of leaving your footwear outside the threshold is not just a matter of wanting to keep interiors clean, it is a long-standing tradition that will cause offence if flouted.

Manners

Lao **social taboos** are sometimes linked to Buddhist beliefs. **Feet** are considered low and unclean – be careful not to step over any part of people who are sitting or lying on the floor, as this is also considered rude. If you do accidentally kick or brush someone with your feet, apologize immediately and smile as you do so. Conversely, people's **heads** are considered sacred and shouldn't be touched.

Besides dressing conservatively, there are other conventions that must be followed when visiting **Buddhist monasteries**. Before entering monastery buildings such as the *sim* or *wihan*, or if you are invited into monks' living quarters, footwear must be removed. Women should never touch Buddhist monks or novices (or their clothes), or hand objects directly to them. When giving something to a monk, the object should be placed on a nearby table or passed to a layman who will then hand it to the monk.

All Buddha images are objects of veneration, so it should go without saying that touching Buddha images disrespectfully is inappropriate. When sitting on the floor of a monastery building that has a Buddha image, never point your feet in the direction of the image. If possible, observe the Lao and imitate the way they sit: in a modified kneeling position with legs pointed away from the image.

Greetings

The lowland Lao traditionally **greet** each other with a *nop* – bringing their hands together at the chin in a prayer-like gesture. After the revolution the *nop* was discouraged, but it now seems to be making a comeback. This graceful gesture is more difficult to execute properly than it may at first appear, however, as the status of the persons giving and returning the *nop* determines how they execute it. Most Lao reserve the *nop* greeting for each other, preferring to shake hands with Westerners, and the only time a Westerner is likely to receive a *nop* is from the staff of posh hotels or fancy restaurants. In any case, if you do receive a *nop* as a gesture of greeting or thank you, it is best to reply with a smile and nod of the head.

The Lao often feel that many foreign visitors seem to be a bit aloof. They have obviously spent a lot of time and money to get so far from home, but once they get to Laos they walk around briskly, looking at the locals, but rarely bothering to smile or greet those they have come so far to see. Foreign visitors who are not grin-stingy will find that a smile and a

sabai di ("hello") will break the ice of initial reservation some locals may have upon seeing a foreigner, and will invariably bring a smile in response.

It's worth bearing in mind that, as in the rest of Asia, showing anger in Laos is rather futile – it'll more likely be met with amusement or the swift departure of the person you're talking to, in order to save face.

Social invitations

Lao people are very **hospitable** and will often go out of their way to help visitors. Especially in rural areas, you may find people inviting you to join them for a meal or to celebrate a birth or marriage. This is a real privilege, and even if you don't wish to stay for long, it's polite to join them and to accept at least one drink if it's offered to you. More than anything, it gives you a chance to experience local life, and gives Lao people a good impression of the tourists who come to their country, and an opportunity to learn more about the world.

Sexual attitudes

Public displays of affection – even just hugging – are considered tasteless by the Lao and are likely to cause offence. Though the gay scene remains very underground in Laos, gay travellers are unlikely to be threatened or hassled. Sexual relations between an unmarried Lao national and a Westerner are officially illegal in Laos – in Vientiane especially, the law prohibiting Lao nationals from sharing hotel rooms with foreigners is sometimes enforced.

Crime and personal safety

Laos is a relatively safe country for travellers, although certain areas remain off-limits because of unexploded ordnance left over from decades of warfare. As a visitor, however, you're an obvious target for thieves (who may include your fellow travellers), so do take necessary precautions.

Carry your passport and other valuables in zipped pockets (or a money belt, if you prefer) and don't leave anything important lying about in your room, particularly when staying in rural bungalows. A few hotels have safes which you may want to use, although you should keep in mind that you never know who has access to the safe. A **padlock** and

DRUGS

In recent years Laos has seen a steady rise of drug tourism. **Ganja** (marijuana) is widely available in Laos, although it's illegal to smoke it. Tourists who buy and use ganja risk substantial "fines" if caught by police, who do not need a warrant to search you or your room. As in Thailand, there have been many instances of locals selling foreigners marijuana and then telling the police. The once-wild drugs scene in Vang Vieng has all but died out (see p.85), but mushrooms and weed are still offered at some backpacker bars in Si Phan Don – either straight up or baked into a dizzying array of "happy" pizzas – but you should bear in mind that travellers have been known to get sick, or robbed, after indulging.

In northern towns, tourists are sometimes approached by **opium** addicts who, in return for cash, offer to take the visitors to a hut or some other private place, where opium pipes will be prepared and smoked. Many Westerners feel the romanticism of doing this all-but-extinct drug is just as appealing as the promise of intoxication, but the opium prepared for tourists is often not opium at all, but **morphine**-laden opium ash that has been mixed with painkillers. The resulting "high" is, for many, several hours of nausea and vomiting. While real **opium** is not as addictive as its derivative, heroin, withdrawal symptoms are similarly painful. Visitors caught smoking opium (or even opium ash) face fines, jail time and deportation.

In addition, it's important to consider the local implications of using drugs in Laos. There remains a serious problem with drug addiction in some rural communities, which local organizations are working hard to address, and using drugs while in the country can encourage local people to do the same, thus undoing a lot of hard work.

chain, or a cable lock, is useful for doors and windows at inexpensive guesthouses and budget hotels and for securing your pack on buses, where you're often separated from your belongings (especially important on VIP buses aimed at tourists, where theft is more common). It's also a good idea to keep a reserve of cash, photocopies of the relevant pages of your passport, insurance details and maybe an "emergency" credit card separate from the rest of your valuables.

As tranquil as Laos can seem, petty theft and serious crimes do happen throughout the country – even on seemingly deserted country roads. Despite improvements in the past few years, petty crime is more common in **Vang Vieng** than just about anywhere else in Laos, with drunk tourists often leaving themselves open to theft and robbery. Although crime rates in **Vientiane** are low, be on your guard in darker streets outside the city centre, and along the river – muggings have occurred. Motorbike-borne thieves ply the city streets and have been known to snatch bags out of the front basket of other motorbikes that they pass.

If you do have anything stolen, you'll need to get the **police** to write up a report in order to claim on your insurance: bring along a Lao speaker to simplify matters if you can. While police generally keep their distance from foreigners, they may try to exact "fines" from visitors for alleged misdemeanours. With a lot of patience, you should be able to resolve most problems, and, if you keep your cool, you may find that you can bargain down such

"fines". It helps to have your passport with you at all times – if you don't, police have greater incentive to ask for money and may even try to bring you to the station. In some instances police may puzzle over your passport for what seems like an awfully long time. Again, such situations are best handled with an ample dose of patience. If your papers are in order, you shouldn't have anything to worry about.

Banditry

With far more serious consequences than petty theft, **banditry** is still a possible (but very small) threat in some parts of Laos. In the past, buses, motorcyclists and private vehicles on certain highways have been held up, their passengers robbed and, in some instances, killed. Because information in Laos is tightly controlled, no one knows exactly if rumoured bandit attacks have actually occurred or if other incidents have happened and gone unreported. Therefore it's always good to check Western government websites such as that of the UK's FCO (Ⓦ fco.gov.uk) for any **travel advice** before heading out into remote regions.

Unexploded ordnance

The **Second Indochina War** left Laos with the dubious distinction of being the most heavily bombed country per capita in the history of warfare. The areas of the country most affected by aerial bombing are along the border of Vietnam ⌐

especially in southern Laos where the border runs parallel to the former Ho Chi Minh Trail; also heavily targeted was Xieng Khuang province in the northeast. Other provinces, far from the border with Vietnam, were the site of land battles in which both sides lobbed artillery and mortar shells at each other. A fair quantity of this ordnance did not explode.

These dangerous relics of the war, known as **UXO** (unexploded ordnance), have been the focus of disposal teams since the 1980s. According to the Lao Government, most areas that tourists are likely to visit have been swept clean of UXO. That said, it always pays to be cautious when in rural areas or when trekking. UXO unearthed during road construction can be pushed onto the shoulder, where it becomes overgrown with weeds and forgotten. Disposal experts say that fast-growing bamboo has been known to unearth UXO, lifting it aloft as the stalk grows and then letting it fall onto a trail that was previously clean. Consequently, it's best to stay on trails and beware any odd-looking metallic objects that you may come across. Picking something up for closer inspection (or giving it a kick to turn it over) can be suicidal. When taking a toilet break during long-distance bus journeys, it's not a good idea to penetrate too deeply into the bush looking for privacy.

In many towns across Laos, locals use old bombs, bomb cases, mortar shells etc for a variety of functions, from demarcating plots of land to decorating their gardens. These will normally (but not always) have been checked by UXO disposal experts, and should pose no threat. Still, it pays to have a healthy respect for all UXO. After all, these are weapons that were designed to kill or maim.

Shopping

One of the pleasures of shopping in a non-industrial country like Laos is the availability of hand-crafted goods. Because items made by hand can only be produced in limited quantities, they are usually sold or bartered in the village in which they were made. Handmade baskets, bolts of cloth and household utensils are best acquired at village level, as everything is cheaper at the source, though it's not all that easy for non-Lao-speaking visitors to turn up and make known what they're after. Provincial markets are the obvious alternative; prices here are usually just a bit more than what you would pay were you to buy directly from village artisans. Of course, if village-made objects make it all the way to the boutiques of Vientiane, their "value" will have multiplied many times over.

As with the rest of Southeast Asia, merchandise often has no price tag and the buyer is expected to make a spirited attempt at **haggling** the quoted price down. Even if an item is sporting a price tag, it's still perfectly acceptable to ask for a discount. Bargaining takes patience and tact, and knowing what an item is really worth is half the battle. The first price quoted will usually be inflated. If you feel the price is way out of line, it is better to just smile and walk away than to squawk in disbelief and argue that the price is unfair – no matter how loud or valid your protestations, nobody will believe that you cannot afford to buy.

On the whole, **Luang Prabang** is better for shopping than Vientiane, with a glut of pricey boutiques selling locally made handicrafts. Note however that in both towns, the vast majority of goods on sale are cheap imports from China and beyond.

Textiles

A surprisingly large number of the ethnic groups that make up the population of Laos produce cloth of their own design, which is turned into men's and women's sarongs, shoulder bags, headscarves and shawls. Traditionally, most textiles stayed within the village where they were woven, but the increasing popularity of Lao textiles with visitors has led urban textile merchants to employ buyers to comb isolated villages for **old textiles** that might be resold at a profit. The result is that many merchants have only a vague idea of where their old textiles are from or which group made them. This doesn't seem to deter foreign buyers, however, and sales are brisk, which has given rise to the practice of boiling new textiles to artificially age them. Some of these so-called antique textiles sell for hundreds of dollars.

To some shopkeepers "old" can mean ten years or so and most will have little idea what the age of a certain piece is, but if you persist in asking, they will often claim an item has been around for a couple of centuries. As textiles are difficult to date, it's best to take such claims with a pinch of salt. All in all, though, it is rare for the local merchants to go to great lengths to deceive customers.

These days, the vast majority of the textiles for sale are **new textiles** specifically made for the tourist market. These may have the same patterns and motifs as the traditional sarongs and so forth, but are cut and sewn into items such as pillowcases. If you're after antique textiles you have to ask; unless you are an expert or have money to burn, it is a good idea to stick to new textiles, which can be had for as little as $5 and are just as pleasing to the eye as the older pieces.

Lao weavers have a long tradition of combining **cotton** and **silk**: a typical piece may have a cotton base with silk details woven into it. Modern pieces of inferior quality substitute synthetic fibres for silk, and some vendors have been known to try to pass off hundred-percent synthetic cloth as silk. Lastly, the synthetic dyes used by most weavers are not colourfast, something to bear in mind when laundering newly purchased textiles.

Silver

Although Thai antique dealers have made off with quite a bit of old Lao **silver** (and marketed it in Thailand as old Thai silver) there is still a fair amount of the stuff floating around. Items to look out for are paraphernalia for **betel chewing**: egg-sized round or oval boxes for storing white lime, cone-shaped containers for holding betel leaves and miniature mortars used to pound areca nuts. Larger silver boxes or bowls with human or animal figures hammered into them were once used in religious ceremonies. C-shaped **bracelets** and anklets are found in a variety of styles. Bracelets and anklets of traditional Lao style, as opposed to hill-tribe design, have a stylized lotus bud on each end.

Hill-tribe silver jewellery (traditionally made by melting down and hammering silver French piastres) is usually bold and heavy – the better to show off one's wealth. With few exceptions, the hill-tribe jewellery being peddled in Laos is the handiwork of the Hmong tribe. In **Luang Prabang**, the old silversmith families that once supplied the monarchy with ceremonial objects are again practising their trade, and their silver creations represent some of the best-value souvenirs to be found in Laos.

Antiques

Thai merchants regularly scour Laos for **antiques** so there are probably more authentic Lao antiques for sale in the malls of Bangkok and Chiang Mai than anywhere in Laos. Conversely, many of the "antiques" for sale in Laos are actually reproductions made in Thailand or Cambodia. This is particularly true in the case of metal Buddhist or Hindu figurines.

Wooden **Buddha images** are often genuine antiques, but were most likely pilfered from some temple or shrine. Refraining from buying them will help discourage this practice. Prospective buyers should also be aware that there is an **official ban** on the export of Buddha images from Laos. Although this is aimed primarily at curbing the theft of large Lao bronze Buddhas from rural monasteries, small images are also included in the ban. That said, it is highly unlikely that Lao officials will confiscate new Buddhas from foreign visitors. The Lao, when acquiring a Buddha image, pay particular attention to the expression on the Buddha's face. Does the Buddha look serene? If so, the image is considered auspicious.

Antique brass weights, sometimes referred to as "**opium weights**", come in a variety of sizes and shapes. Those cast in zoomorphic figures (stylized birds, elephants, lions, etc) are an established collectable and command highprices, sometimes selling for hundreds of dollars. Weights of simpler design, such as those shaped like miniature stupas, are much more affordable and can be bought for just a few dollars in provincial towns.

Opium pipes come in sundry forms as well. Although very few are genuine antiques, the workmanship is generally quite good as they are produced by pipemakers who once supplied Vientiane's now-defunct opium dens. A typical pipe may have a bamboo body, a ceramic bowl and silver or brass ornamentation, and should sell for about $50. During the past few years Laos has been flooded with reproduction opium pipes from Vietnam. These are more ornate than the Laos-made pipes, but aren't worth spending more than $10 or so to buy.

Royalist regalia

With the memories of the war that divided Laos fading, paraphernalia associated with the defunct kingdom is less likely to offend officials of the present regime, though wearing such memorabilia in public would be considered poor form. Brass buttons, badges and medals decorated with the Hindu iconography of the Lao monarchy are sometimes found in gold or silver jewellery and antique shops. Royal Lao Army hat devices depicting Shiva's trident superimposed on Vishnu's discus and brass buttons decorated with Airavata, the three-headed elephant, are typical finds.

Woodcarving, rattan, wicker and bamboo

Until tourism created a demand for souvenirs, nearly all examples of Lao **woodcarving** were religious in nature – for example, the small, antique, wooden Buddha images which are finding their way into curio shops. For those who have bought a stunning, hand-woven textile but are unsure of how to display it, there are ornately **carved hangers** made expressly for this purpose. Workmanship varies, however, so inspect carefully to ensure that there are no splinters or jagged edges which may damage the textile. Keep in mind also that large woodcarvings sometimes crack when transported to less humid climes.

That **baskets** are an important part of traditional Lao culture is reflected in the language: Lao has dozens upon dozens of words for them, and they're used in all spheres of everyday life. Many different forms of basket are used as **backpacks**; those made by the Gie-Trieng tribe in Xekong province are probably the most expertly woven. Baskets are also used for serving food, such as sticky rice. These mini-baskets come with a long loop of string so they can be slung over the shoulder when hiking, as sticky rice is the perfect snack on long treks, road or boat trips. **Mats** made of woven grass or reeds can be found in sizes for one or two people. The one-person mats are dirt-cheap, easily carried when rolled up and make a lot more sense than foam rubber mattresses. Woven mats are especially handy when taking a slow boat down the Mekong, as the passenger holds are often not the cleanest of places. Ordinary sticky rice baskets and mats can be found at any provincial market and should cost no more than a couple of dollars.

Travelling with children

Travelling through Laos with children can be both challenging and fun, but the rewards far outweigh any negatives. The presence of children can help break the ice with locals, especially as the Lao people are so family-focused, but long, bumpy journeys and poor sanitation can make things a struggle at times.

Laos's lack of adequate healthcare facilities is a major concern for parents, so sufficient travel insurance (see p.50) is a must for peace of mind. It's worth taking a first aid set with you, as well as a rehydration solution in case of diarrhoea, which can be dangerous in young children. Rabies is a problem in Laos, so explain to your children the dangers of playing with animals and consider a rabies vaccination before departing.

In tourist areas it should be no problem finding food that kids will **eat**, and dishes like spring rolls, fried rice and *fõe* (see p.34), where chilli is added by the diner, are a good choice for those who may not be used to the spiciness of Lao cuisine.

A major consideration will be the long journeys that are sometimes necessary when travelling around the country – these can be bone-numbing at the best of times, and young children may find them excruciatingly boring. That said, bus journeys are a real "local" experience that can make more of an impression than wandering around temples. It is easy, however, to see a fair amount of the country by sticking to journeys of fewer than six hours.

Most hotels and guesthouses are very accommodating to families, often allowing children to stay for free in their parents' room, or adding an extra bed or cot to the room for a small charge.

If you're travelling with babies, you'll have difficulty finding **nappies** (diapers) throughout Laos. For short journeys, you could bring a supply of nappies from home; for longer trips, consider switching over to washables.

Travel essentials

Costs

Laos is one of the poorest nations is Southeast Asia and consequently one of the cheapest countries to travel in. Your largest expense is likely to be transport, with journeys usually costing between 60,000 and 120,000K; accommodation and food are very inexpensive.

By eating at noodle stalls and cheap restaurants, opting for basic accommodation and travelling by public transport, you can travel in Laos on a **daily budget** of around $20. Staying in more luxurious hotels and resorts, and eating in the best restaurants will push your budget up to a very reasonable $40–60 a day – though you'll struggle to find smart accommodation and restaurants in much of the country. Note, however, that prices are significantly higher in Vientiane, Pakse and Luang Prabang.

While restaurants and some shops have fixed prices, in general merchandise almost never has price tags, and the lack of a fixed pricing scheme can take some getting used to. Prices, unless marked or for food in a market, should usually be negotiated, as should the cost of chartering transport (as opposed to fares on passenger vehicles, which are non-negotiable). Hotel and guesthouse operators are usually open to a little bargaining, particularly during off-peak months.

Bargaining is very much a part of life in Laos, and an art form, requiring a delicate balance of humour, patience and tact. It's important to remain realistic, as vendors will lose interest if you've quoted a price that's way out of line, and to keep a sense of perspective: cut-throat haggling over 1000K only reflects poorly on both buyer and seller. As the Lao in general – with the exception of drivers of vehicles for hire and souvenir sellers in Vientiane and Luang Prabang – are less out to rip off tourists than their counterparts in Thailand and Vietnam, they start off the haggling by quoting a fairly realistic price and expect to come down only a little. It's worth bearing in mind that the country's dependence on imported goods from its neighbours does push prices up – whether for food, toiletries or transport.

Customs

Lao customs regulations limit visitors to five hundred cigarettes and one litre of distilled alcohol per person upon entry, but in practice bags are rarely opened unless a suspiciously large amount of luggage is being brought in. A customs declaration form must be filled out along with the arrival form, but typically nobody bothers to check that the information is correct. There is no limit on the amount of foreign currency you can bring into Laos.

Electricity

Supplied at 220 volts AC. Two-pin sockets taking plugs with flat prongs are the norm. Many smaller towns, including several provincial capitals, have power for only a few hours in the evening or none at all, so it's worth bringing a torch.

Information

Good, reliable information on Laos is hard to come by and, because everything from visa requirements to transport routes is subject to frequent change, your best bet is often to get the latest advice from internet forums, guesthouses and fellow travellers.

The government-run **Lao National Tourism Administration** (LNTA for short; ⓦtourismlaos.org), which has offices around Laos, including Vientiane and Luang Prabang, should be able to supply decent brochures and maps.

Privately owned travel companies such as Green Discovery and Diethelm Travel can provide reliable tourist information in provincial capitals, as well as some free fold-out maps. The best road **map** of the country is the Laos PDR Map published by Golden Triangle Rider and available at bookstores in Thailand, or online at Wgt-rider. com. Other detailed maps of the country are available at bookshops in Vientiane (see p.50). For town maps, in addition to those in this book, Hobo Maps (Whobomaps.com) provides easy-to-use maps of various tourist towns, which are available online or from local bookshops.

ONLINE RESOURCES

ⓦ **travelfish.org** Reliable, no-nonsense website with features, travel tips and accommodation reviews covering Southeast Asia, plus lively Laos forums.

ⓦ **vientianetimes.com** Features news, accommodation listings and links to hundreds of other websites on Laos.

ⓦ **laoembassy.com** Website of the Lao embassy to the US features tourist info and the latest visa regulations.

ⓦ **ecotourismlaos.com** An informative website by the Lao National Tourism Administration that features helpful tips on exploring Laos's national parks.

ⓦ **laos-guide-999.com** Good, locally made website with information on transport, visas and Lao culture.

ⓦ **theboatlanding.laopdr.com** An excellent site on travel in northern Laos. Features information on independent trekking and eco-tourism.

ⓦ **tripadvisor.com** User-generated reviews of hotels, guesthouses and tourist attractions in Laos.

Insurance

It is important to purchase a good travel insurance policy (see box opposite) before travelling that covers against theft, loss and illness or injury. Good medical coverage is particularly important in Laos where the poor healthcare system means that any serious accident or illness while there would most likely require you to travel to Thailand for treatment.

Internet access

Internet cafés are found in most major towns and cities in Laos, though there are still a fair few smaller places that don't have access. Prices are usually around 10,000K per hour; connections can be excruciatingly slow. Almost all Western-style cafés and many hotels and guesthouses across the country now offer free wi-fi. For day-to-day use within towns and cities, a much more reliable option is to use the excellent 3G network, which covers even remote population centres (see p.52).

ROUGH GUIDES TRAVEL INSURANCE

Rough Guides has teamed up with **WorldNomads.com** to offer great travel insurance deals. Policies are available to residents of over 150 countries, with cover for a wide range of adventure sports, 24hr emergency assistance, high levels of medical and evacuation cover and a stream of travel safety information. Roughguides.com users can take advantage of their policies online 24/7, from anywhere in the world – even if you're already travelling. And since plans often change when you're on the road, you can extend your policy and even claim online. Roughguides.com users who buy travel insurance with WorldNomads.com can also leave a positive footprint and donate to a community development project. For more information, go to ⓦroughguides.com/travel-insurance.

Laundry

Most guesthouses and hotels offer a same-day laundry service, and in larger towns a few shops offer laundry service which can be cheaper than what you'll be charged at your accommodation. In either situation, the charge is usually per kilogram. Your clothes may take a beating, so it's best not to entrust prized articles to these services. If you want to wash clothes yourself, you can buy small packets of detergent in many general stores and markets around the country. Hang out your underwear discreetly – women should take particular care, as women's undergarments are believed to have the power to render Buddhist tattoos and amulets powerless.

Money

Lao currency, the **kip**, is available in 100,000K 50,000K, 20,000K, 10,000K, 5000K, 2000K, 1000K and 500K notes; there are no coins in circulation.

Although a law passed in 1990 technically forbids the use of foreign currencies to pay for goods and services in local markets, many tour operators, and more expensive hotels and restaurants quote their prices in dollars (especially common when the price is above 200,000K). Many shops, especially those in more touristy towns, and tourist services will accept Thai baht or US dollars in place of kip, usually at a fairly decent exchange rate, though it makes little sense unless you're paying for something that would require a large amount of kip.

Because of the high denominations of Lao money, it can be rather cumbersome to carry even relatively small amounts of money in kip. It's far easier to carry large sums of money in dollars or baht and to change them as you need to – bear in mind though that larger US notes will get you better exchange rates. It's not possible to convert money to or from kip outside Laos.

Banks and exchange

Banking hours are generally Monday to Friday 8.30am to 3.30pm, with an hour-long lunch break at noon. Exchange rates are fairly uniform throughout the country, though marginally better in larger towns and cities. Most towns have a bank with at least the most basic of exchange facilities – usually dollars and baht – and a wide variety of international currencies can often be changed, including euros and sterling. Moneychangers are common in larger towns, and rates are generally a little lower, though not disproportionately so, than the banks.

Cash and cards

The safest and most convenient way to organize your money in Laos is to travel with a credit and/or debit card. **ATMs** are found in all but the smallest towns, though many charge a small fee per withdrawal, so you might want to avoid making too many small withdrawals. Note that your bank may also charge you for purchases and withdrawals made abroad; check before travelling. In addition to your card, it's worth carrying a supply of American dollars, which can easily be exchanged for Lao kip.

Major **credit cards** are accepted at high-end hotels and restaurants in Vientiane and Luang

KIP AND DOLLARS

Prices in the Guide are predominantly given in kip up to 200,000K – above that level, we've quoted costs in US dollars. This reflects the way things tend to be priced in the country, with more expensive goods, services and accommodation priced in dollars rather than kip – although you will, of course, come across some exceptions to the rule. Unless you're staying in high-end accommodation, or eating at the swankiest restaurants, most of your transactions will be in kip.

Prabang, and in a limited number of other tourist centres. **Cash advances** on Visa cards, and less frequently Mastercard, are possible in some banks in larger towns, though minimum amounts and commission are likely to be imposed.

Travellers' cheques are rarely, if ever, accepted.

Opening hours and public holidays

Hours for government offices are generally Monday to Friday 8am–noon & 1–5pm. Tourist offices throughout the country are theoretically open Mon–Fri 8–11.30am & 1.30–4pm, though in some large towns they're also open at weekends, and offices in small towns often open late and close early. Private businesses usually open and close a bit later, with most opening on Saturday but almost all closed on Sunday. Details of banking hours are given on p.51.

The posted hours on **museums** are not always scrupulously followed outside the major cities and on slow days (almost every day) the curators and staff are often tempted to pack up and head home. Unless a festival is taking place, **monasteries** should only be visited during daylight hours as monks are very early risers and are usually in bed not long after sunset.

Government offices, banks and post offices close for public holidays – a lot of shops, especially in smaller towns, also close for the day.

Phones

The majority of internet cafés now have facilities for international calling, usually through Skype.

Most **mobile phones and smartphones** bought in recent years can be used in Laos, though call, text

---

DIALLING CODES

To call Laos from abroad, dial your international access code, then ☎856 + area code minus first 0 + number. To call abroad from Laos, dial 00, then the relevant country code and the number. Useful country codes include:

Australia ☎61
Ireland ☎353
New Zealand ☎64
South Africa ☎27
UK ☎44
US and Canada ☎1

---

and data charges are high, so if you're planning on using your phone it's worth buying a local SIM card. These are readily available from shops and markets, and for around 35,000K you'll be able to buy a package with enough data to last you several weeks of moderate use. Local network Unitel has excellent 3G coverage in even mid-sized towns. Top-up cards can be purchased in villages across Laos that have even the most basic shop – just look for the flag displaying the network's name.

Regional codes are given throughout the Guide: the "0" must be dialled before all long-distance calls. Some hotels have consecutively numbered phone lines – thus ☎021 221200–5 means that the last digit can be any number between 0 and 5.

Showers

Most hotels and guesthouses in Laos now claim to have hot-water showers – though in reality the water is often disappointingly cold. Traditional Lao showers, sometimes found in accommodation in rural areas, consist of a large, ceramic jar or a cement tub resembling an oversized bathtub without a drain. Standing next to the tub, you use the plastic scoop provided to sluice water over your body. While it may look tempting on a hot day, don't get into these tubs or try to use them for doing your laundry, as the water has to be used by others. In many towns villagers opt for an even more traditional technique – the river. Men usually bathe in their underwear, women in sarongs.

Tampons

Hard to find outside Vientiane and Luang Prabang's minimarkets, which have a very limited selection. Bring supplies.

PUBLIC HOLIDAYS

January 1 New Year's Day
January 6 Pathet Lao Day
January 20 Army Day
March 8 Women's Day
March 22 Lao People's Party Day
April 13–15 Lao New Year
May 1 International Labour Day
June 1 Children's Day
August 13 Lao Issara
August 23 Liberation Day
October 12 Freedom from France Day
December 2 National Day

Time zone

Ignoring daylight-saving time abroad, Laos is 7 hours ahead of London, 15 hours ahead of Vancouver, 12 hours ahead of New York, 3 hours behind Sydney and 5 hours behind Auckland.

Toilets

Squat toilets are the norm throughout Laos, although almost all hotels and guesthouses have Western-style porcelain thrones. Public toilets are not common in Laos, though you'll find them at airports and most bus stations; at the latter a small fee is usually collected. Not all toilets will have toilet paper, so it's worth carrying some with you. Most squat toilets require manual flushing – you'll find a bucket of water with a scoop floating on the surface for this purpose. In some small, rural villages people tend to take to the woods because of a lack of plumbing. On long road trips this is also a perfectly acceptable way to relieve yourself, though keep in mind that many parts of Laos have UXO (see p.46), so it's not wise to wade too far into the bush when the bus stops for a bathroom break.

Travellers with disabilities

For anyone with limited mobility, Laos is a difficult country to explore. Even in the big tourist cities of Luang Prabang and Vientiane, you will find uneven pavements, which lack ramps, and small sets of stairs leading into most restaurants and guesthouses. In smaller towns the situation is even worse – there are often no pavements and most of the roads are dirt tracks.

However, a handful of the newer hotels in Laos (especially in cities) have been built with some regard for disabled guests. The best places have ramps at the front of the building, lifts to all floors of the hotel, and wider doorways that at least allow wheelchair users to pass from one part of the building to another. That said, your chances of getting a room that's been specially adapted for a wheelchair user, complete with grab-rails and a roll-in shower, are close to zero.

Hotels that do make specific allowances for disabled guests include the *3 Nagas* in Luang Prabang (see p.123) and the *Lao Plaza* (see p.73) in Vientiane.

The best way to alleviate transport difficulties is to take internal flights and hire a private minibus with a driver. You should also consider hiring a local tour guide to accompany you on sightseeing trips – a Lao speaker can facilitate access to temples and museums. Flying an international carrier whose planes are suited to your needs is also helpful. Keep in mind that airline companies can cope better if they are expecting you, with a wheelchair provided at airports and staff primed to help.

When preparing for your trip, it's a good idea to pack spares of any clothing or equipment that might be hard to find. If you use a wheelchair, you should have it serviced before you go and carry a repair kit. If you do not use a wheelchair all the time but your walking capabilities are limited, remember that you are likely to need to cover greater distances while travelling (often over rougher terrain and in hotter temperatures) than you are used to.

The following organizations can provide general advice, though little by way of specific advice on the country itself.

USEFUL CONTACTS

UK AND IRELAND

Tourism For All Shap Road Industrial Estate, Shap Road, Kendal, Cumbria LA9 6NZ, ☎ 0845 124 9971, ⓦ tourismforall.org.uk. Provides general advice and information for disabled travellers.
Irish Wheelchair Association Blackheath Drive, Clontarf, Dublin 3 ☎ 018 186400, ⓦ iwa.ie. Useful information provided about travelling abroad with a wheelchair.

US AND CANADA

Access-Able ⓦ access-able.com. Outdated, but still a good online resource for travellers with disabilities.
Mobility International 451Broadway, Eugene, OR 97401, voice and TDD ☎ 541 343 1284, ⓦ miusa.org. Information and referral services, access guides, tours and exchange programmes.
Society for the Accessible Travel and Hospitality (SATH) 347 5th Ave, New York, NY 10016 ☎ 212 447 7284, ⓦ sath.org. Non-profit educational organization that has actively represented travellers with disabilities since 1976.

AUSTRALIA AND NEW ZEALAND

National Disability Services P33 Thesiger Court, Deakin, ACT, 2600 ☎ 02 6283 3200, ⓦ nds.org.au. Provides lists of travel agencies and tour operators for people with disabilities.
Disabled Persons Assembly 4/173–175 Victoria St, Wellington, New Zealand ☎ 048 019100, ⓦ dpa.org.nz. Resource centre with lists of travel agencies and tour operators for people with disabilities.

Vientiane and the northwest

VIENTIANE, OLD TOWN FACADES

1

Vientiane and the northwest

Hugging a wide bend in the Mekong river, Vientiane is more like a large town, dotted with a few grandiose monuments, than the engine room of a nation. However, in the twenty-odd years since Laos reopened its doors to foreign visitors, the city has changed with dizzying rapidity. At the beginning of the 1990s, Vientiane wallowed in an economic stupor brought about by a fifteen-year near-ban on free enterprise and a heavy reliance on Soviet aid. But with the collapse of the Soviet Union, economic restrictions were relaxed; soon afterwards, Vientiane's collection of billboards proclaiming the glories of socialism were outnumbered by advertisements for Pepsi, and the hammer and sickle that had been erected atop the abandoned French cultural centre was removed. Today, with foreign investment pouring in, the city is growing fast, and swish black SUVs easily outnumber tuk-tuks. Along with new shopping malls and luxurious high-rise developments, Vientiane has a thriving tourist economy, and some excellent places to stay. Even so, it remains one of Southeast Asia's quietest and most easily navigable capital cities, and the people have managed to retain their hospitality and sense of humour.

Two days is enough to see Vientiane's main sights, but it pays to stick around longer, and there's plenty to see in the surrounding area. The most popular **day-trip** is to Xieng Khuan, or the "**Buddha Park**", a meadow that's home to more than two hundred concrete Buddhist and Hindu statues, including a 40m-long reclining Buddha. North of Vientiane, the **Ang Nam Ngum Reservoir** attracts locals and foreign visitors alike for relaxing weekend retreats, offering hiking and camping and boat trips to small, half-sunk islands. Off the beaten track and a bit more of an effort to reach is the resort of **Ban Pako**, on the banks of the Nam Ngum River, which offers a rural Lao experience within relatively easy distance of the capital.

Slightly further afield, but still within day-tripping range of Vientiane, is **Vang Vieng,** the small riverside town synonymous with tubing and once notorious for its wild parties. Following a major government crackdown, however, that led to the closure of riverside bars, much of the associated bad behaviour has gone, and although tubing and partying remain a major attraction, the town is now forging a new future as an adventure destination. Set amid spectacular scenery on Route 13, Vang Vieng provides the perfect environment for hiking, kayaking, climbing and caving, and is also a convenient stopover on the spectacularly mountainous ten-hour bus journey from Vientiane to Luang Prabang. An alternative route to Luang Prabang involves travelling

WAT SISAKET

Highlights

❶ Lao National Museum Learn about the heroes of Laos's class struggle as you walk the halls of this crumbling treasure-trove. **See p.64**

❷ Wat Sisaket Vientiane's oldest wat, the only temple spared by the invading Siamese in their 1828 sack of the city. **See p.64**

❸ That Luang Laos's most important religious site, the golden stupa is also the national symbol. **See p.67**

❹ Xieng Khuan The highlight of Vientiane's most popular day-trip destination is a stunningly huge reclining Buddha. **See p.80**

❺ Ang Nam Ngum Reservoir There's fishing, boating and island-hopping in this vast lake north of Vientiane. **See p.84**

❻ Vang Vieng Party in Laos's backpacker capital, or save your strength for caving, mountain biking, rafting and rock climbing in the surrounding countryside. **See p.85**

❼ Elephants Learn about the plight of Sayaboury's most famous creatures at the Elephant Conservation Centre. **See p.97**

HIGHLIGHTS ARE MARKED ON THE MAP ON P.58 & PP.60–61

1

the winding roads of **Sayaboury,** a remote left-bank province famed for its sizeable population of elephants.

Vientiane

High on the list of any visit to **VIENTIANE** should be **Wat Sisaket**, a picturesque Buddhist monastery containing what is thought to be the oldest structure in Vientiane. **Wat Simuang**, however, is the most popular temple with worshippers; it's said the guardian spirit of Vientiane inhabits the sacred stone pillar here. Another top attraction is **That Luang**, Laos's most important religious building, best viewed at sundown when its golden surface glows like a lamp. Aside from temples and stupas, the **museum of Lao art**, housed in the former royal temple of **Haw Pha Kaew**, and the socialist-era **Lao National Museum** are also worth a visit.

As with other urban centres in the region, the majority of Vientiane's merchant class are ethnic Chinese and Vietnamese, whose forefathers emigrated to Laos during the French era. Foreign expatriate workers comprise a significant percentage of the capital's population, which adds a **cosmopolitan** touch to the place and has given rise to a wide choice of places to eat.

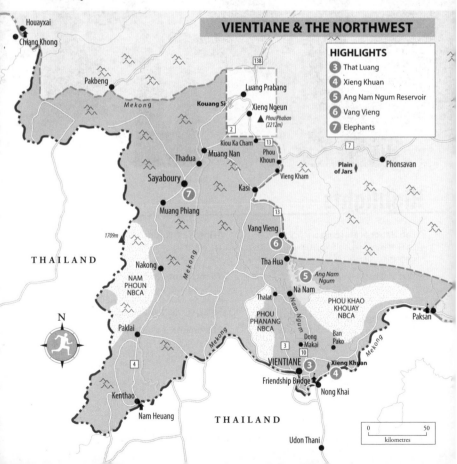

VIENTIANE & THE NORTHWEST

HIGHLIGHTS

3 That Luang
4 Xieng Khuan
5 Ang Nam Ngum Reservoir
6 Vang Vieng
7 Elephants

VIENTIANE ORIENTATION

Three main streets run parallel to the river to form the backbone of the old city centre, cutting across narrower side streets to form an easily deciphered grid. Shaded by tall trees, **Setthathilat Road** is the city's most scenic thoroughfare, particularly the west end with its four monasteries. Along this road and in the immediate area around Nam Phou (see p.64), you'll find the city's greatest concentration of accommodation, restaurants and shops catering to visitors. Further north is **Samsenthai Road**, Vientiane's principal commercial district and site of the imposing *Lao National Cultural Hall* as well as the Lao National Museum, an anachronistic hangover from the days of banner-hoisting socialism. Restaurant-lined **Fa Ngum Road** once ran beside the Mekong but is now separated from it by **Chao Anouvong Park**, built on land recently reclaimed from the river, and further south still, a busy bypass.

Fa Ngum Road roughly follows the course of the river as it bends southeast and skirts behind the Presidential Palace. The palace is off-limits to visitors, but the **Haw Pha Kaew**, which occupies the western corner of the palace compound, has been converted into a museum, housing the largest collection of Lao art and antiquities in the country.

The eastern edge of the city centre is defined by Vientiane's principal thoroughfare and the heart of today's commercial boom, **Lane Xang Avenue**, which begins at the Presidential Palace and marches away from the river past the two **Talat Sao (Morning Market) Malls**. The broad avenue terminates at **Patouxai**, a massive victory arch, around which are scattered numerous embassies, international organizations and government buildings. Just beyond the Patouxai monument, the road forks, its right branch leading off towards **That Luang**, the golden-spired Buddhist stupa and national symbol of Laos.

Brief history

Vientiane's history has been turbulent, as its meagre collection of old buildings suggests. An old settlement, possibly dating back to the eighth century, Vientiane was occupied and subsequently abandoned by the Mon and then the Khmer long before the Lao king Setthathilat moved his **capital** here from Luang Prabang in 1560. Vientiane is actually pronounced "Wiang Jan" (the modern Romanized spelling is a French transliteration), *wiang* being Lao for a "settlement with a stockade", while *jan* means "sandalwood". The wooden ramparts of the "City of Sandalwood" were evidently no match for invaders, for Vientiane was overrun or occupied several times by the Burmese, Chinese and, most spectacularly, the **Siamese**. During one punitive raid in 1828, the Siamese levelled the entire city. For the next four decades, Vientiane was almost completely abandoned.

French arrival

When **French explorers** arrived in 1867, they found the city all but reclaimed by the jungle. Within a few decades, the French controlled most of what is now Laos, Cambodia and Vietnam. When Vientiane was chosen by the French to be the capital of an administrative division of French Indochina, they rebuilt the city and laid out its system of roads. It is from this period, roughly 1899 to 1945, that the city's crumbling collection of French colonial mansions dates.

The end of the First Indochina War between France and Vietnam in 1954 saw a flood of **Vietnamese refugees** enter Vientiane from Ho Chi Minh's newly independent Democratic Republic of Vietnam. As North Vietnamese troops began to infiltrate into South Vietnam while simultaneously occupying large areas of northeastern Laos, the US started pouring massive amounts of unregulated aid into Vientiane, causing widespread corruption among government and military officials. In August 1960, a disgruntled army captain, who resented the vast difference in lifestyles between his high-living superiors and his hard-bitten troops, staged a successful **coup d'état**. Four months later, during the Battle of Vientiane, two Lao factions (one supplied by the US and the other by the USSR) managed to level whole blocks of the city with mortars and artillery.

1

The Vietnam War

As the **war in Vietnam** steadily escalated with growing US involvement, Laos was pulled deeper into the conflict, but for most of the war, Vientiane was like an island of calm surrounded by violent seas. A steady influx of refugees arrived from the outer provinces, the population of the capital swelled, and rows of squatters' shanties appeared along the tree-lined avenues, contrasting sharply with the Mercedes-Benz automobiles of wartime profiteers.

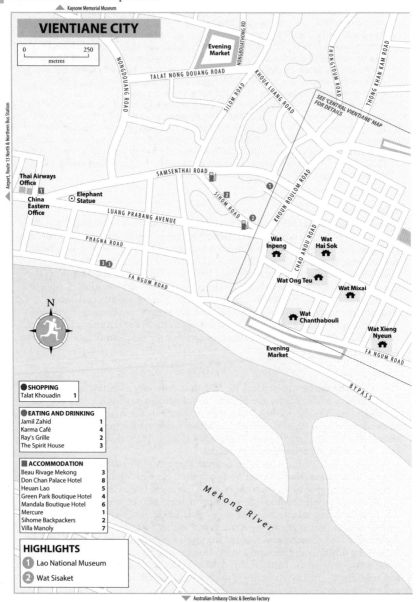

VIENTIANE CITY

0 — 250 metres

▲ Kaysone Memorial Museum

Thai Airways Office

China Eastern Office

Elephant Statue

◀ Airport, Route 13 North & Northern Bus Station

Evening Market

NONGBOUATHONG RD

THONGTOUM ROAD

THONG KHAN KAM ROAD

TALAT NONG DOUANG ROAD

NONGDOUANG ROAD

SILOM ROAD

KHOUA LUANG ROAD

SEE 'CENTRAL VIENTIANE' MAP FOR DETAILS

SAMSENTHAI ROAD

SIHOM ROAD

LUANG PRABANG AVENUE

KHOUN BOULOM ROAD

CHAO ANOU ROAD

PHAGNA ROAD

FA NGUM ROAD

Wat Inpeng

Wat Hai Sok

Wat Ong Teu

Wat Mixai

Wat Chanthabouli

Wat Xieng Nyeun

FA NGUM ROAD

Evening Market

BYPASS

N

Mekong River

● SHOPPING

Talat Khouadin	1

● EATING AND DRINKING

Jamil Zahid	1
Karma Café	4
Ray's Grille	2
The Spirit House	3

■ ACCOMMODATION

Beau Rivage Mekong	3
Don Chan Palace Hotel	8
Heuan Lao	5
Green Park Boutique Hotel	4
Mandala Boutique Hotel	6
Mercure	1
Sihome Backpackers	2
Villa Manoly	7

HIGHLIGHTS

① Lao National Museum

② Wat Sisaket

▼ Australian Embassy Clinic & Beerlao Factory

After the fall of Saigon in 1975, the **Lao communists** suddenly gained power and, with coaching from the Vietnamese, set out to create the Lao People's Democratic Republic. Thieves, prostitutes and other undesirables were rounded up and held captive on two small islands in the nearby Ang Nam Ngum Reservoir and, although revolutionary fervour never reached the extremes seen in China or Cambodia, many in Vientiane found it necessary to escape across the Mekong. These were replaced by immigrants from the former "liberated zone" in northeastern Laos, further changing Vientiane's ethnic make-up.

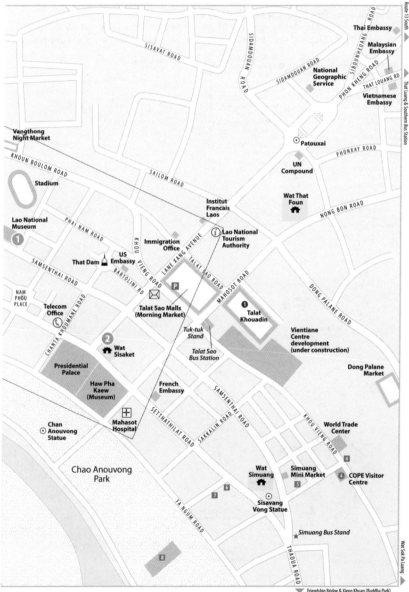

1

Socialism and capitalism

The 1980s were a time of quiet stagnation. Soviet aid eased the transition to **socialism**, but the majority of Lao with any education were in some form of exile, either attending "re-education camps" or squatting in Thai refugee camps, awaiting resettlement in a third country. Grand plans for progress were announced by the communist government and then promptly forgotten. Not until the collapse of the Soviet Union in 1991 and the suspension of Soviet aid was the government forced to rethink its opinions of capitalism. A number of **economic reforms** were implemented, leading to an explosion of new ventures and businesses.

In 1994, the first bridge to span the Mekong river between Laos and Thailand was completed. Dubbed the "**Friendship Bridge**", it marked a new era of cooperation

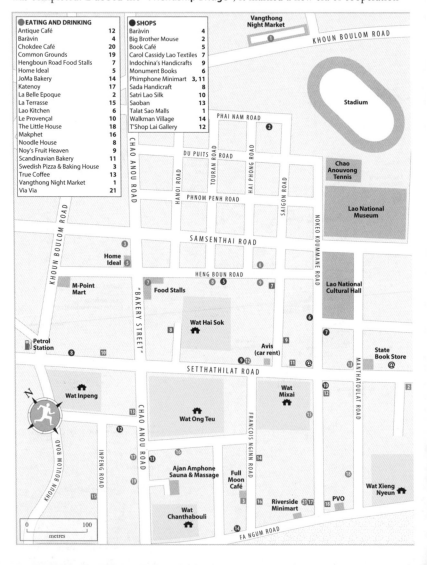

● EATING AND DRINKING	
Antique Café	12
Baràvin	4
Chokdee Café	20
Common Grounds	19
Hengboun Road Food Stalls	7
Home Ideal	5
JoMa Bakery	14
Katenoy	17
La Belle Epoque	2
La Terrasse	15
Lao Kitchen	6
Le Provençal	10
The Little House	18
Makphet	16
Noodle House	8
Noy's Fruit Heaven	9
Scandinavian Bakery	11
Swedish Pizza & Baking House	3
True Coffee	13
Vangthong Night Market	1
Via Via	21

● SHOPS	
Baràvin	4
Big Brother Mouse	2
Book Café	5
Carol Cassidy Lao Textiles	7
Indochina's Handicrafts	9
Monument Books	6
Phimphone Minimart	3, 11
Sada Handicraft	8
Satri Lao Silk	10
Saoban	13
Talat Sao Malls	1
Walkman Village	14
T'Shop Lai Gallery	12

1

between the former enemies. Thai entrepreneurs were soon arriving in Vientiane to search for economic potential. French colonial mansions were restored for use as offices, and scores of venerable old trees were cut down in road-widening projects to accommodate the ever-multiplying number of cars and motorbikes.

In 2009, Vientiane hosted the 25th Southeast Asian Games, attracting more foreign investment and renewing debate about the city's rampant development. Vast new banks and hotels have since opened across the city, particularly on Lane Xang Avenue. With a sky-scraping, Chinese-funded entertainment complex now planned for the area east of Chao Anouvong Park, the changes – both good and bad – look set to keep on coming.

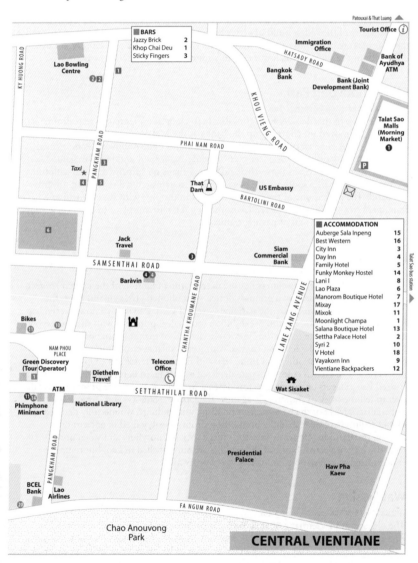

CENTRAL VIENTIANE

1

Nam Phou

With a few exceptions, most of Vientiane's sights are within comfortable walking distance of **Nam Phou Place**. The city's most obvious meeting point, Nam Phou was once the centre of a roundabout, but the renovation of the fountain and the blocking off of half the roundabout created a pleasant public space where locals and visitors could congregate and cool off after sunset. However, recent building sprees have left the square feeling crowded, with new restaurants and bars hastily erected around the fountain itself. The best places to eat here (see p.74) are the older ones, established on the outer edge of the roundabout long before the recent flurry of construction.

The district surrounding the fountain, also known as **Nam Phou**, is the city's oldest. Although the roads and grid system of the district were devised by the French, most of the buildings were constructed during the free-wheeling days of American aid in the 1950s. Many of the oldest buildings have been remodelled in the last decade or so, and their facades are plain and uninteresting; an exception is the **National Library**, located due south of the square, which was carefully restored with Australian assistance.

Chao Anouvong Park

Between Fa Ngum Rd and the Mekong river • Free

Until the start of this decade, Fa Ngum Road ran alongside Vientiane's waterfront. Then diggers moved in, churning up the banks of the Mekong to create new space for development. A large tract of this land was turned into **Chao Anouvong Park**, named after the last king of Lane Xang (see p.266), who fought for – and failed to gain – independence from Siam (now Thailand). It's perhaps no surprise that the sculpture of Anou, on the park's southeastern edge, appears to gaze across the Mekong towards Thailand. The park is one of the few green spaces in the city, with sweet-smelling frangipani trees and neatly ordered lawns making it a pleasant place to unwind, as long as you don't mind the roar of passing traffic.

Lao National Museum

Samsenthai Rd • Daily except public holidays 8am–noon & 1–4pm • 10,000K

The dusty **Lao National Museum** is housed in the former mansion of the French *résident supérieur* and set in overgrown grounds dotted with plumeria (frangipani) trees, the delicate blossoms of which are the national flower of Laos. Previously known as the Lao Revolutionary Museum, the dingy exhibition rooms deal primarily with the events, both ancient and recent, that led to the "inevitable victory" of the proletariat in 1975. Inside, Laos's past is crudely depicted on canvas, with scenes such as crimson-clad Lao patriots of yore liberating the motherland from Thai and Burmese "feudalists". Upstairs there are more crude oils: French colonialists are depicted as hair-faced ogres bullwhipping tightly trussed Lao villagers or tossing Lao tots down a well. Black-and-white **photographs** take over to tell the story of the struggle against "the Japanese fascists" and "American imperialists". Most of the best artefacts on display, including a wonderfully detailed **Khmer sculpture of Ganesh** and a bronze frog-drum, possibly used in ancient rain-making rituals, didn't fit neatly into the official socialist storyline, and were, until recently, very neglected. Some of the exhibits are only labelled in Lao, but there are enough English translations to make a visit worthwhile.

Wat Sisaket

Setthathilat Rd • Daily 8am–noon & 1–4pm • 5000K

The oldest wat in Vientiane, **Wat Sisaket** was constructed by King Anouvong (Chao Anou) in 1818, and was the site of a ceremony in which Lao lords and nobles swore an oath of loyalty to the king. During the 1828 sack of Vientiane by the Siamese, this was

WAT IS THAT?

The **wat**, or Buddhist **monastery**, is the centrepiece of most villages populated by ethnic Lao. A contingent of monks and novices lives in each wat, providing the laypeople with an outlet for **merit-making** (see p.283). The wat also serves as a hub for social gatherings and, during annual festivals and Buddhist holy days, a venue for entertainment.

Sometimes referred to as a "temple" in English, a wat is actually composed of a number of religious and secular structures, some of which could also be described as a temple. The *sim* is usually the grandest structure in the monastery grounds, as it houses the monastery's principal Buddha images, as well as being the place where monks are ordained. The *that*, or **stupa**, is generally a pyramid or bell-shaped structure which contains holy relics, usually a cache of small Buddhas. Occasionally, a *that* will be the reputed repository of a splinter of bone belonging to the historic Buddha himself, while miniature stupas, or *that kaduk*, contain the ashes of deceased adherents. The *haw tai* is a solid structure, usually raised high off the ground, for storing palm-leaf manuscripts, and *kuti* are monks' quarters. Because the latter two buildings are not considered as important as other religious structures in the monastery grounds, and are thus most likely to exude that "timeless Asia" charm. Minor buildings sometimes found at a wat include a bell tower and a **sala**, or open-air pavilion. Many monasteries also have a venerable specimen of a bodhi (*Ficus religiosa*), a wonderfully shady tree of spade-shaped leaves that is said to have sheltered the Buddha while he meditated his way to enlightenment.

Because the wat and resident monks depend on adherents for support, the extravagance of a monastery's **decoration** is directly related to the amount of cash flow in the host village or town. In poor villages, the wat may consist of just a *sim*, which will be a large but simple hut-like structure, raised on stilts without any ornamentation. The only clue to the outsider that this is a monastery will be the freshly laundered monks' robes hanging out to dry alongside a piece of junk metal or war scrap, such as an old artillery-shell casing, which when struck serves as a bell to wake the monks or call them to assemble.

the only monastery not put to the torch and, once the smoke had cleared, the Siamese brought the surviving Lao nobility here and made them swear another oath of loyalty, this time to their new overlords. Later, in 1893, the whole ceremony was repeated again at this very same wat before new masters – the French.

Surrounded by a tile-roofed cloister, the *sim* contains some charming **murals** similar in style to those found at Bangkok's Wat Phra Kaew. The murals, together with the niches in the upper walls containing small Buddha images, and the ornate ceiling, are best taken in while kneeling on the floor (taking care not to point your feet towards the altar). The Buddha images on the altar are not particularly notable, but a splendidly ornate *hao thian*, or candle holder, of carved wood situated before the altar is an example of nineteenth-century Lao woodcarving at its best.

Outside, the interior walls of the **cloister** echo those of the *sim*, with countless niches from which peer diminutive Buddhas in twos and threes. Lining the galleries are larger images that survived the destruction of 1828 and, in a locker at the western wall, a heap of Buddhas that did not. The shaded galleries are a cool and pleasant place to linger and soak up the atmosphere. Breaching the wall that runs along Lane Xang Avenue, the structure with the multi-tiered roof is the monastery's former **library** (closed to the public), where its palm-leaf manuscripts were once kept.

Haw Pha Kaew

Setthathilat Rd • Daily 8am–noon & 1–4pm • 5000K

Haw Pha Kaew was once the king's personal Buddhist temple, but now functions as a **museum of art and antiquities**. Said to date from the mid-sixteenth century, the structure was destroyed by marauding Siamese during the sack of Vientiane in 1828 and was later earmarked for restoration by the French. The temple is named for the

1

Emerald Buddha, or Pha Kaew, which, along with the Pha Bang (see box, p.111), the most sacred Buddha image in Laos, was pilfered by the Siamese in 1779 and carried off to their capital. The Pha Bang was eventually returned to Laos and is enshrined in its namesake city of Luang Prabang, but the Pha Kaew remains in Bangkok to this day, much to the resentment of Lao Buddhists.

The museum houses the finest collection of Lao art in the country. **Bronze Buddhas,** many looted of the inlay that once decorated their eyes, line the terrace surrounding the building. Inside are some exquisite works, one of the most striking being a Buddha in the "Beckoning Rain" pose (standing with arms to the sides and fingers pointing to the ground) and sporting a jewel-encrusted navel. Also of note are a pair of eighteenth-century terracotta *apsara*, or celestial dancers, and a highly detailed "naga throne" from Xieng Khuang that once served as a pedestal for a Buddha image. Next to the throne stands an elaborate candleholder of ornately carved wood and almost identical to one still in use at Wat Sisaket. An arched metal rod attached to the wood is where the lighted candles were placed.

Outsized bronze **statues** of a kowtowing Lao boy and girl on the lawn outside the museum were once part of a tableau that included the statue of explorer Auguste Pavie. The Frenchman's statue is now located inside the French embassy compound across the street. Sheltered under an adjacent pavilion is a sample stone urn from the Plain of Jars, but this small, broken jar is a rather poor specimen and not really typical of those at the site.

Presidential Palace

Just west of Haw Pha Kaew along Setthathilat Road is the **Presidential Palace,** a rather unimpressive French Beaux Arts-style structure, built to house the French colonial governor, and nowadays used mainly for government ceremonies. Tourists aren't allowed inside, but plenty stop for photos outside the gate.

Wat Simuang

Roughly 500m southeast of Haw Pha Kaew, down Setthathilat Rd • Daily sunrise–sunset • Free

While Vientiane has its share of Buddhist monasteries, **Wat Simuang** stands out in terms of the number of worshippers it receives. Numerous pavement stalls stationed outside the walls give some indication of its popularity and sell all the ingredients for a proper tray of offerings (flowers, fruit, incense and candles). The monastery itself was built on an ancient Khmer site, the ruins of which are piled behind the *sim* and consist of laterite bricks with traces of stucco ornamentation.

The sim

The *sim* of Wat Simuang houses the city's *lak meaung*, a sacred stone pillar. It is believed that the guardian spirit of Vientiane inhabits the pillar, which was consecrated with a human sacrifice at the time of the city's founding. Covered with gold leaf and wrapped in sacred cloth, the pillar is the centrepiece of an altar crowded with Buddha images. That great multitudes of worshippers come here is evident from a glance at the ceiling, coal-black with a thick coating of soot, which is constantly rising from sputtering candles and smouldering joss sticks.

By quietly taking a seat on the floor you can observe the **rituals** of devotees seeking answers or favours. Two baby-sized, crude images resting on their own pillows are the main focus of the worshippers' attention. After a question is posed or a favour requested, the devotee attempts to lift one of the images while kneeling towards the altar. Being able to lift the image three times over one's head is considered an auspicious sign. Worshippers whose wishes are granted must return and appease the guardian spirit with an offering; marigolds, coconuts and bananas are particularly popular tokens of gratitude.

The grounds and around

The **monastery grounds** surrounding the *sim* contain a dozen or so brightly painted sculptures of animals, Buddhist–Hindu deities and mythological figures from Lao legends, making this a favourite playground for local kids.

On a small wedge of land outside the south wall of the monastery towers a monolithic **statue of King Sisavang Vong**, who reigned from 1904 to 1959. The statue survived the revolution, having been executed by a Soviet sculptor and presented to the Lao government in 1972 after a visit to the Soviet Union by King Sisavang Vatthana. Ironically, within a few short years of the statue being erected in 1974, the royalist government collapsed, and the newly installed communist government banished King Sisavang Vatthana and his family to a cave near the Vietnamese border, where they all perished. A plaque that was once attached to the pedestal has long been missing and, if asked, many locals will only be able to say that the massive statue depicts "an old king".

Patouxai

At the northern end of Lane Xang Ave • Daily 8am–4.30pm • 3000K

It has been said that, along with coffee and baguettes, the Lao inherited a taste for pompous town planning from the French. **Lane Xang Avenue**, leading off north from Setthathilat Road, was to be Vientiane's Champs Elysées and **Patouxai**, 1km from the Presidential Palace, its Arc de Triomphe. While it would be impossible to mistake Lane Xang Avenue for Paris's most famous thoroughfare, if you were to stand at a fair distance and squint, you might be able to convince yourself that Patouxai resembles its Parisian inspiration.

Popularly known as *anusawali* (Lao for "monument"), this massive reinforced concrete monument was built in the late 1950s to commemorate casualties of war on the side of the Royal Lao government. The structure, said to have been completed with concrete donated by the US government for the construction of an airport, has been jokingly referred to as "the vertical runway". If the story is true, then Patouxai is also the most notable structure left to show for the millions of dollars of aid that were pumped into Laos during the early years of American involvement in Indochina. After the revolution, the arch was given its current name, which literally means "Victory Gate", and partially redecorated – some Hindu iconography symbolic of the defunct Lao monarchy was chipped away so the communists could feel more comfortable with this behemoth reminder of the detested royalists in their midst.

Patouxai is best visited in the early morning before the structure has had time to absorb much heat from the sun's rays. A handful of vendors selling souvenirs and refreshments are sheltered by a ceiling adorned with **reliefs** of the Hindu deities – Rahu devouring the sun, Vishnu, Brahma, and Indra on Airavata, the three-headed elephant. Decorating the walls just below the ceiling are characters from the Ramayana. Up close, the structure looks somewhat crude and unfinished, but the **view** of Vientiane from the top is worth the climb. Halfway up, in a poorly lit two-storey hallway, there's a market selling textiles, T-shirts and tourist trinkets.

That Luang

Around 4km northeast of Nam Phou, off Nongbone Rd • Daily except public holidays 8am–noon & 1–4pm • 5000K • To reach the stupa from the centre, flag down a sawngthaew heading north along Lane Xang Ave or That Luang Rd (expect to pay 5000K per person)

Depicted on everything from banknotes to buildings, the Buddhist stupa **That Luang** is the most important religious building in Laos, and the country's national symbol. The present building dates from the 1930s and is a reconstruction; the original That Luang is thought to have been built by King Setthathilat in the mid-sixteenth century, and it is his statue that is perched jauntily on a pedestal in front of the stupa.

1

THAT LUANG FESTIVAL

In the days leading up to the full moon in November, the great That Luang stupa in Vientiane comes to resemble the centrepiece of a fairground, with street vendors setting up booths in the open spaces around it. The week-long **That Luang Festival** then kicks off with a mass alms-giving to hundreds of monks and a procession from Wat Simuang to That Luang. Over the next few days, bands and performances occupy a stage near the stupa, and tikhi, a game resembling field hockey, is played. On the last evening, the whole city shows up to process with offerings around That Luang.

Archeological evidence suggests that, like most central and southern Lao Buddhist structures of significance, That Luang was built on top of an ancient Khmer site. What the original Buddhist stupa looked like is a mystery, but a Dutch trader, Gerritt van Wuysthoff, who visited Vientiane in 1641, left an awestruck account of the gold-covered "pyramid" he saw there. Between then and the early nineteenth century, the stupa was embellished and restored periodically, but this ceased after the 1828 Siamese raid which left the capital deserted. When French explorers Francis Garnier and Louis Delaporte stumbled upon That Luang in 1867, it was overgrown by jungle, but still largely intact. A few years later, Chinese-led bandits plundered the stupa looking for gold, and left it a pile of rubble. A photo on display in the National Museum, taken in the late 1800s to commemorate the visit of a group of Frenchmen, gives some indication of the extent of the devastation.

A French attempt at **restoration** was made in 1900, after which the stupa was disparagingly referred to as the "Morin Spike", a snipe at the architect, whose idea of a Buddhist stupa resembled a railroad spike turned on its head. Dissatisfaction with the design eventually led to another attempt in the 1930s. Using sketches done by Delaporte as a model, a re-restoration in brick and stucco was carried out over four years, and what you see today are the results of this effort.

The stupas and cloisters

The tapering **golden spire** of the main stupa is 45m tall and rests on a plinth of stylized lotus petals, which crowns a mound reminiscent of the first-century BC Buddhist stupa at Sanchi, India. The main stupa is surrounded on all sides by a total of thirty short, spiky stupas, which can be reached via any of four gates in the crenellated walls that support the monument. The whole is in turn surrounded by a cloistered wall, vaguely Chinese in style. Within the **cloisters** is a collection of very worn Buddha images, some of which may have been enshrined in the original Khmer temple that once occupied the site. Until recently, only the stupas' spires were "gilded", but with the passing years, more and more gold paint has been applied, so that now even the inner walls and their crenellations are gold. The effect is best seen just before sunset or during the evenings leading up to the **That Luang Festival** (see box above), when the stupa is festooned with strings of lights, and moths the size of sparrows circle and cling to its glowing surface.

COPE Visitor Centre

Khou Vieng Rd, around 1km east of the Talat Sao bus station and roughly opposite *Green Park Boutique Hotel* • ⓦ copelaos.org • Daily 9am–6pm • Free, though donations are appreciated

COPE is a non-profit organization founded primarily to help those whose lives have been affected by unexploded ordnance (UXO; see p.46). You can learn about the organization's work and the continuing challenges faced by Lao UXO victims at this excellent, free-to-visit information centre just east of the city centre. The main exhibition, housed in an old store room, starts by describing how America's secret bombing campaigns during the Vietnam War left Laos littered with unexploded

OPPOSITE THAT LUANG (P.67) >

"bombies". Between 1964 and 1973, more than two million tons of ordnance were dropped on Laos. Around thirty percent of the cluster munitions dropped failed to explode and even today, 25 percent of Lao villages are contaminated by UXO. The tragic result is that since the end of the war, at least 20,000 people have been killed or maimed. Some of those affected tell their stories on TV screens around the exhibition, and bombs hanging from the ceiling give some sense of the scale of the problem. But the centre isn't only about looking back; here you can find out how prosthetic limbs and rehabilitation programmes are giving victims another chance at life, and see how those advances are helping other people too, including those injured in motorbike accidents. The centre also runs a café.

Wat Sok Pa Luang

3km southeast of central Vientiane • Daily sunrise–sunset • Free • The easiest way to get here is by tuk-tuk (20,000K), though if you don't mind braving busy roads, it's also possible to cycle from the centre in around 20min

Originally outside the city limits and surrounded by forest, **Wat Sok Pa Luang** lies in a suburb that spreads out from the highway south to the village of Thadua. The temple is known locally for its herbal saunas, though at the time of writing the saunas were being rebuilt following a major fire. Progress is slow, which means that for now at least, wandering through the shady temple grounds is a peaceful (and mostly tourist-free) experience.

ARRIVAL AND DEPARTURE   VIENTIANE

However you arrive, there's no need to panic if you don't have Lao kip for your trip into town, as taxi drivers will happily accept Thai baht or American dollars.

BY PLANE
Wattay International Airport Vientiane's main airport, and the terminus for most internal flights, is located on Luang Prabang Avenue, roughly 6km west of downtown. Here you can get a thirty-day visa on arrival, and there is a wide range of facilities inside the building, including an ATM, restaurant, duty-free shop and a desk for exchanging currency. Lao Airlines operates several domestic flights out of Vientiane, as well as services to Bangkok and Chiang Mai, Hanoi and Ho Chi Minh City, Seoul, Kunming, Singapore, plus Phnom Penh and Siem Reap.
Airlines Lao Airlines, Pangkham Rd ☎ 021 212057, or at the airport ☎ 021 512028; Lao Skyway, Asean Rd ☎ 021 513022; Thai Airways, Luang Prabang Ave ☎ 021 222527; Vietnam Airlines, Samsenthai Rd, mezzanine floor of the *Lao Plaza Hotel* ☎ 021 217562. The Bangkok Airways office (☎ 021 242557) is also in the *Lao Plaza Hotel*.
Destinations Houayxai (1–2 daily; 55min); Luang Namtha (1 daily; 55min); Luang Prabang (2–4 daily; 50min); Oudomxai (1–2 daily; 50min); Pakse (2 daily; 1hr 15min); Phongsali (2 weekly; 1hr 40min); Phonsavan/Xieng Khuang (1 daily; 30min); Sam Neua (4 weekly; 1hr 30min); Savannakhet (1–3 daily; 55min); Sayaboury (2 weekly; 50min).

GETTING INTO THE CITY
By taxi The easiest way to get to the city centre is by taxi ($7 for a car; $8 for a minivan) – the official booking desk is straight ahead as you emerge from immigration. Prices are

fixed, but if you're travelling alone, try teaming up with other travellers. The staff at the desk should be able to provide you with a map of Vientiane.
By tuk-tuk or jumbo Taking a tuk-tuk or jumbo from across the street (they're not allowed to pick up from the terminal) can be a little cheaper, but you'll need to haggle to save any real cash.
By sawngthaew If money is really tight, just walk a few hundred metres from the terminal out to Luang Prabang Avenue, and hail an eastbound sawngthaew (10,000K). These usually stop at the Talat Sao bus station, but will drop you off anywhere along the route if requested.

TO AND FROM THAILAND VIA THE FRIENDSHIP BRIDGE
The vast majority of tourists entering and leaving Laos use the original Thai–Lao Friendship Bridge (daily 6am–10pm). Completed in 1994, the 1240m-long bridge spans the Mekong river at a point 5km west of Nong Khai in Thailand, and 20km east of Vientiane.

ENTERING LAOS
By bus Buses (15 baht) shuttle passengers across the bridge, leaving every 15–20min. The buses start beyond Thai immigration control at the base of the bridge. You will need to clear Thai customs before boarding the bus and continuing on to Lao immigration on the opposite side of the river, where a thirty-day visa on arrival is available. An "overtime

fee" of $1 may be charged if you cross at the weekend or after 4.30pm. Vehicles may cross the bridge for a fee, but you should have the registration papers with you. On both sides of the bridge you'll find exchange booths and ATMs.

By train It's possible to cross into Laos using the local train that connects Nong Khai in Thailand with Tha Naleng Station, 20km east of downtown Vientiane. Talks of extending the track to allow trains to travel into the city itself have come to nothing, so you'll need to take a tuk-tuk into town; you could join up with other travellers to keep the price low.

Visas Visas on arrival are available at immigration booths on the Lao side. Tuk-tuk drivers on the Lao side seem to charge over the odds, asking for around 100,000K for the run into town. Much cheaper are the public buses (6000K per person), which stop nearby. Just walk past the tuk-tuk drivers and head towards the food stalls on the right-hand side. The #14 bus departs from here when full, taking around thirty minutes to reach Talat Sao bus station, close to the centre of town.

LEAVING LAOS

By bus Bus #14 departs for the Friendship Bridge every 15min from the Talat Sao bus station (6000K). At the bridge, you'll need to pick up a RFID card from the "PayPass" booth (free for pedestrians) before getting stamped out of the country. Use the card to get through the barrier on the other side, and then pay for the shuttle bus to the Thai side (4000K), where visas on arrival are available.

Direct buses from Vientiane to the Thai cities of Nong Khai (6 daily) and Udon Thani (8 daily) are mostly used by Lao and Vientiane-based expats, but they are also a convenient way to get over the Friendship Bridge without having to change vehicles. Buses leave daily for both destinations (roughly every 2hr between 7.30am and 6pm) from Talat Sao bus station. From Nong Khai, overnight buses and trains to Bangkok leave between 6pm and 8pm.

By taxi and tuk-tuk If you're in a hurry, a simpler (and more expensive) alternative to the bus is to charter a tuk-tuk ($10) or taxi (140,000K).

By train Overnight trains to Bangkok leave at 6.20pm from Nong Khai, Thailand. The most convenient option is to take the daily 5pm train directly to Nong Khai from Tha Naleng (20–30 baht), near the Friendship Bridge, though it's recommended that you buy your ticket in advance (most guesthouses can help). Another option is to take the bus to the Friendship Bridge and cross using the public bus (see below); once on the Thai side, hire a share taxi to the train station (20 baht). A number of tour agencies and guesthouses in Vientiane offer train tickets, which include transport across the border to the train station.

BY BUS

In addition to public buses and local sawngthaews, which depart from stations across town, there are countless "VIP"

services running from Vientiane to popular destinations such as Luang Prabang, Vang Vieng and Phonsavan. These tourist services can be booked through most downtown guesthouses and hostels, which also offer sleeper services to destinations in Vietnam, Cambodia, Thailand and China.

Central Bus Station (Talat Sao) Public buses to destinations around Vientiane use the compact main bus station, next to the Morning Market (Talat Sao Malls) on Khou Vieng Road, about 1500m from Nam Phou fountain. From here, it's only a short tuk-tuk ride to all the central hotels and guesthouses.

Destinations Buddha Park (every 15min; 40min); Friendship Bridge (every 15min; 30min); Kasi (1 daily; 6hr); Thalat (hourly; 2hr); Vang Vieng (7 daily; 4hr).

Southern Bus Station Buses to and from the south tend to use the southern bus station, about 9km northeast of the centre on Route 13; when leaving, it's a good idea to book tickets a day ahead with your guesthouse – though you'll pay a small premium for the convenience. Daily buses for Hanoi leave from the southern bus station at 7pm, and should arrive 24 hours later; expect to pay around 230,000K for the long, uncomfortable journey. There are also daily buses to Vinh, Hue and Da Nang at the same time, but buses to Ho Chi Minh City only run on Mondays, Thursdays and Saturdays; departure times change frequently, so check before you travel.

From the southern bus station, a shared tuk-tuk into town costs 20,000K per person, and drivers will usually drop you right outside your guesthouse.

Destinations Attapeu (3 daily; 16hr); Don Khong, Si Phan Don (1 daily; 17hr); Paksan (every 30min; 1–2hr); Pakse (15 daily; 8–13hr); Phonsavan (4 daily; 8–10hr); Savannakhet (9 daily; 8hr); Thakhek (5 daily; 5hr); Xekong (1 daily; 15hr).

Northern Bus Station Most buses to and from towns in the north and northeast (such as Luang Prabang, Phonsavan and Sam Neua) use the northern bus station, around 9km northwest of the city close to the junction with Route 13. Note that depending on your final destination, you may have to go first to Luang Prabang and find buses onward from Luang Prabang's northern bus station. Shared tuk-tuks from the northern bus station to the centre cost around 10,000K.

Destinations Bokeo (3 daily; 30hr); Kenthao (1 daily; 7hr); Luang Namtha (2 daily; 24hr); Luang Prabang (11 daily; 9–11hr); Oudomxai (4 daily; 12–17hr); Paklai (1 daily; 6hr); Phongsali (1 daily; 26hr); Phonsavan (6 daily; 8–10hr); Sam Neua (4 daily; 28–30hr); Sayaboury (3 daily; 8–10hr).

BY SAWNGTHAEW

At the Talat Sao bus station The main staging area for sawngthaews and unmetered taxis is at the western side of the bus station. Here, you'll find both shared sawngthaews for towns around the Vientiane Plain, and vehicles for hire.

1

INFORMATION AND TOURS

Tourist office Lane Xang Avenue, just north of the Talat Sao Malls ☏021 212251. Vientiane's main tourist office has helpful, English-speaking staff who can provide advice, recommendations, maps and the latest bus times. Ask about festivals; staff should be able to tell you what's on in the local area and help you to get there using public transport. Mon–Fri 8.30am–noon & 1.30–4pm.

Maps and books There are a few free city maps available. *The Laos Tourist Map*, published by the Department of Tourism Marketing, offers a decent citywide orientation, a list of sights and a map of the wider area. You can pick up a copy at the tourist office and at shops and hotels across town. For more detailed maps and reading material, the best bets are Monument Books and Book Café (see p.78).

Noticeboards Some of the city's coffee shops, such as Nam Phou's *Scandinavian Bakery* (see p.75), maintain noticeboards, displaying information on everything from film festivals to language classes

Listings For "what's on" info check out the *Vientiane Times* (published daily), which also carries advertisements for restaurant specials.

Travel/tour agencies For help with planning trips, booking tours and arranging transport, contact Jack Travel Laos, Samsenthai Rd (☏021 218721); Green Discovery, Heng Boun Rd (☏021 264528, ⓦgreendiscoverylaos .com); or Lao Travel Service, Lane Xang Ave (☏021 216603–4, ⓦlaotravelservice.laopdr.com).

GETTING AROUND

Tuk-tuks and jumbos A quick and efficient way of getting around, tuk-tuks and jumbos often operate as a kind of bus system within the city (picking up people heading in vaguely the same direction), and charge per person according to how far you're going. Shared tuk-tuks generally ply frequently travelled routes, such as Lane Xang Avenue between the Talat Sao Malls and That Luang, and Luang Prabang Avenue; they charge a flat fee of 5000K. Tuk-tuks can also be rented privately like taxis, though you'll need to bargain with the drivers a bit. Many drivers (especially those parked up on street corners) inflate their prices for foreigners, but figure on paying 10,000K per person for distances of 1–2km, and adding 3000K per kilometre beyond that.

Bicycles Vientiane is a very walkable city, but bicycles are an excellent way of getting around, and can be rented at guesthouses and shops around town for 10,000K per day (you'll need to leave ID or cash as a deposit). There are dozens of places to choose from, but the little shop called Queen's Beauty Tailors (8am–6pm), next to Scandinavian Bakery, has friendly, trustworthy owners. PVO (see below) also has a decent selection.

Motorbikes You can easily find a motorbike or scooter to rent for exploring the areas around Vientiane. Although travel speeds are relatively slow, negotiating Vientiane's cluttered roads at rush hour can take some getting used to

at first. Rental motorbikes in Vientiane are mostly secondhand 100cc step-throughs like the Honda Dream, imported from Thailand. The asking price is usually 70,000K a day, but it's possible to bargain this down, especially if you want it for a few days. Most places ask that you leave a passport as a deposit, but we advise against doing this, as there have been reports of places extorting money out of tourists for "damage". A well-established place in the city centre that accepts a cash deposit ($30) is PVO on Fa Ngum Road (☏021 254354, ⓔlaopvo@hotmail.com).

Buses Downtown Vientiane is too small to support a metropolitan public transport system, but bus routes originating at the main bus station, next to the Morning Market (Talat Sao Malls), do connect Vientiane with nearby places on the Vientiane Plain, such as the Buddha Park.

Taxis Expensive, metered yellow taxis tend to congregate outside Day Inn on Pangkham Road, just north of the *Lao Plaza*. Hailing one of these on the congested city-centre roads can prove tricky. Prices are negotiable and drivers will accept Lao kip, Thai baht or American dollars. If you're on the meter, a one-way trip to the Friendship Bridge will cost you around 140,000K.

Cars Avis (☏021 223867, ⓦavrlaos.com), on Samsenthai Road, rents out cars, though many guesthouses and hotels can also make car-rental arrangements (with or without a driver).

ACCOMMODATION

Vientiane has a wide range of tourist **accommodation**, from cheap backpacker dives to the regal, colonial-style Settha Palace. Most of the city's hotels and guesthouses are located in the rapidly developing area around Nam Phou in the centre of town, but others, especially mid-range hotels, continue to open up beyond here – particularly in the vicinity of Patouxai and on Luang Prabang Avenue, a quick tuk-tuk ride into the centre. **Budget hotels** in the central area are generally housed in renovated older buildings. Rooms at the best budget places tend to fill up very quickly, even in low season. It's not uncommon to see late arrivals desperately pounding the pavements looking for a reasonably priced room, as what's left by that time tends to be towards the top end of the budget range without meriting the price. If you haven't booked online, it's therefore a good idea to check in by noon, when people start checking out. Free **wi-fi** is available in most of the establishments listed here.

CITY CENTRE

★**Auberge Sala Inpeng** 063 Inpeng Rd ☎021 242021, ⊛salalao.com; map pp.62–63. These traditional-style bungalows, built on a secluded plot between much larger buildings, offer a chance to escape the hustle of Vientiane's streets without moving too far from the action. After a quiet night's sleep in the a/c rooms, you can enjoy breakfast on your own balcony overlooking the serene gardens. Friendly staff. $25

City Inn Pangkham Rd, north of Nam Phou Place ☎021 218333, ⊛cityinnvientiane.com; map pp.62–63. Worth splashing out on for warm smiles, floors you can see your face in and bath-tubs big enough to ease away those post-journey aches. Every room here has TV and a/c. Popular with the package-tour crowd, so make sure you book ahead. $60

Day Inn 059/3 Pangkham Rd, behind the Lao Plaza Hotel ☎021 223847, ⊛day-inn-hotel.com; map pp.62–63. This long-established, brightly painted hotel has stood the test of time and is still good value, considering its central location and the size of the daylight-flooded rooms. $55

Family Hotel Pangkham Rd, opposite Day Inn ☎021 260448, ⊛familyhotellaos.com; map pp.62–63. A good mid-range option on a relatively quiet street just north of Nam Phou Place, with singles, doubles and family rooms. *Family Hotel* is a tall, skinny building, which means rooms can be a bit poky, but the lack of space inside is made up for by flat-screen TVs, hot showers and a/c. Single 180,000K, double 220,000K

Funky Monkey Hostel François Ngin Rd ☎021 254181, ⊛funkymonkeyhostel.com; map pp.62–63. Very simple rooms and dorms in a tired-looking building a quick stroll up from the Mekong. Low prices attract young backpackers and solo travellers, who wind up drinking around the lobby's pool table most evenings. Dorm 40,000K, double 120,000K

Lani I 281 Setthathilat Rd, tucked away next to Wat Ong Teu ☎021 215639, ⊛laniguesthouse.com; map pp.62–63. A pleasant, centrally located house, decorated with antiques and handicrafts. All twelve rooms have hot water, but the rooms at the back are gloomy and overpriced. It's worth the extra kip to upgrade to the priciest rooms for the light and space. $45

Lao Plaza Hotel 63 Samsenthai Rd ☎021 265141, ⊛laoplazahotel.com; map pp.62–63. Rooms at this plain, Thai-built business hotel are comfortable, with fluffy pillows and giant armchairs, but are starting to look a little dated, so it's worth pushing for a discount. Swimming pool and airport transfers are included in the rate. $130

Manorom Boutique Hotel Heng Boun Rd ☎021 250748, ⊛manoromboutique.com; map pp.62–63. This skinny shard of a building isn't really a boutique hotel, and the rooms don't quite match up to the grandeur of the lobby. That said, they're fresh and comfortable, and the rate

includes breakfast in the seventh-floor restaurant overlooking town. $40

Mixay 39 Nokeo Koummane Rd ☎021 217023; map pp.62–63. One of the cheapest places in town, with spartan rooms ranging from fan singles to triples rented out bed by bed like dorms, with either attached bathrooms or shared facilities. The double rooms seem better maintained. Two rooms have balconies overlooking the street. Dorm 35,000K, double 100,000K

Mixok 189 Setthathilat Rd ☎021 251606; map pp.62–63. Cheap and central backpacker digs similar to *Mixay*, with singles, triples and dorms. Air-conditioned doubles are also available. With all of these rooms, you can expect some noise from the busy road outside. 130,000K

Moonlight Champa 013 Pangkham Rd ☎021 264114, ⊛moonlight-champa.com; map pp.62–63. Well-kept double and twin rooms in a neatly restored guesthouse near the centre (it was formerly called Soukxana). Each room has an en-suite bathroom and cable TV. Discounts are available for longer stays. 220,000K

Salana Boutique Hotel Chao Anou Rd ☎021 254254 ⊛salanaboutique.com; map pp.62–63. With an unbeatable downtown location and rooms decorated with lengths of Lao silk, Salana is one of Vientiane's classiest hotels. In addition to the on-site spa, Sarila, there's a smart fourth-floor bar serving cold beers and cocktails. $110

★**Settha Palace Hotel** 6 Pangkham Rd ☎021 217581, ⊛setthapalace.com; map pp.62–63. This palatial 1932 building close to the centre of town is a carefully restored relic of colonial-era Vientiane. Filled with French period furniture, the hotel's 29 rooms have all the mod cons, including mini-bar and safe. Elsewhere, you'll find an outstanding pool, beautiful landscaped gardens and a well-run business centre. The published rate is around $200 for a double, though discounts may be available. $207

Syri 2 63/67 Setthathirat Rd ☎021 241345, ✉syri2 @hotmail.com; map pp.62–63. Aquariums, sculptures and vases clutter the reception area of this rather odd place with a Chinese–Lao owner. The rooms are gloomy, but the location is good and the rates are low. Choose a/c over a fan and you'll have to pay an extra 50,000K per night. 60,000K

V Hotel Opposite Via Via on Nokeo Koummane Rd ☎021 255999; map pp.62–63. A tall, modern block near the river, with good-value rooms and decent hot showers. The echoing corridors tend to amplify even the smallest sounds, so noise can be a problem. 200,000K

★**Vayakorn Inn** 19 Hengbounnoy St ☎021 215348, ⊛vayakorn.biz; map pp.62–63. Not to be confused with the *Vayakorn Guesthouse*, which is owned by the same people, this newer hotel is more luxurious. There are beautiful wooden floors and furnishings throughout, and the rooms feature a/c, TV and big corner showers. The only letdown is the size of the private balconies, which are tiny. $35

Vientiane Backpackers Nokeo Koummane Rd ☎020 9748 4227, ⓦvientianebackpackershostel.com; map pp.62–63. Big, shabby dorms in a very central location, with all the usual services on offer, from laundry to bike rental. The rate includes a simple breakfast and access to a computer in the lobby (as well as free wi-fi). Dorm 40,000K

OUTSIDE THE CENTRE

★**Beau Rivage Mekong** Fa Ngum Rd ☎021 243350, ⓦhbrm.com; map pp.60–61. Airy, aqua-blue rooms in a fresh, minimalist-style hotel close to the riverfront. TV and a/c come as standard, but panoramic views of the Mekong cost $12 more. The adjoining bar/restaurant, *The Spirit House* (see p.77), is one of Vientiane's best spots for sunsets. $57

Best Western 2–12 François Ngin Rd, near the Mekong ☎021 216906–9; map pp.62–63. The old *Tai-Pan Hotel* has been given a facelift and is now part of the Best Western group. The 44 rooms here are spacious and smart, and guests have free access to the on-site fitness room, sauna and swimming pool. $75

Don Chan Palace Hotel Fa Ngum Rd ☎021 244288, ⓦdonchanpalacelaopdr.com; map pp.60–61. This massive eleven-storey hotel, built in the middle of the Mekong, marked the beginning of the end of Vientiane's low-rise days. The whole place is rather soulless, but the rooms are comfortable enough and many have superb river views. Facilities include a health spa, swimming pool and a karaoke bar. $120

Green Park Boutique Hotel 248 Khou Vieng Rd ☎021 264097, ⓦgreenparkvientiane.com; map pp.60–61. Set back from busy Khou Vieng Road, the smart rooms at this delightful hotel share pretty frangipani gardens and cool green pool. There's also a business centre and spa on site. The only downside is that the bridge leading to the hotel crosses a smelly sewer. $185

Heuan Lao Off Samsenthai Rd, near Wat Simuang ☎021 216258, ⓔ216258; map pp.60–61. This friendly, rambling guesthouse run by an older couple is located on a quiet lane opposite a park. Around the peaceful courtyard, where cats and dogs relax in the sun, you'll find singles, doubles and triples, all en suite. Double 120,000K

Mandala Boutique Hotel Around 1km east of the centre in Ban Simuang, around the corner from Wat Simuang ☎021 214493, ⓦmandalahotel.asia; map pp.60–61. Attractive former school building on a quiet side street away from the centre, surrounded by shady gardens. The standard rooms are quite simple but the suites come with rain showers, bathtubs and balconies. $80

Mercure Samsenthai Rd ☎021 213570–1, ⓦmercure .com; map pp.60–61. Formerly a *Novotel* and now rebranded as part of the Mercure chain, this four-star hotel is a decent option, though its location away from the city centre isn't ideal and prices are on the high side. The 172 rooms are clean and comfortable nevertheless, and there's a pool, sauna and gym on site. p $92

★**Sihome Backpackers** 056 Sihom Rd, halfway between the two petrol stations ☎020 9551 2668, ⓦsihomebackpackershostel.com; map pp.60–61. The most popular place for young backpackers, with super-cheap bunks, walls covered in murals and a sociable bar area out front. Dorms here are quite cramped, but there's a TV room to stretch out in and private doubles are available. Dorm 60,000K, double 280,000K

Villa Manoly Ban Simuang, next to Honour International School and around the corner from Wat Simuang ☎021 218907, ⓦvilla-manoly.com; map pp.60–61. Indeed a villa, and an attractive place too, with a pleasant upstairs terrace and spacious grounds. The singles and doubles are pretty basic and need freshening up, but they have high ceilings and en-suite hot showers. Just a short walk from the river, it has friendly owners and a lovely outdoor swimming pool. p $35

EATING

The **culinary scene** in Vientiane caters to virtually every taste, from sausage and sauerkraut to Korean BBQ. Vientiane also has a large concentration of French and Italian restaurants, the best of which compare favourably to those in Bangkok. If you plan to head out to the remote provinces for a while, take the opportunity to indulge in the capital's Western culinary offerings before hitting the trail.

FOOD STALLS AND MARKETS

For cheap, home-style cooking, head for the outdoor food stalls found in or around any of the city's markets. Crusty baguettes (*khào jì*) are a speciality of Vientiane, and vendors selling these French-inspired loaves, plain or filled with Lao-style pâté, can be found around town.

Heng Boun Road food stalls Heng Boun Rd, between Khoun Boulom Rd and Chao Anou Rd; map pp.62–63. For cheap, tasty snacks throughout the day and into late evening, try the food carts near the Home Ideal shop on

Heng Boun Road: here you'll find good Lao-style *khào pûn* (noodles with sauce), *tam màk hung* and excellent shakes.

Talat Khouadin Just east of the Talat Sao bus station; map pp.60–61. This dusty, partially covered market is Vientiane's cheapest place to buy fruit, vegetables and the like. Come early to watch locals buying fish and meat. Daily sunrise–sunset.

Vangthong Night Market Along Khoun Boulom Road, north of the National Stadium; map pp.62–63. This narrow, food-focused night market sets up near the

1

bowling alley on Khoun Boulom Road in the early evening and stays open till about 10pm, selling fresh fruit, sweet coconut desserts and *ping kai* (grilled chicken). Daily sunset–around 10pm.

GROCERY STORES AND WINE SHOPS

For many travellers, especially Europeans, one of the great pleasures of returning to Vientiane after a long journey upcountry is the availability of cheeses, wine and other imported goods to accompany those crusty baguettes which are a speciality of the capital.

Baràvin Samsenthai Rd ☎021 217700; map pp.62–63. A well-stocked wine shop in the centre of town, with a good selection of vintages from France, the New World and beyond. There's also a little bar at the front of the shop for trying some of the wines. Daily 8am–8pm.

Home Ideal Heng Boun Rd; map pp.62–63. Central supermarket with a wide selection of cosmetics, food, wine and beer, as well as toys and stationery. Prices here are lower than at most of Vientiane's minimarkets. Daily 9am–10pm.

Phimphone Minimart Setthathilat Rd; map pp.62–63. One of the more expensive places to stock up, Phimphone has a selection of cheeses, wine, imported beer and chocolate, as well as American and British products you won't be able to find elsewhere in Laos. There's another branch on the corner of Samsenthai and Chantha Koumane roads. Mon–Sat 8am–9pm; Sun 10am–6pm.

BAKERIES AND CAFÉS

The legacy of the French is most deliciously apparent in the range of cafés and bakeries that crop up all over town. The coffee served at these places varies, with some offering Lao coffee and some using imported beans. At a good café on Setthathilat Road you'll pay around 25,000K for a breakfast special such as coffee and a couple of croissants.

Antique Café Upstairs at Indochina's Handicrafts (see p.78) on Setthathilat Rd ☎021 223528; map pp.62–63. Above an antique shop, this tiny "café" has space for just four or five customers at a time. With cuckoo clocks, medals and paintings cluttering the walls, it's an atmospheric spot for an iced Lao coffee (20,000K). Daily 8.30am–10.30pm.

Common Grounds Chao Anou Rd ☎021 255057, ⓦfacebook.com/commongroundslaos; map pp.62–63. Little ones love this modern café, which has a children's menu and an enclosed play area out the back. Adults rate the place too: for its tempting cookies and cakes (from 7000K) and the healthy wraps (from 32,000K). Mon–Sat 7am–8pm.

JoMa Bakery Setthathilat Rd, just west of Nam Phou ☎021 215265, ⓦjoma.biz; map pp.62–63. This Canadian-owned café is Vientiane's answer to the big Western coffee chains – right down to the free wi-fi – and its decent breakfasts (from 27,000K) will set you up nicely for a day of tramping around town. The salads are good too,

if a little pricey. There are two other branches in town, plus another in Luang Prabang. Daily 7am–9pm.

Karma Café COPE Visitor Centre (see p.68), Khou Vieng Rd, around 1km east of the Talat Sao bus station and roughly opposite *Green Park Boutique Hotel*; map pp.60–61. A simple, thatched-roof café just outside the main exhibition, doing a good line in Lao coffee and home-made ice cream (10,000K). Profits go towards helping victims of UXO. Daily 8am–6pm.

★**The Little House** Midway along Manthatoulat Rd ☎020 5540 6036, ✉cafelao66@yahoo.co.jp; map pp.62–63. It's hard to spot this cute, Japanese-run coffee house, but your effort will be rewarded with sublime Lao coffee from the Bolaven Plateau (from 19,000K). Enjoy it iced or hot, whichever you prefer, but be sure to order a couple of the home-made chocolate truffles – you won't be disappointed. Daily 8.30am–6.30pm.

Scandinavian Bakery On the northern edge of Nam Phou Place ☎021 215199, ⓦscandinavianbakerylaos .com; map pp.62–63. Vientiane's first European bakery is still going strong, selling huge sandwiches, traditional Swedish cakes and refreshing lemonade (11,000K). Views of the fountain have been all but obscured by new buildings, but the coffee makes up for it. Daily 7am–9pm.

True Coffee Setthathilat Rd; map pp.62–63. City-sized, American-style café serving all the usual caffeine kicks (espresso 14,000K) plus some interesting variations such as English toffee latte and choc-chip-twist coffee. There are five Skype-ready computers inside, with internet access available by the hour (8000K). Daily 8am–6pm.

RESTAURANTS

Most of Vientiane's restaurants open for lunch and then again for dinner, but no-frills places usually stay open throughout the day, closing around 9pm. In most Western restaurants you'll pay on average $4 for each course, and even in more upmarket restaurants you'll rarely spend more than $15 unless you get into the wine. Brunch buffets are on offer at the big international-style hotels like the *Mercure* and *Lao Plaza Hotel* for roughly $10. Although we've split restaurants here into two main categories – Asian and Western – most places offer at least a couple of dishes from both regions.

ASIAN

Jamil Zahid Off Khoun Boulom Rd ☎030 990 9456; map pp.60–61. Tucked down an alley near the western end of Heng Boun Road, this shed-like Indian place does superb Punjabi curries, plus tandoor-cooked naans and tasty dahls. The eccentric owner is a camera fanatic, so expect to have your picture taken and shown on the restaurant's dusty TV screen. Daily 11am–10.30pm.

Katenoy Chao Anou Rd, opposite Nazim ☎020 5539 4290; map pp.62–63. Simple Lao place with plastic chairs and tables set outside on a dusty plot of land, doing cheap

1

fruit shakes (10,000K), draught beer by the jug, and an excellent spicy rice salad with holy basil (20,000K). Daily 6pm–late.

★**Lao Kitchen** Heng Boun Rd ☎021 254332, ☎lao -kitchen.com; map pp.62–63. An excellent, reasonably priced option for first-time visitors who want to experiment with Lao food and know exactly what they're ordering. The house special is a fresh-tasting chicken *larp* (34,000K), but the menu also extends to regional dishes like spicy, Pakse-style sausage, with a good selection of dips to choose from. Daily 11am–10pm.

★**Makphet** Behind Wat Ong Teu, south of Setthathilat Rd ☎021 260587; map pp.62–63. Upscale, not-for-profit restaurant on a quiet backstreet in the centre of town offering a modern take on classic Lao dishes. The place is run by former street kids who were trained up for the job. Hugely popular, especially with business crowds, and it's not unusual for all the tables to be full, even at lunchtime. Bookings advised. Mon–Sat 11am–9pm.

Noodle House Heng Boun Rd ☎021 265000; map pp.62–63. Cool, air-conditioned noodle bar run by the folks behind *Khop Chai Deu* (see below), open at lunchtime only. The noodle-packed menu includes everything from spaghetti to pad Thai, with mains for around 25,000K. Daily noon–3pm.

WESTERN

Chokdee Café Fa Ngum Rd ⓦchokdeecafe.com; map pp.62–63. A statue of Tintin points travellers and expats into this sociable Belgian bar/restaurant. The drinks list features dozens of strong imported beers (from 40,000K) and on Friday and Saturday evenings, moules (cooked in local or Belgian beer) are added to the extensive menu. Mon 4.30–11pm, Tues–Sun 8am–11pm.

La Belle Epoque 6 Pangkham Rd, in the Settha Palace Hotel; map pp.62–63. The classiest act in town, serving French and Lao food (mains from 130,000K) in an elegant dining room. There is nowhere else in Vientiane even remotely like this. Even if you don't dine here, you can have a drink at the bar and soak up the colonial atmosphere.

Daily 6.30–10.30pm.

★**La Terrasse** Nokeo Koummane Rd, near Wat Mixai ☎021 218550; map pp.62–63. This place fills its tables by offering outstanding steaks (around 90,000K), pizzas, Mexican food and salads at prices lower than most of the other Western joints. Seating is in a covered courtyard or chic bar/dining area. Highly recommended. Mon–Sat 11am–2pm & 6–10pm.

Le Provençal Pangkham Rd, facing Nam Phou; map pp.62–63. Cosy little French place tucked away on the northern side of the fountain. The wood-fired pizza is first rate, and there's a good selection of wine available by the carafe or bottle. Steaks cost around 90,000K. Daily 11.30am–2pm & 6–10pm.

Noy's Fruit Heaven Heng Boun Rd ☎030 996 0913; map pp.62–63. Need a fresh fruit fix? This relaxed smoothie bar makes great shakes for 15,000K, blending in plenty of sweet coconuts and bananas. Also does decent Western breakfasts. Daily 7am–7pm.

Ray's Grille 17/1 Sihom Rd, west of the petrol station ☎020 5896 6866; map pp.60–61. There isn't a proper sign outside this no-frills American burger joint, so keep your eyes peeled for the little whiteboard, which has the menu scrawled on it. The house special – a whopping philly cheese steak dripping with gooey cheddar (39,000K) – has tourists and expats coming back for multiple visits. Daily except Sat 11.30am–2pm & 6–9pm.

Swedish Pizza & Baking House Chao Anou Rd ☎021 254041; map pp.62–63. Vientiane's best Scandinavian bakery, with pastries and sweet treats, plus a selection of main courses. High on the menu is the most famous Swedish dish of all: meatballs with lingonberries and mashed potatoes (35,000K). There's another branch on the road to That Luang. Daily 7am–9pm.

Via Via Opposite V Hotel on Nokeo Koummane Rd ☎020 7749 2776; map pp.62–63. Hugely popular with tourists, *Via Via* manages to pull off decent Lao dishes alongside its selection of western staples, including good, Italian-style pizzas (around 55,000K). Jugs of wine and well-made mojitos get solo travellers chatting. Daily 10am–10pm.

DRINKING AND NIGHTLIFE

Vientiane is not a great city for partying. Frequent government crackdowns have hamstrung the development of Vientiane's clubbing scene, especially when it comes to late-night places that appeal to Western visitors. The locals' favourite spots for drinking and dancing are a quick tuk-tuk ride west of the town centre along Luang Prabang Avenue. Most of these places play Thai pop and international dance mixes until 1 or 2am, though some places manage to stay open later. Depending on the night and the venue, you may also be able to catch a covers band or, failing that, some **karaoke**. There's usually no cover charge, but if there is it will include a bottle of Beerlao.

Jazzy Brick Setthathirat Rd; map pp.62–63. Don't worry if it's quiet downstairs; this über-cool jazz bar usually fills up from the top. There's a well-stocked bar, a cocktail list to die for, and a clutch of old-fashioned electrical appliances hanging from the walls, making the vibe more

New Orleans than Vientiane. Whisky cocktails start at 40,000K. Daily 6pm–midnight.

Khop Chai Deu Setthathirat Rd; map pp.62–63. This big, French-period house is by far the most popular hangout for foreign tourists. Downstairs in the patio bar you can get cheap glasses of draught beer (10,000K); up the big spiral staircase you'll find another very pleasant bar on the roof. You can eat here, too – the mixed menu has reasonable Lao and Indian dishes, though the *falang* food (and service) is a bit hit and miss. Daily 9am–11pm.

The Spirit House Fa Ngum Rd, right next to the Beau Rivage Mekong ☎021 243795, ⓦthespirithouselaos .com; map pp.60–61. Well-off travellers flock to *The Spirit House* for delectable cocktails (from 20,000K) and views over the river, broken only by a narrow road. One of the best

places to watch the sun set over Thailand. Daily 7am–midnight.

Sticky Fingers François Nginn Rd ☎021 215 972; map pp.62–63. With a pleasant outdoor seating area opposite the *Best Western* hotel, this small Australian-run bar has picked up a loyal following among expats. A good crowd is almost guaranteed between 6 and 8pm on Wednesdays and Fridays, when the famously good cocktails (from 15,000K) are half-price. Tues–Sun 10am–11pm.

ENTERTAINMENT

More than four hundred and fifty years after superseding Luang Prabang as the centre of political power, Vientiane still lacks the natural **cultural life** of the old royal capital, but a couple of venues offer a taste of Laos's heritage, even if just for the entertainment of foreigners. Vientiane's grassroots cultural life only really reawakens during **festivals**. The best time to get a taste of Lao music is in November during the **That Luang Festival** (see box, p.68), when the nation's best singers and musicians are featured in a string of performances during the two weeks leading up to the festival.

Institut Français Laos Lane Xang Ave ☎021 215764, ⓦif-laos.org; map pp.60–61. This French cultural centre regularly puts on concerts, film screenings (in French) and language courses (see below). There's a café on site, plus a well-stocked library offering internet access and copies of the latest French newspapers.

Lao National Cultural Hall Samsenthai Rd; map pp.62–63. Across from the Lao National Museum, as if

you could miss it, is the gargantuan Lao National Cultural Hall. Opened in 2000, the gilded building houses a giant 1500-seat auditorium and occasionally hosts art exhibitions or performances by dance troupes and circuses. It's not always clear what will be happening at the hall until a few days beforehand, so keep your eyes peeled for the adverts that spring up around town or in the *Vientiane Times*.

SPORTS AND ACTIVITIES

Bike tours Vientiane ByCycle ☎020 5581 2337, ⓦvientianebycycle.com. Set up by Dutch native and long-term Vientiane resident Aline van der Meulen, this company runs guided bicycle tours through seldom-visited parts of the city. Half- and full-day tours are available (from 400,000K including water, snacks, bike rental and lunch).

Bowling Lao Bowling Centre on Khoun Boulom Rd ☎021 223219. To hang out with locals at one of the few places where late-night drinking is possible, try bowling. This place offers a super-retro experience, complete with a 1980s-style scoring system. Each game costs 11,000K (13,000K after 7pm). Open daily 8am–late.

Cooking classes Lao Experiences ☎020 9555 3097, ⓦlao-experiences.com. Runs a half-day "cooking experience" from the *Full Moon Café* on François Ngin Road, with participants preparing – and then enjoying – their own Lao lunch ($35/person).

Health clubs Best Western, François Ngin Rd (80,000K/day, including access to the swimming pool); *Lao Plaza Hotel*, Samsenthai Rd (100,000K/day).

Language courses Institut Français Laos, Lane Xang Ave ☎021 215764, ⓦif-laos.org. Short-term courses and private tutorials are available, including a fifty-hour introduction to the Lao language.

Massage and herbal sauna Ajan Amphone, tucked away behind Wat Chanthabouli on Fa Ngum Road, offers Lao massage (55,000K/hr; daily noon–9pm) plus a soothing herbal sauna; slightly classier is Champa Spa (two branches on Pangkham Road; daily 9am–10pm), which offers an extensive range of massages from 80,000K/hr.

Swimming Non-residents can pay to swim at several hotels around the city. Nicest of all is the deep-blue pool at the *Settha Palace Hotel* ($28/day) but cheaper options include the *Best Western* on François Ngin Road ($7.50/day, including access to the gym), and the *Lao Plaza Hotel*, on Samsenthai Road (120,000K/day).

Tennis Chao Anouvong Tennis, Nokeo Koummane Rd, near the National Stadium. Courts cost 20,000K for 45min during the day, or 30,000K after dark, when the floodlights need to be switched on. Racquet hire is 20,000K per session.

SHOPPING

The Talat Sao area just off Lane Xang Avenue is the best place to begin a shopping tour of the capital. Although there are still covered market stalls here selling Chinese electronics and cheap consumer goods, most of these have been swallowed up by the imposing **Talat Sao Malls** (daily 8am–5pm), which are growing together into one big shopping outlet, each

1

housing a variety of jewellery shops, clothing outlets and banks. At some stage during their visit, most tourists end up browsing the market stalls that occupy the new riverbank area just west of Chao Anouvong Park, marked by dozens of red gazebos. T-shirts, toys, paintings, shoes and gadgets are available, though nearly everything is mass-produced and plasticky, and true bargains are impossible to find. The more interesting textile, souvenir and antique shops are found on **Samsenthai** and **Setthathilat roads** and on the lanes running between them.

ANTIQUES AND REPRODUCTIONS

Antique shops can be found in the Morning Market (Talat Sao Malls) and elsewhere in the centre of Vientiane. As ever, virtually all metal images or figurines of Buddhist or Hindu deities are reproductions from Thailand and Cambodia, though vendors won't admit this. Opium weights, usually seen in antique stores but also found in upscale textile shops, are priced at levels way out of line when compared to the rest of Laos, with merchants asking two to five times more for weights than their counterparts in Luang Prabang and the other provinces. Reproduction opium pipes can be found in the antique shops on Samsenthai Road. The cheapest are gaudy things made in Vietnam from tusk-shaped bone, but if you look patiently you may come across bamboo and brass or silver pipes made locally by a couple of craftsmen who are the sole remaining pipemakers in Southeast Asia.

Indochina's Handicrafts Setthathilat Rd ☏ 021 223528; map pp.62–63. Beautiful antiques shop that positively sags under the weight of all the old watches, paintings, coins, medals and Buddhist amulets filling its dusty cabinets. There's a cosy café upstairs (see p.75) and another branch in Luang Prabang. Daily 8.30am–10pm.

BOOKS

Big Brother Mouse Phai Nam Road, just west of the National Stadium ☏ 021 264513, ⊕ bigbrothermouse .com; map pp.62–63. The Vientiane branch of Big Brother Mouse is run with the same idea as the main shop in Luang Prabang (see p.112). Here you can buy colourful, lightweight children's books in Lao and English (prices start at 10,000K) and then give them away to Lao children when you visit remote villages, where access to educational materials is extremely limited. Mon–Sat 8am–4pm.

Book Café Heng Boun Road; map pp.62–63. This small but well-organized shop has a whole section devoted to learning Lao, plus plenty of English-language novels set in Laos. The proceeds from some of the books sold go to victims of UXO. Daily 8am–8pm.

Monument Books Nokeo Koummane Road ☏ 021 243708, ⊕ monument-books.com; map pp.62–63. Sells Vientiane's largest selection of English-language books. It also offers a subscription service for glossy magazines, and a wide range of detailed maps covering Laos and other parts of Southeast Asia. Mon–Fri 9am–8pm; Sat & Sun 9am–6pm.

RATTAN, WICKER AND BAMBOO

Check the antique stores in and around the Talat Sao Malls and the downtown area for old or rare baskets made by the tribal peoples of Laos, which can sell for as much as $200. Cheap sticky-rice baskets and mats costing $1–3 can be found on market stalls near Talat Sao bus station.

TEXTILES

Once a tremendous bargain, antique Lao weavings are now more expensive in Vientiane than in Thailand. If you're determined to buy old textiles in Vientiane, the Morning Market (Talat Sao Malls) is your best bet. New textiles, however, are another matter. Lao silk and cotton textiles can be purchased in bolts of plain coloured cloth or as ready-made clothing for $2–5 per item. If you're looking to make a smart purchase without shelling out too much cash, Lao shoulder bags, or *nyam*, are a cheap and functional choice. Hand-woven *pha biang*, a long, scarf-like textile, can be found in a wide variety of colours and patterns, and chequered *pha khao ma*, the knee-length men's sarong, are also good buys. The Morning Market (Talat Sao Malls) has the best selection; the merchants here are used to foreign tourists and enjoy a spirited haggle.

Aside from the markets, Vientiane boasts an increasing number of upmarket **shops** and **boutiques** carrying, and sometimes specializing in, Lao textiles. They often have the best range and most attractively displayed products, and, unsurprisingly, the highest prices. Most of these new boutiques and galleries are located **south of Samsenthai Road** between Khoun Boulom and Manthatoulat roads and can be taken in during a single, short walking tour.

Carol Cassidy Lao Textiles Nokeo Koummane Rd ☏ 021 212123, ⊕ laotextiles.com; map pp.62–63. Housed in a French-era mansion, this is the most impressive of Vientiene's textile boutiques, producing hand-woven wall hangings tinted with natural dyes under the supervision of an American designer. Step out the back to see local weavers at work. Mon–Fri 8am–noon & 1–5pm, Sat 8am–noon.

Satri Lao Silk 79/4 Setthathilat Rd ☏ 021 219295; map pp.62–63. Long-running textile shop in the very centre of town, selling a mixture of new and antique Lao silks, plus furniture, jewellery and trinkets. Daily 8am–8pm.

TRAVEL GEAR

Walkman Village Fa Ngum Rd ☏ 021 213609; map pp.62–63. This shop near Chao Anouvong Park is the perfect place to stock up on outdoor gear before a trip into the countryside. Here you'll find camping equipment, torches, waterproof clothing, lighters and rucksacks. Daily 9am–9.30pm.

WOODCARVINGS AND HANDICRAFTS

Unlike Chiang Mai in Thailand, Vientiane is not a centre of woodcarving, and the merchandise on offer tends to be crudely carved and garishly lacquered. The places listed here are exceptions and have some top-quality pieces.

Sada Handicraft Setthathilat Rd, close to the junction with Khoun Boulom Rd; map pp.62–63. This tiny shop is the place to come for wooden carvings, from the simple (a pair of chopsticks) to the very grand (think enormous Buddha images and wall hangings). Mostly dark wood.

Daily 10am–8pm.

★**Saoban** Chao Anou Rd ☎020 5510 0034; map pp.62–63. The Vientiane outlet of Saoban, the social development project founded by Lao activist Sombath Somphone, stocks a wide range of handicrafts, including silver jewellery and bags made by local women. Money raised goes towards empowering disadvantaged communities. Mon–Sat 9am–8pm, Sun 1–8pm.

T'Shop Lai Gallery Inpeng Rd ☎021 223178, ⓦartisanslao.com; map pp.62–63. Ethically produced lotions and potions, plus unique paintings, mosaics and a selection of handicrafts made from coconut shell. Prices are fixed, though, and certainly not cheap. Mon–Sat 8am–10pm, Sun 10am–6pm.

DIRECTORY

Banks and exchange Banks, hotels, guesthouses and shopkeepers all over downtown Vientiane will happily exchange foreign currency. Thai and Lao banks, many of which are located on Lane Xang Avenue, can cash travellers' cheques, but a more convenient option for tourists is bank exchange booths, which can be found on Samsenthai Road as well as on Fa Ngum Road. There are also exchange booths at the Friendship Bridge and the airport. Banque pour le Commerce Extérieur Lao (BCEL), Pangkham Road, has the best exchange rates and the widest range of services, including changing travellers' cheques into US dollars and dollar cash advances.

Courier services DHL Worldwide Express ☎021 214868 or 216830; UPS ☎020 2223 2111.

Embassies and consulates Australia, Thadua Rd ☎021 353800; UK, J. Nehru Rd, ☎030 770 0000; Cambodia, near That Khao, Thadua Rd ☎021 314952; Canada, c/o embassy in Bangkok ☎+66 2 636 0540; China, near Wat Nak Noi, Wat Nak Noi Rd ☎ 021 315100; Indonesia, Kaysone Phomvihane Ave ☎021 413909 or 413910; Ireland, c/o embassy in Kuala Lumpur ☎+60 3 2161 2963; Malaysia, That Luang Rd ☎ 021 414205 or 414206; Myanmar (Burma), Lao-Thai Rd, Ban Wat Nak ☎021 314910; New Zealand, c/o embassy in Bangkok ☎+66 2 254 2530; Philippines, Phonthan Rd ☎021 452490; Singapore, Thadua Rd ☎021 353939; Thailand, Kaysone Phomvihane Ave ☎021 214580; US, Thadua Rd

☎021 267000; Vietnam, near Wat Phaxai, That Luang Rd ☎021 413400–4.

Emergencies Dial ☎190 in case of fire, ☎195 for an ambulance, or ☎1191 for police.

Hospitals and clinics Australian Clinic, Thadua Rd, in the Australian Embassy building ☎021 353840 (weekdays only); French Clinic, Khou Vieng Rd ☎021 214150; Alliance International Medical Centre, Honda Complex, Souphanuvong Road ☎021 513095; Mahosot Hospital, Mahosot Rd ☎021 214018.

Immigration office Hatsady Rd, not far from the tourist office ☎021 212520 (daily 8am–12pm & 1–4pm). Here you can extend your visa for $2/day. Travel agents in town tend to charge $3/day for the same service.

Internet access *True Coffee* on Setthathilat Rd (see p.75) has the fastest computers in town (8000K/hour), but there are dozens of smaller internet cafés dotted all around the city, each charging around 200K a minute and closing at about 10pm.

Laundry Most hotels and guesthouses will wash clothes for you. The going rate across town is 10,000K/kilo, though some hotels try to charge considerably more.

Newspapers The *Vientiane Times* is sold at the big hotels and most minimarkets; the *Bangkok Post* is usually available at the Phimphone minimart on Samsenthai Road.

Pharmacies The best pharmacies are on Mahosot Road, north of the Talat Sao bus station.

Excursions from Vientiane

If you need a break from Vientiane, it's easy enough to get out of the city in under an hour and shuttle around the expansive Vientiane Plain by public transport or on a private tour. The most popular destination for a half-day jaunt is the other-worldly **Buddha Park**, southeast of town, which ties in well with a trip to the **Beerlao Factory**. If you have never seen a "Buddha's footprint" you might consider travelling further east to **Wat Phabat Phonsan**. North of the capital, the huge **Ang Nam Ngum Reservoir** is a pleasant retreat for boating, fishing and swimming, with scores of islands to explore, as well as a casino. At the southern edge of the reservoir is the vast **Phou Khao Khouay NBCA**, which can be visited on an adventure tour from the capital. Downstream on the Nam Ngum River, **Ban Pako** is an eco-tourism lodge that makes a fine day-trip, though most visitors end up staying on to relax for a few days, visiting country villages and exploring nature trails. Of the state-sanctioned tourist destinations on the edge of the city, the **Kaysone Memorial Museum** is the most worthwhile, making an interesting diversion into the personality cults surrounding communist leaders. Further north is the eye-poppingly exotic **Dong Makai Market**, known locally as the best place to buy fresh insects and live animals.

Beerlao factory

12km southeast of downtown Vientiane along Thadua Rd • Bus #14 from the Talat Sao bus station (every 15min) passes by the factory • Tours run on Mon, Wed & Fri 1.30–4.30pm, with an additional slot 9.30–10.30am on Wed morning • 40,000K per person

An interesting stop on the road out to the Buddha Park is the **Beerlao factory**. Not many tourists show up here, but those who do have the chance to join a brief tour of the factory and ask questions about the production process. The highlight, after watching a short promotional video and having a peek around, is gulping down free samples of the nation's favourite drink. Note that tours are only run at certain times of the week. If you arrive outside these times, it may still be possible to look around the Beerlao museum on the south side of the road and have a drink in the bar (a large beer here costs just 8000K). Register at the security check point and you'll be given a temporary visitor's pass.

Buddha Park

25km southeast of downtown Vientiane on the Mekong river • Daily 8am–5pm • 5000K, plus 3000K for cameras • Bus #14 from Vientiane's main bus station (every 15min) is scheduled to stop outside the Buddha Park. A common problem is for the bus to travel as far as the Friendship Bridge, where you will be shepherded into an (overpriced) tuk-tuk for the final few kilometres. If this happens, walk back to the main road and jump into a shared tuk-tuk heading east (it should cost no more than 5000K). It's also possible to charter a tuk-tuk for the round trip from Vientiane (you should be able to get the price down to around 150,000K for a full vehicle, including a 2hr wait)

Xieng Khuan, or the "**Buddha Park**", is surely Laos's quirkiest attraction – a tacky tourist trap to some travellers, one of the most interesting sights in Vientiane to others. This collection of massive ferro-concrete sculptures, dotted around a wide riverside meadow, was created under the direction of Luang Pou Bounleua Soulilat, a self-styled holy man who claimed to have been the disciple of a cave-dwelling Hindu hermit in Vietnam. Upon returning to Laos, Bounleua began the sculpture garden in the late 1950s as a means of spreading his philosophy of life and his ideas about the cosmos. After the revolution, Bounleua was forced to flee across the Mekong to Nong Khai, Thailand, where he established an even more elaborate version of his philosophy in concrete. Ironically, the Lao National Tourism Authority chose Bounleua's sculptures as the symbol of their "Visit Laos Year" campaign, and posters depicting the exiled guru's works can be seen in government offices throughout the country.

Besides the brontosaurian reclining Buddha that dominates the park, there are statues of every conceivable deity in the Hindu-Buddhist pantheon and even a handful of personalities from the old regime. Near the park's entrance is a strange edifice that resembles a giant pumpkin with a dead tree sprouting from its crown. Entering the structure through the gaping maw of devouring time, you can explore representations of the "three planes of existence": hell, earth and heaven. A spiral stairway leads to the roof of the building, which affords good views of the park and river.

1

Kaysone Memorial Museum

6km from downtown Vientiane along Route 13 south • Tues–Sun 8–noon & 1–4.30pm • 5000K • Getting to the museum is easiest by rental motorbike or tuk-tuk. Southbound sawngthaews, departing from the main bus station, pass by the museum

The **Kaysone Memorial Museum** is the most visible attempt of the Lao government to build a personality cult around the shadowy man who, according to Party legend, led the Thirty Year Struggle (see p.280). It lies on the edge of Vientiane, in the former American compound known as **Six Klicks City**.

The Memorial Museum is strikingly modest compared to the mausoleum of Kaysone's Vietnamese counterpart, Ho Chi Minh. Opened in 1994, the museum originally consisted only of the tiny ranch house where Kaysone lived, though a more conventional museum was opened next door a year later. Fronted by a huge statue of the former leader, the museum has plenty of the revolutionary photographs common to other Lao museums, but also features objects from various stages of Kaysone's life: his desk from his Savannakhet school, the winnowing tray on which he was placed during the first days of his life, and his mother's bed, along with a model of Kaysone's Vieng Xai cave, his binoculars, revolver and other items from his time with the resistance movement.

Dong Makai Market

Around 15km north of Vientiane along Route 10 • Daily sunrise to around 7pm • The market is best reached by motorbike or with a private car: follow Route 13 north out of Vientiane, joining Route 10 after around 12km. Route 10 runs straight past the market

Occupying a dusty plot of land just north of the point where routes 10 and 13 converge is **Dong Makai Market**. Well known among locals as the best place to buy fresh insects and live animals (both for cooking and eating), it makes for an eye-opening stop on the road from Vientiane to the Ang Nam Ngum Reservoir. Shaded from the sunlight by drooping lengths of canvas and tarp, many of the stalls here sell dead crickets, grubs and beetles by the bowl, which locals snap up to eat at home. Others have more exotic products on offer, including live snakes that writhe around in polythene bags and little pots of yellow ant eggs, which are used to make soup. A lot of the roots, plants and animals sold here are taken illegally from the surrounding forests, including the Phou Khao Khouay protected area, which lies to the east. Authorities know local people are poor and need food, so they often turn a blind eye to the poaching, but market traders can still be cagey about outsiders taking photos, so be careful where you point your camera.

Wat Phabat Phonsan

80km east of Vientiane, roughly halfway between Vientiane and Paksan • Daily sunrise–sunset • Any public transport bound for Savannakhet, Thakhek or Paksan will pass by Wat Phabat Phonsan; it's about an hour and a half's drive from either Vientiane or Paksan

The somewhat isolated monastery of **Wat Phabat Phonsan** is best known for its "**Buddha's footprint**" embellished with paint and gold leaf. In ancient times, the

---

SIX KLICKS CITY

The former American compound, known during the Second Indochina War as **Six Klicks City**, was named for its location, 6km from the centre of Vientiane. An oasis during the years that the US embassy was the seat of power in Vientiane, Six Klicks City was a slice of suburban Americana with nicely paved roads lined with ranch-style homes and swimming pools out the back. One month after Saigon and Phnom Penh fell in April 1975, Pathet Lao troops surrounded the barbed-wire-enclosed compound, and the American residents inside had nowhere to run. Three days later, the first busload of Americans headed to Wattay Airport, beginning the end of an era.

In December 1975, 264 delegates gathered in the compound's gymnasium and proclaimed the formation of the Lao People's Democratic Republic. Having just emerged from their wartime hideout in the caves of Vieng Xai, the Lao communist party members promptly moved into the American fortress, which was to become Kaysone's headquarters until his death in 1992.

BAN PAKO (LAO PAKO) RESORT

A quick trip you can make out of the capital is to **Ban Pako**, 50km northeast of Vientiane, which has a rustic resort (☎030 9884611, ⓦbanpako.com) on a bend in the Nam Ngum River. Once there you could easily spend a couple of days soaking up the laidback atmosphere at this woodsy getaway, affording ample opportunity for swimming, tubing, birdwatching and day hikes to nearby villages. You can also follow self-guided nature trails, on one of which is a herbal steam bath, modelled on the wood-fired saunas at Wat Sok Pa Luang (see p.70), and near a refreshingly cool spring.

To get to the resort with your own wheels, take Route 13 south from Vientiane and turn left at kilometre 24, where you will see signs for Ban Lao Pako. From here there are two options: leave your vehicle at Ban Somsamai and pay a boatman here for the thirty-minute ride downriver to the resort (30,000K per person), or continue by road, following the signs. Alternatively, there's a direct shuttle bus to the resort (one day's notice required; 85,000K per person each way), which departs from Nam Phou Place in Vientiane at 11am.

Accommodation includes detached riverview bungalows with en-suite facilities and verandas (double room 180,000K). Rooms are limited, so it's best to call ahead for reservations. An **open-air restaurant** overlooking the river serves up Lao staples plus a few decent Western dishes.

sandstone bluff upon which the monastery now sits was submerged by the nearby river and, over time, the swirling currents carved deep bowls into its surface. When the water receded, one of these indentations looked enough like a footprint for it to become enshrined as one of those left behind by the historic Buddha during his wanderings through Laos. Never mind that there is no record of Gautama Buddha ever having got this far east, his footprints have been found all over Laos wherever there is a population of Buddhists.

There is limited accommodation in the vicinity of Wat Phabat Phonsan, so it's best visited as a day-trip or en route to or from the south.

Phou Khao Khouay NBCA

90km northeast of Vientiane · Park entrance fee 5000K per person, plus 5000K per vehicle · Travel from Vientiane as part of a tour, or take the bus bound for Thabok from the southern bus station (every 30min; 30min) and ask to be dropped in Ban Na, where, if you ring ahead, a local guide will meet you

Phou Khao Khouay is basically to Vientiane what Khao Yai National Park is to Bangkok. Straddling three different administrative districts and forming the southern edge of the Ang Nam Ngum Reservoir, the huge NBCA features several large ranges and includes two peaks of over 1600m, one of which, Phou Xang, at 1666m, towers over the southern end of the Nam Ngum Lake. There are also several large **waterfalls**, including Tad Xay, Tad Leuk and Tad Phou Khao Khouay, accessible by road, and a smaller dam and reservoir, Nam Luek Reservoir, which can be reached by motor vehicle from the east. Highlights include **Asian elephants**, **tigers** and **gibbons**.

INFORMATION   PHOU KHAO KHOUAY NBCA

Accommodation There's basic homestay accommodation in Ban Na (to arrange this contact Mr Bounthanom; see below). It's also possible to camp at the Tad Leuk waterfall within the park, where tents are available to rent for 40,000K per night.

Tours Local guide Mr Bounthanom (☎020 2220 8286) is the best person to contact when organizing a trip. He runs tours to the eleven-metre-high Ban Na observation tower

(from 200,000K per person per day), where you can spend the night keeping watch for the wild elephants that pass by. Vientiane-based tour operator Green Discovery (☎021 264528, ⓦgreendiscoverylaos.com) also runs one- and two-day trips into the park from the capital, but unless you club together with other travellers the costs are prohibitively high (a one-day tour for one person costs more than $240).

1

Ang Nam Ngum Reservoir

Ninety kilometres north of Vientiane, the vast **Ang Nam Ngum Reservoir** sits above the northern edge of the Vientiane Plain, where the rice-growing flatlands surrounding the capital meet the mountainous terrain of the north. Created when the Nam Ngum River was dammed in 1971, the deep green waters of the reservoir are dotted with scores of forest-clad islands stretching to a dramatic horizon lined with mountains, their peaks lost in mist. Foreign travellers, usually in a rush to head upcountry, tend to bypass Ang Nam Ngum as they make for nearby Vang Vieng, but those who do stop off discover a pretty 250-square-kilometre expanse of water with islands, secluded beaches and swimming spots, and floating restaurants serving fresh fish dishes just above the water. Day-tripping Lao descend on the scenic reservoir in droves at weekends, hiring out wooden boats for picnic cruises. Guesthouses and hotels listed below should be able to point you in the direction of the best hiking trails.

There are a number of convenient options for visiting Ang Nam Ngum, either as a day-trip from Vientiane or Vang Vieng, or en route between the two; short package trips are also available from travel agents in Vientiane. The most logical base for independent travellers is **NA NAM**, a port of rickety shacks suspended above the water, with a clutch of tourist restaurants, basic accommodation, and a fleet of wooden tourist boats – some seating up to forty passengers.

ARRIVAL AND DEPARTURE   ANG NAM NGUM

BY PUBLIC TRANSPORT

From Vientiane Getting to Ang Nam Ngum by public transport is easy enough. From Vientiane, four government buses depart hourly from the Talat Sao bus station for Thalat. From Thalat, you can get a shared tuk-tuk to the reservoir (30min; 15,000K) or the regular tuk-tuk shuttle service to Na Nam, near the dam on the western shore of the reservoir. If you charter a vehicle for the day in Vientiane or decide to ride a motorbike, you might consider making a scenic detour en route along the quieter Route 10 via Ban Keun.

From Vang Vieng Southbound sawngthaews from Vang Vieng pass right by the town of Tha Hua at the northern end

of the reservoir, or you can switch vehicles at the Phonhong junction and cut in to Thalat and Na Nam.

ON A TOUR

From Vientiane Green Discovery (☎021 264528, ⑩ greendiscoverylaos.com) runs one-day tours to the reservoir, stopping en route at Dong Makai Market, with prices from $69 per person. Solo travellers will need to join up with others to keep costs reasonable.

From Vang Vieng Tour operators offer one- to three-day package tours to the reservoir out of Vang Vieng, which combine hiking, boating and camping.

ACCOMMODATION AND EATING

NA NAM

Long Ngum View Resort Near the port in Na Nam

☎021 214872. Popular with Lao spending a night away from the capital, this simple place just uphill from the port

---

KEEPING THE LIGHTS ON

Built with foreign expertise and funding, the **Ang Nam Ngum Reservoir** set a precedent for the production of **hydroelectricity** in Laos, and it continues to provide power for Vientiane and surrounding villages on the Vientiane Plain. Most of the power, however, flows across the Mekong into Thailand, which has an agreement to purchase Laos's surplus electricity.

At the time the dam was built, the Royalist government had only just plugged Vientiane into the hydroelectric dam before they were forced to cede power to the communist Pathet Lao. In an all too typical example of poor environmental planning, the builders of the dam had flooded a vast area of valuable forest 50m underwater. The rotting vegetation sucked oxygen out of the water and blocked up the turbines, a problem that was later turned into profit by underwater logging ventures, whose frogmen dropped to the reservoir floor to cut submerged trees with underwater saws.

Meanwhile, the new communist government found a novel use for the reservoir. After 1975, prostitutes, thieves and teenagers "infected with foreign ideas" were rounded up from the streets of Vientiane, a Lao Sodom in the eyes of the Pathet Lao, and were confined on islands in the middle of the lake for "re-education".

1

BOAT TRIPS ON THE ANG NAM NGUM RESERVOIR

Taking a boat trip is the best way to get a sense of just how big the reservoir is, but a shortage of small boats means tours tend to be aimed at larger groups. Freelance boatmen down at Na Nam's waterfront restaurants generally ask for 150,000K per hour but are willing to negotiate day rates in the vicinity of 400,000K. Na Nam guesthouses can also arrange **boat tours**. Obviously, the more people you have, the more affordable it becomes.

Beyond simply touring the reservoir, possibilities for boat trips include the secluded beach at Don Keng Phou Vieng – the hour-long trip to which passes the scenic Pha Tao or "star cliff" island; or down to the *DanSaVanh Nam Ngum Resort* (see below). Some of the islands are quite large; Don 516, for instance, supports a community of around five hundred families. To convince a boatman to make the three-hour round-trip to the island you'll need to stump up around 800,000K.

has bungalows and rooms with good views of the water. $20
Nam Ngum On the water's edge in Na Nam ☎ 020 5551 3521. The busiest and best-staffed of the restaurants overlooking the water, with freshly caught reservoir fish cooked in a variety of ways, such as fish *tom yam* (50,000K). Seats at the back have exceptional views of the lake. Daily 7am–8pm.

SOUTHERN SHORE

DanSaVanh Nam Ngum Resort On the reservoir's southern edge ☎ 021 5827 5555, ⓦ dansavanh.com. The largest and least subtle of the attempts to turn the reservoir into a major tourist attraction, DanSaVanh is a huge Chinese-owned hotel complete with casino, golf courses and a marina.

Vang Vieng and around

Change comes slowly to rural Laos, but **VANG VIENG**, the once-sleepy town that reclines on the east bank of the Nam Song River between towering limestone karsts, is something of a rare exception. Not so long ago, the main street was a potholed track, crowds were rare, and accommodation was limited to a handful of guesthouses. Then, as thousands of party-hungry backpackers descended on the self-styled "tubing capital of the world", the Lao government found itself struggling to control an inland version of Thailand's Ko Pha Ngan, complete with the drugs and drunken revelry.

Only in 2012, following the deaths of dozens of foreign tourists – mostly as a result of them being drunk or high on the river – did the government take action. The bars and nightclubs that had grown up around the river were torn down, their vertiginous rope swings and slides dismantled, and tubing all but stopped. When word got out, tourist arrivals fell by as much as seventy percent, and locals who'd taken out loans to build guesthouses and hotels during the boom years were left indebted, with little hope of paying their bills.

Today the place is slowly finding its feet again, with less of a focus on tubing, and new, more wholesome activities and day-trips attracting a different kind of tourist. The days of happy shakes and opium pizzas look to be well and truly over, though frustrated locals, many of whom were reliant on the backpacker trade, have successfully persuaded the authorities to allow a handful of bars to reopen along the river. Tubing undoubtedly remains a big draw, but as the jaw-droppingly beautiful landscape around town opens up to tourists, and more visitors see the appeal of spending a week here cycling, caving, rafting and hiking, there may be another, more positive way for the place to move forward.

Organized day tours, many of which combine both tubing and **caving** with lunch in between, are a fast and convenient way for the uninitiated to get into the Vang Vieng groove: once you've done the tour you can go back for more on your own. It's not hard to find a guided tour – just look for signs posted in restaurants and guesthouses. If you do opt to join a tour, be sure to check how many people will be in the group. Some agents have few qualms about stuffing twenty people into a single sawngthaew, which not only spoils a good walk but can seriously hasten the onset of claustrophobia if you're tramping about several hundred metres underground.

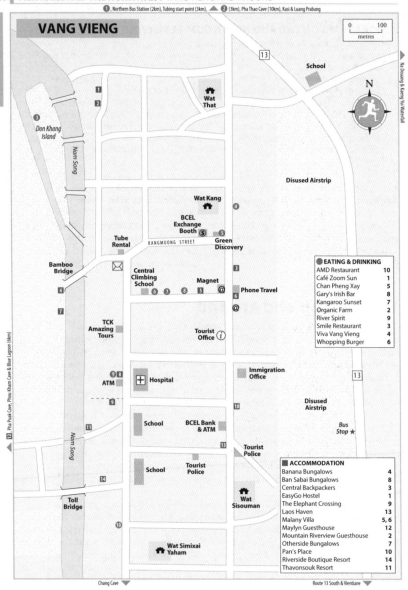

● Northern Bus Station (2km), Tubing start point (3km), ▲ ❷ (3km), Pha Thao Cave (10km), Kasi & Luang Prabang

VANG VIENG

EATING & DRINKING

AMD Restaurant	10
Café Zoom Sun	1
Chan Pheng Xay	5
Gary's Irish Bar	8
Kangaroo Sunset	7
Organic Farm	2
River Spirit	9
Smile Restaurant	3
Viva Vang Vieng	4
Whopping Burger	6

ACCOMMODATION

Banana Bungalows	4
Ban Sabai Bungalows	8
Central Backpackers	3
EasyGo Hostel	1
The Elephant Crossing	9
Laos Haven	13
Malany Villa	5, 6
Maylyn Guesthouse	12
Mountain Riverview Guesthouse	2
Otherside Bungalows	7
Pan's Place	10
Riverside Boutique Resort	14
Thavonsouk Resort	11

Chang Cave ▼   Route 13 South & Vientiane ▼

Chang Cave

Around 1.5km southwest of Vang Vieng • Daily 7.30am–5pm • It costs 2000K to enter the resort (4000K with a bike) plus 15,000K to access the cave

Vang Vieng's best-known cave, **Tham Chang**, has been developed for tourism to such an extent that the proprietors of *Vang Vieng Resort*, whose land you have to cross to get to the cave, levy a fee to enter the resort and again at the cave's entrance. In the nineteenth century, the cave earned its nom de guerre when it was used for defence during an invasion of Chinese Haw from the north ("chang" means steadfast).

Chinese bandits would have an easy run of the place these days, with steep stairs leading up the side of the cliff to the cave mouth. Inside, gaudy coloured lights illuminate cement pathways leading through the cavern, past rock formations that bear an uncanny resemblance to monkeys, frogs, a white elephant and the three-headed elephant, symbol of Lao royalty. Follow the path to the left and you'll wind up at a second cave mouth which affords a bird's-eye view of the valley below. At the base of the cave, cross a stream to find a third cave mouth out of which flows a spring leading into the Nam Song. It's possible to swim up the stream about 50m into this cave, which also has a Buddha image inside. The grassy lawn around the base of the cave is a pleasant spot to catch some rays.

VANG VIENG ACTIVITIES AND TOURS

The countryside around Vang Vieng is full of enough day-trip options to easily fill a week. Scores of caves in limestone karst outcrops, tranquil lowland Lao and minority villages, and Kaeng Yui Waterfall, all make worthy destinations for a rewarding day's hike (if walking isn't your thing, you can rent bicycles or motorbikes from various outlets around town), while the Nam Song River makes for a fun afternoon of **tubing** (see box, p.88), kayaking or rafting – tubes can be rented from the shop near the post office.

If you decide to visit the caves on your own, it's worth getting hold of a plastic map from the tourist office in town (10,000K), which will show you the location of the caves and trails. Otherwise just ask around; everyone in Vang Vieng has their favourite cave, swimming hole or countryside getaway. The local people are more than happy to point you in the right direction, and other travellers will also enthusiastically recommend the best places.

KAYAKING AND RAFTING

Green Discovery Kangmuong St ☏023 511230, ☷greendiscoverylaos.com. Offers a wide range of well-run trips, which mix kayaking with trekking and caving. The "Secret Eden" trip, taking in some spectacular scenery, is available as a one- or two-day excursion. From $28 per person.

TCK Amazing Tours On the main river road ☏023 511691, ☷tckadventureslaos.com. Popular half-day kayaking trips along the Nam Song River, passing some of the bars that tubers drink at, plus quieter stretches of the river. $12 per person.

ROCK CLIMBING

Central Climber School In the centre of town, near Whopping Burger ☏020 5401 8005, ☷phetnakhoneg@hotmail.com. Runs two half-day climbing tours per day (at 9am and 1pm), with English-speaking guides and prices dependent on how much gear you need to borrow.

Green Discovery Kangmuong St ☏023 511230, ☷greendiscoverylaos.com. Half-day, one-day and three-day climbing courses with routes graded from 5a to 8a+. It's also possible to hire gear on a day-by-day basis ($35 per day for a full set of gear for two people).

BALLOONING

Balloons Over Vang Vieng ☏020 9691 8111, ☷laoballooning.com. Hot-air balloon flights offering unrivalled views over Vang Vieng's limestone karsts

from October to April each year. Rides last 40mins, and are bookable through guesthouses and travel agents around town. $70 per person.

ZIP-LINING

Phone Travel Near Central Backpackers in town ☏020 5552 8090, ☷laokim.com. Twice-daily zip-lining tours from the centre of town. Participants are bussed out to Kaeng Yui Waterfall and have the chance to swim after taking on the high wires. $28 per person.

BUGGY TOURS

TCK Amazing Tours On the main river road ☏023 511691, ☷tckadventureslaos.com. From its garage towards the south of town, TCK organizes self-driven tours in powerful dirt buggies, capable of tackling some of the bumpier roads around town. $40 per person.

DIRT BIKING

Uncle Tom's A short walk west of the toll bridge on the western side of the river ☏020 2995 8903, ☷uncletomstrails@hotmail.com. Explore off-road routes around Vang Vieng on good-quality dirt bikes. Previous experience recommended, though lessons are available.

LONGER EXCURSIONS

Aside from a number of organized tours around Vang Vieng itself, there are also one- to three-day excursions to **Ang Nam Ngum Reservoir** that can be booked through most guesthouses.

1

TUBING THE NAM SONG

Love or hate what it's done to the place, **tubing** remains Vang Vieng's premier attraction. In fact, for some people, it's the very reason they ended up in Laos. What started as an inventive way to spend a lazy afternoon floating down the **Nam Song** rapidly evolved into an all-you-can-drink party on the river, and by 2011, the town was thronging with backpackers who came not just to tube, but to party at the clubs that sprang up in town and in the middle of the river.

These days the tubing – and the partying – is more relaxed. Only a few bars now dot the river, and illegal drugs (once sold openly on menus) are seldom seen. For many, drinking is still a big part of the experience, though, with bars offering free shots of *lào-lào* and buy-one-get-one-free deals on whisky. While the rope swings and slides (which, combined with an excess of alcohol, led to a number of fatal accidents) have now disappeared, drinking on the river is still risky, so take care and, if you're a weak swimmer, ask for a **life jacket**.

To avoid getting back after dark, it's best to start tubing early. **Tubes** are available from the lock-up near the post office. There's no need to book so just turn up, pay the fee (55,000K, plus a 60,000K deposit) and a tuk-tuk will drive you to the starting point, 3km north of town near the Organic Mulberry Farm. Tuk-tuks will only depart with at least four people on board, so on quiet days you may have to wait for others to arrive.

A float back into town should take two or three hours from here, but you could easily spend the whole day dancing, drinking and playing mud volleyball at the bars along the way. It's important to leave enough time to get back before dark, however, as it gets cold and it becomes almost impossible to see where you're going in the fast-flowing water. Arrive back late and you will lose your deposit. A good sunblock is essential if you don't want to come out looking like a lobster; the tropical sun is powerful, even on overcast days. And while the tube rental place rents out dry bags, these should not be relied upon to protect phones and other valuables.

Pha Puak Cave

Around 2km west of Vang Vieng; signs point the way • 10,000K

Close to Vang Vieng on the west side of the river lies **Tham Pha Puak**, a cave tucked into a karst encircled by Pha Daeng, or the Red Cliffs. Pha Daeng is considered particularly sacred and some locals even maintain that planes flying over the cliff do so at their peril, no doubt a legend with roots in the Second Indochina War, when Vang Vieng was used as an airbase, known to pilots as Lima Site 6. Although in and of itself nothing special, the cave makes a good short walk or bike ride out of Vang Vieng, and is generally quieter than other caves close to the centre.

Phou Kham Cave and the Blue Lagoon

6km west of Vang Vieng; cross the toll bridge next to *Riverside Boutique Resort* and follow the road to Na Thong, 4km west. Signs will lead you to the car park, where the 10,000K admission fee is collected. If you take a torch, you'll avoid having to rent one (10,000K). A tuk-tuk from the centre to the lagoon should cost no more than 80,000K, including a two-hour wait

Tham Phou Kham makes a rewarding half-day trip that takes in some fine scenery and affords the chance to visit a cave and enjoy a good swim along the way. The path to the entrance is a short, steep climb and is extremely slippery in the rainy season, but there's plenty of bamboo to grab onto on the way up. In the main cavern reclines a bronze Buddha, while there are tunnels branching off the main gallery that you can explore if you have a torch. Tours of the cave cost 50,000K but are not mandatory. On the way to the cave, the bright-blue **lagoon** (actually a stream full of fish) is a great spot for a swim, and you can buy cool beer, fruit and snacks at stalls nearby. Small wooden shelters provide shade, and the well-maintained lawn is a good place to sunbathe, play frisbee or chat with other travellers.

Kaeng Yui Waterfall

Around 6km east of Vang Vieng • To get to the falls from town, cross Route 13 just north of the old airstrip and follow the bumpy road east (a sign points the way) • A 10,000K admission fee is charged when you reach the car park

While it may seem counterintuitive to turn your back on Vang Vieng's majestic karsts, a day spent out east at **Tad Kaeng Yui**, with its twin 30m-high waterfalls, is well worth the trip – especially in the rainy season. Once off the beaten track, Tad Kaeng Yui is now connected to the town centre by a bumpy dirt road, but is still a peaceful spot, nestled in the forest among the hills protecting Vang Vieng's eastern flank. Besides offering a refreshingly cool picnic spot, with small pools of water directly under the falls to lounge in, it rewards the journey with the sense of being smack in the middle of the tropics, miles from anywhere. Along the path to the falls, keep an eye out for reptiles, giant stick insects and butterflies. Tourists arriving at the waterfall on zip-lining trips from town (see p.87) tend to stop for refreshments at the food stalls near the car park, where locals sell cold drinks and fresh coconuts.

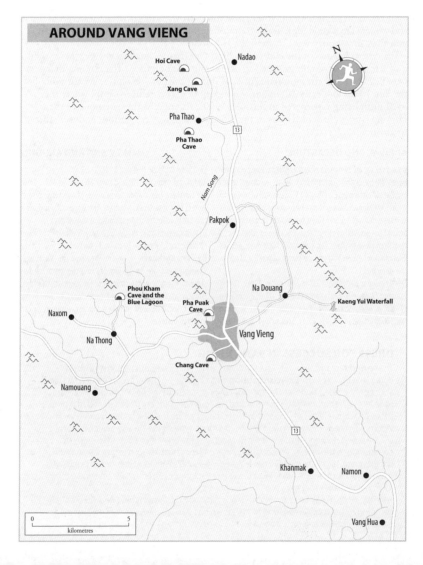

1

Pha Thao Cave

13km north of Vang Vieng; turn left after the bridge just beyond the Kilometre 10 marker on Route 13 – a road sign points the way to the cave – and head for the river. Cross the skinny suspension bridge and you'll reach the village of Pha Thao at the base of a cliff. The cave (10,000K) is hard to spot, so ask locals to point you in the right direction

A descent into **Tham Pha Thao** is the most satisfying caving trip you can make from Vang Vieng. Stretching for more than 2km, the tunnel-like cave is pitch-black and filled with huge and presumably ancient stalactites and stalagmites. It also contains a **swimming hole**, formed in an underground river that winds through the cave. The cave is best visited near the end of the rainy season, when the water level is perfect for a swim in the subterranean pool 800m into the cave. In the height of the dry season, it's possible to go beyond this point and explore the full length of the cave. If you explore the cave during the rainy season, you'll be up to your chest in water at times – so travel light and don't bring along anything that you don't want to get wet. A waterproof torch and camera are a good idea. Tour groups often pull through this cave during the morning, so you may want to go in the afternoon.

The cave is located in the cliff face behind **Pha Thao**, a smallish village where you'll find a few simple restaurants serving drinks and Hmong food. The Hmong living here fled the northern mountains of Laos during the post-revolutionary turmoil of the late 1970s and early 1980s and wound up in a Thai refugee camp, where they lived until being repatriated in the mid-1990s. Essentially, they are some of the Hmong who were denied visas to the US and other Western nations and were forced to go "home".

ARRIVAL AND DEPARTURE

By bus There are two main arrival and departure points for buses. VIP buses and minivans from points north and south use the old airstrip just off Route 13, to the east of town and within walking distance of most accommodation. Hostels and guesthouses around town sell tickets to destinations across Laos (as well as other parts of Southeast Asia). Prices vary from place to place, but only by 20,000K or so, and it's likely that wherever you end up booking, you'll end up on the same bus.

Destinations: Bangkok, Thailand (2 daily; 12hr); Luang Prabang (7 daily; 5–6hr); Pakse (1 daily; 16hr); Phonsavan (1 daily; 6hr); Savannakhet (1 daily; 10hr); Si Phan Don/4000 islands (1 daily; 11hr); Thakhek (1 daily; 9hr);

VANG VIENG AND AROUND

Vientiane (at least 10 daily; 3–4hr).
Additional ordinary, VIP and minivan services leave from the northern bus station, 2km north of the town centre. Tickets for these services bought in town usually include a tuk-tuk transfer from guesthouses in the centre.
Destinations: Luang Prabang (2 daily; 5–6hr); Phonsavan (2 daily; 6hr); Vientiane (9 daily; 3–4hr).
By sawngthaew If you're heading to Vientiane, sawngthaews are an option, leaving the northern bus station every twenty minutes throughout the day, though as they take around four hours to reach the capital, you'd do well to take a quicker, similarly priced minivan instead.

DRESS FOR SUCCESS IN VANG VIENG

The **varied terrain** surrounding Vang Vieng can turn treacherous in a hurry, particularly during the rainy season. **Exercise caution** while wandering through caves and scrambling about on the steep slopes of the karst formations, as serious injuries incurred by foolhardy travellers while tramping about in the area are common. Slippery trails demand that proper shoes be worn – Teva-style sandals with good traction are the best for conquering Vang Vieng's alternately rocky and muddy trails. Bermuda-type shorts are also a good sartorial choice as you may end up knee-deep in water at some point if you intend to enjoy the countryside to the fullest. A re-sealable plastic bag for valuables such as money and your passport is an excellent idea. Do not leave your valuables with local kids or teenagers, who may offer to "look after them for you" while you explore a cave, and make sure you get back to town before dark – robberies have been reported.

Finally, while it may be tempting to wander around in your swimming gear (and it's very common to see travellers walking around town half-naked), always remember that in Laos gratuitous displays of flesh are considered a form of rudeness and disrespect.

INFORMATION

Tourist information Opposite the Agricultural Promotion bank on the main road, just south of the centre wtourismlaos.org. Little English is spoken here, but staff should be able to point you in the direction of local caves and tour companies. They also sell a good plastic map of the town and the surrounding sights (10,000K). Mon–Fri 8am–noon and then 2–4pm.

GETTING AROUND

Most of Vang Vieng's streets are nameless, but getting around this small town is a fairly simple matter. Pushbikes (15,000K/day) and mountain bikes (20,000K/day) can be rented at many places around town. Mopeds are also available at guesthouses and travel shops. Although the cheap, Chinese-made bikes may look tempting at just 30,000K/day, we've heard frequent reports of breakdowns and broken spokes. It's worth the extra money to rent a proper Honda bike (60,000K). Sawngthaews to surrounding villages leave from the stand at the central market. The majority of Vang Vieng's attractions lie on the **west bank** of the Nam Song. There's now a permanent toll bridge crossing the river (4000K return for pedestrians, 6000K for bikes and 10,000K for motorcycles) or, if they haven't been washed away, you can cross for free using the rickety bamboo bridges towards the north of town. The pirogues down by *Thavonsouk Resort* will ferry people across the water for 10,000K. On the other side, Chinese-made tractors trundle along the bumpy paths to nearby villages, acting as makeshift shared taxis that aren't entirely comfortable but are at least faster than walking. You can simply flag them down as you would a bus or tuk-tuk – expect to pay 5000K for journeys of up to 1km, then 2000K for each extra kilometre. If you're looking to explore **areas north or south of town**, you'll find enough local transport in the form of buses and sawngthaews plying Route 13 to get you up and down the highway cheaply. Or, if you prefer something quick and easy, just hire a tuk-tuk (the stand is at the market), which will gladly wait for you for the right price.

ACCOMMODATION

Despite its small size, Vang Vieng is one of the best-value spots for accommodation in the country – it's possible to find a perfectly decent en-suite double here for under $10. On the downside, most of the town's **guesthouses** seem to have been built by the same architect, whose forte is huge, concrete monstrosities with Corinthian columns. Most visitors seem to end up in these cheap but less-than-atmospheric digs in the centre of town. For something with more character, try one of the boutique hotels or bungalow operations along the river, which have views of the Nam Song and mountains beyond.

Banana Bungalows Just north of Otherside Bungalows (see p.92), on the western side of the river ☎020 5501 4937, ✉banana_bungalow@hotmail .com. If you're on a budget and want relative peace and quiet without being too far from the action, these plain bungalows do the job nicely. The cheapest have a shared bathroom, while for 30,000K extra you can upgrade to an en-suite bungalow. 50,000K

Ban Sabai Bungalows Opposite the hospital, towards the south of town ☎020 7755 3225, �🌐inthira.com. Reasonably well-equipped bungalows on stilts, built close to the Nam Song and with shared use of a small pool. Rooms come with a/c and spacious verandas, but are a looking a bit worn. The view from the restaurant (see p.92) is divine. $30

Central Backpackers On the main road, just south of the junction with Kangmuong St ☎023 511593, �🌐vangviengbackpackers.com. Despite the thick-of-it-all location, *Central Backpackers* is actually very good value. Dorms are clean and tidy, with single beds instead of bunks, and the double and triple rooms feel spacious. The ground-floor restaurant isn't great but at least provides a place to meet others. Dorm 30,000K, double 80,000K, triple 120,000K

EasyGo Hostel North of town on the main river road, near Mountain Riverview ☎023 511725, ⍵easygohostel.com. Bargain bamboo dorms and doubles cling to the hillside at this youthful hostel on the road leading to Wat That. It's all a little dingy but the showers are hot, the wi-fi is free and there's a pool table by the entrance. Dorm 23,000K, double 50,000K

The Elephant Crossing At the southern end of the main river road, just south of the hospital ☎023 511232, ⍵theelephantcrossinghotel.com. Although billed as a boutique hotel, this popular place is actually housed in a large concrete building on the edge of the Nam Song. Its 31 well-equipped rooms all have good views over the river and mountains, and the restaurant downstairs is perfect for a quiet meal after a hard day's exploring. Reservations recommended. $45

★**Laos Haven** Just south of the tourist office on the main road through town ☎020 5904 3944, ⍵laoshavenhotel.com. Well run and sparkly clean, Laos Haven is a great mid-range option for couples and young families (family rooms are charged at 100,000K per person). Each room has its own safe, and breakfast is included in the rate. 150,000K

Malany Villa On the same street as Kangaroo Sunset and Gary's Irish Bar ☎023 511083. Cheap, cleanish double rooms in two ugly but central buildings (the second

1

is just to the east, on the main drag). The rate includes free wi-fi. **50,000K**

★ **Maylyn Guesthouse** On the western side of the Nam Song ☎ 020 5560 4095, ⊕ facebook.com/maylyn guesthouse. Rustic bamboo bungalows set around a peaceful, flower-filled garden on the west side of the river, far from the noise of any late-night parties. There's a sociable little chill-out area at the front, and there are several caves nearby. **50,000K**

Mountain Riverview Guesthouse North of the town centre, close to the river ☎ 023 511699. One of the few guesthouses built in the boom years to retain a little bit of character, this place has clean, fan-cooled rooms. Some, like the name suggests, have excellent views of the distant mountains – though you'll pay 20,000K extra for the privilege. **60,000K**

Otherside Bungalows Just south of Banana Bungalows (see p.91), on the western side of the river ☎ 020 5610 6070. The en-suite rooms here are slightly cheaper than those at *Banana Bungalows*, next door, but feel a little damp and drab. Even so, the staff are friendly,

and free tea and coffee helps to sweeten the deal. **60,000K**

Pan's Place At the southern end of the main road ☎ 023 511484, ⊕ pansplacelaos.com. A popular budget pick, *Pan's Place* has a relaxed TV room and a selection of single, double and triple rooms with shared facilities. For 20,000K more, you can bag yourself a room with an en-suite bathroom. **50,000K**

★ **Riverside Boutique Resort** South of town on the road down to the toll bridge ☎ 023 511726, ⊕ riversidevangvieng.com. The slickest, smartest hotel in Vang Vieng, with prices to match. Taking styling cues from ethnic groups across Laos, the fresh, cool rooms here edge a gorgeous turquoise pool, which is framed by limestone karsts on the other side of the river. **$102**

Thavonsouk Resort ☎ 023 511096, ⊕ thavonsouk .com. At the far end of the main river road, south of the hospital. Mid-range bungalows, some with private balconies, enjoying a prime location on the banks of the Nam Song. There are 52 units to choose from, with prices dependent on the size and quality of the bungalow. **$33**

EATING AND DRINKING

Vang Vieng is hardly short of places to eat, but you'll have to search hard to find good food; most **restaurants** have near-identical menus featuring bland tourist munchies. The relatively lax regulations and low start-up costs associated with the town mean foreign-run eating and drinking establishments aren't unusual in Vang Vieng, and it's possible to find anything from vindaloos to fish tacos. Budget travellers tend to eat at the sandwich and pancake stalls around town, or on the main north–south road where there's a whole strip of cheap (some say depressing) restaurants showing *Friends* and *Family Guy* episodes on an endless loop. Apart from these places in the centre of town, there are a few decent restaurants overlooking the river. Now that the clubs on the island in the Nam Song have been closed, parties tend to happen in the centre of town. There are two main **late-night venues**: Viva Vang Vieng (see p.93) and Room 101. They're opposite each other on the main drag, and host cheesy club nights on alternate days. Regardless of which club's night it is, things get lively at around midnight when the other bars close.

★ **AMD Restaurant** South of the hospital along the main river road ☎ 020 5530 1238. Pint-sized, family-run restaurant serving some of the best food in town. The tangy *tom yam* soup (35,000K) is reason enough to make the walk south from the centre, but the tiny open kitchen also turns out good curries, stir-fries and steaks. Daily 7.30am–10pm.

Café Zoom Sun 3km north of town on the road leading to the Organic Mulberry Farm ☎ 020 5610 6536. Near the tubing start point, this café was set up to help local kids get involved with wholesome activities like traditional dancing and weaving. For $3, you can get a coffee and a guided tour of the centre. Tues–Sun 2–7pm.

Chan Pheng Xay Just east of the Green Discovery office on Kangmuong Street ☎ 020 2889 0860. One of the more reliable street-side restaurants in the very centre of town, with reasonable red curries (meat and veggie versions available) for 25,000K. Daily 7am–11pm.

Gary's Irish Bar Just east of Kangaroo Sunset in the centre of town ☎ 030 940 7039, ⊕ garysirishbar.com. Chirpy Irish bar staff and regular live music sessions make Gary's stand out among the cookie-cutter bars in the centre

of town. There's also a good pool table, a dartboard and live football on the TV. Daily 9am–midnight.

Kangaroo Sunset Just west of Gary's Irish Bar in the centre of town. The post-tubing *bar du jour*, with beer pong, free pool and cheap drinks (a large Beerlao costs 10,000K between 7 and 8pm every night) helping to pull in a young farang crowd. Daily 8am–midnight.

Organic Mulberry Farm At the tubing start point (see p.88), 3km north of town ⊕ laofarm.org. It's said tubing started at this farm when the owner encouraged his volunteers to explore the river in a new way. Today it's still the start point for tubing, but is worth stopping off at for its tasty drinks and snacks, based around organic ingredients grown on the farm, including iced mulberry tea (5000K) and a Lao garden salad (20,000K). Daily 7am–9pm.

River Spirit At Ban Sabai Bungalows (see p.91). Good Lao and Thai dishes in an excellent waterfront setting. The extensive menu includes spring rolls with pork (35,000K) and a vegetable larp (28,000K), plus a few western dishes like burgers and steaks. Daily 7.30am–10pm.

Smile Restaurant Towards the north of the island in

the middle of the Nam Song; best accessed using the northernmost bamboo bridge from town. Known as Smile Bar until the government cleared all "bars" from along the river, Smile Restaurant is one of the few surviving spots in the middle of the river where you can swing in a hammock drinking beer (15,000K) or a fruit shake (8000K). As the name of his bar implies, the owner is a happy chappy. Daily 10am–8pm.

Viva Vang Vieng Opposite Room 101 on the main drag. There's little in it between Vang Vieng's two late-night clubs, which both play loud chart hits from the past couple of years. Of the two, Viva is bigger and tends to fill up more quickly. Open until around 2am every other night.

Whopping Burger Next door to the Central Climbing School in the centre of town ⊖whoppingburger @hotmail.co.jp. Funky, Japanese-run restaurant serving tasty burgers (with extraordinarily large buns) while 60s and 70s music blares out. Try the samurai chicken burger, which comes with chunky chips and bundles of fresh coriander (50,000K). Daily 6–11pm.

DIRECTORY

Internet Free wi-fi is available at all but the simplest of guesthouses and restaurants. Computers hooked up to printers and the internet can be found at a dozen different places on the main drag, charging 200K/minute.

Mail The post office (Mon–Fri 8am–11.30am & 1.30–4.30pm) is tucked away near the tube rental shop in the town centre.

Medical facilities Vang Vieng's hospital (24hr) is south of town on the main river road. Small pharmacies are dotted around town, and most staff speak basic English.

Money There's a helpful branch of the BCEL bank (Mon–Sat 8am–noon & 1–4pm) with exchange services and an ATM on the main street opposite the *Dok Khoun I* guesthouse. Other banks include the Lao Development Bank on the town's main north–south road, and an Agricultural Promotion Bank on the same street further south.

The Royal Road: Kasi to Luang Prabang

The quickest route from Vientiane to Luang Prabang is to follow **Route 13** north through the karst mountains of Vang Vieng and up the **old Royal Road** through the mountains north of **Kasi**. Route 13 was laid down by the French in 1943, and although it was improved in the 1960s with American aid, there was very little maintenance on the road until the mid-1990s, when it was properly sealed. Until that time, this rough track of a road took at best a full 24 hours to traverse, and often as long as three days. The highway was finally completed in 1996 after years of toil by Vietnamese road workers, twenty of whom were killed by guerrillas in the process. The breathtaking mountain scenery from Kasi to Luang Prabang makes this one of the most **scenic routes** in all Southeast Asia.

Kasi

KASI is the northernmost town before Route 13 begins its wild 170-kilometre journey along steep ridges and around hairpin bends, with headlong views of rugged valleys and remote mountains as far as the eye can see. The road runs right through the centre of town, forming the main street. The town itself lies in the attractive **Nam Lik river valley** surrounded by rice paddies and low hills, with the occasional karst adding an exotic touch to a pretty landscape. Around Kasi are numerous vast cave systems rumoured to dwarf anything found at Vang Vieng, 60km to the south, but so far plans to develop the Kasi area into a tourist region have come to nought. If the rumours of Olympic-pool-sized cave lakes and caverns large enough to house cathedrals are only half true, then Kasi's hopes of being the next Vang Vieng may some day become a reality. Kasi has a few guesthouses and half-a-dozen decent **places to eat**; buses plying the road between Vientiane and Luang Prabang usually make a lunch stop here.

ARRIVAL AND DEPARTURE   KASI

By bus or minivan Buses from Luang Prabang and Vientiane pull in at a dusty lot, just north of where Route 13 meets the road to Sayaboury. The main strip is within walking distance along Route 13. The journey from Kasi to Luang Prabang costs 80,000K per person, regardless of whether you go by bus or minivan.
Destinations: Luang Prabang (3 daily; 3hr); Vientiane (3 daily; 4hr).

ACCOMMODATION AND EATING

Vanpisit Guesthouse In the centre of town on the main strip ☎ 023 700084. If you need to crash in Kasi, this clean and central place is the best bet. There are three buildings: one is a block that's usually reserved for Chinese and Vietnamese workers and is in considerably worse condition than the other two. The restaurant out front is a popular stop for VIP buses travelling to Luang Prabang, and there are a handful of Western dishes on offer (around 20,000K). **100,000K**

Vieng Kham

Perched on a narrow mountain ridge 39km north of Kasi and just 5km before Phou Khoun, the village of **VIENG KHAM** offers good views to the west of one of Laos's most magnificent **peaks** – a gigantic, lone 2097-metre crag that rises like a giant tooth out of the flatlands below. If you're travelling south, Vieng Kham affords the first view of this breathtaking peak and its more distant companion, which stands at an equally impressive 2089m. Whether you're travelling north or south on Route 13, it's well worth getting a window seat on the west-facing side of the bus in order to photograph these spectacular peaks. South of Vieng Kham there's a long, slow winding descent towards Kasi.

Phou Khoun and Route 7 to Phonsavan

A former French outpost, the mountain village of **PHOU KHOUN**, 44km north of Kasi, is the junction of Route 13 and Route 7. The village has sweeping views of the deep valleys below, and is the main market for people living in isolated villages around the area. Given the mountain location, be warned that the weather can get quite chilly here.

From Phou Khoun, **Route 7** branches off from Route 13 and travels due east across the Xieng Khuang Plateau to **Phonsavan** on the Plain of Jars. This road has been greatly improved in recent years, making it possible to get all the way from Vientiane to Phonsavan in around ten hours, although picking up one of these daily buses at Phou Khoun can prove to be an ordeal: by the time the bus gets here from Vientiane, it is packed, so chances are you'll be standing all the way unless another passenger is prepared to sell you their seat.

ACCOMMODATION AND EATING   PHOU KHOUN

Nang Ouan Just east of the point where Route 13 meets Route 7, a short walk from the market ☎ 020 5534 2375. Bare-bones restaurant, serving fried rice and fragrant noodle soups, loaded with chilli and coriander (15,000K). There's an English menu here. Daily 6am–10pm.

Say Phavong Guesthouse At the junction of routes 13 and 7, diagonally opposite the market ☎ 020 5538 9888. The six rooms here are as basic as it gets, lacking even a fan – but it's generally cool enough in town that you won't need one. Mr Won is friendly enough but speaks little English. **60,000K**

Phou Khoun to Xieng Ngeun

From Phou Khoun, tiny picturesque villages cling to the mountain ridges every 20km or so for the rest of the journey north to Luang Prabang, only a few of them providing tables at which to eat a bowl of *fŏe*. If you're travelling by rented or chartered vehicle, you could try the proper noodle shop at **Pha Keng Noi** (see opposite), a small village

> ### PHOU PHANANG NBCA
> **Phou Phanang NBCA** runs close to Route 13 for 75km, but although tracks lead into the reserve off Route 13, the NBCA is still fairly inaccessible to tourists. However, if you're prepared to rent a four-wheel-drive vehicle or dirt bike from Vientiane, you could try a dirt track running the entire western boundary of the reserve and linking several villages.

perched on a narrow ridge 15km north of Phou Khoun. **Kiou Ka Cham**, 45km north of Phou Khoun, is a larger town, populated by **Hmong**, and located high up in the mountains. It has two very basic guesthouses, several restaurants, tiny pharmacies and general stores selling basic goods and petrol out of old oil drums. To the north, the highway continues to wind through the green-blue mountains, passing ethnic-minority villages and swidden fields cutting bare the hillsides, until it reaches **Xieng Ngeun**, a large settlement, 24km south of Luang Prabang. These days it's a hive of hydropower activity, with three dams in the local area supplying electricity to Thailand. Xieng Ngeun is also an important junction: from here **Route 2** heads southwest 110km to the provincial capital of Sayaboury, on the western side of the Mekong river.

ACCOMMODATION	PHOU KHOUN TO XIENG NGEUN
Duangchavit Opposite the post office in Kiou Ka Cham ☎071 252568. Dark, dingy double rooms and dirty bathrooms mean you should only really stay here if Kijokajam (see below) is already full. Twins are more expensive than doubles at 70,000K. **50,000K**	**Kijokajam** A few doors down from Duangchavit in Kiou Ka Cham ☎071 251571. Eight very basic rooms, each sharing a hot-water bathroom at the end of the corridor and set around a scruffy garden with two caged pet monkeys. **60,000K**

EATING AND DRINKING	
Xom View Thammasa Around 500m north of Pha Keng Noi village along the main road ☎020 9835 9570. This no-frills roadside stop is popular with long-distance	drivers and, if nothing else, serves as a quiet spot to grab a cold drink. Noodle dishes and soups (around 30,000K) are also on offer. Daily 6am–7pm.

The Sayaboury circuit

While the vast majority of visitors use Route 13 between Vientiane and Luang Prabang, it is possible to swing through Laos's northwestern frontier provided you're willing to allow three to four days for the journey. The detour through **SAYABOURY PROVINCE**, the sparsely populated region of rugged valleys and wild elephants on the western side of the Mekong, takes you along a path well off the banana-pancake backpacker circuit. This could soon change; until a few years ago, travelling the route involved using a muddy combination of road and river, with at least part of the journey by boat along the Mekong. Now, the roads have improved to such an extent that boats have stopped running. In any case, the hugely controversial Sayaboury Dam (one of eleven hydroelectric dams planned for the lower Mekong's main stream, and currently being built just east of Sayaboury town) would make navigating this stretch of the river impossible.

Route 2, running the length of Sayaboury Province between Luang Prabang and the bustling border town of **Kenthao**, is especially beautiful, particularly in the rice-growing season (June–Nov), with the electric-green paddies set against a sea of bluish mountains – some as high as 2000m – receding in waves towards Thailand. Whether you travel by bus, by motorbike or with a private car, **Paklai** and **Sayaboury** are the best places to make stopovers. Even with the newly capped roads, journeys can be tortuously slow and in the rainy season especially, washouts and mudslides are common. Needless to say, getting to Sayaboury's remotest corners isn't easy. Secluded caves and waterfalls are out there, but none lies on the tourist route. The region will probably be one of the last places to benefit from the country's improved tourist infrastructure, which is inspiration enough to try this route.

Paklai

PAKLAI, a port town 210km south of Luang Prabang, is the best stopover between Vientiane and Sayaboury. Although not as developed as the border town of Kenthao, 60km to the south, Paklai is bigger, its wooden houses spreading for several kilometres

1

NAM PHOUN NBCA

A 150km-long section of the border with Thailand consists of the massive **Nam Phoun NBCA**, Laos's westernmost bio-conservation area. The chain of mountains forming the park's spine includes peaks as high as 1790m. Two significant streams, the Pouy and the Phoun, flow down from heights above and cross the width of Sayaboury province before flowing into the Mekong. Although the town of Nakong on Route 2 sits right on the edge of the park, the NBCA has yet to be developed for trekking.

along the riverbank. For now, crossing the Mekong here involves using the dilapidated car ferry (motorbikes 5000K, cars 35,000K), but a new bridge may be open around 100m further downriver by the time you read this.

ARRIVAL AND DEPARTURE   PAKLAI

By bus and sawngthaew Now that speedboats have stopped running, the only way to reach Paklai is by road. One slow bus departs Paklai for Vientiane each day at 8.30am (80,000K). Minivans bound for Vientiane leave four times a day from a separate minivan lot, taking around five hours to complete the journey (100,000K). Prices include the ferry crossing. Sawngthaews leave from the market in the morning for the 100km trundle to Sayaboury town, charging 60,000K per passenger (4 daily; 4hr).

To Thailand Four sawngthaews per day leave Paklai's market bound for Kenthao and the border with Thailand at Nam Heuang (daily 8am–4pm, though you may be able to pay an overtime fee to cross at other times). Buses from points north bound for Loei in Thailand can cross the Friendship Bridge, but otherwise you'll be dropped at the border and expected to take a tuk-tuk across. At the time of writing the border was open to foreigners, but there have been reports of it closing unexpectedly. Check ahead. Thai visas are available on arrival, but Lao visas are not.

ACCOMMODATION

Jainhny Guesthouse ☏ 030 946 2014. Just south of the centre on the river road. Cool, welcoming guesthouse with ten good-sized rooms, a friendly owner and gorgeous views of the Mekong. Air-con, if you need it, costs 20,000K extra per night. **50,000K**

SAYABOURY PROVINCE: THE LAO WILD WEST

Something of a Lao Wild West, the remote, densely forested and mountainous **Sayaboury Province** is home to elephants, tigers and the Sumatran rhino. Recognizing it as the perfect place to disappear, CIA operatives active in the Second Indochina War saw Sayaboury as the escape route for **Vang Pao** and his band of Hmong irregulars (see p.276) should their "secret war" go wrong. The untamed nature of the province is perhaps best illustrated by the traditional lifestyle of the **Mabri**, a tribe of nomadic hunter-gatherers numbering only a few hundred, who are known to the Lao as *kha tawng leuang* or "slaves of yellow banana leaves" – the name is derived from the tribal custom of moving on as soon as the leaves of their huts turn yellow.

Some of the villages are so remote that they hardly feel part of Laos, finding it far more convenient to trade with Thai towns across the border, or to simply exist in relatively isolated self-sufficiency. Seizing upon the Lao government's seeming neglect of its far-flung villages, the Thais claimed three Lao villages near the border as their own in a land grab during the 1980s – an incident that sparked two skirmishes between the historic rivals during the course of four years and highlighted the vagueness of the border.

These days the line separating Laos from its larger neighbour has been sketched somewhat more permanently on the map, and it's business as usual for traders on either side, with the border town of **Kenthao** functioning as a gateway for goods flowing across the Nam Huang River. A fair number of smuggled cars, sparkling new and without plates, also pass through here and continue on to Vientiane, where they change hands for a fraction of their tax-heavy cost. Amphetamine production is another thorny cross-border issue, with Thai police accusing clandestine factories on the Lao side of producing *ya ba*, or methamphetamine, which ends up on the streets of the Thai capital Bangkok.

ELEPHANTS IN SAYABOURY

Mention Sayaboury to a Laotian, and more often than not they'll start talking about elephants. Locals have long used the creatures to work the region's rich forests, and today, Sayaboury province still has the country's greatest concentration of elephants – many of them still actively involved in logging. Each February several dozen local pachyderms take a break from their usual routines to join the glitzy three-day **Sayaboury Elephant Festival** (Ⓦ sayabourytourism.com), which includes a "Miss Elephant" contest, dance shows, an elephant banquet and, attracting most attention of all, the coveted Elephant of the Year prize. If you want to visit during the festival, be sure to book accommodation ahead of time – hotels can be booked up for months in advance.

To see elephants in a more natural setting, consider a trip to the **Elephant Conservation Centre** (Ⓦ elephantconservationcenter.com), just west of Sayaboury town, where elephants that were once involved in the logging industry are given the chance to live out their lives more peacefully, offering short rides to visitors. Visitors can stay at the centre on a night-by-night basis (double $70) or volunteer for longer periods of time ($400/week), with the chance to bathe the elephants, learn from local mahouts and meet with the centre's veterinarian. The setting on the edge of a serene lake is superb, but in line with the centre's low-impact philosophy, accommodation is very basic.

Sayaboury

SAYABOURY, a dusty, independent-minded town, sits on the Nam Houng River, with the massive grey-and-white Pha Xang limestone cliffs – so named because they bear a passing resemblance to a herd of elephants in motion – providing a distant backdrop. Today it's real-life elephants that draw the majority of tourists here (see box above).

People from the local **hill tribes** often come down to buy and sell at the town's bustling **market**, spreading out their weird and wonderful range of produce (roots and forest creatures among other things) on swaths of cloth in neat rows around the fringe of the market proper, while members of the Mien tribe run the more established stalls. The textiles available in this section of the market are mostly from Vientiane, so you won't find many treasures here.

ARRIVAL AND DEPARTURE SAYABOURY

By plane The airport, 1km south of town, used to connect Sayaboury with Vientiane, but flights on this route have been suspended indefinitely.

By bus and sawngthaew Sayaboury has two bus stations, one at the southern end of town for vehicles shuttling the 100km road between Sayaboury and Paklai (5 daily; 60,000K), and another at the northern end of town

for vehicles to Vientiane and Luang Prabang. Buses travelling from Luang Prabang to Loei, Thailand, also stop here. Tuk-tuks make the trip into town from both of the bus stations, stopping at the central market (10,000K).

Destinations Luang Prabang (2 daily; 3–4hr); Nam Heuang, for Thailand (1 daily; 4hr); Paklai (at least 5 daily; 3hr); Vientiane (4 daily; 8hr).

ACCOMMODATION AND EATING

Meky In town, around 700m north of the Phongsavanh Bank ☎ 074 211382. The most reliable accommodation option in the town centre, with sixteen half-decent rooms, each with pink bedsheets, a fan, TV, a/c and en-suite bathroom. There's free internet access and coffee in reception. **60,000K**

Nam Tien On the edge of the Nam Tien Lake around 8km southwest of town, near the pier used by the Elephant Conservation Centre. Very good fish dishes (around 50,000K/kilo) served to outdoor tables shaded by

thatched roofs. The lake views make it popular with local officials enjoying day-long karaoke sessions. Handy if you're waiting for the Elephant Conservation Centre's boat to pick you up. Daily 7am–5pm.

Nang Noy In town, opposite the Phongsavanh Bank ☎ 074 211382. The well-run and inexpensive *Nang Noy* is the best bet for food in Sayaboury, with pots of noodle soup bubbling away behind the counter (15,000K). Daily 7am–2pm.

Luang Prabang

WAT XIENG THONG, LUANG PRABANG

Luang Prabang

2

Nestling in a slim valley shaped by lofty, green mountains and cut by the swift Mekong and Khan rivers, Luang Prabang exudes casual grandeur. A tiny mountain kingdom for more than a thousand years and designated a UNESCO World Heritage Site in 1995, the city is endowed with a legacy of ancient red-roofed temples and French–Indochinese architecture, not to mention some of the country's most refined cuisine, its richest culture and its most sacred Buddha image, the Pha Bang. For those familiar with Southeast Asia, the very name Luang Prabang conjures up the classic image of Laos – streets of ochre colonial houses and swaying palms, lines of saffron-robed monks gliding through the morning mist, the sonorous thump of the temple drums before dawn, and longtail boats racing down the Mekong before the river slips out of view through a seam in the mountains.

It is this heritage of Theravada Buddhist temples, French–Indochinese shop houses and **royal mystique** that lends Luang Prabang a pull unmatched by any other city in Laos. While other urban centres in the country are heavily populated by ethnic Vietnamese and Chinese, Luang Prabang is the only city in Laos where ethnic Lao are in the majority. This is not only where the first proto-Lao nation took root, it's also the birthplace of countless Lao rituals and the origin of a line of rulers, including the rulers of Vientiane, Champasak and Lane Xang. Luang Prabang people are tremendously proud of their pivotal role in Lao history. Indeed, they're somewhat known for their cultured ways in the rest of the country; in Lao soap operas, the doctor or the intellectual invariably speaks with a Luang Prabang accent.

Luang Prabang's strict building code, drawn up by UNESCO, keeps it from becoming another modern architectural nightmare. Indeed, after two decades of meticulous restoration, the city's immaculate looks make it feel far removed from the rest of Laos – a state of preservation that has led some detractors to label it a frozen-in-time museum piece. Inevitably, Luang Prabang has lost some of its sleepy charm and dreamy serenity as a result of the ever-growing influx of tourists, with almost every property in the historic centre now serving the travel industry in some form or another, and foreigners now outnumbering locals across much of the old city. An airport expansion completed in 2013, allowing larger planes to fly in and out of Luang Prabang, may well result in the small-town charms of this beautiful city being eroded still further.

Yet, for all the transformations brought by mass tourism, the city remains surprisingly laidback, with none of the hassle associated with other parts of Asia. And the upside of its enormous popularity is manifest in the quality and range of its places to stay and to eat, with a panoply of dreamily romantic, upscale hotels occupying the city's shuttered colonial-era mansions, and a fine array of restaurants – both local and international

TUM TUM CHENG COOKERY SCHOOL, LUANG PRABANG

Highlights

❶ Wat Xieng Thong Laos's most historic wat is one of the jewels of Southeast Asian architecture. **See p.114**

❷ Traditional Arts and Ethnology Centre Visit the TAEC for a fantastic introduction to the clothing and traditions of Laos's ethnic groups. **See p.117**

❸ Ock Pop Tok Take a tour or class at this marvellous textiles centre, a visit to which can be combined with a stroll round bustling Phosy Market. **See p.118**

❹ Xieng Men The dusty paths and village life on the other side of the Mekong feel a world away from the tourist crowds of Sisavangvong Road. **See p.119**

❺ Cookery courses Learn how to cook fragrant Lao cuisine at one of the city's excellent cookery schools. **See p.129**

❻ Kuang Si waterfall This spectacular waterfall is the perfect place to cool off on a hot day. **See p.136**

HIGHLIGHTS ARE MARKED ON THE MAP ON P.102 & PP.104–105

2

– showcasing the area's rich culinary traditions and influences. There's nowhere better for some pampering and recuperation if you've been investigating the rougher charms of the rest of the north.

Most travellers spend only a few days here on a whistle-stop tour of Laos, part of a wider Mekong trip, though the city really demands longer. If time is limited, top priority should go to the **old city**. In a day, you can easily tour the sights, beginning with the sunrise view from **Phousi** mountain and a wander around the lively **morning market**, before heading to the elegant **Royal Palace Museum**, en route to Luang Prabang's most impressive temple, **Wat Xieng Thong**. If you're here for a second day, enjoy some of the sights around Luang Prabang by taking a boat across the Mekong river to the temples of **Xieng Men** or upriver to the **Pak Ou Buddha caves**, followed perhaps by a refreshing dip at one of the area's two major **waterfalls**, Kuang Si and Tad Se.

The most popular time to visit Luang Prabang remains the cooler months of December and January, when the weather is clear and dry – though evenings can be surprisingly chilly. If you can, though, it's well worth coinciding a visit with one of the city's major festivals (see box opposite).

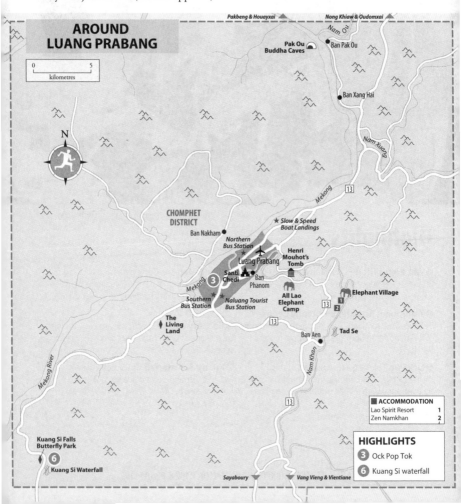

AROUND LUANG PRABANG

Pakbeng & Houayxai

Nong Khiaw & Oudomxai

Nam Ou

Pak Ou Buddha Caves

Ban Pak Ou

Ban Xang Hai

Nam Xuang

Mekong

13

CHOMPHET DISTRICT

★ Slow & Speed Boat Landings

Ban Nakham

Northern Bus Station

Luang Prabang

Henri Mouhot's Tomb

Santi Chedi

Ban Phanom

3

Southern Bus Station

★ Naluang Tourist Bus Station

All Lao Elephant Camp

13

Elephant Village

The Living Land

13

Ban Aen

Tad Se

Nam Khan

Mekong River

Mekong

13

ACCOMMODATION
Lao Spirit Resort — 1
Zen Namkhan — 2

Kuang Si Falls Butterfly Park

6

Kuang Si Waterfall

Sayaboury

Vang Vieng & Vientiane

HIGHLIGHTS
3 Ock Pop Tok
6 Kuang Si waterfall

0 — 5 kilometres

N

LUANG PRABANG FESTIVALS

Luang Prabang's sleepy air is disturbed only at festival time. The most famous festivals last for days and inspire a *lào-lào*-sodden carnival atmosphere that makes it easy to forget that these complex rituals held the very structure of the kingdom in place for centuries. **Lao New Year** (*pi mai lao*) in April is perhaps Luang Prabang's biggest festival, a week-long celebration that begins with a beauty pageant and sees the town (and everyone in it) doused with water – a tradition that has its origins in cleansing rituals designed to wash away the spirits of the old year. On day one, sand stupas are erected in monastery grounds, while the rowdier (and damper) festivities begin with a costumed parade – led by Miss Lao New Year – on day two. Day three dawns with a special *Tak Bat* (see box, p.108) up to the summit of Phousi, followed by private *basi* ceremonies (see box, p.285) across the town in the evening. On day four the Pha Bang (see box, p.111) is carried in a solemn procession led by the city's guardian spirits from the Royal Palace to Wat Mai, where it is ritually bathed to mark the arrival of the new year's spirit (day five), before being returned in another colourful procession to the Royal Palace on the morning of the final day of celebrations.

Near the end of the monsoon, two more holidays bring Luang Prabang to a festive standstill. The city's **boat races** (late August/September) are believed to lure Luang Prabang's fifteen guardian naga (see box, p.242) back into the rivers after high waters and flooded rice paddies have allowed them to escape. The **Festival of Lights** (*Lai Heau Fai*) follows on the full moon in October. In the days leading up to the festival residents build large floats and festoon them with lights. Then, under the full moon, the floats are paraded through the streets, where they are judged for aesthetic merit, and carried down to the Mekong and set atop boats for a second procession on the river. All evening, vendors offer saucer-sized floats made from banana stalks and containing flowers, incense and a candle, which celebrants take down to the river and launch on the current. The Festival of Lights is celebrated concurrently with **Awk Phansa**, the end of the three-month "rains retreat", a time when laypeople donate new robes and other offerings to Buddhist monasteries.

Brief history

Knowledge of Luang Prabang's early history is sketchy, at best. The earliest Lao settlers made their way down the Nam Ou valley sometime after the tenth century, absorbing the territory on which the city lies. At the time, the area was known as Muang Sawa, a settlement thought to have been peopled by the Austroasiatic ancestors of the Lao Theung. According to folklore, this migration of the Lao to Luang Prabang was led by Khoun Lo, who claimed the area for his people and called the settlement **Xieng Dong Xieng Thong**. By the end of the thirteenth century, Xieng Dong Xieng Thong had emerged as one of the chief centres of Lao life in the Upper Mekong region, a principality significant enough to be a vassal state of the great Siamese kingdom of Sukhothai.

Chao Fa Ngum and the advent of Buddhism

It wasn't until the legendary Lao warrior **Fa Ngum** swept down the Nam Ou with a Khmer army in 1353 and captured Xieng Dong Xieng Thong that the town emerged as the heart of a thriving, independent kingdom in its own right. Claiming the throne of his grandfather, Fa Ngum founded the kingdom of **Lane Xang Hom Khao** – the Land of a Million Elephants and the White Parasol – and established the line of kings that was to rule Laos for six centuries.

With Fa Ngum came monks, artisans and learned men from the Khmer court and, according to histories written a century and a half later, a legal code and Theravada Buddhism. Yet Fa Ngum was still very much the fourteenth-century warrior. After his ministers grew weary of his military campaigns and his rather uncivilized habit of taking his subject's wives and daughters as concubines, he was exiled and replaced on the throne by his son, Oun Heuan, during whose peaceful reign the city flourished.

The golden age and Burmese invasion

The sacking of the city in 1478 by the Vietnamese proved a catalyst for the ushering in of the city's **golden age**: striking temples, including the *sim* of Wat Xieng Thong, were built, epic poems composed and sacred texts copied. In 1512, King Visoun brought the **Pha Bang**, a sacred Buddha image, to Xieng Dong Xieng Thong, significant for the identity of the Lao people and the city itself, and a sign that Theravada Buddhism was flourishing.

Wary of encroaching Burmese, King Setthathilat, Visoun's grandson, moved the capital to Vientiane in 1563, leaving the Pha Bang behind and renaming the city after

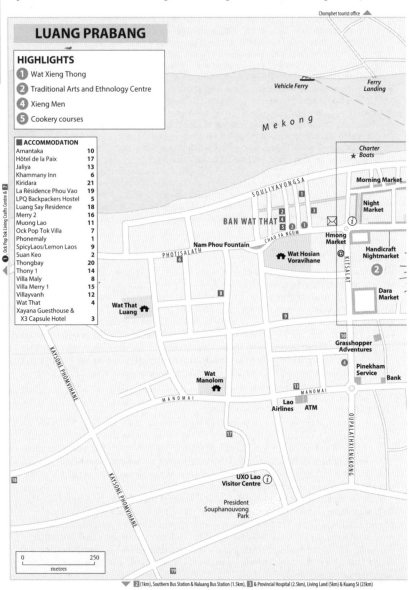

LUANG PRABANG

Chomphet tourist office

HIGHLIGHTS
1. Wat Xieng Thong
2. Traditional Arts and Ethnology Centre
4. Xieng Men
5. Cookery courses

Vehicle Ferry

Ferry Landing

Mekong

Charter Boats

SOULIYAVONGSA

Morning Market

ACCOMMODATION	
Amantaka	10
Hôtel de la Paix	17
Jaliya	13
Khammany Inn	6
Kiridara	21
La Résidence Phou Vao	19
LPQ Backpackers Hostel	5
Luang Say Residence	18
Merry 2	16
Muong Lao	11
Ock Pop Tok Villa	7
Phonemaly	1
SpicyLaos/Lemon Laos	9
Suan Keo	2
Thongbay	20
Thony 1	14
Villa Maly	8
Villa Merry 1	15
Villayvanh	12
Wat That	4
Xayana Guesthouse & X3 Capsule Hotel	3

Ock Pop Tok Living Crafts Centre & 7

Night Market

BAN WAT THAT

CHAO FA NGUM

Hmong Market

Handicraft Nightmarket

Nam Phou Fountain

PHOTISALATH

Wat Hosian Voravihane

Dara Market

KITSALAT

Wat That Luang

Grasshopper Adventures

Pinekham Service

Bank

KAYSONE PHOMVIHANE

Wat Manolom

MANOMAI

Lao Airlines

ATM

MANOMAI

OUPALATHXIENGKONG

UXO Lao Visitor Centre

President Souphanouvong Park

0 — 250
metres

2

the revered image. The Pha Bang may have been known for its protective properties, but they were no match for the might of the Burmese, and Luang Prabang was engulfed by successive **Burmese invasions**, ushering in a period of chaos.

The Kingdom of Luang Prabang, Chinese raids and the French period

With the disintegration of Lane Xang at the turn of the eighteenth century, **Kingkitsalat** became the first king of an independent Luang Prabang. When **French explorers** Doudart de Lagrée and Francis Garnier arrived in 1867, they found a busy

2

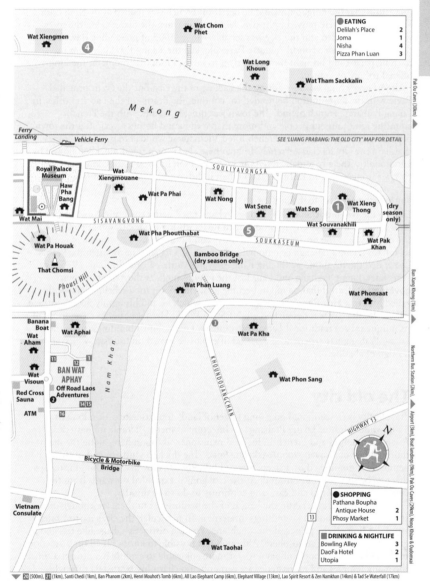

2

market and port town of wooden homes, a town that Garnier called "the most eminent Laotian centre in Indochina". With Luang Prabang firmly in Siam's orbit, the explorers' suggestion that the kingdom would be better off French was scoffed at by King Oun Kham, but they were proved right two decades later when the Siamese left the town virtually undefended and the city was set ablaze by a group of marauding **Haw**. During the siege, French vice-consul Auguste Pavie plucked the ageing Lao king from his burning palace and brought him downriver to safety. From that moment, the king offered tribute to France.

Almost everything was lost during the sacking of the city, but the event provided Pavie with the ammunition he needed to "conquer the hearts" of the Lao and usher in Luang Prabang's **French period**. The town was quickly rebuilt, with the French counting ten thousand people and more than a thousand homes a year after the town's destruction. Within time, the French hired Vietnamese workers to build the homes that lend the city its classic French–Indochinese character, a trend quickly followed by Lao nobility. The city remained remote however: even in 1930 it took longer to travel by river from Saigon to Luang Prabang than it did to travel from Saigon to France.

The Indochinese wars to the present

During the two **Indochina wars**, Luang Prabang fared better than most towns in Laos, though while the city itself remained intact during the fighting that consumed the country over the next two decades, the Second Indochina War ultimately took its toll on Luang Prabang's ceremonial life, which lost its regal heart when the **Pathet Lao** ended the royal line by forcing King Sisavang Vatthana to abdicate in 1975. Two years later, Luang Prabang and Laos lost the king himself, as the new **communist government**, fearful that he might become a rallying point for a rebellion, allegedly exiled him to a Hoa Phan cave, a journey from which he and his family never returned.

In 1995, the city was designated a UNESCO World Heritage Site, in recognition of its unique mix of traditional Lao architecture and old colonial buildings; since then, Luang Prabang has experienced a period of explosive growth in tourism, which shows no sign of abating.

The old city

The **old city** is concentrated on a long finger of land, approximately 1km long by 300m wide. Most of Luang Prabang's architecture of merit – temple monasteries, Asian shop houses and French-influenced mansions – is found here, along the main thoroughfare of **Sisavangvong/Sakkaline Road**. The thicker, southern end of the peninsula is dominated by a steep, forested hill, **Phousi**, crowned by a Buddhist stupa that can be seen for miles around. As the city grew it expanded outwards from the peninsula to the south and east, and continues to do so to this day.

Just four parallel streets run the length of the peninsula, but there are enough cross streets and dead ends to keep things interesting. In particular, the city's narrow **brick lanes**, leading off the principal thoroughfares, retain a distinctly village-like feel and a greater sense of local atmosphere. Although it is possible to knock off all the attractions in the old city in a couple of days, it's far more enjoyable to explore it a little at a time; the many temples and monasteries are certainly too charming be rushed through.

LUANG PRABANG STREET NAMES

Luang Prabang's civic authorities seem to change the city's road names with bewildering regularity, a situation that isn't helped by the fact that many streets change their names numerous times along their length (such as the main street, **Sisavangvong**, which becomes **Sakkaline** closer to the tip of the peninsula, **Chao Fa Ngum** at the opposite end, once it's past the tourist office, and **Photisalath** further west, past the Nam Phou Fountain). This is all made still more confusing by the general lack of street signs. We have given street names where signs are visible on the ground, though you may well see alternative names elsewhere; where signs aren't available we've given the name of the local area (traditional village or "ban"), which is usually called after the local temple. For all this, the city's generally grid-like layout and small size make it easy to navigate.

2

Phousi

Accessed via Sisavangvong Rd (two entrances) or from southeast of Phousi, opposite Khem Khan Food Garden • Daily 7am–6pm • 20,000K

Phousi ("Sacred Hill") is the geographical as well as spiritual centre of the city. Believed to have once harboured a powerful naga who dwelt in its bowels, the hill is also seen as a miniature Mount Meru, the Mount Olympus of Hindu–Buddhist cosmology. Though there is little to see on the hill itself, save for an ancient-looking *sim* at its foot, Phousi is striking from a distance. Indeed, the golden spires of **That Chomsi** at its summit are the first glimpse of the city that many visitors get if they are arriving by plane. Likewise, the peak affords a stunning panorama of the city it crowns, and the shimmering rivers and jungle-clad mountains beyond are mesmerizing. Viewing the **setting sun** from the summit of Phousi has become a kind of tourist ritual, so don't expect to enjoy the moment alone – indeed, early morning is a better time to come, when the city and the hill are more peaceful. A quieter spot from which to watch the sunset is Santi Chedi on a hill due east of Phousi (see p.135), which affords a marvellous view back towards the old city without the crowds.

There are **three approaches** to the summit, meaning you can climb up one route and descend another. The first and most straightforward ascent is via the stairway directly opposite the main gate of the Royal Palace Museum. The second approach, on the other side of the hill, is up a zigzag stairway flanked by whitewashed naga, and can be used for descending to the Nam Khan road. The third and most rambling approach is via **Wat Pha Phouthabat**, near Phousi's northern foot, further east along Sisavangvong Road from the Royal Palace. Most people choose the first ascent, which allows you to first stop at the adjacent **Wat Pa Houak**; from here it's a steep climb through a tunnel of shady plumeria trees to the peak.

Wat Pa Houak

Accessed from Sisavangvong Rd, opposite the Royal Palace • Free, donation recommended

The fine little **Wat Pa Houak** has a charmingly weathered facade, but is mainly of interest for its fascinating nineteenth-century **interior murals**, which appear to depict Luang Prabang as a celestial city. Besides Lao characters in classical costumes, there are Chinese, Persians and Europeans in the city, but it is not clear whether they have come as visitors or invaders.

Wat Pha Phouthabat

Accessed from Sisavangvong Rd, opposite *Sackarinh Guesthouse*

Climbing Phousi via **Wat Pha Phouthabat** affords the most atmosphere. There are actually three monasteries in this compound, one of which is a school for novice monks. The most interesting structure in the compound is the *sim* of **Wat Pa Khe**, a tall, imposing building with an unusual inward-leaning facade. Most noteworthy here is a pair of carved shutters on the window to the left of the main entrance, said to depict seventeenth-century Dutch traders, and on the right-hand (north-facing) wall a similar, if less

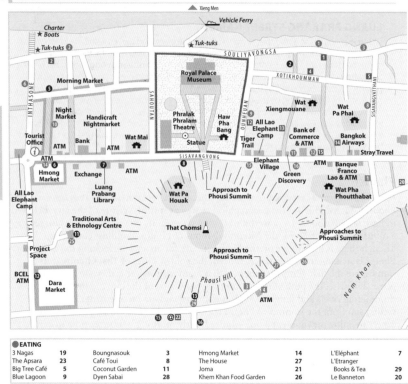

EATING							
3 Nagas	19	Boungnasouk	3	Hmong Market	14	L'Eléphant	7
The Apsara	23	Café Toui	8	The House	27	L'Etranger	
Big Tree Café	5	Coconut Garden	11	Joma	21	Books & Tea	29
Blue Lagoon	9	Dyen Sabai	28	Khem Khan Food Garden	26	Le Banneton	20

well-executed, pair of shutters thought to depict Venetians. Behind and to the left of Wat Pa Khe's *sim* is a stairway leading to a shrine housing the "**Buddha's footprint**" after which Wat Pha Phoutthabat was named. The larger-than-life stylized footprint is complete with the 108 auspicious marks said to be found on the historic Buddha's foot. On festival days, pilgrims make offerings by tossing banknotes into the footprint.

Continuing up the path, you come to a small concrete grotto with an image of Pha Kajai, the Mahayanist deity many Westerners associate with the Buddha. From here, the path meanders past an ever-growing cornucopia of new, gilded Buddhas – some supersize, others named after days of the week – up rather steeply to the summit.

ALMS-GIVING

The daily dawn procession of monks through the streets of the old city has become one of the quintessential images of Luang Prabang and is one of its biggest tourist "attractions". As a result, however, it can feel a little zoo-like, as tourists line up to watch the monks pass, cameras madly clicking to get the best shot.

There's no denying the serene beauty of the alms-giving ceremony, **Tak Bat**, as kneeled locals place sticky rice into the baskets of the passing saffron-robed monks. However, if you do wish to see it, it's important to behave properly – in particular, dress appropriately and modestly, don't make physical contact with the monks, and keep a respectful distance from them. It is possible to join the alms-giving, but locals request that you only do so if it would be meaningful to you. If you do so, buy sticky rice from the morning market beforehand rather than the street vendors who congregate along Sisavangvong Road, as the rice can be of dubious quality.

The Royal Palace (National Museum)

Sisavangvong Rd • Daily except Tues 8–11.30am & 1.30–4pm • 30,000K, guides 50,000K • Handbags and cameras must be left in the locker room to the left of the palace entrance and shoes kept in the rack outside

Occupying a fittingly central location in the old city, between Phousi Hill and the Mekong river, the former **Royal Palace** is now home to the Royal Palace Museum (aka National Museum), preserving the trappings and paraphernalia of Laos's extinguished monarchy. The palace, at the end of a long drive lined with stately palms, was constructed in 1904 by the French and replaced an older, smaller palace of teak and rosewood. The new palace was supposed to be crowned by a European-style steeple, but King Sisavang Vong insisted on modifications, and the graceful stupa-like spire that you see today was substituted, resulting in a tasteful fusion of European and Lao design. Another striking feature is the pediment over the main entrance adorned with a gilt rendition of the symbol of the Lao monarchy: Airavata, the three-headed elephant, being sheltered by the sacred white parasol. This is surrounded by the intertwining bodies of the fifteen guardian naga (see p.242) of Luang Prabang.

The king's reception room

The **king's reception room**, to the right of the entrance hall, is full of huge Gauguinesque canvases portraying what appears to be "a day in the life of old Luang Prabang", with scenes of the city as it appeared in the early twentieth century. The paintings, executed by Alex de Fautereau in 1930, are meant to be viewed at different hours of the day when the light from outside is supposed to illuminate the panels depicting the corresponding time of day.

2

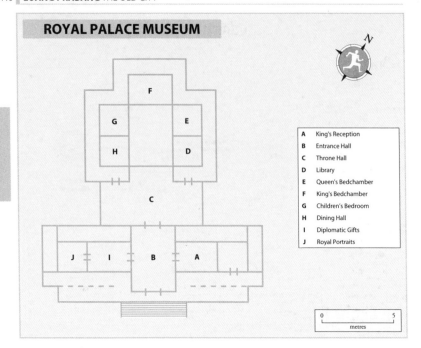

ROYAL PALACE MUSEUM

A   King's Reception
B   Entrance Hall
C   Throne Hall
D   Library
E   Queen's Bedchamber
F   King's Bedchamber
G   Children's Bedroom
H   Dining Hall
I   Diplomatic Gifts
J   Royal Portraits

0   5
metres

The Throne Hall

More impressive is the **Throne Hall**, just beyond the entry hall. Its high walls spangled with mosaics of multicoloured mirrors set in a crimson background, the hall dazzles even in the dim light. These mosaics, along with others at Wat Xieng Thong, were created in the mid-1950s to commemorate the 2500th anniversary of the historic Buddha's passing into nirvana. On display in this room are rare articles of royal regalia: swords with hilts and scabbards of hammered silver and gold, an elaborately decorated fly-whisk and even the king's own howdah (elephant saddle). Also on show is a cache of small crystal, silver and bronze Buddha images taken from the inner chamber of the "watermelon stupa" at Wat Visoun (see p.118). Somehow these treasures escaped the plundering gangs of "Black Flag" Chinese who, led by a White Tai warlord, sacked Luang Prabang in 1887. The stupa was destroyed, rebuilt in 1898, but collapsed in 1914. It was then that the Buddhas were discovered inside.

The royal library

Leaving the Throne Hall via the door on the right, you come to the rather ill-stocked **royal library**, which includes a set of the Jataka presented by the King of Thailand. One cabinet contains the official archives of the Ming and Qing dynasties, a gift from China during the Cultural Revolution. The corridors that surround the rooms at the rear are decorated with sixteen pictures that illustrate the legend of the Ten Wishes of Prince Wetsantara, considered an important epic by Lao Buddhists.

The bedchambers

King Sisavang Vong's bedchamber, located at the very back of the palace, is surprisingly modest. The only thing that looks especially regal – apart from a larger-than-life, moustachioed portrait of Sisavang Vong – is the massive hardwood bed, the headboard of which sports the king's initials and a carved Buddha sheltered by a seven-headed naga.

The footboard bears a rendition of the royal emblem of Laos, this time with a two-tiered parasol. The **children's bedroom** is primarily given over to Lao musical instruments, the most impressive of which is a *khong vong*, a horseshoe-shaped set of gong chimes.

Diplomatic gifts and royal portraits

Of the two final rooms, the near room houses **diplomatic gifts** presented to the Lao people by a handful of nations, as well as the rather tatty-looking flag of the Kingdom of Laos that was given a symbolic ride up into space and back on one of the Apollo missions. Not long afterwards, the Kingdom of Laos ceased to exist. The selection of photos lining the wall includes one of Ho Chi Minh dancing with King Sisavang Vatthana.

In the far room hang **portraits** of Sisavang Vattana, his wife Queen Kham Phoui and their son Prince Vong Savang. These are the only officially displayed portraits of the last members of the six hundred-year-old dynasty anywhere in Laos. Had they not been painted by a Soviet artist they almost certainly would not have survived the years following the revolution. The same goes for the bronze sculpture of King Sisavang Vong in the museum grounds near the front gate. This statue may look familiar if you have already passed through Vientiane, where a larger version stands in the park adjacent to Wat Simuang.

The Haw Phabang

Outside the palace to the right of the main entrance to the compound, the ornate **Haw Phabang** is the new permanent resting place of the **Pha Bang**, the most sacred Buddha image in Laos (see box below). Built in traditional Lao style and awash with gilt adornment, the Haw Phabang was started in 1993, but it was a full two decades before the image was finally installed in 2013, fifty years after the temple was first conceived. Inside the dimly lit, pillared hall, the diminutive Pha Bang, just 83cm high, is enshrined on a richly ornamented, multi-tiered gilded platform, behind a pair of naga, their tails intertwined protectively.

THE PHA BANG

Much more than an ancient image of the Buddha, the **Pha Bang** is the palladium of Laos. The pursuit and enshrining of palladial images has a long history in Southeast Asia, full of intrigue and Byzantine plotting. Like Thailand's Phra Kaew and Burma's Mahamuni Buddha images, the Pha Bang is believed to possess miraculous powers that safeguard the country in which it is enshrined. Formerly, palladial images were thought to legitimize the sovereignty of a king who had one in his possession. Only a pious king with sufficient religious merit could hope to hold onto such an image, and losing it was thought to be proof that a kingdom and its ruler did not deserve to possess it. Thus the histories of certain palladia read like the itinerary of some much coveted sacred sword or holy grail.

According to Lao legend, the Pha Bang image was cast of gold, silver, copper, iron and precious stones. Overseen by the god Indra, who donated gold for its creation, the image was crafted in the heavens above the Himalayas and then delivered to the capital of Sri Lanka. From there the image made its way to Cambodia and then to the city of **Xieng Dong Xieng Thong**, later renamed Luang Prabang (the Great Pha Bang) in its honour. In the early eighteenth century, the Pha Bang was moved to Vientiane, by now the capital. Twice the Siamese invaded Vientiane, capturing the image, and twice they returned it to the Lao, believing that the Pha Bang was bad luck for Siam.

Since 1867, the Pha Bang has been kept in Luang Prabang, where to this day it is considered the most sacred Buddha image in Laos and centrepiece of the Lao New Year festival (see box, p.103). At least, that's the official story. Persistent **rumours** have circulated since the revolution that the authentic Pha Bang was removed from its ornate pedestal and given to the Soviets in return for assistance to the Pathet Lao during the war. The image on display is said to be a copy, while the real Pha Bang is locked away in some vault in Moscow, its powers no longer serving as a talisman for Laos.

Wat Mai

Sisavangvong Rd, just south of the Royal Palace • 10,000K

Wat Mai Suwannaphumaham, or **Wat Mai** for short, has what must surely be Luang Prabang's most photographed *sim* after that of Wat Xieng Thong. The monastery dates from the late eighteenth or early nineteenth century (depending on whom you believe), but it is the *sim*'s relatively modern facade with its gilt stucco reliefs that forms the main focus of attention. Depicting the second-to-last incarnation of the Buddha set amid traditional Lao scenes, the facade was created in the 1960s and has since been restored. Like most examples of modern Lao temple ornamentation, it looks impressive from a distance, but loses some of its lustre up close. During Lao New Year, Wat Mai is a hive of activity, as it is here that the Pha Bang (see box, p.111) is put on display so that the faithful can ritually bathe the image.

Ban Jek

The neighbourhood just north of the former Royal Palace is still known to locals as "**Ban Jek**" or Chinatown, as the rows of shop houses along Sisavangvong Road were once mostly owned by ethnic Chinese shopkeepers – though an alternative name, "Thang Falang" ("white man's way"), sarcastically coined by expats, is a more accurate term these days. Here you'll find some fine examples of Luang Prabang **shop house architecture**, a hybrid of French and Lao features superimposed on the basic South China style that was once the standard throughout urban Southeast Asia. Downstairs was a shop or other place of business, while upstairs the residents lived under a roof of fired-clay shingles supported by brick and stucco walls. This combination kept interior temperatures cool during the hot season and warm during the chilly early morning hours of Luang Prabang's winter. Shuttered windows, introduced by the French, were coupled with transoms of filigreed wood above doors and windows. This allows air to circulate even when doors and windows are bolted shut. Almost all of the shops here are now rented out as tourist businesses of some sort, whether as travel agents, *falang*-friendly restaurants or handicraft-selling boutiques, though for a tourist drag Sisavangvong Road still retains plenty of charm.

Wat Xiengmouane

Xotikhoumman Rd • Training centre showroom 8.30am–10.30am & 11.30am–4pm

Set in leafy, serene grounds and dominated by an elegant *sim* with a Corinthian-pillared facade, **Wat Xiengmouane** is named after its old temple drum which produces a particularly sonorous thump (*xieng mouane* means "jolly sound"). A side building has

---

BIG BROTHER MOUSE

Set up to promote literacy in Laos, **Big Brother Mouse** (Phayaluangmeungchan Rd; ☎071 254937, ✆bigbrothermouse.com) is an excellent scheme that publishes books in Lao and enables young people to gain new skills in reading, writing and computing. Books are still a rare commodity in Laos, so the work that Big Brother Mouse does is vital in helping young Lao people develop new skills and enhance their prospects.

The organization, which is non-profit and Lao-owned, encourages visitors to buy books to take on treks, rather than giving sweets or pens to village children. In addition, tourists can sponsor a book party ($350–450), help young adults practise their English (daily 9am & 5pm; 2hr) or volunteer in the office and shop (vacancies are regularly posted outside the shop). You are welcome to visit the shop and speak to the staff in more detail about their work and what you can do – look for the big cut-out of a mouse outside.

A similar literacy scheme is run at Luang Prabang Library (see p.131).

been converted into a training centre for novice monks to learn traditional arts and crafts, with a showroom displaying items for sale, though the quality of the workmanship is not of the highest order.

Wat Pa Phai

Sisavangvatthani Rd

The principal attraction at **Wat Pa Phai**, the Bamboo Forest Monastery, is the facade of the *sim*, painted and lavishly embellished with stylized naga and peacocks. Inside, on the altar, some hundred-plus Buddha statues are stacked up in rows from the smallest to the biggest, like Russian dolls.

Wat Sene

Sakkaline Rd

Towards the northern end of the peninsula, **Wat Sene** is the first of a row of monasteries that monopolize the west side of the street for nearly two blocks (the others, sharing a single plot, are Wat Sop Sickharam, Wat Ban Phoneheuang and Wat Sirimoungkhoun). Wat Sene is clearly one of the wealthiest in Luang Prabang, with a magnificent *sim* awash with gold stencilling and a beautiful golden chariot in the grounds. Of particular interest is an ornate boat shed housing the monastery's two **longboats**, used in the annual boat race festival, held at the end of the rainy season (see box, p.103). Fittingly, the pediment of the boathouse is decorated with carved wooden naga, the mythical serpentine divinities, which are said to escape during the rains and are enticed back to their protective posts by the races.

Wat Souvanakhili

Sakkaline Rd

South of Sakkaline Road, **Wat Souvanakhili** is a rare example of a Xieng Khuang-style temple. Luang Prabang once boasted at least three temples in this low, squat design, which originated on the windy plains of the province and former kingdom after which the style is named (see p.287). Legend has it that the Chinese "Black Flag" rebels who sacked and looted Luang Prabang in 1887 took special care to destroy Xieng Khuang-style temples because their shape resembled Chinese coffins. It's also said that the Buddha at Wat Souvanakhili broke into a cold sweat in 1958, a dark omen signalling the coming war. The province of Xieng Khuang was heavily bombed during the Second Indochina War, leaving no trace of Xieng Khuang-style architecture there and making the *sim* at Wat Souvanakhili possibly the last surviving example.

Wat Xieng Thong

Entrances on Sakkaline, Kounxoau and Souliyavongsa roads • Daily 6am–6pm • 20,000K

The most historic and enchanting Buddhist monastery in the entire country, **Wat Xieng Thong**, the Golden City Monastery, should not be missed. Near the northernmost tip of the peninsula, the temple compound alone is a delight to wander through, especially early in the morning before the tourist crowds descend on it. The main temple or *sim* was built in 1560 by King Setthathilat (who then promptly moved the capital of the Kingdom of a Million Elephants downriver to Vientiane) and it is this wonderfully graceful building that dominates the monastery when approached from the riverside. Unlike nearly every other temple in Luang Prabang, this *sim* was not razed by Chinese marauders in the nineteenth century and a recent, extensive US-funded project has vividly restored much of its intricate gold stencilling and mosaic work to its original lustre.

WAT XIENG THONG

Longboat Shed
Drum Pavilion
Garden
Funerary Carriage Hall
Tickets
Xieng Thong Road
Stupas
Tickets
Standing Buddha Shrine
SOULIYAVONGSA ROAD
The Mekong River
Elephant Head Drain
Bodhi Tree
Sim
Monks' Quarters
SAKKALINE ROAD
Flame Tree Mosaic
Reclining Buddha Shrine ("Red Chapel")
Sitting Buddha Shrine
Longboat Shed
Stupas
Sitting Buddha Pavilion
Stupas
Tickets
0   5
metres

The sim

You'll need to stand at a distance to get a view of the **roof**, the temple's most outstanding feature. Elegant lines curve and overlap, sweeping nearly to the ground, and evoke a bird with outstretched wings or, as the locals say, a mother hen sheltering her brood. The **walls** of the *sim* are decorated inside and out with stencilled gold motifs on a black or maroon background, which seem to float on the pillars and walls.

Besides stylized floral designs, the motifs depict a variety of tales, including the Lao version of the Ramayana, scenes from the Jataka and stories about the lives of the Buddha, as well as graphic scenes of punishments doled out in the many levels of Buddhist hell. In one of these punishment scenes, on the wall to the right of the main entrance, an adulterous couple is being forced to flee a pack of rabid dogs by climbing a tree studded with wicked thorns. Other unfortunate souls are being cooked in a copper cauldron of boiling oil (for committing murder) or are suspended by a hook through their tongues (guilty of telling lies).

In the rafters above and to the right of the main entrance runs a long, gilded wooden **aqueduct** or trough resembling the shape of a mythical serpent. During Lao New Year, lustral water is poured into a receptacle in the serpent's tail and spouts from its mouth, bathing a Buddha image housed in a wooden pagoda-like structure situated near the altar. A drain in the floor of the pagoda channels the water through pipes under the floor of the *sim* and the water then pours from the mouth of a mirror-spangled **elephant's head** located on the exterior wall.

> ### PALM-LEAF MANUSCRIPTS
> The leafy garden beside Wat Xieng Thong's Funerary Carriage Hall contains some grand bougainvillea, coconut trees and two grey-green fan palms. It was from this species of palm that traditional **palm-leaf manuscripts** were made. Using a stylus to scratch characters onto the palm leaves, monks wrote down Pali-language chants and recorded historical events that affected the kingdom. Before access to paper and cheap printing made palm-leaf manuscripts obsolete, two or three of these trees could be found growing at every wat.

2

Covering the exterior of the back wall of the *sim* is a **mosaic**, said to depict a legendary flame tree that stood on the site when the city was founded. This particular composition is especially beautiful during the Festival of Lights, when the *sim* is decked out with *khom fai dao*, star-shaped lanterns constructed of bamboo and mulberry paper. The flickering candlelight illuminates the tree and animals in the mosaic, making them twinkle magically.

The Standing Buddha Shrine and the Red Chapel
To the left of the *sim*, as you face it, stands a small white-stucco **shrine** containing a standing Buddha image. The purple and gold mirrored mosaics on the pediments of the structure are especially intricate and probably the country's finest example of this kind of ornamentation, which is thought to have originated in Thailand and spread to Myanmar (Burma) as well.

Directly behind the shrine is a larger structure, covered in striking, colourful mosaic pieces depicting village life and known to French art historians as "La Chapelle Rouge", the **Red Chapel**. The sinuous **reclining Buddha** image enshrined within is one of Laos's greatest sculptures in bronze.

The Funerary Carriage Hall
On the other side of the monastery grounds is the **Funerary Carriage Hall** or *haw latsalot*, a rare example of a modern Lao religious structure that manages to impress. Built in 1962, it has wide teakwood panels deeply carved with depictions of Rama, Sita, Ravana and Hanuman, all characters from *Phra Lak Pha Lam*, the Lao version of the Ramayana. Check out the carved window shutters on the building's left side where Hanuman, the King of the Monkeys, is depicted in pursuit of the fairer sex.

Inside, the principal article on display is the *latsalot*, the royal funerary carriage, used to transport the mortal remains of King Sisavang Vong to cremation. The vehicle is built in the form of several bodies of parallel naga, whose jagged fangs and dripping tongues heralded the king's final passage through Luang Prabang. Atop the carriage are three urns of gilded sandalwood, which were used to keep royal corpses in an upright foetal position until the cremation. The urns at the front and rear of the carriage held the remains of the king's father and mother respectively; the centre urn contained the remains of the king, which were cremated in April 1961.

Besides protecting these funerary paraphernalia from the elements, the building houses various **religious relics**. Among these are ornate wooden frames containing images of the Buddha that were given to the monastery as offerings.

Outside the old city
The old city may have the highest concentration of monasteries, but there is plenty of interest beyond, including an excellent museum, over twenty temples, several markets and a choice of scenic walks. **Inthasone Road**, which becomes **Kitsalat Road** east of Sisavangvong Road, divides the old city from the commercial parts of Luang Prabang, which, though newer, still contain plenty of colonial-era mansions.

The most interesting areas within walking distance of the old city for tourists are the old silversmithing district of Ban Wat That, south of Inthasone Road between Chao Fan Ngum Road and the Mekong, now host to some of the city's best-value accommodation; the popular bar and guesthouse area east of Phousi towards the Nam Khan river, where **Wat Visoun** and **Wat Aham** are the most historically important temples; and **across the Nam Khan** river itself, accessed (in dry season) by a rickety bamboo bridge. For some respite from the monastic life, it's well worth hopping on a bike (or hailing a tuk-tuk) for the short ride to **Phosy Market**, the city's biggest and most authentic, and the excellent **Ock Pop Tok** weaving centre, 2km southwest of the old city. Last but perhaps best of all, a boat trip across the Mekong to **Xieng Men**, in **Chomphet district**, will reward you with many venerable riverside temples, as well as a relaxed rural ambience and good views back over the old city.

Traditional Arts and Ethnology Centre

Off Kitsalat Rd • Tues–Sun 9am–6pm • 25,000K • ☎ 071 253364, ⓦ taeclaos.org

Tucked up a steep side road off Kitsalat Road, the small **Traditional Arts and Ethnology Centre (TAEC)** provides an excellent introduction to Laos's ethnic groups, including the Akha, Hmong and Khmu people, among others. Exhibits include numerous items of clothing, such as an amazing Akha Pouly Nyai woman's headdress made up of over three hundred silver ornaments, traditionally worn even when bathing, sleeping and working in fields, as well as household objects and religious artefacts. Annually changing exhibitions keep the centre's displays fresh, and there's an excellent shop (see p.131) and café (see p.127).

Project Space

Kitsalat Rd, opposite TAEC • Daily 9am–6pm • Free • ☎ 071 213091, ⓦ projectspace-luangprabang.com

A one-room, not-for-profit gallery, **Project Space** hosts frequently changing, usually worthwhile art and photography exhibitions by local and international practitioners with a Lao or Southeast Asian theme. It's also sometimes used as a screening venue during the Luang Prabang Film Festival (see box, p.130).

Wat Hosian Voravihane

Chao Fa Ngum Rd

Wat Hosian Voravihane is reached via a stairway flanked by some impressive and undulating seven-headed naga spewing from the mouths of snaggle-toothed *makara*. Elements of the wat suggest influence from northern Thailand, namely the gold-topped *that*. The graceful **stupa** is very similar to examples found in Chiang Mai, Thailand.

Wat That Luang

Off Photisalath Rd

Situated on a low hill 1km southwest of the old city, **Wat That Luang** dates from 1818 and is notable as the last resting place of King Sisavang Vong, whose ashes are said to be interred in the golden stupa in front of the *sim*. The whitewashed *sim itself*, simple yet distinctive in design, largely eschews the rich ornamentation seen on temples elsewhere across the city, except in the lacquering of its heavy timber door and window panels, decorated tympanums and in the fifteen-point *dok so fa* crest surmounting the roof, said to represent Mount Meru.

Wat Visoun

Ban Wat Visoun • 20,000K (includes Wat Aham)

Wat Visoun shares a parcel of land with Wat Aham (see below) on the opposite side of Phousi from the Royal Palace Museum. The monastery's *sim*, as seen in a wood-block print executed by French artist Louis Delaporte in 1873, was once a lavishly decorated example of the all-but-extinct Xieng Khuang style. The original *sim* was razed during the sack of Luang Prabang in 1887 by Chinese bandits, and the bulbous, finial-topped stupa, known as *that makmo* – the **watermelon stupa** – was destroyed as well. The looters made off with treasures stored within, but fortunately didn't take everything. What they left behind is now on display in the throne room of the Royal Palace Museum (see p.109). Wat Visoun's reconstructed *sim* is an unremarkable mix of Luang Prabang and Vientiane styles, but the rebuilt watermelon stupa is still quite unique.

Wat Aham

Ban Wat Aham • 20,000K (includes Wat Visoun)

Next door to Wat Visoun (see above), atmospheric **Wat Aham** features a delightfully diminutive, unrestored *sim*, protected by stucco statues of leering guards and tigers with Cheshire cat smiles, and a couple of mould-blackened *that*, one with a picturesque slant. This wat is associated with *Phu Nyoe* and *Nya Nyoe*, the shaggy, red-faced spirits that are believed to be the founders and protectors of Luang Prabang. Effigies of the two deities head the parade during the Lao New Year festivities in April, and they are believed to inhabit the two venerable **banyan trees** whose shade-giving canopies make this a pleasant place to linger.

UXO Lao Visitor Centre

Behind President Souphanouvong Park, 1km south of the old city • Mon–Fri 8am–noon & 1–4pm • Free, donations welcome • ⓦ uxolao.org

The **UXO Lao Visitor Centre** addresses the devastating impact on Laos of the US's nine-year bombing campaign during the Second Indochina War. The small but well-crafted exhibition lays out the shocking statistics – more ordnance was dropped on the country than was used during the whole of World War II – and outlines the uphill task facing UXO Lao. Despite clearing some three million square metres of land a year, it's estimated that even now it will still take over a hundred years to rid the country of cluster bombs alone.

Ock Pop Tok

Photisalath Rd • Tours every 30min: daily 8.30am–5pm; free • Classes from $59 (half-day) • ☎ 071 212597, ⓦ ockpoptok.com • Free tuk-tuks run during the daytime to the Living Crafts Centre from Ock Pop Tok's shops in the old city (see p.131)

Tucked down a bumpy lane on the banks of the Mekong opposite Phosy Market (see p.132), **Ock Pop Tok** ("East Meets West") offers fascinating guided tours of its **Living Crafts Centre**, which employs thirty expert weavers from local villages. The women work for a decent local wage to their own schedules on looms custom-made for their body sizes. The intricate processes of traditional dyeing and weaving – it takes over three weeks to create a typical wall-hanging – are brought alive by enthusiastic and insightful commentary, and the quality of workmanship on show is superb. The centre also runs excellent **classes and workshops** in natural dyes, weaving and batik, ranging from a few hours up to three days. Each student is allotted a master weaver and a translator, and if you're nimble-fingered enough you should be able to come away with a reasonable two-colour scarf after two days of satisfying toil. You can also stay here at the centre's lovely villa (see p.125) or come for lunch at the breezy riverside *Silk Road Café*.

Across the Mekong: Xieng Men and Chomphet district

Surprisingly few tourists bother to cross the Mekong and explore the sleepy village of **XIENG MEN**, but it's a real delight to escape the crowds and experience village life so close to the city. Although exploring the riverside monasteries here will only take a couple of hours, there's much else to do in largely wooded **Chomphet district**, of which Xieng Men is merely the first village. Ask at the Chomphet tourist office (see below) about mountain biking tours to thirty-metre Hoykhua waterfall (safe for swimming), visits to seldom-visited caves and a two-day trek staying at a local Hmong village.

2

Wat Xiengmene

Just up from the boat landing, follow the narrow lane to the right for 500m through the village • 10,000K

Wat Xiengmene was built in 1592 and extensively rebuilt in modern times, though the *sim* still retains its beautifully carved doors. Inside the *sim*, restored with US money, the most striking feature is a fine naga serpent, glittering with multi-coloured mosaic pieces. The bamboo forest behind the wat conceals a royal cemetery for those members of royalty who, for religious reasons, could not be cremated.

Wat Chom Phet

500m further east along the lane, which becomes a path after 300m • 10,000K

A steep short climb up steps brings you to the timeworn *sim* and stupas of **Wat Chom Phet**. Now fallen into disuse, the whitewashed *sim*'s interior is entirely barren, bar an elaborately carved – if worn – stone altar. At dusk the views of the sunset from here are spectacular, further enhanced by the sounds of the city carrying across the water.

Wat Long Khoun and Wat Tham Sackkalin

300m east beyond Wat Chom Phet along the path • 10,000K, includes guided visit to Wat Tham Sackkalin , for which a tip of around 5000K is expected

Wat Long Khoun is set in peaceful grounds above the river. Very much a working temple, it was once used by Luang Prabang's kings as a pre-coronation retreat involving ritual baths, meditation and reflection. Of note are the two Chinese door guardians painted either side of the main entrance to the *sim*, and the vibrant, colourful Jataka murals within. In one, a group of mohican-topped monks swim for their lives to escape a trio of man-eating fish, while on the back wall, a family of elephants slurps languidly from a waterfall.

Your ticket for Wat Long Khoun includes a guided visit (basically, a kid with a torch) to nearby **Wat Tham Sackkalin**, which is actually a **cave** repository for old and damaged Buddha images. As with Tham Ting upriver (see p.134), this remarkably clammy cave is a focus of activity during Lao New Year, when the residents of Luang Prabang come here to gain merit by ritually bathing the Buddhas. There's not a great deal to see, but it's rather atmospheric and quite fun to scramble over rocks in the dark.

ARRIVAL AND INFORMATION

XIENG MEN AND CHOMPHET DISTRICT

By boat A frequent vehicle ferry (10,000K/person, bikes free, motorbikes 10,000K) runs between Luang Prabang and Xieng Men, leaving from the vehicle ferry landing behind the Royal Palace Museum. For around 20,000K you could also strike a deal with one of the boatmen along the riverbank to be dropped at the main Xieng Men ferry landing and picked up

(assuming the river is high enough) below Wat Long Khoun.

Tourist office Chomphet district's helpful but poorly signed tourist office (Mon–Fri 8–11.30am & 1.30–4pm; ☎ 030 991 0424) is a few hundred metres north of the boat landing; head up to the top of the hill, turn right along the dirt road to Ban Nakham and it's on your right (opposite a temple).

GETTING AROUND

Bike rental Mountain bikes can be rented in Xieng Men for 50,000K/day, or you can bring one on the ferry.
Tours Tours around Chomphet can be arranged with the Chomphet tourist office. You can also contact Mr Bounmy,

the local tourism officer, out of hours (☎ 020 5435 9232). A two-day trek, including guide, food and homestay, will cost from $35/person.

Across the Nam Khan

In the dry season, two bamboo bridges ford the river, one below Wat Pha Phoutthabat (8am–6pm; 5000K), which emerges at Dyen Sabai (see p.128), the other at the tip of the peninsula; in wet season and by bike, cross the motorcycle bridge 500m east of Wat Visoun and turn left at the first big intersection

Although a long walk along the Mekong foreshore and even around the point and back down along the Nam Khan is considered *de rigueur* on any walking tour of the old city, comparatively few tourists make the short hop across the river to the **opposite shore of the Nam Khan**. Here, facing the old city, you can follow (on foot or by bike) the banks of the river to the confluence with the Mekong and then continue along the Mekong shore through several small villages, which see relatively few foreign faces, all the way up to **Ban Don**, where the slow- and speedboat landings are located.

Along the way you can visit a string of old **wats** and **monasteries**, including charmingly worn **Wat Phan Luang**, directly opposite *Dyen Sabai*; atmospheric and

---

LUANG PRABANG ACTIVITIES AND TOURS

Luang Prabang boasts a mind-boggling array of travel agents and tour operators, particularly on Sisavangvong Road, many offering identical trips in and around the city (and further afield). The swift rivers, pretty rural areas and impressive mountains around Luang Prabang afford countless opportunities for adventure sports, including whitewater rafting, mountain biking, kayaking, zip-lining and trekking; many travel agents offer options to combine these with a trip to an elephant sanctuary (see box, p.135). In addition, several operators offer boat tours, which usually work out more expensive, but less hassle than organizing them yourself ad hoc at the boat landings.

Enquiries for tours can be made through your guesthouse or one of the tour agents listed below, though it pays to shop around – and make sure you know exactly what you're paying for when you sign up. Walk-in rates are usually slightly lower than those quoted online, and prices usually depend on the number of people in the group.

TREKKING, KAYAKING AND ADVENTURE SPORTS

★**Green Discovery** Sisavangvong Rd ☎071 212093, ⓦgreendiscoverylaos.com. Adventure-travel specialist with offices throughout the country, Green Discovery has an excellent choice of programmes within Luang Prabang province, from kayaking on the Nam Khan and Nam Xuang rivers (from $49 for a day-trip) and cycling and motorbike tours to rock-climbing, caving and overnight treks (from $77).

★**Tiger Trail** Sisavangvong Rd ☎071 252655, ⓦlaos-adventures.com. With a focus on sustainable tourism, Tiger Trail offers a superlative variety of tour options, including their excellent "Fair Trek" programme, which strives to create positive opportunities for local people. Day-trips in Luang Prabang include hill-tribe trekking ($58) and mountain biking ($52), with overnight treks ($107).

CYCLING AND MOTORBIKE TOUR SPECIALISTS

Grasshopper Adventures Off Kitsalat Rd, behind Dara Market ☎020 2863 4877, ⓦgrasshopper adventures.com. An international operation offering easy guided day tours around the city and along the Mekong (16–20km; $49/person), plus more

adventurous tours further afield, including a five-day trip through tribal hill villages to Vientiane. Helmets included, and tours use German Merida bikes.

Off Road Laos Adventures Ban Wat Visoun ☎020 5981 4423, ⓦoffroad-asia.com. Excellent day and multi-day motorbike trips through remote villages around Luang Prabang and the north. Also offers several one-day mountain biking tours (30–85km), including to Kuang Si (from $59).

BOAT TOURS

Banana Boat Ma Te Sai, Ban Wat Aphay ☎020 2889 4133, ⓦbananaboatlaos.com. Probably the best of the local boat operators (though not the cheapest), running a range of full-day Mekong and Nam Khan trips on twelve-seater vessels, including to Kuang Si via the Xieng Men temples (from $40/person).

Luang Say Cruises Sakkaline Rd ☎071 252553, ⓦluangsay.com. Luxury cruises up the Mekong to Pakbeng and Houayxai, for which it's often possible to get very good last-minute deals (see box, p.198).

Nava Mekong ☎020 5928 5555, ✉info@ navamekong.com. Four-hour lunch cruises up to Pak Ou caves ($25 excluding alcohol). They also run shorter dinner cruises to Xieng Men ($30).

partly ruined **Wat Pa Kha**, which lies a little to the north; and – another 500m on – modern **Wat Phonsaat**, behind which you can garner superb views back across the Nam Khan towards the old city. It's worth continuing at least as far as the handicraft village of **Ban Xang Khong**, 1km further north, where you can stop at the family workshops of weavers and mulberry-paper makers (including a branch of SA Paper Handicrafts; see p.132), and there are a couple of simple cafés serving noodle soup and baguettes.

ARRIVAL AND DEPARTURE　　　　　　　　　　　　　　　LUANG PRABANG　2

BY PLANE

Luang Prabang International Airport If you're flying into the city, be sure to get a window seat on the plane in order to enjoy the stunning bird's-eye views of Luang Prabang. Upgraded and expanded in 2013, Luang Prabang International Airport (LPQ; ⊚ luangprabangairport.com) is situated around 4km northeast of the old city – visitors from most countries are issued with a thirty-day visa on arrival (see p.24), though at busy periods there can be lengthy queues at immigration. There is a foreign exchange booth (24hr), a couple of ATMs and a counter selling prepaid tickets for the minivans that shuttle tourists into the centre (50,000K or 600 baht for up to three people); they can also organize guesthouse accommodation in town. Once you've bought your ticket you'll be ushered to a vehicle and taken directly to your accommodation.

Airlines Lao Airlines (Manomai Rd; ☎071 212172) operates three daily flights to Vientiane, and daily flights to Pakse. Internationally, they fly daily to Bangkok and Chiang Mai and twice weekly to Jinghong, China. Vientiane is also served daily by Lao Central Airlines (☎071 410215) and three times a week by Lao Skyway (☎1441). Bangkok Airways (Sisavangvong Rd; ☎071 253334) has flights twice daily to Bangkok, which is also served by Thai Smile (⊚thaismileair.com) four times a week. Lastly, Vietnam Airlines (☎071 213048) flies twice daily (codesharing with Lao Airlines) to Hanoi and daily to Siem Reap. A tuk-tuk to the airport should cost around 50,000K.

Destinations Bangkok, Thailand (3–4 daily; 1hr 40min); Chiang Mai, Thailand (1 daily; 1hr); Hanoi, Vietnam (2 daily; 1hr); Jinghong, China (2 weekly; 1hr); Pakse (1 daily; 1hr 40min); Siem Reap, Cambodia (1 daily; 1hr 40min); Vientiane (4–5 daily; 40min).

BY BUS AND MINIBUS

Luang Prabang has two public bus stations, plus a third for faster and pricier tourist minibuses and "VIP" international coaches. Tuk-tuks from any station to town cost around 20,000K/person. Though you can buy tickets at the bus stations (get there at least 30min before departure), it's usually easier to get them from one of the tour agencies on Sisavangvong Road. Though this works out more expensive, it will include a transfer from your guesthouse (plus commission for the agent).

Northern bus station Buses from the north arrive at the Northern bus station (☎071 252729), 3km northeast of town, near the airport. Minibuses leave at 9am, 11am and 1pm for Nong Khiaw, or you can take the 8.30am service to Sam Neua, which will stop off en route. The Luang Namtha bus leaves at 9am, and buses for Houayxai (normally marked as Borkeo, the name of the province) at 5.30pm and 7pm, the latter a VIP service.

Destinations Houayxai (Borkeo; 2 daily; 14hr); Luang Namtha (1 daily; 9hr); Nong Khiaw (3 daily; 3hr 30min–4hr); Oudomxai (3 daily; 6hr); Phongsali (1 daily; 13hr); Sam Neua (1–2 daily; 14hr).

Southern bus station Buses from points south along Route 13 stop at the Southern Bus Station (☎071 252066), 3km south of the centre. There are daily buses to Phonsavan (8.30am), two daily to Sayaboury (9am & 2pm) and Vang Vieng (9.30am & 12.30pm), and regular VIP and normal "Express" services to Vientiane (first at 7am), with a VIP sleeper at 8.30pm.

Destinations Phonsavan (1 daily; 10hr); Sayaboury (2 daily; 5–6hr); Vang Vieng (2 daily; 6–7hr); Vientiane (10 daily; 10–12hr); Vinh, Vietnam (1 daily; 22hr).

Naluang tourist bus station Naluang tourist bus station (aka minibus station) is opposite the Southern Bus Station, and serves an ever-expanding list of destinations north, south and international. Tourist buses will normally drop you centrally – often at a guesthouse that the driver has links to, though you're not obliged to stay there. Moving on, you'll save money if you book direct with the bus station itself (☎071 212979, ⊚naluangstation.com); their tickets are cheaper than the agencies in town but still include transfer. More locally, they're also useful for minibuses to Kuang Si (see p.136) and for motorbike rental (see p.122).

Destinations Bangkok, Thailand (1 daily; 22hr); Chiang Mai, Thailand (1 daily; 16hr); Hanoi, Vietnam (6 weekly; 24hr); Jinghong, China (1 daily; 21hr); Kunming, China (1 daily; 26hr); Loei, Thailand (daily; 9hr); Luang Namtha (1 daily; 9hr); Mengla, China (daily; 13hr); Nong Khiaw (1 daily; 3hr); Oudomxai (1 daily; 5hr); Phonsavan (1 daily; 7hr); Vang Vieng (3–5 daily; 5–6hr); Vientiane (2 daily; 10hr); Vinh, Vietnam (6 weekly; 24hr).

BY BOAT

Arrival In 2012, the slow boat pier for services to/from Houayxai and Pakbeng was moved to Ban Don, 10km east of the old city, in a move to benefit the local tuk-tuk drivers; speedboats arrive at the same place. Sawngthaews to town (20,000K/person) should drop you at your accommodation once you've bought a ticket at the booth at the top of the landing. Drivers may try to disgorge you on the edge of the old city – stand your ground. At the time of writing, there were no boat services running on the Nam Ou to Nong Khiaw, though these were rumoured to restart by mid-2014 (with a change of boats at Hat Kip; see p.169); until they were suspended in late 2013, they ran from the old slow boat pier behind the Royal Palace in the old city.

Departures Slow boats depart daily for Pakbeng (110,000K) en route to Houayxai (220,000K) at 8.30am. While you can buy tickets at the navigation office in Ban Don (☎071 212237; arrive at least half an hour early), it's much easier to pick one up from a travel agent in town. Prices are much higher (190,000K to Pakbeng is typical), but will include pick-up from your accommodation; otherwise, a sawngthaew to the pier will cost around 60,000K (for the vehicle). The eight-seater speedboats to Pakbeng (190,000K) and Houayxai (320,000K) theoretically depart at 9am (arrive early to be sure of a seat), though, as they'll only set off when full, often leave (much) later; since there's no guarantee they'll run, some travel agents are reluctant to sell tickets in advance. More advice on travelling on the Mekong is given in the chapter "The far north" (see box, p.198). Note that there are several luxury cruise boats between Luang Prabang and Houayxai, including the beautiful *Luang Say* (see boxes on p.198 & p.120).

Destinations Houayxai (1 daily: slow boat 2 days; speedboat 1 daily, 6–7hr); Pakbeng (1 daily: slow boat 8hr; speedboat 3–4hr).

INFORMATION

Tourist office The main tourist office is on the corner of Sisavangvong and Inthasone roads, opposite the Hmong Market (Mon–Fri 8–11.30am & 1.30–4pm, Sat & Sun 9–11.30am & 1–3.30pm; ☎071 212487, ☯tourism luangprabang.org). It is not always open when it should be, and the large room feels rather understocked for such a popular tourist destination.

Maps Hobo Maps (☯hobomaps.com) produces the most useful maps to both the city and the surrounding area, which you can access for free online. Their indexed city map is also available in printed form from most bookshops and some souvenir shops (20,000K).

GETTING AROUND

Bike rental Although you can comfortably walk everywhere in the old city, bicycles are ideal for exploring the town at large. Most budget guesthouses and a number of shops on Sisavangvong/Sakkaline Road (and the surrounding roads) rent out road bikes for 20,000K per day.

Motorbike and minivan rental Motorbikes – a great way to reach out-of-town attractions – are available to rent from around 120,000K a day from rental shops in the old city, and from Pinekham Service, at the bottom of Kitsalat Road, southeast of the Dara Market (☎071 212922). It's slightly cheaper to book them at the Naluang bus station (see p.121), which also rents out minivans (from $60/day).

Tuk-tuks Tuk-tuks can be surprisingly hard to find when you need one, but there are always congregations outside the tourist office and above the vehicle ferry pier, and in the early morning drivers hang around guesthouse areas waiting for foreigners bound for the bus stations or airport. Tuk-tuk journeys around the city are priced at a flat rate of 20,000K for foreigners, but you'll probably be quoted a higher price and be expected to haggle.

WHERE TO STAY

For most people, a location within the **old city** is the first choice. Here you'll find not only most of the city's best attractions but also many shops and restaurants. While the old city is still home to a dwindling number of budget options, the nicest area to stay for travellers on a budget is in the narrow lanes behind *Joma* café, a short stroll southwest of the old city, between **Chao Fa Ngum Road** and the Mekong, though for a bit more nightlife (such as it is) you may prefer one of the guesthouses around *Lao Lao Garden* and *Utopia*, close to the Nam Khan, **east of Phousi**. If you're looking for upmarket accommodation, you'll find an almost overwhelming choice. If you want a hotel with a swimming pool, however, bear in mind that building controls mean that you'll have to stay outside the old city – many of the most exquisite hotels occupy leafy plots **south of the centre**, beyond Kitsalat Road, though there are a few bargains to be had in this area, as well. Finally, while Luang Prabang is hardly frenetic, for ultimate peace and quiet there are numerous beautiful places to stay in the forested hills **outside the city**, particularly out east off Highway 13 en route to Tad Se waterfall; several of these are attached to popular elephant camps (see box, p.135). Most hotels out of the centre offer free transfer throughout the day.

ACCOMMODATION

Luang Prabang has hundreds of **places to stay**, from simple rooms in inexpensive guesthouses to gorgeous luxury hotels in historic properties, many of which play heavily on a French-colonial theme. While you can spend a fortune on accommodation, it's worth noting that a lot of the cheaper, mid-range places can be just as atmospheric (if not more so) than the fancy hotels. **High season** is December and January (festivals, such as Lao New Year, are also very busy times), but regardless of the season, it's a good idea to **book in advance** if you have a particular establishment in mind or if you'll be arriving in the evening. A good booking site for accommodation, especially for the budget end where few guesthouses have websites or email addresses, is ⓦ luang-prabang-hotels.com. **Prices** in Luang Prabang are a lot higher than elsewhere in the country and it can be hard to find much below 100,000K in high season, though big discounts are often available when business is quiet. **Breakfast** and free bike rental is normally included in the rates at smarter, more upmarket places, as (sometimes) is airport transfer; **free wi-fi** is standard.

2

THE OLD CITY

3 Nagas Sakkaline Rd ☎ 071 253888, ⓦ 3-nagas.com; map pp.108–109. Situated in two buildings on either side of the main road, this intimate boutique hotel is justifiably regarded as one of the city's best. The rooms, beautifully decorated with dark wood and Lao fabrics, are undeniably romantic. Views across the Nam Khan cost a little more. Check the website for internet specials. ‾$260‾

Ammata Kounxoa Rd ☎ 071 212175, ⓔ pphilasouk @yahoo.com; map pp.108–109. This sweet guesthouse, spread across two buildings, is excellent value. The pricier rooms ($45) in the new building come with TV and bathtubs, though all are nicely decorated in dark wood. ‾$35‾

Ancient Luang Prabang Kounxoa Rd ☎ 071 260804, ⓦ ancientluangprabang.com; map pp.108–109. A great-value alternative if *Lotus Villa* (see below) is full, this is one of the most stylish mid-range options in the tranquil northern part of the peninsula. Rooms (each with balcony) are awash with wood furniture and dominated by open stone baths – if you don't know your roommate intimately you soon will. Breakfast included. ‾$65‾

★**The Apsara** Soukkaseum Rd ☎ 071 254670, ⓦ theapsara.com; map pp.108–109. A beautiful small hotel with bags of atmosphere overlooking the Nam Khan. Best are the upstairs rooms ($130), which balance heavy-wood (and authentically creaky) floorboards with brightly coloured bedspreads and curtains, and feature gorgeous bathtubs – in-room but discreetly screened off. Guests can be ferried across the river to use the pool at *The Apsara Rive Droite*, its pricier but less characterful sister property. It also has an excellent modern Asian restaurant (see p.127). ‾$80‾

★**The Belle Rive** Souliyavongsa Rd ☎ 071 260733, ⓦ thebellerive.com; map pp.108–109. An absolutely charming hotel set across three buildings opposite the Mekong. The rooms (all with river views) have been beautifully furnished with dark wood and Oriental touches, such as decorated sinks and local fabrics. The suites in the main building ($160) are split-level and have a slightly more contemporary feel than those in the 1920s annexe. ‾$130‾

★**Lotus Villa** Kounxoa Rd ☎ 071 255050, ⓦ lotus villalaos.com; map pp.108–109. Lovely, light-filled rooms set around a shady courtyard filled with banana trees. The charming staff make you feel instantly at home, and the limitless breakfasts (included) are among the best in the city. The luxurious two-room Orchid Suites ($186) are worth the splurge for the extra space, and include a private balcony. Reserve well in advance. ‾$75‾

★**Mekong Riverview** Souliyavongsa Rd ☎ 071 254900, ⓦ mekongriverview.com; map pp.108–109. The excellent position at the head of the peninsula affords almost all rooms a view of the river, which can be enjoyed from the private balcony. Rooms are large and light, with magnificent hardwood floors; Lao cushions and wall hangings add a splash of colour, and nice touches include fragrant fresh flowers. A no-groups rule adds to the feel of (unstuffy) exclusivity. ‾$220‾

★**Namsok** Sisavangvatthani Rd ☎ 020 2235 4747, ⓔ taetotam@hotmail.com; map pp.108–109. On one of the few streets in the old city where you can still get a room for $10, this friendly place is excellent value, with big and spotless, if rather sparse, wood-floored rooms. For a bit more style (and cash) you can go for one in the block behind with TVs and snazzy black bathrooms. ‾80,000K‾

Pathoumphone Soukkaseum Rd ☎ 071 212946; map pp.108–109. A real bargain, especially considering its location right opposite the Nam Khan, with very friendly owners. Rooms have shared bathrooms and verge on dingy, but you won't find cheaper. Ask for room two, which has a small balcony and views over the river. ‾60,000K‾

Rim Vang Ounheuan Rd ☎ 071 212148; map pp.108–109. The dark, wooden rooms have surprisingly smart bathrooms, but are plain and a little overpriced; however, you can't beat the location, just around the corner from the National Museum. ‾160,000K‾

Sackarinh Off Sisavangvong Rd ☎ 071 254512; map pp.108–109. Tucked down a bustling little alleyway off the main road, with football-loving owners, this friendly guesthouse has petite en-suite rooms with small flat-screen tellies and windows, but no view. ‾$25‾

Sok Dee Off Souliyavongsa Rd ☎ 071 252555; map pp.108–109. A few steps up a brick lane off the Mekong road, this popular guesthouse is a great choice for somewhere a little quieter but still central. Go for one of the

2

rooms upstairs in the main building – bright and welcoming, though the trade-offs are thin walls and periodic lapses in cleanliness. Very handy for breakfast at *Saffron*. **140,000K**

Sopha House Soukkaseum Rd ☎071 253058, ✉sopha-house@gmail.com; map pp.108–109. The huge thatch-walled rooms on the all-wood first floor of this gorgeous old building opposite the Nam Khan ($35) share a delightful balcony overlooking the river, but suffer from poor plumbing; the smaller, more basic rooms downstairs arguably provide better value. **160,000K**

Thaheuame Souliyavongsa Rd ☎020 5508 0903, ✉thaeaume@gmail.com; map pp.108–109. An attractive Mekong-side guesthouse close to the morning market. The larger upstairs rooms ($35) are best, being light and airy with big windows overlooking the river, though it's quieter at the back; all display a touch of style and the welcome is friendly. **$25**

Thanaboun Sisavangvong Rd ☎071 · 260606, ✉thanaboun.gh@gmail.com; map pp.108–109. Rooms here are set back from the main drag and are plain, but attractive. The most atmospheric, yet also the smallest and cheapest, are those off the small courtyard at the back. **150,000K**

Thatsaphone Villa Off Sisavangvong Rd ☎020 5567 1888; map pp.108–109. On a little side street close to Wat Xiengmouane, this lovely guesthouse, set among palm trees, is a great deal for this part of town. Renovated in 2014, the simple rooms are slightly on the small side, but nicely furnished, with flat-screen TVs. **$25**

Victoria Xiengthong Palace Kounxoa Rd ☎071 213200, ⓦvictoriahotels.asia; map pp.108–109. Set in a frangipani-studded compound next to Wat Xieng Thong, the last residence of King Sisavang Vatthana was sumptuously renovated in 2011. On our visit, room decor was understated to the point of slight anonymity, but following a change of ownership, manager Guillermo was working hard to alter that; currently the two-storey suites ($350), with huge jacuzzi baths, offer the best value. Big discounts off-season. **$290**

View Khem Khong Souliyavongsa Rd ☎071 213032, ✉ericsensaoui@msn.com; map pp.108–109. The cheapest rooms here may be rather cramped and without a view, but you won't find many better priced on the Mekong road. There's just one with a river view, though it's considerably more expensive (350,000K). The attached restaurant (see p.128) is good. **140,000K**

★Villa Nagara Soukkaseum Rd ☎071 213120, ⓦvillanagara.com; map pp.108–109. A classy new seven-room place in a delightful wooden house right above the (dry-season only) Nam Khan bamboo bridge. Though the rooms aren't large, each is individually and stylishly decorated to its own colour palette and features lovely Lao fabrics. Breakfast (included) is served on the riverside terrace. **$75**

Villa Senesouk Sakkaline Rd ☎071 212074, ⓦluangphabang.com/senesouk; map pp.108–109. Sweet, immaculately kept rooms decorated with Lao masks and figurines in a large house opposite Wat Sene. For an extra $10 you can procure a balcony overlooking the temple, but best are the large, wood-panelled rooms in a separate building behind, with private sit-outs onto a peaceful courtyard ($50). **$30**

Xieng Mouane Xotikhoumman Rd ☎071 252152, ✉xiengmouane@yahoo.com; map pp.108–109. In an elegant hundred-year-old family home with historic connections (check out the sepia-tinted photos by the entrance), this guesthouse has a peaceful location opposite Wat Xiengmouane. Good-sized rooms feature bright Lao fabrics and the occasional heirloom. **$35**

AROUND CHAO FA NGUM ROAD

LPQ Backpackers Hostel Off Chao Fa Ngum Rd ☎020 9113 8686; map pp.104–105. On the nicest and leafiest of the little lanes leading to the river, this hostel has slightly squished dorms but smart bathrooms with top-notch showers, and a chilled-out movies room. Avoid the overpriced, box-like private rooms downstairs, though. Breakfast included. Dorm **50,000K**, double **120,000K**

Phonemaly Off Chao Fa Ngum Rd ☎071 253504; map pp.104–105. Two charming wooden buildings, lit at night with lanterns, provide some of the most atmospheric accommodation on a lane full of guesthouses. Cute rooms are large and come with comfy beds. **150,000K**

Suan Keo Off Chao Fa Ngum Rd ☎071 254404; map pp.104–105. Flowery bedspreads enliven the good-sized rooms at this peaceful, ever-popular guesthouse. You'll have to be quick to nab one of the two lovely wooden rooms upstairs. Good value. **100,000K**

Wat That Off Chao Fa Ngum Rd ☎071 212913, ⓦwatthatguesthouse.net; map pp.104–105. A very pleasant guesthouse set across two buildings on either side of a pretty lane. Ask for the big, wooden room upstairs at the back of the lovely traditional Lao house next to *LPQ*; the bigger building opposite is more expensive (rooms 150,000K), but has a gorgeous wooden balcony. Big discounts off-season. **100,000K**

Xayana Guesthouse & X3 Capsule Hotel Off Chao Fa Ngum Rd ☎071 260680, ⓦmylaohome.com; map pp.104–105. The doubles at this modern guesthouse are disappointingly basic and cramped; come here instead for the snug dorms, which have surprisingly large beds. Dorm **40,000K**, double **100,000K**

EAST OF PHOUSI

Chitlatda Ban Wat Aham ☎071 212227; map pp.108–109. Behind a bank of internet terminals, the cheapest rooms at this friendly, popular guesthouse are windowless and cell-like, but clean and en-suite. The wood-floored rooms upstairs are lighter and bigger (with TVs), but almost twice the price. **60,000K**

Merry 2/Villa Merry 1 Ban Wat Aphay ☎071 254445/ ☎071 252325, ⓦvilla-merry-guesthouse.com; map pp.104–105. There's a range of rooms on offer at popular *Merry 2*, on a little lane leading down to the Nam Khan. The cheapest are slightly dingy, but clean enough – much better to head upstairs where an extra 20,000K will get you an en-suite, gleaming wood floors and (perhaps) a shared balcony. Smarter still are the large family rooms in the connected annexe, though for this money ($40) you'd be better continuing down the lane to *Villa Merry 1*, in a gorgeous spot on the river. **60,000K**

Muong Lao Ban Wat Aphay ☎071 252741, ⓔthavone9@gmail.com; map pp.104–105. The rooms at this good-value, friendly guesthouse opposite Wat Visoun are simple, but very pleasant, and the old-fashioned, all-wood rooms upstairs have a nice shared balcony overlooking the temple. There's also an attractive outside restaurant. **140,000K**

Thony 1 Ban Wat Aphay ☎071 212805, ⓦthony1 guesthouse.com; map pp.104–105. The highlight of a stay here is the lovely communal area overlooking the river where you can enjoy a cold beer. The wood-panelled river-view rooms are the nicest, if a little overpriced ($35), though if you're on a budget the smaller viewless rooms aren't a bad option. **100,000K**

Villayvanh Ban Wat Aphay ☎071 252757; map pp.104–105. Nestling among coconut palms down the warren of lanes leading to *Utopia*, this welcoming little guesthouse is a real find. Rooms (with TV) are immaculately maintained; the wood-floored ones at the back feel slightly newer. Free tea and coffee all day. **120,000K**

SOUTH OF THE CENTRE

Amantaka Kitsalat Rd ☎071 860333, ⓦamanresorts .com; map pp.104–105. The old hospital provides a fantastic setting for Luang Prabang's most exclusive hotel. The huge, high-ceilinged suites – many of which have private pools – provide a cool retreat from the city and have been elegantly furnished. Afternoon tea is served daily in the library, and the spa is a blissful treat. **$800**

Hôtel de la Paix Off Manomai Rd, 1km south of the centre ☎071 260777, ⓦhoteldelapaixlp.com; map pp.104–105. Set around a leafy quadrangle within the forbidding high walls of the town's surprisingly attractive former prison compound – the lack of signs adding to the air of exclusivity – the sister hotel to the *3 Nagas* offers luxury aplenty and a great sense of seclusion. Vast suites feel Zen-like in their minimalism, with a muted palette of greys that nods to its former function – yet with private plunge pools (with some rooms), private gardens (with all), a cookery school, gorgeous spa and a seemingly endless pool, this is one place you wouldn't mind doing time. **$504**

Jaliya Manomai Rd ☎071 252154; map pp.104–105. Facing onto a lovely private garden and tucked well away from the road, the rooms at this old-fashioned, peaceful place are all very clean and comfortable, with TVs. Good value. **120,000K**

★**Khammany Inn** Photisalath Rd ☎020 9529 3925, ⓔkhammanyhostel@gmail.com; map pp.104–105. Professionally run and immaculately kept, this sociable place, a 10min walk from the old city, is hugely popular with backpackers and justifiably so. Ask for one of the smaller basement dorms – from the first-floor 16-bedder there's a two-storey hop down to the bathroom. Breakfast included. Dorm **45,000K**, double **160,000K**

Kiridara Highway 13, 1.5km south of the centre ☎071 261888, ⓦsnhcollection.com/kiridara; map pp.104–105. Perhaps the most architecturally striking – from a distance at least – of all Luang Prabang's hotels, set in a series of pitch-roofed, Lao-style pavilions that climb the forested slopes of Phou Wen, *Kiridara* is often one of the first glimpses of the city from the air. Rooms feature timber floors, stone walls and well-chosen Lao fabrics, though views of the city are side on from all but the suites ($336). The infinity pool and the spa are big plus points, but overall it perhaps lacks the finesse (and high price tag) of the city's very top properties. **$192**

★**La Résidence Phou Vao** At the eastern end of Kaysone Phomvihane Rd, 1.5km south of the centre ☎071 212530, ⓦresidencephouvao.com; map pp.104–105. A beautiful, sophisticated hotel that lives up to its expensive price tag. All of the huge, wood-heavy rooms have private balconies, some with views of Phousi in the distance, and are sumptuously decorated. The spa, with pavilions set among the lush grounds, is a heavenly retreat, and the swimming pool is welcome respite after the heat of the city. A shuttle runs into town on demand (and hourly in the evenings), or it's just a 20min walk to the centre. **$650**

★**Luang Say Residence** 2km south of the centre ☎071 260891, ⓦluangsayresidence.com; map pp.104–105. Set in gorgeous colonial-style villas amid palm and banana-leaf gardens, this exquisite luxury hotel unashamedly summons all the spirit and exotic mystery of imperial Indochine – despite only dating back to 2010. The huge, light suites, with columns and big bay windows, are irresistibly decadent, and highlights include top-class French cuisine at the *Belle-Epoque* restaurant and afternoon tea in the Henri Mouhot-dedicated *1861 Bar*. Guests have use of the spa at *Phou Vao*. **$530**

★**Ock Pop Tok Villa** Photisalath Rd, 2km southwest of the centre ☎071 212597, ⓦockpoptok.com; map pp.104–105. Blending beautiful textiles and classic Luang Prabang style, the four rooms at the Living Crafts Centre's new villa are full of colour and winning details (such as Akha-headdress lampshades). Though a bit out of town, it's ideal for a class (see p.118), circuit of Phosy Market (see p.132) or

2

– from the more expensive riverside rooms – just to sit and ponder this lazy stretch of the Mekong. Breakfast is served in the centre's excellent *Silk Road Café*, and there's free transfer to the centre – or grab a bike and cycle yourself. **$60**

SpicyLaos/Lemon Laos ☎020 2255 5539; map pp.104–105. Prone to periodic identity crises (hence the twin names), this long-established backpacker joint has cheap, but not hugely cheerful accommodation in very dark dorms – so great for escaping the heat, or recovering from a Beerlao hangover. There's a large patio and a great communal vibe. Dorm from 30,000K, double 70,000K

★**Thongbay** 500m down a track off Highway 13, 2km southeast of the old city ☎071 253234, ⓦthongbay -guesthouses.com; map pp.104–105. The sixteen rustic, wood-and-thatch bungalows here are set in a beautiful garden, with the best looking over the Nam Khan. Though a bit of a distance from the centre, the peaceful location more than makes up for it, and there are bikes and a regular shuttle to get you into town. It would be easy, however, to lose hours lounging on your balcony watching the villagers tend their vegetable gardens on the opposite bank. Breakfast included. **$55**

Villa Maly Off Photisalath Rd ☎071 253903, ⓦvilla -maly.com; map p.104–105. Just a 10min walk from the old city, this exclusive property has a real colonial feel. The spacious rooms, decorated in pastel shades, ooze class and refinement, and the lovely pool area is a real bonus. **$347**

OUT OF THE CITY

★**Lao Spirit Resort** Ban Xieng Lom, 15km east of Luang Prabang ☎020 5855 3133, ⓦlao-spirit.com; map pp.104–105. A really special place, alive with birdsong and tucked away among jungle on the banks of the Nam Khan. The six gorgeous bungalows have oodles of space, open-air showers and large balconies perfect for soaking up the river views. Delicious meals are served throughout the day in the restaurant and various trips can be arranged, including to the nearby Elephant Village (see box, p.135). **$140**

Zen Namkhan Ban Xieng Lom, 15km east of Luang Prabang ☎020 5557 1120, ⓦzennamkhanresort.com; map pp.104–105. A tranquil resort in forested surroundings high in the hills above the Nam Khan. The attractive wooden bungalows play on a Japanese theme, with paper lanterns and *torii*-shaped headboards, and draws include daily yoga, a Japanese spa and a natural-feel "eco" pool. **$145**

EATING

Thanks to the huge growth in tourism, Luang Prabang boasts more **restaurants** than anywhere else in the country outside the capital, and dining out is unquestionably one of the highlights of the city. It's the perfect place to experience the richness and variety of Lao cuisine (see box below), though thanks to the ever-expanding number of expats making Luang Prabang their home you can find high-quality international food here, too – particularly French, though also other European and Asian cuisines. Many of the city's top dining spots cluster in the northern part of the peninsula, along Sakkaline and Soukkaseum roads; for cheaper – but often equally tasty – meals, make for the delightful riverside restaurants along the Mekong riverfront, which is also the ideal spot to be at sunset. Another of the city's joys is its clutch of French-style **café-bakeries**, the best of which produce cakes and pastries that would easily pass muster in Paris. Finally, though Luang Prabang lacks the **street food** scene you find in Thailand, the night market and Hmong market are ideal spots to linger for a cheap fill, as much for the atmosphere and the chance to chew the cud with other travellers as for the quality of the food on offer.

LUANG PRABANG CUISINE

Luang Prabang is a city that prides itself on its food. Some dishes are unique to the royal city, and others are simply done better here than elsewhere – all of which conspires to make this the town in which to dig into **Lao food** with a sense of mission, despite the wide availability of international cuisine.

At the top of your list should be **or lam**, a bittersweet meat soup made with chilli wood, lemongrass, aubergine and dill. Another local speciality, **jaew bong**, a condiment of red chillies, shallots, garlic and dried buffalo skin, is an excellent accompaniment for crispy *khai paen*, a highly nutritious **river weed** that's first sundried with sesame seeds, garlic and chilli, then fried in oil.

Phak nam, a type of **watercress** particular to the area, is a common sight in Luang Prabang's markets (see p.131), and is widely used in salads. The most common style appears on menus either as "watercress salad" or "Luang Prabang salad" and is in fact quite similar to a Western salad – a light alternative to the meat salads more commonly served in Lao restaurants. Locals even add a twist to the Lao staple, *tam màk hung* (**papaya salad**): the distinctive Luang Prabang flavour of this dish comes from the addition of crab juice.

STREET FOOD AND SNACKS

Hmong Market On the corner of Sisavangvong and Kitsalat roads; map pp.108–109. Baguettes, Lao coffee and fresh fruit shakes are sold throughout the day at the Hmong Market, and during the evenings you'll also find someone selling delicious *kanom krok* (little coconut and rice pancakes) here. Daily 9am–9pm.

Night market Off Sisavangvong Rd; map pp.108–109. The best way to dine for next to nothing is to head to the buffet stalls set up down the narrow side street next to the *Ancient Luang Prabang* hotel and join the communal tables, sampling local treats in a casual, buzzing atmosphere. Just 10,000K will buy you as much rice, noodles and veg as you can cram onto a plate, then order tasty meat or fish grills and beer separately. Daily 5–10pm.

CAFÉS

Delilah's Place Chao Fa Ngum Rd ☎071 254988; map pp.104–105. A chilled-out café-restaurant with ethnic-cushion-strewn benches and a couple of candlelit roadside tables out front. Come for a pancake (20,000K) and cup of strong Lao coffee at breakfast time, and choose from the menu of tasty Lao specials, such as *oua kai* (lemongrass stuffed with onions and veg; 25,000K) later on. Daily 7am–10pm.

Joma Branches on Chao Fa Ngum Rd (map pp.104–105) and Soukkaseum Rd (map pp.108–109) ☎071 260920, ☯joma.biz. Perennially popular, though really you could be anywhere in the world. A good choice if you're craving a Western breakfast or lunch, with granola, bagels (from 18,000K), sandwiches and cakes on offer, plus a range of coffees and fruit juices. The Nam Khan branch is the nicer of the two, with a sun-trap veranda and seating by the river. Daily 7am–9pm.

★Le Banneton Sakkaline Rd ☎020 5464 9189; map pp.108–109. Situated a little up from Wat Sene, this superb café-boulangerie feels decidedly French, with an excellent choice of patisseries, including the best croissants in town, plus delicious baguettes and good coffee. Breakfast sets from 40,000K. Daily 6.30am–6pm.

Le Café Ban Vat Sene Sakkaline Rd ☎071 252482, ☯elephant-restau.com; map pp.108–109. This charming café, with its artfully distressed exterior and cool, fan-spun interior, is a wonderful place to lose a few hours, whether over a lunchtime baguette (around 40,000K) or an afternoon coffee with one of their delicious cakes – including a heavenly banana tatin (24,000K). Daily 6.30am–10pm.

L'Etranger Books & Tea Ban Wat Aphay ☎071 260248; map pp.108–109. The tables outside this great little bookshop (see p.131) are perfect for a refreshing drink while you watch the world go by (local mulberry green tea 15,000K), though the food is so-so. A small room upstairs

hosts an interesting exhibition on Lao culture and life, and movies are shown nightly (see p.130). Daily 7am–10pm.

Le Patio Café Traditional Arts and Ethnology Centre, Kitsalat Rd ☎071 253364, ☯elephant-restau.com; map pp.108–109. The veranda café of the 1920s colonial mansion that houses the TAEC (see p.117) is a handsome, genteel place for lunch after a spin round the exhibition, with an interesting and reasonably priced menu of tribal-influenced Lao dishes (Hmong pork belly, for instance, or Akha meatballs; both 28,000K) and baguettes from 30,000K. Tues–Sun 9am–6pm.

★Saffron Branches on Souliyavongsa and Inthasone roads ☎020 5458 7134, ☯saffroncoffee.com; map pp.108–109. The best place in town for a pulse-quickening espresso, either inside among sepia photos and jazz music, or (at the Souliyavongsa branch) outside on the terrace overlooking the Mekong. There's a good range of breakfasts, including a delicious granola bowl (20,000K), and you can also buy their own locally grown coffee here. Daily 7am–9pm.

RESTAURANTS

THE OLD CITY

★3 Nagas Sakkaline Rd ☎071 253888, ☯3-nagas .com; map pp.108–109. One of the best places in town for Lao food – beautifully prepared and presented – with an atmospheric dining room that opens onto Sakkaline Road. Try the exquisite *larp* with sliced Mekong fish (56,000K) or the lemongrass stuffed with pork (60,000K). The wine list is excellent, and the boozy cocktails (Lao sling 50,000k) to die for. Daily 6.30am–10.30pm.

★The Apsara Soukkaseum Rd ☎071 254670, ☯theapsara.com; map pp.108–109. Head chef Luke bristles at the word, but the fusion cooking at this lovely hotel's excellent restaurant is some of the city's best, with a short menu combining Southeast Asian ingredients with Aussie flair. Lunch covers local classics for around 50,000K, while dinner is a bit more adventurous and might include smoked fish with betel leaf (45,000K) and slow-cooked buffalo cheeks (90,000K). Daily 11.30am–3pm & 6–9.30pm.

Big Tree Café Souliyavongsa Rd ☎020 7777 6748, ☯bigtreecafe.com; map pp.108–109. One of many places on this stretch of the Mekong with terraced seating overlooking the river, this cute gallery-cum-restaurant serves an interesting variety of Western, Korean and Lao food, and has breakfast sets starting from 40,000K. Mon–Sat 8.30am–9.30pm.

Blue Lagoon Ounheuan Rd ☎071 253698, ☯blue-lagoon-restaurant.com; map pp.108–109. Popular with expats, the best seats here are in the atmospheric garden courtyard. The mixed European (mainly Swiss) and Asian menu is a little pricy (*larp* 78,000K; buffalo fillet with Gruyère and *rösti* 136,000K), but the presentation and service is absolutely superb. Daily 10am–10.30pm.

2

2

Boungnasouk Souliyavongsa Rd ☎071 212749; map pp.108–109. The menu here features a wider selection of Lao and Asian food than most restaurants on this strip, including a delicious, herb-filled beef *larp* (30,000K). Head for the seating on the lower terrace for good views of the river. Daily 8am–9pm.

Café Toui Sisavangvatthani Rd ☎020 5657 6763, ⓦ cafetoui.com; map pp.108–109. A small, intimate place with a couple of pavement tables. The menu is predominantly Lao, though the baguettes make this an excellent lunch stop; the highlight is the set Lao menu that offers a taster of local dishes including *mok pa* and *larp* for 80,000K. There's also Twinings tea for those craving a cuppa. Daily 10am–10pm.

Coconut Garden Sisavangvong Rd ☎071 260436, ⓦ elephant-restau.com; map pp.108–109. The most atmospheric choice on this stretch of the main road, with a lantern-lit courtyard, coconut palms and ambient music. The Lao dishes are very tasty, if a little on the small side – try the *kranab pa* (grilled river fish stuffed with pork and herbs and wrapped in a banana leaf (48,000K). Daily 8am–11.30pm.

L'Eléphant Sathouyaithao Rd ☎071 252482, ⓦ elephant-restau.com; map pp.108–109. Situated in a beautiful colonial building, this acclaimed, upmarket restaurant is the kind of place where you almost expect to see Humphrey Bogart stroll in. The menu is predominantly French, so expect the likes of frogs' legs *provençale* (115,000K) and duck breast with dauphinoise potatoes (150,000K), though (more reasonably priced) Lao essentials are covered as well. Daily noon–2.30pm & 6–10.30pm.

Luang Prabang Bakery Sisavangvong Rd ☎020 5557 0384, ⓦ lpbgh.com; map pp.108–109. This surprisingly smart little place has an extensive menu that encompasses pizza, sandwiches and a good choice of Lao dishes, plus a tempting selection of baked goods; they also set up a night-time cake stall nearby outside the *Ancient Luang Prabang*. Most mains 60,000–70,000K. Daily 10am–10pm.

Nazim Sisavangvong Rd ☎071 253493; map pp.108–109. A simple but decent, friendly and ever-popular Indian restaurant serving a good range of north and south Indian veg (from 20,000K) and non-veg (from 32,000K) curries. Sometimes open for breakfast. Daily 11am–11pm.

Riverside Barbecue Souliyavongsa Rd ☎020 5599 9945; map pp.108–109. By far the most popular spot by the Mekong, this big, bustling *sin dad* joint packs in hundreds every night, attracted more by the trestle tables bulging with help-yourself meat, fish and veg than by the constant power ballad soundtrack. Obliging waiters are on hand to help you perfect your barbecue technique. All-inclusive buffet (excluding alcohol) 60,000K. Daily 6–10pm.

Rosella Fusion Soukkaseum Rd ☎020 7777 5753; map pp.108–109. Sandwiched between some of the city's biggest culinary hitters on the Nam Khan riverside, this charming family-run place more than holds its own, with some deliciously fragrant Lao cooking served in generous portions (mains 35,000–40,000K). Owner Dith formerly worked as head barman at *Amantaka*, and as you'd expect the cocktails are excellent too – try the house rosella (hibiscus). Daily 11am–9.30pm.

Tamarind Soukkaseum Rd ☎020 7777 0484, ⓦ tamarindlaos.com; map pp.108–109. This small and very popular Nam Khan-side restaurant has a well-deserved reputation for some of the best Lao food in town. It's definitely worth splashing out on one of their "feast" menus, which allow you to experience a more authentically local side of Lao food (from 90,000K/person). They also run a very good cooking school (see box, p.129). Book ahead. Mon–Sat 11am–11pm.

★**Tamnak Lao** Sakkaline Rd ☎071 252525, ⓦ tamnaklao.net; map pp.108–109. Though it's popular with tour groups, this shouldn't put you off, as the Lao menu here is more extensive than elsewhere in the city and the food full of flavour. The stir-fried fish with Chinese mushrooms and ginger (55,000K) and delectably spiced *or lam* (50,000K) are highly recommended. Daily 9am–10pm.

★**Tangor** Sisavangvong Rd ☎071 260761, ⓦ letangor .com; map pp.108–109. Opened in 2013, *Tangor* is so French there's a good chance you'll be served by a waiter in cravat. Unsurprisingly, the pricey food is excellent too, from baked Camembert to tarte tartin. Try the ceviche (80,000K as a main), given added zing by lemongrass and basil and so fresh it's almost swimming. The street-facing terrace is a popular people-watching spot. Daily 11.30am–11pm (kitchen closes at 9.45pm); closed 1 Sat per month.

★**Un Petit Nid** Sakkaline Rd ☎071 260686, ⓦ unpetitnid.com; map pp.108–109. This cute "biblio bistro" set slightly back from the main road makes a nice retreat throughout the day; try the *khào pûn* (noodle soup with coconut milk, potatoes and galangal; 25,000K) or, if you're feeling indulgent, one of the steaks (75,000K). Daily 7.30am–9.30pm.

View Khem Khong Souliyavongsa Rd ☎071 213032; map pp.108–109. A lovely outdoor restaurant right on the banks of the Mekong river, with candle-lit tables and big white umbrellas. The menu is quite extensive and the food inexpensive and delicious (*or lam* 30,000K). One of the best of the riverside options. Daily 7am–9pm.

OUTSIDE THE OLD CITY

★**Dyen Sabai** Ban Phan Luang, across the Nam Khan ☎020 5104817, ⓦ dyensabai.com; map pp.108–109. Arguably the most atmospheric place in town, with bamboo "huts" scattered with cushions overlooking the

COOKERY COURSES

Luang Prabang is a great place to learn more about Lao food, with several cookery schools offering a range of introductory classes. You can choose between full-day courses, which usually include a tour of the market to learn about Lao ingredients and making your own lunch (and/or dinner), or shorter evening courses, which mainly focus on cooking demonstrations.

★**Tamarind** Kitsalat Rd ☎020 7777 0484, ⊛tamarindlaos.com. The excellent one-day class begins with a fascinating tour of Phosy Market (see p.132) before the group heads to the peaceful lakeside cooking school where you learn six Lao dishes – such as lemongrass stuffed with chicken, *môk pa* and *jaew*. Day class Mon–Sat 9am–3pm (280,000K); evening class Mon–Fri 4–8pm (210,000K).

Tum Tum Cheng Sakkaline Rd ☎020 2242 5499, ⊛tumtumcheng.wicked-web.biz. A shorter course than most, where you can learn how to prepare many of the more unusual Lao ingredients and more about the royal cuisine of Luang Prabang. Daily: day class 8.30am–2pm (250,000K); evening class 5–8pm (230,000K).

2

river. The *sin dad* (from 70,000K for two) is reason enough to cross the river, but the delicious cocktails (happy hour noon–7pm) and relaxed vibe will keep you here for much longer. During dry season, cross at the bamboo bridge (5000K from 8am to 6pm) near Wat Pha Phoutthabat; in wet season a small boat ferries people across from the same point – look for the boat captain at the top of the steps. Dry season: daily 8am–11.30pm; wet season: Mon–Sat noon–11pm.

The House Ban Aphay ☎071 255021, ⊛thehouselaos .com; map pp.108–109. A relaxed Belgian–French bar-restaurant, with a cosy interior, beer garden and *pétanque* court. Flemish specialities on offer include *stoofvlees* (76,000K), and the range of beers encompasses Chimay (Bleue 84,000K) and Duval (58,000K) – perfect (if pricey) if you're craving a change from Beerlao. Daily 5–10.30pm.

Khem Khan Food Garden Ban Aphay ☎020 5221 4794; map pp.108–109. High on the bank of the Nam

Khan river behind Phousi, this is a great venue for traditional Lao food, with lovely views of the Nam Kham. The *keng kai màk nao*, a soup served with chicken, and the *sai oua* sausages (both 40,000K) are standouts. Daily 8am–10pm.

Nisha Kitsalat Rd ☎071 253746; map pp.104–105. A short hop from the Dara Market, a no-frills Indian that dishes up Luang Prabang's best south Indian veg curries – try the *malai kofta* (16,000K) or *aloo baingan* (13,000K) – though there's also the obligatory *chicken tikka masala* for the meaty-minded. Daily 9am–11pm.

Pizza Phan Luan Khoundouangchan Rd, Ban Phan Luang ☎020 5577 1203; map pp.104–105. Tucked down a candlelit alleyway behind an English school, this chilled-out, candlelit garden restaurant across the bamboo bridge (see p.117) is the unlikely venue for arguably the city's best wood-fired pizza. Pizza Margherita 45,000K, glass of wine 30,000K. Tues–Sun 5.30–10pm.

DRINKING AND NIGHTLIFE

The town's riverfront restaurants are the best places to sip a cool drink at sunset, but the most hopping **bar** area is south of the old city between Phousi and the Nam Khan. Don't expect amazing nightlife – thanks to a town curfew they all close at 11.30pm.

Bowling Alley 4km southwest of town, past the Southern bus station ☎020 5511 0033; map pp.104–105. Believe it or not, the place to be after the bars close is the ten-pin bowling alley. A game costs 20,000K/person (after 6pm) but really, as evidenced by the quality of play, it's the Beerlao (15,000K) that everyone's here for. Tuk-tuks wait outside *Lao Lao Garden* and *Utopia* at chucking-out time to take you there. Daily noon–2am.

DaoFa Hotel 3km south of town, near the Southern bus station ☎071 260789; map pp.104–105. If you're looking for something with more of a local spin, head over to Luang Prabang's premier nightclub, tucked down an alleyway beside a hotel – a dark, smoky and sweaty affair

with oil-drum tables and cans of Carlsberg for 15,000K. There are live bands early evening, then DJs and a blink-and-you-miss it disco before bedtime. You can also rent a private karaoke booth (150,000K/3hr) to try to replicate that tortured-cat Lao karaoke sound. Daily 8.30pm–midnight.

Hive Ban Aphay ☎020 5999 5370, ⊛hivebarlaos.com; map pp.108–109. A popular, if rather brash, bar, with DJs and an epic happy hour (noon–7pm) of two-for-one cocktails (25,000K). A hip-hop and "Ethnik" fashion show (Tues–Sat from 7pm) displays clothes from Laos's various ethnic groups in conjunction with nearby Kōpnoï (see p.131). Daily 7am–11.30pm.

2

★**Icon Klub** Off Sisavangvong Rd, near Wat Pha Phoutthabat ☎071 254905, ⓦiconklub.com; map pp.108–109. A cosy little bar run by Hungarian Lisa, with an eclectic decor and a good line in homespun cocktails (40,0000–50,000K). One of Luang Prabang's most convivial late(ish)-opening options, so popular with Westerners propping up the bar over a nightcap. Sometimes runs events and periodically closes for several weeks at a time. Daily 5.30–11.30pm.

Lao Lao Garden Ban Aphay ☎020 7777 4414; map pp.108–109. A large, hugely atmospheric garden bar – a great place to chill out over a Lao barbecue (49,000K) under the lanterns, before things pick up later on. The huge drinks menu includes a range of rather potent two-for-one cocktails from 20,000K, and large Beerlao for 14,000K. Daily 8am–11.30pm.

S Bar Ban Aphay ☎020 5466 5757; map pp.108–109.

With a drinks menu printed on 12" vinyl, this moodily lit new kid on the block thinks of itself as a cooler, more cosmopolitan alternative to the competition along the main bar strip. It's quickly become famous for its burgers (55,000K), though the sushi and "Lao tapas" are well worth a try too. Daily noon–11.30pm.

★**Utopia** Ban Wat Aphay, by the Nam Khan ☎020 2388 1771, ⓦutopialuangprabang.com; map pp.104–105. "Zen by day, groovy by night" is *Utopia's* philosophy – and it's a real winner. With stunning river views, rustic-tropical decor, and a good food and booze menu, not to mention early morning yoga, "beach" volleyball, DJ evenings and BBQ-in-a-bomb nights, there's enough to make your visit last all day. It's on the river, east of Wat Visoun – just follow the signs from the main road. Daily 8am–11.30pm.

ENTERTAINMENT

THEATRE

Phralak Phralam Theatre Royal Palace Museum ⓦphralakphralam.com. A building in the grounds of the Royal Palace Museum serves as the home of the Royal Ballet Theatre, which gives performances four nights a week (Mon, Wed, Fri & Sat 6pm; 100,000–150,000/person depending on the seat). The shows include excerpts from the Lao version of the Ramayana, a mock Lao wedding ceremony, as well as some Lao interpretations of the dances of their tribal neighbours. The glittering costumes are stunning, and the traditional

Lao music will be playing in your head long into the night.

FILM

There are no cinemas in Luang Prabang, but *L'Etranger* (see p.131) shows quality films nightly at 7pm above the bookshop; there's no charge, but you are expected to buy food or a drink. Movies are also shown most nights at *Xayana Guesthouse* and *LPQ Backpackers* (see p.124). Real buffs should aim to arrive in the city for the Luang Prabang Film Festival (see p.130).

SHOPPING

As the royal capital of Laos, Luang Prabang was traditionally a centre for skilled **artisans** from around the former kingdom. Weavers, gold- and silversmiths, painters, sculptors of bronze, wood and ivory all held a place of importance in old Luang Prabang, and the most gifted artisans were awarded royal patronage. After the revolution these arts were seen as decadent and officially suppressed, while the artisans associated with the former royalty were shunned. Unable to practise their trade, many drifted to more acceptable occupations or fled the country. These days, with the boom in tourism, the traditional arts have been experiencing a revival, and there is a wide array of different crafts on sale – as well as the usual selection of tourist junk. **Silver** and **textiles**, in particular, can be good buys in Luang Prabang, but only if you buy from the right people and haggle. The biggest tourist draw remains the **handicraft nightmarket**. In addition, numerous shops along Sisavangvong and the surrounding roads sell textiles and other crafts.

LUANG PRABANG FILM FESTIVAL

Launched in 2010, the **Luang Prabang Film Festival** (ⓦlpfilmfest.org) was set up to celebrate film-making in Southeast Asia, with the hope of encouraging a film industry in Laos. Running over five days in December, the festival showcases films from all ten ASEAN countries, in outdoor locations such as the handicraft market, and is aimed at both locals and tourists, with free (first-come, first-served) seating for all. Following the festival, a smaller programme of films is toured around other major provinces in the country. Both events are supplemented by educational projects throughout the year in order to support film-making (still very much in its infancy) in Laos.

BOOKSHOPS

Many guesthouses and cafés have small book exchanges.

L'Etranger Books & Tea Ban Aphay ☎071 260248; map pp.108–109. The best second-hand bookshop in town (plus a number of new books), including some foreign fiction and a good selection on Laos. Also lends books for a minimal fee, serves food and drinks (see p.126), and screens recent films nightly. Daily 7am–10pm.

Luang Prabang Library Sisavangvong Rd ☎071 254813; map pp.108–109. The small bookshop next to Luang Prabang's rather meagrely stocked public library has a book exchange, plus a few travel guides and other Laos-related titles on sale, the profits from which help support teacher-training scholarships for girls who volunteer in the shop. Visitors can also buy Lao-language school books for their library boat project – pop the books in the "book bag" next to the counter, and once it's full (100 titles) the books are taken by boat to any of 75 local villages along the Mekong and its tributaries; see ⓦcommunitylearning international.org for more. Mon–Fri 8am–5pm, Sat & Sun 9am–4pm.

Monument Books Sathouyaithiao Rd ☎071 254954, ⓦmonument-books.com/laos.php; map pp.108–109. A great little bookshop stocking a good range of magazines, local and international fiction and non-fiction, travel guides, maps and children's books. Mon–Fri 9am–9pm, Sat 9am–7pm.

Yensabai Books & Art Wat Ban Aphay ☎071 260 1955; map pp.108–109. A small range of books (largely secondhand) to buy and borrow, plus maps, coffee and art. Daily 8am–10pm.

CLOTHES, TEXTILES AND HANDICRAFTS

Traditional textiles are practically Luang Prabang's signature product. Both antique and new textiles can be bought here, and the city has many upscale boutiques specializing in high-quality Lao textiles – look for the "Handmade in Luang Prabang" label (see ⓦluangprabang handicraft.org for more).

Anakha The Blue House, Sakkaline Rd ☎020 5875 4990; map pp.108–109. A classy and inviting boutique selling a fine range of linen homeware and elegant silk women's clothing, ideal for perfecting that Catherine Deneuve-in-*Indochine* look. Daily 9.30am–10pm.

Kōpnoï Ban Aphay ☎071 260248, ⓦkopnoi.com; map pp.108–109. This excellent shop sells a small but select range of fair-trade Lao textiles from around the country, including beautiful silk scarves. It also carries an eclectic range of other gift and household items, including Khmu-made bamboo straws (80,000K for 12), cushions, lamps and jewellery. The exhibition space upstairs, which showcases local art, is worth a quick browse. Daily 8am–9pm.

Mulberries Souliyavongsa Rd ☎071 254594, ⓦmulberries.org; map pp.108–109. Beautiful fabric and clothing from this fair-trade company, as well as mulberry tea and smellies. Also has a silk farm and training centre in Phonsavan.

★**Ock Pop Tok** Branches on Sakkaline Rd ☎071 254406 and Sathouyaithiao Rd ☎071 253219, ⓦockpoptok.com; map pp.108–109. Though the textiles here are a little pricey, there's no denying the quality of the work, which surpasses most of what's on offer elsewhere in town. All of the products have been made in Laos – either at the shop's Living Crafts Centre (see p.118) or through their Village Weaver Projects which support local communities. The Passa Paa range (ⓦpassa-paa.com) at the new Sakkaline Road branch is particularly worth a look. Colourful Hmong toy animals from $5. Daily 8am–8pm.

TAEC Kitsalat Rd ☎071 253364, ⓦtaeclaos.org; map pp.108–109. The excellent shop at the museum (see p.117) sells a wonderful collection of reasonably priced handicrafts, with half of the shop's income going back to village producers. Tues–Sun 9am–6pm.

MARKETS

Dara Market Kitsalat Rd; map pp.108–109. A rather sanitized modern precinct offering a varied range of products, from mobile phones to Western clothing, with a few Lao handicrafts stalls and silversmiths at the back. Daily 8am–5pm.

Handicraft market Sisavangvong Road between the tourist office and the Royal Palace Museum; map pp.108–109. From embroidered bedspreads and brightly coloured shoulder bags to *lào-láo*, lanterns and the obligatory Beerlao T-shirts, this is the city's most famous market and you're bound to find something that appeals. A lot of what is sold is much of a muchness, and a high proportion is actually from Thailand and China, but nonetheless it's fun to browse and it's possible to get some good bargains. Be prepared to haggle (see p.47).

Hmong market On the corner of Sisavangvong and Kitsalat roads; map pp.108–109. During the day, a small number of stalls set up close to the nightmarket – much of the produce is the same, though there's a little less pressure from sellers. Also a good place for snacks (see p.127). Daily 7am–9pm.

Morning market Between Inthasone Rd and the Royal Palace Museum; map pp.108–109. On a street parallel to Sisavangvong Rd and the river, the crammed-in stalls here sell a whole range of produce, from bug-eyed fish and scrawny chicken feet to piles of bright-green veg and little round aubergines. Get there early to experience it at its best – by 10am, most of the stalls have started packing up. Daily 6–10am.

2

★**Phosy Market** Photisalath Rd, 2km southwest of the centre ☎071 253730; map pp.104–105. The city's main market provides a welcome taste of real daily life in Luang Prabang away from the tourists. This huge, largely covered market sells almost everything you can think of, from machetes to mobiles to giant Miffys. The meat section is alive with the sound of cleavers, and it's a good place to pick up snacks, such as bags of spicy and delicious dried, fried mushrooms. Daily 7am–5pm.

MULBERRY-PAPER

SA Paper Handicrafts Off Souliyavongsa Rd ☎020 7777 7613; map pp.108–109. Tucked down a tiny lane opposite Wat Xiengmouane, this is one of a number of shops selling colourful, traditional mulberry-paper lanterns, including collapsible models, plus books, cards and photo albums. Daily 9am–9pm.

SILVER, JEWELLERY AND ANTIQUES

New silver of superior quality can and should be bought directly from Luang Prabang's expert silversmiths. There are several shops attached to workshops in Ban Wat That,

the traditional silversmithing district southwest of the old city between Chao Fa Ngum Road and the Mekong, though opening hours are erratic. Other silversmiths are located near the Royal Palace, opposite Wat Aham and in the Dara Market. Items to look out for include paraphernalia for betel chewing, boxes or bowls and jewellery. With a few exceptions, the hill-tribe jewellery peddled in Luang Prabang is the handiwork of the Hmong. All of these articles are sold in the shops on Sisavangvong/Sakkaline Road.

Garden of Eden Opposite Dyen Sabai, across the Nam Khan ☎020 2822 9059; map pp.108–109. A cute little jewellery shack across the bamboo bridge, with items from 39,000K, though the real attraction is the free jewellery classes run by the friendly owner: choose your materials and she'll teach you how to tailor to her designs. Daily 9am–11pm.

Pathana Boupha Antique House Opposite Wat Visoun, east of Phousi ☎071 212262; map pp.104–105. This lovely colonial building is one of the best places to head to for antiques, as well as silverware, ethnic jewellery and handicrafts. Daily 8.30am–7pm.

DIRECTORY

Banks and exchange Luang Prabang has ATMs in all the main tourist areas, including several on Sisavangvong Road. There are a number of moneychangers on Sisavongvong Road, and most banks – of which there are again several on Sisavangvong Road – will exchange the usual range of currencies.

Hospitals and clinics The best place for emergencies is the provincial hospital, 4km southwest of the old city (☎071 252026), though for anything serious you'll need to go to Thailand.

Internet and wi-fi Most of the travel agents on Sisavangvong Road have internet connections for around 100K/min. Almost all the hotels and guesthouses and many of the restaurants have free wi-fi.

Laundry Most hotels and guesthouses will wash clothes for you – expect to pay around 8000–10,000K/kilo.

Massage and herbal sauna The Red Cross, opposite Wat Visoun (☎071 252856; daily 8am–8pm), has traditional Lao massage at 40,000K/hr (reserve ahead) and an excellent sauna (from 5pm only) for 10,000K. Proceeds go to help poor villagers. For a wider choice of massages in

more comfortable surroundings, Spa Garden, Kounxoa Rd (☎071 212325; daily 9am–9.30pm) is highly recommended – try the "Mystic Lao Massage" (1hr; 60,000K) or an aromatherapy massage (150,000K).

Pharmacies Bouaphanh Pharmacie on Sakkaline Road (daily 8.30am–1pm & 2–8pm; ☎071 252252) speaks decent English and is reasonably well stocked, as is Poppy Pharmacy on Sisavongvong Road. Otherwise, try Dara Market.

Post office The GPO is on Chao Fa Ngum Road, near the junction with Inthasone Road (Mon–Fri 8am–noon & 1–5pm, Sat 8am–noon).

Phone services Some of the travel agents on Sisavangvong Road will sell you a Lao SIM card (see p.52), and will help you install it on your phone. Most internet cafés have facilities for Skype.

Yoga Luang Prabang Yoga (🌐 luangprabangyoga.org) is a cooperative of yoga teachers who run a variety of classes in some of the city's most attractive locations. The current schedule includes a 1hr session most mornings at *Utopia* (see p.130; Mon–Sat 7.30am; 30,000K), while evening classes alternate between *Utopia* and Ock Pop Tok (see p.118).

Excursions from Luang Prabang

Once you've exhausted Luang Prabang's many monasteries and temples, you'll still find many more attractions in the surrounding countryside. All can be visited as a half-day trip – either by a tour through a travel agent or by chartering a tuk-tuk or boat for the

trip – though if you're feeling energetic you could also tackle some of them by bike. North along the Nam Khan River, the popular **Pak Ou caves** trip is worth considering if you haven't had a chance to travel the Mekong by boat, though for most travellers the caves' appeal is trumped by the picturesque **waterfalls** of **Tad Se** (east of the city) and **Kuang Si** (south), both of which are lovely spots for a picnic and splashing around in turquoise waters. Just a few kilometres east of Luang Prabang, en route to Tad Se, there are a few low-key attractions around the village of **Ban Phanom**, which can easily be covered by road bike. Finally, Luang Prabang's gorgeous hinterland has almost limitless possibilities for trekking, kayaking, mountain biking and other outdoor activities. Travel agents often combine one or more of these (see box, p.120) with a trip to one of the hugely popular elephant camps near town (see box opposite).

The Pak Ou Buddha Caves and around

Daily 8am–sunset • 20,000K

Numerous caves punctuate the dramatic limestone cliffs around **Pak Ou** – the confluence of the Mekong and Nam Ou rivers, around 30km north of the city – of which the two "Buddha Caves" of **Tham Ting** and **Tham Phoum** are the best known. These caves have been used for centuries as a repository for old Buddha images that can no longer be venerated on an altar, either because they are damaged to the point of disfigurement or simply because newer images have crowded them out. In former times, before the caves became a tourist attraction, the inhabitants of Luang Prabang didn't give much thought to the caves or their contents except during **Lao New Year**, when boatloads of townsfolk would make the pilgrimage upriver and ritually bathe the semi-abandoned Buddhas to gain merit. The practice survives to this day and is worth seeing if you happen to be around. If not, the caves still deserve an hour or so, if only to gaze at the eerie scene of hundreds upon hundreds of serenely smiling images covered in dust and cobwebs. Tham Ting, the lower cave, just above the water's surface, is more of a large grotto and is light enough to explore without an artificial light source. The upper cave, a steep five-minute climb up steps, is unlit, so bring a torch.

The Whisky Village

Most boat trips to Pak Ou include a stop at **BAN XANG HAI**, the so-called "**Whisky Village**", some 6km back downriver towards the city. It's a bit of a tourist trap, the village's narrow lanes almost exclusively lined with identikit textile and souvenir shops interspersed with a few stalls selling the locally made *lào-láo* for which it's now famous, but after you've seen a cave-full of Buddhas you may be ready for a good, stiff drink.

ARRIVAL AND DEPARTURE   THE PAK OU CAVES AND AROUND

By boat Boat trips (70,000K/person) can be arranged with the boatmen at the bottom of Inthasone Road – most boats leave around 8.30am. Travel agents in town charge around 100,000K/person, including pick-up. Later in the day you'll probably need to charter one yourself (300,000K per six-person boat, but be prepared to haggle).

By bus It's also possible to make the journey by road – the caves lie around 9km off Highway 13 – though it's a lot less scenic. Tuk-tuks charge 250,000K (for up to five people) to Ban Pak Ou, though you'll still need to take a boat across the Mekong (25,000K/person) to reach the caves.

Ban Phanom and around

Ban Phanom is easily reached by bike by heading south from Phousi past Wat Visoun, parallel to the Nam Khan, and turning left at Highway 13 (after 1.5km); after 500m, turn right uphill off the Highway on to the Ban Phanom Road – you pass Santi Chedi (see opposite) first, from where it's 1km (downhill) to Ban Phanom

About 4km east of the old city, **BAN PHANOM** attracts its share of the tourist dollar through its pedigree as a former royal weaving village. If you take the time to wander

2

ELEPHANT CAMPS

By far the most popular activity outside Luang Prabang is a visit to one of the numerous **elephant camps** that have proliferated around town in recent years. Taking their lead from the Elephant Conservation Centre in Sayaboury (see box, p.97), these provide homes for selected pachyderms in their retirement from the logging industry. Not all the camps are everything they're cracked up to be: avoid anywhere advertising elephant "shows" and try to find out how many people the elephant has to carry (more than two on its back – plus mahout – is a no-no) and its workload, which shouldn't total more than four hours per day. The best sanctuaries provide good veterinarian care for the animals and a strictly regulated work load. Trips tend to include not just the chance to ride an elephant but also to help bathe the animals, and some camps run courses teaching mahout skills. For more advice, see Ⓦ elefantasia.org.

All Lao Elephant Camp Offices on Sisavangvong Rd and on the corner of Cha Fa Ngum and Inthasone roads ☎071 253522 or 254548, Ⓦalllaoservice.com. The largest of the elephant camps, around 7km east of the city. Most popular are its one- to six-day mahout courses (two days $170/ person, including accommodation), though a vast range of trips are offered combining elephant rides ($50/person for 90min) with trekking, kayaking, bamboo rafting and so on. Guests on multi-day courses stay at the camp's *Mahout Resort*, on the banks of the Nam Khan.

Elephant Village Sisavangvong Rd ☎071 260012, Ⓦelephantvillage-laos.com. Regarded by many as the most ethically responsible of the elephant camps, this German-owned operation currently has nine rehabilitated former logging elephants (plus one baby) which they're careful not to overwork, and trains and employs local villagers as mahouts and guides. The Elephant Village camp, 14km east of town, occupies a beautiful position on the Nam Khan close to Tad Se (see p.136). A half-day "Elephant Experience" costs $46/ person; other options include a full-day trip combining a five-kilometre ride with a trek along the beautiful Trail of Falls ($77/person). The more expensive overnight packages involve a luxurious stay at the Victorian-expedition-themed *Shangri Lao Explorer Camp* (Ⓦshangri-lao.com) on site. Book well in advance.

its quaint, red-dirt streets you'll find a few independent textile shops, as well as women hard at work weaving in the relatively cool space beneath their raised, traditional wooden homes.

Santi Chedi

Site open access 24hr; *sim* open daily 8–10am & 1.30–4.30pm • Free • The best way to get here is by bike (see p.122) – though be prepared for a steep final slog up to the chedi

About 3km east of town, and 1km west of Ban Phanom, stands Luang Prabang's largest religious monument. Constructed in 1988 and christened **Santi Chedi**, or "Peace Stupa", this modern, concrete pagoda is best known for its mural-splashed interior, though its carved windows are great works of art in themselves. However, the main reason to come up here is for the impressive **views** of Phousi and the Nam Khan River, which needless to say are especially attractive at sunset, as is Santi Chedi itself when its golden surface catches the glow of the setting sun – most impressive from a distance.

Henri Mouhot's tomb

Leaving Ban Phanom, take the right fork and follow the Nam Khan road for 3.5km, eventually joining the Highway 13 bypass; the memorial is a 5min walk from the road and clearly signposted

Four kilometres up the Nam Khan from Ban Phanom is the final resting place of **Henri Mouhot**, the Anglophile French naturalist and explorer best known as the "discoverer" of Angkor Wat. A simple whitewashed memorial, made from stone donated by the Lao king Tiantha and erected by the Mekong Commission in 1867, marks the spot, about 20m from the river's edge in a dried-up tributary.

2

THE LIVING LAND

If you've ever wondered how sticky rice, the ubiquitous Laos staple, ends up on your plate, then book a trip to **The Living Land** (❶020 5519 9208, ❿livinglandlao.com), a twenty-acre rice and vegetable farm around 5km south of the centre of Luang Prabang on the edge of town. Visitors are given a fun, hands-on demo of the fourteen-stage process of rice cultivation, including how to guide a water buffalo-drawn plough – muddy work in wet season – culminating in a "rice *dégustation*". The community farm supports seven families, and proceeds go towards helping local kids through college. Half-day trips (8.30am–noon) cost around $45, including transfer, and should be booked a day in advance.

Tad Se

Daily 8am–5.30pm • 15,000K • ❶030 923 0236 • zip line ❶020 5429 0848, ❿flightofthenature.com; half-day trips from $45 (including transfer); book in advance and check for deals with the travel agents in town • Tuk-tuks charge a flat-rate of 150,000K for 1–5 people to Ban Aen, from where it's 10min by boat to the falls (10,000K each for 2 people or 20,000K for 1)

Around 18km east of Luang Prabang, the wide **Tad Se** waterfall wanders down a gradual slope, serenely cascading through trees and easing through a dozen clear-blue pools like some elaborate Zen meditation, until it finally flows into the Nam Khan river. Although it doesn't quite possess the drama of Kuang Si (see p.136), it's still a beautiful place, made all the more enchanting by the short approach by boat along a tranquil section of the river from the village of Ban Aen. The pools here aren't as good for swimming as those at Kuang Si, but they're fine for a refreshing dip. There are a couple of simple restaurants and snack outlets on site.

Though you can climb to the upper falls up a steep (and occasionally slippery) trail, the most exhilarating way to experience them, best booked in advance, is via **zip line** through the forest canopy – a chain of fourteen wires links twenty platforms spanning the falls, the longest, at the summit, nearly 400m in length. You can also ride (and bathe with) rather bored-looking elephants if you wish.

During the dry season, water levels at Tad Se can be rather low so check locally before travelling out there during this period.

Kuang Si and around

Daily 8am–5pm • 20,000K • ❶071 212068 • **Bear rescue centre** daily 8.30–5pm • Free (with entry ticket to falls) • ❿freethebears.org.au

One of the best day-trips from Luang Prabang is to **Kuang Si** waterfall, 25km southwest of the city, a picturesque, multi-level affair that tumbles 60m before spilling through a series of milky, aquamarine pools perfect for swimming. The spray from the falls keeps the surrounding grounds cool even at midday, making it an ideal spot for a picnic – tables are scattered across the site and very popular with local families, giving the falls a fun, festive feel. Swimming is allowed in several of the lower pools, but the most popular is the second tier, where there are basic changing facilities and, gazed upon by bemused locals, Westerners often amuse themselves for hours leaping into the soft, cool water via a rope swing suspended from an overhanging tree. From here it's a five-minute walk past more tumbling cascades to the spectacular main drop. A steep path on the opposite side of the falls leads to the top in about thirty minutes, though it can get quite slippery, so be very careful – and don't attempt it in wet season.

The path from the entrance to the falls leads past a small, Australian-owned **bear sanctuary**, home to a few sun and Asiatic black bears rescued from the illegal meat and medicine trade by the Lao government. Numerous restaurants and food stalls crowd the entrance to the park and there's a simple café inside.

Kuang Si Falls Butterfly Park

Around 500m back along the main road to Luang Prabang from the main falls • Daily 10am–5pm • 30,000K

The forests around Kuang Si are famed for their myriad colourful butterflies, with up to fifty species flexing their wings here in wet season. Opened in 2014 by a young Dutch couple, the prettily landscaped **Kuang Si Falls Butterfly Park** gathers up to a thousand Lepidoptera at any one time beneath a big bamboo-strutted enclosure. The falls continue their descent through the gardens, eventually tumbling into the Mekong some 5km north, and there are pools for swimming here, too. A café on site sells coffee and home-made cakes and sandwiches.

ARRIVAL AND DEPARTURE   KUANG SI AND AROUND

By minibus A cheap way of reaching Kuang Si is to take a tour by minibus, booked via a tour agency or direct with Naluang bus station (see p.121). Buses leave daily at noon and 2pm (45min; 60,000K), though this leaves you with only two hours at the falls.

By tuk-tuk Taking a tuk-tuk can be the most economical way to go if you can assemble a group – drivers charge around 50,000K per person for a group of four to five people; otherwise you should be able to charter a

vehicle for a little less.

By boat The slowest but most scenic route is by boat from the old city down the Mekong river – boatmen congregate at the bottom of Inthasone Road and at the tip of the peninsula near Wat Xieng Thong, and charge 100,000K per person return (for six people). The final portion of the journey is by tuk-tuk, which should be included in the cost, though check this before setting out.

2

The northeast

PLAIN OF JARS

The northeast

The remote northeast of Laos was, until recently, difficult to reach, owing to mountainous terrain and poor roads, which largely kept it isolated from tourism. Despite great improvements to the infrastructure – it's now possible to reach Sam Neua in less than a day from Luang Prabang, with no change of bus – the region remains one of the least-visited parts of the country due, partly, to being short on typical tourist sights, and because it doesn't fit too neatly with the typical north–south itinerary. However, there's a real frontier friendliness among the inhabitants, who come from more than two dozen ethnic groups, and it's a great area (especially north of Phonsavan) in which to feel as though you're getting off the beaten track. In addition, history, both ancient and modern, feels particularly tangible in the area.

Topographically diverse, the northeast region extends from the towering peaks that border the Vientiane Plain, across the Xieng Khuang Plateau, over the jagged backbone of the Annamite Mountains, and into the watershed of the Nam Xam river, which flows into Vietnam. The area encompasses **Hua Phan** and **Xieng Khuang provinces**, and part of **northern Luang Prabang province**. Historically, this swathe of Laos was the domain of two independent principalities – the Tai federation of Sipsong Chao Tai in Hua Phan and the Phuan Kingdom of Xieng Khuang. Sandwiched between expansive empires to the west and east, both entities struggled to maintain their sovereignty until the late nineteenth century, when the French finally folded most of their territory into unified Laos.

The kings of the defunct royal house of **Xieng Khuang** came from the same family tree as those of Luang Prabang, both kingdoms claiming descent from Khoun Borom, the celebrated first ancestor of numerous Tai–Lao legends. Yet, unlike in Luang Prabang, few physical traces of Xieng Khuang's splendour survive. In the place of the distinctive Xieng Khuang-style temples are bomb craters doubling as fishing holes and houses erected on piles crafted from bomb casings – reminders that this was one of the most heavily bombed pieces of real estate in the world, and a testimony to the rugged perseverance of the Phuan, Black Tai, Hmong and Khmu peoples who inhabit the province. Much of the bombing was directed at the strategic **Plain of Jars**, which takes its name from the fields of ancient, giant funerary urns that are the northeast's main tourist draw. For most visitors a trip to the region means little more than a flying visit to Xieng Khuang's provincial capital **Phonsavan** to see the Jar sites, sometimes coupled with a quick side trip to nearby **Muang Khoun**, the former royal seat of Xieng Khuang, where a handful of ruins whisper of the kingdom's vanished glory.

It's remarkable that even with greatly improved roads, few travellers make the journey to **Hua Phan**, an impenetrable sea of rugged green mountaintops lost in mist and shallow valleys, far from the Mekong river and the traditional centres of lowland Lao life. The only provincial centre in Laos east of the Annamites is Hua Phan's capital **Sam Neua**, a

BUDDHA AT MUANG KHOUN

Highlights

❶ Plain of Jars Fields of ancient giant stone urns scattered across the Xieng Khuang Plateau stand as witnesses to a vanished civilization. **See p.148**

❷ Muang Khoun Travel back in time to the ancient kingdom of Xieng Khuang where temple ruins and a giant Buddha are all that remain of a once proud kingdom. **See p.150**

❸ The Muang Kham hinterland The village of Muang Kham is the launching point for trips to

caves, hot springs and visits to Hmong, Khmu, Black Tai and Phuan villages. **See p.151**

❹ Vieng Xai The incredible limestone karst scenery that surrounds this small town provided the perfect hiding place for the Pathet Lao during much of their Thirty Year Struggle. **See p.158**

❺ Route 1 From Nam Neun junction to Nong Khiaw, ride across the rooftop of Indochina to one of the least-visited parts of the country. **See p.160**

HIGHLIGHTS ARE MARKED ON THE MAP ON P.142

frontier town closer to Hanoi than Vientiane, a proximity that lends it a distinctly Vietnamese flavour. This lightly populated region is home to more than twenty ethnic groups, most of them Tai, including the Black, Red and White Tai, all of whom share a distinctly Hua Phan character – a fortitude shaped by the remote mountainous terrain and by years spent living in the heart of the **Pathet Lao's liberated zone**. After the Pathet Lao rose to power in 1975, the communists further exploited Hua Phan's isolation by transforming their liberated zone into a massive prison camp. Thousands of former Royal Lao soldiers were interred in the province's notorious re-education camps. Hua Phan's wartime history has been etched into the land at **Vieng Xai**, a short ride from Sam Neua. Dozens of **caves** hidden in the sawtoothed limestone karsts of Vieng Xai served as the headquarters for the Pathet Lao during their Thirty Year Struggle.

Xieng Khuang and the Plain of Jars

Xieng Khuang province lies at the crossroads of important trade routes leading north to China, south to Thailand and east to Vietnam, and has been coveted throughout the centuries by rival Southeast Asian empires. Xieng Khuang, hemmed in by a ring of dramatic mountains, including the country's tallest peak, Phu Bia, is best known for

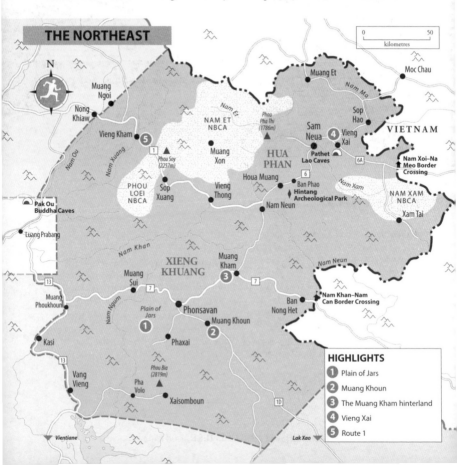

HIGHLIGHTS

1. Plain of Jars
2. Muang Khoun
3. The Muang Kham hinterland
4. Vieng Xai
5. Route 1

SAFETY IN XIENG KHUANG

Although **bandits or insurgents** once gave Xieng Khuang province an uncertain reputation, today the more immediate danger comes from the **mines**, **bomblets** and **bombs** that litter the province. The main Jar sites have been cleared of Unexploded Ordnance (UXO), but it's important to stick to the paths, and not to pick up or kick any object if you don't know what it is.

the treeless flatlands and crater-ridden landscape of the **Plain of Jars**. A plateau of grassy meadows and low rolling hills situated at the centre of the province, the Plain takes its name from the clusters of chest-high funerary urns found there. For people with a deep interest in archeology and Southeast Asian history the jars are worth the journey to Xieng Khuang, but for some tourists they are something of an anticlimax. However, their other-worldliness, against the flat barren landscape of the area, retains a certain mystique, and by choosing your guide wisely it's possible to get a lot more out of a visit here.

As the flattest area in northern Laos, the Plain of Jars is also a natural gathering point for **armies** – a fact not lost on military commanders of the early kingdoms of Lane Xang, Vietnam and Siam and later the Soviet Union, France and America, the Viet Minh, the Pathet Lao and the Lao Royalists. Fought over dearly in the Second Indochina War, the region was bombed extensively between 1964 and 1973, transforming the Plain into a wasteland, which leaves a lasting impression on those who fly over it into **Phonsavan**, the province's capital and main base for exploring the area.

Brief history
Even the **legends** surrounding the jars reveal how thoroughly life in Xieng Khuang has been overshadowed by **war**, with local lore telling of how the jars were created to hold rice wine by an army of giants to celebrate a military victory. Although the identity of the civilization that built the jars remains a mystery, local folk tales telling of the arrival of the Phuan people (see p.289), the lowland Lao group that still dominates the ethnic make-up of the area today, date back as far as the seventh century, when the divine Tai–Lao first ancestor Khoun Borom (see p.260) sent his seventh and youngest son, Chet Chuong, to rule over the Tai peoples of Xieng Khuang. Although the time frame for this version of events may be a bit premature, Xieng Khuang was nonetheless one of the earlier areas settled by Tai peoples in Laos, and by the fourteenth century, an independent **Phuan principality**, known as Xieng Khuang and centred on modern-day **Muang Khoun**, had already begun to flourish here.

The Kingdom of Xieng Khuang
While the **Kingdom of Xieng Khuang** had the wealth to build exquisite pagodas, it never amassed the might necessary to become a regional power. Sandwiched between the great empires lying to its east and west, Phuan kings maintained a semblance of independence over the years by offering tribute to Vietnam and Lane Xang and eventually Siam. Whatever price the royal house paid, however, it was not enough to keep Xieng Khuang from being repeatedly annexed, overrun and forcibly depopulated, beginning with the invading armies of the **Vietnamese** on their way back from sacking Luang Prabang in the late 1470s through to the Second Indochina War, when nearly every village in the province was obliterated.

In 1869, warrior horsemen from southern **China** raced across the plain, slaughtering villagers or carrying them off into captivity. These Black Flag bandits pillaged the riches of the kingdom and plundered the contents of the jars. Those who fled didn't get far: Lao and Thai soldiers on their way to Xieng Khuang to quell the invasion rounded up the refugees and frogmarched them through the jungle to the Chao Phraya River Valley in Siam, where they became slaves to Thai lords. The tortuous march lasted over a month, with many dying along the way, lost to sickness and starvation. In two generations, Siamese armies and Chinese bandits reduced the population by three-quarters through death and forced migration. The Phuan state never recovered.

French rule

Xieng Khuang enjoyed better protection from its neighbours with the arrival of the **French**, who considered the province's temperate climate – which can be downright cold by any measure for several months of the year – suitable for European settlement and plantation agriculture. The primary cash crop, however, was **opium**, a trade the French quickly moved to control (see p.268). Muang Khoun was chosen as the French provincial capital and the devastated former royal seat of the defunct kingdom was transformed into an architectural gem of French Indochinese villas and shop houses, which might have rivalled the charm of Luang Prabang and Savannakhet had Xieng Khuang not returned to its familiar role as battleground a few decades later.

The Second Indochina War

One hundred years after the carnage of the Chinese bandits, American planes wreaked destruction that was equally indiscriminate, levelling towns and forcing villagers to take to the forest, as the two sides in the **Second Indochina War** waged a bitter battle for control of the Plain of Jars, which represented a back door to northern Vietnam. Throughout much of the 1960s, Xieng Khuang was the site of a seesaw war, with the Royalist side led by Hmong General Vang Pao gaining the upper hand in the rainy season and the communist side launching offensives in the dry months.

Xieng Khuang today

Today, villages have been rebuilt and fields replanted. Many of the valley-dwelling, wet-rice farmers, as well as a majority of the townsfolk in Phonsavan, are descendants of the Phuan kingdom. In addition to the Lao, the Phuan are joined by a third lowland group, the Black Tai, and also the Khmu – a Lao Theung group who ruled the lowlands until they were forced into the hills with the arrival of the Tai groups over a thousand years ago – and a significant population of Hmong, who arrived in Laos from China in the nineteenth century and now make up roughly a third of the provincial population.

Phonsavan

The capital of Xieng Khuang province, **PHONSAVAN** obliterated during the Second Indochina War and hastily rebuilt in its aftermath, has only now, almost four decades after the end of conflict, begun to recover economically. The bomb-casing collections in many guesthouse lobbies are grim galleries reflecting the area's tragic past when possession of the strategic plain was seen as the key to control of Laos. It was the new communist government that designated Phonsavan the new provincial capital, and parked Laos's fledgling collection of Soviet MiGs nearby, a smug reminder of who won the battle for this bitterly contested area.

THE HMONG IN XIENG KHUANG

With much of the literature of the province's historical Phuan kingdom (see p.143) destroyed and many of the customs lost, **Hmong culture** and festivals have come to play an important role in Xieng Khuang life. Boun Phao Hmong, or the Festival of the Hmong, celebrated throughout the province in November, draws overseas Hmong back each year for an event featuring water buffalo and bull-fights. In December, Hmong New Year, a time for young Hmong to find a husband or wife, is celebrated, as is the lowland Lao festival of Boun Haw Khao, a two-day holiday in which food is offered to the dead. It has a distinctly Xieng Khuang flavour, however, with the addition of horse races, horses being especially prized by villagers who work Xieng Khuang's far-flung fields.

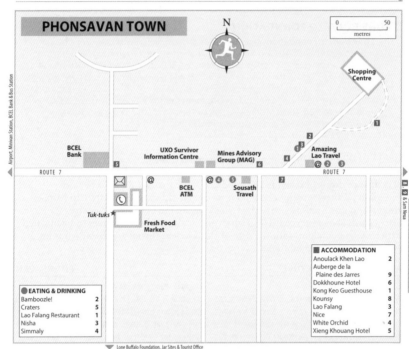

Lone Buffalo Foundation, Jar Sites & Tourist Office

The town you see today, laid out on a rather grand scale and extending south of Route 7, is a modern **reconstruction** that lacks any real character, though, as the wide boulevards attest, local officials have very big plans for this little place. Driving them on is the international interest in the world-famous Jar sites scattered around the perimeter of the plain. Tourism has given the town new life: bombs at the Jar sites have been cleared away and Khoun Cheuam's jar – the largest of the scores of jars in the area – stares down from tourism posters across the country. Although most visitors come only to see the Jar sites, the Xieng Khuang Plateau is a place of great natural beauty and its backroads and villages are well worth exploring.

Mines Advisory Group

Opposite the restaurant *Simmaly* on Route 7 · Mon–Fri 8am–8pm, Sat & Sun 4–8pm; films daily at 4.30pm, 5.30pm & 6.30pm · Free, donations welcome · W maginternational.org

If you're visiting the Plain of Jars, be sure to stop in at the **Mines Advisory Group (MAG)**, which is carrying out vital work, not only in deactivating UXO but in educating and informing local people, especially farmers and those involved in the scrap metal trade. An informative display provides an introduction to the work they are doing, with photographs making vividly clear the horrifying risks that UXO pose to local lives. Free films are shown every evening; this is a great opportunity to find out more about the UXO situation and the work that MAG does.

UXO Survivor Information Centre

Just west of the Mines Advisory Group on Route 7 · Mon & Tues 8am–4pm, Wed–Sun noon–8pm · Free, donations welcome · W facebook.com/qlacenter

The colourful **UXO Survivor Information Centre**, run by a local non-profit group, acts as a kind of museum, providing visitors with a down-to-earth look at the challenges

3

LONE BUFFALO FOUNDATION

The **Lone Buffalo Foundation** (🅦facebook.com/lonebuffalo) gives kids in Xieng Khuang Province access to free English lessons. The organization was set up following the death of a respected local English teacher called Manophet (Lone Buffalo), and aims to empower local children (eighty percent of the students are ethnic Hmong) by teaching them a new language, developing their social skills and helping them to get involved with new sports and activities. You can visit the foundation's **English Development Centre**, located just east of the tourist office, to find out more about the group's work and help students practise their newly acquired language skills. The centre is open Monday–Friday 4.15–8pm.

faced by UXO survivors. The eye-opening exhibits include a map showing the extent of the areas still affected by UXO (around a third of the two million tonnes of ordnance dropped remains unexploded), while signboards describe post-explosion problems, such as how poor roads and old vehicles conspire to hamper attempts to save victims' lives. Most shocking are the information centre's blackboards showing recent UXO survivors. Sadly, the list continues to be updated with new names, along with the date of the accident (many are recent) and the extent of the victims' injuries.

ARRIVAL AND DEPARTURE   PHONSAVAN

BY PLANE

Wattay International Airport At the time of writing, Lao Airlines (☎ 061 312027) was only operating flights to and from Vientiane (1 daily; 30min). Landing at the airport, you'll need a tuk-tuk (20,000K per person) for the 5km ride into town, though you may be able to get a free lift with one of the hotel reps waiting in arrivals. Note that the airport is most commonly called "Xieng Khuang" rather than Phonsavan.

BY BUS

Buses arrive at/depart from several stations across town. When leaving Phonsavan, you may prefer to book your ticket a day in advance at the *Lao Falang Restaurant* (see p.147); the owner takes a cut of around 20,000K on each booking, but will arrange tuk-tuk transport to the bus station for you, or even have the bus pull up outside your guesthouse. Note that now Route 1D is open, it's possible to travel between Vientiane and Phonsavan without having to go via Vang Vieng.

Inter-provincial bus station The main inter-provincial bus station handling arrivals from Vientiane,

Luang Prabang and Vang Vieng is 4km west of the centre on Route 7; tuk-tuks (10,000–15,000K per person) will ferry you into town. Buses bound for Vietnam also leave from here at 6.30am each morning (except Tues), crossing the border at Nam Khan–Nam Can; it takes around 10hr to reach Vinh (150,000K), from where connections to Hanoi are available.

Destinations Luang Prabang (1 daily; 8hr); Paksan (3 daily; 6–8hr); Phou Khoun (1 daily; 10hr); Sam Neua (1 daily; 10hr); Vang Vieng (1 daily; 6hr); Vientiane (5 daily; 9hr); Vinh, Vietnam (1 daily except Tues; 10hr).

Bounmixay bus station The Bounmixay bus station, south of the tourist office on route 1D, is where the majority of buses travelling from Vientiane come to a stop.

Destinations Pakse (1 daily; 16hr); Vientiane (7 daily; 8hr).

Minivan station Minivans connecting Phonsavan with Laos's three main tourist centres depart early in the morning from a lot in the centre of town, just off Route 7.

Destinations Luang Prabang (1 daily; 7hr); Vang Vieng (1 daily; 5hr); Vientiane (1 daily; 8hr).

INFORMATION

Tourist information The tourist office (daily 8–11.30am & 1.30–4pm), with old bombs outside the door, is rather inconveniently situated in the southern part of town, a couple of kilometres away from most accommodation. Staff can provide you with plenty of information on local tours, but may not actually have the prices, or be able to get you booked onto a tour. For that, your best bet is to visit a couple of the many tour operators lining Route 7 to get a good idea of what's

on offer.

Services There's a BCEL ATM on Route 7; the main branch, with currency exchange services, is situated about 1km to the west on the same road (daily 8.30am–3.30pm). Most travel agents and some guesthouses will also change money. There's an **internet** café next to the restaurant *Simmaly* (daily 7am–10pm), charging 10,000K per hour. Alternatively, *Lao Falang Restaurant* has free wi-fi.

ACCOMMODATION

Anoulack Khen Lao Just north of Route 7, on the road leading to the shopping centre ☎061 213599. A smart, large hotel, tucked away off the main road. The big, bright rooms are impressive for the price, and the attached bathrooms are spick and span. Rates include breakfast. 220,000K

Auberge de la Plaine des Jarres 1.5km south of town, on the hill ☎030 517 0282, ⓦplainedesjarres .com. This rustic lodge is set in landscaped grounds surrounded by pine trees and bougainvillea, with wonderful sweeping views over the town and surrounding countryside. Accommodation is in wooden cabins that feel more alpine than Lao, with rather thin walls and hard beds, but this is definitely the most picturesque setting in Phonsavan. Popular with tour groups, so book ahead. 400,000K

Dokkhoune Hotel Just west of White Orchid on Route 7 ☎020 234 2555. With a lobby full of decorative UXO and good views of the mountains from the hallways, this four-floor block is in a good central location. The large, but dull, rooms are a bit of a disappointment, though not bad value. 80,000K

★**Kong Keo Guesthouse** 200m north of Route 7 (follow the dirt track that starts just north of the Lao Falang Restaurant) ☎055 211354, ⓔkongkeojar @hotmail.com. The best and quirkiest choice for budget travellers. Rooms are rather small, beds are lumpy and the bathrooms pretty poky, but the overall vibe of the place more than makes up for it, with a cool bar-restaurant and a garden littered with UXO. In addition to tours, they can arrange visas for Cambodia, China and Vietnam. 60,000K

Kounsy At the far eastern end of the main drag, near the junction ☎061 211170. This guesthouse has a number of basic, rather dark rooms, though they're cosier than many others on Route 7. 70,000K

Lao Falang Above Lao Falang Restaurant, just north of the hotel White Orchid ☎020 2221 2456. The cheapest place to crash for the night, with basic dorm beds above a restaurant that serves food and beer to a mostly Western crowd. Automatic motorbikes are available here for 100,000K/day. Dorm 30,000K

Nice Directly opposite White Orchid on Route 7 ☎061 312454. Comfortable little en-suite rooms off a lantern-strung outdoor hallway. The staff are helpful and the place is in a good location close to the best restaurants, but bear in mind that it gets chilly during the winter. 70,000K

White Orchid On the cnr of Route 7 and the road leading to the shopping centre ☎061 312403. This friendly, family-run place, just off the main road, is an excellent choice. Rooms are a little dark, but decent value and very clean. Travel and tour information (and bookings) can be provided by the helpful staff, though prices tend to be higher than other places nearby. 80,000K

Xieng Khouang Hotel Route 7 ☎061 213567, ⓔxiengkhouanghotel@gmail.com. A big, modern block that lacks soul and a welcoming smile, but redeems itself slightly with clean rooms and white sheets. The rooms highest up have good views over town. 160,000K

EATING AND DRINKING

The little fresh-food **market** behind the post office is well worth a wander, the amount and variety of the produce on sale giving a good indication of just how much people's lives here have improved since the government quietly swept communist economics under the rug. As with most markets in Laos, it's a great choice for a quick, cheap lunch, or to stock up on fruit and snacks before a long bus journey. Restaurant-wise, there are a fair few places to eat on the main road, though you won't exactly be spoilt for choice. The most atmospheric place for a drink is the bar at *Kong Keo* (see above).

Bamboozle! Route 7, just west of Nisha ☎030 952 3913. Bamboo-bedecked, *falang*-friendly restaurant with a menu that mixes Western dishes with cheaper Asian staples (the Lao noodle soup is just 15,000K). A great place to meet other travellers and find out about charitable initiatives in the area (five percent of the restaurant's profits go towards the Lone Buffalo Foundation (see p.146). Daily 7am–11pm.

Craters East of Simmaly on Route 7 ☎020 780 5775. A relaxed place with UXO lined up outside and old weaponry decorating the interior. The menu offers everything you would expect from a travellers' café, including Western breakfasts (from 14,000K), club sandwiches (32,000K) and a few good Asian dishes, including a tangy *tom yam* (29,000K). Daily 6.30am–10pm.

Lao Falang Restaurant Just north of the White Orchid hotel ☎554 06868. Not really recommended for its food (mains around 30,000K), as service is so slow, but this is still a good place to grab a Beerlao and mingle with other travellers. Each night at 6pm the owner screens a film about the American bombing of Laos. Daily 6.30am–11.30pm.

Nisha Just east of Bamboozle! on Route 7 ☎020 9826 6023. Bare-bones Indian place serving great *dosa*, alongside the usual assortment of curries. In the mornings it's popular with backpackers, who come for the good banana *roti* (12,000K). Daily 6am–9.30pm.

Simmaly Opposite the Mines Advisory Group on Route 7 ☎030 572 7430. There's no finery, but this Chinese-run restaurant is always full of a good mix of locals and tourists. Portions are large and prices cheap, with great spicy soups and fried rice dishes going for 10,000K. Daily 7am–10pm.

The Plain of Jars

Many visitors mistake the Jar sites for the **PLAIN OF JARS** and vice versa. The latter is a broad rolling plain covering an area roughly 15km across at the centre of the Xieng Khuang Plateau, which sits high above the Mekong and the Vientiane Plain. The ancient **Jar sites** scattered around the perimeter of the plain led the French to name the region the Plaine de Jars – the PDJ to the American pilots who flew over it. Topographically, the plain is something like the hole in a doughnut with concentric rings of increasingly high mountain peaks around it. Although the jars are the main tourist attraction of Xieng Khuang Province, there's much more to see here. The Plain itself offers beautiful scenery, which most visitors, obsessed with seeing the jars, completely overlook. Away from the main highway there are countless backroads to explore as well as friendly **Phuan and Hmong villages**, where it may feel like you're the first foreigner the children have seen.

The presence of the jars attests to the fact that Xieng Khuang, with its access to key regional trade routes, its wide, flat spaces and temperate climate, has been considered prime real estate in mainland Southeast Asia for centuries, but the story of the plain as a **transit route** for ancient man has yet to be told. As a natural corridor between the coasts of southern China and the vast plains of Korat beyond the Mekong, the Plain of Jars has certainly seen the passage of many tribes and races, perhaps even groups of *Homo erectus*, who ranged from northern China to Java between one million and 250,000 years ago.

The Jar sites

The **Jar sites** are among the most important prehistoric archeological sites in Southeast Asia. Clusters of stone jars thought to be two thousand years old, along with seemingly older stone pillars, are scattered across the Plain and also in other parts of Xieng Khuang and Hua Phan province. The largest urns measure 2m in height and weigh as much as ten

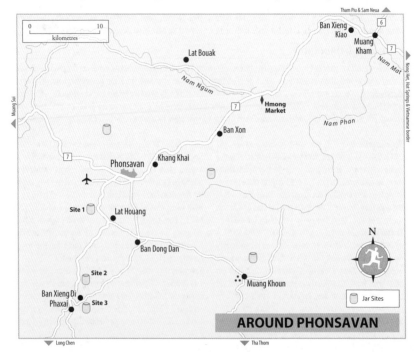

AROUND PHONSAVAN

tonnes. Little is known about the **Iron Age megalithic civilization** that created these artefacts; war and revolution kept archeologists from working on the sites for decades. By the time French archeologist Madeleine Colani began excavating at the Jar sites in the 1930s, most of the urns had been looted, although she did find bronze and iron tools as well as coloured glass beads, bronze bracelets and cowrie shells. Colani theorized that the jars were **funerary urns**, originally holding cremated remains. More recent discoveries have revealed underground burial chambers, further supporting Colani's theory.

Of the dozens of Jar sites, twelve are currently open to tourists, though the **three main sites** are those most commonly visited on tours. The closest one to Phonsavan, known as Site 1, just 2km southwest of town, has over two hundred jars. Sites 2 and 3 are much more scenic and are located about 10km southwest of the market village of **Lat Houang**, which is 10km south of Phonsavan, on the road to Muang Khoun.

Site 1

Site 1 or **Thong Hai Hin** ("Stone Jar Plain") is the most visited of the sites. Following the path from the car park to the jars, you'll quickly come to **Hai Cheaum** ("Cheaum Jar"), a massive jar 2m high that was named after the Tai–Lao hero of lore, who is celebrated in one version of the jar myth as the liberator of the people of the Plain of Jars from a cruel overlord named Chao Angka. Legend has it that the jars were made to ferment rice wine to celebrate the victory; as the jars bear a passing resemblance to *lào hái* jars used today, the liquor-loving locals didn't have to stretch their imaginations too far to come up with this theory. Walk downhill a little way and you'll find yourself amid another group of jars, one of which has a crude human shape carved onto it.

In the hill off to the left is a large **cave** that the Pathet Lao used during the war, and which, according to local legend, was used as a kiln to cast the jars. Erosion has carved two holes in the roof of the cave – natural chimneys that make the cavern a worthy kiln of sorts. Colani suggests that the cave was used as a crematorium: in and around the cave she found the remains of what she believed to be commoners not lucky enough to be interred in the stone funeral urns, which were reserved, she argued, for the ashes of the nobility.

Site 2

The turn-off for **site 2** is 3km south of site 1 at Lat Houang, along the main Phonsavan–Muang Khoun road. Zipping across the flats surrounding Lat Sen, the town that played host to the old French airstrip, towards Phaxai and the Jar sites, you'll pass narrow dirt runways on the grassy meadows and hillsides. These clearings are used by hunters to trap swallows in nets that they trigger from camouflaged huts at one end of the strip; smoky fires bring bugs to the surface of the clearing, attracting the swallows. The most skilful hunters can catch several hundred birds on a good day, netting a tidy sum.

Ten kilometres on from the turn-off at Lat Houang, you turn left along a dirt track – a road in slightly worse condition than the Phaxai road – and follow it for 2km through a village just large enough to support a tiny monastery, until you wind up at two adjacent hills, one on either side of the road. Nearly a hundred jars are scattered across the twin hills here, lending the site the name **Hai Hin Phou Salato** ("Salato Hill Stone Jar Site").

Site 3

The gateway to Site 3, the most atmospheric of the three Jar sites, lies in the village of Ban Xieng Di, 4km up the Phaxai road on the left. Large Lao Phuan houses line the way to Wat Xieng Di, a simple wooden monastery, 1km from the turn-off, where you'll find the path leading to **Hai Hin Lat Khai**, also known as Hai Hin Xieng Di. There's a depressing, bomb-damaged Buddha here that the guides like to point out. Pick up the path at the back corner of the monastery compound, which hops a stream and cuts uphill through several fields before arriving at a clearing with more than a hundred jars and sweeping views of the surrounding countryside.

ESSENTIALS

THE JAR SITES

Admission to site 1 is 15,000K, while sites 2 and 3 cost 10,000K each. It's possible to visit the Jar sites independently by **chartering a tuk-tuk** (expect to pay around 150,000K for a half-day) or by **renting a motorbike** (70,000–100,000K/day) or bicycle (20,000K/day). However, it's highly recommended you go with a guide in order to gain a better understanding of the history and myths surrounding the sites, in addition to learning more about how UXO is affecting the area.

TOURS

The most popular tour, and one that's offered by every travel agent and guesthouse in Phonsavan, is one that takes in sites 1, 2 and 3 (around 150,000K/person, excluding admission fees), though in all honesty you'll probably find that visiting one site is more than enough. As many places offer the same tour, it can be hard to know just how well informed your guide will be. We've listed a couple of recommended operators below.

Amazing Lao Travel Just west of Bamboozle! on Route 7 ☎061 260026, ⓦamazinglao.com. This well-established outfit on the main road has a good range of options for groups, for whom discounts are often available. If you're travelling solo contact the office and they'll try to find a tour for you to join.

Sousath Travel At Bombie's Bar on Route 7 ☎020 2967213, ⓔrasapet_lao@yahoo.com. For something a little different, try Southath Travel, whose itineraries mix trips to the usual Jar sites with the chance to see lesser-visited war relics, including rusting tanks, a landing site used by American "Ravens" and some impressive B52 bomb craters. Tours start at 200,000K, based on a group of four.

Muang Khoun (Old Xieng Khuang)

A ghost of its former self, **MUANG KHOUN**, old Xieng Khuang, 35km southeast of Phonsavan, was once the royal seat of the minor kingdom Xieng Khuang, renowned in the sixteenth century for its 62 opulent stupas, whose sides were said to be covered in treasure. Years of bloody invasions by Thai and Vietnamese soldiers, pillaging by Chinese bandits in the nineteenth century and a monsoon of bombs that lasted nearly a decade during the Second Indochina War taxed this town so heavily that by the time the air raids stopped next to nothing was left of the kingdom's exquisite temples. The town was all but abandoned, and centuries of history were drawn to a close. All that remains of the kingdom's former glory is an elegant Buddha image towering over ruined columns of brick at Wat Phia, and That Dam, both of which bear the scars of the events that ended Xieng Khuang's centuries of rich history. Although the town has been rebuilt and renamed, it has taken a back seat to Phonsavan, and, with little in the way of amenities for travellers – there are a few *fŏe* shops around the market, but no hotel – it's most convenient to visit Muang Khoun as a day-trip.

That Dam

A long row of low-slung wooden shop houses springs up along the road from Phonsavan in the shadow of towering **That Dam**, signalling your arrival in Muang Khoun. A path alongside the market leads up to the blackened hilltop stupa, the base of which has been tunnelled straight through to the other side by treasure seekers hoping to find more than a simple bone of the Enlightened One inside. A British surveyor who travelled through the area in the service of the Siamese king in 1884 – shortly after the invasions by Chinese Haw – surmised that the bandits pillaged the stupa, making off with 7000 rupees' weight of gold.

Wat Phia

Continuing on the main road beyond the market, you'll pass the ruins of a villa, the only reminder that this town was once a temperate French outpost of ochre colonial villas and shop houses, and arrive at the ruins of sixteenth-century **Wat Phia**. Brick columns reach skywards around a seated Buddha of impressive size, a mere hint at the temple architecture for which the city was renowned.

The more recent temple of **Wat Siphoum**, the uninspiring structure nearest the market, bears little trace of the old designs for which the city's monasteries were known and serves notice of how much of Xieng Khuang's culture has been lost.

Muang Kham and around

Many of the ethnic groups that populate Xieng Khuang are well represented in the area between Phonsavan and **MUANG KHAM,** a large village to the northeast. A trip out to Muang Kham – formerly known as Chomthong – and its nearby hot springs makes an interesting excursion. Several sights around the village are included on the itineraries of day-tours out of Phonsavan, and though none is worth a special journey in its own right, collectively they're a good excuse to see more of rural Xieng Khuang province.

Phonsavan to Muang Kham

Route 7 winds through valleys hemmed by hills bursting with *dok bua khom* – yellow flowers that are crushed into a natural fertilizer for vegetable gardens – passing dusty Khmu, Black Tai, Phuan and Hmong villages, with their wooden huts. Leaving Phonsavan, you first pass through **Khang Khai**, the town that became the seat of Prince Souvannaphouma's neutralist government after the Battle of Vientiane in December 1960, before arriving in **Ban Xon Tai**, 12km north of Phonsavan, where two village women etched the name of their hometown into Pathet Lao lore when they shot down an American plane during the war. Apparently armed with little more than rifles, the heroines inspired the addition of the adjectives "patriotic" and "brave" to generations-old songs praising the beauty of Xieng Khuang women.

Fourteen kilometres further on, you'll pass through the Hmong village of Tha Cho before arriving in **Daen Thong**, 12km further on, a village peopled by Khmu, a midland tribe that makes up around seven percent of Xieng Khuang's population. Widely considered to be among the original inhabitants of Laos, the ancestors of the Khmu are thought by some to have built the funerary urns scattered across the Plain of Jars. The next village, **Ban Lao**, was settled by Black Tai (Tai Dam), who fled to Laos several decades ago from Dien Bien Phu, the Vietnamese valley where the final battle of the First Indochina War was fought. After a further 7km, a dirt track forks off to the east leading to another Black Tai village, **Ban Xieng Kiao**, while the main road continues over a bridge spanning the Nam Mat stream and winds its way into **Muang Kham**.

Tham Piu

4km north of Muang Kham; the turn-off for the cave lies on the left-hand side of Route 6 – follow the road 1500m to the stairs at the foot of the hill

A number of tours from Phonsavan now include a sombre pilgrimage to **Tham Piu**, a cave in which hundreds seeking refuge from the wartime bombing were killed when a fighter plane fired a rocket into the grotto. At the foot of the hill you'll find a steep set of stairs climbing up to the wide mouth of the cave. Only blackened rock testifies to the tragic incident.

Baw Nam Hon Nyai

Around 20km from Muang Kham along Route 7; after passing through the tiny Na Ba market and crossing a bridge, turn right at Ban Nam Dien – 16km from Muang Kham – and head for the cliffs to find the spring. The road ends at the resort's gate, 3.5km away from Route 7 • Entrance fee 5000K, bath 5000K • Many travel agents in Phonsavan will be able to add a visit to the hot springs onto a morning at the Jar sites – expect to pay around $35 for the entire trip.

From Muang Kham, Route 7 east towards the Vietnamese border leads you to two **hot springs**, Baw Nam Hon Lek and **Baw Nam Hon Nyai** – "Little Hot Spring" and "Big Hot Spring". The smaller of the two isn't worth a visit, but **Baw Nam Hon Nyai** has been converted into a resort of sorts. The spring fills a swampy green pond of no remarkable beauty, but blooming flowers in the rainy season attract Phonsavan couples, who make the trip out on weekends to picnic and canoodle. A crude piping system draws the spring's steamy water to the site's main attraction: the **hot baths**, which are situated in a long shed among a small cluster of rustic bungalows. A warm bath – there are two large tubs per private room – is certainly worth the trip during Xieng Khuang's chilly winters.

Muang Sui

From Phonsavan, Route 7 winds west towards the mountainous edge of the Plain of Jars and then begins working its way through the mountains to the outpost of Muang Phoukhoun on Route 13. This section of the French-built highway – a favourite target of Hmong insurgents as recently as the 1990s – grinds through pine-topped hills and steep-banked stream beds for 48km to **MUANG SUI**. Roughly at the halfway mark, the road fords the Nam Ngum as the river builds up steam en route to the Nam Ngum Dam, and then passes a pair of villages populated by Hmong, who were forcibly resettled here in the late 1990s.

Once a significant village known for its temples, Muang Sui was yet another casualty of the intense fighting in Xieng Khuang province. Now rebuilt alongside **Nong Tang**, a pretty lake hemmed in by stubby limestone karsts and praised for its serenity in local folk songs, it's a sleepy town of wooden shop houses and a small market. Nearby is **Tham Pha**, a forest cave that shelters a Buddha image and a *that*. One kilometre from town, an old 1500m-long landing strip, in a state of disuse, cuts across Route 7 as it begins its 90km journey towards Muang Phoukhoun.

Basic accommodation is available in the town, though most people who make the trip out here do so in conjunction with a tour of the Plain of Jars.

Hua Phan province

Sparsely populated **Hua Phan province** is a sea of misty mountains, dotted with isolated bowl-like valleys. The country's northeasternmost province, it's also one of the most spectacularly beautiful provinces in all of Laos, with some of the north's highest mountains, a large number of diverse ethnic groups, extensive forest cover and one of Laos's largest NBCAs. There are also enough caves, waterfalls and limestone karst scenery to give Vang Vieng hoteliers sleepless nights: you only need to drive the road in from Nam Neun to realize what amazing tourist potential Hua Phan has. The problem of course is infrastructure – though roads are now greatly improved, there are still very few of them, and unless they're travelling through to or from Vietnam, very few travellers make the effort to see the area.

Travelling beyond **Sam Neua** – the chilly provincial capital – is a more attractive option than it used to be now that the **Na Meo border crossing** gives overland access to Thanh Hoa province in Vietnam. Regular buses from Sam Neua travel up to the border, though you'll need to already have a Vietnamese visa in order to make the crossing.

Brief history

Difficult terrain and the province's proximity to Vietnam made Hua Phan the perfect headquarters for the Pathet Lao, who operated out of the caves that honeycomb the karst formations in Vieng Xai for the better part of their Thirty Year Struggle. Along with Phongsali (see p.175), Hua Phan was set aside as a regroupment area for the communist forces under the Geneva agreements of 1954. While the province formed the backbone of the Pathet Lao's liberated zone, not all of Hua Phan was under communist control: for years, the 1786m mountain peak of **Phou Pha Thi** was crowned by a "blind bombing" device to guide air raids on Hanoi (see box, p.157).

The real muscle behind the Pathet Lao during the war, **Vietnam**, retains much political and economic control over Hua Phan, and a steady flow of Vietnamese goods, electricity, merchants and construction workers arrives in the Lao province via three border points – one of which is open to foreign travellers.

Hua Phan is predominantly populated by various Tai groups – Red, Black, Neua and White – and, in the towns, migrants from Vietnam and China. With more than twenty **ethnic groups** in the mix, it's perhaps not surprising that even residents from neighbouring Xieng Khuang complain about the difficulty of understanding Hua Phan dialect. During the centuries before French rule, the area was part of a Black Tai principality, known as the Sipsong Chao Tai, which spanned the present-day Lao–Vietnamese border. The principality fell under the sway of the lowland Lao kingdoms of Luang Prabang, Xieng Khuang and Vientiane and under the control of the greater powers that in turn controlled them – Siam and Vietnam. Stone pillars (known as Suan Hin), located several kilometres off Route 6 near Houa Muang, suggest that the area was a hub of some forgotten culture long before Tai–Lao and Vietnamese rulers squabbled over this region.

Sam Neua

You could be forgiven for thinking that you'd crossed into Vietnam on descending into **SAM NEUA**, the provincial capital and the only sizeable Lao town east of the Annamite Mountains. Unlike the rest of Laos, which drains west into the Mekong, all of Hua Phan province's rivers flow southeast to the Gulf of Tonkin – Sam Neua itself sits in the narrow Nam Xam river valley. If you want to feel like you're in the middle of nowhere, Sam Neua fits the bill, sitting in a bowl surrounded by low, pleasant hills with the narrow river rushing through its centre.

Although there's little to occupy the traveller in Sam Neua, save absorbing the rugged frontier atmosphere of this most un-Lao outpost, the place serves as a comfortable base for the Pathet Lao Caves in Vieng Xai, or a stopover on the push to northern Vietnam. Perhaps the best reason to visit Sam Neua, however, is to explore the surrounding

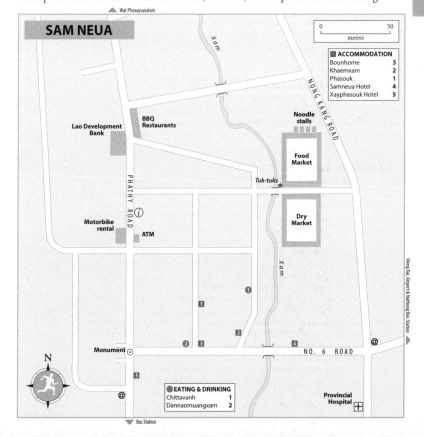

SAM NEUA

0 — 50 metres

ACCOMMODATION
Bounhome	3
Khaemxam	2
Phasouk	1
Samneua Hotel	4
Xayphasouk Hotel	5

Wat Phoxaysanalam

Lao Development Bank

BBQ Restaurants

Noodle stalls

Food Market

Tuk-tuks

Dry Market

Motorbike rental

ATM

PHATHY ROAD

NONG KANG ROAD

Xam

Monument

NO. 6 ROAD

Vieng Xai, Airport & Nathong Bus Station

EATING & DRINKING
Chittavanh	1
Dannaomuangxam	2

Provincial Hospital

Bus Station

N

countryside – the excellent tourist office can provide up-to-date information about transport options, or to really explore, you could rent a motorbike. Aside from the tourist office and a small number of guesthouses, tourist infrastructure in Sam Neua is quite limited, and you're likely to be regarded as something of a novelty, even in the centre of town. Be warned that this area can be a lot colder than the rest of the country, so a sweater and long trousers come in very handy if you're planning on stopping here, especially during winter.

Phathy Road

The main street is the two-kilometre-long, four-lane **Phathy Road** – a huge central boulevard lined with institutional-looking government buildings and bearing the unmistakable mark of the Vietnamese, who rebuilt the town after the war. It does seem remarkably empty, however, as though the city were destined for great things that never quite materialized.

There are almost no cultural sites, but you can walk up Phathy Road to the **victory monument**, an easy climb that affords a good view of the valley, and a bit further on, near the main street's end, to **Wat Phoxaysanalam**. Construction of the wat began in 1958 and took nearly a decade to complete, whereupon it was almost immediately destroyed by the bombing. The modest structure that now stands here was completed in the 1980s. It was until very recently the only wat in town and there are only a handful of resident monks. As journalist Christopher Kremmer (see p.302) wrote in *Stalking the Elephant Kings*: "if you're tired of seeing monks in Laos, come to Sam Neua". The town's three other pre-war wats, including the two-hundred-year-old Xieng Khuang-style Wat Inpeng, were never rebuilt. The sad little spires along Phathy Road leading up to the wat indicate where these holy sites once were.

The food market

Sam Neua's food **market**, on the eastern side of the river, is a good place to get a feel for the province's character. Vietnamese goods, many of which are bought by merchants at weekend border markets in Xieng Khoun and Na Maew, flood the stalls in a display of vegetables, meats and the occasional severed dog head. The market buzzes throughout the day, its vendors bundled against the cold with their heads wrapped in colourful scarves, a

---

SAM NEUA TEXTILES

Experts on **Lao textiles** all seem to agree that the most sophisticated pieces, in terms of both design and colour scheme, are produced in the region around **Sam Neua**. A fashion revolution followed the political revolution in 1975, when the victorious communists abandoned their headquarters near Sam Neua and moved into Vientiane. The wives of the new leaders enthusiastically sported the Tai Daeng styles of Sam Neua, and it wasn't long before the look caught on. Today the bold, spidery patterns of Sam Neua textiles are a favourite all over Laos.

Among Lao textiles, the work of the Tai Daeng and Tai Nua stand out. Classified by ethnologists as "tribal Tai", these ethnic groups are related culturally and linguistically to the lowland Lao. However, unlike the lowland Lao, they are animists for the most part, though Mahayana Buddhist influence can be seen in their textile motifs. These groups believe that death is the most important rite of passage in a person's life, and the funeral ceremony is correspondingly elaborate. To prepare for it, a woman will weave a special skirt to wear to the grave. A geometric design woven into the waistband of the skirt will serve to ward off spirits that might attempt to block her passage into the "Garden of Golden Mangoes". Another significant textile used by the Sam Neua cultures is a "shaman's shawl", worn by spirit mediums while performing healing ceremonies. Symbols on these shawls are remarkably similar to those found on bronze frog-drums of the sixth-century BC Dong-son culture which was centred in northern Vietnam. Other motifs found on Sam Neua textiles include the swastika, a Hindu symbol that was adopted by Mahayana Buddhism, and the stylized "third eye". Perhaps the most striking and the most "Lao" of the Sam Neua motifs are realistic naga imprinted in the textiles by tie-dyeing.

sartorial twist that most likely lent the province its name – "Hua Phan" means "wrapped head". It's a great place to head to for a cheap bowl of *föe*, or to try some local snacks.

The dry market

Just south of the food market is Sam Neua's **dry market**. Here you'll find all manner of individual stalls selling various goods, including a minor smattering of Lao **textiles**, although much of the best stuff gets sent directly to Luang Prabang or Vientiane. Although a lot of cloth is produced in Hua Phan, it's all made in people's homes, not factories. The area around the dry market houses all kinds of electrical shops bulging with refrigerators, televisions, rice-cookers, bicycles and home karaoke systems.

ARRIVAL AND DEPARTURE   SAM NEUA

By bus There are two bus stations in Sam Neua; a tuk-tuk from either into the centre should cost 20,000K.

Main bus station Long-distance buses arrive at/depart from the main bus station, around 1km south of town just off Route 6. Buses for Vietnam also depart from here daily at 8am, stopping at Thanh Hoa (180,000K) and continuing on to Hanoi (300,000K). Arrive at the bus station by 7am to ensure you get a ticket and remember that you'll need a pre-arranged visa to enter Vietnam.

Destinations Luang Prabang (2 daily; 13–14hr); Nong Khiaw (2 daily; 12hr); Phonsavan (3 daily; 8hr); Thanh Hoa, Vietnam (1 daily; 9hr); Vieng Thong (1 daily; 5hr); Vientiane, via Phonsavan (3 daily, 18–20hr); Vientiane, via Luang Prabang (1 daily; 25hr).

Nathong bus station Buses serving destinations within the province use Nathong bus station, to the east of town. Each morning from Tuesday to Sunday, buses run from here to Thanh Hoa in Vietnam. Daily sawngthaews also run to the border at Na Meo (50,000K), though you may struggle to find onward transport on the Vietnamese side. Each morning, sawngthaews run from the Nathong bus station to the caves at Vieng Xai (see p.158), but note that, as sawngthaews rarely run in the opposite direction during the afternoon, you may end up having to stay overnight. Destinations: Muang Et (1 daily; 5hr); Na Meo (1 daily; 3hr); Thanh Hoa, Vietnam (1 daily except Mon; 9hr); Vieng Xai (2 daily; 50min); Xam Tai (1 daily; 5hr);

INFORMATION

Tourist office The tourist office (Mon–Fri 8–11.30am & 1.30–4pm) is situated on Phathy Road, the main boulevard in town; the very helpful, English-speaking staff can advise on visiting the area, including Vieng Xai, nearby waterfalls and hot springs, and have the most up-to-date information on bus and sawngthaew times.

Services Also on Phathy Road, the Lao Development Bank changes US dollars, Thai baht and sterling, and can also provide cash advances. Some guesthouses offer wi-fi, and you can also access the internet (150K/min) at the shop just east of *Samneua Hotel*.

GETTING AROUND

Motorbike rental A shop just south of the tourist office offers motorbikes for 60,000K per day, though the staff speak little English.

Tuk-tuk Drivers tend to wait near the bridge closest to the dry market, and at the bus stations. Expect to pay 10,000K per person for journeys within town.

ACCOMMODATION

Accommodation in Sam Neua varies very little in price and quality; most guesthouses and hotels have grand reception areas full of Chinese-style wooden furnishings, which then lead to rather dark and disappointing rooms. On the plus side, most places offer free tea and fruit, which is especially welcome during the winter.

Bounhome In the centre of town on Route 6, just east of the Dannaomuangxam restaurant ☎064 312223. Housed in a modern building, with smallish but clean rooms. The more expensive rooms, with en-suite bathrooms, are on the ground floor, while guests on the top floor use a (somewhat inconvenient) shared bathroom and toilet downstairs. Double 80,000K, single 70,000K

Khaemxam In the town centre, just west of the river ☎064 312111. This family-run hotel is good value, and among budget travellers is the most popular place to stay. Rooms are a decent size and pleasant, if basic, with a choice between en-suite and shared bath. 70,000K

Phasouk On the quiet alley leading north from Bounhome ☎064 312479. Tidy, cared-for rooms with frilly pink curtains, spread across four echoing floors. The shared landings lead out onto decent balconies, but when the owner hangs her washing out you may struggle to find space to relax. 80,000K

Samneua Hotel Just east of the river on Route 6 ☎020 509 4444. This grand peach-coloured building is well located on the eastern edge of the river. All rooms are en suite and have TVs, though they can feel rather cramped owing to the large, decorative wooden beds. There's a popular restaurant around the back. **100,000K**

Xayphasouk Hotel South of the monument on the road to the bus station ☎020 5576 6644, ✉xayphasoukhotel@gmail.com. This glass-fronted hotel has the most expensive rooms in town, but is also one of the few buildings with warm rooms during the winter. The doubles here are smart and business-like, with gleaming floors and free wi-fi. The staff are helpful, though limited English is spoken. **150,000K**

EATING AND DRINKING

Sam Neua is no place for fine dining, but it has a couple of half-decent places for a bite to eat. Expect to wait a while for your food – most places are just a two-person operation. In addition to the restaurants listed below, you could try the northern end of the food market, where half-a-dozen ladies sell steaming hot *föe* with or without meat from the adjacent stalls (10,000–15,000K). On the road running north of the tourist office you'll find a few BBQ places, which grill chicken nightly.

Chittavanh North of Khaemxam, on the river ☎061 213777. On the ground floor of the guesthouse of the same name, Chittavanh does reasonable noodle soups with duck or beef (both 15,000K) and some cheap Western options, allowing you to piece together a simple breakfast. At night, it's popular with Chinese drinkers. Daily 6.30am–11pm.

Dannaomuangxam Just west of Bounhome on Route 6 ☎020 2880 2887. This family-run place is a good choice throughout the day, serving cornflakes and fried eggs for breakfast, and tasty pork and chicken soups for dinner (20,000K). Daily 7am–11pm.

Phou Pha Thi

35km northwest of Sam Neua • Contact the Sam Neua tourist office for information about reaching the mountain, though renting a motorbike may be your best bet

Phou Pha Thi, a 1786m-high limestone mountain, is the tallest peak in northern Hua Phan and the most distinctive mountain in the province: a broad-based massif, with a near-vertical summit. The Nam Xam river, which flows through the centre of Sam Neua and all the way to the Gulf of Tonkin, runs directly down from the peak's southern flanks.

Phou Pha Thi is famous for being an important Lima Site during the **Second Indochina War** when the CIA and Special Forces set up a navigation radar tower on the summit. As this secret mountain base, run by the CIA and guarded by three hundred Thai mercenaries, was in the very heart of Pathet Lao territory, the story of its eventual capture and destruction is the stuff of local legend (see box opposite). Note that you can't actually climb the mountain at present.

Hintang Archeological Park

64km south of Sam Neua, signposted off Route 6 • Best reached by motorbike, but if you want to use public transport, take a bus or sawngthaew from Sam Neua's main bus station towards Phonsavan (roughly hourly 7am–2pm; 20,000K) and get off at Ban Phao. The stones are a 6km walk away along the dirt road.

Located just off Route 6, 6km southwest of Ban Phao, **Hintang Archeological Park** is home to the **Suan Hin** or "Stone Garden". Surrounded by forest, the megalithic stone gardens consist of large slabs of rock that have been stood upright and arranged in circles. The age and origin of the sites as well as the culture that created them remain a mystery, though the pillars have been linked by archeologists to the stone funerary urns of the Plain of Jars and it's thought that they're approximately two thousand years old.

Nam Xam NBCA

Around 85km southeast of Sam Neua, to the south of Route 6A • The park can only be reached by four-wheel-drive vehicles; ask about trips at the tourist office in Sam Neua.

The hilly **Nam Xam NBCA** is spread over around 700 square kilometres. The conservation area basically encompasses a broad bend in the **Nam Xam river** where it makes a lengthy

THE FALL OF PHOU PHA THI

In a decision that would prove to be the turning point of the war in Laos, US President Lyndon Johnson ordered the installation of a navigational beacon to guide air strikes against the North Vietnamese atop **Phou Pha Thi**. Here, US air force cargo helicopters dropped off the components of the device, code-named Commando Club, which was assembled a few hundred metres from fields growing some of the best opium in Laos. Hmong soliders, not known for their ability to defend fixed positions, were assigned to protect the latest in military wizardry.

A few weeks before Commando Club became operational in late 1967, a couple of monks were caught on the summit of Phou Pha Thi carrying cameras and sketch-books; they were Vietnamese spies, and soon after Commando Club began directing its all-weather, high-altitude air strikes on the Hanoi valley, two Soviet-built biplanes, dark-green museum pieces with cloth-covered wings and wooden propellers jury-rigged to fire mortar shells, buzzed the site – the only time during the war that the North Vietnamese attacked a target with biplanes. The planes were shot down, but the Vietnamese, provoked by this high-profile site that threatened their security, moved more troops into Laos. By the time North Vietnamese commandos scaled the summit with grappling hooks and ropes to take the position on March 10, 1968, the nineteen Americans operating Commando Club knew the end was near.

The **fall of Phou Pha Thi** was typical of the lack of unified command that plagued the US' war in Laos. As historian Roger Warner wrote in *Shooting at the Moon*: "The radar installation belonged to the air force, but the CIA was supposed to defend it. The CIA couldn't defend it as it chose, because the ambassador didn't want unauthorized weapons on the mountaintop. Kept from direct accountability for its own men, the air force lost interest, even though it had proposed the installation in the first place, and, on the mountain itself, nothing held the villagers from wandering where they pleased, including to the little opium patch near the summit, which they harvested just as they always had."

Phou Pha Thi also signalled a shift in the demands the US placed on its Hmong allies: they were no longer being armed to defend their own mountaintops, but were now pawns of the war in Vietnam. Eight Americans were pulled off Phou Pha Thi, leaving eleven dead or missing – the beginning of prolonged confusion, as Warner indicates, over the fate of Americans missing in action in Laos, and for whom the search actively continues today.

detour around two large mountains within the NBCA, before extending over to the Vietnamese border to the east that comprises the park's eastern boundary. The tallest peak is located in the centre of the park and is 1741m. The eastern area of the park is said to provide a habitat for elephants, bears, tigers and gibbons.

The road from Sam Neua to Vieng Xai

The road heading east out of Sam Neua passes through the Striped Hmong village of **Ban Houa Khang** before descending into a valley of rice fields surrounded by shaggy karsts – the first glimpse of the heart of Pathet Lao territory. Passing through the lowland Lao town of **Ban Muang Liat** and the Hmong village of **Houai Na**, you'll arrive at a fork, 21km from Sam Neua. Bearing left leads to Sop Hao and Xieng Khoun on the old French road to Hanoi, right to **Vieng Xai**, 8km away, and eventually the Vietnamese border town of Na Meo.

Nam Nua waterfall

Three kilometres down the Vieng Xai road you'll come to a bridge over a swift-flowing stream, and from here a track leads off left to the top of a 70m waterfall, **Tad Nam Nua**, most stunning during the wet season. Cutting away from the path, it's possible to scramble along the rocks and riverbank to a viewpoint at the crest of the falls. The classic frontal view is harder to attain: back at the junction, take the Sop Hao road for roughly 2km where you'll find a track leading for over 1km through paddies and eventually across a stream and a sticky thicket of bamboo.

Vieng Xai

Arriving in **VIENG XAI** ("City of Victory"), you wouldn't know the Pathet Lao and their communist allies in Vietnam had won the Second Indochina War. Sprawled across a valley surrounded by the cave-riddled karst formations used by the Pathet Lao as their wartime headquarters, Vieng Xai was cobbled together by comrades from Russia, North Korea and Vietnam as well as labourers from Hua Phan's notorious re-education camps (see box opposite). In 1973, at the end of the war, there were plans to make Vieng Xai the heart of the newly socialist nation, but in the end Laos's socialist friends could not be convinced to foot the bill to turn a backwater into a gleaming new capital, and so the Pathet Lao leadership decamped to Vientiane. With time, Vieng Xai couldn't even compete with nearby Sam Neua as a provincial hub. People moved out and many buildings fell into a state of crumbling decay. These days, the town has a slow, dusty charm, complemented by its stunning backdrop of limestone karsts.

Very few travellers stay in Vieng Xai, most preferring to see the caves (see below) as a **day-trip** from Sam Neua, which has much better food and accommodation. However, if you can afford the time, the scenic countryside and ambience around Vieng Xai reward further exploration, evoking Guilin in China.

The Pathet Lao caves

When American air force Chief of Staff General Curtis LeMay jested that the US would bomb the enemy "back to the Stone Age", he hadn't realized that living like cavemen would prove to be the key to the survival of the North Vietnamese Army and Pathet Lao during the heaviest aerial bombardment in history. Like Vang Vieng in central Laos and Mahaxai in the south, the limestone karst formations in the valleys east of Sam Neua are pockmarked with **caves** and crevices – which proved a perfect hideout for the Pathet Lao's parallel government. **Viet Minh** army units began using t he caves and enlarging them in the early 1950s while fighting the French in the days before Dien Bien Phu. Soon, the Lao leftists had joined the Vietnamese underground, and by the middle of the 1960s, Vieng Xai and the surrounding area had become a troglodyte city of thousands living in the more than one hundred caves. The caves – some at the foot of hills, others high up, hidden by surrounding escarpments and accessible only by scaling steps cut into sheer rock faces – were an impregnable fortress, but even poking your head outside could prove deadly as craters near the caves attest.

The inhabitants of the caves followed a routine of sleeping by day and working at night in the fields outside (animals had to be dark-coloured in order to remain undetected by the enemy) or in the caves themselves: caverns held weaving mills, printing presses and workshops where American bombs and worn-out trucks were upgraded into farming tools and appliances. On Saturdays, adults would take a break and attend **classes** consisting of professional, cultural and political courses as well as lessons in algebra, geometry and geography.

The conclusion of the war didn't bring the hardships experienced in the caves to an end: what changed were the inhabitants. After 1975, the caves became a "**re-education**

VISITING THE PATHET LAO CAVES

Around a dozen caves are open to the public, and the only way to visit them is by **guided tour**, which takes about two hours. Guided tours are run by the Caves Visitor Centre at 9am & 1pm (60,000K). Outside of these times, it's possible to arrange for a private tour, which costs an additional 50,000K per group. The guides can be a little hit and miss, but the audio tour (included in the entry fee) is excellent, with accounts from people who lived in the caves really bringing them to life. In order to get the most out of the tour, it's recommended you rent a bike (or charter a tuk-tuk or minivan; see p.160) – this will allow you to see more caves, as some of them are quite spread out, but it does depend on everyone in your group renting one. Bikes are available to rent from the Caves Visitor Centre for 15,000K .

RE-EDUCATION CAMPS

The first group of prisoners to be transported to **re-education camps** – the Pathet Lao's means of neutralizing its wartime enemies – arrived by invitation in full military dress months before the communist takeover in December 1975. After receiving letters signed by Prince Souvannaphouma, seventy high-ranking Royal Lao Army officers and provincial governors came to what they thought would be an important meeting and were whisked off to the Plain of Jars, where they were fêted with a banquet and a movie. Any hope of a uniquely Lao solution to the Second Indochina War ended there, as these officials were shortly thereafter flown off to Hua Phan, where they were stripped of their rank and separated into small work parties. In the following months, thousands of civil servants and army officers voluntarily entered the re-education centres in Hua Phan, Attapeu and Phongsali after being assured the "seminars" would last only a few weeks. With their opponents safely out of the way in the most remote corners of the country, or having opted already to flee to Thailand, the Pathet Lao moved ahead with the final stage of their bloodless takeover virtually unopposed.

Joined later by thousands more who arrived somewhat less willingly, the internees were turned loose in the fenceless camps, which were heavily guarded and hemmed in by the extreme geographical features of the Lao wilderness, and left to forage for food and build their own shelters out of bamboo. Each morning, a bell was rung at 5am and the prisoners were assigned a job for the day – cutting wood in the jungles, building roads, working in the fields. In the evenings, self-criticism and political indoctrination sessions were held. Although there was no physical torture, mindless rules were established in order to control the captives, who were never allowed to settle into one place. The cumulative effect of the "re-education", according to a former Royal Lao Army officer, who spent thirteen years in a Hua Phan camp, was a sort of "brainwashing". Life in the camps was hard – the officer is certain that he only made it because of a Green Beret survival course he attended in the US – and many ran off or died of malaria.

Drug addicts, prostitutes and other "anti-social" elements were also rounded up and shuttled off to **Ang Nam Ngum** near Vang Vieng (see p.84), where an estimated three thousand people were placed on "Boy Island" and "Girl Island". In 1977, the **royal family** too was arrested and banished to Camp 01 at Sop Hao, in Hua Phan, where the king and crown prince reportedly died of starvation two weeks apart in May 1978. The queen is said to have died in 1981, and, like her husband and son before her, was buried in an unmarked grave outside the camp. The only government acknowledgement of their deaths came a decade later, when Party Secretary General Kaysone mentioned in an aside during a visit to Paris that the king had died of old age.

There are **no official figures** for the number of people who were interned in the camps, but estimates based on reports by former inmates and their families suggest that at the height of the camps, in 1978–79, the number of internees may have been as high as fifty thousand. Whatever willingness supporters of the Royalist regime had to work with the new government quickly evaporated when it became clear that those interned in the camps weren't coming home anytime soon. Confronted with the prospect of being sent off for re-education, more than three hundred thousand people, nearly a tenth of Laos's population, fled the country.

The first group of prisoners, low-ranking members of the former regime, was **released** in 1980, and despite finally being deemed fit to live in socialist Laos, many took the first chance they got to cross the Mekong. As the 1980s wore on, more and more prisoners were gradually released under pressure from Western nations and Amnesty International, which reported that in 1985 seven thousand people remained in the camps, a number which had dwindled to 33 by March 1991. The camps may now be empty, but as of 2013, the Lao government still had at least three prisoners of conscience and two political prisoners locked up. Previously, Amnesty International described Laos as "a country which has a zero-tolerance policy towards dissent in any form".

camp" for functionaries of the Royal Lao government – from the lowliest foot soldier to the former king (see box above).

Inside the caves

Each of the caves, most named after the Pathet Lao leaders who lived there, had multiple exits, an office and sleeping quarters, as well as an emergency chamber for use in case of chemical-weapons attacks (these chambers were kitted out with a Soviet oxygen machine and a metal door of the sort you'd find on an old submarine).

Tours often begin with the large cave of **Kaysone Phomvihane** (see p.216), who became leader of the Lao communist movement at its formation in 1955, and remained unchallenged in his post as head of the Lao People's Democratic Republic from its inception in 1975 until his death in 1992. Born in Savannakhet of a Lao mother and a Vietnamese father, Kaysone spent far more time in Vieng Xai than the Pathet Lao's face man, Prince Souphanouvong. While the Red Prince was off playing Vientiane's game of cat-and-mouse politics, Kaysone stayed in Hua Phan, attending frequent meetings in Hanoi – a risky two-day journey from Vieng Xai – with North Vietnamese leaders Ho Chi Minh and General Vo Nguyen Giap, the legendary military strategist behind the French defeat at Dien Bien Phu.

One of the most fascinating caves is **Xanglot Cave**, a huge natural cave which housed a large concert hall where rallies and meetings were held, alongside festivals and musical and dance performances. It's fascinating to imagine the residents attempting to maintain some semblance of normal life while living in these extraordinary conditions.

ARRIVAL AND INFORMATION
VIENG XAI

By sawngthaew Sawngthaews bound for Vieng Xai leave Sam Neua's Nathong bus station at 7am and 9am each morning, or when full (20,000K per person; 50min) and arrive in front of Vieng Xai's market. Returning to Sam Neua on the same day is tricky, as the last sawngthaew can be as early as 1pm, and occasionally it won't run at all if there are not enough passengers.

By tuk-tuk or minivan If you want to visit Vieng Xai for the day, the most practical option is to ask staff at the tourist office to arrange transport for you. A return tuk-tuk transfer from Sam Neua to Vieng Xai, including waiting time, should cost no more than 250,000K. For 300,000K you can make the same journey in a minivan. With either option, the driver will happily shuttle you between the caves you visit during the tour, which means you'll avoid a long walk or having to rent a bike.

Caves Visitor Centre To get to the visitor centre in Vieng Xai (☎064 314321, ⊛visit-viengxay.com; daily 8am–noon & 1–4pm), turn right out of the market and follow the main road for about five minutes until you reach a monument, where the road splits in two. Bear left – the office is on the right a few minutes later.

ACCOMMODATION AND EATING

Aside from the bowls of *fŏe* rustled up during the daytime by the **noodle stalls** at the small market, satisfying meals can be hard to come by in Vieng Xai. If you're planning to stay for more than one night you may want to bring supplies from Sam Neua's market.

Naxay Guesthouse Directly opposite the Caves Visitor Centre ☎064 314330. The small en-suite huts at Naxay are the most convenient choice for an overnight stay in Vieng Xai, with a lovely garden area in which to relax. <u>80,000K</u>

Sabaidee Odisha A ten-minute walk north of the Caves Visitor Centre, just beyond the ATM ☎020 2385 0594. You'll find a very broad selection of warming curries and chais at this shabby but welcoming Indian restaurant (mixed vegetable curry 15,000K), along with a few Lao dishes. Daily 7am–9pm.

Nam Neun to Nong Khiaw

The journey from **Nam Neun** to **Nong Khiaw** along **Route 1** is one of northern Laos's great road journeys, crossing numerous mountain ranges and valleys. These days, you're most likely to travel directly from Sam Neua to Nong Khiaw or Luang Prabang (twelve and fourteen hours, respectively), but if you want to experience local Lao life then it's worth considering stopping en route, though don't expect much more than basic accommodation and noodle shops.

Nam Neun

Until relatively recently, travelling through the region meant stopping at the village of **NAM NEUN** for a change of vehicles, usually overnight. Now, the longest you're likely to stop is for an extended break – two or three restaurants cater to travellers in transit with bowls of instant noodles and warm drinks. The town is set in a steep valley perched above the swift-flowing **Nam Neun river** – spanned here by a sturdy Russian-built bridge – which flows out of the Nam Et NBCA and eventually empties into the Gulf of Tonkin at Vinh in Vietnam. From here, Route 1 winds through the mountains towards Vieng Thong.

Vieng Thong

VIENG THONG, sometimes referred to by its old name **Muang Hiam**, lies in the upper valley of the Nam Khan river, which sweeps across the wide swathe of rice fields on the town's western flank. The town itself winds along the bottom of the narrow river valley and its main street begs for a high-noon shoot-out. These days, it's unlikely that you'll stop here for anything more than a food and toilet break on the long journey from Sam Neua to Nong Khiaw, but if you do find yourself hanging around here for a bus, or while waiting to join the Nam Nern Night Safari (see below), the 1km walk to the nearby **hot springs** is a pleasant diversion. While the pools are large enough for a good soak, they're far too hot; a tiny pool near the main road is cooler and a popular spot for villagers to bring their infants for a warm bath. There are a number of cheap guesthouses near the dry market, plus the usual noodle shops – to get here, turn left down Route 1 from the bus stop until you come to a T-junction; the centre of town lies just to the right.

Southeast through Phou Loei NBCA

West of Vieng Thong, Route 1 labours up forested hills and through ethnic minority villages, with their rough huts precariously perched along the ridges above a sea of mountains. The **scenery** is simply spectacular, with row upon row of mountain ranges extending into the distance.

Route 1 passes through **Phou Loei NBCA** (National Biodiversity Conservation Area), covering an area of 1465 square kilometres. In the high, mountainous divide separating Luang Prabang, Hua Phan and Xieng Khuang provinces, the park consists of north–south ranges, with its highest peak, **Phou Soy** at 2257m, at the northern end. Almost bordering Phou Loei is stunning **Nam Et NBCA**, an area of 1915 square kilometres that runs right up to the Vietnamese border in the north. Currently, the only way to visit the park is on the **Nam Nern Night Safari** (ⓦ namet.org/namnern; 2,000,000K/person), a two-day tour co-developed by the Wildlife Conservation Society. The trip, which departs from Vieng Thong and includes basic accommodation in traditional-style huts, gives visitors the chance to birdwatch, track wildlife and learn about the medicinal properties of the park's diverse flora.

THE NAM KHAN RIVER

After the long overland loop to reach Vieng Thong, it's strange to think that the river flowing swiftly past the town ends its journey in distant Luang Prabang. Starting from the Nam Et NBCA north of Vieng Thong, the **Nam Khan river** heads southwest between two ranges of high mountains, over difficult rapids and through dense jungles. The entire area is a big blank on most maps and no passenger boats travel this length of the river. If you're interested in exploring the part of the river that's already made it onto tourist itineraries, speak to Green Discovery or Tiger Trail (see p.120) in Luang Prabang. Both companies run half- and full-day kayaking expeditions from just outside the city, usually including a stop for lunch and a swim at Tad Se (see p.136). Prices depend on the number of people taking part.

The far north

KAYAKING ON THE NAM HA RIVER

The far north

While history has seen the rise and fall of a Lao dynasty enthroned at Luang Prabang, the elevated northern fringes of the former kingdom have remained relatively isolated until recent times. Decades of war and neglect have done their part to keep this stunning area of Southeast Asia from developing, and although inward investment from neighbouring China is beginning to transform the landscape in places, the north still retains ways of life that have virtually vanished in neighbouring countries. While the fertile valleys of the Upper Mekong and its tributaries have for centuries been the domain of the Buddhist lowland Lao, the hills and mountains to the north have been the preserve of a scattering of animist tribal peoples, including the Hmong, Mien, Khmu and Akha. It is largely the chance to experience first-hand these near-pristine cultures that draws visitors to the region today.

4

Many people come this far north in order to take the amazing boat trip along the **Nam Ou river**. In recent years, boat traffic has dwindled, owing not just to improved roads but also to Chinese dam construction, but whether reached by road or river, the town of **Nong Khiaw** makes a spectacular introduction to the far north, nestling among some of the region's most dramatic scenery, with limestone mountains all around and excellent opportunities for exploration. It's also the sole gateway to tiny **Muang Ngoi**, an hour north by river and long a favourite with visitors to the region wanting to kick back for a few days. From Nong Khiaw or Muang Ngoi it's a stunning two-day journey by boat, overnighting at the rough-and-ready river port of **Muang Khoua** – a key waypoint for travellers bound for Vietnam – to **Phongsali**, the principal (and eponymously named) town of a mountainous province that's every bit as untamed as you might imagine of somewhere so remote. With an old town that feels as though it hasn't changed for decades and a relatively new trekking scene, Phongsali makes an appealing base from which to visit hill tribes that retain a very traditional way of life. Improved transport means that it's now easier to explore the region than ever before, though you can still expect long journeys on endlessly windy roads.

A long day's drive south of Phongsali – but a relatively straightforward hop from Nong Khiaw – is **Oudomxai**, a fast-developing provincial capital and important transport hub; from here it's possible to connect to most other places in northern Laos, as well as Vientiane. Though Oudomxai itself has little to detain visitors for long, it's just an hour's drive from the enchanting village of **Muang La**, home to one of the region's most magical places to stay. The most popular northern town is undoubtedly

Highlights

❶ Nong Khiaw Surrounded by stunning limestone peaks and straddling the Nam Ou, idyllic Nong Khiaw is the perfect place to lose a few days. **See p.167**

❷ Boat trips on the Nam Ou The spectacularly scenic stretch of the river between Nong Khiaw and Muang Khoua is flanked by jagged karst and (for now) remains undisturbed by Chinese dam projects. **See p.169**

❸ Trekking around Phongsali This quietly charming town is the perfect base for exploring the vast tropical forests and diverse traditional

cultures of Laos's remote northernmost province. **See p.177**

❹ Muang La With hot springs, a historic temple and a gorgeous setting, serene Muang La is an ideal day-trip from Oudomxai. **See p.184**

❺ Nam Ha NBCA Hike, kayak or raft, but don't miss this stunning national park near the trekking centre of Luang Namtha. **See p.187**

❻ The Gibbon Experience Hurtle through primary forest by zip line, a thrilling way to experience Bokeo Nature Reserve. **See p.196**

HIGHLIGHTS ARE MARKED ON THE MAP ON P.166

the tourist centre of **Luang Namtha**, a good place to relax for a few days if you're after some home comforts, and a popular base for trekking, owing to its comfortable and excellent-value accommodation and easy access to nearby tribal villages. More laidback is the low-key centre of **Muang Sing**, reached by a stunning road journey northwest through **Nam Ha NBCA**, a pristine and beautiful protected area of the country. Both Muang Sing and **Muang Long**, a small but bustling centre still almost untouched by the tourist industry, are ripe for trekking opportunities in the surrounding countryside.

While boat traffic on the rivers isn't quite what it used to be, the border town of **Houayxai** is the popular starting point for the memorable boat trip down the Mekong, via the port town of **Pakbeng**, to gracious Luang Prabang. It's also the starting point for the fantastic **Gibbon Experience**, which provides a great opportunity to explore the jungle, on foot and by zip line.

Many visitors see comparatively little of the region, travelling from the Thai border down to Luang Prabang on the Mekong, perhaps swinging first up to Luang Namtha for a couple of days' trekking, and then maybe travelling up to Nong Khiaw and Muang Ngoi from Luang Prabang. But if you've got time, the area deserves further exploration – venture a little off the beaten track and you'll almost certainly be rewarded with adventures experienced by surprisingly few.

THE FAR NORTH

HIGHLIGHTS

1. Nong Khiaw
2. Boat trips on the Nam Ou
3. Trekking around Phongsali
4. Muang La
5. Nam Ha NBCA
6. The Gibbon Experience

The Nam Ou River Valley

Starting on the China border, the **Nam Ou** drains all of Phongsali province and flows down through western Luang Prabang province to meet the Mekong above Luang Prabang. Much of the Phongsali province watershed is devoid of roads and still well covered with old-growth forests, and despite the threat from ongoing dam construction (see below), for now the river and its many tributaries remain in many ways much as they were when nineteenth-century French explorers passed through.

The main urban centre of the upper Nam Ou is **Phongsali**, though the town itself lies an hour's drive west of the river, with dusty **Hat Sa** effectively acting as its port. The other two towns of significance on the Nam Ou are Muang Khoua and Nong Khiaw: **Muang Khoua** sits astride the river, an important staging post between Oudomxai and the Vietnamese border, while **Nong Khiaw** is located where Route 1 crosses the river on its way from Oudomxai to Hua Phan province in the extreme northeast. All of the towns listed in this section can be reached by both road and river – though as yet there are no bus services to tiny **Muang Ngoi**. Undoubtedly, however, the river is the more enjoyable option.

Nong Khiaw

Resting at the foot of a striking red-faced cliff, amid towering blue-green limestone escarpments, the dusty town of **NONG KHIAW**, on the banks of the Nam Ou river, lies smack in the middle of some of the most dramatic scenery in Indochina. There's not a great deal to the town itself, but the relatively slow pace of tourist development here has allowed it to retain its village-like charm; it's a great place to lose a few days, preferably watching the river from your own private balcony, and makes a good base for **day-trips** in the scenic surrounding countryside (see box, p.170).

Nong Khiaw is spread over either side of the long bridge that stretches over the Nam Ou. At the northern end of the bridge, you'll find the boat mooring, a few guesthouses and the more local side of town, which extends for around 1.5km along the dusty main street parallel to Route 1. Across the bridge, are the majority of guesthouses and restaurants.

Morning market

Main road through town, next to the primary school • Mon–Fri & Sun 6–7.30am, Sat 6–8.30am

Nong Khiaw's **morning market** is worth an early start any day of the week, but it's at its biggest on Saturdays, when villagers – mainly Hmong tribeswomen – travel as far as 25km to show their wares. Some bring live animals to be slaughtered and eaten, a grizzly introduction to the highland taste for locally sourced wild meat.

DAM LIES: SINOHYDRO AND THE NAM OU

One of only two rivers in Laos navigable for most of their extent – the other is the Mekong itself – the **Nam Ou** ("Rice Bowl River") is the lifeblood of the subsistence arable farmers and fisher folk who live along its banks. Sadly, their way of life is under severe threat – as is the future of the river itself as the region's principal artery – by a $2 billion project, under way since 2011, to **dam** the river along three-quarters of its 450km length. Under the terms of the agreement, the Lao government has granted Chinese construction giant **Sinohydro** development rights for the whole of the Nam Ou basin until 2026, after which (once, cynics suggest, the dams begin to deteriorate) ownership returns to Laos. Three dams are already under construction – due for completion in 2018 – with four more in the pipeline. Though Sinohydro's impact assessments have been kept secret, the potential environmental consequences on the region (which includes the hitherto pristine ecosystem of Phou Den Din NBCA; see box, p.179) are catastrophic, with Nam Ou's 84 fish species under particular threat. Local communities meanwhile, many of which have been or will be forced to resettle, have been kept in the dark about Sinohydro's plans, or fed misinformation, with compensation for loss of land and livelihood minimal or in some cases non-existent. For more information, see ⓦ internationalrivers.org.

Nong Khiaw View Point

500m south of the bridge along Route 1 • Daily 6.30am–3.30pm • 20,000K • Bring suitable footwear

South of the bridge, a path leads off the main road up through thick jungle to the **Nong Khiaw View Point** atop Phou Phadeng, which gives stunning 360-degree views. The steep but rewarding ninety-minute climb is best tackled in dry season (Oct–March); in April views tend to be obscured as farmers burn off their rice fields, and the trails are sometimes closed in the rains. It's essential to stick to the cleared path as the area is still blighted by unexploded ordnance.

Pathok Caves

2.5km south of Nong Khiaw along Route 1 • Daily 7am–5pm • 5000K • Bring a torch or hire one from the hut (5000K)

It's an easy walk or cycle south from town to the **Pathok Caves**, where villagers hid from shelling during the Second Indochina War. Set among steeply rising limestone karsts, the caves are indicated by a small blue sign on the right; buy your ticket from the little wooden hut before the bamboo bridge and you're then free to explore by yourself, though insistent local children will likely follow you to act as guides (and will expect a tip). There are two surprisingly extensive (and very dark) cave systems here: the first is easy to spot from the path, accessed up a steep concrete stairwell. On exiting, follow the path round to the right for a few hundred metres to find the second cave, which is more claustrophobic and atmospheric.

ARRIVAL AND DEPARTURE   NONG KHIAW

By boat The boat landing is on the north side of the river, from where it's a 5–10min walk to most accommodation. Boats leave for Muang Ngoi at 11am and 2pm (1hr; 25,000K); one of the morning boats will sometimes continue to Muang Khoua (6hr; 120,000K) if there's enough demand (usually five people). Tickets should be bought at the ticket office at least half an hour beforehand. At the time of writing there were no passenger boats to Luang Prabang (8hr; 150,000K), though services were rumoured to restart as far as the dam works at Hat Kip, 2hr downriver, by mid-2014, where (when assuming water levels are high enough)

you'll need to change on to another boat, or take a bus to Luang Prabang; in the meantime it's possible to charter a boat (650,000K) to Hat Kip. Before they were suspended, boats left at 11am (8hr; 150,000K); if they're running, head down to the boat ticket office the day before you plan to travel to sign up (if there aren't enough people – usually sixteen – you'll either have to charter or go by bus).

By bus The bus station is situated on the northwestern edge of town, a 15min walk from the bridge (tuk-tuk 10,000K). All buses depart from here, though a minibus comes down to the boat landing to meet boats from Muang Ngoi, and will

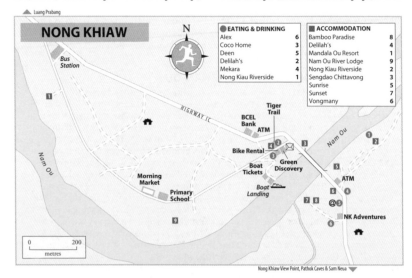

▲ Luang Prabang

NONG KHIAW N

● EATING & DRINKING	
Alex	6
Coco Home	3
Deen	5
Delilah's	2
Mekara	4
Nong Kiau Riverside	1

■ ACCOMMODATION	
Bamboo Paradise	8
Delilah's	4
Mandala Ou Resort	1
Nam Ou River Lodge	9
Nong Kiau Riverside	2
Sengdao Chittavong	3
Sunrise	5
Sunset	7
Vongmany	6

Bus Station

HIGHWAY 1C

BCEL Bank
ATM
Tiger Trail

Bike Rental
Boat Tickets
Green Discovery
Nam Ou
ATM

Morning Market
Primary School
Boat Landing

@

NK Adventures

0   200
metres

4

BOATS ON THE NAM OU

The wildly scenic boat journey up (or down) the Nam Ou has long been one of northern Laos's unmissable highlights. With the future of long-distance travel on the river, already diminished by improved roads, under threat from dam projects (see box, p.167), however, now is the time to come before it's too late.

Suspended in 2013, boat services should have resumed for the southern leg of the journey, between Luang Prabang and **Nong Khiaw**, by the time you read this, though may be dependent on water levels – they may not run during the dry season. Closer to Luang Prabang, where the river follows Route 13, extensive logging and slash-and-burn agriculture have stripped the surrounding mountains: only where the slopes are too rocky or too steep for cultivation have stands of forest been left intact. In an effort at reforestation, however, rows of young teak trees, recognizable by their enormous leaves, have been planted. After the road leaves the river, the scenery takes a turn for the spectacular, with vertical limestone peaks and pristine little white-sand beaches. It's likely you'll need to change boats at Hat Kip, around two hours downriver of Nong Khiaw, to get around the Nam Ou Dam 2 works when passenger services resume.

Upriver from Nong Khiaw the scenery continues to impress, possibly even surpassing that of the stretch below Nong Khiaw, the river snaking through impenetrable jungle. Because many of the surrounding mountains are simply too steep for slash-and-burn agriculture, the forests have been left virtually untouched. When the river is not too high and fast, this leg is also blessed with shelves of squeaky-clean beach, perfect for admiring the dramatic scenery. However, this primeval landscape lasts only a third of the distance to **Muang Khoua** before the topography flattens out a little and the lush landscape is replaced in part by arable hills with a beaten, domesticated air about them. You'll pass a few Vietnamese gold-panning mills along the stretch. The journey between Nong Khiaw and Muang Khoua takes five to six hours.

Beyond Muang Khoua, it's another 100km – via Nam Ou Dam 5 (see p.174) – to **Hat Sa**, the last town of any size on the Nam Ou until Ou Tai, close to the Chinese border at Lan Tui. The mountainous scenery along the narrowing river on the Muang Khoua–Hat Sa leg may be a little less dramatic than around Nong Khiaw, but the journey is nonetheless impressive and peaceful, and the surrounding forest rich in birdlife.

Passenger boats continuing up the Nam Ou beyond Hat Sa are few and far between, but it is possible to charter a boat with an agent (such as Amazing Lao Travel in Phongsali; see box, p.177) to explore Laos's northernmost corner. North of Hat Sa there's little formal accommodation, but it should be possible to find lodging in villages.

4

take passengers up to the bus station. Most guesthouses can also book you onto minibus services, which include pick-up from where you're staying. Buses depart for Luang Prabang at 8.30am, 10am and noon, with a pricier minibus leaving at 1.30pm. The Oudomxai bus leaves at 11am, though note the Sam Neua service doesn't pass through every day. Occasionally minibuses run as far as Luang Namtha, so it's worth asking around if you want to go that far.

Destinations Luang Prabang (3–4 daily; 3–4hr); Oudomxai (daily; 4hr); Sam Neua (usually daily; 12hr).

INFORMATION

Services Most of the guesthouses and restaurants have free wi-fi, but the only place to get online without your own device is *Deen* restaurant, which has a computer terminal available for 250K/min. There's a branch of BCEL with an ATM up on the highway, plus a second ATM across the bridge.

GETTING AROUND

Mountain bikes Mountain bikes can be hired from the shop next to *Coco Home* (daily 7am–6pm; 30,000K/day or 50,000K for two; ☎ 020 9800 3044), where they'll also give advice on local routes.

ACCOMMODATION

Bamboo Paradise On the southern side of the bridge; take the first turning (a dirt track) to the right ☎ 020 5554 5286. The original bamboo-thatch rooms (60,000K) here each have appealing hammock-slung private balconies at right angles to the river. Cool, cement-floored rooms in the newer building above (70,000K) are bigger and enjoy wider views, though balconies are shared. Bigger still (yet also cheapest) are the plain, viewless rooms at the back. All are good value. **50,000K̲**

Delilah's North side of the bridge, on the main street

NONG KHIAW TRIPS AND ACTIVITIES

Nong Khiaw has half-a-dozen **tour operators**, three of which are excellent. All offer trekking, kayaking, rafting and mountain-biking trips in the surrounding countryside. They can also arrange private buses and charter boats along the Nam Ou.

★**Green Discovery** Main street, north of the river ☎071 810081, ⊛greendiscoverylaos.com. A long-established operator with impeccable eco credentials, offering a particularly good range of cycling (from $40) and kayaking trips (from $41), and there are dozens of options for "multi-sport" two- and three-day trips.

★**NK Adventures** South of the river ☎020 5868 6068, ⊜bounhome68@hotmail.com. Nong Khiaw's best locally owned outfit is run by very helpful and forward-thinking Home, and offers very good value. His most popular day excursion begins with a boat journey upriver to visit two tribal villages, followed by a hike

through rice fields and lunch at a waterfall, returning to Nong Khiaw by kayak or boat (from $22 for six people, up to $35 for two). Two-day treks, staying with a Hmong or Khmu family, start from $55.

★**Tiger Trail** In the same building as Delilah's, north of the river ☎071 252655, ⊛laos-adventures .com. Tiger Trail offers an impressive range of day and overnight treks, including the highly recommended "100 Waterfalls" one-day trek, which begins with a beautiful journey on the Nam Ou before hiking through streams and rice paddies to the eponymous waterfalls ($63).

☎020 5439 5686. Nong Khiaw's cheapest accommodation, above the café-restaurant of the same name (see opposite), has a couple of small dorms (double bed an extra 10,000K) and a small double with shared bathroom. Dorm 35,000K, double 55,000K

★**Mandala Ou Resort** Off the main street, 200m southeast of the bus station ☎020 2881 1039, ⊛mandala-ou.com. Opened in 2013, Nong Khiaw's most stylish place to stay occupies a gorgeous, tranquil position on the river. Rustic-chic rooms feature big cement beds and bathrooms, nice personal touches (with items sourced from British owner Nic's travels around the north) and private sit-outs. Breakfasts (with warm, fresh bread and croissants) are excellent; the romantic, lantern-lit restaurant is a great spot for a well-mixed sundowner; and there's nowhere better in town than the infinity pool — Nong Khiaw's first and only — to soak up the views. Free bikes. 560

Nam Ou River Lodge Off the main street, 800m southeast of the bus station ☎020 5537 9661, ⊛namouriverlodge.com. Spacious, whitewashed, if rather sparse, rooms in a two-storey building with a shared terrace and big views across the river. Sinking into the hammock in the cute little bamboo-thatch bar is a welcome way to end the day. Good value and very handy for the morning market. 100,000K

Nong Kiau Riverside South side of the bridge ☎071 810004, ⊛nongkiau.com. These huge wood and thatch bungalows, set a little off the main road, have incredible views of the karsts and the bridge, and are beautifully decorated with dark-wood furniture. Each bungalow has a

wide private balcony that you could easily lose days on, and the large, cool restaurant serves excellent Lao food (see opposite). Rates include breakfast. 556

Sengdao Chittavong North side of the bridge ☎030 923 7089. Conveniently located by the bridge, this tranquil place has big bamboo huts, each with a balcony, neatly arranged around a long, pretty garden. There's also a nice, breezy restaurant that looks over the river. 80,000K

Sunrise On the southern side of the bridge ☎030 985 3899. A collection of simple, clean, bamboo-thatch bungalows on the river, all with hammocks and balconies (shared in the cheapest rooms, which also have squat toilets). 60,000K

Sunset South side of the bridge, first turning to the right (past Bamboo Paradise) ☎071 810033. Though it has arguably the best situated bungalows in Nong Khiaw, with amazing views over the river, this former favourite is looking a little tired these days, and rates are overpriced compared with what you can get elsewhere. Nonetheless, the on-site restaurant is the perfect place to finish the day with a cold Beerlao. 150,000K

Vongmany South of the bridge ☎020 5499 0787, ⊜khammanh495@yahoo.com. This tall, brand-new guesthouse, behind the popular *Vongmany* restaurant, looks a little out of place among the other more ramshackle properties along the river, though the modern rooms are surprisingly basic and simple. There are good views from the hammock-strewn wraparound balcony (the best attract a 40,000K premium), though overall it lacks the character of elsewhere in town. 80,000K

EATING AND DRINKING

Alex South side of the bridge, on the same lane as Bamboo Paradise. A rustic, bamboo-walled place that's widely agreed to provide the best Thai–Lao cooking in town

(mains 15,000–25,000K), though the care they show in preparation tends to show in painfully slow service. Also offers packed lunches and daily specials. Daily 6am–10pm.

★Coco Home Main street, just up from the boat landing ☎020 2367 7818. This leafy, Thai-run restaurant-bar-beer-garden has a pool table, good sounds and lots of hideaway corners in which to chill. The cute wooden movie room upstairs is usually full of supine travellers catching the twice-nightly film showings (6 & 8pm). Sometimes closes out of season. Daily 7am–10.30pm.

Deen South side of the bridge ☎020 2214 8895, ⓦ deenfoodnongkiaulaos.net. A simple and sweet little Indian restaurant, offering a huge range of veg (from 10,000K) and non-veg (from 20,000K) curries, served piping hot. Daily 7am–10pm.

Delilah's North side of the bridge, on the main street ☎020 5439 5686. A popular traveller's café that's a congenial spot for breakfast, with home-made bread and yogurt plus a three-egg "power" omelette (25,000K).

Also offers good coffee and cakes, plus desserts in the evening, which might include banoffee pie and flambéed bananas. Daily 7.30am–10.30pm.

Mekara South side of the bridge ☎030 923 0591. The widest selection of Lao food in Nong Khiaw, particularly good for its authentic curries (Paneng curry 25,000K), served in generous portions. The thatched roof, fairy lights and ambient music make it an atmospheric choice for dinner, though service can be slow and on occasion surly. Daily 7am–10pm.

Nong Kiau Riverside South side of the bridge ☎071 810004, ⓦ nongkiau.com. Nong Khiaw's smartest restaurant, in a breezy wooden pavilion right above the water with superlative views, serves excellent Lao food, including a delicious *mók pa* (37,000K) and Lao sausages (25,000K). Unfortunately, service can be very slow. Daily 7am–10pm.

Muang Ngoi

Strung out along a single dirt track, tiny **MUANG NGOI** is idyllically set amid beautiful scenery on the banks of the Nam Ou. It's long been an attractive spot for backpackers, many of whom end up whiling days away here. Just an hour's boat ride north of Nong Khiaw, the village – until 2013 only accessible by river – has a real edge-of-the-world feel. Although it's easy enough to just hang out here sipping coffee and swinging in a hammock (as, indeed, most people do), there are a lot of **activities** on offer, including trekking to nearby hill-tribe villages, exploring the dirt tracks that thread out of town by mountain bike, canoeing on the river and organized fishing trips. However, wandering the main street, especially during high season, you can't help but feel this sleepy little place has been somewhat ambushed by tourism, with every second property seeming to be a guesthouse or a travellers' café.

Note that, at the time of writing, there was no internet access in Muang Ngoi – though this may well have changed by the time you read this – and the guesthouses are your only option for changing money (at poor rates); it's best to bring enough cash to cover your stay.

Tham Kang Caves

10,000K • The caves are a 20–30min walk from the village; from the main street turn left after *Neem* restaurant and follow the path across the bridge past the school and sports field

One excursion that you can take without a tour guide is to the nearby **Tham Kang Cave**; it's very dark so take a torch. Formerly the district capital, Muang Ngoi was almost obliterated during the Second Indochina War, and villagers took refuge from bombing raids in this huge cave. The town was left uninhabited after the war, when local services (and much of the populace) were moved to the new town of Nong Khiaw.

ARRIVAL AND GETTING AROUND   MUANG NGOI

By boat Although Muang Ngoi is now accessible by road, the only public transport is by boat. Boats arrive at the village's northern end; the ticket office (open 8–9.30am) is situated just uphill from the boat landing, on the first path to the left. If you head straight on, you will meet the village's main street. Leaving Muang Ngoi, boats depart at 9.30am to both Nong Khiaw (25,000K; 1hr) and Muang Khoua (100,000K; 4–5hr); for the latter,

you'll need to sign up on a board at the ticket office in advance – be prepared to wait a day or two if there aren't enough people travelling (theoretically ten – though it's usually possible to negotiate if there are a few of you).

Mountain bikes Good-quality mountain bikes can be rented from the shop in front of *Phonevaly Guesthouse*, though they're expensive (60,000K/day).

TOURS

Lao Youth Travel On the path up from the boat landing, just beyond Lattanavongsa ☎030 200 5385, ⓦlaoyouthtravel.com. Muang Ngoi's most professional outfit, with the most extensive range of options, from a half-day kayaking trip to a local waterfall ($22) to two-day ($59) and three-day ($98) treks visiting local villages; prices are based on groups of four to six people. Trips are best organized in advance via the Luang Prabang branch (☎071 253340).

Mr Kongkeo Signposted 250m south of the boat landing ☎020 2202 3296. Mr Kongkeo, the local English teacher, is a useful source of information and can organize trips including a two-day overnight trek visiting local Hmong and Khmu villages ($44 each for two people), bamboo rafting on the river (2hr 30min; $10/person) and trips to the local caves.

ACCOMMODATION

Almost all of Muang Ngoi's accommodation is in wooden bungalows, many of which have wonderful river views that make up for their basic interiors. As you head up from the boat landing you'll be approached by a number of guesthouse owners – it's worth having a look at what they have to offer, as new places spring up regularly.

Alounemai Down a side alley away from the river, 150m south of the boat landing ☎020 2386 3255. Though it may not overlook the river, this is one of Muang Ngoi's most atmospheric options. The spacious rooms are set around a lush garden, and the on-site *Sky Bar* has a purpose-built pizza oven (though it's not fired up every evening). 50,000K

Lattanavongsa Just up from the boat landing, on the left ☎020 2236 2444. This is a justifiably popular guesthouse, with four very clean, large rooms in a low wooden bungalow. They also have a number of newer bungalows at Lattanavongsa 1 set around a palm-and-flower-filled compound, just up the road (100,000K), with proper hot-water showers, though they lack river views. 80,000K

★**Lertkeo** 350m south of the boat landing ☎020 7730 5041. With fantastic views across the river, this new guesthouse is as upmarket as Muang Ngoi gets. The five sturdily built concrete bungalows feature lovely balconies and immaculate bathrooms with genuinely hot showers. The only drawback is that the bungalows are a little packed together. 100,000K

Nicksa's Place 200m south of the boat landing. Tiny, basic thatched bungalows, though the setting, among beautiful flowers and with gorgeous views of the river, makes it feel a little special. 50,000K

Ning Ning 15m from the boat landing, up a short path to the left ☎020 388 0122. With its neat picket

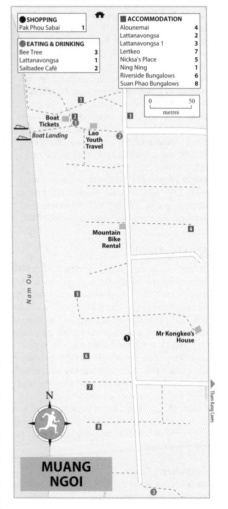

● SHOPPING		
Pak Phou Sabai		1

● EATING & DRINKING		
Bee Tree		3
Lattanavongsa		1
Saibadee Café		2

■ ACCOMMODATION		
Alounemai		4
Lattanavongsa		2
Lattanavongsa 1		3
Lertkeo		7
Nicksa's Place		5
Ning Ning		1
Riverside Bungalows		6
Suan Phao Bungalows		8

Boat Tickets
Boat Landing
Lao Youth Travel
Mountain Bike Rental
Nam Ou
Mr Kongkeo's House
N
Tham Kang Caves

MUANG NGOI

fence, net curtains and crisp, white bed linen, *Ning Ning* feels a very proper and orderly sort of place. Tucked away in a shady garden, the immaculate thatched wooden bungalows are among the village's biggest and best. Its restaurant perches in a peerless position above the river, and the owner's family are chatty and friendly. 120,000K

Riverside Bungalows 300m south of the boat landing ☎020 2214 8777, ⓔpdvbungalows@gmail .com. Though you pay a little more here than for similarly ramshackle bungalows along the strip, what you lose in pennies you gain in good hot showers, *two* hammocks per balcony and the best mattresses in town. The Lao–Swedish owners sometimes have "beach" barbecues up at the *Riverbeach Bar*, north of the boat landing. **80,000K**

Suan Phao Bungalows 400m south of the boat landing ☎ 020 2266 9940. Though not the sturdiest of

bungalows, these are light and very well maintained, with hammock-slung terraces. Ask to see a few, however, as some can be a little damp. **50,000K**

EATING AND DRINKING

Virtually all of the town's bungalow operations serve **food**, with *Ning Ning*, *Alounemai* and *Riverbeach* (see oppsoite) all providing particularly atmospheric surroundings. Some of the restaurants have coordinated their happy-hour periods to span much of the day – if you were so inclined you could merrily spend an increasingly foggy-minded afternoon hopping from place to place. Sleepy by day, Muang Ngoi is positively supine by nightfall, and you can take most of the quoted opening hours listed below with a pinch of salt: on a quiet night many places will have packed up for bed by 8.30pm.

Bee Tree 450m south from the boat landing ☎ 030 208 4877. Right at the bottom end of the village, this attractive, lantern-lit restaurant, with seating on bamboo sofas and jazzy sounds, offers the village's best Lao food. It's pricier than elsewhere in town, with mains around 35,000K, but the spicing is good and ingredients fresh. Also has cocktails from 30,000K. Daily 11.30am–11.30pm.

Lattanavongsa Just up from the boat landing, on the left ☎ 020 2236 2444. The restaurant attached to this guesthouse is one of the nicest in town, with a breezy

balcony overlooking the boat landing; pancakes and sandwiches cost around 15,000K, and Lao curries 20,000–25,000K. A good place to spend the evening over a cold Beerlao. Daily 7am–10.30pm.

Saibadee Café At the top of the path up from the boat landing. This cute corner café overlooking the street is one of several offering popular all-you-can-eat breakfast buffets (25,000K), though for fresher food pick something off the menu (hot baguettes 15,000K). Daily 6.30am–10pm.

SHOPPING

Pak Phou Sabai 250m south from the boat landing ☎ 020 9993 8527. This chilled-out but well-organized new book exchange-café-shop sells a fascinating range of local products, from Muang Ngoi rice, Mekong river weed

and Lao coffee to stencilled artwork and handmade scarves. Also organizes cookery classes with local women. Daily 8am–9pm.

Muang Khoua

Located on the left bank of the Nam Ou where the highway from Oudomxai crosses the river via a new concrete bridge on its way to Vietnam, **MUANG KHOUA** is an important crossroads and outpost in southern Phongsali province. The town itself is built on a steep hillside where the Nam Phak river enters the Nam Ou, and is famous for its precarious-looking wooden suspension bridge, which connects Muang Khoua with the village of Natoun. If you follow the road uphill from the boat landing, it leads to the main road – both are crammed with old shop houses, though many have been replaced with modern constructions. A left turn off the main road will take you to the small daily market.

Though there's not a great deal to see in Muang Khoua, it does have a certain charm, and some travellers end up staying for a couple of days to explore the rugged and hilly surrounding countryside further. For most visitors, however, it's just a stopover en route to Hat Sa (for Phongsali) on the river, or to or from Vietnam via the border crossing at Dien Bien Phu.

The suspension bridge

The bridge is surprisingly hard to find: at the top of the boat landing road, turn left down the main street (past the tourist office) to the T-junction where it meets the main highway; cross the road and head straight on down a track, signposted B. Salongxay

A stroll out across the high, swaying **suspension bridge** – shared with speeding motorbikes – is worth it for the view, but is a stomach-fluttering experience and not for the vertigo-prone. Wandering around the dusty, ramshackle hamlet of Ban Natoun across the bridge you'll feel like you've dropped back half a century or so.

4

ARRIVAL AND DEPARTURE

MUANG KHOUA

By boat Boats leave from the boat landing at around 9am most days for Muang Ngoi (100,000K; 4–5hr) and Nong Khiaw (120,000K; 6hr), and at around 10am heading north to the Nam Ou Dam 5 works at Muang Samphan (3–4hr), the first leg of the journey up to Hat Sa, for Phongsali (8–9hr; 130,000K to Hat Sa). You'll have to pay more if there's not a full complement of passengers. At Muang Samphan, you're bundled into the back of a pick-up truck (15min; 10,000K) for the transfer to the boat for Hat Sa (3hr) on the other side of the dam. Note that there's nowhere to buy food until Hat Sa, so bring supplies. It's possible to charter a boat either up- or downriver for upwards of one million kip.

By bus The bus station is 3km west of the centre of town (5000K in a shared sawngthaew). Buses run to Oudomxai

from the bus station three times daily (8am, noon & 3pm; 3hr). To reach Phongsali by road you'll need to first take the 8am bus to Pak Nam Noi (see p.179; 1hr), where a Phongsali-bound service from Oudomxai passes through at around 9.30am (7hr).

To Vietnam The road to Dien Bien Phu in Vietnam via the border crossing at Sop Houn/Tay Trang was relaid in 2012, and the journey is now possible in as little as 4hr. There is a 6am bus, but the most convenient service currently leaves at around 10.30am from outside Muang Khoua's tourist office, arriving in Dien Bien Phu around 3pm, though it's best to check times with the tourist office the day before. Note that you will need to already have your Vietnamese visa to make this crossing.

INFORMATION AND TOURS

Tourist office Muang Khoua's tourist office (Mon–Fri 8–11.30am & 1.30–4pm; ☎088 210098, ⌨phongsaly .net) is situated on the main road, a 5min walk up from the boat landing, and has a useful hand-drawn map of the town on the wall. The very helpful local tourism officer, Mr

Bounma, can organize treks to visit Akha Pouli and Khmu villages (800,000K for two people, including homestay), and can be contacted out of hours (☎020 5802 1794).

Internet Internet access is available at *Chaleunsouk* guesthouse (10,000K/hr).

ACCOMMODATION AND EATING

Muang Khoua has a number of **guesthouses**; unless you're heading straight for the *Nam Ou*, your best option on arrival is to follow the road uphill from the boat landing. There are no great culinary treats in Muang Khoua – the market is the best choice for a decent *föe* or takeaway lunch. The trio of **restaurants** on the way up from the boat landing have great views of the river and are good for a Beerlao, though the food is pretty grotty; *Saifon* is probably the best of them.

Chaleunsouk 5min walk up from the boat landing ☎030 932088. One of the nicest choices in town, with clean, cool rooms featuring oversized beds with decorated headboards; ask to see a few rooms, as they vary in size. The reception area also sells handicrafts, and there's a nice communal veranda. 60,000K

Manhchai Next to the tourist office ☎020 2201 6810. Right opposite the overpriced *Sernnaly Hotel*, this vision in pink is one of the smartest options. The sizeable rooms have flatscreen TVs, though the mattresses are rather hard. They claim to have free wi-fi (currently unique for Muang Khoua), though the owner is reluctant to part with the password unless you're staying. 100,000K

Manotham Ban Natoun, across the suspension bridge ☎020 5588 0058. Muang Khoua's most atmospheric place to stay, above the Nam Phak, with terrific views over town and across to the wooden bridge from the communal terrace – though rooms are basic

and dark, with saggy beds. The guesthouse is easy to miss – turn left after the suspension bridge and follow the road for 100m, past the yellow house on the right; look for the tiny sign. 50,000K

Nam Ou Above the boat landing – look for steps to the left leading up to it ☎088 210844. Muang Khoua's most popular backpacker choice, with rather cell-like rooms that feel a little flimsy. The shared bathrooms are pretty dingy, but those with private bath (50,000K) are a bit better. The sociable terrace restaurant, overlooking the river, is the travellers' favourite for dinner, with Vietnamese noodles (18,000K) and an insanely garlicky *larp* (30,000K). 40,000K

Nang Mien Next to Chaleunsouk Guesthouse ☎020 2284 5474. This small, bare-bones restaurant has a great local feel, and serves up a well-spiced fried rice (15,000K) and a gorgeous Lao-style yellow curry (25,000K). Daily 7am–9pm.

Hat Sa

The scruffy village of **HAT SA** consists of barely sixty homes, most of which are constructed from the ubiquitous bamboo and palm thatch, although concrete construction has reached even this remote outpost. Most travellers bypass Hat Sa, since they're either in a hurry to start downriver or to press on to Phongsali, 20km away, but Hat Sa and the villages further up the Nam Ou are about as far off the beaten track as you can get and are worth exploring, especially if you find Nong Khiaw and Muang Ngoi too touristy and are looking for something a little bit different. Amazing Lao Travel in Phongsali (see box, p.177) can offer advice.

ARRIVAL AND DEPARTURE   HAT SA

By boat Hat Sa is reached in 8–9hr by passenger boat from Muang Khoua, via the dam at Muang Samphan (see p.174). Regular passenger boats only really go this far, though if you're interested in exploring the Nam Ou further north it's worth enquiring here; alternatively you can book a tour from Phongsali.

By sawngthaew The boat from Muang Samphan arrives too late for passengers to catch the public sawngthaew (noon) to Phongsali (1hr), so you'll need to charter one. This costs 15000K per person if full; otherwise you'll need to negotiate (as a guide, 40,000K per person for six people travelling).

Phongsali and around

Perched just below the peak of Phou Fa ("Sky Mountain"), **PHONGSALI** looks and feels every bit the principal town of Laos's northernmost province – though in fact it no longer has provincial capital status, having lost that honour to comparatively insignificant Boun Neua (see p.179). The altitude gained becomes apparent once the sun drops below the horizon and the chill sets in; on clear nights, as soon as the lights go out, the view of the heavens is unparalleled. The crisp air seems to amplify the stellar glow and the Milky Way is splashed across the sky like a giant, luminescent cloud.

Phongsali's prosperous air, which owes much to the town's proximity to China, comes as quite a change of scene if you've travelled upstream along the Nam Ou. Despite being a large town, tourism remains in its infancy here. Though at first you may wonder where you've ended up, soon enough the cool mountain air and stunning surrounding countryside will work their charm on you. With the trekking scene still fairly low-key, the town is a great place to do an overnight trip to the province's fascinating **hill-tribe** villages. It's also a useful stopping point for intrepid travellers en route to the Chinese border crossing at Lan Tui, opened to foreigners in 2013.

A wide slice of terrain wedged between China's Yunnan and Vietnam's Lai Chau provinces, Phongsali province would surely indeed be a part of China today were it not for the covetous nineteenth-century French. During the Second Indochina War, Phongsali came under heavy Chinese influence, a fact evident in the fortress-like

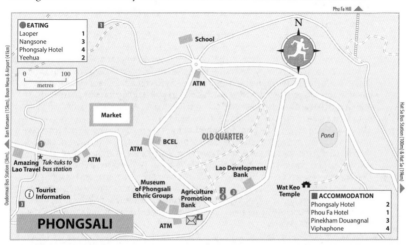

former Chinese consulate, now the *Phou Fa Hotel* (see p.178). It was during this time also that much of the province was stripped of its hardwood forests, compensation for China's support for the Pathet Lao. The town's inhabitants are made up of the Theravada Buddhist, Tibeto-Burman-speaking Phu Noi people and the Chinese Haw, descendants of Yunnanese traders who annually drove caravans of pack-ponies south into old Siam.

The old quarter

On a slope directly behind the *Phongsaly Hotel* – regarded as the dead centre of town – is Phongsali's **old quarter**. A wander through these friendly but medieval-looking lanes is like stepping back in time. Interspersed among the squat houses, some still of mud bricks and rough-hewn planks, are a few architectural standouts, including one distinctly Chinese building with a beautifully carved wooden facade that looks like it belongs on the backstreets of old Kunming. The quarter's three main streets run parallel for a stretch and then converge at a large basketball court, from which leads Phongsali's main commercial thoroughfare, a tidy street of low shop houses, some with roofs constructed of oil drums hammered flat and laid out like shingles.

TREKKING ETIQUETTE

While it is possible to organize trekking on your own, it is safer, more rewarding and – assuming you use a registered agency – of greater benefit to local communities to book it via an **agent**. Registered outfits will donate a significant percentage of your fee to the local villages, usually both as direct contributions to village funds and as money for development; you should always check where your money goes in advance, and trustworthy organizations will always be open to sharing this information.

If you book with a reliable agency, your experience will be greatly enhanced by having a local **guide** and **interpreter**. Though standards of English can vary, a good guide will be able to explain customs and activities that you might otherwise find incomprehensible and can help you to interact with the hill folk, who may be unaccustomed to or apprehensive of outsiders. If you do decide to do a trek independently, using a bit of common sense and following a few rules should make for a smooth, memorable visit.

(1) Never trek alone. While Laos is a relatively safe country in terms of violent crime, there have been **robberies** of Western tourists in remote areas. Owing to the government's total control of the Lao media, word of these incidents is suppressed, making it impossible to ascertain just how much risk is involved in solo trekking. Encountering armed men while hiking through the woods does not mean you are going to be robbed – they are more likely to be hunting – but it is best to treat all such encounters with caution. If you are approached by armed men and robbery is clearly their intent, do NOT resist.

(2) Most hill-tribe peoples are animists. **Offerings** to the spirits, often bits of food, left in what may seem like an odd place, should never be touched or tampered with.

(3) The Akha are known for the elaborate **gates** which they construct at the entrances to their villages. Far from being merely decorative, the gates are designed to demarcate the boundaries between the human and spirit worlds. If you come across a spirit gate at the entrance to a village, you should find another way to walk, skirting the village to avoid disrupting it while it is being "cleansed" of bad spirits. It goes without saying that climbing onto such a gate to pose for a photograph is poor form.

(4) Many hill folk are willing to be **photographed**, but, just like everyone else, do not appreciate snap-and-run tactics. Old women, particularly of the Hmong and Mien tribes, are not always keen on having their picture taken. You should always make clear to a potential subject that you wish to photograph them and to gauge their response before taking a photo.

(5) Don't give out sweets or pens to village children, which often leads to them begging the same things off future tourists, and insults the self-sufficient nature of these tribal peoples. Likewise, the indiscriminate handing out of **medicine**, particularly antibiotics, does more harm than good. Unless you are a trained doctor, you should never attempt to administer medical care to hill people.

TREKKING AND TRIPS FROM PHONGSALI

The main attraction of a visit to Phongsali is the opportunity to **trek** in this beautiful region, home to 28 different ethnic groups. One of the advantages of making it this far is that, on longer treks at least, there's a good chance that some of the tribes you'll encounter will have had little contact with foreigners before. Many of the treks around Phongsali start in or near Boun Neua or Boun Tai, which can be used as alternative bases (see p.179). Depending on the trek, you may witness a *basi* ceremony, go swimming in local creeks – and will almost certainly consume a lot of *lào-láo*. Prices vary according to the size of the group, and will include food, accommodation, (almost always) guide fees, though not always transport. Note that "walk-in" rates are usually cheaper than prices quoted online – though of course if you book at the last minute you run the risk of having to hang around for a day or two for others to join the tour. Both of the main operators in town are strong on **responsible tourism**, and are happy to demonstrate where your trekking fees go.

If you don't fancy an organized trek, renting a **motorbike** is a great way to see the local countryside. Vehicles can be rented from Amazing Lao Travel and *Yeehua* guesthouse. The tourist office has a couple of mountain bikes for rent (50,000K/day).

TOUR OPERATORS

Amazing Lao Travel ☎ 088 210594, ⓦ explore phongsalylaos.com. The main private tour operator in town runs a wide range of treks, of one to five days' duration. One-day trips start at 250,000K per person, though more rewarding are two- and three-day overnight treks (from 600,000K/880,000K/person), visiting more isolated tribes. Treks range as far as Ou Tai and Ou Neua, in Laos's very northern corner, and boat trips up the Nam Ou include one to Dam 6,

with an opportunity to meet displaced villagers.

Tourist office See p.178. Popular treks organized by the tourist office include the two-day Jungle Trek from Boun Neua through pristine forest, staying overnight with high-dwelling Akha Pixo tribespeople (from 400,000K), and the challenging three-day Multiethnic trek from Boun Tai, where you'll receive a massage at an Akha Eupa village (from 618,000K). Chief tourism officer, Mr Khamphanh (☎ 020 2844 9939), can be contacted out of hours.

Situated on the opposite bank of the town's green bathing pond is **Wat Kaeo**, the local monastery.

Museum of Phongsaly Ethnic Groups

On the main street • Mon–Fri 8–11.30am & 1.30–4.30pm • 10,000K

Anyone interested in seeing what Phongsali's ethnic groups dressed like before the influx of cheap Western-style clothing from China should pay a visit to the excellent **Museum of Phongsaly Ethnic Groups**. This three-room display of tribal costumes and artefacts is brought to life by detailed explanations in English. Most fascinating is the second room, which covers talismans, divinity and birth and death rites, with a table piled high with food and cigarettes to illustrate the *basi* (see box, p.285).

Phou Fa hill

Daily 7.30am–5.30pm • Summit entrance charge 5000K • The access path is a 5min walk from the big roundabout at the entrance to town, just past the *Daopufor* Restaurant

It's worth making the stiff, but not unpleasant, walk up the forested hillside of **Phou Fa** hill, the top of which is crowned by a modern stupa and offers excellent views over the town and surrounding countryside on a clear day. A picnic stop halfway up makes a good lunch spot. As an alternative to the eight-hundred-odd steps, you can descend along the bike track that starts just beyond the TV tower at the summit.

Ban Komaen

Boun Neua road • Day-trips (6hr of walking) can be arranged with the tourist office or Amazing Lao Travel (from 154,000K, including lunch and guide)

One of the most popular day hikes from Phongsali is to **Ban Komaen**, the so-called four-hundred-year-old tea plantation, high up in the hills around 15km from town.

The tea trees here, some of which reach 6m, are said to be some of the oldest in the world. In season, the leaves are picked high on the trees by Phu Noi women, and then packed into bamboo cylinders and sold in cigar-shaped tubes.

ARRIVAL AND DEPARTURE

By plane Lao Skyway runs a twice-weekly service (Tues & Sat; 1hr 40min) from Vientiane to Boun Neua airport, 41km west of Phongsali. Tickets (one million kip) can be bought from the airline office in the *Viphaphone* guesthouse (☎ 088 210999), or online, and cover transfer from Phongsali to the airport.

By sawngthaew Sawngthaews from Hat Sa stop at the small Hat Sa bus stop just under 1km east of town, from where it's an easy downhill walk to the centre; alternatively, sawngthaews charge 7000K from here to the tuk-tuk stand in the centre, or 10,000K to drop off at one of the guesthouses. Moving on, a sawngthaew departs from the Hat Sa bus stop at 8am (get there by 7.30am) for the boat departure from Hat Sa, which usually leaves once the sawngthaew arrives. Note that if there aren't enough passengers at Hat Sa, your only option will be to charter a boat or try again the next day.

By bus Buses from Oudomxai arrive at the Oudomxai bus station, 3km west of town, from where you can get a sawngthaew to the turning for the tourist office in the centre (7000K). Leaving Phongsali, sawngthaews set off

PHONGSALI AND AROUND

from the same point at 7am for the Oudomxai bus station for the 8am departure to Oudomxai (7–8hr). The fastest bus to Vientiane is the 2pm VIP service, though cheaper, slower buses also leave at 8.15am and 11am.

To China It's currently a two-day trip to China via the Lan Tui–Meng Kang border checkpoint, newly accessible to foreigners, right at the far northern tip of Laos. Take the 9am bus to Ou Tai (via Boun Neua, see opposite; 5–6hr), where you'll need to stay overnight – there are a few simple guesthouses – and then the 9am bus the following day direct to Jiangcheng (4–5hr), the first major town into China, 33km north of Lan Tui. The mountainous road is narrow and tough going and may be impassable in the rains, though it's due to be widened and paved by 2017, which should make the journey possible in a day. From Jiangcheng, you can arrange onward transport to Pu'er and Kunming.

Destinations Boun Neua (3–4 daily; 1hr 30min); Boun Tai (daily; 3hr); Hat Sa (daily; 1hr); Muang Khoua (daily; 7hr); Oudomxai (daily; 7–8hr); Ou Tai (daily; 5–6hr); Vientiane (3 daily; 25–27hr).

INFORMATION

Tourist office The helpful tourist office (Mon–Fri 8–11.30am & 1.30–4.30pm; ☎ 088 210098, ⓦ phongsaly .net) is situated just south of the main road. They can

provide good information about the town and transport options, as well as a useful map, and offer a range of treks and tours (see box, p.177).

ACCOMMODATION

Accommodation in Phongsali caters mostly to Chinese workers; standards of upkeep are low and prices high for what you get. Be warned that you're likely to be woken up by the government announcements broadcast on loudspeakers around town first thing. All the hotels and guesthouses have free wi-fi.

Phongsaly Hotel In the centre of town ☎ 088 210042. A rather soulless Chinese hotel, but well situated in the centre of town, with large rooms with flatscreen TVs and decent bathrooms. **100,000K**

Phou Fa Hotel A 5min walk (signposted) from the main roundabout on the way into town ☎ 088 210031, ✉ phoufahotel@gmail.com. Situated on a hill with great views over the town, this is regarded as Phongsali's most upmarket place to stay – not that there's much competition. The initial impression of its institutional exterior isn't great (it's been compared to an abandoned gulag), but the rooms at the far end of the complex, which are set around a sweet garden, are nice enough, with gold bedspreads, decorated

headboards, TV and hot showers; some bathrooms are let down by poor plumbing, however. **200,000K**

Pinekham Douangnal Just along the lane from the tourist office ☎ 020 299 9924. Phongsali's newest guesthouse, occupying a fetching mauve-coloured building, is one of the best options. Pleasant tile-floored rooms have big beds and decent bathrooms. **80,000K**

Viphaphone In the centre of town ☎ 088 210999. New flooring has brightened up the largish rooms at this rather characterless three-storey hotel, and the mattresses are better than some in town. The best rooms are those at the back, with views of the mountains. **80,000K**

EATING

Most of the **restaurants** in Phongsali are Chinese, where dishes are served in large portions intended for sharing – eat out in a group if you can. As usual, you can get bowls of *fŏe* in the market, tucked away off the main street.

PHOU DEN DIN NBCA

Phou Den Din is Laos's northernmost NBCA and runs along the Vietnamese border for over 100km. The scenery here is rugged and mountainous, rising up to the peaks in the Phou Den Din range, which reach heights of over 1800m and form the border with Vietnam. The 2220-square-kilometre park is said to contain Asian elephants and Asiatic black bears as well as, possibly, leopards and tigers. This is one of Laos's most inaccessible NBCAs, though it can be reached by boat up the Nam Ou, or on foot. Your best option is to speak to the tourist office or Amazing Lao Travel in Phongsali for up-to-date information.

★**Laoper** Just north of the central tuk-tuk stand ☎ 020 5548 1444. Without doubt this simple family-run restaurant offers the best cooking in Phongsali. There's no menu – just point at whatever ingredients in the kitchen take your fancy (or make the appropriate animal noises), and trust them to cook up a Yunnan-style feast. Mains 30,000–35,000K. Daily 5–9.30pm.

Nangsone Just east of Phongsaly Hotel. With its gingham tablecloths and pot plants, this cute little café is the only place geared towards Western tourists, and the best option for a sit-down breakfast. Apple or banana pancakes are excellent (20,000K), and big bowls of fried rice go from 20,000K. Daily 6am–9pm.

Phongsaly Hotel In the centre of town ☎ 088 210042.

The large, impersonal restaurant on the ground floor of this hotel has a rather mysterious Chinese menu that includes psychedelic-sounding dishes such as "wool blood flourishing" and "sauce detonation eggplant". For the less adventurous, there are plenty of other options, including plain old "bad pepper fried beef" (30,000K). Huge portions. Daily 6.30am–9.30pm.

Yeehua Near the market ☎ 088 210186. Attached to Phongsali's cheapest guesthouse, this no-frills but very friendly restaurant may be the only place in town serving Lao dishes – the pork larp (35,000K) is very tasty, but watch out for the chillies. Daily 6.30am–9.30pm.

Phongsali to Oudomxai

The road between Phongsali and Oudomxai has improved in recent years, though sections of the eight-hour journey are still bone-shaking. They're mitigated by the stunning scenery, however, and on the way you stop at a couple of small towns – **Boun Neua** and **Boun Tai** – which can be used as alternative trekking bases to Phongsali.

This road passes through some prime **Akha territory**, and the tribal women use the thoroughfare to hike between villages and conduct trade. A few of the villages actually straddle the road and afford fleeting snapshots of Akha life: women displaying glittering headdresses and betel-stained smiles, men shouldering long-barrelled muskets, and gaggles of gaping kids clad only in a layer of ochre-coloured dust. You may find that your bus driver stops to buy (or for his passengers to buy) various furry mammals (such as civet cats, bamboo rats and porcupines), which are hung up like prizes at the side of the road, and generally bought to be eaten. It may not be particularly appetizing to the Western eye (or, indeed, legal) but it's a fascinating glimpse of rural life that you don't necessarily experience elsewhere in the country.

The northern taste for exotic wild meats reaches its zenith at **Pak Nam Noi**, a tiny crossroads village, 136km south of Phongsali, but just 33km west of Muang Khoua (see p.173); twice a month (around the full- and half-moons) it hosts a special morning market, which you should avoid if you're prone to squeamishness. South of Pak Nam Noi, the road follows the forested valley of the Nam Phak river through mainly **Khmu** villages to beautiful Muang La, 28km north of Oudomxai (see p.184).

Boun Neua

With Phongsali town hemmed in by mountains with limited scope for expansion, small, unlovely **BOUN NEUA**, 41km west, is the unlikely new recipient of provincial capital status. The principally Tai Leu town sits crucially close to the Chinese border and is developing as a hub, with Phongsali's airport (see p.178) and links to China north via Ou Tai (see p.178) and southwest via Ban Yo and Pakha, though the latter crossing is not open to foreigners. It's principally of interest, however, for its trekking possibilities, visiting Akha and Phu Noi villages, which can be organized with the local tourist office.

Boun Tai

Around 90km south of Phongsali, midway towards Oudomxai, the large, spread-out village of **Boun Tai** is populated by lowland Lao and often frequented by the inhabitants of nearby Akha villages. Treks can be organized here visiting a remarkable array of remote Akha groups, including Eupa and Mouchi. Buses stop on the site of a ruined **French fortress**, a short walk north of the village **market**, best known for its finely attired Tai Dam ladies (who prefer not to be photographed).

ARRIVAL AND INFORMATION

By bus The daily (8am) Phongsali–Oudomxai bus passes through Boun Neua (1hr 30min), Boun Tai (3hr 30min) and Pak Nam Noi (5hr 30min); Phongsali–Boun Neua services are more frequent. There are two early morning services from Boun Neua to Ou Tai. At Pak Nam Noi, you can pick up buses originating in Oudomxai bound for Muang Khoua (3 daily; 1hr) and Vietnam (daily; 5hr).

PHONGSALI TO OUDOMXAI

Tourist offices There are helpful tourist offices at Boun Neua (☎ 020 5670 0526) and Boun Tai (☎ 020 5592 4442, ⌨ bountaitrekking.com), each located at the town's bus station, though they're not always staffed when they should be (Mon–Fri 8–11.30am & 1.30–4.30pm). It's well worth ringing in advance (these mobile numbers can be called out of hours) for advice on trekking and exploring local villages.

ACCOMMODATION

BOUN NEUA

Hao Xayalath 1km north along the Ou Tai road from the bus station ☎ 020 5519 4166. Though there's a basic guesthouse in the bus station compound, this new villa on the edge of town is the nicest place to stay, with broad staircases and airy corridors. The cheaper rooms upstairs are the best deal, though all are clean and en-suite, with hot showers. **60,000K**

BOUN TAI

Hongthong Hotel 700m along the track opposite the bus station ☎ 020 2239 8753. Rather grand, attractive

pink hotel on the edge of the village. All the rooms have high ceilings and hot showers; VIP rooms are the most salubrious, big and carpeted, if slightly musty (120,000K). The restaurant serves decent Lao food. **60,000K**

PAK NAM NOI

Sinsai By the Namnoy Bridge ☎ 030 996 9344. Simple, friendly guesthouse in a pink block near the bus stop – handy for the morning market, just across the bridge. Small rooms have cold showers but some have wonderful views over the Namnoy River. **50,000K**

Oudomxai and around

Any prolonged travel in the north will eventually involve a stop at the large, bustling town of **OUDOMXAI**, an important transport hub at the junction of routes 2 and 13. Fast developing as the economic centre for the north, with Chinese making up twenty percent of the population, the town has an energy about it that you don't often find in Laos – the giant TV screens and interminable traffic in the centre come as quite a change of scene after the sleepy settlements further north. Most travellers treat Oudomxai as a stopover, but there's enough in and around the town to warrant hanging around for a day or two.

There are two hills in the centre of town, either side of the main road. The museum atop Phu Sai, to the east, isn't worth the entry fee, but there are good views out across town at the top of the steps. **Wat Phu That**, west of the main road, is crowned by a golden stupa, behind which a giant Buddha statue casts a serene eye across the surrounding hills.

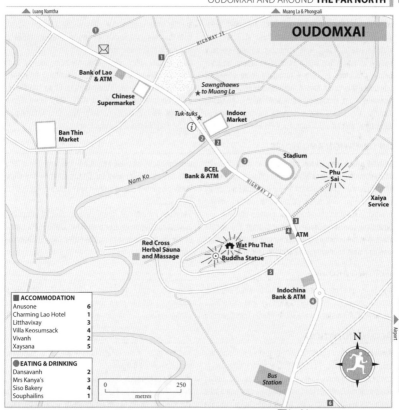

Ban Thin Market

Daily 7am–6pm • 1.5km northwest of the bus station; cross the river and turn left at the big Chinese supermarket

Not for the faint of heart, Oudomxai's **fresh market** represents a fascinating slice of local life. Behind the trestle tables bursting with fresh fruit and veg, the chaotic meat and fish market displays a stomach-turning spread of Lao delicacies – legal and illegal – from wobbly slabs of blood cake to a post-apocalyptic collection of shrivelled, dried and smoked wildlife.

Red Cross Herbal Sauna and Massage

Daily 2–7.30pm • Massage 40,000K/hr, sauna 12,000K • ☎ 081 312391 • Turn left off the main road, 700m north of the bus station – follow the signs

One of the best ways to spend your time in Oudomxai is with a visit to the **Red Cross Herbal Sauna and Massage** – the perfect way to relax after a bone-numbing bus journey. The money goes towards supporting the Red Cross's work in helping and educating local people.

ARRIVAL AND DEPARTURE   OUDOMXAI AND AROUND

By air Flights are operated between Vientiane and Oudomxai (50min) daily by Lao Airlines and twice weekly by Lao Skyway. The airport is 1km southeast of town; tuk-tuks will run into the centre (10,000K), though you could easily walk. There's a Lao Airlines agency at *Litthavixay* guesthouse.
By bus Oudomxai's bus station is situated a 15min walk southeast of the town centre. Walk north (left) out of the bus station to find most of the town's hotels and

guesthouses. The town has excellent transport links, including daily direct services to both China (via Boten) and Vietnam (via Tay Trang). Note that buses can often get very busy – aim to arrive at the bus station around an hour before departure as they occasionally leave ahead of schedule if they're full. Most departures take place between 8am and 10am, though for some destinations, like Luang Namtha and Luang Prabang, there are also afternoon departures around 2.30/3pm; for Vientiane, the best bet are the more comfortable VIP services (2pm and 4pm). Note that Houayxai usually appears on schedules as Bokeo (the name of the province).

Destinations Dien Bien Phu, Vietnam (daily; 7hr); Houayxai (Bokeo; daily; 7hr); Luang Namtha (3 daily; 4hr); Luang Prabang (3 daily; 5hr); Mengla, China (via Boten, daily; 6hr); Muang Khoua (3 daily; 4hr); Nong Khiaw (1 daily; 4hr); Pakbeng (2 daily; 3hr 30min); Phongsali (daily; 8hr); Vientiane (4 daily; 15hr).

INFORMATION AND TOURS

Tourist office The well-run, helpful tourist office (Mon–Fri 8am–noon & 2–5pm; ☎ 081 212483, ⓦ oudomxay.info) is situated on the northern side of the river, opposite the indoor market, and has a selection of printed matter on the town and province, plus information on transport connections.

Tours The tourist office runs a range of tours and one- to three-day treks, including a walking tour of the town and one-day visits to nearby Akha villages. One of the natural highlights of Oudomxai province is the huge Chom Ong cave system, 45km west of Oudomxai; two-day trips, involving some trekking and a stay at a Khmu village, start from 350,000K.

Services For internet, there are a number of computers available at *Litthavixay* (see below) for 8000K/hr. For a dose of free wi-fi, your best bet is the coffee shop at *Charming Lao Hotel*.

GETTING AROUND

By bike and motorbike Road bikes (30,000K/day), decent mountain bikes (60,000K/day) and motorbikes (Chinese 80,000K/day, Honda 100,000K/day) can be rented from Xaiya Service (daily 8am–7.30pm; ☎ 020 9959 5995), 300m east off the main road (turn right just south of *Litthavixay*).

ACCOMMODATION

Anusone Down a small side street just across from the bus station ☎ 030 513 0777. The rooms here are in concrete bungalows, set around a pleasant family compound off the main road. Though quite dark and a little worn around the edges, it's not a bad choice if you're making an early start in the morning. Hot water costs 20,000K extra. 50,000K

Charming Lao Hotel Highway 2, just off the main road through town ☎ 081 212881, ⓦ charminglaohotel .com. Opened in 2012, Oudomxai's plushest spot overlooks an attractive park at the top end of the town. Big, carpeted rooms come with comfy mattresses, wood furniture and flatscreen tellies; if they're a little functional for the price, stone-floored bathrooms add a bit of interest. There's also a spa, coffee shop and pleasant restaurant, serving mainly Lao food (7–10pm). $50

Litthavixay Main road, 500m north of the bus station ☎ 081 212175, ⓔ litthavixay@yahoo.com. Arguably the best deal in town, with bright, very clean rooms, all with TV and en suite. Internet access is available in the large reception area. 80,000K

Villa Keosumsack Opposite Litthavixay Guesthouse, main road ☎ 081 312170, ⓔ seumsack@hotmail.com. The spacious rooms in this rather ornate wooden building, set a little back off the main drag, have a touch of class about them, with colourful fabric bed runners and timber floors. An open terrace at the front is a nice vantage-point from which to survey the street's goings-on. 160,000K

Vivanh Just south of the bridge, 900m north of the bus station ☎ 081 212219. A really sweet little guesthouse offering big, sparkling rooms with TV and brightly coloured bedspreads; the female staff are very welcoming and friendly. 60,000K

Xaysana Left off the main road, 400m north of the bus station ☎ 020 251 5737. An attractive, scrupulously well-maintained hotel on a quiet street behind Wat Phu That. The big, bright rooms, up a rather grand wooden staircase, have high ceilings and pretty curtains. Excellent value. 80,000K

EATING AND DRINKING

There are lots of places to eat on the main road, including a number of Chinese restaurants and the usual *fõe* places around the bus station. For **breakfast**, the bus station is the best option, with women selling baguettes, *khào lãm* and bags of fruit.

Dansavanh Next to the tourist office ☎ 081 212696. The riverside terrace of this weird, mausoleum-like Chinese hotel – formerly the town's poshest – is the most picturesque place for a Beerlao (though that's not saying much). Daily 3–11pm.

Mrs Kanya's Right off the main road, 800m north of the

bus station ☎ 020 5568 1110. Locals swear this big, bustling restaurant is Oudomxai's top choice for authentic Lao food. Grab a seat at one of the shared tables and choose one of the wonderfully sour soups (30,000K) and *larp* (50,000K), though bear in mind that anything with beef is likely to come with big slabs of tripe. Huge portions. Daily 6am–10pm.

Siso Bakery *Main road, 300m north of the bus station* ☎ 020 2822 2298. This sweet little shop is a good place to stop for breakfast or lunch on your way to or from the bus station, with fresh brioches and baguettes from 12,000K. Daily 7am–7pm.

Souphailins Just off the main road, 400m north of the tourist office (past the post office) ☎ 020 606 2474. Half concealed behind thick vegetation, this gorgeous little palm-thatch restaurant feels like it's been transported from the hills, a world away from the busy Oudomxai traffic. The *falang*-friendly northern Lao menu encompasses Western breakfasts and a good selection of vegetarian dishes, though the food can be bland unless you ask for spice. Fried chicken with cashew nuts 30,000K. Daily 6am–9pm.

Muang La

Picturesquely set amid lush paddies on the banks of the Nam Phak River, the tranquil, predominantly Tai Leu village of **Muang La** is famous for its sacred Pha Singkham Buddha, and makes an attractive day-trip from Oudomxai, or – with some superb accommodation – an alternative base. The village is also renowned for **hot springs**, which retain a constant 43°C and bubble up at various points alongside the river. The most popular bathing spot for locals is the stone-walled pool by *Muang La Resort's* wooden suspension bridge, though for more privacy try the indoor or outdoor baths at *Hotel Lhakham*.

Pha Singkham Temple

5000K

Situated on a low hill near *Muang La Resort*, the modern **Pha Singkham Temple** is home to one of the most venerated and potent Buddha images in Laos. Its story is a fascinating one of Tolkienesque proportions, the ancient Buddha – according to legend, one of the five originals cast in Sri Lanka – having survived numerous misadventures, from being sunk during a river battle at nearby Pak Nam Noi to narrowly avoiding destruction during the Indochinese War (luckily, the statue had been stashed in a nearby cave). The Buddha's special gift is one of wish fulfillment: simply ask the statue what you desire and your wish will be granted – though if it does, woe betide you if you fail to return within a year to make a contribution to the temple.

ARRIVAL AND DEPARTURE   MUANG LA

By sawngthaew Sawngthaews for Muang La depart at 8am from Oudomxai's sawngthaew stand, just north of the river, returning at around 4pm (50min).

By tuk-tuk Tuk-tuks leave on demand from the tuk-tuk stand, near the indoor market (if you arrive about 9–10am you should find one to share).

INFORMATION AND TOURS

Tourist office The tourist office is in the bus station (Mon–Fri 8–11.30am & 1.30–4.30pm; ☎ 030 928 3726, ⓦ oudomxay.info).

Tours Oudomxai's tourist office runs full- and half-day tours to Muang La, visiting the temple and springs (half-day from 125,000K/person, including transport and lunch).

ACCOMMODATION AND EATING

★**Hotel Lhakam** *1km from the bus station* ☎ 020 5884 1561, ✉ lhakhamhotel@gmail.com. The budget alternative to the *Muang La Resort* is superb value, boasting spacious, high-ceilinged rooms with balconies above the rushing waters of the Nam Phak. As well as a riverside terrace restaurant, the hotel has its own hot baths, which are open to guests and non-guests alike (daily 4–9pm; 25,000K; reserve in advance). Breakfast included. **125,000K**

★**Muang La Resort** *500m from the bus station*

☎ 021 243446, ⓦ muangla.com. Set in lush tropical gardens in a peerless position by the river, this blissful retreat is one of the most luxurious places to stay in northern Laos. The huge, naga-themed suites, in half-timbered villas, are exquisitely furnished and feature acres of polished wood. Guests can soak up the river views from private hot tubs, drawn from the local springs and raised off the ground. Most visitors stay as part of a two- or three-night package, which includes a choice of well-thought-out activities and trips. **$331**

Luang Namtha and around

Surrounded by forested hills that remain lush even when the rest of the countryside is a dusty brown in the hot season, **LUANG NAMTHA** is the north's most touristy town, though it still has a quiet local charm. The town is a popular base from which to access beautiful **Nam Ha NBCA** (see box, p.187), with a whole range of activities available, from rafting and kayaking on the Nam Tha River to trekking to hill-tribe villages.

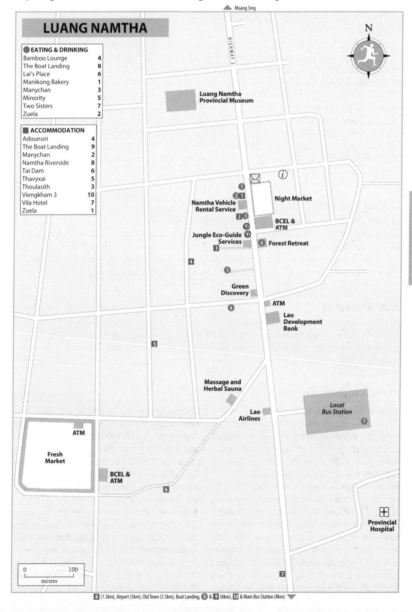

LUANG NAMTHA

Muang Sing

HIGHWAY 3

● EATING & DRINKING
Bamboo Lounge	4
The Boat Landing	8
Lai's Place	6
Manikong Bakery	1
Manychan	3
Minority	5
Two Sisters	7
Zuela	2

■ ACCOMMODATION
Adounsiri	4
The Boat Landing	9
Manychan	2
Namtha Riverside	8
Tai Dam	6
Thavyxai	5
Thoulasith	3
Viengkham 3	10
Vila Hotel	7
Zuela	1

N

Luang Namtha
Provincial Museum

Night Market

Namtha Vehicle
Rental Service

BCEL &
ATM

Jungle Eco-Guide
Services

Forest Retreat

Green
Discovery

ATM

Lao
Development
Bank

Massage and
Herbal Sauna

Local
Bus Station

Lao
Airlines

ATM

Fresh
Market

BCEL &
ATM

Provincial
Hospital

0   100
metres

8 (1.5km), Airport (5km), Old Town (5.5km), Boat Landing, 8 & 9 (6km), 10 & Main Bus Station (8km)

4

BIKE RIDES FROM LUANG NAMTHA

The best way to spend a day in Luang Namtha is to rent a mountain bike and explore the local area – the map usually provided with rental bikes details some good routes, or download the Luang Namtha area map from ⊕hobomaps.com. One of the best routes (around 20km in total) takes you south through the old town to *The Boat Landing* (a good stop for lunch), from where you head east across the Nam Tha into the Black Tai villages of **Ban Pasak**, **Ban Pong** and **Ban Tongkwa**, following dusty streets through paddy fields. The last stretch is on a generally very quiet main road, which loops past a few more villages before taking you back to the town.

Pancake flat, Luang Namtha stretches for over 10km along Highway 3. Most of the tourist services are situated at the top end of town, 7km north of the **old town** – exploring the latter gives an idea of what Luang Namtha was like before the advent of tourism. It's a great place in which to rent a bicycle or motorbike – just a few kilometres' ride will take you into small traditional dusty-street villages, surrounded by rice paddies and grazing buffalo.

Luang Namtha was heavily contested during Laos's civil war and was razed to the ground. Once the fighting stopped, the surrounding hills were stripped of their trees and the mammoth logs were trucked away to China. Today, the once devastated and depopulated valley is thriving again, and from the lush surroundings you'd be hard-pressed to believe how recently it had taken place.

Luang Namtha Provincial Museum

Highway 3, two blocks north of the tourist office • Mon–Fri 8.30am–5pm • 5000K

In the town itself, the only formal attraction is the **Luang Namtha Provincial Museum**, housed in the grand Lao–Vietnam Friendship Centre. You'll find displays of traditional hill-tribe costumes and artefacts, bronze drums, a model depicting battles that took place in the area during the civil war and a rusty collection of weaponry.

Night market

Opposite Manychan on the main street • Daily 5–10pm

Luang Namtha's **night market** is a little disappointing, though it's a good choice for a cheap dinner (see p.188) and is a popular evening hangout for tourists. The main bulk is made up of a rather tacky mix of clothes, houseware and pirate DVDs aimed largely at a local crowd.

ARRIVAL AND DEPARTURE

LUANG NAMTHA

By air The airport is close to the old town, about 6km south of the main town; expect to pay around 10,000K per person in a shared tuk-tuk. There are five flights a week from Vientiane (1hr), three with Lao Airlines and two with Lao Skyway. Lao Airlines (⊕ 086 212072) has an office on the main street, just south of the main concentration of guesthouses.

By bus The main bus station is situated 11km south of the new town; a shared tuk-tuk to the centre should cost 10,000K. Buses from within the province, including Muang Sing and Muang Long, as well as from Boten, on the Chinese border, arrive at the local bus station, just south of the centre, from where it's a short walk to most guesthouses. Tickets for all buses can be bought directly at the bus station or, for a surcharge of around 20,000K, from travel agents and guesthouses; the price includes transfer to the bus station.

To China The easiest way for travellers with a valid visa to cross into China is to take the 8am direct bus all the way to Jinghong (8hr), via Mengla (5hr), from the main bus station. Services also run throughout the morning (every 90min from 8.30am) from the local bus station to the Boten–Mon Han border crossing (open daily 7am–4pm), but you'll need to change buses here and at Mengla to reach Jinghong this way.

Destinations from main bus station Dien Bien Phu, Vietnam (daily; 11hr); Houayxai (Bokeo; 2 daily; 4hr); Jinghong, China (daily; 8hr); Luang Prabang (daily; 9hr); Oudomxai (3 daily; 4–5hr); Vang Vieng (daily; 14hr); Vientiane (2 daily; 19hr).

Destinations from local bus station Boten, China (6 daily; 2hr); Muang Long (daily; 4hr); Muang Sing (5–6 daily; 2hr); Nalae (2 daily; 3hr).

By boat The Nam Tha is navigable from Luang Namtha all the way downriver to Houayxai from about July until November or December. Passenger boats no longer travel this route, so you'll need to charter your own. The most convenient option is to speak to one of the better tour operators in town, such as Green Discovery (see below), which offers packages starting at $122 per person (based on six or more people travelling), or one million kip for the whole boat. You may get a slightly better price if you charter a boat outright directly with a boatman; the boat landing is behind *The Boat Landing* guesthouse, about 6km south of the new town (see p.188). The journey takes two days, overnighting in Ban Khonkham at the boatman's house. Note that the boats travelling on this route have no roof, so be prepared to get a little wet. In the dry season (roughly January to June), the Nam Tha is unnavigable from Luang Namtha, and trips start downstream at Nalae, 70km south (3hr by road). Buses run to Nalae (en route to Vieng Phouka), but your best bet is still to speak to someone at Green Discovery to arrange boat transport.

INFORMATION

Tourist office The tourist office (Mon–Fri 8–11.30am & 1.30–4pm; ☎ 086 211534, ⓦ luangnamtha-tourism -laos.org) is situated one street east of the main road, behind the night market. As well as organizing treks and tours they can provide information on self-guided walking and cycling trips from town, plus bus and air timetables.

Online Forest Retreat (see below) runs a useful website and blog about the town and environs (ⓦ luang namthaguide.com).

GETTING AROUND

By tuk-tuk Most tourists stick to the new town, where most of the tourist accommodation is found. Should you want to go further afield, there're always a number of tuk-tuks hanging around on the main road.

By bike and motorbike Many of the guesthouses and several rental shops on the main street rent out bicycles and motorbikes, including Namtha Vehicle Rental Service, just north of *Manychan* (local bike 10,000K; mountain bike 15,000K; 125cc motorbike 40,000–60,000K).

TOURS AND ACTIVITIES

Though Luang Namtha has a few cowboys, there are some excellent outfits (all operating from offices on the main strip) running reliably well-organized and ethical treks, which benefit the local villagers, as well as tourists. Not all the trips leave daily, and you'll probably find that your choice is limited by those that have already been signed up for by other travellers – be sure to arrange one as soon as you arrive or, better still, book in advance. Note that for all treks and activities, the price you pay is dependent on the number of people on it, and you should make sure that if you're visiting a local village, a percentage of the money you pay goes towards supporting the community.

Forest Retreat ☎ 020 5568 0031, ⓦ forestretreatlaos .com. Since opening in 2011, this Kiwi-run operator has established a strong reputation for its huge range of trips and activities, from cookery courses to "cultural immersion", plus plenty of rafting, kayaking, biking and "multisport" options. They're very strong on ecotourism and run various interesting projects benefiting local communities.

★ **Green Discovery** ☎ 086 211484, ⓦ greendiscovery laos.com. Generally agreed to be the best-set-up operation in town (and also the priciest), offering an

NAM HA NBCA

Established in 1993, the **Nam Ha NBCA** is one of Laos's most convenient conservation areas, easily accessible from Luang Namtha. Covering 2224 square kilometres contiguous with the Xieng Yong Protected Area in Yunnan, China, the park straddles two high mountain chains and boasts two peaks in excess of 2000m. The NBCA is an important biological habitat for many forest creatures, including 33 species of mammals and 288 species of birds. However, it's unlikely you'll see much in the way of wildlife on a trek into the park – though the forest teems with birdsong. The best known of the park's rivers are the **Nam Ha** and the **Nam Tha**, both of which are developed for kayaking and rafting trips, though the latter is possible only for a few months of the year in wet season.

Within the NBCA itself are some 25 **hill-tribe villages**, the most populous ethnic groups being Akha, Hmong, Khmu and Lantaen, and multi-day **trekking tours** between these settlements are also possible. Note that trekking in the NBCA must be booked through a licensed agent (see above).

excellent range of trips and treks, from a two-day kayaking adventure on the Nam Tha (from $69), to two-day mountain bike rides to Muang Sing (from $94) and overnight treks into Nam Ha NBCA, staying at hill-tribe villages (from $62/person in a group of eight up to $112 each for two). They are committed to low-impact, eco-conscious tourism, using local staff, and the office staff will help you choose the right trip for you.

★**Jungle Eco-Guide Services** ☎086 212025, ⓦthejungle-ecotour-laos.com. The best locally owned

outfit (and a little cheaper than some of the competition), with a network of nine well-maintained trails through the NBCA, plus kayaking and boating options on the Nam Tha River and more. Their tough but exhilarating three-day Jungle Camp Adventure Trek tramps through ninety-percent primary forest, rich in wildlife, with fishing and swimming stops en route (from $70). Other unusual treks include a two-day Lahu homestay and their Akha Camp trip, using the services of an Akha guide with a fine talent for mimicking birds (both from $44).

ACCOMMODATION

Luang Namtha has the best selection of **accommodation** north of Luang Prabang, and standards are generally very high. Most of the following are situated north of the local bus station in the new town. Note that many guesthouses get full by early evening, so it's worth booking ahead if you know you'll be arriving later in the day.

Adounsiri One street west of the main road ☎020 2299 1898. In a leafy plot on a side street parallel to the main road, this popular guesthouse has simple but very pleasant rooms, some of which are off a sweet communal terrace. 60,000K

★**The Boat Landing** 6km south of the centre ☎086 312398, ⓦtheboatlanding.com. This justifiably well-regarded eco-resort is excellent value, with utterly charming bamboo-thatch bungalows scattered among a flower- and butterfly-filled garden overlooking the Nam Tha river. The beautiful, peaceful location is the perfect base for exploring the area (Green Discovery tours can be booked here), though some may find it a bit too far from town. The on-site restaurant offers superlative local cuisine (see opposite). Rates include breakfast. $47

Manychan Opposite the night market ☎020 2292 7878. Situated in a tall building behind the restaurant of the same name (see opposite), the simple, tile-floored, en-suite rooms here are a popular choice, though they lack the character of *Thoulasith* or *Zuela* either side. 60,000K

Namtha Riverside Down a dirt track off the main road, 2km south of the centre ☎086 212025, ⓔinfo @thejungle-ecotour.com. Set in lush, well-tended gardens on the banks of the Nam Tha, these spacious bamboo-thatch huts are good value, with modern bathrooms (showers can be solar-powered when the weather's up to it) and a touch of style. Rates include breakfast and mountain-bike rental. $25

Tai Dam 200m east of the main market ☎020 2239 0552. A lovely, tranquil little place tucked down a dirt track west off the main drag, with rustic but sweet, round-roofed bungalows

overlooking paddy fields. No English spoken. 50,000K

★**Thavyxai** Two streets west of the main road ☎030 511 0292. In a giant-columned building with airy, high-ceilinged rooms, *Thavyxai* both looks and feels grander than its rates suggest. The terrace at the back is a lovely place to gaze over the rooftops and soak up the sun. Good English spoken and excellent value. 60,000K

★**Thoulasith** Main street ☎086 212166, ⓦthoulasith-guesthouse.com. Set just off the main street in a graceful building facing onto a garden, with large, bright rooms and arguably the best bathrooms in town. The pick of the bunch are the rooms upstairs, which face onto a lovely balcony. Luang Namtha's top budget choice. 80,000K

Viengkham 3 Opposite the main bus station, 11km south of the centre ☎020 2377 7100. Should you arrive late at night or be catching an early bus, the high-ceilinged rooms in this new salmon-pink block are a much nicer alternative to the bus station guesthouse. Surprisingly peaceful. 60,000K

Vila Hotel 400m south of the local bus station ☎086 312425, ⓦvilaguesthouse.com. A pleasant and relaxing mid-range place set in a leafy green compound and housing pretty, wooden rooms with more stylish bathrooms than most (though with rather hard beds). Staff are charming and there's a good restaurant on site. Popular with tour groups. 150,000K

Zuela Opposite the night market ☎020 5588 6694, ⓦzuela.asia. One of most comfortable places to stay in town, with large, brick-lined rooms in two gorgeous wooden buildings, set back from the main drag, and a pleasant restaurant. 80,000K

EATING AND DRINKING

During the day, the **fresh market** is a great place for a cheap bowl of *fŏe* and you can also buy small portions of *larp* and other dishes here. At night, the main street fills with the scent of grilled meat from the **night market** (see p.186) – there are a number of tables in the central compound where you can enjoy the food over a cold beer, and be sure to try the delicious sweet sticky rice with grated coconut for dessert.

★**Bamboo Lounge** Main street ☎020 5568 0031, ⊛forestretreatlaos.com. Attached to the Forest Retreat trekking office, this Kiwi-run, eco-themed bar–restaurant is always the busiest place on the strip. The genuine wood-fired pizzas (50,000–90,000K), baked in an oven out front, are an indulgent treat, and pastas, risottos, sandwiches and daily specials are also on offer. A good choice at either end of the day, with excellent coffee and cocktails (Lao daiquiri 15,000K). Daily 7am–11.30pm.

★**The Boat Landing** 6km south of the centre ☎086 312398, ⊛theboatlanding.com. The Boat Landing's rustic restaurant is a great place to sample quality Lao food, with plenty of jeows (dips) on offer, including a local speciality with sweet rattan (8000K). Try the tongue-tingling Akha ginger chicken soup with chilli, garlic, mint and shallots (38,000K), accompanied by one of their speciality fresh juices. During high season Green Discovery runs a nightly tuk-tuk to the restaurant from the centre of town – pop into the office for more details. Daily 7am–9pm.

Lai's Place Off the main street (no phone). This simple, Black Tai-run restaurant off the main drag is one of the best places in town for Lao food, the menu encompassing a good selection of jeows (served with sticky rice, from 15,000K) and a few dishes of tribal origin. The owner was trained in cooking some Western dishes up at Forest Retreat, and also turns out a mean burger (from 20,000K). Daily 7am–9pm.

★**Manikong Bakery** Opposite the night market ☎020 2235 4446. With its cute gingham tablecloths and friendly welcome, this efficient new bakery–café is a great breakfast choice, with fresh croissants and muffins, plus

sets from 35,000K. The ham, egg and cheese bagel (25,000K) will set you up for the day, and there are also the usual Asian and Western dishes for later on. Daily 6.30am–10pm.

Manychan Opposite the night market ☎020 2292 7878. A relaxed place, popular throughout the day, offering a good range of Lao food and some interesting French-influenced Western dishes such as steak with blue-cheese sauce (55,000K). The fruit shakes are particularly delicious (10,000K). Daily 6.30am–10.30pm.

Minority Down a small path off the main street ☎020 299 8224. A cute wooden restaurant, run by a Tai Dam family, who collect traditional recipes from different tribes in the region, including the Khmu and Akha. Some dishes are better than others, but all are interesting and worth a try. Rattan-shoot and banana-flower soup 25,000K. Daily 7am–10.30pm.

Two Sisters Local bus station ☎020 2239 2222. It may not be the most obvious location for a restaurant recommendation, but this sweet place, decorated with birds' nests, antlers and local basketry, is a good lunch stop, especially if you're hanging around for a bus. The beef noodle soup (10,000K) is lovely, and there's a good variety of other dishes including larp (40,000K). Daily 8am–11pm.

Zuela Opposite the night market ☎020 5588 6694. The restaurant attached to the guesthouse of the same name is a good choice for breakfast, serving a delicious muesli with loads of fresh fruit and yoghurt for 20,000K. There's the usual range of Western and local dishes on offer for lunch and dinner, and the courtyard is a lovely place to relax over a Beerlao. Daily 6.30am–10.30pm.

DIRECTORY

Internet There are various internet cafés on the main road, including Green Mountain and Smile Internet, which has Skype facilities (12,000K/hr). All the guesthouses have free wi-fi.

Massage and herbal sauna A number of places offer Lao sauna and massage, of which the best (unnamed but

signed "Herbal Sauna and Massage") is just west of the main street, down the lane leading to Tai Dam Guesthouse and the main market (☎020 5548 8077; daily 4–10pm; sauna 14,000K, massage 50,000K)

Post office Main street, just north of the night market (daily 8am–noon & 1–4pm).

Muang Sing

In the centre of a flat plain surrounded by high mountains, **MUANG SING** developed a low-key trekking scene in the 1990s and 2000s, providing a nice alternative to Luang Namtha, 60km southeast. In recent years, however, tourism has waned significantly as the surrounding land is increasingly given over to Chinese-run plantations, and local guesthouse owners realize in turn they can make more money renting out to seasonal workers than the occasional Western traveller. Nonetheless, with a handsome main street of wonky-balconied Tai Leu houses and a famous morning market, the town is still a pleasant base, though the choice of accommodation is limited.

Though Muang Sing is fairly spread out, most tourist facilities are clustered on the main road. You can explore the surrounding **countryside** and traditional villages on foot or by motorbike or bicycle. However, to get the most out of the area, join a

one- to three-day **trek** through the surrounding mountains to remote and unspoilt villages where life has barely changed in centuries (see box, p.191).

Lying within the boundaries of the region known as the Golden Triangle, Muang Sing has a long connection with **opium**. During the late French colonial era, the town became an important collection point and way-station for the French colonial government's opium monopoly, and even as late as the 1990s, opium dens reappeared for a while to cater to the brief tourist rush. As in Thailand, however, opium eradication programmes have had significant success, and opium production is now a fraction of what it was twenty years ago.

The morning market

Opposite the bus station in the northwest of town, about 700m north of the tourist office • Daily 6am–6pm

The principal sight in Muang Sing is its large **morning market**. Clustered around the gates you'll find women sat in neat rows selling mounds of fruit and vegetables, beyond which is the covered food market, a good spot to pick up snacks, such as melt-in-the-mouth fried bananas. The market is famous for its colourfully dressed vendors, though nowadays the locals are more likely to be wearing tracksuits and Nike knock-offs. A few tribal ladies sell textiles at the far end of the food market, though expect some hard selling, even if you're just looking. If you want to take a photo of a vendor, it's only polite to buy something first and ask permission. The market kicks off very early, just after sunrise, and though goods are on sale throughout the day, it's best to get there before 10am in order to see the best of it.

The Tribal Museum

On the main road, north of the tourist office • Mon–Fri 8–11.30am & 1.30–4pm • 5000K, Akha film 5000K

Occupying a simple but elegant wooden building on the main road, the **Tribal Museum** has a well-explained collection of tribal costumes, plus local textiles, basketware and (upstairs) a few desultory Buddhas. For an extra fee, you can watch a documentary on the Akha's role in opium cultivation, and how they've adjusted to life without it.

Wat Sing Jai

Next to the Tribal Museum, on the main road

The town's principal temple is the brightly restored **Wat Sing Jai**, which has a wonderfully rustic *sim* painted in festive hues and festooned with long, colourful prayer flags. If you come in the morning there's usually a lot of activity, mostly the village ladies coming to pray and make offerings – at other times, the temple is often locked.

ARRIVAL AND DEPARTURE   MUANG SING

By bus The bus station is in the northwest of town opposite the morning market, though you should be able to ask your bus driver to let you off on the main road. From the bus station, it's just a 5min walk to the main road – turn left out of the compound, then left again at the first major intersection; this will eventually bring you onto the main road, next to the Tribal Museum. Alternatively, shared tuk-tuks charge 10,000K to the guesthouses (minimum 30,000K).

Destinations Luang Namtha (6 daily; 2hr); Muang Long (4 daily; 2hr).

INFORMATION

Tourist office The Muang Sing Tourism Office (Mon–Fri 8–11.30am & 1.30–4.30pm; ☎ 086 213021) can issue you with a useful map of the town, and carries some informative printed leaflets, but is largely concerned with booking people on tours and treks (see box below).

Chief tourism officer Mr Xaiyaseng can be contacted on ☎ 020 5578 6824) out of hours.
Internet Internet access is available at the tourist office (10,000K/hr).

GETTING AROUND

By bike and motorbike The Biking Man (☎ 030 526 4881, ✉ tigermantrek@gmail.com) is a small agency opposite the tourist office which has a few local bikes (20,000K – but not much use unless you don't plan to leave town), mountain bikes (50,000K) and motorbikes (80,000K) for rent.

ACCOMMODATION AND EATING

Muang Sing's **guesthouses** were in a state of flux at the time of writing, with several having recently shut and others block-booked to Chinese workers. The choice of places to eat is far from overwhelming, though there are a couple of simple noodle places on the main street. During the day, your best bet is at the **morning market**, where you can get decent bowls of *fŏe* and stock up on snacks for bus journeys. An unsuccessful attempt to copy the project in Luang Namtha, the

---

TREKKING AND BIKING FROM MUANG SING

The flat, triangular plain in which Muang Sing is located is watered by the Nam Youan River, which flows down from China, along with numerous other streams. Scores of **hill-tribe settlements** are located in the valley basin and all through the surrounding mountains; ethnic groups in the region include Tai Leu, Tai Dam, Akha, Mien, Hmong and others.

There are several reliable agencies in town, offering a range of **treks** in the area, plus one- and two-day **biking** trips on the flat valley roads. As ever, you will probably find that what trip you do is dependent on what other people are signed up for, and prices vary according to the number of people – if you can get a group of four or more together in advance your options will be greater.

TOUR OPERATORS
The Akha Experience Next to the tourist office ☎ 020 5535 3318, ✉ akhaexp@gmail.com. Newly set up by former Exotissimo guide Xay, this small agency offers a well-thought-out, activity-filled three-day trek, staying in local Akha villages (from $108/person).
Muang Sing Tourism Office (see above). Trips include a two-day trek, staying a night in an Akha village, costing 380,000–600,000K, plus a one-day trip to Xieng Kok (from 200,000K).

Phou Iu Travel Phou Iu II Guesthouse ☎ 020 2239 0195, ⊚ phouiu-ecotourism-laos.com. The best established of the local tour operators, with a fine range of treks, of one (from 170,000K) to three days' (from 620,000K) duration, and bike tours, including a one-day, 30km ride to visit several ethnic tribes (from 280,000K). Their moderately challenging two-day "Old Falang's Trail" trek (from 450,000K) climbs through forested mountains in the Nam Ha NBCA, ending in Luang Namtha.

moribund **night market** (daily 5–10pm) in the centre of town occupies a far bigger plot than it requires (the site of the original fresh market), but is useful for its small collection of grilled meat, noodle and drinks stalls.

Adima 8km north of town, on the road to the Chinese frontier ☎ 020 5519 7768, ⊛ adima-guesthouse.com. The nicest place to stay around Muang Sing, with big, brick A-frame bungalows in a gorgeous setting overlooking paddy fields. The grass-roofed restaurant makes an ideal lunchtime destination on a bike ride, but book ahead. There are Akha and Yao villages nearby, accessible on (self-guided) walks. **60,000K**

Chanthimmeng East of the main road ☎ 030 511 0834. A smart, modern guesthouse, with cool, high-ceilinged rooms and hot showers that are actually hot. Ask for a room that looks out over the paddy fields at the back. If open, its rustic pavilion restaurant is a lovely place to soak up the views with a Beerlao. **70,000K**

Phou Iu II Down a dirt track, west off the main road ☎ 020 5598 5557, ⊛ muangsingtravel.com. Muang Sing's most upmarket accommodation, with a variety of bamboo-thatch bungalows set around a delightful garden compound, though they're pricey for what you get. The cheapest have hard beds and concrete pillows; much more comfy are the brighter, carpeted mid-range rooms ($31). The $56 bungalows are incredibly overpriced. Treks can be booked at the agency here (see box, p.191), and there's a restaurant and bikes for rent. **140,000K**

Sing Cha Lern West of the main road, opposite Phou Iu II ☎ 020 2883 4884. Rather institutional hotel, modern yet already looking worn, catering mainly to Chinese customers, though the new Chinese restaurant facing the main street is promising. **60,000K**

Taï Lu Main road ☎ 020 5503 8844. A rather picturesque wooden building built in the Tai Leu style, the town's original hotel was on the point of moving at the time of writing, the owner planning to move both rooms (around 50,000K) and restaurant to the (similarly attractive) building opposite. The cheery restaurant, its tables dressed with lacy tablecloths, will probably look much the same, with a promising menu full of *jeows* and local specialities, most of which are usually unavailable. Banana-flower soup 30,000K. Daily 7am–9pm.

The Akha Road: Muang Sing to Xieng Kok

The road that stretches west of Muang Sing towards the Burmese frontier passes through one of Laos's least-visited regions. While the peaceful, largely agricultural scenery belies it, the history of this region is tied to the production of illicit drugs: opium, heroin and, more recently, methamphetamine. It is believed that most meth, known locally as *ya ba* or *ya máa* ("crazy medicine"), is produced in labs across the border in Myanmar (Burma), but smugglers use routes through Laos on their way south to Bangkok, a principal market and distribution point for the drug, which finds its way to nightclubs all over Southeast Asia. Travellers are unlikely to see any indication of this activity from the road, however, except for the occasional conspicuously large mansion built with profiteering money. Indeed, the landscape in this remote corner of Laos has changed significantly in recent years, forest cover giving way increasingly to vast plantations of banana, sugar cane and long broom grass, for export to China.

While the Lao government has mundanely designated this 75-km stretch of road **Route 17**, a more apt designation might be the **Akha Road**, given the high density of Akha villages through which it passes. The Akha of this isolated region have had little contact with the lowland Lao, and this is reflected in their dress. Indeed, the area is one of the few in Laos where you will see Akha men still wearing their traditional headgear: disc-shaped red turbans or tall hats festooned with seed-beads. Though paved for the first few kilometres west of Muang Sing, the road is poor outside villages, and it's a bumpy ride – while there are daily buses, many people choose to travel this route by motorbike. The main stop between Muang Sing and **Xieng Kok**, on the Burmese frontier, is **Muang Long**, long known as an excellent base for **trekking**.

Muang Long

Small but bustling **MUANG LONG** is an up-and-coming town, much developed in recent years by Chinese commercial interests. Though the town itself has few "sights", there is superb trekking in its unspoilt hinterland, heavily populated by Akha tribes who continue a very traditional way of life. If you don't mind basic food and facilities, then Muang Long is the place for you. The town lies in a flat, narrow valley bottom, with the Nam Ma river flowing right down the valley to enter the Mekong at Xieng Kok. Two tributaries intersect the Nam Ma right at the junction of Muang Long: the Nam Dok Long flows down from the north while the larger Nam Luang river enters from deep in the mountains to the south. Together, the two river valleys form corridors into the mountains north and south of Muang Long – an area ripe for exploring on foot or by motorbike. There are several easy areas to explore around Muang Long, which can be done as **day-trips** – speak to the tourist office for more information, or to book a tour (see p.191).

The morning market
Daily 5.30am–6pm

At dawn a parade of tribal peoples comes down from the hills to trade at the large central **market**, in the centre of town. Unlike Muang Sing, many still wear tribal dress. Besides the usual basketloads of peppers, tubers and gourds, villagers bring pieces of rare eaglewood, which they gather from the dense forest. This resinous wood, used in Middle Eastern countries in the manufacture of perfumes and incense, is warehoused here before being shipped off to Bangkok, where it fetches astonishingly high prices at shops in the small Arab quarter off Bangkok's Sukhumvit Road. Though there's some activity in the market all day, as ever it's best visited early in the morning or in late afternoon.

ARRIVAL AND DEPARTURE   MUANG LONG   4

By bus The bus station is 500m east of the main market area, to which it's an easy stroll: continue along the road and turn right at the second junction to reach the market. Though there is a timetable, buses tend to leave on demand and you may be forced to hang about; it's possible to charter in both directions. The bus for Xieng Kok is scheduled to leave at noon; the road, narrow and unpaved, is truly dismal.

Destinations Luang Namtha (daily; 3hr 30min); Muang Sing (3 daily; 1hr 30min); Xieng Kok (daily; 50min).

INFORMATION AND TOURS

Tourist office The tiny tourist office (Mon–Fri 8am–11.30am & 1.30–4pm; ☎020 5588 5655, ⓦ muanglongtourismoffice.weebly.com) is 200m west along the main highway from the market street turning. It's seldom open when it claims to be, but can be contacted in advance for advice on exploring the local area and river transport from Xieng Kok to Houayxai.

Tours The tourist office can organize treks of one to five days' duration, staying in local Akha, Hmong or Lahou villages, plus motorbike trips (though you'll need to bring your own); one-day tours start at 160,000K per person, two days at 310,000K per person. Based at the tourist office but available beyond its usual limited opening hours, Da Luthasmee (☎020 5588 0410, ✉daluck999@hotmail.com) is a friendly and helpful source of information.

Services There's a branch of Lao Development Bank, with an ATM, close to the market, but as yet nowhere to check internet in town.

ACCOMMODATION AND EATING

Henghom On the main highway, 300m west of the bus station ☎030 920 1755. Occupying a cheerful banana-yellow block, the town's newest guesthouse has big, high-ceilinged rooms with hot showers and free tea and coffee. **60,000K**

Kungna 200m east of the bus station ☎020 5578 6585. Overlooking paddy fields on the way into town, this attractive bamboo terrace restaurant is the most picturesque spot for a beer or meal, with a simple menu of soups and stir-fries (around 30,000K). Equally nice sister restaurant *Dansavanh*, closer into town, should have reopened by the time you read this. Daily 7am–10pm.

Siseng Just down a side street opposite the Agricultural Promotions Bank ☎020 5556 0225. Great for an early-morning stumble to the market, this tiddly guesthouse is the most central option, with surprisingly big (if bare) rooms with attached squat loos. The basic restaurant next door is good for a quick noodle soup. **60,000K**

Thatsany On the main highway, just west of Henghom Guesthouse ☎020 5534 8337. Muang Long's nicest place to stay is set back from the road on a verdant plot filled with birdsong. The best rooms front on to a communal veranda in the powder-blue building at the back. **60,000K**

Xieng Kok

A sleepy frontier village on a remote stretch of the Mekong, **XIENG KOK** is the last river port for cargo vessels coming down from China. The village has a ramshackle charm, not least because few tourists make the trip this far. The Upper Mekong scenery here is fantastic, the narrowing river fast-flowing and studded with islets of craggy stone, and the region's remoteness gives it a real wilderness feel. Xieng Kok is right on the border with Myanmar (Burma), and though the crossing isn't open to foreigners, around 15km upstream from the village the first **Lao–Myanmar Friendship Bridge** is due to be completed in 2015, which should in time see an improvement in the roads – and ultimately, perhaps, one day the inviting prospect of travel between the two countries.

Two kilometres back along the main road towards Muang Long, the old town – **Ban Xiengkok Keo** – is an attractive Tai Leu settlement of two-storey wooden houses. In the centre of the village, one belongs to master craftsman Mr Ou, an elderly gent who makes beautiful swords used in shamanic ceremonies, which he is happy to show visitors.

ARRIVAL AND DEPARTURE XIENG KOK

By bus Minibuses from Muang Long (daily; 50min) do a loop of the town and will drop you off at the boat landing. The minibus back leaves when full – sometime after 2pm.

By boat From Xieng Kok it is possible to travel downriver along the Mekong towards Houayxai. Speedboats no longer run since a spate of attacks by armed gangs from the Burmese side of the river in 2012, but some 20–30 cargo boats normally pass through each day. Speak to one of the boat owners getting their papers stamped at the immigration office above the boat landing (just below

Xieng Kok Resort) to arrange a ride. Ban Mom is the only Lao village between Xieng Kok and Houayxai with tourist accommodation, from which it's a 2hr journey by sawngthaew to Houayxai, though it may be worth continuing to Tonpheung, from which sawngthaews run more frequently. Occasionally, early morning passenger boats run to Ban Mom (250,000K; 5hr) and Tonpheung (300,000K; 6–7hr); speak to the tourist office in Muang Long to find out the latest situation.

ACCOMMODATION AND EATING

Daosavanh 20m to the right from the boat landing ☎ 020 239 5443. In case *Xieng Kok Resort* has been block-booked by Chinese traders, the town's other guesthouse is okay for a night. The dark, windowless rooms have squat loos and cold showers, but the welcome is friendly. __50,000K__

Xieng Kok Resort Above the boat landing ☎ 030 920 0356. On the embankment overlooking the river and

landing, the worn but charming *Xieng Kok Resort* is the main place to stay. The self-contained wooden bungalows, with low beds, nets and TVs, all have en-suite bathrooms (with Western loos and solar-powered showers) and sit-outs overlooking the Mekong. In the restaurant, the English-language menu, so old and crumpled it appears to be written on parchment, will leave you scratching your head at dishes like "convenient" and "fry the potato silk". __50,000K__

Houayxai

HOUAYXAI, sandwiched between the Mekong and a range of hills, is the first introduction many visitors have to Laos, lying across the border from Thailand. It was long an important crossroads for Chinese merchants from Yunnan who, driving caravans of pack-ponies laden with tea, silk and opium, would pass through Houayxai on their way south to Chiang Mai, and again on the return north with their loads of gold, silver and ivory. Today, Chinese goods are still much in evidence, but exotic cargos of silks and opium have been replaced by dirt-cheap hand tools and brittle plastic wares that are floated down the Mekong by the barge-load.

Most tourists hurry through Houayxai, either rushing across the new **Thai–Lao Friendship Bridge** to Thailand at the end of their visas or heading straight from the border or bus station to the pier for the slow boat downriver to Luang Prabang. Despite

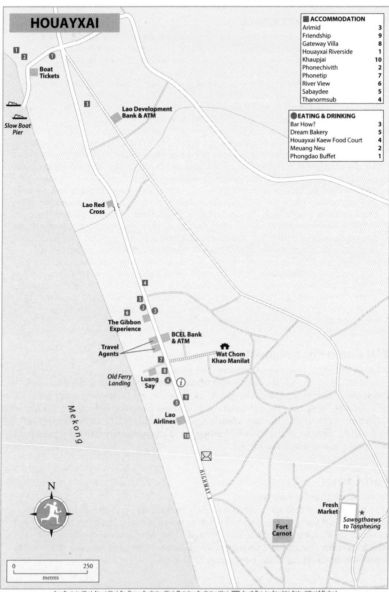

HOUAYXAI

ACCOMMODATION

Arimid	3
Friendship	9
Gateway Villa	8
Houayxai Riverside	1
Khaupjai	10
Phonechivith	2
Phonetip	7
River View	6
Sabaydee	5
Thanormsub	4

EATING & DRINKING

Bar How?	3
Dream Bakery	5
Houayxai Kaew Food Court	4
Meuang Neu	2
Phongdao Buffet	1

Boat Tickets

Slow Boat Pier

Lao Development Bank & ATM

Lao Red Cross

The Gibbon Experience

Travel Agents

BCEL Bank & ATM

Wat Chom Khao Manilat

Old Ferry Landing

Luang Say

Lao Airlines

Mekong

N

Fresh Market

Sawngthaews to Tonpheung

Fort Carnot

HIGHWAY 1

0   250
metres

4

Speedboat pier (3km), Airport (5km), Keo Champa Bus Station (5km), Phetarloun Bus Station (6km), ▼ Fourth Thai–Lao Friendship Bridge (10km) & Thailand

being a border town, it's not completely devoid of charm, though the main reason to stop here now is to take part in the acclaimed **Gibbon Experience** (see box, p.196).

Most accommodation and travel services are clustered around the old ferry landing where the (now locals-only) boats from Chiang Khong dock. From a tourist perspective this is still the main centre of interest, though much of the town's commerce is shifting south towards the bus stations and new town.

4

THE GIBBON EXPERIENCE

One of the country's pioneering eco-tourism projects has been set up around 80km out of Houayxai along Route 3 in Bokeo Nature Reserve, a pristine area of jungle that had previously been inaccessible to tourists. The excellent **Gibbon Experience** (☎084 212021, ⓦ gibbonexperience.org) offers a uniquely exhilarating way of exploring the reserve, combining trekking (with guides) with **zip-lining** long stretches across the forest canopy; some wires are in excess of 500m in length. It's unlike anything else on offer in Laos, and has quickly become a must-do among backpackers (and others), despite its high price tag.

Groups of no more than eight spend either one or two nights in the reserve, on one of three trips. There are two three-day options, running on alternate days: the more adventurous "**Waterfall**", which involves two to three hours of trekking a day and thus gets you further into the reserve; and the "**Classic**", which despite being a little more relaxed (with only an hour and a half of walking), offers the greater chance of seeing wildlife – don't expect to see the eponymous, critically endangered black crested gibbon, though you may hear them calling in the early morning. For those short on time, a third alternative, the recently added "**Express**" runs every day, and in order to condense the whole experience into two days, involves the most zip-lining of any of the trips. Nights are spent in the specially crafted **tree houses**, high up off the forest floor.

At $310 for three nights and $190 for two, the Gibbon Experience is expensive, but worth the splurge. Costs include all meals, accommodation, local guides and transport out to and back from Houayxai. **Guides** can be hit and miss – complaints about indifference and lack of English are common – but most people say that the overall experience makes up for this. It's hugely popular and **bookings** should be made well in advance via the website, though in low season it's sometimes possible to walk into the Houayxai office (on the main street, just north of the old ferry landing; daily 8am–7pm) and join up for the next morning. You're advised to bring a torch, good trekking boots, loo roll, a fully charged camera battery (there's no electricity) and plenty of mosquito repellent.

Wat Chom Khao Manilat

Off the main street, reached by stairs immediately opposite the old ferry landing

Houayxai's main sight is the hilltop **Wat Chom Khao Manilat**, with a tall, Shan-style drum tower and, to the left of the gaudy, modern *sim*, a picturesquely weathered teakwood building now used as a classroom for novice monks. Behind the *sim* is a collection of *heuan pha*, literally "cloth houses", originally built to store belongings of the dead. The top of the stairway leading up to the monastery from the main road is a good place to watch the sun set.

Fort Carnot

1km southeast of Wat Chom Khao Manilat (signposted)

It's worth ambling through Houayxai's sleepy backstreets up to the weather-beaten remains of **Fort Carnot**, built by the French at the turn of the last century. There's not much to see except a pair of watchtowers and a couple of low dorm blocks, one of which has been restored and converted into a visitor centre, but you can climb to the top of the far tower for a fine view across to Thailand.

Red Cross Herbal Sauna and Lao Massage

500m north of the old ferry landing, just beyond the bridge • Massage (Mon–Fri 1.30–9pm, Sat & Sun 10.30am–9pm) from 35,000K, sauna (daily 4–8.30pm only) 10,000K; special wellness programme 110,000K • ☎084 211935

In a cute little wooden house a little midway between the old ferry landing and the slowboat pier, the **Lao Red Cross** has a herbal sauna and offers a range of traditional treatments. Choose between body, foot and herbal massages (or packages involving combinations of the three), or pamper yourself with a special, three-hour wellness programme.

CROSSING INTO THAILAND

With the opening in 2013 of the grand **Fourth Thai–Lao Friendship Bridge** (daily 6am–10pm), 11km south of the old ferry landing, foreigners are no longer permitted to use the river crossing to Chiang Khong. The easiest way to cross the border is to take a sawngthaew to the new bus station and pick up one of the direct VIP services direct to Chiang Rai (57,000K), via Chiang Khong, which leave at 8am, 9am, 4pm and 5pm. Alternatively, take a sawngthaew to the bridge (20,000K), from where (after Lao immigration) buses shuttle across to Thai immigration (7000K) – visas are available on arrival – then a tuk-tuk to Chiang Khong (150–200 baht); from here you can catch direct buses to Chiang Rai and Chiang Mai. There are banks and an information point at the bridge.

ARRIVAL AND DEPARTURE   HOUAYXAI

BY PLANE

Houayxai's airport is 6km south of the centre. Flights to Vientiane (55min) are operated daily by Lao Airlines and twice weekly with Lao Skyway. Chances are you'll need to charter a sawngthaew to town (50,000K). Lao Airlines has an office next to *Khaupjai* guesthouse, just south of the old ferry landing (☎ 084 211026).

BY BUS

Houayxai has two bus stations, around 1km apart. Domestic VIP and international buses, including services from Chiang Rai, arrive at the swish new private bus (Phetarloun) station, 7km south of the centre. Normal buses arrive at the old (Keo Champa) bus station, 6km south of the centre. Sawngthaews from either bus station cost 10,000K per person to the centre of town. You can buy tickets for onward travel through tour agencies in Houayxai; these cost a bit more than buying direct from the bus station, as transfer is included. If you're in a hurry to get to Luang Prabang (and don't fancy the speedboat) the best option is the overnight VIP service at 6pm from the new bus station. Note that most buses to Houayxai are marked "Bokeo" or "Borkeo", the name of the province.

Destinations from the new bus station Chiang Khong, Thailand (4 daily; 30min); Chiang Rai, Thailand (4 daily; 3hr); Dien Bien Phu, Vietnam (6 weekly; 15hr); Jinghong, China (6 weekly; 12hr); Kunming, China (daily; 17hr); Luang Namtha (daily; 3hr 30min); Luang Prabang (daily; 12hr); Mengla, China (6 weekly; 8hr); Vang Vieng (daily; 17hr); Vientiane (daily; 21hr).

Destinations from the old bus station Luang Namtha (2 daily; 4hr); Luang Prabang (daily; 13hr); Oudomxai (daily; 8hr); Vientiane (daily; 23hr).

BY BOAT

By slow boat The slow boat pier is about 1km north of the old ferry landing. Boats depart for Pakbeng (110,000K), midway to Luang Prabang (220,000K), at 11.30am; arrive at least 30min early to ensure a seat. Tickets can be bought directly from the ticket office at the pier (opens 8am), or from travel agents on the main road; the price for the latter will include commission and a tuk-tuk ride to the pier, so anticipate paying a little more.

Destinations Luang Prabang (daily; 2 days); Pakbeng (daily; 7hr).

By speedboat The speedboat pier is 4km downriver of the centre (tuk-tuk 15,000K). Boats for Pakbeng (170,000K) and Luang Prabang (340,000K) theoretically depart at 9.30am, but leave when full – get there well in advance (and conversely be prepared for a wait), or book via an agent in town.

Destinations Luang Prabang (daily; 6–7hr); Pakbeng (daily; 3–4hr).

To Xieng Kok There are no regular services upriver to Xieng Kok. You need to take a sawngthaew from the main market, 1km southeast of the old ferry landing, to Tonpheung, where you should be able to arrange transport by cargo boat (see p.194). Less frequent sawngthaews continue on to Ban Mom, further upriver (and at the end of the road), where there is basic accommodation.

INFORMATION

Tourist information The tourist office (Mon–Fri 8.30am–noon & 1.30–4pm; ☎ 084 211162), just south of the old ferry landing, has some useful information boards but is mainly interested in pointing customers towards its tours.

Internet The *Gateway Villa Hotel* at the top of the old ferry landing has internet terminals (10,000K/hr).

ACCOMMODATION

There's a lot of accommodation on offer in Houayxai – if possible, arrive before noon, as a lot of the better places fill up early. For now most remain clustered around the old ferry landing, though there a few good options around the slow boat landing, 1km north.

DOWN THE MEKONG

Although it's now a well-worn tourist route, many travellers agree that the two-day journey by **slow boat** (*heua sa*) along the Mekong from Houayxai to the old royal capital of Luang Prabang, stopping overnight at the village of Pakbeng, is one of those definitive Southeast Asian experiences. Originally, these antiquated diesel-powered boats were primarily for cargo and the occasional Lao passengers who relied on them for trade and transport. Although the boats can be very full, these days it's a fairly comfortable journey, with seating generally on cushioned wooden benches or reclining "airline" seating, and enough space to wander around, play cards, read Kindles and so on. Drinks and a few snacks are on sale on board – though you'd do better to bring your own provisions – and there are Western loos. Big bags are normally stored down in the hold at the back. It can be chilly on board, at least in winter, so bring warm clothing.

Whether you consider taking one of the **speedboats** (*heua wai*) between Houayxai and Luang Prabang, which stop in Pakbeng for lunch, depends on how risk averse you are. Skimming across the water at speeds of up to 60kph, or even faster, these cramped eight-seater crafts cut hours off journey times, but there's no doubt that the exhilarating ride is a great deal less comfortable and more dangerous – deaths have been reported, though the vast majority of journeys pass off incident-free. Life vests and crash helmets are provided – the latter most useful as protection against the wind and engine noise.

A couple of **luxury boats** also make the journey down the Mekong, the pick of which is *Luang Say* (Luang Prabang ☎071 252553, Houayxai ☎084 212092; ⓦ luangsay.com). The price ($506/person in high season) includes overnight accommodation at the *Luang Say Lodge* in Pakbeng (see p.201), meals and drinks, plus stops at Pak Ou Buddha Caves (see p.134) and minority villages along the way. It's well worth enquiring about last-minute deals (which, if available, begin a week before the boat leaves), particularly in low season, which can drop as low as $216 heading upriver from Luang Prabang.

Arimid Just south of the slow boat landing ☎084 211040. A collection of a dozen basic but attractive two-room bungalows, quite pleasant if a bit squeezed together, with en-suite bathrooms, plus a very cheap restaurant. If you're looking for something with Lao flavour, or are planning on staying in Houayxai a few days, this is a good choice. **80,000K**

Friendship 100m south of the old ferry landing ☎084 211219. One of the cheapest options. Rooms are dark with rather hard beds but have pretty bedspreads – though you wouldn't ask whoever chose the colour scheme to decorate your house. **60,000K**

Gateway Villa At the top of the old ferry landing ☎084 212180, ⓔ gatewayhotel.laos@hotmail.com. The smartest hotel in the centre attracts mainly Chinese custom, but is still friendlier to Western visitors than many places up north. The small doubles are a good deal for single travellers. Sometimes fills up with groups. Breakfast and a/c included. **100,000K**

Khaupjai 200m south of the old ferry landing ☎020 5568 3164. Sparklingly clean new guesthouse with comfy beds and showers that point straight into the lavatory bowl, so you can perform all your morning ablutions at the same time. Nonetheless, the rooms are probably the best maintained along the strip. **120,000K**

Phonechivith/Houayxai Riverside Above the slow boat pier ☎084 211765, ⓦ houayxairiverside.com. Sister properties set in a pair of striking ochre-orange buildings just above the slow boat landing. Enlivened by Lao fabrics, the rooms at *Phonechivith Guesthouse*, off a shared veranda, demonstrate a touch more class than down in town. Next-door *Houayxai Riverside Hotel* is the nicest in town, where you can gaze out of big picture windows overlooking the Mekong from your swish, comfy pad. The wooden terrace restaurant right on the water offers all kinds of soups, salads and fried dishes. Also organizes bus travel to Thailand. *Phonechivith* **100,000K**, *Houayxai Riverside* **$35**

Phonetip At the top of the old ferry landing ☎084 211084. The cheapest rooms here are rather cramped, with shared bathrooms, but an extra 20,000K will buy you a bit more space and an en suite. There's a communal balcony overlooking the street, and some rooms have views down to the river. **40,000K**

★**River View** Behind the Meuang Neu restaurant, 100m north of the old ferry landing ☎030 903 0993. A very popular place with spacious, well-maintained rooms in a long, three-story block leading down to the river. Shaded by tall palm trees, the raised garden terrace at the back is one of the most atmospheric places to contemplate the sunset with a Beerlao. **80,000K**

★**Sabaydee** 200m north of the old ferry landing ☎020 5692 9458. This modern hotel boasts big, spotlessly clean rooms, with a terrace at the top that offers terrific views of the Mekong. A friendly welcome and the best deal in town. **90,000K**

Thanormsub 250m north of the ferry landing ☎ 084 211095. This blue-roofed house has fourteen very clean, tiled rooms with fetchingly pink, if slightly cramped, bathrooms. No views, but the staff are friendly and it's fairly quiet. **90,000K**

EATING AND DRINKING

Bar How? 150m north of the old ferry landing ☎ 020 5516 7220. With its bottle-lined walls, good music and ambient lighting, this relaxed place almost has the feel of a wine bar. It's a favourite with backpackers for its cold Beerlao, cocktails (mojito 30,000K) and reasonably priced Lao, Thai and *falang* food (*tôm yam* 35,000K, steaks 60,000K). Daily 6am–11pm.

Dream Bakery 100m south of the old ferry landing. A cheerful and inviting bakery-café with big wooden chairs and colourful tablecloths. Coffee comes from the Bolaven plateau and the cakes and pastries (blueberry pie 10,000K, strudel 12,000K) are more than passable. Daily 7am–8pm.

Houayxai Kaew Food Court Next to Gateway Villa Hotel ☎ 084 212180. Sleek and modern, this restaurant looks a bit out of place in Houayxai. But with its helpful picture menu of mainly Chinese and Thai specialities and (occasional) live music, it's a good spot to unwind; *larp* 35,000K. Daily 7am–9pm.

Meuang Neu Riverview Guesthouse, 100m north of the old ferry landing ☎ 020 5568 4257. A travellers' favourite with a rustic feel, which serves a largely Western menu including pizzas (from 55,000K) and desserts like fried banana in chocolate sauce. Also a good place to pick up a sandwich before a long boat or bus journey south. The garden restaurant is a lovely spot at dusk (see p.198). Daily 6am–11pm.

Phongdao Buffet Just up from the slow boat landing, on the right ☎ 020 9665 7444. Westerners normally pass straight by this unassuming locals' place, but it does the best *sin dad* (Lao barbecue) in town, the buffet table groaning under the weight of fresh meat, veg, fish and seafood. Daily 5–10pm.

Pakbeng

The ramshackle river port of **PAKBENG** is the halfway point between Houayxai and Luang Prabang, and the only town of any size along the 300km stretch of river between them. As tourist vessels don't travel the Mekong after dark, a night here is unavoidable if you're travelling by slow boat. Although first impressions of the town are generally unfavourable, Pakbeng is actually a very interesting place, with a distinctly northern Laos feel about it. Once extremely poor, it is now growing rapidly, a change of fortune owing to its role as an important **trading post**; goods from China and Thailand come down the river from Houayxai and then make their way up into the interior from here. Tourism has also been a big boon for the town, with the slow boats disgorging hundreds of hungry backpackers a day.

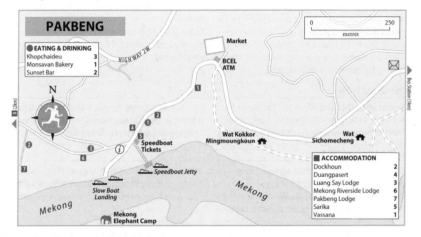

Most tourists to Pakbeng come by slow boat, arriving late and leaving early in the morning, the two times of day when it's at its least appealing, with touts (who can be pushy by Lao, if not general Southeast Asian standards) hanging around at the boat landings and in restaurants and guesthouse doorways. Stick around for a day or so to see the town without the night-time hordes, when it reverts to its relaxed, sleepy self and exhibits a low-key charm.

Many people think the port area around the landing *is* Pakbeng, but the real town lies past the top of the hill and stretches for a good kilometre along the main road that follows the Mekong before turning north towards Oudomxai. Just beyond the last of the guesthouses, en route into town (about 500m east of the boat landings), the **market** is worth an early morning wander, though these days the Hmong women and children who frequent it have largely abandoned traditional dress. Beyond here are two pleasant *wats*: **Wat Kokkor Mingmoungkoun**, which has a pretty and elegant *sim*, and a few hundred metres further on, **Wat Sichomecheng**, which sits high on a bluff above the Mekong in the centre of town.

Mekong Elephant Camp

Rides from $47, treks from $55 • ☎ 020 5557 0577, ⓦ mekongelephantcamp.com

Stretching up the jungle-clad hillside on the opposite shore of the river, the **Mekong Elephant Camp** attempts to lure travellers into staying beyond the obligatory single night – in the morning you can usually see (and hear) one or two of the camp's eight elephants grazing along the bank. Run by *Pakbeng Lodge* (see p.201), the camp offers various day packages, ranging from straightforward elephant rides (combined with a bathing session) to a challenging three-hour uphill trek on foot through primary forest, descending on your pachyderm's shoulders and concluding the day with a swim.

ARRIVAL AND DEPARTURE   PAKBENG

By slow boat Slow boats stop at the landing at the bottom of the port road, a short walk from the guesthouses. You may find that young boys offer to help you lug your bag uphill – negotiate a fee for this beforehand. Moving on, boats usually depart around 9.30am to Luang Prabang, and about 8.30am to Houayxai – it's best to check times locally the night before. Arrive at least 30min early to ensure a seat, particularly heading downriver. Tickets are sold on board. Some captains stop briefly at the caves at Pak Ou (see p.134) before Luang Prabang, charging each passenger who disembarks for a look a few thousand kip extra. This works out cheaper than chartering a boat from Luang Prabang, but leaves little time for exploring.

Destinations Houayxai (daily; 8hr); Luang Prabang (daily; 7hr).

By speedboat Speedboats pull up to the floating speedboat landing, close to the slow boat landing. Boats heading both up- and downriver normally depart around 9am, though will only leave when full; buy tickets from the booth at the top of the speedboat landing.

Destinations Houayxai (daily; 3hr); Luang Prabang (daily; 3hr).

By bus Buses run twice daily to Oudomxai (4hr) from the bus station, 2km northeast of the boat landings (5000K in a shared tuk-tuk).

INFORMATION

Tourist office The tourist office (Mon–Fri 8am–11.30pm & 2–4pm; ☎ 030 928 3725, ⓦ oudomxay.info) is easily visible at the top of the boat landing. There is a useful map

you can take a picture of, and it offers various trips, including to the Khamtan Budda Cave, where villagers sheltered during the Second Indochina War.

ACCOMMODATION

Once the boat pulls in, don't waste any time securing a **room**. Travellers arriving off the slow boat are usually greeted by countless touts for the town's guesthouses – you're best off searching for accommodation yourself to avoid being overcharged. From the landing, the majority of guesthouses are just up the hill to the right, though there are a few more stylish options if you head to the left, away from town.

Dockhoun 100m east at the top of the landings ☎ 081 212540. Good-sized rooms with colourful bedspreads in a vivid green building, but the real advantage is the lovely restaurant, bedecked with hanging baskets and boasting superlative views of the river. **100,000K**

Duangpasert Just east at the top of the landings ☎ 081 212624. Friendly place that's more clued up than most along the port road. For river views go for one of the upstairs rooms, though downstairs you have the advantage of a big (shared) terrace; all rooms have high ceilings and hot showers. Also has a bakery. **100,000K**

★ **Luang Say Lodge** 3km west of the boat landings ☎ 081 212296, ⓦ luangsay.com. Eighteen luxury Lao-style bungalows by the river, featuring all mod cons. On stilts, the bungalows are connected by a beautifully built covered walkway which leads to the reception. The resort even has its own boat pier and fancy restaurant with uniformed staff. The outdoor patio bar, with a view of the Mekong, is a great place for a sundowner. Half-board **$76**

★ **Mekong Riverside Lodge** 100m west of the landings ☎ 020 5517 1068, ⓦ www.mekongriverside lodge.com. Raised on stilts, with bamboo-weave walls and rattan furniture, these stylish wooden bungalows provide a welcome mid-range alternative to Pakbeng's identikit guesthouses. Best of all are the gorgeous private sit-outs, poised right above the water and ideal for watching the elephants on the opposite bank over a leisurely breakfast (included). **$50**

Pakbeng Lodge 500m west of the landings ☎ 081 212304, ⓦ pakbenglodge.com. An upmarket hideaway, French-owned and -operated, set amid thick foliage with its own pier on the western edge of town. It's worth paying extra for the super-stylish deluxe rooms ($150), high above the Mekong, with huge sliding doors opening out on to a magnificent panorama. Has a strong community ethos – including a clinic offering free healthcare for locals. Half-board. **$125**

Sarika At the top of the speedboat landing ☎ 081 212306. In a plum position very close to the landings, this is one of the best options. Whitewashed rooms are smallish but well maintained and feature nice wood trims. No balconies but some have views down to the Mekong. **100,000K**

Vassana 300m east of the boat landings ☎ 081 212302. Despite its unpromising exterior, this is actually one of the smarter guesthouses along the main strip. For once, some thought has gone into the colour scheme, and rooms have big, comfy beds, sparkling bathrooms and (very Lao this) reclining chairs ripped straight out of vans. No views, though. **80,000K**

EATING AND DRINKING

A lot of the guesthouses have restaurants, serving a fairly predictable mix of Western and Lao/Thai dishes, mitigated to some extent by fine river views; competition for custom along the main strip is fierce. An hour or so before the slow boats arrive, and again the next morning, a few stalls up from the landing put steaks, sausages and chicken on to grill – a tastier sandwich option for the onward boat journey than the baguettes sold by the numerous guesthouse bakeries.

Khopchaideu 100m west of the landings, opposite Mekong Riverside Lodge ☎ 020 5171 7068. Away from the main drag, this Bangladeshi-run place is the better of town's two curry houses, and focuses on heavy north Indian non-veg cuisine. Dishes are slightly one-size-fits-all, but pretty tasty; chicken tikka masala (27,000K).

Monsavan Bakery 100m east of the landings ☎ 020 577 1935. Festooned with Beerlao flags, this cool and breezy restaurant–bakery opposite the (slightly overpriced) *Monsavan Guesthouse* is a good place for a breakfast bagel (with cream cheese 25,000K) or bowl of muesli (25,000K). Daily 6am–10.30pm.

Sunset Bar Pakbeng Lodge, 500m west of the landings ☎ 081 212304, ⓦ pakbenglodge.com. The lantern-lit upper terrace bar at *Pakbeng Lodge* is hands down the nicest place within walking distance of town to soak up the views over a sunset cocktail (from 50,000K). Dinner, served here or in the inviting main restaurant, is a set Thai–Lao menu ($12; best to reserve). Daily till 10pm.

4

South central Laos

THAT ING HANG

5

South central Laos

Many travellers see very little of south central Laos, spending just a night or two in the principal towns of Thakhek or Savannakhet before pressing on to the far south or crossing the border into Vietnam. However, if you're willing to take time out from the more popular north and south of the country you'll find that there is much more to the region than the main Mekong towns, which are slowly awakening from their post-colonial slumber. In this part of the country, explorers are rewarded handsomely: by warm smiles and friendly shouts of "sabaidee", by the otherworldly beauty of the vast caves that edge the Khammouane Limestone NBCA near Thakhek, and by glimpses of the massive Nakai-Nam Theun NBCA, the largest of all Laos's conservation areas.

The three narrow provinces that dominate this part of Laos, namely **Bolikhamxai**, **Khammouane** and **Savannakhet**, are squeezed between mainland Southeast Asia's two most formidable geographical barriers: the Mekong river and the Annamite Mountains. The **Mekong** has long served as a lifeline for the inhabitants of this stretch of the interior, providing food and a thoroughfare for trade and transport. In the late nineteenth century, European colonialism turned the life-giving "Mother of Waters" into a political boundary, and the Lao on its west bank were incorporated into Siam. During the 1970s and 1980s, the river became a further political and economic divide, when short-lived but draconian post-revolutionary policies forced large numbers of the inhabitants of the towns along this stretch of the Mekong, primarily ethnic Vietnamese and Chinese, to flee across the river into Thailand.

East of the river, the elevation gradually increases, culminating in the rugged **Annamite Mountains**, which, throughout much of recorded history, have divided Indochina culturally into two camps, Indian influence prevailing west of the chain and that of China dominating the east. Until very recently these mountains made up one of the region's least inhabited areas and were teeming with wildlife, including some of Asia's rarest and most endangered species, such as the tiger, Javan rhinoceros and Indian elephant. In recent years, however, this area has been the target of heavy logging, and some observers claim that the damage done to the forest since the start of the new millennium is irreversible.

As might be expected, the three principal settlements and provincial capitals of south central Laos – Paksan, Thakhek and Savannakhet – are all on the Mekong. **Paksan**, the smallest of these, lies at the mouth of the Xan river, which flows down from the 2620-metre Phou Xaxum on the Xieng Khuang Plateau. Thanks to the opening of a Thai–Lao Friendship Bridge just north of town, the old casino town of **Thakhek** is seeing an increase in foreign visitors. East of Thakhek is a dramatic landscape of imposing and impossibly vertical mountains of the kind often depicted in old Chinese scroll paintings, which forms the southern boundary of the

COLONIAL HOUSES AND TUK-TUK IN THAKHEK

Highlights

❶ Mahaxai Caves Whether you choose to go it alone or join an organized tour, you can enjoy excellent hiking, cycling and cave-exploring near Thakhek. **See p.212**

❷ Kong Lo Cave This seven-kilometre stretch of underground river in the Khammouane Limestone NBCA is one of Asia's most unusual and enchanting spots for kayaking. **See p.214**

❸ Trekking near Savannakhet Splendid trekking just a short drive from the French–Indochinese shop houses of the south's colonial

gem, with the chance to spot monkeys and hornbills. **See p.217**

❹ That Ing Hang This revered sixteenth-century Buddhist stupa next to the Mekong provides a great excuse for a bicycle ride out of Savannakhet, especially during the annual festival. **See p.218**

❺ Ho Chi Minh Trail Numerous relics of the famous clandestine highway – rusting tanks, downed helicopters and the like – can still be visited en route to Vietnam. **See p.221**

HIGHLIGHTS ARE MARKED ON THE MAP ON P.206

5

Khammouane Limestone NBCA. Easily visited on a day-trip from Thakhek, these awesome limestone formations are riddled with labyrinthine tunnels and caverns. **Savannakhet** has been described as southern Laos's equivalent of Luang Prabang, its inhabitants living comfortably among architectural heirlooms handed down by the French.

Aside from the main north–south artery of **Route 13**, central Laos has three important highways – Routes 8, 12 and 9 – which cross the region from west to east, connecting the Mekong River Valley with the provincial interior, and extending beyond into Vietnam. The northernmost highway, **Route 8** – served by daily buses from Vientiane – snakes up through mountains, rainforests and the Phu Pha Maan "stone forest" before winding down to the city of Vinh on the Gulf of Tonkin. The middle route, **Route 12**, begins at Thakhek and crosses the Annamites, connecting with Vietnam's Highway 15 and the coastal city of **Dong Hoi**. Southernmost of the three is **Route 9**, currently served by daily buses connecting Savannakhet with **Dong Ha**, **Da Nang** and **Hué** in Vietnam. If and when plans for a 220km-long high-speed railway between Savannakhet and the Vietnamese border at Lao Bao come to fruition (estimates say trains will be running by 2017), journey times will plummet.

Near **Xepon**, Route 9 bisects another route of more recent vintage: the **Ho Chi Minh Trail**. Actually a network of parallel roads and paths, the trail was used by the North Vietnamese Army to infiltrate and finally subdue its southern neighbour. The area is still littered with lots of war junk, some of it dangerous. The best way to view these rusting relics is to use Xepon as a base, making trips to nearby Muang Phin and Ban Dong.

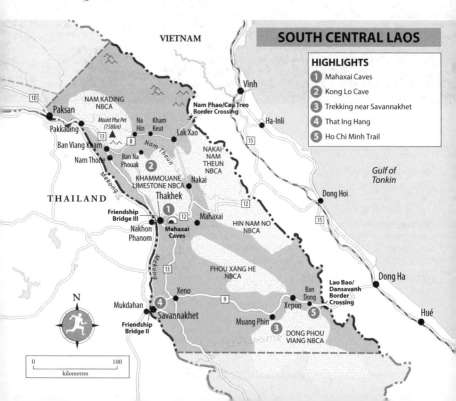

SOUTH CENTRAL LAOS

HIGHLIGHTS

1. Mahaxai Caves
2. Kong Lo Cave
3. Trekking near Savannakhet
4. That Ing Hang
5. Ho Chi Minh Trail

Paksan and around

Route 13 passes through **PAKSAN**, capital of Bolikhamxai province and the northernmost major settlement on the narrow neck of Laos, but few travellers actually stop over in this small, sleepy Mekong town, and the ferry crossing to and from **Beung Kan** in Thailand is still little used, despite being open to foreigners (Lao visas are not available on arrival). But there is another reason you may end up here: work on Route 1D is now complete, making it possible to travel from the south of Laos to the Plain of Jars without needing to detour through Vientiane. It's a convenient mid-way stop at the convergence of two rivers, with one particularly welcoming guesthouse and enough noodle shops to keep your belly full on an overnight stay.

Nam Kading NBCA

Forty kilometres southeast of Paksan, **Nam Kading NBCA** is Bolikhamxai Province's largest conservation area and a place of dramatic scenic beauty. Running parallel to the Mekong and encompassing 1740 square kilometres, the park has a chain of mountains down its length, the highest peak being the 1588-metre **Mount Pha Pet**, which can clearly be viewed as you travel Route 13. Unfortunately, this is likely to be as intimate a glimpse as you'll get, as facilities for visitors are extremely limited.

Pakkading

Behind the ridge on the eastern boundary of the **Nam Kading NBCA**, the **Nam Mouan** and **Nam Theun** rivers converge to form the **Nam Kading**, so named because the waterfalls where the Nam Theun spills off the plateau are said to make a "kading" sound – the sound of a water buffalo's bell. The Nam Kading flows out through a gap in the mountains to join the Mekong at the village of **PAKKADING**. There are a number of good fish **restaurants** on the highway here, making it a favourite lunch spot for truckers and travellers plying Route 13.

To the east of Pakkading, the highway crosses a Russian-built bridge and heads south out of town. Drivers often pause to light a cigarette before crossing the bridge, and then respectfully toss the lit cigarette into the swift waters below, an offering to appease the feisty water serpent believed to live at the river's mouth. Every year a buffalo is sacrificed to the water serpent, though the offerings weren't enough to spare the lives of a Russian engineer and several Lao workers who died during construction of the bridge.

ARRIVAL AND INFORMATION

PAKSAN AND AROUND

By bus The bus station is just off Route 13, west of the bridge that crosses the Nam Xan and close to the busy market. However, this bus station is mostly used by sawngthaews running short-distance journeys within the local area. Services to points north and south tend to drive slowly through the middle of town, tooting their horns and stopping to let passengers jump aboard. To catch a bus, your best bet is to wait on Route 13 outside *Paksan Hotel* –there are plenty of services to Vientiane, Savannakhet and Phonsavan passing by from around 6.30am in the morning.

Services The Lao Development bank, next to the bus station, changes money.

ACCOMMODATION AND EATING

BK Guesthouse Around 500m south of Paksan Hotel (walk down the road just opposite the hotel's entrance) ☏ 054 212638. Calm, well-run place with cheap rooms and a quiet garden, where tall star-fruit trees provide shade and snacks. The place is taken care of by a welcoming, English-speaking host. Double with fan <u>50,000K</u>, a/c <u>70,000K</u>

Paksan Hotel On Route 13, around 800m east of the bus station ☏ 054 791333. Pretty enough from the outside, but something of a disappointment once you step through the door. The double rooms in the block at the back are reasonable value, however. <u>70,000K</u>

Saynamxan Restaurant On Route 13, on the west side of the bridge crossing the Nam Xan. The longest-established of Paksan's proper sit-down restaurants has a huge terrace overlooking the Nam Xan. Meals don't quite match the views, but make a nice change from the noodle shops in town. Daily 8am–10pm.

5

Route 8 towards Vietnam

At the tiny junction town of **Ban Vieng Kham**, 47km south of Pakkading, **Route 8** begins its journey over the Annamite Mountains to Vietnam. These days the majority of travellers pass through here on direct, air-conditioned buses running the Vientiane–Vinh route, but if you have time it's worth pausing at the spectacularly located village of **Na Hin**, a handy access point for Kong Lo Cave (see p.214), or at the frontier town of **Lak Xao** – the closest settlement of any size to the Vietnamese border.

Na Hin

Tracing a centuries-old trading route to Vietnam, Route 8 zigzags through hilly countryside, dotted with woods and tiny stream valleys, the southern horizon punctuated by black-topped limestone pillars draped in lush vegetation. An hour's drive along this route from Ban Vieng Kham takes you to the village of **NA HIN**, which sprang up during the construction of the **Theun-Hin Boun Dam**, completed in 1998. The hydroelectric potential of the area is vigorously demonstrated during the monsoon season, when the rains recharge a medley of waterfalls on the surrounding hillsides. The densely forested hill guarding the valley's southeastern side alone supports as many as six sizeable falls, all visible from the highway. Today Na Hin has found a new lease of life as a gateway into the Phou Hin Poun NBCA, more popularly known as the **Khammouane Limestone NBCA** (see p.214).

ARRIVAL AND DEPARTURE   NA HIN

By bus From Na Hin there are daily connections to Vieng Kham, Vientiane and Thakhek. If you're heading east to Lak Xao and the Vietnamese border, any bus travelling along Route 8 from Vientiane should stop for you.

ACCOMMODATION

Sainamhai Resort 3.5km south of town ☎ 020 2249 8989, ⓦ sainamhairesort.com. If you choose to stay in Na Hin, check out *Sainamhai Resort*, which has gorgeous riverside bungalows and good trekking right on its doorstep. It's also possible to rent a motorbike here for the trip to Kong Lo Cave (see p.214). **224,000K**

Lak Xao

Like many towns along Route 8, **Lak Xao** is dusty and uninviting, with nothing in the way of attractions. Still, it makes a handy stopover if you're travelling east to Vietnam (see box below), with a handful of reasonable guesthouses spread out on Route 8 and Route 1E.

THE NAM PHAO/CAU TREO BORDER CROSSING

If you've come as far east as Lak Xao and want to use the **Nam Phao/Cau Treo** border crossing into Vietnam, your best option is to hop into a shared tuk-tuk (20,000K) at the main market for the 35km journey to the border (40min). If you're crossing into Laos from Vietnam, there's usually a tuk-tuk on hand, but you may well have to charter it outright (expect to pay 100,000K to Lak Xao).

Crossing the border (daily; roughly 8am–5pm) can be a hassle, so it's best to start your journey early to ensure you don't end up stuck at the border. On the Vietnamese side there's usually a small army of touts ready to pull you into a van headed for Vinh. Neither immigration post is near a town of any size; the settlement on the Vietnamese side of the border is **Cau Treo**, 105km west of Vinh on Highway 8.

A relatively stress-free way to get across this border is by taking one of the nightly Vinh-bound buses from Vientiane (160,000K; see p.71) or Thakhek (90,000K; see p.210).

Lao visas on arrival are available at this border, but you'll need to arrange Vietnamese visas in advance. There is a Vietnamese embassy in Vientiane (see p.79).

By sawngthaew Sawngthaews depart from the bus station just east of Route 8 when full, bound for Thakhek (4hr) and the Nam Phao/Cau Treo border crossing (40min).

Thakhek and around

Less visited than Savannakhet to the south, **THAKHEK**, capital of Khammouane province, is gradually gaining popularity as the best base to explore the nearby **Mahaxai Caves** and karst formations, and the massive **Khammouane Limestone NBCA**. It is also a good entry point into Laos from Nakhon Phanom in Thailand, as well as being a handy place to break the long journey down Route 13 to Savannakhet.

Take a short walk out from the town square and you'll find crumbling French villas, overgrown gardens, and, despite the ever-present roar of kids on mopeds, an almost haunted atmosphere pervading the too-wide streets. It's hard to believe that during the Second Indochina War, Thakhek was a sort of Havana on the Mekong, with visiting Thais flocking to its riverbank casino. These days, it's Nakhon Phanom on the opposite bank that's the big metropolis, though since the opening of the third Thai–Lao Friendship Bridge in 2011, the town has caught up with its neighbour somewhat, with investors from Vietnam and China clamouring to build new hotels, offices and factories.

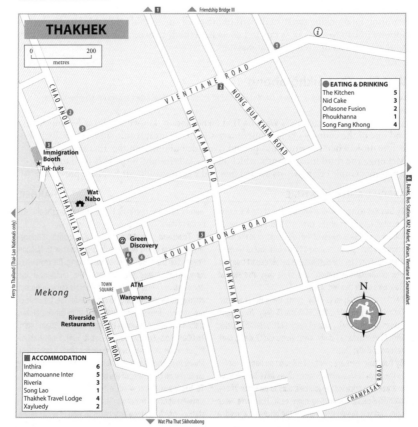

THAKHEK

0 — 200 metres

EATING & DRINKING
The Kitchen	5
Nid Cake	3
Orlasone Fusion	2
Phoukhanna	1
Song Fang Khong	4

Immigration Booth
Tuk-tuks

Wat Nabo

Green Discovery

Mekong

TOWN SQUARE   ATM
Wangwang

Riverside Restaurants

N

ACCOMMODATION
Inthira	6
Khamouanne Inter	5
Riveria	3
Song Lao	1
Thakhek Travel Lodge	4
Xayluedy	2

Friendship Bridge III

Wat Pha That Sikhotabong

5

Brief history

Thakhek's roots date back to the Chenla and Funan empires. The name Thakhek, which means "Visitor's Landing", is relatively new, but is a reference to the town's importance as far back as the eighth century. As Sikhotabong, and later Lakhon, Thakhek was a principality spanning both banks of the Mekong, and a hub for trade routes connecting civilizations in Vietnam, Thailand and Cambodia. Its former spiritual centre, the shrine of That Phanom, is now in present-day Thailand and is still the holiest site in ethnically Lao northeastern Thailand. When the kingdom of Lane Xang was formed under the leadership of Fa Ngum in the fourteenth century, Sikhotabong's governor oversaw the southern extent of the Lao empire.

Under the French, the town became an administrative outpost with a bustling Vietnamese community: the colonial administration thought that an influx of Vietnamese workers was the key to finally turning a profit on their sparsely populated Lao territory. By the 1940s, the town was 85 percent Vietnamese. After the revolution, large numbers of these Vietnamese families fled across the Mekong to Nakhon Phanom on the opposite bank, with the result that until recently, Thakhek remained a sleepy backwater.

The old centre

There are a few nice colonial-era buildings around Thakhek's overgrown town square, and on **Chao Anou Road**, north of the square, is a fine row of 1920s shop houses featuring interlocking swastika designs of moulded stucco (although this Hindu motif appears in Lao weaving, it is rare in Lao architecture). Between Chao Anou and Setthathilat is a large temple, Wat Nabo.

Wat Pha That Sikhotabong

6km south of Thakhek • Daily sunrise–sunset • 5000K • Easily reached by bike or motorbike. Expect to pay a tuk-tuk driver 50,000K, including an hour's wait.

Thakhek's main attraction is **Wat Pha That Sikhotabong**, known locally as Muang Kao, and one of the country's holiest pilgrimage sites. It's a great scenic spot, especially just before dusk, when the sun slinks behind riverside buildings on the Thai side of the Mekong. The third lunar month, which usually falls in July, is the best time to visit, when the temple celebrates its annual *bun* and a carnival-like atmosphere prevails.

ARRIVAL AND DEPARTURE

THAKHEK

By bus Bus passengers disembark either at the Kilometre 2 Market (2km east of the riverbank), at the junction of Route 12 and 13 (4km east of the riverbank), or at the inter-provincial bus station, around 4.5km northeast of town on Route 13. Buses for the destinations below depart from the inter-provincial bus station, and some may also stop at Thakhek's other two bus stops.

Destinations Attapeu (2 daily; 10hr); Dong Hoi (4 weekly; 7hr); Hanoi (1 weekly; 24hr); Mahaxai (5 daily; 2hr 30min); Paksan (6 daily; 4hr); Pakse (4 daily; 9hr); Salavan (2 daily; 5hr); Savannakhet (3 daily; 4hr); Vientiane (7 daily; 8hr); Xekong (2 daily; 7hr).

By tuk-tuk There are plenty of tuk-tuks on hand – useful, as the town is sprawling. Rogue drivers have been known to agree one price for the journey, only to pull over after a kilometre or so, demanding more cash. Hold firm, keep calm and you should get there for the price you agreed. A

journey from the riverbank to the bus station should cost no more than 30,000K.

To Thailand The third Thai–Lao Friendship Bridge, around 14km north of town, links Thakhek with Nakhon Phanom on the western side of the Mekong. The cross-river ferry, which leaves Thakhek from the ramp near the Immigration Office, is reserved for locals only, so do not attempt to leave Laos here. To cross the bridge, take one of the regular buses from Thakhek's inter-provincial bus station to Nakhon Phanom (roughly hourly 7.30am–4pm; 18,000K Mon–Fri, 20,000K on Sat & Sun). From Nakhon Phanom bus terminal, buses leave for Ubon Ratchathani, Mukdahan, Khon Kaen and Nong Khai. Visas are available on arrival on both sides of the bridge.

To Vietnam If you want to travel east to Vietnam, the simplest option is to head to Thakhek's inter-provincial bus station, which has regular services to Vinh (daily at 7am &

8pm; 90,000K), plus less frequent services to Da Nang (Mon & Fri at 8pm; 120,000K); Hué (Mon, Wed, Thurs & Sat at 7am & 8pm; 90,000K); and Hanoi (Saturday only; 160,000K).

INFORMATION

Tourist office Vientiane Road, north of the centre ☎051 212512. This excellent tourist office is by far the best place for information on the local area, and staff can help you organize eco-tours and treks with English-speaking guides. Daily 8am–11.30am & 1–4.30pm.

Services To change money, head for the Lao Development Bank opposite the Kilometre 2 Market; there's also a kiosk run by the same bank at the ferry pier. Internet access is available at a shop just north of the Inthira (daily 8am–10pm), charging 5000K/hr.

GETTING AROUND

Bike rental Bicycles are available from various guesthouses (20,000K/day) for getting around town.
Motorbike rental Wangwang, a small shop just west of the ATM on the town square, has motorbikes for exploring the Mahaxai caves and karst formations. Manual bikes cost 60,000K/day, automatics are 100,000/day.

ACCOMMODATION

Inthira Chao Anou Rd, just off the town square ☎051 251237, ⬤inthirahotels.com. Thakhek's first proper boutique hotel actually comprises two restored colonial-era trading houses in the heart of town. Each room has a modern, studio feel with lots of polished wood, plus a minibar, TV and a/c. The two big rooms at the front of the building have balconies with views of the square. There's a very good restaurant on the ground floor (see below). $29
Khamouanne Inter Kouvolavong Rd, 300m east of the river ☎051 212171. Newly spruced up with bright-green paint (but still with the same kitsch 3D floor tiles), this guesthouse is the best budget option near the river. Ask to see a few rooms before checking in, as quality and cleanliness varies. 80,000K
Riveria Setthathilat Rd, opposite the Immigration Office ☎051 250000, ⬤hotelriveriathakhek.com. The swankiest place in town, the *Riveria* has a range of double and twin rooms – some with million-dollar views of the Mekong – and modern facilities, including a business centre and banqueting hall. Helpful staff; in-room wi-fi and big buffet breakfast included in the room rate. $65

Song Lao On a quiet street north of Phouhanna (follow the yellow signs) ☎030 530520. A little out of town and more peaceful as a result, Song Lao has lovely double rooms in a long, wood-clad building facing a fragrant garden. There are also a couple of VIP bungalows at the far end (150,000K). 120,000K
Thakhek Travel Lodge Up a side road halfway between the Kilometre 2 and 3 markets ☎051 212931, ✉thakhektravellodge@gmail.com. Despite being a long walk from the river, this three-storey guesthouse is the most popular budget option in town. It features basic dormitories and fan rooms with shared facilities, as well as a/c en-suite rooms, all reasonably priced. They also rent out bicycles, motorbikes and vans, and run tours. Dorm 30,000K, double 60,000K
Xayluedy On Vientiane Rd, west of the tourist office ☎020 2217 8222. If it's a fresh, tidy room you're after, look no further than this new, glass-fronted block. There are two types of rooms available but both have a/c, wi-fi and a flatscreen TV, so unless you need lots of space, go for the cheaper option. 130,000K

EATING AND DRINKING

Thakhek is no centre of culinary excellence, but eating options have diversified in recent years, and there are now a few decent restaurants around town. In addition to these, pancake stalls set up across from the *Inthira* each evening, and there are usually a few stalls selling fresh fruit, cold drinks and sugar cane on the riverfront.

The Kitchen At the Inthira on Chao Anou Rd ☎051 251237, ⬤inthirahotels.com. The restaurant on the ground-floor of the *Inthira* serves consistently good Asian and Western dishes from a clean, shop-front kitchen. Pizzas, cocktails and cheeseburgers (38,000K) are all on offer, and it's worth trying the "explorer" set menu (85,000K), which features a good mix of Lao classics. Daily 7.30am–10pm.
Nid Cake On Vientiane Road, a short walk from the junction with Chao Anou Rd ☎020 5565 1008. The home-made cakes here are super sweet (in both senses of

the word), and can be enjoyed in a shaded shop front dotted with cute gnomes. Cakes from 5000K; ice creams also available. Daily 7am–10pm.
★**Orlasone Fusion** Chao Anou Rd, north of the junction with Vientiane Rd ☎020 5522 2409. There's a very good reason why locals flock to this open-air grill restaurant of an evening. Fresh slivers of beef, pork and seafood are delivered raw for diners to cook and then dip in the deliciously spicy sauces. Braver visitors may like to order a plate of heart or liver to go with the rest of their meal. Daily 4–11.30pm.

5

ORGANIZED TOURS AROUND THAKHEK

Good tours of the **caves near Thakhek** are run by **Green Discovery**, which has a helpful desk on the ground floor of the *Inthira* (daily 8am–9pm; ⓦ greendiscovery.org). Among the trips on offer is a half-day excursion to the Buddha Cave, 17km to the northeast of town, which contains more than 220 bronze Buddha images ($30 per person, based on two people taking the tour). A longer, full-day tour adds in a visit to Tham Nong Paseum, a 400-metre-long cave with an underground river ($80 per person, based on two people taking the tour). A much cheaper option is to visit the caves independently and hire a kayak for some paddling around when you get there (100,000K for up to three people). The tourist office in Thakhek (see p.211) can advise you on getting there by sawngthaew.

Green Discovery also runs longer trips to the northern end of the **Khammouane Limestone NBCA**, including a three-day excursion to **Kong Lo Cave**, which involves a good mix of cycling, trekking and kayaking, and includes meals and accommodation ($451 per person if two people take the tour). Bear in mind that if you're heading to Vientiane later on your travels, tours from there tend to be slightly cheaper, and the choice of companies much wider.

★ **Phoukhanna** Vientiane Rd, east of Xayluedy ☎ 020 216 8088. One of the quirkiest places to drink in town, with probably the cheapest beer too (a big Beerlao is a steal at just 8000K). Late evening is the best time to go, when young locals arrive to sing along to the loud music, drinking and snacking in thatched huts strewn with fairy lights. Daily until 11.30pm.

Song Fang Khong Kouvolavong Rd, just north of the square ☎ 020 5403 3350. Surprisingly authentic dishes from the country on the other side of the Mekong, prepared by a Thai chef. It's a small operation with a tiny corner kitchen, so you'll have to wait a while for your *som tam* (10,000K), especially at busy times. Daily 10am–11pm.

Mahaxai Caves

East of Thakhek, Route 12 is swallowed up by a surreal landscape of karst formations. Hidden among the sea of jagged limestone hills are the **Mahaxai Caves**, many of which lie within the Khammouane Limestone NBCA. A number of the more easily accessible caves are popular both with Lao families on a weekend picnic and with foreign tourists. These more visited caves line the Thakhek–Mahaxai road, the furthest one only about 20km from Thakhek. The best caves here are spectacular and a day-trip out to explore them is a must if you're staying in Thakhek.

Tham Ban Tham

Ban Tham • 3000K

To find this cave, turn south down the dirt road that leads off Route 12 towards **Ban Tham**, a small village nestling at the base of the first limestone escarpment. The gaping mouth of the tautologically named **Tham Ban Tham** ("tham" meaning "cave") should be visible from the highway. Cut through the village to find the concrete stairs leading up to the cave, which contains a shrine, centred on a sizeable Buddha image. Perched partway up the side of the hill, Tham Ban Tham offers a commanding view of the surroundings, and is particularly pretty at sunset. If you've come with a local, ask to see the shrine to Ganesh, an elephantine rock hidden in a tunnel within the main cavern. From Ban Tham, follow the road cutting north to get back on the main road.

Tham Xieng Liap and Tha Falang

Free

Just before the second wooden bridge along the Thakhek–Mahaxai road, roughly 17km from Thakhek, a dirt path on the right leads to **Tham Xieng Liap**. After 300m the trail reaches a stream, which flows into the entrance of the cave on the opposite bank (during the monsoon, the water level may be too high to enter the cave). While not the most inspiring cave, Tham Xieng Liap is a pleasant stop chiefly for its seclusion and the novelty of scrambling across a stream full of rocks into the half-submerged cave mouth.

Further east along the main road is the disappointing **Tha Falang,** reputedly a favourite spot during colonial times with Thakhek's French residents, who would come here to picnic by a stream.

Tham Sa Pha In
Free

Drink vendors set up shop in the recesses of two cliffs 100m beyond the turn-off for Tha Falang, signposting the path leading to **Tham Sa Pha In**, which is without question the best of the caves. A small sign on the left points towards the path leading to the cave, a short walk from the main road. Look for the bamboo gate to find the cave entrance. The cave was renamed for the Hindu god Indra after the Second Indochina War, when villagers claimed to see the Hindu deity's image reflected in the pool. Illuminated by an inaccessible opening in the ceiling of the cave, the pool glows emerald green, the colour of Indra's skin. You can pause to light a candle by the shrine in the back of the cave before clambering down to sit by the pool, where swifts dive-bombing the surface and the drone of insects conspire to give the deep cavern an otherworldly atmosphere.

Tham En
20,000K

The most visited of Mahaxai's caves, **Tham En**, named for the large number of sparrows that are said to inhabit the cave and popular for what the Lao call its natural air conditioning, lies another 4km up the road; it's easily located by the gate, where an official collects the entrance fee. A concrete stairway takes you deep into the tunnel mouth, but there is still plenty of room to clamber around on the rocks and climb up to one of the several cave mouths that offer great views of the forest outside. On weekends, the cave is packed with day-tripping locals picnicking and playing cards.

ARRIVAL AND INFORMATION   MAHAXAI CAVES

By motorbike and tuk-tuk The easiest way to reach the caves is by renting a motorbike (from 60,000K/day) or chartering a tuk-tuk from Thakhek (expect to pay around 250,000K for a full day, including fuel).

By public transport Some visitors prefer to catch a Mahaxai-bound bus to the caves and then explore on foot. Public transport can be tricky, however: pick-ups and buses travel the road frequently enough in the morning, but to get back, you'll have to flag down one of the buses or pick-ups coming from Mahaxai – of which there are several a day – although you can't count on catching one late in the afternoon.

On foot If you want to do a walking tour of the caves, a good starting point is Tham Ban Tham, on the road to Mahaxai, 7km from Thakhek; from here you can walk to Tham En (see above), taking in other caves en route, a 12km walk in all.

Mahaxai

Fifty kilometres east of the Mahaxai Caves lies the beautifully situated town of **MAHAXAI**, engulfed in limestone karst formations, on the banks of the Xe Bang Fai river. A bumpy 50km drive from Thakhek, this lively little town lacks sights of its own, but is nevertheless a charming place offering visitors enchanted by the strange beauty of Khammouane's karst formations a chance to soak up the surroundings at a more measured pace.

Hiring a **boat** to cruise the river, which stretches from the mountainous Vietnamese border to the Mekong, can be a bit of a chore – ask by the river or around town – but if you can swing it, a two-hour round-trip by motorized pirogue is scenic in either direction, with the upstream route taking in stunning cliffs and the downstream option skimming through gentle rapids, past submerged water buffalo and villagers catching fish. Most **cave** touring originates in Thakhek, but the area surrounding Mahaxai is also honeycombed with caves.

ARRIVAL AND DEPARTURE   **MAHAXAI**

By bus and pick-up Buses and pick-ups from Thakhek (5 daily; 2hr) grind to a halt at the central market, next to an old tin-roofed temple.

Khammouane Limestone NBCA

The most accessible of Khammouane province's three NBCAs is the Phou Hin Poun NBCA, more popularly known as the **Khammouane Limestone NBCA** and home to a dizzying array of wildlife, including elephants, tigers and macaques. Unlike the neighbouring Nakai-Nam Theun and Hin Nam No NBCAs to the east, the Khammouane Limestone NBCA can be accessed by road or river from a number of approaches, making it the most practical and affordable of the three to visit.

The best way to experience the park is on an organized **tour**; a do-it-yourself tour won't allow you to penetrate the interior of the park to the degree a professionally organized expedition can. The chief highlight of many of the tours is the journey by kayak through the wonderfully dramatic **Kong Lo Cave**, a natural 7km river tunnel through a limestone karst mountain into a hidden valley. Bring a torch and some rubber flip-flops as it can be necessary to wade through the shallower stretches of the river.

ARRIVAL AND DEPARTURE   **KHAMMOUANE LIMESTONE NBCA**

By bus It's possible (if complicated) to get as far as Kong Lo Cave using public transport. A sawngthaew leaves Phetmany Market in Thakhek each morning at around 7.30am, bound for Lak Xao. Ask to get off at Khoun Kham, and change to a southbound sawngthaew for the final stretch to Kong Lo Cave. Getting back to Thakhek on the same day is impossible, so plan on staying there for at least one night.

On a tour Organized tours within Khammouane Limestone NBCA operate out of Thakhek (see p.212) and Vientiane (see p.72), and generally include kayaking, hiking and **village stays**. Do-it-yourself tours from Thakhek are also easily arranged and affordable – contact the tourist office in Thakhek.

ACCOMMODATION

L'Auberge Sala Hine Boun On the banks of the Nam Hin Poun river; it's reached by taking a tuk-tuk from Na Hin (on Route 8) to Ban Na Phouak on the northern boundary of the NBCA, and then a boat up the Nam Hin Poun ($15; 2hr) ☎020 755220, ⓦsalalao.com. This eco-resort within the park has comfortable bungalows and is within easy day-hiking distance of a number of hill-tribe villages, Tham Thieng cave and Kong Lo Cave. Kayak excursions through the underground river can be arranged here, though a cheaper option, especially if you're travelling solo, is to arrive at the cave with your own transport and wait until you can split the cost of a longtail boat and driver (around $10) with other sightseers. **$23**

Savannakhet

SAVANNAKHET (known locally as "Savan") is one of the country's largest cities, and the surrounding area that makes up Savannakhet province, stretching from the Mekong river to the Annamite Mountains, is Laos's most populous region; for centuries the inhabitants fought off designs on their territory from both Vietnam and Thailand. The city is also south central Laos's most visited provincial capital, its popularity with travellers due in part to its central location on the overland route between Vientiane and Pakse and between Thailand and Vietnam, the two countries linked to each other by a 240km-long road originally carved by the French. At the time of writing, work had just begun on a high-speed rail line linking Savannakhet with the Vietnamese border town of Lao Bao. The controversial project would slash journey times between Thailand and Vietnam and, critics say, leave Laos with a crippling debt to repay.

Aside from being an important junction, Savannakhet also possesses very impressive **architecture**, and is a major staging post for **jungle treks** and cycling tours.

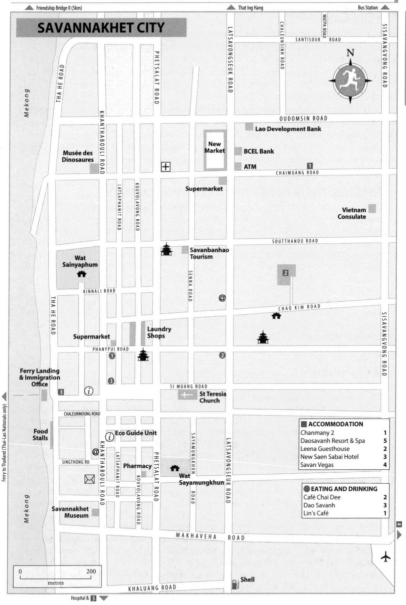

SAVANNAKHET CITY

ACCOMMODATION
Chanmany 2	1
Daosavanh Resort & Spa	5
Leena Guesthouse	2
New Saen Sabai Hotel	3
Savan Vegas	4

EATING AND DRINKING
Café Chai Dee	2
Dao Savanh	3
Lin's Café	1

Savannakhet's inhabitants, as travellers who have recently arrived from Vietnam are quick to note, are much mellower than their neighbours east of the Annamite Mountains, despite the fact that a large percentage of the town's population is ethnic Vietnamese, descendants of entrepreneurs who migrated to Laos during French rule. Most have been living here for generations and consider themselves to be more Lao than Vietnamese in habit and temperament.

5

The Old City

Savannakhet's **town square** was the heart of the French settlement, the surrounding neat grid streets reserved for the villas of French officials and the shop houses of Vietnamese merchants. One of the best areas for a stroll or spin on a bike to see old buildings is the district of tree-lined streets and former French administrative offices south of the post office. The old town also has several pleasant wats and a few Chinese temples worth a wander.

The **Old French Quarter** boasts some fine examples of European-inspired architecture, though most of this looks much more ancient than it really is – it's doubtful that any of these crumbling structures predate the early twentieth century. The main square is dominated by the octagonal spire of **St Teresia Catholic Church**, built in 1930, its thick masonry walls keeping the interior blessedly cool even on the hottest of days.

KAYSONE: THE MAN BEHIND THE BAMBOO CURTAIN

When Lao prime minister and communist leader **Kaysone Phomvihane** died in 1992, party leaders commissioned 150 bronze statues of him, which have since been erected in pavilions across the country. Whether these busts are a faithful portrayal of Kaysone remains irrelevant to most Lao, since from 1958 until 1975, the leader of the People's Revolutionary Party was rarely seen in public. Only now that the state has begun remaking itself in his image is the cloud of secrecy surrounding him dissipating, but the lack of biographical details about his life makes it difficult to discern the private Kaysone from the state-cultivated one.

What is known is that Kaysone was born in Savannakhet in 1920, the only son of a Vietnamese civil servant father and a Lao mother. As a teenager he left for Hanoi, where he studied at a law school under the name of Nguyen Tri Quoc before dropping out to devote himself to the life of a revolutionary. By 1945, he had attracted the attention of North Vietnamese leader Ho Chi Minh, who instructed him to return home and infiltrate a Lao nationalist movement supported by the American Office of Strategic Services, a forerunner of the CIA.

Later that year, Kaysone and his followers deferred to the leadership of **Prince Souphanouvong**, whom he followed to Bangkok after the French returned to power in 1946. Soon after, Kaysone joined the newly formed Committee for Resistance in the East, coordinating anti-French guerrilla raids along the Lao–Vietnamese border and responsible for liaisons with the Viet Minh, a tie that was to earn him the trust of the North Vietnamese, who eventually recruited him into the Indochinese Communist Party (ICP). After training at the Viet Minh's military academy, Kaysone became commander of the Latsavong brigade, the guerrilla unit in southeastern Laos that marked the beginnings of the Lao People's Liberation Army. By 1950, Kaysone had been named defence minister in the Pathet Lao resistance government, where he spent four years recruiting and training members for the Pathet Lao's fighting force, of which he formally became commander in 1954. When the Lao People's Revolutionary Party formed in 1955, Kaysone became secretary general – a post he would hold for the next 37 years. His control of the revolutionary movement was further solidified in 1959 when Souphanouvong and other Pathet Lao leaders were jailed in Vientiane. Though Kaysone relinquished his post as commander of the army in 1962, he continued to direct military strategy until the end of the Thirty Year Struggle in 1975.

It was only fitting that Kaysone – a man who disdained the perquisites of military rank, indeed who was never even referred to by rank – should emerge as the first prime minister of the Lao People's Democratic Republic in December 1975. For the next seventeen years, Kaysone firmly held the reins of power in Laos and, among diplomats, earned a reputation as a clever man, eager to learn and willing to acknowledge his mistakes. He earned praise for ditching botched policies and initiating economic reforms, and by the time of his death at the age of 72, Kaysone's Laos hardly fitted the mould of a typical socialist country at all.

Since his **death**, the image of Kaysone's greying hair and full face has been employed by a party reaching out for symbols of nationalism. But more striking than the party's decision to transform Kaysone into a "man of the people", who relished simple food, are the pedestals upon which his bust has been placed. Shaded by red and gold pavilions topped by tiered parasols, Kaysone's monuments exude something of the regal splendour once reserved for the Theravada Buddhist monarchs who ruled over the kingdom of Lane Xang.

SAVANNAKHET ACTIVITIES AND TRIPS

Savannakhet Province is packed with options for environmentally sensitive trekking, cycling and wildlife tours – many of them still in their infancy. Staff at the **Eco Guide Unit** on Latsaphanit Road (Mon–Fri 8–11.30am & 1.30–4pm; ☎041 214203, ⓦsavannakhet-trekking .com) can offer advice on what's available and find you an English-speaking guide. The exceptionally helpful team here can organize a range of one- to five-day community-based treks, as well as guided cycling tours. Options for two-wheeled exploration include a one-day cycling tour to That Ing Hang (see p.218) with stops along the way to see weavers at work (around 200,0000 per person), and a longer two-day cycling trip with the chance to stay in a Lao home overnight (around 500,000K per person). The three-day "Katang Trail" trek (Nov–May only) is more focused on local culture and wildlife, with a good chance of spotting hornbills and monkeys in the Dong Phu Vieng protected area (around 1,500,000K per person). Prices are dependent on the number of people taking part.

If you'd rather save cash, a **self-guided tour** is a practical alternative. The main tourist office (see p.218) has an excellent series of free leaflets providing information on local street food (including prices and descriptions) and the locations of historic buildings, allowing you to explore the city at your own pace. A bike or motorbike ride in any direction from the centre gives an opportunity to view the difference in lifestyles between the ethnic Vietnamese of the town and the ethnic Lao in the countryside. As you head out, brick and stucco give way to teak and bamboo, while rows of shade trees come to an abrupt halt and fruit trees – mango, guava and papaya – begin to appear in every yard.

Vietnamese and Chinese joss houses and schools in the area attest to the wealth and influence of Savannakhet's merchant class, who came to the town in search of business opportunities. They left after the revolution, taking their money and entrepreneurial skills with them, and only recently have foreign investors begun to return.

Wat Sainyaphum
Tha He Road • Daily sunrise–sunset • Free

Just north of the ferry landing, on the road running along the Mekong, sits **Wat Sainyaphum**, Savannakhet's largest Buddhist monastery. Nearly all the structures at the wat, save for the school building in the northwest corner of the compound, have been restored in garish, circus-like hues. It is worth a visit, however, especially if you are looking for a serene, shady spot to while away the afternoon.

Musée des Dinosaures
North of Wat Sainyaphum, on Khanthabouli Rd • Daily 8am–noon & 1–4pm • 10,000K

Set up with help from French paleontologists, the **Musée des Dinosaures** showcases finds from digs around Savannakhet. It's a dusty, unloved little space, but the museum's latest discovery is intriguing enough to warrant a quick visit. The bones of a huge crocodile-like species named *Laosakalumensis laosensis* were uncovered around 145km southeast of the city, and are now displayed for visitors to see. Museum workers, showing off their exciting find, often encourage tourists to hold the fossilized bones.

Savannakhet Museum
Kanthabouli Rd, just south of the post office • Daily 8.30–11.30am & 1.30–4pm • 5000K

The unkempt **Savannakhet Museum** displays an odd collection of exhibits, including rusting guns and mines from the Second Indochina War and a couple of two-thousand-year-old bronze kettle drums recently discovered in Savannakhet Province. The drums were designed and made by the Dong Son people of northern Vietnam, and their presence here hints at the existence of an ancient trade route between the two regions. Entering the museum, be sure to look out for the huge gold bust of Kaysone, Savannakhet's most revered native son (see p.216).

5

That Ing Hang

Around 15km northeast of Savannakhet; follow Route 9 north for 12km, where a sign points to the right; follow this road for 3.5km to the stupa • Daily 8am–6pm • 5000K • A round-trip from the centre in a tuk tuk should cost 100,000K

A much-revered Buddhist stupa dating from the sixteenth century (although some locals claim it's over a thousand years old), **That Ing Hang** is located just outside Savannakhet and can be reached easily by bike, motorcycle or tuk-tuk. The stupa is covered in crude yet appealing stucco work, and the well-manicured courtyard that surrounds it offers a pleasant opportunity for a stroll and photographs.

The stupa is best visited during its annual festival in February when thousands make the pilgrimage, camping in its grounds. During the celebrations, the door to a small chamber at the base of the stupa is opened, and male devotees queue up to make offerings to the Buddha images inside. By custom, women are prohibited from entering this inner sanctum.

ARRIVAL AND DEPARTURE

SAVANNAKHET

By plane The airport is on the southeastern side of the town, off Makhaveha Road, a few blocks from the centre. Regular Lao Airlines (☎041 212140, ☏laoairlines.com) flights connect Savannakhet with Vientiane (2 daily Mon–Fri; 1hr) and Pakse (5 weekly; 30min).

By bus Most buses offload at the station on the north side of the town, with tuk-tuks on hand to make the 2km run into the city centre (10,000K).

Destinations Attapeu (2 daily; 10hr); Da Nang (1 daily; 13hr); Dansavanh/Lao Bao (3 daily; 6hr); Dong Ha, Vietnam (daily; 7hr); Don Khong, for Si Phan Don (1 daily; 7hr); Hué, Vietnam (1 daily; 13hr); Pakse (9 daily; 5hr); Salavan (1 daily; 8hr); Thakhek (at least 7 daily; 8hr); Vientiane (8 daily; 8–9hr); Xekong (1 daily; 5hr).

By sawngthaew From the New Market in the middle of town sawngthaews depart throughout the morning for destinations on Route 9. Note that these services may also call at (or even depart from) the road outside the main bus station. Arrive at the station early for the best chance of getting to your destination.

Destinations Dansavanh/Lao Bao (4 daily; 4hr); Muang Phin (4 daily; 3hr); Xepon (6 daily; 4hr).

To Thailand Ferries run between Savannakhet and Mukdahan in Thailand, but this crossing is reserved for Thai and Lao nationals. Tourists must use the 1.6km-long Friendship Bridge II, 5km north of Savannakhet, which has connected the two cities since 2007. Buses bound for Mukdahan leave Savannakhet's main bus terminal (12 daily; 14,000K), stopping at Thai immigration, where visas on arrival are available. The 40min bus ride ends at Mukdahan's main bus station, a short ride from the town centre.

To Vietnam A daily bus to Vietnam leaves Savannakhet at 10pm. Different cities are served, including Dong Ha, Hué and Da Nang (80,000–110,000K), depending on the day of the week you travel. A VIP bus bound for Dong Ha (Mon–Fri; 7hr) leaves the bus station at 10.30am. Note that even "direct" buses usually require a vehicle change (or a long wait) at the border. Local buses leave Savannakhet's bus station for the Lao Bao border (6hr) at 7.30am, 9am and noon each day.

INFORMATION

Tourist office The very well equipped tourist office, west of the main square (Mon–Fri 8–11.30am & 1.30–4pm ☎041 212755) can help with general enquiries, but if you want to go trekking in Savannakhet province, make a beeline for the Eco Guide Unit (see box, p.217), around the corner on Latsaphanit Road.

GETTING AROUND

Tuk-tuks As Savannakhet is incredibly spread out, you may find tuk-tuks easier than trying to walk the long blocks outside the old quarter, especially on hot days. Tuk-tuks can be flagged down around town and cost 10,000K for short distances within the centre.

Bike rental Bicycles are another excellent way of seeing the town and can be rented at hotels and guesthouses around town, including *Leena Guesthouse* (10,000K/day).

ACCOMMODATION

Savannakhet has a very good range of **accommodation**, including family-run guesthouses, business hotels and even a Vegas-style casino. Generally, the most atmospheric and convenient area to stay is in the old city, but don't expect to find charming guesthouses in colonial buildings as in Luang Prabang. Most of the best modern options are scattered on the wide streets outside the immediate vicinity of the old city, but these places can be inconvenient if you don't have your own transport.

5

Chanmany 2 East of the market, just off Chaimuang Rd ☏041 213992. Not really geared towards Western backpackers, but a great budget choice all the same, Chanmany 2 has fresh en-suite doubles in two quiet, peach-coloured buildings. No English spoken. **60,000K**

Daosavanh Resort & Spa Tha He Rd, south of the hospital ☏041 252188, ⓦdaosavanh.com. The most luxurious and best-equipped hotel in Savannakhet sprawls alongside the main river road. Many of the rooms and suites face the hotel's glistening blue pool, which is surrounded by mature fruit trees. The resort has its own spa, gym and restaurant, and non-guests can pay to use the pool (100,000K/day). **575,000K**

Leena Guesthouse Head 200m east along Chao Kim Rd, off Latsavongseuk Rd, and follow the signs ☏041 212404. Two worn but comfortable buildings in a quiet residential area, offering en-suite rooms, some with a/c, hot water and TV. There's a pleasant restaurant serving

Western breakfasts downstairs, and a huge wat and a Chinese temple nearby. **50,000K**, a/c **90,000K**

New Saen Sabai Hotel Just opposite the ferry landing on Tha He Road ☏041 252601, ⓔnewsaensabai99 @gmail.com. This modern block has relatively smart rooms with carpeted floors, small balconies, glass hand basins and decent corner showers. Rooms are a little overpriced, so you may like to ask for a reduction, but the location is undoubtedly good. **250,000K**

Savan Vegas Nongdeune Village, just south of the airport ☏041 252200, ⓦsavanvegas.com. Plans to transform Savannakhet into the new "Lao Vegas" don't seem to have materialized, leaving this place as the only resort on The Strip. This vast, brash, international-class hotel has a range of rooms, all with high-end fixtures and fittings. Non-guests are welcome to try their luck at the tables and slots (Thai baht only). **400,000K**

EATING

The food and service at Savannakhet's **travellers' cafés** are passable, but the town does have some very good street food. One famous local noodle dish worth seeking out is *baw bun* (Vietnamese rice noodles served with chopped-up spring rolls and beef). Vietnamese spring rolls are also quite good here. Other local delights include bamboo shoots and watermelon and *sin Savannakhet* – sweet, dried, roasted beef. Head to the tourist office to pick up a free leaflet providing information on local food.

Café Chai Dee Latsavongseuk Rd ☏020 5988 6767, ⓦcafechaidee.com. Chilled café-restaurant turning out a mix of Western and Japanese dishes, plus *lào-láo* mojitos (24,000K) and red wine by the glass (20,000K). There's also a book exchange, and handmade local crafts are offered for sale. Daily except Fri 8.30am–9pm.

Dao Savanh On the northwestern side of the town square ☏041 260888. French cuisine par excellence at this beautifully restored colonial house right in the heart of town. Try the delicious set menu featuring green garden

salad, beef bourguignon and ice cream for dessert (65,000K). Daily except Tues 10am–9.30pm.

★**Lin's Café** Latsaphanit Rd, just north of the town square ☏020 9988 1630. An ideal spot for a coffee or coconut milkshake (10,000K), with free wi-fi, a stack of the latest newspapers and a wide selection of books about Laos. The food menu runs from organic salads to homemade veggie curries, and upstairs there's a small exhibition about the history of the region. Daily except Wed 8.30am–8pm.

DIRECTORY

Banks and exchange The Lao Development Bank and the BCEL are near the intersection of Latsavongseuk and Oudomsin roads, the former facing Oudomsin Road and the latter facing Latsavongseuk Road.

Consulates Vietnam: on Sisavangvong Road (Mon–Fri 7.30–11am & 1.30–4pm; ☏041 212418).

Hospitals and clinics The biggest hospital is located on Khanthabouli Road, near the provincial museum.

Internet access A handful of internet places can be found around town. The gaming shop on Latsavongseuk Road, just across from the turn-off to *Leena Guesthouse*, has computers available for 4000K/hr (daily 7am–11pm). Otherwise, most guesthouses and Western-style cafés have free wi-fi.

Laundry You'll get a fast and cheap service at the laundry shops on Kouvolavong Road, north of the town square.

East to Xepon and the Vietnam border

From Savannakhet, **Route 9** heads east through a series of drab and dusty towns, passing Muang Phin and then Xepon, where it begins its climb up into the Annamite Mountains. The road ends its Lao journey at the **Lao Bao pass**, before crossing into Vietnam and continuing down to **Dong Ha**, where it joins Highway 1. The French completed the road in 1930, as part of an Indochinese road network intended to link

5

Mekong towns with the Vietnamese coast, bringing in Vietnamese migrants and trucking out Lao produce. Today, the Thais, too, have an interest in Route 9 as a trade corridor, linking their relatively poor northeastern provinces with the port of Da Nang in Vietnam. When a new rail route linking Thailand with Vietnam opens towards the end of this decade (see p.206), the importance of the route will increase even further.

While most travellers barrel through on direct buses to and from Vietnam, the frontier is not without sites of interest. As you approach **Muang Phin**, Route 9 begins to cross the north–south arteries of the **Ho Chi Minh Trail**, a network of dirt paths and roads that spread throughout southeastern Laos, running from the Mu Gia Pass in Bolikhamxai province south through Attapeu and into Cambodia. While much of the debris from the war lies off the beaten track, some of these war relics are easily accessible. Another place worth stopping at to explore the surrounding area is the rebuilt market town of **Xepon**, which, along with neighbouring towns, is populated predominantly by Phu Tai people, a lowland Lao group.

Muang Phin

You'll know you've reached **MUANG PHIN**, roughly 160km east of Savannakhet, when you spot the massive Vietnamese–Lao friendship monument. The golden rendering of a Pathet Lao and North Vietnamese soldier dwarfs the town, whose run-down appearance attests to Muang Phin's unfortunate position on one of the fronts during the war.

Xepon

A ramshackle village in the foothills of the Annamite Mountains, 40km from the Vietnamese border, **XEPON** is a handy stopover en route to Vietnam or Savannakhet. It's such a small town that even the market fails to generate much of a buzz. The original town of Xepon was destroyed during the war – along with every house of the district's two hundred villages – and was later rebuilt here 6km west of its original location, on the opposite bank of the Xe Banghiang river. The old city (written as "Tchepone" on some old maps) had been captured by communist forces in 1960 and became an important outpost on the Ho Chi Minh Trail. As such, it was the target of a joint South Vietnamese and American invasion in 1971 (see box, p.279), aimed at disrupting the flow of troops and supplies headed for communist forces in South Vietnam.

ARRIVAL AND INFORMATION   XEPON

By bus Buses plying Route 9 drop passengers at the market towards the western end of town. From here, they run to and from Dansavanh/Lao Bao (4 daily; 1hr), Muang Phin (4 daily; 1hr) and Savannakhet (4 daily; 4hr).

VIETNAMESE INFLUENCE

Ties between Muang Phin and **Vietnam** go back a long way. During much of the eighteenth and nineteenth centuries, the area's Phu Tai inhabitants paid tribute to the court in Hué. In the middle of the nineteenth century, the Vietnamese rulers, having just wrapped up a war with Siam, were content to exact a light tribute of wax and elephant tusks from the Phu Tai, preferring to leave the Tai minority's territory as a loose buffer zone between regional powers. By this point, Vietnamese merchants, following the traditional trading route across the Lao Bao pass, were already arriving in Muang Phin with cooking pans, iron, salt and fish sauce, and returning east with cows and water buffaloes in tow. A story told by an early French visitor to the town attests to the business acumen of one of these merchants. Upon arriving in town, the merchant found prices too high, but was reluctant to return home without making a good profit. With a quick conversion to Buddhism the merchant's problem was solved: he shaved his head and shacked up in the local temple where he could defray his expenses until prices dropped, at which point the merchant donned a wig, bought up a few buffalo and hightailed it back to Hué.

By sawngthaew Any sawngthaew passing through Xepon will stop at the market (you may have to flag it down). From here it's possible to get to Ban Dong (see below), though getting there and back on the same day can be tricky, as there are few Savannakhet-bound sawnthaews running in the afternoon. Sawngthaews leave the market for the Lao Bao border post throughout the day (20,000K).

Exchange services There's a Western Union branch at the eastern end of Xepon's main drag (Mon–Fri 8am–3.30pm).

Motorbike rental You won't find an official rental place in Xepon, but the guys at the motorbike shop near the bus station may be willing to let you rent one of their old bikes for the run into Ban Dong.

ACCOMMODATION AND EATING

There's a surprisingly large number of cheap guesthouses in Xepon, but they're all pretty similar, with hastily assembled en-suite rooms in bland concrete buildings. The food scene is limited: your best bet is to head to one of the noodle shops opposite the bus station, which do tasty pork noodles for 15,000K, or try the market, where you'll find fresh fruit, bread and snacks.

Vieng Xay Just to the east of the market, on the opposite side of the road ☎ 041 214895. One of the more central options, with cheap double rooms and a small "tourist office" beside the lobby (no English is spoken), where a folder from the tourist office in Savannakhet gives you the latest information on transport to and from Vietnam. **50,000K**

The Ho Chi Minh Trail at Ban Dong

If you're travelling by public transport, the best time to visit Ban Dong is in the morning, as there are so few late-afternoon buses plying this stretch of highway; the most reliable way to reach the village is by motorbike

As you head east out of Xepon, the highway gradually climbs through the foothills of the Annamite chain, passing bomb craters – often obscured by brush – and unexploded ordnance, dragged to the roadside by villagers clearing their land. Women squat by the road with their intricately woven baskets, selling bamboo shoots – a local speciality. The area's abundant bamboo crop is in fact partially a by-product of the spraying of defoliants by American forces who hoped to expose the arteries of the Ho Chi Minh Trail: hardy bamboo is quick to take root in areas of deforestation.

Rows of drink shops, competing to quench the thirst of Vietnamese truckers, signal your arrival in **BAN DONG**, a popular stop on any tour of the **Ho Chi Minh Trail**. Villagers are slowly growing accustomed to tourists poking around for a glimpse of the Republic of Vietnam's American-made tanks left over from one of America's most ignominious defeats during the war, at the battle known as **Lam Son 719**. Ban Dong was cleared of unexploded war debris in 1998, but if you're travelling independently it's still a good idea to ask a villager to show you to the remaining war relics, as you should always take extra care when leaving a well-worn path.

Dansavanh

Pushing east from Ban Dong, tiny ethnic minority villages hug the roadside until you come to **DANSAVANH**, the last town on the Lao side of the pass. For a relatively remote border town, Dansavanh is actually quite tourist-friendly, though few people stick around long to explore – preferring instead to continue on to Vietnam.

ARRIVAL AND DEPARTURE   DANSAVANH

By bus or sawngthaew There are regular buses from Dansavanh to Muang Phin (4 daily; 2hr), Savannakhet (4 daily; 4hr) and Xepon (4 daily; 1hr). There are also sawngthaews running to Savannakhet until the early afternoon (40,000K); these may be just as quick as the bus or take much longer, depending on how often the driver decides to stop en route.

To Vietnam Crossing the Dansavanh/Lao Bao border (7am–10pm) can take time, so it pays to head for the Lao immigration post early in the morning if possible. Note that overnight buses from Savannakhet to the border tend to arrive at the border at around 3am, which means you may have to wait for the border to open before crossing. Remember, travellers wanting to enter Vietnam must arrange a visa in advance. On the Vietnamese side, there are motorcycle taxis to take you down the hill to Lao Bao town where buses leave for Khe Sanh and Dong Ha; from here bus or train connections can be made to Hanoi and Hué.

The far south

SI PHAN DON

The far south

Tropical, tranquil and steeped in ancient history: the tail end of Laos is popular for a reason. Anchored by the provinces of Champasak, Xekong, Attapeu and Salavan, the region lay at the crossroads of the great empires that ruled Southeast Asia centuries ago – Champa, Chenla and Angkor. Today, its proximity to Thailand, Cambodia and Vietnam makes it a favourite stop among backpackers, who come here for lazy islands, crashing waterfalls and ancient, sun-scorched temples. The far south conveniently divides into two sections, dictated primarily by topography, with Pakse, the region's most important market town, as the main hub. In the west, the Mekong river cuts Champasak province roughly in half, while further east, the fertile highlands of the Bolaven Plateau separate the Mekong corridor from the rugged Annamite Mountains that form Laos's border with Vietnam.

There are dozens of ancient Khmer temples scattered throughout the lush tropical forests that skirt the Mekong, the most famous of which, **Wat Phou**, is the spiritual centre of the region and the main tourist attraction in southern Laos. An imposing reminder of the Angkorian empire that once dominated much of Southeast Asia, Wat Phou is one of the most impressive Khmer ruins outside Cambodia, and lies a few kilometres from the town of **Champasak**, the former royal seat of the defunct Lao kingdom of the same name.

From here it makes sense to follow the river south until you reach **Si Phan Don** – or "Four Thousand Islands" – where the Mekong's 1993km journey through Laos rushes to a thundering conclusion in a series of picturesque **waterfalls**. As the region's name suggests, there are thousands of sandy islands cluttering the river, many of them home to long-established ethnic Lao villages, but just three – **Don Khong**, **Don Det** and **Don Khon** – have been properly developed for tourists.

Much of the area east of the Mekong lies off the beaten track, with travel here often involving long, bumpy journeys to spots of raw natural beauty. Easier to explore is the **Bolaven Plateau**, just east of Pakse, with its rich agricultural bounty and crashing waterfalls. Historically, the isolation of this region made it an ideal place for insurgents to hide out – from anti-French rebels to the North Vietnamese in the Second Indochina War. The latter transformed trails and roads along Laos's eastern edge into the Ho Chi Minh Trail, which American forces and their allies later subjected to some of the most intensive bombing in history. By braving the primitive transport links between the far-flung villages of Salavan, Xekong and Attapeu, you'll witness the resilience of the land, still home to a diverse variety of wildlife.

Pakse, the region's commercial and transport hub, provides the most convenient **gateway** to the far south, with travellers arriving either from Savannakhet or from

OLD FRENCH COLONIAL MANSION IN CHAMPASAK

Highlights

❶ Champasak Unwind in this sleepy town on the Mekong, taking time to explore temples, sacred mountains and ancient Khmer ruins. **See p.233**

❷ Wat Phou The most harmonious Khmer ruin outside Cambodia, this fifteen-century-old hillside landmark exudes a serenity lost in overrun Siem Reap. **See p.236**

❸ Si Phan Don – the "Four Thousand Islands" Discover crashing waterfalls and crumbling colonial buildings on these beautiful tropical islands, or spend your days stretched out in a riverside hammock. **See p.241**

❹ Dolphin-watching off Khon Island Try to spot endangered Irrawaddy freshwater dolphins in one of their last surviving habitats. **See p.247**

❺ Explore the Bolaven Plateau Ascend the Bolaven Plateau for cool breezes, towering hundred-metre falls and the freshest tea and coffee around. **See p.250**

❻ Tad Lo A relaxed backpacker scene is growing up around the base of these falls, whose clear swimming holes are invitingly cool. **See p.252**

HIGHLIGHTS ARE MARKED ON THE MAP ON P.226

Thailand via the Chong Mek border crossing. It's also possible to arrive from Stung Treng in Cambodia by road (see p.249), or from Vientiane by air.

The most pleasant **time of year** to visit the region is during the cool season (Nov–Feb), when the rivers and waterfalls are in full spate and the scenery is at its greenest.

Brief history

The **early history** of the far south remains a hot topic of debate among archeologists. Although the ruins of an ancient city buried near Champasak (and not far from Wat Phou) indicate that the area was the centre of a thriving civilization as early as the fifth century, no one seems sure if the town was part of **Champa**, a Hinduized kingdom that ruled parts of central Vietnam for more than fourteen centuries, or the **Chenla** kingdom, which is thought to have been located near the Mekong river in present-day northern Cambodia, extending through what is now southern Laos. The **Khmer** were the first people to leave a clear imprint on the area, and the temple ruins that survive throughout the far south along the Mekong river suggest the region was an important part of the Khmer empire from the eighth to the twelfth century, when the Angkor empire was at its height. It is also thought that the better part of southern Laos was

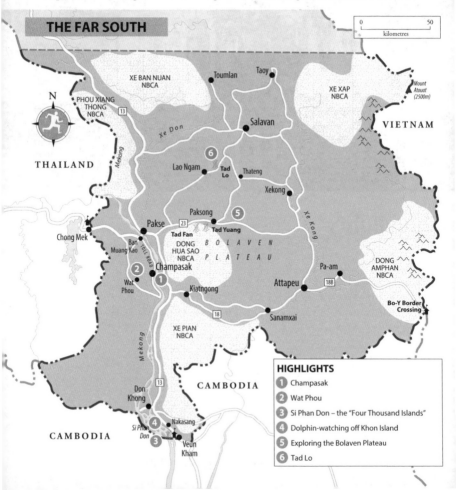

THE FAR SOUTH

0   50
kilometres

THAILAND

VIETNAM

Mount Atouot (2500m)

XE BAN NUAN NBCA
Toumlan
Taoy
XE XAP NBCA

PHOU XIANG THONG NBCA

Xe Don

Salavan

N

Lao Ngam   Tad Lo   Thateng

6

Xekong

Chong Mek

Pakse

Paksong

5

Ban Muang Kao   Tad Fan   Tad Yuang

DONG HUA SAO NBCA

B O L A V E N
P L A T E A U

Xe Kong

2

Champasak

1

Wat Phou

Kiatngong

Attapeu

Pa-am

DONG AMPHAN NBCA

Bo-Y Border Crossing

XE PIAN NBCA

Sanamxai

Mekong

Don Khong

CAMBODIA

4   Nakasang

Si Phan Don

3

Veun Kham

CAMBODIA

HIGHLIGHTS

1. Champasak
2. Wat Phou
3. Si Phan Don – the "Four Thousand Islands"
4. Dolphin-watching off Khon Island
5. Exploring the Bolaven Plateau
6. Tad Lo

dominated by ethnic Khmer, in particular the **Mon–Khmer ethnic groups** that still inhabit the Bolaven Plateau region and the Annamite Mountains.

The Lao Kingdom of Champasak

The **ethnic Lao** are relative newcomers to the region, having made their way slowly south along the Mekong as Angkor's power, and its hold over present-day southern Laos, waned. By the early sixteenth century, King Phothisalat was spending much of his time in Vientiane and eventually, in 1563, the capital of Lane Xang was shifted from Luang Prabang to Vientiane. While the origins of the first ethnic Lao principality in the Champasak region are unclear, legends trace the roots of the **Lao kingdom of Champasak** back to Nang Pao, a queen said to have ruled during the mid-seventeenth century. The story goes that **Nang Pao** was seduced by a prince from a nearby kingdom and gave birth out of wedlock, initiating a sex scandal for which she has been remembered ever since. The queen supposedly acknowledged her mistake by decreeing that every unwed mother must pay for her sin by sacrificing a buffalo to appease the spirits, a tradition continued into the late 1980s by unwed mothers, known as "Nang Pao's daughters", from some of the ethnic groups in the area. Legend has it that Nang Pao's actual daughter, Nang Peng, ceded rule over the kingdom to a holy man, who in turn sought out **Soi Sisamouth**, a descendant of Souligna Vongsa, the last great king of Lane Xang, and made him king in 1713.

Soi Sisamouth ascended the throne of an independent southern kingdom centred on present-day Champasak, near Wat Phou, and extended its influence to include part of present-day Thailand, as well as Salavan and Attapeu. But the king and his successor only managed to maintain a tenuous independence and, after its capital was captured by Siamese forces in 1778, Champasak was reduced to being a **vassal of Siam**, and so it remained until the French arrived more than one hundred years later, claiming all territory east of the Mekong river.

Division and reunification

Caught between French ambition and a still-powerful Siam, Champasak was split in half – a situation which lasted until 1904, when a Franco–Siamese treaty reunited its territories. Following this, Champasak's king, Kam Souk, had to travel to Pakse to swear his allegiance to France.

In 1946, Kam Souk's son, **Prince Boun Oum na Champasak**, renounced his claim to the throne of a sovereign Champasak (in exchange for the title of Inspector General for life) and recognized the king of Luang Prabang as the royal head of a unified Laos, effectively ending the Champasak royal line. When he fled Laos after the communist takeover in the mid-1970s, the Prince said the kingdom was doomed from the start because of Nang Pao's misdemeanour: "With an unmarried mother as queen, everything started so badly that the game was lost before it began."

Pakse

Capitalizing on its location at the confluence of the Xe Don and the Mekong rivers, roughly halfway between the Thai border and the fertile Bolaven Plateau, **PAKSE** is the far south's biggest city. For travellers, the place is mostly a convenient stopover en route to Si Phan Don and Wat Phou, though it's also a more comfortable base than Paksong for exploration of the Bolaven Plateau and nearby NBCAs, and the border crossing to Thailand just west at Chong Mek makes Pakse a logical entry or exit point for travellers making a north–south tour of Laos.

Unlike other major Mekong towns, Pakse is not an old city. Rather it has risen in prominence, from relatively recent beginnings a hundred years ago as a French administrative centre, to being the region's most important market town, attracting

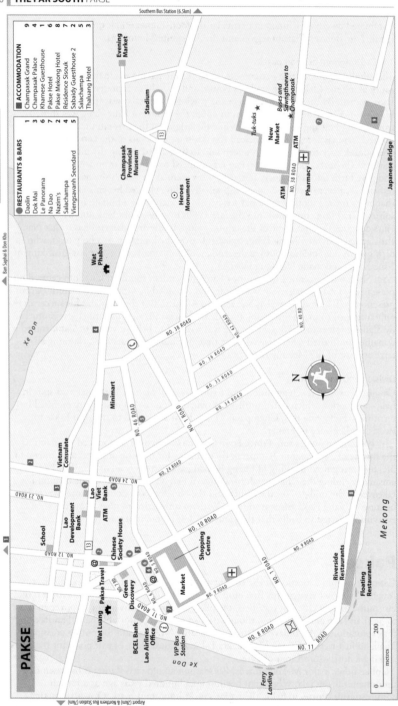

PAKSE

Southern Bus Station (6.5km)

Airport (2km) & Northern Bus Station (7km)

Ban Saphai & Don Kho

Xe Don

Mekong

Xe Don

Japanese Bridge

● RESTAURANTS & BARS	
Daolin	1
Dok Mai	3
Le Panorama	6
Na Dao	7
Nazim's	2
Salachampa	4
Viengsavanh Seendard	5

■ ACCOMMODATION	
Champasak Grand	9
Champasak Palace	4
Khamese Guesthouse	1
Pakse Hotel	6
Pakse Mekong Hotel	8
Résidence Sisouk	7
Sabaidy Guesthouse 2	2
Salachampa	5
Thaluang Hotel	3

Evening Market

Stadium

Champasak Provincial Museum

Heroes Monument

Wat Phabat

New Market

Tuk-tuks

Buses and Sawngthaews to Champasak

ATM

ATM

Pharmacy

Vietnam Consulate

Minimart

Lao Development Bank

Lao Viet Bank

ATM

School

Chinese Society House

Green Discovery

Pakse Travel

Wat Luang

BCEL Bank

Lao Airlines Office

VIP Bus Station

Market

Shopping Centre

Riverside Restaurants

Floating Restaurants

Ferry Landing

NO. 23 ROAD
NO. 12 ROAD
NO. 24 ROAD
NO. 46 ROAD
NO. 38 ROAD
NO. 36 ROAD
NO. 35 ROAD
NO. 34 ROAD
NO. 1 ROAD
NO. 43 ROAD
NO. 42 ROAD
NO. 48 ROAD
NO. 10 ROAD
NO. 9 ROAD
NO. 1 ROAD
NO. 11 ROAD
NO. 8 ROAD
NO. 9 ROAD
NO. 38 ROAD
NO. 11 ROAD

N

0   200
metres

traders from Salavan, Attapeu, Xekong and Si Phan Don, as well as from Thailand. The diverse and rapidly growing population of Vietnamese, Lao and Chinese today numbers some eighty thousand.

Nestling between the Mekong and a bend of the Xe Don, Pakse's centre, where you'll find the market and most of the hotels and restaurants, is surrounded by water on three sides. For some reason the streets in the centre of the city have all been laid out diagonally, but it's such a small place that finding your way around isn't a problem. Along No. 11 Road, the street that follows the Xe Don, are a few remaining examples of crumbling Franco–Chinese **shop houses** and the town's main temple, **Wat Luang**. Turning away from the river here, you'll soon find yourself by the big new **Champasak Plaza Shopping Centre**, built on the site of the old market that was razed by fire in 1998.

As more and more tourists make their way south to Pakse, the number of **day-trip options** has begun to grow. **Ban Saphai**, a silk-weaving village north of the city, offers the chance to see villagers weaving *sin* according to age-old practices, and experience life in a traditional town on the island of **Don Kho** in the middle of the Mekong. In the hills south of the city, the villagers of **Kiatngong** raise elephants, which can be hired for trekking, while nearby **Ban Phapho** presents the opportunity to observe elephants being trained for work in the forest. Other sights, such as the coffee plantations and waterfalls of **Bolaven Plateau** (see p.250), can also be taken in on day-trips from Pakse.

Chinese Society House

On No. 5 Road near *Salachampa*

For one of the few surviving examples of colonial architecture in the far south, be sure to check out the **Chinese Society House**, yet another French-era building. With many of the town's French-influenced buildings in disrepair or already replaced by modern shop houses, the Society House, beautifully renovated in 1998, is an elegant example of a style on the way out in rapidly modernizing Pakse.

Champasak Palace Hotel

On the northern edge of Route 13, west of Wat Phabat

To some the **Champasak Palace Hotel** is majestic, pretty even; to others it's a brash eyesore that resembles an ugly wedding cake. One thing is certain: it's one of the few prominent reminders of the late Prince Boun Oum na Champasak, a colourful character who was the heir to the Champasak kingdom and one of the most influential southerners of the last century. Legend has it that Boun Oum needed a palace this size so that he could accommodate his many concubines. The palace, left incomplete after the one-time prime minister wound up on the wrong side of history and left for France in the 1970s, was converted into a hotel (see p.232) by Thai investors, who retained its original wooden fittings, tiled pillars and high ceilings. The stucco motifs on the gables depicting the country's post-revolutionary zeal were not in the prince's original plans.

Champasak Provincial Museum

1.5km east of the town centre on Route 13 • Mon–Fri 8–11.30am & 1.30–4pm • 10,000K

The **Champasak Provincial Museum**, located in a bright-white building, is home to some fine examples of ornately carved pre-Angkorian sandstone **lintels**, taken from sites around the province. It's worth swinging by the museum if you've already walked or cycled this far east, but it's easy to leave the place feeling slightly underwhelmed.

The New Market

Just off No. 38 Road, around 2km southeast of the centre

Even if you don't need to buy anything, the huge **New Market** (Talat Dao Heuang) is
well worth a visit. Along with the usual array of mounds of tobacco, plastic ware and
live chickens, specialities available at the market include tea, coffee and a variety of fruit
and vegetables, much of this from the bountiful Bolaven Plateau, as well as fish from
the islands of Si Phan Don, including gigantic golden carp featherbacks, and the
fermented fish paste known as *pa dàek*, sold out of ceramic jars.

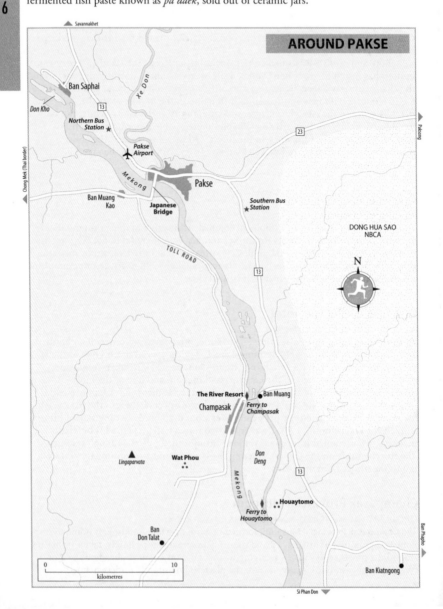

Ban Saphai

15km north of Pakse, a few kilometres west of Route 13 · Regular sawngthaews depart from the sawngthaew lot at Pakse's New Market, and stop at the market in the centre of town; check to see when they return to Pakse, as transport along the route is limited.

BAN SAPHAI is a sizeable village on the left bank of the Mekong river, where women weave on traditional hand looms in the shade of their family house. Their textiles are sold in one or two shops in the village market, or, if you prefer, you can negotiate with one of the weavers directly, although there's nothing here that you won't find in Pakse. Most visitors only stay for a quick look around, primarily using the village as a staging post for boat trips to the island of Don Kho.

6

Don Kho

Across the water from Ban Saphai · Take a sawngthaew to Ban Saphai and then hire a boat from the riverbank to ferry you across and back (40,000K for up to four people).

The villagers of **DON KHO**, a shady island located directly across the river from Ban Saphai, are well known for their talent at the loom. Rather than spending time in Ban Saphai, you might well opt to head straight here, as the friendliness of the villagers and the meandering dirt paths along the Mekong make for a pleasant, surprisingly relaxing visit. If you decide to stay, you'll find a small guesthouse on the island (30,000K) and bikes can be rented for 20,000K per day.

ARRIVAL AND DEPARTURE   PAKSE

By plane The airport lies 2km northwest of the city on Route 13, and is served by tuk-tuks on hand to greet flights. The Lao Airlines office is on No. 11 Road, near the BCEL Bank (Mon–Fri 8–11.30am & 1.30–4.30pm; ☏031 212152).

Destinations Luang Prabang (1 daily; 1hr 40min); Savannakhet (1 daily; 30min); Vientiane (2 daily; 50min).

By boat Route 13 is now such an easy drive that public boats have stopped running south from Pakse. Tourist boats (60,000K each way) run between Pakse and Champasak when demand is strong enough. To book, contact *Sabaidy Guesthouse 2* (see p.232).

By bus Long-distance buses pull in at stations around the city. Generally speaking, services to and from the north use

the Northern Bus Station, 7km north of the city on Route 13, while those to and from the south and east pull up at the Southern Bus Station, 8km southeast of town on Route 13 at the big T-junction; tuk-tuks from either bus station into town cost around 20,000K. The VIP Bus Station, just south of the tourist office on No. 11 Road, is for buses to Vientiane, Cambodia and Thailand.

Destinations Attapeu (10 daily; 4–5hr); Bangkok, Thailand (1 daily; 15hr); Phnom Penh, Cambodia (1 daily; 16hr); Salavan (9 daily; 3hr); Savannakhet (5 daily; 5hr); Siem Reap, Cambodia (1 daily; 16hr); Si Phan Don (1 daily; 2hr 30min); Tad Lo (4 daily; 3hr); Thakhek (5 daily; 8hr); Ubon Ratchathani, Thailand (2 daily; 3hr); Vientiane (at least 15 daily; 10–16hr); Xekong (10 daily; 2–4hr).

TOURS FROM PAKSE

Pakse's location, combined with its well-developed tourist infrastructure, means there's an excellent range of tours and day-trips on offer.

Tourist office (see p.232). The main tourist office is a very good place to start. Trips here include three days of trekking in the Xe Pian NBCA, an excursion that mixes kayaking, hiking and camping with plenty of opportunities for wildlife spotting ($180 per person based on two sharing).

Green Discovery ⓦgreendiscovery.org. Runs one-, two- and three-day trips to ride the elephants at Kiatngong, with prices from $97 per person, based on two people taking the trip. The same company also runs one-day trips to the Bolaven Plateau, taking in some of the region's most impressive waterfalls

(around $86 per person).

Pakse Travel No. 12 Rd Ⓦpaksetravel.com. A local company that organizes minivan excursions to Wat Phou and Si Phan Don, and can also arrange onward travel to Cambodia, Thailand and Vietnam.

Vat Phou Cruises No. 11 Rd, across from the tourist office Ⓦvatphou.com. Runs luxurious river cruises down the lower Mekong, taking three days to travel from Pakse to Wat Phou and back. The company's office in Pakse, located just across from the tourist office, offers last-minute rates that are significantly cheaper than the prices listed online.

6

By sawngthaew The busy sawngthaew lot on the eastern side of the New Market serves local destinations, including Champasak (2hr; 20,000K) and Vang Tao, where you can cross to the Thai town of Chong Mek. Daily sawngthaews to Paksong (1hr; 20,000K) and the three main islands of Si Phan Don (3hr; 50,000K) also leave the Southern Bus Station 9am–3.30pm.

Destinations Ban Saphai (roughly hourly; 30min); Champasak (roughly hourly; 2hr); Paksong (3 daily; 1hr); Si Phan Don (roughly hourly; 3hr); Vang Tao, for Thailand (roughly hourly; 50min).

To Thailand The easiest way to cross the border at Vang Tao (daily 5am–8pm) is to board one of the VIP buses bound for Ubon Ratchathani (80,000K), which leave Pakse twice a day. A cheaper, slower and more complex option is to take a sawngthaew from the New Market to the border (20,000K). After you've crossed into Thailand, local sawngthaews will be waiting to shuttle you to the town of Phibun Mangsahan, where you can transfer to buses to Ubon Ratchathani, which has an airport and plentiful road and rail links. Whichever way you're crossing, Lao and Thai visas are available on arrival at the border.

INFORMATION

Tourist office The Provincial Tourism Office is on No. 11 Road, near the Xe Don River (Mon–Fri 8am–noon & 1.30–4pm; ☎ 031 212021), and has bus timetables displayed on a touchscreen computer, as well as information on treks (see box, p.231).

GETTING AROUND

By tuk-tuk Pakse is compact enough to get around on foot, but for getting out to the bus stations or the museum, tuk-tuks and jumbos can be flagged down just about anywhere, especially on Route 13, which serves as the town's main boulevard. Expect to pay 10,000K per person for short inner-city journeys.

By bike or motorcycle Guesthouses and cafés around town rent out bikes (15,000K/day) and motorbikes (60,000K/day).

ACCOMMODATION

Pakse isn't chock-full of cheap hotels, but there's something to choose from in nearly every price bracket. Note that **budget hotels** are very poor value compared with the north of the country – a basic double room with its own en-suite bathroom, which might cost 60,000K in Vientiane, can go for as much as 100,000K or more in Pakse.

Champasak Grand South of the New Market, next to the Japanese Bridge ☎ 031 255111, ⚲ champasak grand.com. More luxurious than the *Champasak Palace*, with prices to match. It's a way out of town, and pretty soulless, but $80 buys you a modern room with spectacular river views, a quality buffet breakfast, and access to the blissfully cool pool. Minibar, a/c & TV. **$80**

Champasak Palace Route 13, just west of Wat Phabat ☎ 031 212263, ⚲ champasakpalacehotel.com. Though he didn't actually live here, this extraordinary building was once a palace built for Prince Boun Oum, who fled to France after the 1975 revolution. Royal-sized rooms lead onto wide terraces with sweeping views of the Xe Don river. The cheapest rooms in the ugly "new" block out back are best avoided in favour of those in the main hotel ($35). No longer the fanciest place in town, but still the most atmospheric. **$25**

Khamese Guesthouse Up a narrow track off No. 21 Rd, north of the school ☎ 030 571 2963. The cheapest double rooms in town can be found at this very basic riverside guesthouse, which has lovely views over the Xe Don. For 30,000K you get a mattress on the floor of a box room, plus access to a shared (cold) shower. More expensive en-suite rooms (60,000K) are available. **30,000K**

★**Pakse Hotel** No. 5 Rd, near the shopping centre ☎ 031 212131, ⚲ hotelpakse.com. The city's best-value mid-range hotel, offering spotlessly clean rooms in a central location. This former cinema is well managed by Jérôme, a Frenchman, and food served in the panoramic rooftop restaurant is good, if a little pricey. "Eco" rooms are cheapest, but you'll have to forgo a view of the city. Bookings advised. **250,000K**

Pakse Mekong Hotel No. 11 Rd ☎ 020 2230 9889. Gleaming-new, Lao-run hotel, just across the road from the Mekong, and a short stroll to the dozens of riverside restaurants. The good-sized double and twin rooms here have desks, TVs and free wi-fi, while the lobby has free-to-use computers. **$28**

Résidence Sisouk Just across from the tourist office ☎ 031 214716, ⚲ residence-sisouk.com. Hardwood floors and inspirational photos from around Laos add character to this central boutique hotel. Rooms are comfy and stylish, with plush white linen and free wi-fi, and there's a coffee shop attached. **$50**

Sabaidy Guesthouse 2 No. 24 Rd ☎ 031 212992. All budget travellers seem to head straight to this guesthouse, sited in a quiet, old residential area. Rooms are clean if spartan, and the dorm is the best in town. Dorm **40,000K**, double (shared bathroom) **80,000K**

Salachampa No. 10 Rd, near Champasak Plaza ☎ 031 212273. An elegant, restored French villa, with teak floors, verandas and a sitting room filled with antique furniture.

All rooms have bathrooms and a/c, but spurn the cheaper modern cottages on offer; rooms in the old building are spacious, with high ceilings. **150,000**

Thaluang Hotel At the northern end of No. 24 Rd

☎ 031 251399. Set around a compound full of leafy plants, rooms here are a little cramped and full of cobwebs, especially at the cheaper end, and beds are quite hard, so it's worth splashing out a little if you can. **70,000K**

EATING AND DRINKING

Pakse has the best range of **restaurants** south of Vientiane, largely owing to the number of foreigners working here and its mix of ethnic Vietnamese, Chinese and Lao communities. Most of the town's better restaurants are found in the centre, in the triangular-shaped area traced by roads 1, 10 and 13. South of here, along the Mekong, are dozens of similarly priced restaurants with great views over the water, selling everything from grilled duck to Thai food.

6

Daolin At the junction of Route 13 and No. 24 Rd ☎ 020 5573 3199. Positively bustling most of the day, Daolin lures people in with low prices and reliable backpacker food that's prepared in an open kitchen. Apart from the usual noodle dishes and cheese baguettes (15,000K), there's decent local coffee and gooey ice-cream sundaes (20,000K). Daily 6.30am–9pm.

Dok Mai No. 24 Rd, south of Route 13 ☎ 020 9800 8652. It's not quite like being in Italy, but the pasta dishes (from 30,000K) served at this skinny restaurant are pretty good, and drizzled with proper extra virgin olive oil. A quick warning: there's no pizza on the menu. Daily 11am–11pm.

Le Panorama On the top floor of Pakse Hotel. Worth a visit for the views across Pakse, *Le Panorama* is probably the most romantic spot in town, serving Asian and European dishes. The service and food don't quite match the ambience, but considering the location, the prices (mains around 45,000K) aren't too bad. Daily 4.30–11.30pm.

Na Dao North of the Champasak Grand on No. 16W Rd ☎ 031 255558. The classiest act in town, Na Dao serves a

delicious range of French dishes (think rib-eye steak and duck with fruit; mains around 85,000K) in stylish modern surroundings. Good wine list. Mon–Sat 11am–1.30pm & 6.30–10pm.

★ **Nazim's** No.12 Rd, just south of Route 13 ☎ 020 7760 5060. A very well-managed branch of Laos's most popular Indian restaurant chain, serving affordable meat and veggie curries (from 9000K per dish). Wash down the chillies with an ice-cold mango lassi. Daily 7.30am–10pm.

Salachampa Attached to the Salachampa (the entrance is on No. 12 Rd) ☎ 031 212273. Sip draught Beerlao (8000K/glass) in the shade of tall palm and papaya trees. The food isn't anything special, but there are some reasonably priced Lao dishes (watered down for western taste buds) to accompany the beer. Mon–Sat 6–10pm.

Viengsavanh Seendard Just south of No. 46 Rd ☎ 031 212388. A no-nonsense place that wins over locals with very tasty, inexpensive, barbecued meat that's fantastic with cold beer. The beef set, including lime, salad, dips and instant noodles, costs 50,000K. Daily 5–10pm.

DIRECTORY

Consulates Vietnam, on No. 24 Rd (Mon–Fri 8–11am & 2–4.30pm; ☎ 031 212824).

Hospital South of the shopping centre on No. 9 Rd.

Internet access Internet cafés come and go; your best

bet is *Sedone* (daily 8am–6pm; 5000K/hr), just south of *Pakse Hotel*. Otherwise, most hotels and tourist-oriented restaurants have free wi-fi.

Champasak and around

From Pakse, daily sawngthaews head south to the charming riverside town of **CHAMPASAK**, past misty green mountains and riverbanks loaded with palm trees. Meandering for 4km along the right bank of the Mekong, Champasak serves as a gateway to **Wat Phou** and other **Khmer ruins**. Although it is easily possible to visit Wat Phou as a day-trip from Pakse, there is plenty of cheap accommodation available in Champasak, and basing yourself here allows you to take in the sights at a leisurely pace. With its old wooden houses, three temples, Khmer ruins, mountains and river-boat trips, plus guesthouses and good food, it's easy to imagine Champasak becoming another Muang Ngoi in no time.

Brief history

Champasak's pace is so decidedly leisurely that it's difficult to imagine it as the capital of a once bustling kingdom, whose territory stretched from the Annamite Mountains into present-day Thailand. However, when France's Mekong expedition, led by

Doudart de Lagrée and Francis Garnier, arrived in 1866, they found it to be the most important city in the south, a status later usurped by Pakse when it became a French administrative centre. These days, the quiet cluster of ten villages that constitutes Champasak makes Pakse seem like a pulsing metropolis.

Palace of Prince Boun Oum

On the main road, downstream from what is probably the least-used roundabout in Laos, two elegant **French mansions**, tanned a pale yellow by the tropical sun, stand out from the traditional wooden shop houses. The first mansion belonged to the former **palace of Prince Boun Oum na Champasak**. Although in 1946 he renounced claims to sovereignty over the former kingdom of Champasak, Boun Oum retained his royal title and continued to perform his ritual duties as a Buddhist monarch until he fled the country prior to the Pathet Lao takeover; he died in France in 1980. During Lao New Year, Boun Oum performed purification rites at the town's temples to expel evil spirits, and on the final day of celebrations he would preside over ceremonies at this palace, in which a *maw thiam*, or medium, called the spirits of Champasak's past rulers, and a *basi* ceremony was held. Since the advent of the new government, however, the pageantry has been abandoned and New Year ceremonies in this former royal seat have become a strictly family affair.

As is the case with the nagas in front of Boun Oum's house, which were taken from Wat Phou, the area's most exquisite **pre-Angkorian relics** wound up in the late prince's private collection, some of which is now on display at Wat Phou's small museum.

ARRIVAL AND DEPARTURE | CHAMPASAK

By bus and sawngthaew Sawngthaews from Pakse should let you off at Champasak's tiny roundabout, towards the north of town. They may drop you at the *Anouxa Hotel*, 1km north of the roundabout, claiming you're in the centre of town; it's a peaceful enough location, but the bungalows here are overpriced. Three sawngthaews run through Champasak each morning (between 6.30am and 9am), charging 20,000K for the journey to Pakse. For bus connections to and from Si Phan Don, you'll need to cross the river to Ban Muang (7000K). Tickets to Si Phan Don sold at the tourist office in Champasak (70,000K) include a pick-up from your hotel, the ferry crossing and a minibus ride to either Ban Hat Xai Khoun or Nakasang, where you can catch a boat to the islands.

By boat If there is sufficient demand, two or three Pakse-bound tourist boats leave the dock, roughly 2km north of town, each day (the first is at 1pm), taking two hours to reach Pakse (70,000K). Travelling to Si Phan Don by boat is an altogether more complicated process. Unless lots of other travellers have the same idea, you'll need to hire the entire boat for the six-hour journey, and stump up around $250. To get yourself on either of these services, call in at the tourist office.

INFORMATION

Tourist office The tourist office, just off the roundabout (no phone; Mon–Fri 8am–11.30am and 2–4.30pm; also open weekends in high season with same hours), has a few useful maps and handouts, and is the best place to arrange bus rides and boat trips. Staff here are very helpful and are working hard with limited resources to develop new treks and tours in the area – ask for details, as by the time you read this, they may be up and running.

Services You'll find almost everything you need near Champasak's roundabout, including a bank, 100m to the west, where there's an ATM and exchange desk.

GETTING AROUND

By bike and motorbike The Inthira (see p.235) rents out bicycles (15,000K) and motorbikes (80,000K), as do most of the guesthouses in Champasak.

By tuk-tuk Tuk-tuks can be hired for trips to Wat Phou. You may not be able to find one on the street, so just ask at any guesthouse.

ACCOMMODATION AND EATING

Champasak With Love North of the roundabout ☎ 030 926 5926. Fresh and funky with its own terrace and a tree swing, *Champasak With Love* stands out among the town's riverside restaurants. The iced coffee (15,000K) is very good, but the food menu is a little uninspiring. Free wi-fi. Daily 7am–10pm.

Inthira Around 500m south of the roundabout ☎031 511011, ⊛inthirahotels.com. Comfortable, central accommodation with a hint of Lao styling. The best rooms – duplex suites with their own peaceful balconies – are pricey at $79 a night. Although it rarely seems busy, the hotel's restaurant, with a pool table on its first-floor terrace, is a safe bet for curries, pizzas, salads and cocktails (25,000K 6–8pm daily). Daily 7am–10pm. $49

Khamphouy South of the roundabout ☎020 2227 9922, ⊜gnesthouse@hotmail.com. None of the furniture matches, but this very welcoming, old-school guesthouse has good-value double and twin rooms in two separate buildings. Free wi-fi and tea, and a little lobby lounge full of books all help to seal the deal. 40,000K

★**The River Resort** 3.5km north of Champasak, on the Mekong ☎020 5685 0198, ⊛theriverresortlaos .com. For luxury in southern Laos this riverside hideaway is without rival. The twenty Lao–Japanese-style rooms, with outdoor showers and fan-cooled terraces, occupy an incredibly serene stretch of the Mekong's western edge, and are separated from one another by lush gardens of banana plants, organic rice paddies and majestically tall trees. The resort has its own spa and a panoramic restaurant overseen by a Thai chef. $119

Vongpaseud Just south of the Inthira ☎031 920038. Super-low prices make this place the top choice among budget travellers. Rooms here are dingy but en-suite, with hot water 20,000K extra per night. Breakfast is served on the creaking deck out back, which has splendid Mekong views. 30,000K

ENTERTAINMENT

Theatre d'Ombres de Champassak At Salachampa Restaurant, next to the tourist office ☎020 5508 1109. With French support and puppets rediscovered after forty years hidden in a local wat, fourteen local musicians, artists and singers have begun performing together. On Tuesdays and Fridays, the troupe re-enacts part of the Ramayana

---

THE LEGACY OF THE ANGKORIAN EMPIRE

In the mid-nineteenth century, French explorers began stumbling across the **monumental ruins** of a centuries-dead empire that had once blanketed mainland Southeast Asia. When word of these jungle-clad "lost cities" reached Europe, the intrigued populace assumed they must have been the work of expatriate Romans or perhaps some far-wandering tribe of Israelites. But as French exploration and colonization of Indochina expanded, scholars began to acknowledge they were the work of a highly sophisticated Southeast Asian culture.

The Khmer, whose descendants inhabit **Cambodia** today, controlled a vast empire that stretched north to Vientiane in Laos and as far west as the present-day border of Thailand and Burma. From its capital, located at Angkor in what is now northwestern Cambodia, a long line of kings reigned with absolute authority, each striving to build a monument to his own greatness which would outdo all previous monarchs. With cultural trappings inherited from earlier Khmer kingdoms, which in turn had borrowed heavily from Indian merchants that once dominated trade throughout Southeast Asia, the Khmer rulers at Angkor venerated deities from the **Hindu** and **Buddhist** pantheons. Eventually, a new and uniquely Khmer cult was born, the *devaraja* or god-king, which propagated the belief that a Khmer king was actually an incarnation of a certain Hindu deity on earth. Most of the Khmer kings of Angkor identified with the god Shiva, although Suryavarman II, builder of **Angkor Wat**, the most magnificent of all Khmer monuments, fancied himself an earthly incarnation of Vishnu.

In 1177, around 27 years after the death of Suryavarman II, armies from the rival kingdom of Champa took advantage of political instability and sacked Angkor, leaving the empire in disarray. After some years of chaos, **Jayavarman VII** took control of the leaderless Khmer people, embracing Mahayana Buddhism and expanding his empire to include much of present-day Thailand, Vietnam and Laos. But the days of Khmer glory were numbered. Soon after the death of Jayavarman VII the empire began to decline and by 1432 was so weak that the **Siamese**, who had previously served as mercenaries for the Khmer in their campaigns against Champa, were also able to give Angkor a thorough sacking. The Siamese pillaged the great stone temples of the Angkorian god-kings and force-marched members of the royal Khmer court, including the king's personal retinue of classical dancers, musicians, artisans and astrologers, back to Ayutthaya, then the capital of Siam. To this day, much of what Thais perceive as Thai culture, from the sinuous moves of classical dancers to the flowery language of the royal Thai court, was actually acquired from the Khmer. When the Angkorian empire collapsed, Siam moved in to fill the power vacuum and much of the Khmer culture absorbed by the Siamese was passed on to the Lao.

6

using shadow puppets, and on Wednesdays and Saturdays they add music and sound effects to a silent movie filmed in northern Laos by the team behind the original *King King movie*. Shows start at 8pm and admission is 50,000K.

Wat Phou

8km southwest of Champasak • Daily 8am–4.30pm • 35,000K • Tuk-tuks can be hired in Champasak (80,000K for a return trip), and will wait for you while you visit the ruins. If you're on your own and can't find anyone to share a ride with, rent a bike from town (15,000K) – it's a flat, pleasant ride.

One of the most evocative Khmer ruins outside Cambodia's borders, **Wat Phou** should be at the top of your southern Laos must-see list. It's not hard to see why the lush river valley here, dominated by an imposing 1500m-tall mountain, has been considered prime real estate for nearly two thousand years by a variety of peoples, in particular the Khmer. The surrounding forests are rich with wildlife, including the rare Asiatic black bear. The pristine state of the environment – it is without question one of the most scenic landscapes chosen by the Khmer for any of their temples – was a major factor in UNESCO's decision to name the area a World Heritage site.

Wat Phou ("Mountain Monastery" in Lao) is actually a series of ruined temples and shrines dating from the sixth to the twelfth centuries. Although the site is now associated with Theravada Buddhism, sandstone reliefs indicate that the ruins were once a **Hindu place of worship**. When viewed from the Mekong, it's clear why the site was chosen. A phallic stone outcropping, easily seen among the range's line of forested peaks, would have made the site especially auspicious to worshippers of Shiva, a Hindu god that is often symbolized by a phallus.

Archeologists tend to disagree on who the original founders of the site were and when it was first consecrated. The oldest parts of the ruins are thought to date back to the sixth century and were most likely built by the **ancient Khmer**, although some experts claim to see a connection to Champa. Whatever the case, the site is still considered highly sacred to the ethnic Lao who inhabit the region today, and is the focus of a **festival** in February, attracting thousands of Lao and Thai pilgrims annually.

The site

At the entrance to the site, a small **museum** houses pieces of sculpture found among the ruins as well as some said to have belonged to Prince Boun Oum. The **stone causeway** leading up to the first set of ruins was once lined with low stone pillars, the tips of which were formed into a stylized lotus bud. On either side of the causeway

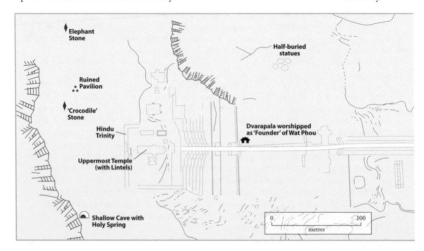

there would have been reservoirs known in Khmer as *baray*. As ancient Khmer architecture is rich in symbols, it is surmised that these pools represented the oceans that surrounded the mythical Mount Meru, home of the gods of the Hindu pantheon.

Just beyond the causeway, on either side of the path, two megalithic structures of sandstone and laterite mirror each other. According to local lore, they are segregated **palaces**, one for men and the other for women. Archeologists are sceptical though, pointing out that stone was reserved for constructing places of worship, and, even if this hadn't been the case, the vast interiors of both buildings were roofless and would have afforded little shelter. The structure on the right as you approach is the best preserved. Its carved relief of Shiva and his consort Uma riding the sacred bull Nandi is the best to be found on either building.

The stairways

As the path begins to climb, you come upon jagged stairways of sandstone blocks. Plumeria (frangipani) trees line the way, giving welcome shade and littering the worn stones with delicate blooms known in Lao as *dok champa*, the national flower of Laos. At the foot of the second stairway is a shrine to the legendary founder of Wat Phou. The statue is much venerated and, during the annual pilgrimage, is bedecked with offerings of flowers, incense and candles. When and why this one statue has come to be venerated in such a fashion is unknown, and once again, local folklore and archeological record diverge.

Continuing up the stairs, you come upon the final set of ruins, surrounded by mammoth mango trees. This uppermost temple contains the finest examples of **decorative stone lintels** (see box, p.239) in Laos. Although much has been damaged or is missing, sketches made by Georges Traipont, a French surveyor who visited the temple complex in the waning years of the nineteenth century, show the temple to have changed little since then. On the exterior walls flanking the east entrance are the images of *dvarapalas* and *devatas*, or female divinities, in high relief. On the altar, inside the sanctuary, stand **four Buddha images**, looking like a congress of benevolent space aliens. Doorways on each side of them lead to an empty room with walls of brick; it is thought that these walls constitute the oldest structure on the site, dating back to the sixth century.

To the right of the temple is a Lao Buddha of comparatively modern vintage, and just behind the temple is a relief carved into a half-buried slab of stone, depicting the Hindu trinity – a multi-armed, multi-headed Shiva (standing) is flanked by Brahma (left) and Vishnu (right).

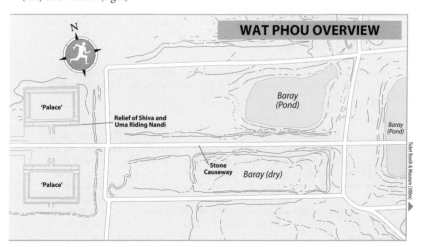

WAT PHOU OVERVIEW

'Palace'

Relief of Shiva and Uma Riding Nandi

Baray (Pond)

Baray (Pond)

Stone Causeway

Baray (dry)

'Palace'

Ticket Booth & Museum (300m)

6

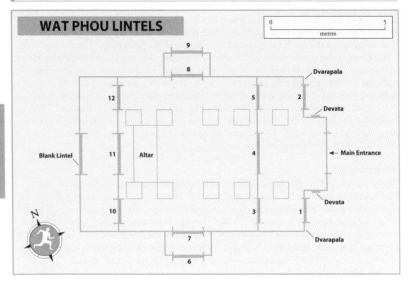

WAT PHOU LINTELS

0 _____ 5
metres

9
8
Dvarapala
12
5
2
Devata
Blank Lintel
11
Altar
4
◄— Main Entrance
Devata
10
3
1
N
7
Dvarapala
6

The cave

Continuing up the hill behind the temple, you'll come to a **shallow cave**, the floor of which is muddy from the constant drip of water that collects on its ceiling. This water is considered highly sacred, as it has trickled down from the peak of Lingaparvata. In former times, a system of stone pipes directed the run-off to the temple, where it bathed the enshrined Shivalinga. By tradition, this water was utilized in ceremonies for the coronation of Khmer kings and later the kings of Siam. Even today, Lao pilgrims will dip their fingers into a cistern located in the cave and ritually anoint themselves, although this is something foreign visitors should respectfully avoid.

The crocodile and elephant stones

If you follow the base of the cliff in a northerly direction, a bit of sleuthing will lead you to the enigmatic **crocodile stone**, which may have been used as an altar for pre-Angkor-period human sacrifices, though there is no hard evidence that ritual sacrifice was a part of the ceremonies that took place here. Nearby is a pile of sandstone rubble that once formed a pavilion and is thought by archeologists to be one of the oldest structures on the site. A few metres away to the north is the **elephant stone**, a huge, moss-covered boulder carved with the face of an elephant. This carving is relatively recent, probably dating from the nineteenth century.

Lingaparvata

If you were to hike straight up the mountain to the **summit of Lingaparvata**, it would take two days of rigorous climbing over vertical cliff faces and dense forest. In 1997, an Italian team of archeologists did just that. On the very tip of the natural phallic outcropping that is the peak of the mountain, they discovered a small Shivalinga of carved stone. Sadly, the archeologists found it necessary to remove this artefact that had crowned the sacred mountain for untold centuries, catching raindrops that would eventually filter down to the cave of lustral waters at the foot of the mountain. The trophy now rests in the small museum at the entrance to Wat Phou.

Hong Nang Sida Temple

1km south of Wat Phou (a trail runs between the two sites)

Hong Nang Sida is a small twelfth-century Khmer temple, built on an ancient thoroughfare that once stretched from Wat Phou to Angkor Wat. This little-visited ruin can be taken in in just a few minutes: the dimensions of Hong Nang Sida are modest compared with those of Wat Phou, and very few of the sandstone blocks from which it was constructed are adorned with carvings. Still, as with Wat Phou, the warm light on the venerable stone walls is particularly magical during sunrise and sunset.

6

Houaytomo Temple

Around 15km southeast of Champasak • Hire a pirogue at the tourist office in Champasak for the return trip south along the river (250,000K) • 10,000K

If your thirst for Khmer temples has yet to be quenched, a visit to **Houaytomo**, a tenth-century temple, is an option. Best visited as a day-trip from Champasak, the ruin is set in the midst of a lush forest on the banks of a stream, for which it is named. Also known by various other names, including Oum Muang, the temple is thought to have been dedicated to the consort of Shiva in her form as Rudani, and was "discovered" by Frenchman Etienne Edmond Lunet de Lajonquière early in the twentieth century.

DECORATIVE LINTELS AT WAT PHOU

The importance of the **decorative lintel** in Khmer art cannot be overstated. Here, more than anywhere else, Khmer artisans were free to display their superb stone-carving skills. Their imaginative depictions of deities, divinities, characters and events from Hindu and Buddhist mythology are recognized as some of the most exquisite art ever created. Early examples date from the seventh century, and as the styles and motifs have evolved over the centuries, experts are able to date lintels by comparing them to known works. The lintels at Wat Phou are listed below; the numbers correspond to those on the map (see opposite).

1 The god Krishna defeats the naga Kaliya In this story from the Bhagavad Purana, Krishna defeats Kaliya, a menacing water serpent that has been terrorizing villagers.

2 The god Vishnu riding the bird-man Garuda Although Vishnu on Garuda was a common theme in Khmer art, images of the two were rarely depicted on lintels.

3 Indra riding Airavata Despite being a Hindu god, Indra holds a significant place in Theravada Buddhist mythology. Until the Lao revolution Airavata, the three-headed elephant, was the official symbol of the Lao monarchy.

4 Indra on Airavata A larger and more detailed depiction of #3.

5 Deity atop Kala Although this deity is very commonly depicted on lintels, it is uncertain just who it is supposed to be. As the deity is holding a mace and sitting in the "royal ease" pose, perhaps it depicts a generic king or ruler.

6 Deity atop Kala (see #5) On the portico above the lintel is what is left of a scene from the Churning of the Sea of Milk myth, a contest between gods and demons for possession of the elixir of immortality. This scene is depicted most spectacularly on the bas-reliefs at Angkor Wat in Cambodia.

7 Krishna killing Kamsa From the Bhagavad Purana, a gruesome depiction of Krishna tearing his uncle in half. According to this myth, it was foretold that King Kamsa's death would come at the hands of one of his own family members. This prophecy launched the king on an orgy of killing which was only halted when his nephew put him to death.

8 Deity atop Kala (see #5)

9 Deity atop Kala (see #5) On the ruined portico above this lintel are the remains of a depiction of the god Vishnu in his incarnation as Narayana, reclining in cosmic slumber as he floats atop a naga on the waters of a vast primordial ocean.

10 Shiva as a rishi atop Kala Shiva is depicted as a wandering ascetic, perched above Kala.

11 Deity atop Kala (see #5) This lintel has been badly damaged, possibly by looters trying to remove part of the sculpture for the thriving stolen-antiquities trade in Thailand.

12 Deity atop Kala (see #5)

Xe Pian NBCA

Just southeast of Houaytomo and running the entire length of Route 13 all the way to Si Phan Don is the **Xe Pian NBCA**, roughly triangular in shape and bounded by Route 18 to the north. Although many tourists travel right alongside it for almost 150km en route to Don Khong, few are aware they are right next to Laos's southernmost NBCA and one of the country's largest (2400 square kilometres) nature reserves. The terrain here is mostly plains, although there are mixed deciduous forests and several peaks between 300m and 800m. In the east, the **Xe Kong** flows into Cambodia through the park, and tigers, elephants, leopards and **rhinoceros** may survive here. The best way to visit the NBCA is from Pakse, where tour companies can organize treks through the park (see p.231), including trips to the "elephant village" of **Kiatngong** and the enigmatic ruins atop **Phou Asa**, nearby.

Kiatngong and Phou Asa

50km southeast of Pakse • Elephant treks to Phou Asa about $10 • The best way to get here is by your own transport: travel agents in Pakse (see p.231) rent out vans and pick-ups, charging around $80 for a full day, including a driver and petrol, but you may be able to get a better price by chartering a sawngthaew from the New Market

Located approximately 50km southeast of Pakse, **KIATNGONG** is one of several villages in the area whose inhabitants keep **elephants**. In recent years, it's become possible for tourists to hire out elephants for treks up nearby **Phou Asa**, a jungle-clad hill with some mysterious ruins atop its summit. Phou Asa is thought to date back to the nineteenth century, and the site's layout suggests it was possibly used as a fort, though archeologists admit that the crudely stacked stone walls and pillars are an enigma. Local villagers, believing the ruins to be the remains of an ancient Buddhist monastery, periodically make pilgrimages to the site to leave offerings at a "Buddha's footprint" carved into a low cliff below the ruins. From the summit, commanding views of the surrounding dense jungle, rice fields and villages lend credence to the fort hypothesis. The best time to come is at dusk, when spectacular sunsets can be enjoyed. Some wooden cottages have been built for tour groups that overnight in the village; if you want to stay here independently, be sure to speak to the tourist office in Pakse first (see p.232).

Ban Phapho

20km from Kiatngong • Can be visited in one day together with Kiatngong if you charter a vehicle from Pakse

Ban Phapho, like Kiatngong, has a history of training of elephants for the timber trade. As in Kiatngong, elephant trekking can be arranged at the village, although Ban Phapho lacks the picturesque ruins and views that make Kiatngong the more popular destination. It has some basic accommodation with shared facilities – the tourist office in Pakse should be able to help you arrange a stay here.

THE CHANGING ROLE OF ELEPHANTS

Elephants have traditionally been used by the people of Kiatngong to haul timber and rice. Villages located far in the interior used to hire Kiatngong's elephants and mahouts to carry their rice harvest to main roads, where it could be transferred to trucks. Recently, though, new roads have made this mode of transport all but obsolete and mahouts have begun selling off their elephants. The last time villagers organized a hunt to round up wild elephants was in 1988, and many are turning to water buffalo as a more practical beast of burden. A steady stream of potential elephant trekkers, however, will ensure that at least for the time being, villagers here will continue to keep elephants as their ancestors did for centuries.

Si Phan Don (Four Thousand Islands)

In Laos's deepest south, just north of the border with Cambodia, the muddy stream of the Mekong is shattered into a 14km-wide web of rivulets, creating a landlocked archipelago. Known as **SI PHAN DON**, or Four Thousand Islands, this labyrinth of islets, rocks and sandbars has acted as a kind of bell jar, preserving traditional southern lowland Lao culture from outside influences. Island villages were largely unaffected by the French or American wars, and the islanders' customs and folk ways have been

6

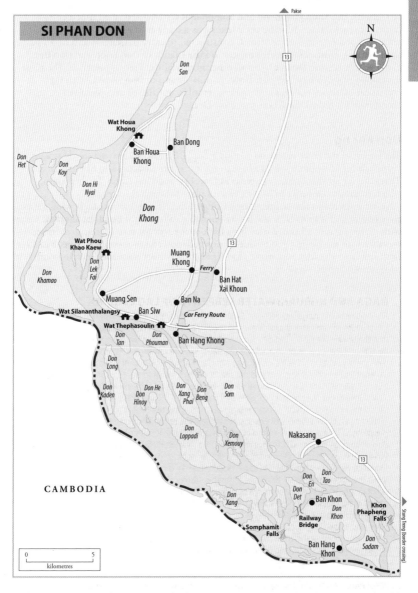

passed down uninterrupted since ancient times. As might be expected, the Mekong river plays a vital role in the lives of local inhabitants, with the vast majority of island families fishing for a living. Ecological awareness among locals is high by Lao standards, with nearly half of the villages in the district participating in voluntary fisheries conservation programmes.

The archipelago is also home to rare wetland flora and fauna, including an endangered species of freshwater **dolphin**, which it's sometimes possible to glimpse during the dry season. Southeast Asia's largest – and what many consider to be most spectacular – **waterfalls** are also located here. The area's biggest sightseeing attractions, the **Khon Phapheng** and **Somphamit** waterfalls, dashed nineteenth-century French hopes of using the Mekong as a trade artery into China. The remnants of a French-built railroad, constructed to carry passengers and cargo past these roaring obstacles, can still be seen on the islands of **Don Khon** and **Don Det**, along with a rusting locomotive and other ghosts of the French presence. The most developed place to base yourself is the popular island of **Don Khong**, with its collection of quaint villages and ancient temples, but there's also plenty of accommodation on Don Khon and Don Det.

Don Khong

The largest of the Four Thousand Islands group, **DON KHONG** draws a steady stream of visitors, most of whom use it as a base to explore other attractions in Si Phan Don. That said, it's nowhere near as popular as Don Det and Don Khon, further south, which means it's far easier to find a peaceful place to watch the sunset.

Now connected to the mainland by a bridge, Don Khong is surprisingly wide for a river island, and is known locally for its venerable collection of **Buddhist temples**, some with visible signs of a history stretching back to the sixth or seventh century. These, together with the island's good-value accommodation and interesting cuisine, based on fresh fish from the Mekong, make Don Khong the perfect place for indulging both adventurous and lazy moods.

NAGA AND NGEUAK: WATER SERPENTS OF LAO LEGEND

The origins of the **naga** are debated. Snake cults are thought to have existed in Southeast Asia long before the arrival of Buddhism in the region, particularly in Cambodia, so it is possible that this snake-like icon is indigenous. Another possibility is that the naga is a cultural migrant from Hindu India. In Hindu mythology, the naga, Sanskrit for serpent, is sometimes associated with the god Vishnu in his incarnation as Narayana, a cosmic dreamer reclining on the body of a giant naga and floating on an endless sea. Buddhism adopted the icon, and a story relates how, while meditating, the historic Buddha was sheltered by a seven-headed naga during a violent rainstorm. In Laos, it is probable that the present-day form of the naga, called *nak* or *phayanak* in Lao, is a fusion of both indigenous and imported beliefs.

The naga is both a symbol of water and its life-giving properties, and a protector of the Lao people. An old legend is still related of how a naga residing in a hole below Vientiane's That Dam stupa was known to rise up at critical moments and unleash itself upon foreign invaders. While the naga is mainly a benign figure, a similar water serpent, the **ngeuak**, is especially feared by Lao fishermen. Believed to devour the flesh of drowning victims, ngeuak are said to infest the waters around Si Phan Don. As for the existence of naga in modern-day Laos, the Lao point to "proof" that can be seen in a photograph displayed in some homes, restaurants and places of business. The photo shows a line of American soldiers displaying a freshly caught deep-sea fish that is several metres long; some copies of the photograph have the Lao words *nang phayanak* (Lady Naga) printed below. Skeptics argue the picture is of a giant oarfish, found off the west coast of the US in the 1990s, but many Lao still believe that the photo depicts a naga captured in the Mekong by American soldiers during the Second Indochina War.

CLOCKWISE FROM TOP LEFT COFFEE BEANS IN BOLAVEN (SEE BOX, P.253); TAD FAN WATERFALL (P.250); WAT PHOU SITE OVERVIEW (P.236) >

Don Khong has only three settlements of any size, the port town of **Muang Sen** on the island's west coast, the east-coast town of **MUANG KHONG**, where most of the accommodation and cafés are situated (see map, p.245), and the smaller town of **Ban Houa Khong**, where slow boats from Pakse moor. Like all Si Phan Don settlements, both Muang Sen's and Muang Khong's homes and shops cling to the bank of the Mekong for kilometres, but barely penetrate the interior, which is primarily reserved for rice fields. The best way to explore Don Khong and experience the traditional sights and sounds of riverside living is to rent a **bicycle** or motorbike from one of the guesthouses and set off along the road that circles the island. Don Khong's flat terrain and almost complete absence of motor vehicles make for ideal cycling conditions. For touring, the island can be neatly divided into **two loops**, southern and northern, each beginning at Muang Khong, or done all in one big loop.

Southern loop

Picturesque villages and almost completely flat roads make the **southern loop**, roughly 20km long, the more popular of the two itineraries. Follow the river road south from Muang Khong (taking care to stick to the narrow path along the river, not the road that parallels it slightly inland) until, a couple of kilometres south, you reach the little village of **Ban Na**, where the real scenery begins. Navigating the trail as it snakes between thickets of bamboo, you'll pass traditional southern Lao wooden houses trimmed with painted highlights of white and royal blue.

Approaching the tail of the island you'll emerge onto a paved road. The vast bridge you see on your left-hand side stretches for more than 700m, and cost nearly US$35 million to complete. Follow the road around to the far end of the bridge, and continue west along the road, passing rice paddies and the swishing tails of dusty water buffalos. Tall trees provide welcome shade as you pass through **Ban Siw**. Worth a look is the village monastery, **Wat Silananthalangsy**; the recently restored *sim* lacks charm, but a school building at the back of the compound has been left in a wonderfully decrepit state. This is often the case in Laos, as Buddhist laymen believe that much more merit is acquired by donating money towards the restoration of a structure that shelters Buddha images than by rebuilding a mere school for novice monks.

As you continue on from here, the number of houses lining the road continues to grow until you reach Muang Sen, a sleepy port with a popular floating restaurant. While there is nothing to see in the town, it's a recommended stop for rest and refreshment before heading east via the shade-stingy 8km stretch of very potholed road that leads back to Muang Khong.

Northern loop

The long, sometimes shadeless, route of the **northern loop** rewards handsomely with access to a serene forest monastery. The total distance of approximately 35km is best covered by **motorbike**; in the hot season, industrial-strength sunblock and a wide-brimmed hat are a must.

Starting from Muang Khong, you begin by heading due west on the road that bisects the island. During the hot season the plain of fallow rice paddies that makes up much of the island's interior looks and feels like a stretch of the Kalahari. After the rains break and rice paddies are planted, the scenery is quite beautiful.

Wat Phou Khao Kaew

Just before **Muang Sen**, turn right at the crossroads and head north; follow this road up and over a low gradient and after about 4km you'll pass a steep, bridge-like hump in the road. Keep going another 1500m and you'll notice large black boulders beginning to appear off to the left. Keeping your eyes left, you'll see a narrow trail that leads up to a ridge of the same black stone and, on the top of the hill, a large reclining Buddha. Park your bike at the foot of the ridge, and, following the trail up another 200m to the right, you'll spot a cluster of monks' quarters constructed of weathered teak. These structures belong to **Wat Phou Khao Kaew**, an evocative little forest monastery situated atop a river-sculpted stone bluff overlooking the Mekong. The centrepiece is a **brick stupa**; a fractured pre-Angkorian stone lintel found at the base of the stupa would, assuming it was once fixed to it, date the structure to the middle of the seventh century. Sadly, large parts of the original stupa have been haphazardly covered over with concrete and painted red and gold.

Nearby sits a charming miniature *sim*, flanked by plumeria trees. A curious collection of carved wooden deities, which somehow found their way downriver from Myanmar (Burma), decorates the ledges running around the building. If you want to have a look at the inside of the *sim*, ask one of the resident monks to unlock the door for you, or you can peer through the windows on either side of the main entrance, which faces the river.

Ban Houa Khong

If, after a look round Wat Phou Khao Kaew, you're still feeling energetic, continue another 6km north to **Ban Houa Khong**, on the outskirts of which stands the modest **residence of Khamtay Siphandone**, former revolutionary and ex-prime minister. Not far away is a **monastery** that has been restored to reflect the status of the village's most important part-time inhabitant. The wat is not all that remarkable, except perhaps for the collection of artefacts in the main temple. Sharing the altar with rows of Buddha images is a gargoyle-like object, actually a *somasutra* from an ancient Khmer temple, used to channel lustral water onto an enshrined Shivalinga. Next to the altar is a display case filled with small Buddha images and other dusty relics.

Tham Phou Khiaw

Pushing on from Ban Houa Khong, follow the road east to Ban Dong and then south to Muang Khong, a journey totalling 13km. On arriving at the northern outskirts of Muang Khong, just before reaching the high school, you pass a trail bordered with white stones, which leads to **Tham Phou Khiaw**, or Green Mountain Cave. Although it has gained quite a reputation among travellers, based no doubt on the obscurity of its location, the cave is no Lost City of Gold: in reality, it's a shallow grotto sheltering one

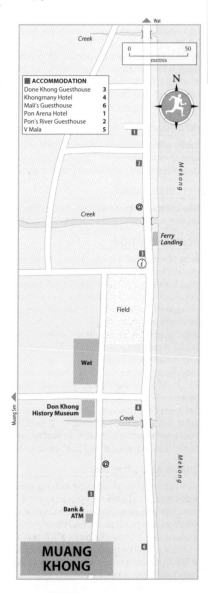

6

▲ Wat

Creek

0   50
metres

N

■ **ACCOMMODATION**
Done Khong Guesthouse	3
Khongmany Hotel	4
Mali's Guesthouse	6
Pon Arena Hotel	1
Pon's River Guesthouse	2
V Mala	5

Mekong

Creek

@

Ferry Landing

ℹ

Field

Wat

Muang Sen

Don Khong History Museum

Creek

@

Mekong

Bank & ATM

MUANG KHONG

termite-riddled Buddha and a number of clay pots containing crude votive tablets, each with an image of the Buddha pressed into it. Unless you're here during the Lao New Year celebrations, when islanders visit the site to make offerings and ritually bathe the images, or the Bun Bang Fai festival, a month later, when bamboo skyrockets are launched in a rain-making ritual, it's not really worth the effort.

ARRIVAL AND DEPARTURE   DON KHONG

By boat Boats dock in the middle of Muang Khong, near Done Khong Guesthouse. Boats to Don Khon and Don Det depart from the same spot daily at 8.30am (1hr 30min) and cost 40,000K; arrange through the guesthouses the day before.

By bus or sawngthaew A total of six public buses to Don Khong, as well as numerous sawngthaews (3hr; 50,000K), leave from Pakse's Southern Bus Station daily, stopping at Ban Hat Xai Khoun to allow passengers to cross the Mekong by boat. The chances of getting a public bus from Ban Hat

Xai Khoun back to Pakse are pretty slim, but if you want to chance your arm, cross the river by pirogue (15,000K) and wait for one to pass by on Route 13.

By tourist bus A more reliable option is to take one of the tourist buses operated by companies in Pakse and Champasak (both 70,000K). Often, the tickets include the boat transfer from Ban Hat Xai Khoun to Muang Khong, but check when buying. Leaving Don Khong is easy; almost every guesthouse in Muang Khong sells tickets to major cities in Laos, Thailand and Cambodia, with prices including boat transfers.

INFORMATION

Tourist office There's a tourist office just south of Done Khong Guesthouse (Mon–Fri 8–11.30am & 2–4.30pm). Staff can provide timetables and book onward transport for you.

Internet Most guesthouses offer free wi-fi. Otherwise, try the internet café just north of V Mala (200K/minute).

GETTING AROUND

Bike and motorbike rental Several of the guesthouses and shops in Muang Khong offer bicycles for rent (10,000K/

day); the shop beside Pon's River Guesthouse also rents out motorbikes (50,000K/day).

ACCOMMODATION   MUANG KHONG, DON KHONG

Done Khong Guesthouse Just across the road from the ferry landing ☎031 214010. This long-established place, in a very handy location near the dock, has basic en-suite rooms (those at the front share a little terrace), plus a popular restaurant and very friendly staff who speak both English and French. 70,000K

Mali's Guesthouse 250m south of the ferry landing ☎030 534 6621, ⚲maliguesthouse.com. Quaint double rooms looked after by a charming, English-speaking lady, and separated from the riverfront by a well-kept garden. TV, a/c and a tiny, shared plunge pool. Rates include breakfast and laundry. 200,000K

Pon Arena Hotel 50m north of Pon's River Guesthouse ☎031 515018, ⚲ponarenahotel.com. A bit of an eyesore, but comfortable all the same, this hotel has smart rooms, the most expensive of which have views across the

Mekong. Rooms in the new block, with an infinity pool near the river, cost $85 per night. Breakfast is included in the rate. $45

★ **Pon's River Guesthouse** 150m north of the ferry landing ☎020 2227 0037, ⚲ponsriverguesthouse -donkhong.com. A great place to stay, with tidy en-suite rooms and a very popular restaurant downstairs. TV and a/c are available for an extra 20,000K. The manager is well connected locally (his brother owns Pon Arena Hotel) and can arrange a variety of tours. 60,000K

V Mala Just north of the ATM on the main north–south road ☎020 9754 5787. Simple, but surprisingly stylish, these timber-floored rooms are located in a rust-red wooden house one street back from the river. Bathrooms are shared, but there are separate facilities for men and women. Good value. 50,000K

EATING AND DRINKING

All of Don Khong's guesthouses serve food, and, as you might expect, **fish** is the island's staple. The islanders have dozens of recipes, all worthy of a place on your plate – from the traditional làp pa (a Lao-style salad of minced fish mixed with garlic, chillies, shallots and fish sauce) to fish steamed in coconut milk – but whatever you do, be sure to try the island speciality, mók pa. Steamed in banana leaves, this sublime fish dish has the consistency of custard and takes an hour or more to prepare. The people of Si Phan Don are very proud of their láo-láo, which has gained a reputation nationally as one of the best **rice whiskies** in Laos. For those who haven't taken a liking to Lao white lightning, you're in luck: Muang Khong has devised a gentler blend known as the "Lao cocktail", a mix of wild honey and láo-láo served over ice with a dash of lime.

Don Khon and Don Det

Tropical islands in the classic sense, **DON KHON** and **DON DET** are fringed with swaying coconut palms and inhabited by easy-going, sarong-clad villagers. Located south of Don Khong, the islands are especially stunning during the rainy season when rice paddies in the interior have been ploughed and planted in soothing hues of jade and emerald. Besides being a picturesque little haven to while away a few days, the islands, linked by a bridge, provide opportunities for some leisurely trekking, cycling and tubing. As yet, there only a handful of motor vehicles on the islands, making them one of the precious few places in Southeast Asia not harried by the growl and whine of motorbikes. There is, however, a fee of 25,000K (payable at the bridge) to cross between the islands, but this includes access to Somphamit Falls.

6

Ban Khon

A delightfully sleepy place with a timeless feel about it, **BAN KHON**, located on Don Khon at the eastern end of the bridge, is the largest settlement on either island and has the most upmarket accommodation (see p.249). Quaintly decrepit French-era buildings with terracotta tile roofs add some colonial colour to the village's collection of rustic homes of wood, bamboo and thatch. A short walk west of the old railroad bridge, past the ticket booth, stands the village monastery, **Wat Khon Tai**. Hidden behind the newly built *sim* is the laterite foundation of what was once a Khmer temple dedicated to the god Shiva. As with several Buddhist temples in southern Laos, this one was built on the ruins of an ancient Hindu holy site, suggesting that the otherwise humble Ban Khon is around 1000 years old. On a pedestal nearby stands a Shivalinga, which was probably enshrined in the original Khmer temple. Because Khmer Shivalinga are usually simple and lack the intricate carving for which Khmer art is famous, they are rarely the target of art thieves and so stand a better chance of remaining on or near their original place of enshrinement.

Somphamit Falls

Taking the southwestern path behind Wat Khon Tai, you'll soon be aware of a low, almost inaudible purr that gradually becomes a roar the further you proceed. After following the path for around 1500m, you'll come to a ticket checkpoint (tickets for the old French bridge are valid here) and then, a low cliff overlooking **Somphamit Falls**, a series of high rapids that crashes through a jagged gorge. Fishermen can sometimes be seen carefully negotiating rickety bamboo catwalks suspended above the violently churning waters.

ACTIVITIES IN DON KHON AND DON DET

One of Don Khon's most popular activities is a boat trip in search of the **Irrawaddy dolphins** that can occasionally be spotted off the southern side of the island. Take the railroad trail for 4km through rice paddies and thick forest to the village of **Ban Hang Khon**, the jumping-off point for dolphin-spotting excursions. The April–May dry season, when the Mekong is at its lowest, is the best time of year to catch a glimpse of this highly endangered species. The dolphins tend to congregate in a deep-water pool, and boats can be chartered from the village to see them (60,000K for a one-hour trip), depending on the number of people, and you're obliged to pay for the boat regardless of whether you see any dolphins). During the rest of the year, chances of seeing the dolphins decrease, as deeper water allows them more range. Recent efforts to protect the dolphins have seen the number in this region increase from thirty in 1993 to around 75 today, but their future here is still uncertain (see box, p.248).

Following the success of **tubing** in Vang Vieng, enterprising islanders on the northern side of Don Det have started renting out tubes (15,000K/day). The sandy beach at the island's northern tip is the favoured jumping off point, but you should be aware of the strong currents – and parasites – found in these waters.

The old railroad

To see the remnants of Laos's **old French railroad**, head south from the old railroad bridge. A short distance back from the bridge lies the rusting locomotive that once hauled French goods and passengers between piers on Don Khon and Don Det, bypassing the falls and rapids that block this stretch of the river. Nearby, behind thick brush bordering rice fields, is an overgrown **Christian cemetery** that includes the neglected tomb of a long-forgotten French family that died on the same day in 1922 – some say murdered by their Vietnamese domestics. It is actually possible to follow the former railroad all the way across both islands; however, with the exception of two alarmingly precarious bridges constructed from railroad scrap and lengths of rail recycled as fences, there are few signs that a railway ever existed.

Ban Hua Det

Walk from Don Khon to Don Det, following the 3km elevated trail that runs north from the railway bridge, and you'll arrive at the bustling backpacker enclave of **Ban Hua Det**, at the northern end of the island. Here, dozens of tourist-friendly **guesthouses, bungalows and restaurants** have sprung up just a stone's throw from an incongruous industrial structure once used for hoisting cargo from the train onto awaiting boats; it's all that remains of the railroad's northern terminus. In just a few short years the place has grown into a mini version of Koh Phangan, and construction continues apace to keep up with the influx of visitors, many of whom arrive here for the joints and happy shakes that local bars sell openly. Needless to say, if you'd rather be woken up by the crowing of a rooster than the screech of a band saw or partying backpacker, stay further south.

Khon Phapheng Falls

30,000K • Most tourists visit the falls as a package from Don Khong (see p.249), but it is also possible to get here by motorbike (take the bike across the river using the car ferry and ride south along Route 13)

Despite technically being the largest waterfall in Southeast Asia, **Khon Phapheng**, to the east of Don Khon, is not all that spectacular. Indeed, it's best described as a low but wide rock shelf that just happens to have a huge volume of water running over it. The drop is highest during the March–May dry season and becomes much less spectacular when the river level rises during the rainy season. Still, the sight of all that water crashing down on its way to Cambodia is quite mesmerizing, and a well-built tourist pavilion above the falls provides an ideal place to sit and enjoy the view. There's also no shortage of food shacks serving snacks.

THE IRRAWADDY DOLPHIN

If there's one creature that's exempted from a Lao diet famous for consuming everything that hops, flies, swims or crawls, it's the rare **Irrawaddy dolphin**, which has been known to make its way upstream from Cambodia to frolic in the waters of Si Phan Don. Bluish-grey and up to 2.5m long, the freshwater dolphins are looked upon by islanders as reincarnated humans with a human spirit – an idea that's been etched into local lore by folk songs and stories of dolphins rescuing people from the jaws of crocodiles. But sadly, the dolphins themselves may soon be no more than legend.

Over the past hundred years their population in the Mekong has dwindled from thousands to around 75, and as few as ten now inhabit the area near Don Khon. Gill-net fishing and, across the border in Cambodia, the use of poison, electricity and explosives have caused dolphin **numbers to plummet**. In the past, fishermen were reluctant to cut costly nets to free entangled dolphins, causing them to drown, but this no longer happens, as Lao villagers are now compensated for their nets – part of an initiative begun by the Lao Community Fisheries and Dolphin Protection Project. A more pressing threat to the dolphins' survival is the vast Don Sahong dam, currently being built south of Don Khon, which scientists believe could change the river's hydrological balance forever.

ARRIVAL AND DEPARTURE

By public transport Unusually for Laos, using public transport to get from Don Khong to Don Khon and Don Det isn't significantly cheaper than going with a direct boat service aimed at tourists. By the time you've paid to get across the river to Ban Hat Xai Khoun (15,000K), waited for a bus to Nakasang, and then paid for the boat to Don Khon or Don Det, you'll be struggling to justify the extra hassle.

On a tour It is possible to visit Don Khon and Don Det plus the waterfall at Khon Phapheng as a day-trip from Don Khong, although Don Khon alone is worth a few days' visit. Muang Khong's guesthouses and restaurants offer boat trips (60,000K/person) that take you to see the waterfalls

DON KHON AND DON DET

and the defunct railroad. A more costly one-day tour (150,000K) includes transport to Khon Phapheng Falls and a shot at seeing Irrawaddy dolphins (see p.248).

On to Cambodia Although buses run to the border, the easiest way to get into Cambodia via the Veun Kham crossing is to take a direct bus (daily; 5hr; $17–18) that leaves either from the islands or from Pakse to Stung Treng (see p.231) – minibuses are usually your best option, and direct tickets are also available to Siem Reap (1 daily; 14hr) and Phnom Penh (1 daily; 11hr). Cambodian and Lao visas are available on arrival. Immigration officials on both sides ask for a $1–2 fee to stamp your passport, in addition to a visa fee.

ACCOMMODATION AND EATING

Although Don Khon was the first island to take off with backpackers, Don Det has now surpassed its larger neighbour in popularity, and has taken on a distinctly Vang Vieng feel. There's not a huge difference in **accommodation** on the two islands, and where you stay is largely a matter of shopping around for a bungalow or room to suit your taste and budget. On **Don Khon**, most of the bungalows are located near Ban Khon on the north end of the island. Bungalow places are scattered all the way around **Don Det**, but the north side of the island has by far the highest concentration. In fact, this part of the island can get so busy in high season that it's difficult to cycle down its winding dirt streets. Food, not accommodation, is the real money-earner here, and every bungalow place has a **restaurant** serving (quite average) Lao food and the usual traveller's fare, so you may want to take some of your meals at the bungalow you're staying at.

DON KHON

Sala Done Khone Next door to Mr Bounh's ☎031 260940, ⓦsalalao.com. The rooms in this converted French-era bungalow, which was once a hospital, feature a/c and hot-water showers. Further down the road there are stylish floating rooms with vaulted ceilings, separate daybeds and balconies just inches above the water. $50

Seng Ahloune Just east of the bridge ☎031 260934, ⓦsengahloune.com. Very close to the old French bridge and popular with tour groups, this big restaurant has bright bungalows lining the waterfront. They're not especially cheap, but are quiet and central with polished wooden floors and roomy shower areas. $40

Somphamit Just west of the Sala Done Khong hotel on the main river road ☎020 526 2491. Comfortable riverside bamboo bungalows equipped with fans and wide, shared terraces with decent hammocks. All of the rooms are en-suite, which may explain why some of them are a little musty. Ask to see a couple before dumping your bags. 60,000K

Sunset Paradise Guesthouse The easternmost guesthouse on the main riverside path in Ban Khon (no phone). Spacious and solid, these wooden bungalows face one another across a peaceful garden, just back from the river. The helpful staff speak English and French, and there's good food at the restaurant overlooking the water. 100,000K

DON DET

Bountip's Eastside Guesthouse On the east coast of the island, south of the Crazy Gecko restaurant ☎054 813900. Exceptionally cheap bungalows that just happen

to be located in a very peaceful coconut grove by the water's edge. It's a bit of a walk from the centre of Ban Hua Det, however, and you'll have to share a tatty cold-water bathroom. 30,000K

Crazy Gecko Sunrise side, south of Don Det Bungalows. This laidback riverfront restaurant, with a terrace strewn with swinging lanterns and tropical plants, stands out for its varied menu, which dares to deviate from fried rice and pancakes. Dishes include a lightly spiced pumpkin burger (20,000K) and tasty Lao soups. Daily 7am–9.30pm.

Don Det Bungalows On the east coast of the island, around 1.2km south of the centre of Ban Hua Det ☎020 2300 4959. For something quiet and relatively classy, try these comfy bungalows, which have swooping Lao-style rooflines and cocoon-like hammocks. There's a reasonable restaurant on the other side of the path. 130,000K

Keo Inpeng Towards the northern end of the island off Ban Hua Det's main drag (no phone). Hard to spot off the main drag (look for the small sign on the right as you walk south from the beach), Keo Inpeng has good-value en-suite rooms in a modern block that's surrounded by marigolds. 60,000K

The Last Resort On the west side of the island, around 750m from town ⓦfacebook.com/lastresortdondet. This self-styled travellers' community was started by a former banker from the UK. Thatched wigwams sleeping two to four people are set around a sociable garden that's home to a fire pit and an open-air cinema. Organic herbs and vegetables grown on site are used in communal meals each night. 60,000K

Little Eden Ban Hua Det, just west of the northernmost beach ⓦ littleedenguesthouse-dondet.com. Mature banana plants signal your arrival at the village's smartest resort, which has shiny-clean rooms. If you can afford to push the boat out, go for one of the brighter deluxe rooms (70,000K extra). 250,000K

Santiphab Right next to the railroad bridge on Don Det. Decent en-suite bungalows are available at this long-running place at the northern end of the old French bridge, with views across to Don Khon on the other side of the babbling river. 40,000K

6 The Bolaven Plateau

As gradual as Route 23's eastwardly climb out of Pakse is, there's no mistaking when you've reached the **Bolaven Plateau**, roughly 30km from Pakse. The suffocating heat of the Mekong Valley yields to a refreshingly cool breeze, and coffee and tea plantations, exulting in the rich soil, begin cropping up along either side of the highway. Hilly, roughly circular in shape, and with an average altitude of 600m, the high plateau has rivers running off in all directions and then plunging out of lush forests along the Bolaven's edges in a series of spectacular **waterfalls**, some more than 100m high, before eventually finding their way to the Mekong. Four provincial capitals – Pakse, Salavan, Xekong and Attapeu – surround the Bolaven, while the main settlement on the plateau itself is the town of **Paksong**.

The French, recognizing the fertility of the terrain, cleared wide swathes of forests and planted strawberries, coffee, tea and cardamom. Although it was cardamom that provided the south's chief export during colonial times, coffee is the crop that dominates the plateau these days, earning the well-paved highway that links Pakse with Paksong the moniker the **Coffee Road**.

Long before the French planted their first coffee crop, midland **hill tribes** were practising swidden agriculture on the plateau. Today, twelve ethnic groups, including lowland Lao, Laven, Alak, Suay and Taoy, live in the area. Given that ethnic minorities are in the majority here, it's only fitting that the plateau takes its name from one of these groups, the **Laven**.

One of the easiest waterfalls to access here is **Tad Lo** on the forested northern edge of the plateau, a spot increasingly popular with budget travellers looking for somewhere pleasant to relax for a few days and enjoy the plateau's cool climate. You can lounge in the pools of the Xe Set river below the waterfall and do some elephant trekking to nearby tribal villages. South of Route 23 between Pakse and Paksong is the **Dong Hua Sao NBCA**, containing the **Tad Fan Waterfall**. Paksong was levelled in bombing raids during the war and has not been able to rekindle the charm it once possessed.

Lak Sao-et, the tiny village 21km from Pakse along Route 23, is an important junction for **bus transfers** – there are connections here for Tad Lo and Salavan in the northeast, and for Paksong and beyond.

Dong Hua Sao NBCA

Located in the southwest quarter of the Bolaven Plateau, **Dong Hua Sao** is the only NBCA up on the plateau itself. It's home to some of the most spectacular waterfalls in the country, including the picture-perfect cascades of Tad Fan and Tad Yuang, which can be visited independently or as part of a day-trip from Pakse.

Tad Fan

Off Route 23 en route from Pakse to Paksong; turn right at the Kilometre 38 marker onto a dirt road leading to Tad Fane Resort • 5000K, plus 3000K for a vehicle • If you're travelling by bus, ask to be let off at Tad Fan, and walk the dirt road in

Falling water enthusiasts will get a kick out of **Tad Fan**, a twin cascade some 100m high, set amid primeval jungle that stretches as far as the eye can see. Arriving at Tad Fan, pay at the kiosk and walk through Tad Fane Resort. Paths will guide you to a viewpoint on the edge of a cliff that overlooks the falls. A trail leads down to a better vantage point, but it's not advisable to attempt this slippery path during the rainy season, as it's a long drop down into the abyss.

Tad Yuang

Off Route 23 from Pakse to Paksong, signposted 1km east of Tad Fan; follow the dirt track for 800m to reach the falls • 10,000K, plus 5000K for a car

Head east from Tad Fan for 1km along the main road and you'll see signs for **Tad Yuang**, a spectacular dual cascade that's popular with picnicking locals and tourists. The dirt track from the main road is very bumpy (so take care if you're riding a motorbike). You'll need to climb down some steep steps to reach the swimming hole below the falls. When we last visited the only accommodation here – a cluster of bungalows at the top of the falls – was closed. If you want to stay nearby, try Tad Fane Resort (see below).

ACCOMMODATION	DONG HUA SAO NBCA
TAD FAN	Lao-style rooms near the falls (though there are plans to build
Tad Fane Resort At the Tad Fan falls ☎ 020 5531400. This	more). They're a touch on the costly side, but the view from
well-run little resort has a restaurant and fourteen nicely built	the surrounding gardens is one of the best in all of Laos. ___$32

Paksong

Laos's famed coffee capital, **PAKSONG**, some 60km east of Pakse, was rebuilt after the war and is finally finding a market for its traditional cash crop. Those searching for some epicentre of coffee culture will be disappointed, but arriving on the plateau from the baking lowlands, especially during the torrid March–May hot season, will make you wonder how a bit of altitude can turn the cruel midday sun into a shoulder-warming friend.

The temperate weather and amiable locals notwithstanding, Paksong's sights are almost nil. The **town** itself is a small collection of mould-blackened concrete shop houses lining wide, dust-scoured streets, which wouldn't look out of place on the set of a spaghetti Western. A gatepost at the entrance of the market is possibly the only structure in town to have survived the war. Beyond it is a depressing block of ramshackle shops and noodle stands. Despite the bleakness of the town, the surrounding countryside and **coffee plantations** provide some diverting scenery, especially during March and April when the coffee trees are covered with intoxicatingly fragrant white blossoms.

ARRIVAL AND DEPARTURE   PAKSONG

By bus and sawngthaew Buses from Xekong and Attapeu pass through the town, and sawngthaews arriving and departing from Pakse (20,000K) pull up at the market. Your best chance of catching one of these is to get to the market first thing, as connections tend to tail off by early afternoon.

Destinations: Attapeu (2 daily; 5hr); Pakse (3 daily; 1hr); Xekong (2 daily; 5hr).

ACCOMMODATION AND EATING

Paksong is still starved of good accommodation and, for as long as tour operators in Pakse continue to run cheap day-trips to the Plateau, that situation looks unlikely to change. For food, check out the row of restaurants opposite *Savanna Guesthouse*, which do cheap grilled food, or the noodle stands at the market.

Savanna Guesthouse About 500m northeast of the market, next door to the Paksong guesthouse ☎ 020 579 0613. The best option within easy walking distance of the market, *Savanna* has en-suite rooms in a modern, single-storey building. All come with hot water and TV, and larger rooms are available for 20,000K extra. __**80,000K**__

Tad Lo

Around 90km northeast of Pakse and 30km southwest of Salavan

In the past few years the area around **Tad Lo**, a 10m-high waterfall on the banks of the Xe Set, has been attracting a growing stream of backpackers. The cheap guesthouses and restaurants in the village just downstream of the main waterfall (there are three along this section of the river) provide everything visitors need for a few days' relaxation. In the hot season, the pools surrounding **Tad Hang**, the falls closest to the guesthouses, are a refreshing escape from the heat. Large boulders in the river shade a few surprisingly deep swimming holes and are perfect spots for lounging in the sun. For a long, scenic walk that takes in all three falls, follow the well-marked trail that runs around the back of *Tad Lo Lodge*. The tourist office on the road to the falls can hook you up with a guide for this walk if you'd prefer not to do it alone. If you do decide to swim, take care and be sure to clear the water before darkness, when the floodgates of a dam upstream sometimes unleash a torrent of water without warning.

ARRIVAL AND DEPARTURE   TAD LO

By bus and tuk-tuk The road between Pakse and Salavan is now almost completely sealed, making journeys a lot quicker than they used to be. The turn-off for Tad Lo is 88km northeast of Pakse, just beyond the village of Lao Ngam. Buses will drop you at the turn-off, where a market, general stores and an ATM crowd the mouth of the 1.5km road that leads to Tad Hang, the lower falls, which can be reached by tuk-tuk (10,000K/person). When it comes to leaving Tad Lo, guesthouses near the falls will take you back to the highway for 10,000K, where you can pick up a morning bus to Salavan or Pakse.

ACCOMMODATION AND EATING   TAD LO

★ **Café Em** Next door to the tourist office on the road to the falls ☎020 5633 4637, ✉ema.g@gmx.at. Wonderful little outdoor coffee shop using organic, freshly roasted Arabica beans from the Bolaven Plateau. The breakfast, with Austrian-style coffee and honey-smothered pancakes (25,000K), is a great way to start the day. Daily 6am–7pm.

★ **Palamei Guesthouse** At the T-junction in the middle of the village, just east of the tourist office ☎030 962 0192. The superb-value rooms at this family-run garden guesthouse are very clean and well looked after. Cheaper rooms share a bathroom, while more expensive ones (60,000K) have en-suite facilities. If you want the chance to chat with locals, join the family for dinner (they charge 30,000K/person, and you can help with the cooking if you prefer).

Sabai Sabai Just west of the tourist office ☎020 9858 9266. Bamboo-built, backpacker-friendly guesthouse, which has some of the cheapest – and simplest – dorm beds we've seen in Laos. Downstairs there's a restaurant serving cheap food (grilled chicken and chips 15,000K), and a shop selling local handicrafts. Also motorbike rental, BBQ parties, and free wi-fi for customers. No set opening hours. Dorm 15,000K, single 25,000K, double 35,000K

Tad Lo Lodge On a hill overlooking Tad Hang ☎031 214184, ⊛tadlolodge.com. If you want to be near the falls, splash out on this resort, which has bungalows just steps from the water's edge (you can choose which side of the river you want to stay on). $47

Tim Opposite the school library on the road to the falls ☎034 211885, ✉soulidet@gmail.com. This long-running place has reasonable doubles and twins with shared facilities, but compared with others nearby they feel poor value. Downstairs there's a restaurant (daily 7am–10pm) serving simple backpacker grub (fried rice 15,000K). It also offers internet access and a book exchange. 50,000K

Salavan, Xekong and Attapeu provinces

Salavan, **Xekong** and **Attapeu**, cut off from the Mekong River Valley by the Bolaven Plateau and made remote by the rugged jigsaw of the Annamite Mountains, are some of the least-visited provinces in Laos. Until recently, poor infrastructure and the scars of war conspired to keep the region isolated. With the Ho Chi Minh Trail streaming across their borders, these provinces were victims of some of the heaviest bombing during the Second Indochina War. Villages were decimated, roads destroyed and in some places the dangerous litter of battle still lies about. Yet these factors kept the

6

LAO JAVA

In the early twentieth century, the French were looking for ways to make their newest chunk of Indochina profitable. Laos had become a disappointment when the grand scheme of using the Mekong as a trade link to China turned out to be impractical, but the French soon had other plans. Would **coffee**, which had been successfully introduced to Vietnam, also thrive in Laos? It seemed worth a try. Saplings were brought from the orchards around Buon Me Thuot in Vietnam and planted at varying degrees of elevation. From the banks of the Mekong on up to the Bolaven Plateau, rows of arabica and robusta were carefully nursed. After four years, the first harvest saw mixed results: coffee at lower elevations failed to fruit, but planters on the Bolaven were rewarded for their patience.

By the 1940s, **coffee plantations** covered the plateau. But then war and revolution intervened, and by the 1980s, the once painstakingly tended trees had gone wild. However, interest in Lao coffee has been rekindled over the last decade and the old plantations have benefited from foreign investment. A blight-resistant strain of arabica was recently introduced from Costa Rica, and the Association des Exportateurs du Café Lao is hoping to increase annual coffee production and make Lao coffee known to aficionados around the globe.

Although coffee made its way to Laos via Vietnam, the **coffee-drinking etiquette** and accoutrements of Laos have a flavour all their own. The tin-drip, used in Vietnam to filter coffee into a glass, is rare in Laos; the Lao favour pouring hot water through a sock-like bag filled with ground coffee.

densely forested mountains of Attapeu and Xekong pristine until the beginning of this century. Today, intense **logging** is turning parts of this once rich ecosystem into a moonscape. For the time being, however, the provinces are still home to a variety of wildlife and numerous ethnic minority villages.

Arcing around the **Bolaven Plateau**, these provinces can be seen in a convenient clockwise loop from Pakse. From Lak Sao-et (see p.250), 21km east of Pakse, head northeast for roughly 100km along well-maintained Route 20 towards Salavan, where bus connections are available for the paved 90km trip to **Xekong** via **Thateng**, the dusty northern gateway to the Bolaven Plateau. Just east of the plateau, Xekong provides a handy if uninspiring stopover en route to **Attapeu**, capital of Laos's southeasternmost province. From Attapeu, it's a pleasant haul back to Pakse up the eastern flank of the Bolaven and through the coffee plantations surrounding Paksong. Unfortunately, public buses have yet to start travelling impassable Route 18, the shortcut to Si Phan Don, which shadows the southern edge of the Plateau.

Salavan

Located on a flank of the former Ho Chi Minh Trail north of the Bolaven Plateau, Salavan province was held by the Royal Lao government until 1970, when an NVA push to consolidate control over the Trail drove the Royalists out. The provincial capital, also called **SALAVAN**, was, thanks to its proximity to the Trail, all but obliterated during the war by B-52 strikes. It wasn't until the late 1980s that rebuilding began; in the interim, the province was used as a re-education camp in which high-ranking RLA officers were given plots of land to till, many dying of malaria.

Today, Salavan town is a peaceful backwater, scorched in the hot season by desert-like winds. Many new buildings of permanent materials, including towering banks, have replaced the rickety wooden structures that were the norm up until the 1990s, and nowadays you'd need a guide with knowledge of what the old town looked like in order to glimpse any evidence of Salavan's tumultuous history. Unless you are simply looking for a very out-of-the-way place to hang out, there isn't much reason to gravitate here, though the town can be used as a base to explore Mon–Khmer villages in the area. There are few sit-down restaurants, although stalls at the town market sell fruit, noodles and sticky rice.

By bus and sawngthaew Buses and sawngthaews pulling in at Salavan's dusty bus station, west of the centre, connect the town with Vientiane, Savannakhet, Thakhek and towns around the Bolaven Plateau, including Pakse (30,000K) and Attapeu (50,000K).

Destinations Lao Ngam, for Tad Lo (at least 2 daily; 1hr 30min); Pakse (at least 2 daily; 3hr); Savannakhet (4 daily;

4hr); Taoy (1 daily; 4–5hr); Thateng (2 daily; 1hr); Xekong (at least 1 daily; 4hr).

Services A short stroll west of the market on Route 15 you'll find a branch of Lao Development Bank (it's the tallest building around), which exchanges cash and has an ATM out front.

6

ACCOMMODATION

Jindavone Just east of the market on Route 15 ☏ 034 211065. A popular choice with local officials and army men, Jindavone scores points for value and location. The smallish rooms are more expensive than those at *Thipphaphone*, next door, but have TV, air-con and clean showers. **90,000K**

Thipphaphone Just east of the market on Route 15 ☏ 034 211063. Cheap, central option with rather sloppily maintained doubles that have grubby walls and en-suite bathrooms. Unless you're really on a budget, you'd be better off at *Jindavone*, next door. **60,000K**

Thateng

A dusty junction of threadbare markets and crooked wooden houses with thatch roofs, **THATENG** was where the French commissioner to Salavan, Jean Dauplay, "the father of Lao coffee", chose to settle in the 1920s. Sadly, Thateng's strategic location as the gateway to the plateau, a grip on which was considered key to controlling the bulk of the far south, made it a prime target for American bombs. The town was basically wiped out, and although villagers returned after the war, the place is nowadays little more than an unappealing transit point.

Xekong

In 1984, a wide expanse of jungle was cleared of trees and graded flat in order to found the town of **XEKONG**. Created partly because the nearby town of Ban Phon was deemed no longer habitable owing to unexploded ordnance, Xekong, some 50km east of Thateng, is now the capital of a new province, created when Attapeu was divided in

---

DAM AND BLAST: THE XE KONG

The **Xe Kong** is one of Laos's great rivers, starting high in the Annamite Mountains from the eastern flanks of the 2500-metre-high Mount Atouat and flowing southwestwards around the southern edge of the Bolaven Plateau. It enters Cambodia via the Xe Pian NBCA, eventually joining the Mekong river in that country, north of Stung Treng.

During the Second Indochina War, US aircraft struck at the threads of the Ho Chi Minh Trail running parallel to the river, hoping to disrupt the endless tide of men and supplies streaming southwards. Bombs invariably wound up in the river and the resulting explosions sent scores of fish floating belly-up to the surface, unintentional war reparations quickly collected by villagers living amid a battlefield. Today's depleted fish catches are still blamed on the war, but more modern fishing equipment has surely had an impact, as has the use of explosives for catching fish, a technique that was utilized by Vietnamese soldiers during the war and remains part of the Cambodian fisherman's arsenal along some stretches of the river. One victim of such high-impact methods, the **Irrawaddy dolphin** (see p.248), until the 1980s a frequent visitor to Attapeu's maze of rivers in the rainy season, now rarely visits these waters.

Another major threat to the Xe Kong is the region's increasing reliance on **hydropower**; at the time of writing up to seventeen dams were being planned along the river and its tributaries. Critics have warned that unless these projects are correctly managed, forests and fish stocks could be decimated, with serious consequences for the twenty or so ethnic groups living in the surrounding area, whose way of life is dependent on a healthy river.

half. There's little to see or do in the town itself, which sits alongside the meandering Xe Kong (see box, p.254), and for some of the intrepid travellers that make it here, that's where the appeal lies. Xekong is a small, working town, without any of the usual tourist trappings.

Three major branches of the **Ho Chi Minh Trail** snaked through the jungle surrounding Xekong, and consequently this area was one of the most heavily bombed in Laos. Animist tribal peoples living in the adjacent hills, under constant threat of attack from the sky, erected talismans above their huts to ward off falling bombs. Some of these tribes produce **hand-woven textiles** that are highly sought-after by collectors. Decorative patterns feature traditional motifs such as animals and plants, alongside stylized fighter planes and bombs of obvious inspiration.

Despite the dropping of bombs and defoliants, the area is host to a surprisingly large and varied **wildlife** population, with bears, gibbons, tigers and elephants all said to be roaming the forested hills. However, your chances of getting close to any wildlife are slim: the astonishing amount of **UXO** that blankets this province makes exploration extremely dicey. Disposal teams have concluded that Xekong will be losing people to UXO for decades to come. Despite this, the average traveller has little to worry about if a few simple rules are followed (see p.47). The number-one rule is to stay on well-worn paths, even when passing through a village.

As if the danger of UXO weren't enough, there is a disturbing beasty lurking in Xekong's waterways: the *pa pao*, an innocuous-looking blowfish with a piranha-like appetite and, according to locals, a particular fondness for lopping off the tip of the male member.

ARRIVAL AND DEPARTURE   XEKONG

By bus Buses to and from Pakse and other towns around the Bolaven Plateau operate from the bus station, about 4km out of town; a handful of tuk-tuks await arriving buses and will ferry you into the centre for 10,000K.
Destinations Attapeu (2 daily; 2hr); Pakse (8 daily; 2–4hr); Salavan (at least 1 daily; 4hr); Vientiane (8 daily; 15hr).

INFORMATION

Tourist information The best place for tourist information is *Phathip Restaurant*, south of the post office on the road running closest to the river.

Services The Lao Development Bank, which changes money, is east of the post office. Further east still, around the market, you'll find plenty of ATMs.

ACCOMMODATION AND EATING

Phathip Restaurant Near the post office. The best place for delicious Vietnamese food, including vegetable-packed (but very salty) noodle soups (10,000K). The menu – in English, Swedish, French and Lao – has plenty of info on exploring the surrounding area. Daily 7am–7pm.

Sekong Hotel Just across from Phathip Restaurant on the road nearest the river ☎ 038 211039. Get past the grumpy dogs guarding the yard out front and this hotel has reasonably comfortable en-suite doubles, as well as more expensive "VIP" rooms (100,000K). The walls are a little nicotine-stained throughout, but otherwise it's not bad value. **50,000K**

Woman Fever Kosment Center Guest House Just across from Phathip Restaurant on the road nearest the river ☎ 020 5638 286. There's little English spoken at this rickety old guesthouse (which might explain the barmy name), though the rooms – which share squat toilets at the end of the building – are very cheap. **40,000K**

Attapeu

A leafy settlement of almost twenty thousand people, most of whom are Vietnamese, Chinese or lowland Lao, remote **ATTAPEU** occupies a bend in the Xe Kong just south of where it is joined by the **Xe Kaman**. Access to the town is much improved, with frequent buses plying the paved road that links it to Pakse, and it's a pleasant destination compared with the hot and dusty towns of Xekong and Salavan.

Attapeu is no warehouse of tourist attractions: the way to enjoy this town is by leisurely wandering in its rambling lanes, absorbing the easy-going pace and chatting with the genial residents. In the evening, head to the southern end of town, where the Xe Kong pauses to flow east to west, and the high riverbank invites you to catch a sunset over the river. The only real sight is Attapeu's main **wat**, which occupies a massive block in the heart of town. On the northern side of the compound, standing out among the gaudy modern temple architecture, there's also a handsome French-style monastery school building.

If you're arriving by bus on Route 18B, note the monument at the bus station, commemorating Lao–Vietnamese cooperation during the war. The monument, depicting Pathet Lao and NVA soldiers waving flags and Kalashnikov rifles aloft, is a near copy of the one in Muang Phin, Savannakhet province. Not surprisingly, it was built by the Vietnamese.

Brief history

It was near Attapeu, the capital of Laos's southeasternmost province, that the Ho Chi Minh Trail diverged, with one artery running south towards Cambodia and the other into South Vietnam. But despite being the final staging point in Laos for North Vietnamese supplies, Attapeu somehow eluded the grave effects of war that wiped other southern cities off the map. That the town remains an oasis among rugged mountains perhaps reflects what some American military advisors mocked as the reluctance of the Royal Lao Army, which controlled Attapeu in the late 1960s, to engage their opponents in battle – a trait that prompted the Americans to nickname the Royalist troops "the Fastest Army Running", a moniker derived from the army's old French acronym FAR. When the Pathet Lao announced that they intended to take the city in April 1970, Royal Lao troops lived up to their reputation and fled. Five years later, the Pathet Lao made the entire province a **re-education camp** (see p.159), resettling

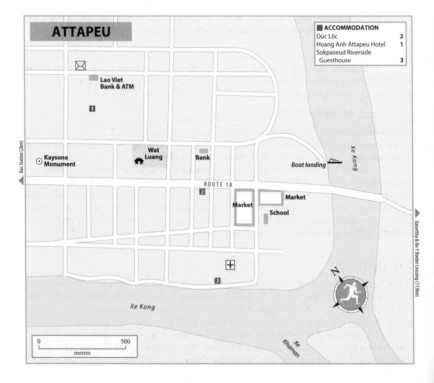

THE BO Y BORDER CROSSING

There's a border crossing with Vietnam at the end of Route 18B, 113km east of Attapeu. Five minibuses leave Attapeu each morning (hourly from 6am) crossing the border at **Bo Y** after a winding, three-hour drive. You can buy tickets in advance from the **Dúc Lôc hotel** (see below). By the time you read this, direct shuttle buses to the border may well be running from Attapeu's main bus station, but for now, you'll have to buy a ticket that takes you all the way to Vietnam (80,000K to Kon Tum, though tickets to Ngoc Hoi and Gia Lai are also available). Tickets to other Vietnamese destinations via Bo Y, including Da Nang and Hué, can be bought in Pakse. To cross into Vietnam, you must have arranged your visa before arrival at the border.

6

political enemies and forbidding them to leave the province for years. The Pathet Lao perhaps thought it only fitting to punish opponents with a dose of what they had had to endure, living in the country's remotest areas during their Thirty Year Struggle; what better place than one which, even by nineteenth-century Lao standards, was known for its "extreme unhealthiness", as reported by French explorer François Jules Harmand, who visited Attapeu in 1877. This reputation festers to this day, with Attapeu registering one of the country's highest rates of malaria.

Such tumultuous history lends new currency to the old legend surrounding Attapeu's name. When the first lowland Lao immigrants to the region asked the indigenous people what the name of their town was, the latter thought the Lao were pointing to a pile of water buffalo dung, or *itkapu* in their language, and responded accordingly. With a slight change in pronunciation to accommodate the Lao accent, the town of "buffalo shit" was born.

ARRIVAL AND INFORMATION   ATTAPEU

By bus Arriving by bus, you'll find yourself on the northwestern outskirts of the city, 4km from the centre. The bus station is served by frequent buses from Pakse, with shared tuk-tuks on hand for the run into town (10,000K/person).
Destinations Pakse (at least 5 daily; 4–7hr); Vientiane (4

daily; 16hr); via Paksong (2 daily; 5hr); Xekong (2 daily; 2hr).
Services There's a branch of the Lao Viet Bank, along with an ATM, right outside the *Hoang Anh Attapeu Hotel*. You can change money at a couple of places within 20m or so of the *Dúc Lôc hotel*.

ACCOMMODATION AND EATING

There's a surprisingly good range of new guesthouses and hotels in Attapeu, most of them aimed at Vietnamese visitors. This makes it easy to find somewhere cheap and comfortable to rest your head for the night. Eating well is harder, with few proper sit-down restaurants to enjoy a good meal at. You can try the downstairs restaurant at *Dúc Lôc* (see below), or head to one of the bars near the riverfront – though these are more about beer and karaoke than decent dinners.

Dúc Lôc On the south side of Route 18, in the city centre ☎020 9982 2334. Very well run Vietnamese place close to the market, and convenient if you're heading to the Bo-Y border crossing (buses leave from right outside the door). The wood-panelled rooms feel very fresh, with TV and a/c to boot. Downstairs there's a restaurant serving good Vietnamese food (a bowl of pho will cost you 10,000K). **80,000K**
Hoang Anh Attapeu Hotel Just north of Wat Luang ☎036 210035. This vast, minimalist hotel has the nicest rooms in town. Along with a squidgy white bed and tiled

bathroom with rain shower, the cheapest doubles have tiny balconies, some overlooking the resort's tennis courts. **300,000K**
Sokpaseud Riverside Guesthouse South of the centre along the main river road ☎030 999 0773. Slightly twee, this mansion-like guesthouse just across the road from the *Xe Kong* is an excellent budget choice. Chandeliers hang from the wooden ceilings, there's a breezy landing overlooking the water, and the rooms are unexpectedly good for the money. **80,000K**

DETAILS OF CARVING FROM WAT PHOU

Contexts

History

Laos as a unified state within its present geographical boundaries has only existed for little more than one hundred years. Its national history stretches back six centuries to the legendary kingdom of Lane Xang, a rival to the empires of mainland Southeast Asia until it splintered into a cluster of weak principalities dominated by their more powerful neighbours.

The beginnings

As long as forty thousand years ago, Laos was inhabited by **hunter-gatherers** who lived in relatively permanent sites and used tools made of stone, wood and bamboo, not terribly different from many of those still in use in rural Lao villages today. By 8000 BC, these peoples had become **farmers**, growing beans, peas and rice and domesticating animals. Excavations at a site in present-day northeastern Thailand reveal that copper and bronze work in the region dates back four thousand years – as early as anywhere in the world. **Ironworking** was the next step forward, and by 500 BC the inhabitants of the Khorat Plateau in northeastern Thailand were using ploughs with iron tips, pulled by water buffalo, to cultivate wet rice.

The **earliest indigenous culture** in Laos to have been investigated by archeologists was that of an Iron Age megalithic people who lived in what is now Xieng Khuang province on the Plain of Jars. These people built stone pillars which were positioned next to underground burial chambers, and large stone funerary urns to hold the ashes of their dead. The civilization is thought to have progressed from crafting the three-metre-tall stone slabs to the massive jars after the development of iron tools. Bronze objects as well as beads foreign to the region suggest that the civilization was a wealthy one and lay at the centre of trade routes to China, Vietnam and points south. However, very little else is known about this people and what became of them.

By this time, broad linguistic and cultural groups were beginning to emerge in Southeast Asia. Small villages were developing and between them there was regular communication and trade in such items as pottery, salt and metal tools. The early inhabitants of Laos and the surrounding parts of central and southern Indochina spoke Austroasiatic languages such as Mon and Khmer, while the ancestors of the lowland Lao spoke proto-Tai languages, and were still living in the river valleys of southeastern China. What is known about this group of **Tai** people comes mostly from documents written by their neighbours. Tai peoples described in early Chinese documents were valley- and lowland-dwelling subsistence farmers who typically cultivated wet rice and vegetables and, unlike the Chinese and Vietnamese, lived in houses built on piles. They reared water buffalo less for use as beasts of burden than as symbols of wealth and status or for use in ritual.

The **Tai villages** of the first millennium AD were probably much like the villages of rural Laos today, and would have consisted of a small cluster of households sharing

Iron Age	First century AD	Ninth century
The earliest known indigenous culture in Laos emerges on the Plain of Jars	Indian traders introduce Buddhism to Southeast Asia	The Hindu Khmer Empire of Angkor builds dozens of temples across the region

THE MYTH OF THE BIRTH OF THE LAO

In the early days, when humankind grew unruly and refused to honour the gods, the **chief of the gods** flooded the earth. Three lords managed to survive the flood, floating up to heaven on a raft. They paid homage to the chief of the gods, and once the floods had subsided the lords returned to earth in the vicinity of Dien Bien Phu with a water buffalo, which helped them sow the rice fields in the plain. When the buffalo died, a large vine bearing three gourds grew from its nostrils, and from the gourds came shouts and cries. One of the lords pierced the gourds with a hot poker and a mass of people struggled out of the blackened holes. These were the **Lao Theung**, the Lao of the hillsides. Seeing their plight, a second lord cut more holes with a chisel and from these larger openings emerged the **Lao**. The lords taught the Lao how to grow rice and build homes, but when the population grew too big, the chief of the gods sent his son, **Khoun Borom**, to earth.

Descending to earth on an elephant with crossed tusks, Khoun Borom brought with him teachers and courtiers, teaching the Lao how to make tools and schooling them in the arts of dance and music. After a prosperous reign of 25 years, Khoun Borom sent his seven sons to rule over the Tai–Lao world. The eldest went to **Luang Prabang** and the others to Xieng Khuang, Chiang Mai, Xishuangbanna (in southwestern China), Ayutthaya and regions of lower Burma and northern Vietnam.

labour during harvests. A need for mutual protection against outside forces most likely drove such villages together into larger units known as *muang* – a term which refers to both a group of villages and the central town in a network of villages.

With the lowlands to the east and northeast densely settled by Vietnamese and Chinese populations, the Tai peoples slowly **migrated** west and southwest into northern Laos and southern Yunnan, and eventually as far as Assam in northeastern India, displacing the sparse indigenous population of Austronesian and Austroasiatic groups and forcing them into the less desirable upland areas – where their descendants still live today. This migration is reflected in the Lao legend of Khoun Borom (see box above). By the ninth century, the Tai were spread across upland Southeast Asia and surrounded by **Nanchao**, a well-organized military state located in southwestern China; a Vietnamese state on the verge of independence from China; Champa, an Indianized kingdom on the coast of Vietnam; Angkorian Cambodia; and the Mon and Pyu kingdoms of Burma.

Indianized influences

From the first century AD, Indian traders made their way east through Southeast Asia by land and by sea en route to China. Hinduized enclaves sprang up along the coast of Indochina and later inland civilizations developed in Burma, Cambodia and Thailand. It was these classical **Indianized civilizations** along with individual Indian traders and travelling monks, rather than Chinese culture, that would shape the identity of the Lao, an influence evident today in the sharp difference between the Tai groups who underwent Indianization, became Buddhist and incorporated Pali and Sanskrit words into their languages, and those that did not.

The foundation of Buddhist civilization in Thailand and Laos was laid by a unique Theravada Buddhist cultural complex known as **Dvaravati**. This civilization grew up to

1353	1512	1563
Exiled prince Fa Ngum establishes the Lane Xang Hom Khao Empire	The golden Buddha image, the Pha Bang, is brought to Xieng Dong Xieng Thong (now Luang Prabang)	The capital is moved to Vientiane, but the Pha Bang is left behind, and Luang Prabang is renamed after it

dominate the Central Plain of Thailand for several centuries, although more as a cultural influence than an empire. Sites found across Thailand and Laos suggest Dvaravati was a prosperous, expansive civilization that flourished between the sixth and ninth centuries. The sites appear to have been most densely clustered around the lower Chao Phraya River Valley of Thailand, along what were regular routes of communication and trade, which contributed to the spread of Buddhism in the area. This is evidenced by the discovery of eleventh- and twelfth-century relics in Luang Prabang and near Phonhong on the Vientiane Plain, the earliest Buddhist statuary yet discovered in these parts of Laos.

The Khmer

By the end of the ninth century, Dvaravati's influence over central Southeast Asia was rapidly being eclipsed by the **Khmer Empire** of Angkor. At its height, this empire extended from its core of Cambodia and the southern half of northeastern Thailand into Vietnam, central Thailand and Laos, where the Khmer built dozens of Angkor-style temple complexes. As a result of this expansion, the Khmer gained control over important trade routes between India and China. The empire was held together by an extensive network of communications and institutions, as well as a system of highways linking key centres of the empire, traces of which are visible between Wat Phou and Angkor.

As the empire grew, Khmer governors, who were sometimes princes with ties to the royal house at Angkor, were placed in control of newly acquired areas, bringing with them tax collectors, judges, scribes and monks and ordering the construction of enormous religious monuments. The people then living in what is now southern Laos were probably predominantly Khmer as far north as Savannakhet, although by the eleventh and twelfth centuries, ethnic Tai made up a significant portion of the population on the fringes of the Angkor empire.

Early Tai principalities

The first record of contact between the Khmer empire and a Tai state occurred sometime after the seventh century near Chiang Saen in far northern Thailand, where a Tai state known as **Yonok** emerged along the Mekong river in the vicinity of Bokeo province. By the late tenth century, Buddhism was blossoming in Yonok, transforming the localized Buddhism into an institutionalized religious tradition with ties to the civilizations of the Mon and Ceylon. It was around this time that the Tai were beginning to move onto the lowland plains, suitable for extensive cultivation of rice.

Though the origin of the first Lao principalities is ill-defined to say the least, it appears that the first significant Tai centres in what is now Laos took root in the north, at Luang Prabang and Xieng Khuang, both of which are identified in legends as areas ruled by the sons of Khoun Borom.

By the thirteenth century, Luang Prabang, along with Chiang Saen, Jinghong (the Tai Leu capital located in Yunnan) and a Black Tai centre near the Da River in Vietnam, had emerged as one of the chief Tai centres of the Upper Mekong, an area settled by people who called themselves **Lao** and lived under the threat of invasion from Nanchao and Vietnam. A century later, Luang Prabang, then known as Xieng Dong Xieng Thong,

1637–94	1778	1893	World War II
The reign of Sourinyavongsa, and the Golden Age of Lane Xang	Troops from the kingdom of Siam take Vientiane	For half a century, Laos is a French colony, and the country's present borders take shape	The Japanese occupy Laos and station troops throughout the region

had become but one of many small Lao principalities that existed on the fringes of two larger Tai states that had emerged: **Lan Na**, centred on Chiang Mai, and **Sukhothai**, the principality which is viewed as the cornerstone in Thailand's development. These states had capitalized on the collapse of the region's classical Indianized empires, Angkor and Pagan, their growth fuelled by large bases of rice land and manpower. Inscriptions from the Siamese *muang* of Sukhothai indicate that Lao rulers from Xieng Dong Xieng Thong were paying tribute to the Sukhothai by the late thirteenth century.

Yet even as the sun began to set on Angkor in the thirteenth century, the Khmer empire's most lasting impact on its still nebulous northern neighbour was to come in the form of a helping hand to the young exile who was to transform the petty Lao principalities scattered across Laos and portions of Thailand into a power in mainland Southeast Asia.

The rise of Lane Xang

Legends tell of a young prince named Fa Ngum, who belonged to the ruling family of Xieng Dong Xieng, being cast out of the fledgling Lao principality. But in 1351 he returned, backed by an army provided by the Khmer court at Angkor, and began fighting his way up the Mekong Valley atop a war elephant. After subduing the lower Mekong Valley, Sikhotabong (present-day Thakhek) and Kham Keut (near Lak Sao), Fa Ngum proceeded to the Plain of Jars where, with the aid of an exiled Phuan prince, he captured Muang Phuan, the capital of the principality of Xieng Khuang.

In 1353, Fa Ngum returned to Xieng Dong Xieng Thong, where he ascended the throne and began the reign considered the cornerstone in Laos's development. Fa Ngum called his new kingdom **Lane Xang Hom Khao**, the Kingdom of a Million Elephants and the White Parasol, a name signifying military might and royal prestige. For two decades he continued to expand Lane Xang, creating a decentralized state with hubs in Xieng Khuang, Sikhotabong and Vientiane. All three of these *muang* were virtually autonomous, but they each helped Lane Xang by contributing revenue and manpower – the greatest asset in a sparsely populated land.

With Fa Ngum and his Khmer queen, Kaew Keng Nya, came Cambodian monks and artisans, a new civil administrative system and a code of laws. It's fairly certain Buddhism also flourished during Fa Ngum's reign, growing further with the arrival of his second queen, Kaew Lot Fa.

Although Fa Ngum was a strong leader, after twenty years on the throne and following some internal strife, he was ousted by his ministers. In 1373 the succession passed to his only son, **Oun Heuan**, who ruled for 43 years, ushering in an era of peace during which the city flourished. Oun Heuan is remembered as Samsenthai or king of Three Hundred Thousand Tai, a name signifying the number of Lao men available to Lane Xang for labour and military service. After Oun Heuan's death, a period of bitter political infighting began – with eight kings in 22 years – which left the kingdom severely weakened.

The leading ministers of Lane Xang restored stability by offering the throne to the ruler of Vientiane, Vangburi (1438–79), the only surviving son of Oun Heuan. Whereas Fa Ngum had merely tipped his hat to Theravada Buddhism, Vangburi was a devout Buddhist. He took the Buddhist name Sainyachakkaphat upon his coronation

1945	1946	1947
Prince Phetsarath deposes the pro-French king and forms the Lao Issara, or "Free Laos" government	French reoccupation forces take Vientiane and Luang Prabang. Thousands of Lao Issara supporters flee to Thailand	The Lao Issara, supported by Ho Chi Minh's Viet Minh, launches raids on French garrisons

and promptly appointed new abbots in key monasteries. Theravada Buddhism, slower to take hold east of the Mekong at first, now served to legitimize the rule of the kings of Lane Xang. In return for the king's patronage the monks taught that the king ruled because he possessed superior moral merit.

Sainyachakkaphat took pains to return Lane Xang to its former glory, but his rule was not to last. **Vietnam**, angered by Lane Xang's betrayal of the Vietnamese struggle against the occupying forces of China's Ming Dynasty and further provoked by a Phuan revolt against Vietnamese control over Muang Phuan, invaded Lane Xang in 1479. Five columns of Vietnamese troops swept through Xieng Dong Xieng Thong and Sainyachakkaphat, humiliated, abdicated and fled. The Lao king's younger brother, Souvanna Banlang, regrouped the Lao troops and eventually chased off the Vietnamese, whose final retort was the sacking of Muang Phuan on their way home.

Xieng Dong Xieng Thong's destruction proved to be a catalyst for Lane Xang's first golden age, a century when the civil administration was fine-tuned, striking temples were built and epic poems composed.

The kingdom of the Pha Bang

Souvanna Banlang's three successors – La Saen Thai (1486–96), Somphou (1496–1500) and Visoun (1500–20) – ruled over a peaceful and prosperous Lane Xang, their reigns marked by strengthened ties and an upswing in trade with Ayutthaya. The wealth generated by trade went into the adornment of Xieng Dong Xieng Thong. These rulers also reorganized the government, which served to make the kingdom more stable than it had ever been before.

Buddhism flourished, under **Visoun** in particular, as monks took up residence in the city and the monasteries became centres of literary culture, where sacred Pali texts were studied. It was also during his reign that the Lao Buddhist world-view came together. Visoun ordered the composition of the *Nithan Khoun Borom*, which brought together legends concerning the origin of the Lao, Khoun Borom and the founding of Xieng Dong Xieng Thong – complete with grand stories of Fa Ngum's deeds – and placed these tales within the framework of Theravada Buddhism. Arguably, Visoun's most important act was bringing the **Pha Bang** to Xieng Dong Xieng Thong from Vientiane in 1512, a defining event in the development of Lao identity. The golden Buddha image, installed at Wat Visoun, became the palladium of the ruling dynasty and the symbol of unity and power of the kingdom itself.

Whereas Visoun and his immediate predecessors had ruled over a peaceful state concerned primarily with domestic affairs, Visoun's son Phothisalat and grandson Setthathilat had major ambitions for Lane Xang, which they saw as being the equal of Ayutthaya. **Phothisalat** (1520–47) was a man driven by profound piety. He gave generously to the monastic order and left his mark on the spiritual life of Xieng Dong Xieng Thong when, in 1527, he broke with local traditions and banned the practice of animism, ordering the destruction of associated religious buildings. In pursuit of his expansionist aspirations, Phothisalat established a wide network of regional relations, which included taking a Lan Na princess as his queen. He chose to reside at Vientiane, which had the advantage of being closer to the trade routes linking Lane Xang with Vietnam, Ayutthaya and Cambodia. Vientiane was also closer to the population centre

1949	1950	1953
France concedes greater independence to the Vientiane government. The Lao Issara disbands	Souphanouvong founds the resistance group Pathet Lao ("the Land of the Lao"), calling for an independent Laos	The Viet Minh seize parts of Laos for the Pathet Lao

of the expanding Lao world: with the downfall of Angkor in the previous century, the Lao had begun to shift into the middle Mekong Valley and onto the Khorat Plateau where the land was flatter and more fertile.

Phothisalat's aggressiveness contributed to the souring of relations with Ayutthaya. Tensions between the neighbours flared up over the now weakened state of Lan Na; Lane Xang prevailed, and Phothisalat's son **Setthathilat** (1548–71) assumed the throne at Chiang Mai in 1546. He quickly hurried home, however, after the death of his father, who was crushed beneath his elephant during a display of his riding skills. In his hasty departure, Setthathilat nonetheless managed to pilfer Lan Na's talismanic Emerald Buddha, the sacred **Pha Kaew** that today is the palladium of the ruling line in Bangkok.

The Burmese invasions

Setthathilat was only 14 when, in 1548, he assumed the throne of Lane Xang. But the young king's hold over Lan Na gradually slipped away, as internal disputes in Chiang Mai and the rise of a powerful Burmese kingdom in the west dashed hopes of a greater Lao state unifying Lane Xang and Lan Na. Wary of the growing **Burmese threat**, Setthathilat reacted defensively. In 1563, he officially moved his capital to Vientiane and quickly set about building brick ramparts around the city. In deference to Xieng Dong Xieng Thong, the Pha Bang was left behind and the city was renamed after the revered image, while the Emerald Buddha was placed in the newly constructed Haw Pha Kaew in Vientiane.

Lane Xang managed to forge an alliance with Ayutthaya, but the Tai states proved no match for the armies of the Burmese warrior-kings who reduced Lan Na, Ayutthaya and Lane Xang to vassalage in a matter of a decade, and sacked Vientiane in 1565. The invaders were eventually repelled by a guerrilla campaign led by the king. After reclaiming Vientiane, Setthathilat renovated That Phanom in Sikhotabong and built That Luang in the capital, in an effort to lift the morale of his vassals in the central Mekong; they had misgivings about being ruled by a royal line whose roots were in Luang Prabang, especially one that was taxing their resources by waging a costly war.

By the end of 1569, Lane Xang was the only Tai power remaining. Burma once again set its sights on Vientiane, which fell for the second time, and once again Setthathilat regained his capital – but this time the heavy demands on the *muang* of the central Mekong brought resentment to boiling point. Setthathilat was lured into a campaign against the mountain peoples of the south by the powerful ruler of Sikhotabong, and was never seen again. The king's downfall revealed a major weakness in Lane Xang: the monarchy still depended on the loyalty of its vassals, but the latter no longer felt any strong allegiance to the king or to Lane Xang. With the death of Setthathilat, Lane Xang plunged into turmoil as the Burmese retook Vientiane and extended their rule to the Vietnamese frontier. By the early 1580s the kingdom was in such disarray that no king sat on the throne for nearly a decade. It would take half a century for Lane Xang to recover.

Sourinyavongsa and the Golden Age

The decisive character who returned stability to Lane Xang and eventually ushered in its **Golden Age** was Sourinyavongsa (1637–94). Although rarely seen in public, he was a popular king who ruled over a peaceful and prosperous kingdom. The **first Europeans** to reach Lane Xang, a mission from the Dutch East India Company led by Gerritt van

1954	1955–60	1961
The Geneva conference reaffirms Lao independence under the Royal Lao Government; the Pathet Lao is allotted two provinces	The US and Soviet Union arm opposing sides, and the country becomes increasingly unstable	A coalition government is formed. Foreign forces agree to leave Laos but ignore their promises, keeping Laos at war

Wuysthoff and a party of Jesuits, arrived during Sourinyavongsa's reign to find a flourishing Buddhist kingdom whose wealth was poured into the construction of religious monuments and the monastic order. Monks – more numerous than the soldiers of Germany, as one visitor observed – came from as far as Cambodia and Burma to Vientiane, which had emerged as a regional centre of Buddhist studies.

Sourinyavongsa ensured his reign was peaceful by aligning Lane Xang with neighbouring powers through marriage, although he did not hesitate to resort to force when necessary – after all it was a violent struggle among relatives that won him the throne in the first place. When the ruler of Xieng Khuang refused to offer his daughter in marriage to Sourinyavongsa, Lane Xang invaded Xieng Khuang, seizing the woman in question and taking several thousand captives, who were resettled near the capital. Thereafter Xieng Khuang paid regular tribute to Vientiane and was forced to break off its relationship with Vietnam. Sourinyavongsa took the daughter of the Vietnamese emperor as a concubine and established the boundaries between the two states in a treaty with Vietnam which identified all people living in houses on piles as Lao subjects and all living in homes that rested on the ground as Vietnamese. The frontier with Ayutthaya remained unchanged, with both countries respecting the border established by Setthathilat between the Mekong and the Chao Phraya rivers. Lane Xang was left holding sway over the northern and eastern portions of the Khorat Plateau.

Sourinyavongsa avoided the bitter rivalries that contributed to the downfall of Setthathilat, by striking a balance between the regional interests of the kingdom. He appeased the powerful families of the central Mekong by dividing the powers of state among three chief ministers – the minister of the palace conducted foreign relations and ran the royal secretariat; a second commanded the army and oversaw Vientiane; and a third, the viceroy, the powerful ruler of Sikhotabong, ruled the south.

While the new balance of power provided the stability Lane Xang needed to flourish, no provisions were made to maintain that stability after the king's death. In the end, the kingdom paid the price for Sourinyavongsa's stern brand of justice: the king had executed his only son for adultery, leaving no obvious heir to the throne when he died in 1694. Once again there was a political crisis, but this time around, the country's three regions went their separate ways.

The division of Lane Xang

In 1698, Vientiane was taken over by **Setthathilat II**, a Lane Xang prince who returned from exile in Vietnam to establish a new kingdom. Very soon, however, **Setthathilat** had trouble on his northern flank. Sourinyavongsa's grandsons – Kingkitsalat and Inthasom – had fled Vientiane to Chiang Hung (present-day Jinghong in Yunnan) some years before and sought assistance from their mother's relatives in Sipsong Pa Na. With the aid of a cousin, the princes raised an army, captured Luang Prabang in 1706 and soon after marched on Vientiane. Setthathilat appealed for help from Ayutthaya. The king of Ayutthaya negotiated a division of the territory at the bend in the Mekong, south of Paklai, making Kingkitsalat the first ruler of an independent Luang Prabang kingdom, and leaving Setthathilat to rule over Vientiane.

Meanwhile, in the south, a new ruling house had emerged at **Champasak**. The prince, sometimes said to be a long lost son of Sourinyavongsa, assumed the throne as King Soi

1964–73	1974
"Armed reconnaissance" flights begin against the North Vietnamese. The US secretly drops more than two million tonnes of bombs on Laos	A new coalition government is formed in Laos, including both Souvannaphouma and Souphanouvong

Sisamouth in 1713. Thus the new ruling lines of each of the three major principalities, Luang Prabang, Vientiane and Champasak, could claim, however tenuously, some link to Fa Ngum and, by extension, to Khoun Borom. Family ties notwithstanding, it didn't take long for these isolated principalities of inland Southeast Asia to be at each other's throats, making these weak states easy prey for their larger neighbours. The rivalry between Luang Prabang and Vientiane was particularly bitter, deteriorating further when a second wave of Burmese invasions swept across the Tai world in the 1760s and forces from Vientiane aligned with the invaders and helped sack Luang Prabang.

Ayutthaya, which had flourished since the last wave of Burmese invasions, was next. The Burmese breached the walls and took the city in 1767, razing everything to the ground and hauling off tens of thousands of prisoners. The city was abandoned, but with remarkable speed the Siamese built a new kingdom, one that was to succeed at the expense of the Lao states.

The rise of Siam

Under the charismatic leadership of King Taksin, a military genius, the **Siamese** quickly rebuilt their kingdom downriver from Ayutthaya near Bangkok, and within a decade had retaken its territory, conquered Lan Na, and were prepared to expand to the east to secure its perimeter. Taking advantage of a peaceful Burma and a distracted Vietnam, twenty thousand Siamese soldiers set out towards Vientiane in 1778.

A second army of ten thousand swept east through Cambodia and, after conquering first Champasak and then Sikhotabong, turned north and marched on Vientiane. Here, the two Siamese forces met before the ramparts of Vientiane and were joined by a battalion from Luang Prabang bent on revenge. The city fell, and hundreds of prisoners, including the royal family, were dragged back to Siam and forcibly resettled on the plains north of the Siamese capital. The two Buddha image palladia of Lane Xang, the Pha Bang – which had been relocated to Vientiane by Setthathilat II in 1705 – and the Pha Kaew, were hauled off as well and enshrined in Thonburi (that part of Bangkok west of the Chao Phraya River). By reducing Champasak and Vientiane to vassal states and bringing Luang Prabang into an unequal alliance, Siam had extended its empire to the Annamite Mountains and forced the Lao world to adjust to a predominantly Bangkok-centred existence for the next century.

Anou's rebellion

The captured Lao princes returned to Vientiane as vassal kings, beginning with Nanthasen (1782–92). He brought with him the Pha Bang, which the Siamese king had decided was bad luck for his kingdom. Nanthasen didn't waste time in rekindling the old conflict with Luang Prabang, which his forces conquered in 1792. But Siam was wary of allowing any of the Lao vassal states to improve their position at the expense of another, and so recalled Nanthasen. He was replaced by Inthavong (1792–1804), the elder brother of the accomplished general Anou, who served as viceroy and led Lao armies to fight in the name of Siam in battles with Burma. By the time of Inthavong's death at the turn of the century, Vientiane had begun to pay tribute to Vietnam and, when **Anou** (1804–28) was chosen to ascend to the throne, he immediately notified the Vietnamese.

1975	1977
After communist victories in Phnom Penh and Saigon, Pathet Lao forces take Vientiane in a bloodless coup. The Lao People's Democratic Republic (PDR) is proclaimed	The royal family are arrested and exiled to Hua Phan province, ending the centuries-old Lao monarchy

Siam became increasingly alarmed by Vietnam's growing influence, and, worried that Vietnam had its eye on Champasak, decided to run the risk of turning Anou into a powerful, and potentially dangerous, vassal by appointing Yo (1819–27), Anou's son, to the Champasak throne. Anou, who envisioned restoring Lane Xang to its former glory, made good on Bangkok's fears. On the pretence of coming to Siam's aid in the event of an attack by the British, who had by this time established a presence in Burma, Anou's and Yo's troops advanced across the Khorat Plateau early in 1827, and by late February had come within a few days' march of Bangkok. However, Anou misjudged the strength of the Siamese, who struck back fiercely, capturing Yo and sacking Vientiane. Anou fled to Vietnam. When he returned to Vientiane with a small force several months later, fighting broke out which resulted in Anou's capture. Siamese forces destroyed every building in the capital, save for Wat Sisaket, and dragged the entire population back to Thailand, where they were resettled. Vientiane was abandoned to the jungle; it was still in ruins when French explorers arrived four decades later. Anou was the last Lao ruler to attempt to liberate the former territories of Lane Xang.

During the decades that followed Anou's defeat, Siam and Vietnam jockeyed for control over the fragmented Lao *muang*. By force and diplomacy, Siam depopulated the area east of the Mekong, particularly in south central Laos, leaving a wasteland of burned villages and rice fields. Only Luang Prabang managed to stay intact. **Xieng Khuang** represented the greatest source of conflict in the struggle, effectively operating as a back door for a Siamese invasion of Vietnam.

By the middle of the nineteenth century, the Lao territories had become a buffer zone between the two powers. Siam was dominant in the Mekong Valley; the Vietnamese held sway in the east; joint control was exercised over what was left of Muang Phuan. This balancing act was soon upset, however, by **marauding Chinese**, remnants of Chinese rebellions, who swept through the northern Lao territories on horseback in the 1870s and 1880s. Siam, its position in Laos endangered by the incursions, launched a series of military expeditions. The last of these campaigns backfired, leading to the sacking of Luang Prabang and eventually to Siam's loss of Laos to the French.

French conquest

As the nineteenth century wore on, French governments became increasingly imperialistic. With Britain threatening to dominate trade with China, France saw Vietnam, and by extension Laos, as a potential route into the resource-rich Yunnan region. By the time the Mekong Exploration Commission of 1867–68 set off from Saigon for Laos and Yunnan, **Cochinchina** (present-day southern Vietnam) was already a French possession. Interest in Laos, quickly waned however, after the explorers found that significant stretches of the river were unnavigable.

It wasn't until the 1880s, when French explorer **Auguste Pavie** began trekking across Laos in search of political alliances and trade routes, that interest in the country was rekindled. As vice-consul in Luang Prabang, Pavie was the chief advocate of France's extension of the Indochina empire to the banks of the Mekong. He won an important ally for France by rescuing the northern kingdom's ageing king Oun Kham almost singlehandedly when the city, left virtually undefended by the Siamese, was torched in 1887 by a White Tai leader from Sipsong Chao Tai, out for revenge against Siam.

1992	1997	2007
Diplomatic relations are re-established with the US	Laos becomes a member of the Association of Southeast Asian Nations (ASEAN)	In the US, ten members of the Hmong minority are arrested and accused of trying to overthrow the Lao government

Pavie's effort led the king to state: "[Luang Prabang] is not a conquest of Siam. Luang Prabang, wanting protection against all attacks, voluntarily offered its tribute. Now through Siam's interference, our ruin is complete… we will offer tribute to France…"

The relentless efforts of Pavie, coupled with gunboat diplomacy in Bangkok, eventually forced Siam to relinquish its claim to all territory east of the Mekong in 1893, although not before nearly sparking a war between Siam, Britain and France. Britain and France eventually settled on the Mekong river as the boundary between British Burma and French Laos and agreed to guarantee Siamese independence in the Chao Phraya River Valley in order to ensure a buffer zone between the two Western powers.

French rule

For half a century, Laos was ruled as a **French colony**. The boundaries with Burma, China and Vietnam that were adopted – essentially the limits of the Mekong watershed – were carved with indifference to the complex existing political structures and ethnic groupings. In short, the borders meant nothing to the peoples of Laos. After initially dividing the Lao territories into three regions administered from Vietnam, the French eventually settled on **Vientiane** as their administrative capital and split the country up into eleven provinces, with the kingdom of Luang Prabang as a nominal protectorate.

After France realized that the Mekong was a poor transport route and that explorers' claims of an Eldorado were but a pipe dream, Laos became the neglected backwater of its Southeast Asian acquisitions. Accordingly, the French presence in Laos was minimal. The French made do with limited administrative manpower by simply floating their administration on top of existing feudal court structures. The royal houses of Xieng Khuang, Champasak and Luang Prabang – Vientiane's ruling line had been eliminated after Anou's defeat – were preserved, although France reduced the status of the rulers of Xieng Khuang and Champasak to that of governors and reserved the right to approve the successors to all three houses. Outside the cities, the French established an administrative system that pitted various ethnic groups against one another, effectively deflecting resentment away from themselves.

In order to cover the cost of administration, France imposed heavy **taxes** on opium, alcohol and salt, levied a head tax on males between 18 and 60, and required all adult males to perform unpaid *corvée* labour. Often required to walk days to work sites far from their villages, while supplying their own food, villagers sometimes responded by simply clearing out of an area altogether, returning once the project was completed. Such measures provoked **revolts**, some led by messianic religious figures, with the first large uprising beginning on the Bolaven Plateau in 1901 (see box opposite). It seems these disturbances were more in response to central government intrusion into rural life and the disruption of old orders than they were specifically anti-French. It's telling, however, that most of these uprisings occurred among upland peoples, upon whom the French made harsher demands and for whose customs they showed less respect. Later, these revolts were construed as forerunners of the nationalist Lao Issara and Pathet Lao movements.

While explorers' reports that Laos was teeming with **natural resources** proved overly optimistic, the French did manage to exploit, among other things, tin deposits near Thakhek and teak trees, which were cut and floated down the Mekong, and introduced coffee. France's chief agricultural exports were cardamom from the Bolaven Plateau area

2009	2011
Around four thousand Hmong are deported back to Laos from refugee camps in northern Thailand	Two tropical storms cause severe flooding, killing at least 27 people and washing away roads and villages

THE BOLAVEN REVOLT

A chanting mob, two-thousand strong, descended on Savannakhet in April 1902, convinced by a holy man that any bullets fired at them would be miraculously transformed into frangipani flowers. Three times they attacked, and each time they were mown down by troops from France's "Garde Indigène". The rout, which left 150 dead, marked the climax of the so-called **Holy Man's Revolt**, which had its origins with the arrival of the French in 1893 and simmered on for many years afterwards in the highlands of the south.

The French brought with them administrative changes and increased taxation, and reshuffled the traditional relationships that had guided life in Laos for generations. At first, resistance was textbook Lao. Villagers avoided direct confrontation, preferring to make their displeasure about the new order known through passive means: villages undercounted their populations, adapted a generally uncooperative attitude, or simply left. The first serious opposition didn't arise until eight years after the French employed gunboat diplomacy to wrest control of Lao territory from Siam.

When **Ong Kaew**, an Alak tribesman believed to possess supernatural powers, prophesied that "the end of the world as we know it" was nigh, he found willing listeners among midland tribes living along the plateau, chafing under increased taxes and *corvée* labour demands instituted by the French commissioner of Salavan. Sensing that Ong Kaew was gaining too much influence, the commissioner ordered the burning of a pagoda erected in the holy man's honour. This only served to increase support for Ong Kaew, and in April 1901 he and a band of rebels attacked the commissioner and his guard. Soon after, nearly all of the Bolaven region was in revolt.

By 1902, the revolt had spilled across the Mekong and briefly gained the support of older lowland Lao families, who felt threatened by the collapse of the social and economic order to which they were accustomed. After the disastrous march on Savannakhet, Ong Kaew and another Lao Theung leader, **Ong Kommadam**, whose son would later continue to resist the French and ultimately become a Pathet Lao leader, retreated across the Xe Kong as villages were burned and less fortunate leaders rounded up and executed. But the defeat at Savannakhet and renewed attempts by France to pacify the Bolaven region did little to dispel the holy man's popularity, and it took a new commissioner at Salavan, **Jean Dauplay**, to force Ong Kaew to surrender in 1907. Three years later, with the holy man's influence over the Bolaven inhabitants as strong as ever, Dauplay arrested Ong Kaew, who died "during a jail break" the next day. The revolt was effectively over.

Not all was lost during the insurrection. French authorities were careful to place more of the burden on lowland Lao when they raised taxes in 1914, and Ong Kaew had unwittingly sown the seeds for what the Pathet Lao would later claim to be the stirrings of Lao nationalism.

and, from the highlands of Xieng Khuang, **opium**, a product that was later allegedly used by the CIA and the Pathet Lao to finance their respective war efforts.

Trade was in the hands of Chinese merchants, as it had been for centuries. Goods followed traditional routes from Laos and the west bank of the Mekong across the Khorat Plateau towards Bangkok and away from French Vietnam. The same Chinese merchants who exported cardamom, sticklac and benzoin, skins and ivory to the trading houses of the Siamese capital were already importing cheap British and German products by the time the French established themselves in Laos.

With trade flowing towards Bangkok, minimal exports and a depleted population providing an insufficient tax base, the colony remained dependent on **federal subsidies**.

2012	2013	2014
Prominent community development worker Sombath Somphone is abducted in Vientiane. The Lao government denies responsibility	Laos joins the World Trade Organization	Work begins on the first major train line through Laos, linking Thailand with Vietnam

The French hoped to remedy these problems by building roads and, eventually, a railway from the Vietnamese coast – a project derailed first by the Great Depression and then by World War II – and by encouraging mass Vietnamese migration, in order to tackle the age-old problem of too much land and too few people. Had it not been for World War II, the French may well have succeeded in making the Lao a minority in their own land, in which case Laos might not exist today.

For all its talk of the "civilizing mission" of their particular brand of imperialism, France appeared to have no mission in Laos, other than to deny territory to the British. Elsewhere in Indochina, the French built schools, universities, a railway network and an extensive highway system, and though they did construct a skeletal highway system linking Laos with Vietnam and rebuilt monuments destroyed by the Siamese in the early 1800s, few improvements were made to Laos's educational or healthcare systems.

World War II

The initial fallout from events in Europe in 1940 was the **Japanese occupation** of Laos. Vichy France was left responsible for the administration of Indochina and gave the Japanese the right to move and station troops throughout the region. Sensing an opportunity to avenge its defeat of 1893, Siam, renamed **Thailand** in 1939, seized the west-bank territories of Sayaboury and Champasak, leaving the Lao angry with both the Thai for encroaching on their territory and the French for failing to defend the country.

To counter the appeal of Thai nationalist propaganda, the French encouraged a weak **nationalism** among the Lao elite. They nurtured a renaissance of literature, theatre, music and dance, while supporting patriotic rallies and the creation of a national development programme. Schools were built, the healthcare system improved and the first Lao newspaper was published. Colonial officials raised concerns that these steps were arousing dangerous sentiments; they were to be proved right, although it would be left to the Japanese to shatter the illusion of French power and provide the spark for Lao independence.

In March 1945, the Japanese staged a pre-emptive strike to neutralize French forces in Indochina, imprisoning French soldiers and civil servants, and proclaiming an end to France's colonial regimes. Japanese forces reached Luang Prabang the following month and made Sisavang Vong, the pro-French king, declare independence, forcing his hand by hauling off the crown prince to Saigon. Somewhat less reluctantly, **Phetsarath**, who could trace his family line back to Anou, the last king of Vientiane, became prime minister. The eldest of three remarkable brothers who would profoundly affect Lao history, Phetsarath was now the second most powerful political figure after the king.

Free Laos

Nationalists across Indochina moved to take advantage of the power vacuum created by the end of World War II and **Japan's surrender**. In Laos, an independent-minded Lao elite formed a government which became known as the Lao Issara, literally "**Free Laos**", while next door Ho Chi Minh proclaimed the establishment of the Democratic Republic of Vietnam.

The rapid awakening of the Lao elite after years of French rule left them factionalized, with support split between opposition to the Japanese and opposition to the French. A power struggle ensued as King Sisavang Vong welcomed the return of the French and Phetsarath reaffirmed the independence of Laos and declared the union of the Kingdom of Luang Prabang and the territory of Champasak in a single, independent Kingdom of Laos. The king repudiated Phetsarath by dismissing him as prime minister and viceroy on October 10, 1945.

In response, the newly constituted **Lao Issara government** deposed the king two days later. This new government, which based itself in Vientiane, contained some of the key figures who would dominate politics in Laos over the course of the next few decades, including Phetsarath's younger brothers Souvannaphouma and Souphanouvong, both educated in Paris. Before joining the new government in Vientiane as Minister of Foreign Affairs and Chief of the Liberation Army, **Souphanouvong** was flown to Hanoi by an American general, where he met with, and earned the support of, Ho Chi Minh. He returned with a contingent of Viet Minh soldiers – the first instance of Vietnamese armed support for a Lao nationalist movement – and swore to continue the struggle until an independent Laos had been won.

The **Potsdam Agreement** marking the end of World War II failed to recognize the Lao Issara government. Under the terms of the agreement, the Japanese surrender was accepted by the British to the south, who facilitated the return of French occupation forces. In March 1946 French forces, along with their Lao allies, made their way slowly up the Mekong Valley. Lao Issara volunteers, led by Souphanouvong and assisted by the Viet Minh, resisted the French near Thakhek, but the French successfully reoccupied Vientiane in April 1946 and Luang Prabang three weeks later. Thousands of Lao Issara supporters and Vietnamese fled to Thailand, where Prince Phetsarath established a government-in-exile in Bangkok. Although Souphanouvong repeated US President Franklin Roosevelt's statement that the French should not be allowed to return to Indochina, the US and Britain did not offer the Lao Issara support.

The Kingdom of Laos

In 1947, the newly constituted **Kingdom of Laos** began to take shape. Prince Boun Oum of Champasak, who had helped the French in the south, renounced his claim to a separate southern kingdom, strengthening the French position in Vientiane and paving the way for Laos to be unified under the royal house of Luang Prabang. The territories west of the Mekong were restored, elections for a Constituent Assembly were held and a new constitution proclaimed. The members of the new government, which was a decidedly pro-French body, were drawn from the elite that had benefited from the French presence all along. The government lacked cohesion, however, and the king opted to remain in Luang Prabang rather than move to Vientiane.

The French by now were increasingly bogged down in their struggle with the **Viet Minh,** which had erupted in December 1946 and would become known as the First Indochina War. What had begun as a police action had rapidly become a costly "war without borders", which was to last eight years and cost the lives of 93,000 on the French side and an estimated 200,000 Viet Minh supporters. Vietnamese nationalists coordinated and participated in Lao Issara guerrilla raids, led by Souphanouvong, on French convoys and garrisons. The Viet Minh's influence over Souphanouvong took its toll on the unity of the Lao Issara, and by May 1949 the rift had become irreparable; Souphanouvong was removed from his post. In July, France appealed to moderate elements of the Lao Issara by conceding greater authority to the Vientiane government. The Lao Issara announced its dissolution. As Souvannaphouma, along with two dozen moderate Lao Issara leaders, returned to Vientiane on board a French transport plane, Souphanouvong set out from Bangkok on foot for Viet Minh headquarters. Meanwhile, the leader of the movement, Phetsarath, remained behind, refusing to return to Laos until 1957, when his title of viceroy was finally restored by the king.

The Pathet Lao

When Souphanouvong arrived at Viet Minh headquarters in Tonkin in late 1949, he was warmly welcomed by Ho Chi Minh, who had ambitious plans for him. Souphanouvong, who sought only arms and money, also received some advice from Vo

Nguyen Giap, the legendary Vietnamese general who would later defeat the French at Dien Bien Phu. In the course of the meeting, Giap told Souphanouvong to keep away from towns, saying "Remember, those who rule the countryside rule the country."

While the moderate members of the dissolved Lao Issara joined the new **Royal Lao Government** (RLG) in 1950, Souphanouvong founded his own government, which saw itself as the successor to the Lao Issara. In August 1950, in a far corner of northern Laos, Souphanouvong presided over the **First Resistance Congress**, which was supervised by the Viet Minh. The Congress adopted a twelve-point manifesto, at the bottom of which appeared the notation "**Pathet Lao**", literally "the Land of the Lao". This became the name by which his resistance group was to be known. The manifesto called for a truly independent and unified Laos to be governed by a coalition government with the RLG, and the Pathet Lao pledged cooperation with the Vietnamese and Khmer in the common struggle against the French.

The Pathet Lao then focused on recruiting members in northern and eastern Laos. Cadres moved into remote villages, promoting literacy, building schools and organizing village militias. Kaysone Phomvihane directed the Committee for the Organization of the Party, which recruited new cadres, until the **Lao People's Party** was formally established in 1955.

The First Indochina War

By the early 1950s, the **First Indochina War** had engulfed the region. Chinese military aid flowed to the Viet Minh, while the US, smarting from the fall of China to the communists, supported France. After the routing of the nationalists in China and the outbreak of the Korean War, the French could portray, with greater success, their struggle against the Viet Minh not as a colonial war but as a fight in defence of the "Free World".

For the Viet Minh, Laos was an extension of their battle against the French. Twice in 1953 they staged major invasions of Laos, seizing large areas of the country before turning them over to the Pathet Lao.

By this point, Souphanouvong had formally established the headquarters of the resistance government in **Sam Neua**, which lay at the heart of an extensive "liberated zone"; meanwhile in Paris, Souvannaphouma was pressing the French for complete independence. By the time this was granted in October 1953, however, Laos was a divided country, with large areas controlled by the Pathet Lao and the rest of the country under the RLG.

Taunted by the Viet Minh invasions of Laos, which France was obliged by treaty to defend, General Henri Navarre, the French Commander-in-Chief in Indochina, ordered the French Expeditionary Force's parachute battalion to establish a massive base in **Dien Bien Phu** in November 1953. Navarre reasoned that by creating a camp in this isolated valley along the traditional invasion route of Laos, he could force the Viet Minh into an open battle – while at the same time protecting Laos – and end the war in eighteen months. The war did end, but not quite as he expected. The Viet Minh encircled the valley and began a bloody assault that lasted 59 days and cost the lives of twenty thousand Viet Minh soldiers. The French were forced to surrender on May 7, 1954. Their efforts to restore the pre-World War II status quo in Indochina had collapsed.

The Geneva Conference

On May 8, the nine delegations attending the **Geneva Conference** called to discuss the situation in Korea shifted their focus to Indochina. The government in Vientiane was represented by Phoui Sananikone, the scion of Vientiane's leading family and a leader of the anti-Japanese resistance in northern Laos during World War II. The Viet Minh arrived with a young Lao by the name of Nouhak Phoumsavanh, who proposed that the Pathet Lao resistance government of which he was a member be represented as well. Phoui defended the sovereignty of the Vientiane government and the proposal was rejected. The conference's final declaration included Phoui's proclamation that the RLG would not pursue a policy of aggression nor would it allow a foreign power to use its soil for hostile purposes. The **Agreement on the Cessation of Hostilities** was signed on July 20 – by the Viet Minh and France – which in addition to a ceasefire also called for a regrouping of opposing forces, leading to elections in two years.

Although Laos was reaffirmed as a unitary, independent state with a single government, the Pathet Lao did manage to win de facto recognition as an insurgency group and were allotted the provinces of Phongsali and Hua Phan in which to regroup.

America intervenes

The **US** had since 1950 been funding an estimated seventy percent of the French war effort in Indochina. In 1951, the US signed an economic aid agreement with the government of Phoui Sananikone which aimed to speed up the development of a free and independent Laos. After the 1954 Geneva Accords, which the US did not sign, considering them a sell-out to international communism, strengthening the anti-communist governments of Indochina became a priority for President Dwight Eisenhower's administration. The withdrawal of the French military left a power vacuum on the edge of a historically expansionist state, a worrisome state of affairs in the eyes of the US.

As of 1955, the US was financing most of the Lao government budget and completely bankrolling the Royal Lao Army, countering the Viet Minh, which was shouldering the entire cost of the Pathet Lao's army. Feeling that the French were not taking their responsibility of training the Lao army seriously enough, the US skirted the terms of the Geneva agreement by training select officers in Thailand and by equipping and expanding the police force. Other funds went into churning out propaganda, building roads and communications networks, and propping up the kip. The Americans bought truckloads of the local currency above the black market rate, burned the notes and gave the government US dollars in exchange.

For the next eight years, the US spent more on foreign aid to Laos per capita than it did on any other Southeast Asian country, though the overwhelming majority of the aid was military. As US dollars poured into the country, the army grew increasingly powerful and existing rivalries between leading families were reinforced, with the clans more concerned with improving their social standing than exercising responsible power. Fretting over recent communist takeovers around the world, US policies were motivated by the fear of the so-called **Domino Effect**. As President Eisenhower prepared to turn over the helm to John F. Kennedy, he told his successor: "If Laos is lost to the free world, in the long run we will lose all of Southeast Asia."

The quest for unity and neutrality

After Geneva, the priority of the RLG was to regain control of the two Pathet Lao provinces so that elections could be held in accordance with the peace settlement. But when elections finally went ahead in December 1955, it was without the Pathet Lao, disgruntled at being refused its demands for changes to the electoral law and freedom for its front organization, the Lao Patriotic Front (behind which stood the Lao People's Party), to operate as a political party. The elections resulted in the formation of a government led by **Prince Souvannaphouma**, who entered into negotiations with his half-brother Souphanouvong in the belief that national unity and neutrality were the key to the preservation of the state. The two sides cut a deal in November 1957 to include two Pathet Lao members in a coalition government in exchange for the reintegration of Hua Phan and Phongsali into the rest of Laos.

Left alone, it seemed, the people of Laos could work out their problems, or so Souvannaphouma thought. However, when elections the following May gave leftist candidates 21 seats in the National Assembly, the US embassy and the CIA actively promoted the creation of the right-wing Committee for the Defence of National Interests, known as the CDNI, and withheld aid from Souvannaphouma's government, forcing its collapse in July. Power in Vientiane had shifted from the National Assembly to the American Embassy.

With the collapse of the government, any hope for a neutral, united Laos was rapidly disintegrating. After a right-wing government – led by **Phoui Sananikone** – took charge in August, the truce put in place by the Geneva Accords began to unravel. Civil war seemed inevitable. In January, claiming that a North Vietnamese invasion was imminent, Phoui demanded and received emergency powers for a year, effectively shutting the Pathet Lao out of Vientiane's political arena and opening the door for the Royal Lao Army to gain control of the Ministry of Defence. A ruthless and powerful military figure, **General Phoumi Nosavan**, assumed the post of vice minister of defence. The story goes that in 1949 he drew matchsticks to decide between staying on with Prince Souphanouvong in his alliance with the Viet Minh or travelling to Vientiane to cooperate with French forces. A decade later, no such indecision hampered Phoumi as he eagerly auditioned for the role of strongman. Immediately stepping up harassment of the Pathet Lao's political front, he did not disappoint the Americans.

After negotiations to integrate two Pathet Lao battalions into the Royal Lao Army stalled, one battalion slipped back to Hua Phan, where the communist forces were preparing to resume their insurgency. The government considered the leftist troops to be in rebellion and responded by arresting Pathet Lao leaders in Vientiane, including Souphanouvong. As skirmishes signalled a return to the battlefield, the country's two most powerful political figures, Prince Phetsarath and King Sisavang Vong, died within a fortnight of each other in October 1959.

Phoumi's coup and the growth of the Pathet Lao

Phoui's failure to rein in the increasingly powerful military had sown the seeds for his ousting. With a helping hand from the vehemently anti-communist CDNI, General Phoumi, by now in charge of the ministry of defence, staged a **coup** in December. His troops took to the streets of Vientiane under the pretext, yet again, of a Pathet Lao attack. Although Phoumi failed to take charge of the newly formed government, it was nonetheless controlled by the military and staunchly aligned with the US and Thailand. Rigged elections held in April left the leftists without a seat, much to the satisfaction of the US.

The **corruption** of the generals and politicians in Vientiane and the purge of communist cadres in the countryside gave the Pathet Lao propaganda machine ample material with which to win hearts and minds. With Souphanouvong biding his time in jail, Kaysone Phomvihane, as head of Pathet Lao military operations, expanded his control over the organization's leadership. Communist forces were active throughout most of the country, and by 1960 roughly twenty percent of the population was no longer under government control.

Although the Royal Lao Army generals were far too concerned with vying for influence to worry about the communists' successes in indoctrinating the rural population, the men guarding Souphanouvong and his comrades certainly took note. As the new government – one which was set on a show trial for the Red Prince – was taking shape, all fifteen Pathet Lao prisoners, along with their guards, slipped off in the night. Souphanouvong began his now legendary 500km march to Pathet Lao headquarters in Hua Phan.

The Laotian crisis

The Pathet Lao weren't the only ones fed up with the self-serving politicians and generals in Vientiane. In August 1960, a disgruntled 26-year-old army captain named

Kong Le seized control of Vientiane, much to the surprise of the US and the Cabinet, whose ministers were away in Luang Prabang. Proclaiming himself a neutralist, Kong Le called for an end to "Lao killing Lao" and an end to foreign interference in the affairs of the country. He then invited Souvannaphouma to lead a new government.

As Laos began to split apart, the Pathet Lao seized more territory. Phoumi regrouped what troops he could in Savannakhet, where he gained the backing of the CIA. Planes belonging to Air America, a civilian contract airline that was later revealed to be a front for the CIA, began flying into Savannakhet with arms and bundles of money.

In November, Phoumi's men, coordinated by American advisors and assisted by a group of crack Thai troops, began a march on Vientiane, as Moscow and Washington – both of whom saw Laos as an excellent place from which to control Southeast Asia – looked on. The Soviet Union began airlifting supplies to Kong Le's neutralist forces in the capital. Laos was now at the heart of a Cold War showdown.

By the time Phoumi's troops reached Vientiane in December, the neutralists had allied themselves with the Pathet Lao and the Viet Minh. With both sides reluctant to spill Lao blood, a sloppy battle ensued which was won by the rightists. The neutralists retreated north and eventually joined Pathet Lao forces on the Plain of Jars. Souvannaphouma, who fled for Phnom Penh before the battle, was formally ousted as prime minister by King Sisavang Vatthana and replaced by Prince Boun Oum of Champasak.

But by March 1961, as a neutralist–Pathet Lao offensive got under way, President Kennedy announced American support for a **political settlement** involving the neutralization of Laos. This was an acknowledgement that America saw military victory as unlikely given the incompetence and reluctance to fight on the part of the Royal Lao Army, something that Kennedy sensed when he first met the diminutive Phoumi and commented, "if that's our strongman, we're in trouble". With Cuba, Berlin and numerous other hotspots on the radar, Washington worried about spreading itself too thinly. The president concluded his March 23rd speech on the "Laotian Crisis" saying: "All we want in Laos is peace, not war; a truly neutral government, not a Cold War pawn; a settlement concluded at the conference table and not on the battlefield."

The US had already begun to hedge its bets, however. Lao army troops were training in Thailand, US army advisers had arrived with new weapons and a handful of planes, and the CIA launched Operation Momentum (see p.276), which established a **clandestine army** recruited from the Hmong.

Two months after Kennedy's speech, a **second conference** was convened at **Geneva**, but despite the determination of the Soviet Union and the US to neutralize tensions over Laos, it took a year and a decisive defeat for the Royalist army at Luang Namtha before the feuding Lao factions reached an agreement on the formation of a **second coalition government**. The second coalition, however, was a failure, dissolving after the April 1963 assassination of a neutralist cabinet member. Fearing arrest or assassination, Pathet Lao ministers fled the capital.

The tacit agreement

Following the second round in Geneva, Washington's priority was South Vietnam, where, by 1962, it already had ten thousand military advisers and support troops. By October 1962 American and Soviet military personnel had withdrawn from Laos, but only forty North Vietnamese had cleared the checkpoints, leaving an estimated five thousand troops in Laos.

The country was being drawn increasingly into the **Second Indochina War**, as North Vietnam and the US undermined its neutrality in the pursuit of their agendas in Vietnam. Lao territory was a crucial part of the North Vietnamese war effort. They could not risk allowing the US to use northern Laos, in particular the Plain of Jars, to threaten North Vietnam and they needed to control the mountainous eastern corridor

VANG PAO AND THE CIA'S SECRET HMONG ARMY

Soon after Soviet aircraft began dropping weapons and supplies by parachute to Pathet Lao and neutralist forces stationed on the Plain of Jars in December 1960, a Central Intelligence Agency operative by the name of Bill Lair boarded an H-34 helicopter in Vientiane and flew off into the mountains of Xieng Khuang in search of **Vang Pao**, a little-known Royal Lao Army lieutenant-colonel. With Laos in the midst of a crisis that held the rapt attention of the world's superpowers, the 30-year-old Hmong officer was holding out against the communist forces who had taken over the Plain of Jars and the surrounding hillsides, an area heavily populated by Hmong. Lair and Vang Pao had been preparing for this meeting, albeit unknowingly, for a decade. The Texan had spent the better part of the 1950s training members of Thailand's national police in guerrilla warfare, a measure taken against the perceived threat of an invasion by communist China. Vang Pao, meanwhile, had been earning his reputation as a ruthless and clever soldier by leading raids against North Vietnamese forces stationed in Laos, first as a police officer and later as a member of a group of French-trained hill-tribe irregulars.

As retold in Second Indochina War correspondent Jane Hamilton-Merritt's *Tragic Mountains*, Vang Pao made clear in his meeting with Lair that the Hmong and the US shared a common enemy: "For me, I can't live with communism. I must either leave or fight. I prefer to fight." In the cool of a hillside thatch hut, the seeds of the CIA's so-called **secret army** were sown. To Lair and Vang Pao, American and Hmong needs were a perfect fit. The US provided weapons and training for the indigenous population, who were led by one of their own in a fight for their own cause.

The **Hmong** were naturals as guerrilla soldiers. Determined to defend their homeland, they knew the terrain and could run circles around the Pathet Lao and the North Vietnamese. After a three-day crash course in the weapons of modern warfare, Vang Pao's initial force of several hundred soldiers won their first battle, ambushing a curious band of Pathet Lao who had tracked the supplies descending from Air America planes by parachute. Operation Momentum, as the project was known, was a success. The clandestine army developed into an effective **guerrilla fighting force**, their numbers swelling to twenty thousand over the course of the decade. Hmong soldiers rescued downed American pilots, learned to fly fighter planes and bravely marched into battle, often trailed by their wives and children. Most importantly, Vang Pao's slapdash band of irregulars were all that stood between the Mekong and the North Vietnamese.

At first, US costs were low and Americans few and far between, a far cry from the battle next door in Vietnam. But a low-cost, home-grown war run out of the hip pocket of a lone CIA agent wasn't what the US military had in mind for Laos. As the 1960s progressed, the war in Laos escalated, advisors flooded the American ranks, and the role of air power grew to criminal proportions, and with it the role of the Hmong. Although they were best at guerrilla warfare, the Hmong were increasingly involved in set-piece, conventional battles against a determined North Vietnamese force; an estimated 25 percent of the Hmong who enlisted to fight were killed in battle.

By 1968, Vang Pao's forces were no longer fighting for their homeland, they were fighting for the US, pawns of the **war in Vietnam**. The institutionalization of the Laos war had reduced Operation Momentum to a bloated recruitment programme churning out war-weary Hmong mercenaries. Half a world away in Washington DC, former ambassador to Vientiane William Sullivan, questioned in Senate hearings as to whether the US had any responsibility for the well-being of Vang Pao and his people, made it painfully clear where the Hmong stood: "No formal obligation upon the US; no."

of southern Laos in order to move soldiers and supplies to South Vietnam along the Ho Chi Minh Trail (see opposite). The US saw no option but to challenge North Vietnam's strategy. Eventually, all sides with a stake in Laos came to the same conclusion about the Geneva Accords: while they would have loved to point an accusing finger at the opposition's violations of the agreement, they had much more to gain by quietly pursuing their own agendas. So the right-wing Lao, the Americans and the Thais on the one side and the Pathet Lao, the North Vietnamese and their Chinese and Soviet backers on the other tacitly agreed to pretend to abide by the accords, guaranteeing Laos's neutrality while keeping the country at war.

Even after the collapse of the second coalition government in 1963, patriotic Souvannaphouma was determined to keep the vision of a neutral Laos alive. After negotiations with the Chinese and Vietnamese failed, he returned to Vientiane and on April 18, 1964, he announced his plans to resign, prompting Phoumi's rightist rivals to launch a surprise coup the next day. But within a few days, the prince was back in power and the generals were out.

Excluded from the new government, the Pathet Lao went on the offensive, chasing Kong Le's remaining neutralists off the Plain of Jars and into an alliance with Vang Pao and his Hmong army. The communist offensive fitted neatly into what would become the standard seesaw pattern of fighting in northern Laos, in which each side went on the offensive when the season best suited them.

But in the spring of 1964, the communists came up against a whole new enemy: **airpower**. Single-prop T-28 aircraft hammered at communist positions, scaring off their soldiers who had never faced aeroplanes before. Within a matter of weeks, T-28 bombing runs were joined by US jets, which were sent over Laos as they happened to be in the neighbourhood. Once the bombing began, Washington apparently decided it wasn't such a bad idea. And although the bombing campaign would be reported for years by Pathet Lao and North Vietnamese radio, it would take five years before the US public heard anything about it.

Escalation

In 1964, with the US pushing hard for an **escalation of the bombing**, Souvannaphouma, prodded by the US embassy, declared that the North Vietnamese were using the eastern flank of Laos to send combatants and supplies to South Vietnam along what would become known as the **Ho Chi Minh Trail**. He then gave the go-ahead for what were euphemistically known as "armed reconnaissance" flights over Laos, permission that essentially became a blank cheque for the US to bomb wherever it pleased.

The war was intensifying next door in **Vietnam**, too. US President Lyndon B. Johnson, facing an election in November 1964, did not want to be the president who lost against the communists. After the USS *Maddox* came under attack off the coast of North Vietnam, US senators passed the **Gulf of Tonkin Resolution**, which became Johnson's justification for the Vietnam War. No such resolution was passed regarding Laos; after all, the country was "neutral".

When Ambassador William Sullivan assumed his post in Vientiane near the end of 1964, his assignment was to wage war while maintaining the fiction of the Geneva Accords. He came to the Lao capital aware of US plans for Operation Rolling Thunder – a sustained carpet-bombing campaign against North Vietnam designed to go "after the manure pile" rather than simply swatting flies, as the Commander of the US Air Force, General Curtis Le May, eloquently put it. Even before the Vietnam operation began, Sullivan established his own programmes for Laos, called **Operation Barrel Roll** in the north and **Operation Steel Tiger** in the south.

Sullivan set the tone for the US campaign in Laos – ground troops were kept out (apart from reconnaissance missions and raids on the Ho Chi Minh Trail area) and military planes had to take off outside the country. The war took place in total secrecy. As British journalist Christopher Robbins wrote in *The Ravens*, based on interviews with pilots who fought in "the Other Theatre", "There was another war even nastier than the one in Vietnam, and so secret that the location of the country in which it was being fought was classified… The men who chose to fight in it were handpicked volunteers, and anyone accepted for a tour seemed to disappear as if from the face of the earth."

From 1964 until the ceasefire of February 1973, US planes flew 580,944 sorties – or 177 a day – over Laos and dropped 2,093,100 tonnes of bombs – equivalent to one planeload of bombs every eight minutes around the clock for nine years – making Laos the most heavily bombed country per capita in the history of warfare.

The turning point: 1968

On March 10, 1968, communist forces overran a strategic limestone massif in Hua Phan which the US had crowned with a high-tech bombing guidance device that directed attacks on Hanoi and was guarded by Hmong troops. The **fall of Phou Pha Thi** (see box, p.157) underscored the lack of unified command that plagued the various US factions – the embassy, the CIA and the air force – responsible for fighting the Laos War.

According to Roger Warner in his book *Shooting at the Moon*, while some involved in directing the US war effort thought the US had erred by provoking the North Vietnamese with the installation of this direct threat to Hanoi's security, others argued that the North Vietnamese escalation in Laos was simply a part of the same intensive effort that produced the January 31 **Tet Offensive**, in which a combined force of seventy thousand communists violated a truce to launch attacks on more than a hundred cities across South Vietnam. In a Washington reeling from Tet, which brought with it the popular perception that the communists were winning the war in Vietnam, President Johnson vetoed requests for a massive troop expansion, and on March 31 he suspended bombing north of the Twentieth Parallel to jump-start the peace talks in Paris that would grind on for five years. By the year's end the bombing had completely ended.

The suspension of bombing in Vietnam was terrible news for Laos, as the US Air Force's reaction was to send more planes over Laos than ever before. Swarms of planes circled the country, homing in on their targets their targets with the help of a new breed of forward air controllers known as Ravens, introduced in the wake of the Phou Pha Thi disaster. These pilots, dressed in civilian clothes, flew single-engine Cessna propeller planes, with a hill-tribe translator in the backseat to communicate with ground forces, guiding up to three hundred American sorties per day. The early days of Operation Momentum, when the CIA quietly waged a grassroots guerrilla war, were a distant memory.

Nixon's presidency

In order to facilitate pulling out of Southeast Asia while saving face for the US, President **Nixon** initiated a policy of "**Vietnamization**". This involved a gradual withdrawal of US forces coupled with an intensification of the air war and more material support, as well as pursuing communist sanctuaries with greater intensity in the hope that South Vietnam could hold its own against the North.

The first major test of this strategy was the US' **invasion of Cambodia**, which lay at the end of the Ho Chi Minh Trail. Until 1970, Cambodia, under the leadership of Prince Norodom Sihanouk, had stayed neutral in the war. Neutrality for Sihanouk, however, meant allowing the North Vietnamese to operate on Cambodian soil and the US to bomb the North Vietnamese with B-52s. On March 18, 1970, a right-wing pro-US general named Lon Nol replaced Sihanouk in a coup and, two weeks later, US and South Vietnamese troops invaded the regions of the country nearest South Vietnam.

The operation set off a political uproar in the US, and massive **anti-war demonstrations** spread across the country. Politically, the Cambodian "incursion", as it was termed, and subsequent protests prompted the US Congress to pass a measure forbidding the use of American ground troops in Cambodia and Laos. Had they not, US ground troops might have taken part in **Lam Son 719** (see p.279) – one of the most disastrous operations undertaken by the US in the whole of the war. Backed by American air power, 20,000 South Vietnamese troops drove across the Annamite Mountains in the hope of cutting North Vietnamese supply lines near Xepon. The move proved catastrophic. Five thousand South Vietnamese were killed or wounded, 176 Americans died and more than one hundred US army helicopters were shot down, with an estimated six hundred more damaged. It became clear that even with massive US support, the South Vietnamese didn't stand a chance, pushing US policymakers closer to the realization that the war was a lost cause.

OPERATION LAM SON 719

On the outskirts of the village of Ban Dong on Route 9 sit two rusting American tanks, all that remains of a massive invasion and series of battles that have become a mere footnote in the history of the decade-long American military debacle in Indochina.

In 1971 President Nixon, anticipating a massive campaign by North Vietnamese troops against South Vietnam the following year (which happened to be an election year in the US), ordered an attack on the Ho Chi Minh Trail to cut off supplies to communist forces. Although a congressional amendment had been passed the previous year prohibiting US ground troops from crossing the border from Vietnam into Laos and Cambodia, the US command saw it as an opportunity to test the strengths of Vietnamization, the policy of turning the ground war over to the South Vietnamese.

For the operation, code-named **Lam Son 719**, it was decided that ARVN (Army of the Republic of Vietnam) troops were to invade Laos and block the trail with the backing of US air support. The objective was Xepon, a town straddled by the Trail, which was some 30–40km wide at this point. Nixon's national security advisor, Henry Kissinger, was later to lament that "the operation, conceived in doubt and assailed by scepticism, proceeded in confusion".

In early February 1971, ARVN troops and tanks pushed across the border at Lao Bao and followed Route 9 into Laos. Like a caterpillar trying to ford a column of red ants, the South Vietnamese troops were soon engulfed by North Vietnamese (NVA) regulars, who were superior in number. Ordered by President Thieu of South Vietnam to halt if there were more than three thousand casualties, ARVN officers stopped halfway to Xepon and engaged the NVA in a series of battles that lasted over a month. US air support proved ineffectual, and by mid-March scenes of frightened ARVN troops drastically retreating were being broadcast around the world. In an official Lao account of the battle, a list of "units of Saigon puppet troops wiped out on Highway 9" included four regiments of armoured cavalry destroyed between the Vietnam border and Ban Dong.

The US realized that as long as it fought in Indochina, it would continue to give the Soviet Union and China reason to cooperate. By July 1971, Nixon seemed ready to sacrifice South Vietnam – and by extension Laos and Cambodia – in order to create an opening with China.

On January 27, 1973, the US, North Vietnam, South Vietnam and the Viet Cong at last signed the **Paris Accords**, under the terms of which a ceasefire was established and all remaining American troops were to be repatriated by April. In reality the accords would accomplish little more than smoothing the US withdrawal from Indochina.

The Pathet Lao takeover

Souvannaphouma wanted assurances from the Americans that the North Vietnamese would pull their troops out of Laos. But the Vietnamese had never acknowledged having troops in Laos in the first place and the US had already committed itself to a withdrawal. The North Vietnamese knew this left them in a position of power and decided to stay in Laos and Cambodia until a new government was established in Vientiane. When the Vientiane government and the Pathet Lao eventually signed an agreement of reconciliation, neither US nor North Vietnamese signatures were present.

Continued negotiations resulted in the formation of a **third coalition government** in April 1974, with leftists taking half the ministerial portfolios and the remainder going to the right. But when Phnom Penh and then Saigon fell to communist forces in April 1975, a complete communist takeover in Laos appeared a foregone conclusion.

By August 23, a band of fifty women soldiers had symbolically "liberated" Vientiane. Vang Pao was persuaded to leave Laos by the US, whose representatives were also pulling out. A mass exodus of Hmong towards Thailand followed; an estimated thirty thousand Hmong had died during the war.

Lowland Lao generals of the Royalist side usually cooperated with the new government. Thousands of civil servants and military officers went willingly to re-education camps (see box, p.159) in remote corners of the country after being told these "seminars" would only last a few weeks.

The absence of right-wing figures opened the door to further Pathet Lao advances which culminated in a **National Congress of People's Representatives** on December 2, 1975, when the congress proclaimed the Lao People's Democratic Republic and accepted the abdication of King Sisavang Vatthana.

The Lao People's Democratic Republic

The **Thirty Year Struggle**, with its roots in the short-lived Lao Issara government, was over. The man in charge was the little-known party secretary-general **Kaysone**, who was named prime minister. The man who had been the face of the Pathet Lao all along, Souphanouvong, assumed the role of president, essentially becoming a figurehead – after all, it wouldn't do to have a communist country run by a French-educated prince.

Unlike their comrades in Vietnam and Cambodia, the Pathet Lao took power in a **bloodless coup**. After overthrowing the government of Souvannaphouma and abolishing royalty, the Pathet Lao named the prince and the king as advisors to the new government and demonstrated further flexibility by inviting the US to maintain its embassy in Vientiane.

The Pathet Lao's goodwill ended there, however, as they continued to round up civil servants and military personnel with ties to the Royalists until as many as fifty thousand people were in **re-education camps** (see box, p.159). Many, on their release, left the country. By the mid-1980s Laos had lost ten percent of its population – including an overwhelming majority of its educated class.

Considerable problems faced the new government, which took over a country stripped of money and resources. The **economy** was now a shambles, crippled by the termination of US aid, runaway inflation and the closure of the border with Thailand – the country's primary source of imports, which resulted in severe food shortages. Thirty-five thousand ethnic Vietnamese and Chinese – the traditional merchants of the country – boarded up their shops in Vientiane and crossed the Mekong. Intent on ushering in a socialist state, the Pathet Lao followed **Eastern bloc models**: they collectivized farms, centralized control of prices and nationalized what little industry there was. The government required long-haired teenagers to get haircuts and women to wear traditional skirts in an effort to develop Lao socialist men and women. Prostitutes and petty thieves were shipped off to re-education camps of their own on islands in the middle of Ang Nam Ngum.

As living standards declined within Laos and the number of refugees in camps in Thailand swelled, **opponents of the regime** found ready recruits. The Thailand-based Lao National Revolutionary Front produced anti-government propaganda and sent sabotage teams into Laos, while remnants of the Hmong secret army went on the offensive in northern Laos, capturing a town on the outskirts of Luang Prabang in March 1977. Fearing that opponents might rally around the figure of the king, the government arrested the royal family and banished them to Hua Phan, where the king, queen and crown prince died, something officially acknowledged only in 1990.

Vietnamese forces helped quell the Hmong revolt, and in July, Vientiane and Hanoi signed a 25-year **Treaty of Friendship and Cooperation** which formalized Vietnamese political, economic and military assistance, including the stationing of more than thirty thousand Vietnamese troops in Laos over the next decade. Relations were also close with the Soviet Union, which sent hundreds of technicians and advisers to Laos, drawing it firmly within the Soviet sphere of influence.

The new thinking

By 1979, external and internal difficulties facing the new government forced it to re-evaluate its policies; as a result, its agricultural cooperative programme was suspended and a less rigid form of socialism was adopted. After ten years of power, in December 1985, Laos was still dependent on foreign aid and it remained one of the world's poorest countries. The time had come, in the eyes of Kaysone, for a change.

After overcoming opponents of reform, Kaysone was able to implement the **New Economic Mechanism**, approved by the Fourth Party Congress in November 1986, which essentially introduced a market economy. Without an upheaval among the party's leaders – many of whom had worked together since their days in the Indochinese Communist Party in the 1940s – the ageing hardliners of the Pathet Lao embarked on a series of reforms, generally known as *jintannakan mai* or the New Thinking, which was as thorough as anything to be found in Eastern Europe at the time. By the late 1980s, the centralized socialist economy had been largely dismantled. Farmers could own their own land and sell their crops at free-market prices, state-owned businesses had to make a profit or close their doors and wholly owned foreign investment projects, protected against nationalization, were authorized.

Political changes did not accompany the economic reforms, however. Local elections held in 1988 – the first since 1975 – and subsequent national elections in 1989 did provide some popular legitimacy for the government, but candidates were approved by the party prior to polls. And although the re-education camps were wound down, the government continued to deal strictly with **dissent**.

Discontent was eased when the economy opened up, raising living standards and making material goods more abundant. Government intrusion into people's lives was also reduced, and by the late 1980s, the Mekong was again a two-way street. Lao refugees were invited to return, and Western tourists began to visit the country.

In 1991, the Fifth Party Congress endorsed the long-awaited **Constitution**, which guaranteed basic freedoms and the right to private ownership of property. The congress served to indicate that the party was no longer above the law when one member of the politburo was demoted for corruption. Economic reform also received an endorsement, with the party replacing the communist red star in the national crest with the That Luang stupa and eliminating the word "socialism" from the national motto.

The 1992 **death of Kaysone**, who had led the communist movement since the inception of the Lao People's Party in 1955, presented a serious challenge to the regime, but a smooth transition, resulting in the appointment of **Nouhak Phoumsavanh** as state president and **Khamtay Siphandone**, the prime minister, as president of the party, ensured the government's political stability.

Regional integration

As communism began to collapse in Eastern Europe and Vietnam began to withdraw its forces from Laos, the government strengthened ties with Thailand and with other capitalist countries, notably Japan, Australia and Sweden. Cooperation with the US in the search for missing US servicemen on Lao soil and control of the opium trade improved the relationship with the US, culminating in the re-establishment of full ambassadorial relations in 1992. With the collapse of the Soviet Union in 1991, Laos also began to smooth over difficulties with China which had arisen as a result of Vientiane's alliance with the USSR and Vietnam. China has in fact emerged as Laos's most important foreign military ally, as well as a powerful economic force on Laos's northern border. Thus, by the early 1990s, Laos enjoyed relatively good relations with all its border countries, allowing it to slip back into its familiar role of a crossroads between contending regional powers.

The Australian-financed **Friendship Bridge** to Thailand – opened in 1994 outside Vientiane – as well as membership in the **Association of Southeast Asian Nations** in July

1997 were two important signs that Laos had finally begun to shake off decades of isolation. But for the **Sixth Party Congress**, the Friendship Bridge to Thailand symbolized the way in which the New Thinking was being corrupted, as economic reforms brought a host of new problems, including corruption, gambling dens, brothels and increased crime. The conservative policies introduced by the congress indicated the party intended to slow the pace of reforms and would attempt to contain the fallout from "socially evil outside influences", in part by appealing to traditional Lao values.

Economic reforms, with the accompanying social problems, increased official corruption and growing income disparity, represented a great challenge to internal order in the eyes of the party. The party clung to this view despite the fact that in the mid-1990s and again in the first few years of the new millennium, there was a slight upswing in insurgent activities, reportedly by the group known as the Chao Fa, perhaps owing to anger at government attempts to **resettle** highland groups. The official reason for resettlement was to put an end to opium cultivation and slash-and-burn agriculture, and bring far-flung villagers closer to hospitals and schools. The consequences in some cases proved fatal for the highlanders, who contracted valley-related diseases such as malaria.

Laos today

Former Minister of Defence **Choummaly Sayasone** took the reigns of power from Khamtay Siphandone in June 2006. **Sayasone** is the first post-revolution leader of Laos who is not a member of the ageing old guard, but he has been firmly committed to maintaining the status quo. With absolutely no possibility of a home-grown opposition leader coming to the forefront, the government is under little pressure to initiate serious political reforms.

Despite nations like China, Vietnam and Thailand pumping millions of dollars into new roads, rail links and hydroelectric projects – and rewards from the subsequent sale of hydropower to those neighbours – Laos continues to rank among the region's poorest and least developed countries. More than a quarter of the adult population is illiterate, access to safe drinking water is unreliable, and the country continues to languish near the bottom of World Health Organization rankings. In the meantime, Laos continues to shrewdly manipulate international governments, as well as non-governmental organizations, in order to keep aid flowing in, while human rights abuses continue to be overlooked.

In late 2009, as Vientiane geared up to host the 25th **Southeast Asian Games**, around four thousand Hmong were deported back to Laos from refugee camps in northern Thailand. The move was widely criticized by the UN, who were, along with the Hmong themselves, concerned that they might face retribution for their involvement in the Second Indochina War. Following the deportations, there were reports of the Hmong refugees being forced into signing "confessions", and the majority of the refugees were sent to an apparently heavily guarded "resettlement area", with limited access to adequate food and supplies.

Laos's reputation took another blow in December 2012, when the prominent Lao development worker **Sombath Somphone** was abducted in Vientiane. CCTV footage of the incident was circulated widely online, leading human rights groups such as Amnesty International to call for his safe return. The Lao government quickly denied involvement in the incident. At the time of writing, his whereabouts remain unknown.

The future for Laos is growth. Tourism continues to develop, bringing with it much-needed investment, and global trade links look set to increase, thanks partly to Laos's accession to the World Trade Organization, completed in February 2013. Though, with powerful nations like China funding the projects that are most likely to have a profound effect on economies and environments – such as the high-speed rail link from Kunming to Thailand, expected to be up and running by 2019 – it may be outsiders, rather than the people of Laos, who determine the country's destiny.

Religion and belief systems

The multiplicity of belief systems in Laos mirrors the complexity of its ethnic make-up. Theravada Buddhism is the majority religion, practised by approximately two-thirds of the population, followed by animism and ancestor worship. The remainder practise Mahayana Buddhism and Taoism, and a small percentage of the population follow Christianity or Islam.

Buddhism

Lao legend has it that Buddhism came to Laos in the fourteenth century, but archeological evidence suggests that Buddhism existed in parts of what is now Laos as early as the eighth century. **Theravada Buddhism**, sometimes referred to as the "southern school" of Buddhism owing to its geographic spread, is prevalent in Sri Lanka, Myanmar (Burma), Thailand and Cambodia as well as Laos. The vast majority of lowland-dwelling ethnic Lao, whose numbers make up over half of the population of Laos, are adherents of Theravada Buddhism, as are other ethnic groups such as the Tai Leu, Phuan and Phu Noi, plus a fraction of the tribal Tai groups, such as the Phu Tai, Tai Daeng and Tai Dam. Lao-style Theravada Buddhism is a fascinating blend of indigenous and borrowed beliefs and rituals. During Laos's many years of vassaldom to the various kingdoms made up of lands that now lie within Thai borders, many outside religious beliefs and customs found their way into the Lao royal courts of Luang Prabang, Vientiane and Champasak and, from there, into the valleys of the interior via the tributaries of the Mekong river. The Hindu customs and beliefs that were adopted by the Thai after their sack of Angkor, in what is now Cambodia, were also passed on, in diluted form, to Laos.

Later, Chinese and Vietnamese immigrants brought with them **Mahayana Buddhism**, the so-called "northern school" of Buddhism. As the immigrants prospered and assimilated, the images of their gods found their way into urban monasteries. Go into one of these monasteries today and, alongside images of the Buddha, you may well see a representation of a Hindu god such as Ganesh or a Mahayana Buddhist deity such as Kuan Yin.

The ideological rift between the two Buddhist schools is as vast as the one that divides Catholicism and Protestantism. Theravada Buddhism is the more austere of the two and has been described as having an "every man for himself" philosophy, that is to say, each individual adherent is believed to be responsible for his or her own accumulation of merit or sin. Mahayana Buddhism is more of a "group effort", with adherents praying for divine assistance from *bodhisattva*, near-Buddhas who have postponed their enlightenment in order to serve as the compassionate protectors of all mankind.

For most Lao Buddhists, religion in everyday life revolves around the all-important practice of **making merit**, or *het bun*. This accumulation of merit is paramount to a Theravada Buddhist's spiritual strategy, a way to dilute the destructive effects of any sin that may have been accrued by bad deeds, while at the same time ensuring that the next incarnation will be better than the present one. Many of the holidays in the Lao calendar are associated with Buddhist festivals and give the visitor a chance to observe the practice of merit-making, whether it be ritually bathing Buddha images or donating new robes to monks. Making merit is accomplished most readily by giving **alms** to Buddhist monks and novices. This enchanting practice can be witnessed just after dawn, when barefoot monks solemnly walk through the neighbourhood or village surrounding their monasteries in order to collect offerings of food from laypeople. Merit thus acquired is believed to bring the giver good fortune in this life and the next, and also to dilute the destructive effects of sin that may have been accumulated. Male adherents may also make merit for themselves and their families by taking vows and becoming a novice monk for a limited period of time. Even more merit may be acquired by becoming an ordained disciple of the Buddha.

Animism and ancestor worship

Predating Buddhism in Laos, **animism** is the belief that natural objects – such as hills, trees, large rocks or plots of land – are inhabited by spiritual entities or possess supernatural powers. While the Buddhist Lao still harbour vestiges of these beliefs, some midland and highland tribal peoples are exclusively animist.

An easily recognized example of animism among Buddhists is the practice of erecting a **spirit house** on plots of land. Ordinarily found in a corner of a piece of property, a spirit house is the customary abode of the *jao bawn*, or spirit of the site, and resembles a miniature house or sometimes a model of Mount Meru, the Hindu Mount Olympus, atop a pedestal. The idea is to make the spirit house a more habitable place than the dwellings for humans located on the same plot of land; naturally, if the *jao bawn* is comfortable in its digs, it is less likely to cause trouble for people living in the vicinity. Offerings to keep the spirit of the site propitiated may include flowers, incense, candles or sweets. A much simpler offering to *jao bawn* that visitors may note is the practice of pressing spirit offerings of sticky rice against trees or rocks. Another manifestation of animism that can be readily seen is the **talaew**, a six-pointed star made from strips of bamboo and placed over doors and gates or in rice fields. The device is thought to bar evil spirits from entering and doing harm.

After the revolution, the communists discouraged many animist practices, such as the annual sacrifice of water buffalo in tribal villages in the south, believing that such worship wasted resources and held back the progress of the nation. As with Buddhism, animism quickly revived once official suppression was relaxed.

Ancestor worship in different forms is also practised by many of the highland tribes that migrated to Laos from China, including the Akha, Hmong and Mien. Practices

---

THE MONKHOOD

Most ethnic Lao men become novice monks at some time in their lives, usually before marriage. Monks take **vows** to uphold no less than 227 precepts. These range from abstinence from sexual relations, alcohol and the wearing of any sort of ornamentation to more arcane rules such as a prohibition on urinating while standing upright (so as not to soil robes). Laos's history of social upheaval and a generally relaxed attitude towards rules, however, have meant that, especially in rural monasteries, not all of the precepts are strictly adhered to. For most Lao males, the time spent wearing a robe is short, usually no more than three months or so during the rainy season. Interestingly, a man who has yet to do time in a monastery is referred to as *dip* or "unripe", alluding to the fact that many Lao don't consider a man complete without some time spent in the monastery; before the advent of public schools, lessons in reading and writing at the monastery were about all the education the average Lao could hope for.

As the state religion, Buddhism enjoyed royal patronage up until the time of the **revolution**. In the years leading up to the revolution, the communists cleverly used Buddhist monks, many of whom were unhappy with widespread government corruption, as instruments for diffusing propaganda. Once the cause had been won, however, the communists moved to gain total control, banning the practice of alms-giving. This effectively made it impossible to remain a monk, as it is against Buddhist precepts for monks to cultivate plants or raise animals for food. The move backfired, however, as laypeople were shocked at the new regime's heavy-handed treatment of the monkhood and resented being deprived of any opportunity to make merit. Popular outcry forced the government to rescind the draconian measures, but only after large numbers of monks fled to Thailand or abandoned their robes and became laymen. Today, the study of Marxist–Leninist theory is still mandatory for all monks, but Lao Buddhism has made a strong comeback and economic reforms and liberalization have helped to increase the numbers of men in the monkhood to pre-revolution levels.

THE BASI

While travelling in Laos, you'll probably come across many lowland Lao wearing one or more bracelets of white thread around their wrists. This is a sign that the wearer has recently taken part in a **basi**, the quintessential Lao ceremony of **animist** bent, which is performed throughout the year. Also known as *sukhuan*, the ceremony is supposed to reunite the body's multiple souls, which are thought to succumb to wanderlust and depart from the body every now and again. *Basi* ceremonies are held during Lao New Year as well as being an important part of weddings, births and farewell parties.

Before the ceremony can be performed, an auspicious time must be gleaned from an astrologer, and a *phakhuan* – made from rolled banana leaves and resembling a miniature Christmas tree – must be prepared. The *phakhuan* is decorated with marigolds and other flowers, and draped with white threads. This arrangement sits in a silver bowl filled with husked rice, which is placed in the centre of a mat laid out on the floor. Participants sit in a circle around the *phakhuan* and offerings of food and liquor are placed near it. These are used to entice the absent souls to return. An animist **priest**, known as a *maw phawn* or "wish-doctor", presides over the ceremony, inviting the souls to return with a mixture of Pali and Lao chants. The white threads that are draped over the *phakhuan* are then removed and tied around the wrists of the participants while blessings are invoked. During the *basi* ceremony performed at Lao New Year, each thread tied around the wrist may be accompanied by a shot of rice liquor, and this sometimes leads to an impromptu *lam wong*, or "circle dance", performed by euphoric participants.

While trips operating from major tourist centres may include the chance to experience a *basi* ceremony, these have always been set up especially for the benefit of visitors. Alternatively, you may find yourself invited to partake in one if you travel out to more remote towns and villages, where locals are often keen for foreigners to join the party.

vary, but all believe that the spirits of deceased ancestors have the ability to affect the lives of their descendants. The ancestors are thought to be rather helpless and dependent on the living for earthly comforts; they reward descendants who remember them with offerings, but can become harmful if neglected.

Other beliefs

The Mien also worship **Taoist** deities, painted images of which are traditionally displayed on the Mien altar. **Hinduism**, or Brahmanism, was first introduced to what is now southern and central Laos by the Khmer, who adopted many Hindu traditions and beliefs from Indian traders who began arriving in the ports of Southeast Asia in the first century AD. While the Laos' recognition of Hindu divinities is minimal compared with that of their Thai cousins, two such deities, namely the multi-armed, four-faced **Brahma** and the green-skinned **Indra**, have become icons in the Theravada Buddhist pantheon and so are commonly depicted in Lao monasteries. Images of **Ganesh**, the so-called elephant god, can be found on the premises of some Buddhist monasteries and shrines, particularly in the south. The *shivalinga*, or stone phallus symbolizing the god **Shiva**, was commonly enshrined at ancient Khmer temples and, because many Lao Buddhist monasteries were built on top of ancient Khmer sites, the *shivalinga* and other bits of Khmer statuary are often found on Buddhist altars, particularly in the south.

Christianity arrived in Laos in 1642 in the form of an Italian Jesuit missionary but, according to his journal, he was far from successful. Not until the French colonial period did Christian missionaries scramble to make converts throughout Laos. A significant number of Laos's ethnic Vietnamese population is Catholic and the largest concentration of Catholics is found in southern Laos, particularly Savannakhet, which boasts the country's most elaborate Catholic church. Lao Christians also fared badly after the revolution. Because the communists saw Christianity as "Western", and therefore potentially subversive missionaries were expelled and churches closed.

Arts and temple architecture

The vast majority of works of art created in Laos – sculpture, painting, architecture, even decorative motifs on jewellery – are inspired by Buddhism, with the important exception of Lao textiles. The motivation behind much Theravada Buddhist art relies heavily on the concept of making merit. Wealthy patrons looking to acquire religious merit and dilute an accumulation of sins can do so by commissioning the crafting of an image of the Buddha or by financing the building or restoration of any of the structures found in monastery grounds.

Owing to Laos's distance from lucrative trade routes and its tumultuous history, the patronage of the religious arts never reached the heights that were attained in neighbouring Cambodia, Thailand and Burma. Nevertheless, a style did develop that is distinctively Lao and, although the number of works which exhibit a high degree of refinement is rather small, Lao art makes up for it with a vigour and whimsy that rarely fails to charm.

Sculpture

The historic Buddha was a prince who gave up his wealth and birthright in order to pursue the "middle path" – a philosophy of moderation – towards enlightenment. Just before his death, the Buddha was said to have discouraged his followers from making images of him, saying that it was his teachings that should be worshipped, not a likeness of him. For a time after the Buddha's passing, Buddhists used **symbolic imagery** to recall the enlightened one. An empty throne or a royal parasol was sometimes depicted commemorating the Buddha's decision to abandon his life of luxury and seek the path to enlightenment.

However, human nature being what it is, adherents needed something more concrete. The **first images of the Buddha** were probably made several centuries after the Buddha's death. By that time, no living artist had actually seen the Buddha, but a list of physical traits said to be unique to the Buddha had been passed down. The result of this list of fairly rigid attributes is that Buddha images from all over Asia share much the same characteristics. Lao images are no different and many of their seemingly bizarre features, toes of equal length for instance, are due to the strictness with which the aesthetic canon has been followed. In much the same vein, the attitude of the Buddha's arms and hands, or *mudra*, are rich with **symbolism** and must be depicted accurately if they are to be understood. Most of these gestures correspond to Buddhist theory or to events that occurred during the Buddha's lifetime. Besides the standard gestures and poses, the Lao have invented a couple of their own. One is a standing Buddha with arms to its sides and fingers pointing downwards, known as the "Beckoning Rain" pose. Buddhas with this *mudra* are found only in Laos and parts of northern Thailand. A similar standing Buddha with arms crossed at the wrists is also a Lao-invented *mudra*, known as "Contemplating the Tree of Enlightenment". The most sacred Buddha image in the country, the Pha Bang (see p.111), is also a standing Buddha, this time with arms held out in a blocking gesture, known as the "Dispelling Fear" pose.

One *mudra* in particular is especially popular with the Lao. This is found on Buddhas sitting in a half-lotus position, with the left hand resting palm-upward on the image's lap and the right hand extended down and touching the earth with the fingertips. Known as "Victory Over Mara", this pose commemorates the historic Buddha's triumph over Mara the Tempter, a Satan-like figure that tried unsuccessfully to distract the Buddha from his path to enlightenment.

The best place to see sculpted images of the Buddha is on an altar in a Buddhist temple's main *sim*. Typically, a massive central image, usually constructed of brick and stucco, is flanked by numerous smaller images cast from bronze or carved from hardwood. In Luang Prabang, the Pha Bang undeniably gets the most attention, but the superb reclining Buddha enshrined in a small "chapel" at Wat Xieng Thong is perhaps the best example of Lao sculpture to be found in the country.

Temple architecture

Of all Lao architectural elements, the *that*, or **stupa**, is probably easiest for the visitor to appreciate. This is due mainly to the fact that it is at once readily recognizable and varied in design. The concept of the stupa – a monument atop a reliquary containing sacred relics of the Buddha – originated in India and spread throughout Asia. In each country where Buddhism took root, the local architects and artisans put their own ideas to work when designing a stupa, and thus the bell-shaped stupas of Sri Lanka have little in common stylistically with the multistoreyed "pagoda" stupas found in China and Japan. Vientiane's That Luang stupa, the national symbol of Laos, is a fusion of aggressive angles and graceful curves that make it quite different from designs predominant in neighbouring countries (although stupas in this style can also be found in the northeast of Thailand where ethnic Lao predominate). This design of stupa is probably the greatest single Lao contribution to Buddhist architecture.

Within a typical Lao wat there are a number of buildings serving different functions, but it is the *sim*, the structure in which the monastery's principal Buddha image is enshrined, that gets the most attention from Lao architects and artisans. Lao *sim* have two main styles: the **Vientiane style** owes much to the Bangkok school of architecture, while the **Luang Prabang style** shares characteristics with that of Chiang Mai in northern Thailand. From a distance, the difference between the two styles is easily discerned. The roof of a Vientiane-style *sim* is high and steep, while a Luang Prabang-style roof gently slopes nearly to the ground.

Variations on *sim* design were produced by the Phuan and Tai Leu ethnic groups. The rare **Xieng Khuang style**, once found in the province of the same name, is low and squat, designed to withstand the weather of the windswept Plain of Jars. The handiwork of the Phuan people, this style barely survived Laos's violent history – the only remaining example lies outside of the province at Wat Khili in Luang Prabang (see p.114). Examples of architecture produced by the Tai Leu are very similar to that found in the Xishuangbanna region of China's Yunnan province. The *sim* at Muang Sing's Wat Sing Jai (see p.191) is a picturesque example of the Tai Leu style.

Decorative features on the *sim* and other structures found at a Lao wat are in a variety of mediums. Carved wood, moulded stucco and, to a lesser extent, mirrored-glass mosaics typically ornament the exterior while, inside, detailed murals cover entire walls. Doors and windows of the *sim* are often made from teakwood, ornately carved with the figures of celestial beings or demons upon a background of stylized flames or floral forms known as *lai lao* – "Lao pattern". The structure's wooden pediments – triangular segments of the upper facade that support the roof – are another place to look for pleasing examples of *lai lao*, along with carved depictions of Hindu deities such as Kala and Indra atop Airavata. Many of these motifs have origins in ancient Khmer ornamentation, such as that found at Wat Phou in Champasak province. Lao stuccowork is sometimes gilt-covered and almost always looks better from a distance. The use of stucco for ornamentation was introduced to Laos by the Khmer or possibly the Mon, but the methods and designs of Lao stuccowork owe more to the Tai Yuan of what is now northern Thailand. Likewise, the use of mirrored glass also came to Laos via Thailand. The mosaics at Wat Xieng Thong are Laos's most famous example of ornamentation using this medium but the works are modern, having been created in the late 1950s. Lao murals are meant to be read like a story and those found on the walls of the *sim* usually depict one of the tales from the Jataka tales, the Lao version of the Ramayana (see p.299), or scenes of local life.

The Lao belief that religious merit can be made by **restoring** old monastery buildings ensures that nearly all Lao *sim* are restored every fifty years or so. The artisans who restore these buildings are under little pressure to be true to an earlier design. Indeed, it is believed that the more lavish the new design, the more merit is likely to be made by the patron who commissioned the restoration. The result is that much of the decoration on Buddhist buildings in Laos is nowhere near as old as the structure it adorns.

Textiles

The matrilineal society of the lowland Lao and tribal Tai meant that when a man married, he immediately set up house on the property of his new bride's parents. Sometimes this entailed leaving his home village and subsequently, when this couple's son came of age, he would do the same. With such a custom, men's roots in a village were never deep and this was reflected by their simple dress: it told almost nothing of a man's background. Women, on the other hand, were the heirs to a weaving tradition that reflected their ethnic and geographical origins. Techniques improved with each new generation and were passed on.

Each **ethnic group** had its own particular patterns and colours, which varied from village to village but were still recognizable as belonging to that group. Sometimes, as with the Tai Daeng, these variations were great – indeed, one could fill a hefty book with the myriad designs found in Tai Daeng weaving. According to experts, the "grammar" of a textile can be read to reveal not only the ethnicity of the wearer, but also her marital and financial status. Because all women in a village wove and wore similar patterns and a woman normally wore only what she herself had made, it was apparent at a glance who had mastered the art of weaving – a highly desirable skill in the eyes of young men looking for a prospective bride. Not surprisingly, a woman's most striking apparel was saved for festival days when all the young men from the village and beyond would be in attendance.

The many years of war in Laos had a predictable effect on textile weaving, with the heavy looms too heavy for fleeing refugees to take with them. By sad coincidence, peace in Laos was accompanied by the introduction of inexpensive, mass-produced textiles. The importance that Lao mothers once placed on teaching their daughters the secrets of the loom rapidly faded. As a result, antique pieces have become highly sought-after collectables, and museums as far afield as Australia have hired textile experts to scour Lao villages for examples of nineteenth- and early twentieth-century Lao weaving. In recent years, a few companies have been encouraging villagers to return to their traditional weaving with fair-trade and cooperative initiatives that gives both weaver and tourist the opportunity to benefit from the traditional skill.

Laos's ethnic mosaic

While many of Southeast Asia's nations are ethnically diverse, Laos is one of the few that is still visibly so. That is to say, it is one of the last countries whose minorities have not been totally assimilated into the culture of the majority.

In an effort at categorization, the Lao government officially divides the population into three groups. Which group an ethnicity fits into is determined by the **elevation** at which that ethnicity dwells; thus many unrelated ethnic groups may be grouped together if they reside at one elevation. This method of categorization may be seen as a tenuous majority's subtle means of proclaiming cultural superiority over its sizeable population of minorities while at the same time trying to bring them into the fold.

The lowland Lao

The so-called **Lao Loum** (or lowland Lao) live at the lowest elevations and on the land best suited for cultivation. For the most part, they are the **ethnic Lao**, a people related to the Thai of Thailand and the Shan of Burma. The lowland Lao make up between fifty and sixty percent of the population, and are the group for which the country is named. They, like their Thai and Shan cousins, prefer to inhabit river valleys, live in dwellings that are raised above the ground, and are adherents of Theravada Buddhism. Laos is by no means the only place where ethnic Lao dwell. Most of Thailand's northeastern region is populated with ethnic Lao and, owing to internal migration patterns caused by economic factors, Bangkok has the largest concentration of ethnic Lao anywhere. This fact is not lost on the Lao of Laos who feel that history has deprived them of much of their original territory.

Of all the ethnicities found in Laos, the culture of the lowland Lao is dominant, mainly because it is they who hold political power. Their language is the official language, their religion is the state religion and their holy days are the official holidays. As access to a reliable water source is key to survival and water is abundant in the river valleys, the ethnic Lao have prospered. They have been able to devote their free time – that time not spent securing food – to the arts and entertainment, and their culture has become richer for it. Among the cultural traits by which the Lao define themselves are the cultivation and consumption of sticky rice as a staple, the taking part in the animist ceremony known as *basi* (see p.285), and the playing of the reed instrument called the *khaen*.

Akin to the ethnic Lao are the Tai Leu, Phuan and Phu Tai, found in the northwest, the northeast and mid-south respectively. The **Tai Leu** of Laos are originally from China's Xishuangbanna region in southern Yunnan, where nowadays they are known as the "Dai minority". In Laos, their settlements stretch from the Chinese border with Luang Namtha province, through Oudomxai and into Sayaboury; Muang Sing is perhaps the Tai Leu settlement visitors are most likely to encounter. The Tai Leu are Theravada Buddhists and, like the Lao, they placate animist spirits. They are known to perform a ceremony similar to the *basi* ceremony which is supposed to reunite the wayward souls of their water buffalo. They are also skilled weavers whose work is in demand from other groups that do not weave, such as the Khmu.

The **Phuan** were also once a recognized kingdom, but are now largely forgotten. The kingdom's territory, formerly located in the province of Xieng Khuang (the capital of which was formerly known as Muang Phuan), was at once coveted by the Siamese and Vietnamese. Aggression from both sides as well as from Chinese Haw bandits left it in ruins and the populace scattered.

The Phuan are Theravada Buddhists, but once observed an impromptu holy day known as *kam fa*. When the first thunder of the season was heard, all labours ceased and villagers avoided any activity that might cause even the slightest noise. The village's fortune was then divined based on the direction from which the thunder was heard.

The **Phu Tai** of Savannakhet and Khammouane provinces are also found in the northeast of Thailand. They are Theravada Buddhists and have assimilated into Lao culture to a high degree, although it is still possible to recognize them by their dress on festival days. The predominant colours of the Phu Tai shawls and skirts are an electric purple and orange with yellow and lime-green highlights.

The "tribal Tai"

Other Tai peoples related to the Lao are the so-called **tribal Tai**, who live in river valleys at slightly higher elevations and are mostly animists. These include the rather mysteriously named Tai Daeng (Red Tai), Tai Khao (White Tai) and Tai Dam (Black Tai). Theories about nomenclature vary. It is commonly surmised that the names were derived from the predominant colour of the womenfolk's dress, but others have suggested that the groups were named after the river valleys in northern Vietnam where they were thought to have originated. These Tai groups were once loosely united in a political alliance called the **Sipsong Chao Tai** or the Twelve Tai Principalities, spread over an area that covers parts of northwestern Vietnam and northeastern Laos. The traditional centre was present-day **Dien Bien Phu** in Vietnam, known to the Tai as Muang Theng. When the French returned to Indochina after World War II, they attempted to establish a "Tai Federation" encompassing the area of the old Principalities. The plan was short-circuited by Ho Chi Minh who, after defeating the French, was able to manipulate divisions between the Tai groups in order to gain total control.

The **Tai Dam** are found in large numbers in Hua Phan and Xieng Khuang provinces, but also inhabit northern Laos as far west as Luang Namtha. Principally animists, they have a system of Vietnamese-influenced surnames that indicate political and social status. The women are easily recognized by their distinctive dress: long-sleeved, tight-fitting blouses in bright, solid colours with a row of butterfly-shaped silver buttons down the front and a long, indigo-coloured skirt. The outfit is completed with a bonnet-like headcloth of indigo with red trim.

Mon–Khmer groups

The ethnic Lao believe themselves and their ethnic kin to have inhabited an area that is present-day Dien Bien Phu in Vietnam before migrating into what is now Laos. Interestingly, there is historical evidence to support their legends. As the Lao moved southwards they displaced the original inhabitants of the region. Known officially as the **Lao Theung** (*theung* is Lao for "above"), but colloquially known as the *kha* ("slaves"), these peoples were forced to resettle at higher elevations where water was more scarce and life decidedly more difficult.

The Khmu

The **Khmu** of northern Laos are thought to number around 350,000, making them one of the largest minority groups in Laos. Speakers of a Mon–Khmer language, they have assimilated to a high degree and are practically indistinguishable from the ethnic Lao to outsiders. Their origins are obscure. Some theorize that the Khmu originally inhabited China's Xishuangbanna region in southern Yunnan and migrated south into northern Laos long before the arrival of the Lao. The Khmu themselves tell legends of their being northern Laos's first inhabitants and of having founded Luang Prabang. Interestingly, royal ceremonies once performed annually by the Lao king at Luang Prabang symbolically acknowledged the Khmu's original ownership of the land. The Khmu are known for their honesty and diligence, though in the past they were easily duped by the lowland Lao into performing menial labour for little compensation. Their lack of sophistication in business matters and seeming complacency with their lot in life probably led to their being referred to as "slaves" by the lowland Lao. Unlike other groups in Laos, the Khmu are not known for their weaving skills and so customarily traded labour for cloth. The traditional Khmu village has four cemeteries: one for adults who died normal deaths, one for those who died violent or unnatural deaths, one for children and one for mutes.

A large spirit house located outside the village gates attests to the Khmu belief in **animism**. Spirits are thought to inhabit animals, rice and even money. Visitors to the village must call from outside the village gate, enquiring whether or not a temporary village taboo is in place. If so, then a visitor may not enter, and water, food and a mat to rest on will be brought out by the villagers. If there is no taboo in effect, male visitors may lodge in the village common-house if an overnight stay is planned, but may not sleep in the house of another family unless a blood sacrifice is made to the ancestors. There is no ban on women visitors staying the night in a Khmu household as it is thought to be the property of the women residents.

The village common-house also serves as a home for adolescent boys, and it is there that they learn how to weave baskets and make animal traps as well as become familiar with the village folklore and taboos. The boys may learn that the sound of the barking deer is an ill omen when a man is gathering materials with which to build a house, or that it is wrong to bring meat into the village from an animal that has been killed by a tiger or has died on its own. Young Khmu men seem to be prone to wanderlust, often leaving their villages to seek work in the lowlands. Their high rate of intermarriage with other groups during their forays for employment has contributed to their assimilation.

The Htin and the Mabri

Another Mon–Khmer-speaking group which inhabits the north, particularly Sayaboury province, are the **Htin**. They excel at fashioning household implements, particularly baskets and fish traps, from bamboo (owing to a partial cultural ban on the use of any kind of metal), and are known for their vast knowledge of the different species of bamboo and their respective uses.

Linguistically related to the Khmu and Htin are the **Mabri**, Laos's least numerous and least developed minority. Thought to number less than one hundred, the Mabri have a taboo on tilling the soil which has kept them semi-nomadic and impoverished. Half a century ago they were nomadic hunter-gatherers who customarily moved camp as soon as the leaves on the branches that comprised their temporary shelters began to turn yellow. Known to the Lao as *kha tawng leuang* ("slaves of the yellow banana leaves") or simply *khon pa* ("jungle people"), the Mabri were thought by some to be naked savages or even ghosts, and wild tales were circulated about their fantastic hunting skills and ability to vanish into the forest without a trace. The Mabri were said to worship their long spears, making offerings and performing dances for their weapons to bring luck with the hunt. Within the last few decades, however, they have given up their nomadic lifestyle and many now work for other groups, often performing menial tasks in exchange for food or clothing.

The Laven and the Gie-Trieng

The Bolaven Plateau in southern Laos is named for the **Laven** people, yet another Mon–Khmer-speaking group whose presence predates that of the Lao. The Laven were very quick to assimilate the ways of the southern Lao, so much so that a French expansionist and amateur ethnologist who explored the plateau in the 1870s found it difficult to tell the two apart. Besides the Laven, other Mon–Khmer-speaking minorities are found in the south, particularly in Savannakhet, Salavan and Xekong provinces. Among these are the **Bru**, who have raised the level of building animal traps and snares to a fine art. The Bru have devised traps to catch, and sometimes kill, everything from mice to elephants, including a booby-trap that thrusts a spear into the victim.

The **Gie-Trieng** of Xekong are one of the most isolated of all the tribal peoples, having been pushed deep into the bush by the rival Sedang tribe. The Gie-Trieng are expert basket weavers and their tightly woven quivers, smoked a deep mahogany colour, are highly prized by collectors. The **Nge**, also of Xekong, produce textiles bearing a legacy of the Ho Chi Minh Trail that snaked through their territory and of American efforts to bomb it out of existence. Designs on woven shoulder bags feature stylized bombs and fighter planes, and men's loincloths are decorated with rows of tiny lead beads, fashioned from the munitions junk that litters the region.

The Alak and the Katu

The **Alak** and **Katu** have of late been brought to the attention of outsiders by Lao tour agencies who are eager to cash in on the tribal custom of sacrificing water buffalo, in a ceremony reminiscent of the final scene in the film *Apocalypse Now*. The Katu are said to be a very warlike people and, as recently as the 1950s, carried out human sacrifices to placate spirits and ensure a good harvest. The ethnic Lao firmly believe that these southern Mon–Khmer groups are adept at black magic, and advise visitors to keep a cake of fragrant soap on their person to foil the sorcery of tribal witchdoctors.

The hill tribes

The **Lao Soung** (literally, the "high Lao") are comparative newcomers to Laos, having migrated from China at the beginning of the nineteenth century and settled on the only land available to them, at elevations over 1000m above sea level. Among them are the country's most colourfully dressed ethnic groups, including the Hmong, Mien, Lahu and Akha. For many visitors, the opportunity to visit a hill-tribe village is the highlight of a trip to Laos. Despite the prevalence of Western clothing these days, most villages appear not to have changed for centuries.

The Hmong

Most numerous among the Lao Soung are the **Hmong**, their clothing some of the most colourful to be found in Laos. The ethnic group (within which a number of sub-groups, known by the colour of their clothes, ie Red Hmong and Black Hmong) are particularly known for their silver; Hmong babies receive their first silver necklace at the age of one month, and by the time they are adults they will have several kilos of silver jewellery, most of which is cached until special occasions such as Hmong New Year. Interestingly, their written language uses Roman letters – though it's hardly surprising considering it was devised by Western missionaries.

As many Hmong fought on the side of the Royal Lao Government during the war, the tribe has been persecuted since the Revolution; pogroms caused many to flee for refugee camps in Thailand, from where some three hundred thousand were able to make their way to the US. The 2009 deportation of thousands of Hmong from Thailand back to Laos (see p.282) received international criticism. Within Laos, Hmong use of slash-and-burn agriculture has given the government an excuse to resettle them at lower elevations. Tight controls on the media mean that unrest among the Hmong and Lao military drives against them are rarely reported.

The Lahu

The **Lahu** inhabit areas of northwestern Laos, as well as Thailand and Myanmar (Burma). A branch of the tribe known as the Lahu Na, or Black Lahu, are known first and foremost for their hunting skills. Formerly they used crossbows but now they manufacture their own muzzle-loading rifles which they use to hunt birds and rodents. Old American M1 carbines and Chinese-made Kalashnikov rifles are used to bring down larger game, and Lahu hunters are sometimes seen at the side of the road displaying freshly killed wildlife for sale, though the practice is increasingly less acceptable in the eyes of both government and local people.

The Mien

Linguistically related to the Hmong, the **Mien** also immigrated into Laos from China, but their culture is much more Sinicized; the Mien use Chinese characters to write and worship Taoist deities. Like the Hmong, they cultivate opium, which they trade for salt and other necessities that are not easily obtained at high elevations, and are known to be astute traders. It's estimated that nearly half the country's Mien population fled after the communist victory. Today Sayaboury province, northwest of Vientiane, has the largest population of Mien in Laos. The costume of Mien women is perhaps Laos's most exotic, involving intricately embroidered pantaloons worn with a coat and turban of indigo blue. The most striking feature is a woolly red boa, attached to the collar and running down the front of their coats.

The Akha

The **Akha** are another of the highlands' stunning dressers; look out for the Akha women's distinctive headgear, covered with rows of silver baubles and coins. Speakers of a Tibeto–Burman language, the Akha began migrating south from China's Yunnan province to escape the mayhem of the mid-nineteenth-century Muslim Rebellion. This was followed by another exodus after the Chinese communist victory in 1949 and again during the Cultural Revolution. They now inhabit parts of Vietnam, Myanmar (Burma) and Thailand as well as Laos, where they are found mainly in Phongsali and Luang Namtha provinces.

Akha villages are easily distinguished by their elaborate "spirit gate". This gate is hung with woven bamboo "stars" that block spirits, as well as crude male and female effigies with exaggerated genitalia. The Akha are animists and, like the Hmong, rely on a village shaman and his rituals to help solve problems of health and fertility or provide protection against malevolent spirits. The Akha raise dogs as pets as well as for food, but do not eat their own pets; dogs that will be slaughtered for their meat are bought or traded from another village.

The Akha are fond of singing and often do so while on long walks to the fields or while working. Some songs are specially sung for fieldwork but love ballads and a sort of "Akha blues" – songs about struggling through life while surrounded by rich neighbours – are also popular.

The environment

A landlocked state in the heart of tropical Southeast Asia, Laos covers a land area of nearly 237,000 square kilometres, a size comparable to that of England. Laos is dominated by rugged highlands cut by narrow river valleys and shares in two of Southeast Asia's most prominent geographical features: the Annamite Mountains and the Mekong river, with the Mekong picking up more than half of its water flow during its nearly 2000km journey through Laos.

With a heat and humidity typical of a tropical region, Laos's climate nourishes a natural wealth of wildlife that includes rare or endangered species. Early French explorers marvelled at the sheer beauty of Laos's landscape, as they dodged tigers and collected samples of strange and wonderful insects. Indeed, the country's former name, the Kingdom of a Million Elephants, boasts of these tropical riches. In the recent past, Laos has surprised the scientific world with a number of new species of plant or animal life discovered or rediscovered in the country's forests and rivers. Sadly, Laos's natural wonders have been greatly diminished since the late nineteenth century – there are at most a thousand or so elephants roaming the country's frontiers today, and the forest continues to shrink each year. Despite the efforts of a handful of concerned international groups, the Lao government's efforts at **conservation** have been half-hearted and ineffectual. Lucrative **logging** and **mining** contracts have been awarded to Chinese and Vietnamese firms, bringing riches to government and military officials but leaving the environment much poorer as a result. Likewise, the **damming** of Lao rivers to generate hydroelectricity that can be sold to neighbouring countries is seen as a way for Laos to generate capital, but the ill effects that dams and the reservoirs behind them have on the environment are often ignored (see p.298).

Agriculture

Agriculture plays a significant role in Laos's economy as the vast majority of people in Laos live off the land. Rice, as the cornerstone of the Lao diet, accounts for eighty percent of agricultural land. For the most part, farmers employ one of two cultivation systems when growing rice. In the lowlands, farmers generally practise the wet-field paddy system, while swidden cultivation (also known as shifting or slash-and-burn agriculture) is primarily employed in the highlands. Large level areas along the Vientiane Plain, in Savannakhet and in Champasak are perhaps the areas best suited for extensive paddy rice cultivation in the country, and these places have not surprisingly emerged as the country's population centres. Other crops include cardamom, coffee, corn, cotton, fruit, peanuts, soybeans, mung beans, sugarcane, sweet potatoes, tobacco and various vegetables.

Swidden cultivation techniques practised by the Lao Theung and Lao Soung date back thousands of years and vary from group to group, with some peoples living in permanent villages around which they rotate cultivation within a large swath of forest, and others shifting their settlements from hillside to hillside. Nearly all midland and upland groups rely on swidden rice cultivation. Given the destruction of vast tracts of forest every year due to this method (a sight that visitors to the north during the months of March to May cannot fail to notice), there is a move towards educating farmers and villagers in the hope that they can adopt less destructive methods – conversely, however, some say that this practice keeps the soil fertile and the forests in balance.

The Lao government has used shifting agriculture among tribal peoples, especially the Hmong, as a reason to forcibly **resettle** thousand of highland families. The stated policy is to protect forest habitats and to bring hill peoples closer to community resources such as hospitals and schools. While this may have been beneficial for forests, the effects on resettled peoples are often no less than disastrous.

The Mekong

With a limited land base for agriculture, it's no surprise that **freshwater ecosystems** are of massive importance to Laos. The heart and soul of Laos's freshwater ecosystems is the **Mekong river**, the longest river in Southeast Asia, and the tenth largest in the world, carrying 475,000 million cubic metres to the sea each year. With the beginnings of its 4180km journey in a frozen stream high up in the Plateau of Tibet, the Mekong travels the entire length of Laos before slipping through Cambodia and fanning out into the "Nine Dragons" that constitute the river's delta in Vietnam. The Mekong is joined by fourteen major tributaries during the course of its 1993km journey through Laos. Nearly all the rivers and mountain streams in the country eventually find their way into the Mekong, as ninety percent of Laos drains into the river.

Rural life revolves around the Mekong River System, which encompasses everything from the myriad mountain streams to the flooded rice paddies to the river itself. It generates power, waters crops, provides a place to bathe and is an all-important source of fish. In most of lowland Laos, as well as in many parts of the highlands, fish and other aquatic animals provide more than seventy percent of the animal protein in people's diet. Nowhere in Laos is this more evident than in the country's southernmost tip, where almost every family fishes and every meal includes something from the Mother of Waters. It is in this region that the Mekong expands to attain its greatest width – 14km at the height of the rainy season – and journeys through the country's best known **wetlands**: Si Phan Don and the Khone Falls (see p.297).

Forests

The country is dominated by mixed **deciduous forests**, in which trees survive lengthy periods of minimal rainfall by shedding their leaves in order to conserve water. Tall, pale-barked **dipterocarps**, a group of tropical hardwoods prized for their timber, tower over these monsoon forests, ranging in height from ten to forty metres. Natural stands of teak, rosewood and mahogany were once common features of Laos's deciduous forests, though these much sought-after hardwoods, considered ideal material for building everything from furniture to the decks of yachts, have been substantially reduced in number.

Bamboo, hardly in short supply, thrives in Laos's monsoon climate and appears in more varieties in Laos than in any other country with the exception of two of Laos's neighbours, China and Thailand. Growing at astonishing rates during the rainy season, bamboo rules the understorey of the deciduous forests, surviving in soils too poor for many other types of vegetation and dominating secondary forests – those areas where a new generation of plants has grown up after forest has been stripped bare by swidden agriculture, rampant logging or the harsh excesses of chemical defoliants. Flexible bamboo is used by the Lao for making everything from houses to Laos's national musical instrument, the *khaen*, while bamboo shoots find their way into a variety of Lao dishes. Other, less common forest types in Laos include dry dipterocarp forests, noteworthy for their more open canopies and found along the arid plateaus of southern Laos; and rare old growth pine forests and semi-evergreen and hill evergreen forests, the latter soaked by frequent rainfall and possessing moss-covered forest floors and dense undergrowth.

Conservation zones and wetlands

In the early 1990s, the government of Laos established a system of **National Biodiversity Conservation Areas** throughout the country, which put under protection more than twelve percent of the country's total land area, one of the highest ratios in the world. However, that has not stopped the Lao government from leasing logging and mining concessions within NBCAs. Forests have been particularly damaged in the south along the Vietnamese border – where until recently never-before-seen species were turning up – and in the northeast.

As yet only parts of the conservation areas are accessible and open for tourism – such as the caves of the Khammouane Limestone NBCA near Thakhek; most are well off the beaten track. A survey of some of the more interesting areas follows.

Southern Laos

Flush against the Vietnam border in Khammouane and Bolikhamxai provinces and to the south of Lak Xao, the **Nakai–Nam Theun** is without question one of the world's more important biodiversity areas. Indeed, many of the last large mammals to be discovered or rediscovered worldwide inhabit this area. A lost world of evergreen forests, savanna and jagged, mist-shrouded peaks, the Nakai–Nam Theun is one of the richest wildlife and forest areas remaining in Southeast Asia. It is best known for the discovery of the saola, a large mammal resembling a shaggy brown and white deer with spindly horns, and the giant-antlered muntjac and the black muntjac, as well as the rediscovery of the Indochinese warty pig.

Once a royal hunting reserve, this area is now the largest single "protected" area in Laos, extending over 3700 square kilometres, with an elevation ranging from 500m on the Nakai Plateau to mountain peaks of well over 2000m, and is home to at least eleven globally threatened large mammal species. Its forests provide habitat for most of the mainland Southeast Asia fauna, including such rare animals as tiger, lesser slow loris, clouded leopard – a small tree-dwelling cat which hunts birds and monkeys by night – Asiatic black bear and elephant. More than four hundred bird species, among them the endangered white-winged duck, crested argus, beautiful nuthatch and greater spotted eagle, have been recorded here, the highest diversity of any site surveyed in Laos. The area is also noteworthy for its forests, composed of stands of wet and dry evergreen, cypress forest, old growth pine, found only in parts of Southeast Asia, and riverside forest – all of which are regionally threatened habitats. Nakai–Nam Theun is also treasured for its four river systems. However, their hydroelectric potential now figures large in national development plans, which have consequences for the wildlife of the surrounding area, not to mention the livelihood of local people.

Further south, spectacular waterfalls plunge from soaring escarpments cloaked with pristine evergreen forests in **Dong Hua Sao**, a 910-square-kilometre zone to the east of Pakse and the south of Paksong, which encompasses a flat, upland area along the Bolaven – of immense floral and faunal interest – and the lowlands along the Plateau's southern flank. With its habitat further diversified by the presence of sandstone flats and wetlands, Dong Hua Sao is home to nearly 250 species of birds, including the rare Siamese fireback, green peafowl and red-collared woodpecker as well as primates, including the endangered douc langur and gibbons, sun bear and the world's largest species of wild cattle, the gaur, once a prized trophy among big game hunters during colonial times.

Shadowing the Laos–Cambodia border and spanning the southern stretches of Attapeu and Champasak provinces, the **Xe Pian** is for the most part covered by semi-evergreen forest, interspersed with tracts of dry dipterocarp forest. Wetlands and riverine systems are also an important feature of the Xe Pian, which takes its name from the snaking Xe Pian River that bisects the reserve's eastern and southern flatlands. As home to eight threatened bird species, the protected area is of global significance for wildlife conservation and supports numerous lowland bird species as well as a wealth of migrants. Woolly-necked storks and nesting sarus cranes are both thought to inhabit the wetlands of the Xe Pian.

Gibbons also fill the central forests of the Xe Pian with their unmistakable hooting, and villagers have reported seeing kouprey, the elusive grey forest ox whose global population is thought to number no more than three hundred, hog deer and Eld's deer. Black bears, sun bears, peacocks, leopards and otters, hunted for their skins which are sold to Cambodians, have also been spotted in the area, as have two rare river creatures: the Irrawaddy dolphin, which is said to still pay seasonal visits to the Xe Pian, and the Siamese crocodile, already extinct in most Southeast Asian rivers.

Just west of the Xe Pian lie two **wetlands** of regional significance, Si Phan Don and the Khone Falls. Here, the Mekong concludes its journey through Laos, swirling past the countless outcroppings of soil and rocks that constitute the "Four Thousand Islands" of the region's name. Considered the richest fishing grounds in Laos, Si Phan Don possesses large tracts of seasonally flooded forest, along the banks of the Mekong and on the dots of land in between, which constitute a crucial spawning ground for the unknown number of fish species inhabiting this portion of the river. At the southern tip of Si Phan Don – and the entire country for that matter – lie the Khone Falls, an 8km-wide series of channels composed of waterfalls and rapids flowing between rocky islands. The falls, which begin 5km north of the Cambodian border, are a vital passageway for the Mekong's many species of migratory fish.

The seasonally flooded islands here are also an important sanctuary for **birds** and represent one of the last nesting areas of the river tern, greater thick-knees and river lapwing, all of which appear as the water level begins to recede in January. The trees of the wetlands' flooded forests also provide perches for thick-billed pigeons, pied hornbills and green imperial pigeons and offer a welcome spot for blue-tailed bee-eaters to rest after one of their aerial insect chases. The area is also one of the rare places in Southeast Asia visited by red-headed and white-rumped vultures, whose numbers are on the decline owing to hunting and a shortage of food, caused partly by the fact that Laos now has fewer tigers, whose leftovers make a favourite vulture snack. Other rare or endangered birds making the rounds in the area are the grey-headed fish eagle, the woolly-necked stork and the giant ibis.

Beneath the surface, Laos's lower Mekong area possesses a stunning array of **fish species**, including giant golden carp, featherbacks, eels and freshwater rays that grow well over a metre in length, fish that climb the Khone Falls by sucking their way up the rocks with their lips and the mysterious *ba leum,* a fish weighing 200kg that fishermen attempt to snare with the entrails of dogs attached to a hook at the end of a 30m length of rope. Long the jewel of the Mekong, the blunt-nosed Irrawaddy dolphin is now critically endangered.

Central and northern Laos

East of Ang Nam Ngum and less than two hours' drive from Vientiane, centrally located **Phou Khao Khouay** is perhaps the most accessible of the conservation zones. In this often-steep upland area large tracts of evergreen forests dominate the valleys and hillsides, while coniferous and scrub forests flourish in the thin soils masking sandstone bedrock formations at higher elevation.

In the far northern corner of northeastern Hua Phan province, elephants roam the bamboo forests of **Nam Et** protected area, more than half of which lies 1000m above sea level. Nam Et has been severely affected by shifting cultivation which has left the area with relatively little dense forest. It remains an important refuge for bears, endangered cats, such as the clouded leopard and tiger, wild cattle, and dhole, the rare, reddish wild dogs that hunt in packs. To the southwest of Nam Et, **Phou Loei**, occupying more than 1400 square kilometres in Luang Prabang and Hua Phan provinces, is one of the most important wildlife and evergreen forest conservation areas in northern Laos. Composed of rugged highlands, most of which are well over 1000m, and cut by the Nam Khan and Nam Xuang rivers, Phou Loei has a significant amount of bamboo forests and grasslands resulting from swidden cultivation – still the primary form of agriculture among villagers living in the area. Hunting and fishing with poison present further challenges to managing this NBCA, whose wildlife includes silver pheasants, banteng, hog deer, bears and cats, as do the creation of new settlements in far-flung areas noted for their pristine forests.

Environmental issues

In its rush to develop by capitalizing on key natural resources, primarily its wetlands and forests, Laos must come to terms with a number of critical, often interrelated, **environmental issues**. Perhaps the greatest source of concern for conservationists is Laos's many **hydroelectric dam** projects. It is no secret that dams have the potential to cause a serious negative impact on the environment, yet for Laos, the Mekong and its tributaries, with an estimated hydroelectric potential of more than 18,000 megawatts – more than half the river's total estimated potential – represent an alluring means for generating much-needed foreign exchange. Dams, in the view of the International Union for the Conservation of Nature, are not necessarily incompatible with conservation goals; instead, they represent a critical challenge to the integration of conservation and development objectives. The $1.2 billion, 1070-megawatt Nam Theun 2 Dam, which began operation in spring 2010, is a case in point. The creation of the dam led to local villages being resettled (a process, which, some claim, still hasn't been adequately completed), and has undoubtedly impacted on the Nakai–Nam Theun and other local conservation areas. It's feared much larger projects such as the hugely controversial Sayaboury Dam (see p.95), now under construction, could wreck entire ecosystems, and destroy the livelihoods of many thousands of local inhabitants. Supporters, however, claim that projects like this, through the amount of money and foreign investment involved, will help communities across Laos to develop.

Laos's potential for hydropower development is inextricably linked to its forests, which protect the catchments that provide the water that ultimately generate the energy. **Deforestation** is a major problem, with the country's primary forest cover having steadily declined over the past five decades from an estimated seventy percent at the time of the French withdrawal from Indochina to roughly ten percent today. Laos's forests are threatened by the clearing of lowland forest for permanent agriculture, the use of chemical defoliants during the Second Indochina War, infrastructure development, shifting agriculture, new settlements and logging; large companies from Asian countries continue to win logging concessions from the government.

Developing and enforcing a set of regulations governing logging is a difficult task given the government's limited resources and the vast tracts of forest spread through the country; simply designating biodiversity conservation zones isn't enough to preserve the country's natural wealth.

Deforestation places increasing pressure on Laos's rural population, who rely on the forest for food, firewood, construction materials, herbs, medicine and a host of other things. The declining forests also threaten Laos's wildlife, which is already struggling to survive other intense pressures, including **hunting** and the **wildlife trade**. The level of hunting has increased in recent decades, the result of the increased availability of guns and explosives, improved access to previously remote areas via newly cut logging roads and the exorbitant prices that rare and endangered species fetch on international markets. The gathering of forest products is also on the rise. While much of the wildlife trade is for local food consumption and use in traditional medicine, large quantities of wildlife and wildlife products are sold to Thailand, Vietnam and China. Thus, while posters and pamphlets warning villagers against hunting vulnerable species are visible in government offices and noodle shops throughout the country, elephant ivory, bear paws, pangolin scales, turtle shells, rare types of orchids and bird bills – all highly valued items in this cross-border trade – continue to find their way onto restaurant tables in Hanoi and into traditional medicines in Bangkok and Hong Kong.

Literature and myths

Classical Lao literature has its roots in the Jataka tales, a collection of 547 stories about the Buddha's previous lives. The tales recount the events and experiences which led to his incarnation as Siddhartha Gautama, the prince who sought the meaning of life and attained enlightenment. Penned in India and Sri Lanka, they spread with Buddhism to Southeast Asia.

Of more direct impact on Lao literature were an additional fifty tales that employed the same basic theme as the Jataka. Known as the **Panyasa Jataka**, these were perhaps composed by the Mon and abridged by the Tai Yuan of Lan Na, a kingdom centred around Chiang Mai in what is now northern Thailand. Contacts between Chiang Mai and Luang Prabang resulted in the Panyasa Jataka arriving in Laos where the stories were modified and expanded. Eventually the Lao versions came to differ significantly from the Tai Yuan versions, in that the former deviated from strict religious themes and became more entertaining, even to the point of having some sexual content.

Two types of story emerged: prose and poetic. Prose stories contained much Pali, the language of the Theravada Buddhist scriptures, and were written in a script called *phasa tham*, or Dharma language. These would have been comprehensible only to monks who had studied the language. Much more popular with lay-people were the poetic stories, written using the Lao script and containing mostly Lao vocabulary. As Lao is a tonal language, these poems did not rhyme as poetry composed in English sometimes does. Instead, tones and alliteration were used to produce a rhythm. Both types of stories were recorded by writing on the fronds of a certain kind of palm with a stylus, and some of the longer versions made use of hundreds of palm leaves. These surprisingly durable palm-leaf manuscripts were kept in a special library in the monastery grounds or sometimes in private homes. Occasionally, the stories were copied anew, but there was no pressure on the scrivener, usually a monk, to remain true to the original. The result was literally hundreds of versions and variations of these

THE RAMAYANA

Of the Indian literature to become established in Southeast Asia, the Hindu **Ramayana** is by far the best known. This epic poem, with its host of vivid characters possessing comic-book hero attributes, arrived in Southeast Asia during its "Indianization" at the hands of Hindu traders. In the original, Hanuman, the King of the Monkeys, assists the god Rama in rescuing his wife Sita from the many-headed, multi-armed demon Ravana.

Once the Ramayana became established in Southeast Asia, however, it didn't take long for local variations to emerge. The inhabitants of Java, Bali, Burma, Cambodia and Thailand all composed their own distinct versions and eventually the story spread from coastal areas into the Indochinese hinterland. Although a version of the poem was well known to the Khmer who once inhabited what is now southern Laos, the Ramayana's introduction to the ethnic Lao came much later via Siam.

French colonization brought scholars who, perhaps because they were already familiar with the Khmer version of the poem, tended to overemphasize the Ramayana's significance to Lao literature, proclaiming it Laos's most important work. Later, Indian scholars, eager to aggrandize the influence of Indian culture in a country they considered an outpost of "Greater India", echoed French opinions. In fact, the Lao version of the Ramayana, known as **Pha Lak Pha Lam**, was never popular at the village level. Suitably modified to suit Lao tastes, it did, however, become a favourite of the Lao court. This popularity is reflected in depictions of the Ramayana in murals and reliefs found at Buddhist monasteries, especially those that were patronized by the monarchy.

stories that not only taught values but also contained a wealth of information about traditional Lao society. During certain festivals, villagers would gather at the local monastery or in a private home to hear the stories read aloud and in this way some favourites eventually emerged. The *Sang Sin Sai* in particular is felt by many Lao to be the pinnacle of Lao literature. As with all of these stories, the plot takes a back seat to the poetry itself and the author is obscure. Attributed to "Pangkham", the story is almost certainly the product of many authors and editors.

A tradition of oral folk tales known as **Xieng Miang**, after the name of the central character, were eventually transcribed as both poetry and prose. The stories seem to be almost the opposite of the Jataka-style morality tales: Xieng Miang is a lazy but clever trickster who enjoys outwitting authority figures, especially the king. In a typical exploit he covets the king's prized cat and so decides to kidnap it. Once he has the cat safely home, Xieng Miang teaches it to shun the fresh fish it is accustomed to by beating the cat every time it nears a fish placed on the floor. The cat soon learns to eat rice and when the king arrives to claim his cat, Xieng Miang "proves" it doesn't belong to the king by letting the cat choose between a plate of rice and plate of fish. Knowing that going near the fish will bring on a beating, the cat chooses the rice and the king goes home empty-handed. The stories of Xieng Miang remain popular today among Lao children, and work recently began on creating animated short films about the character, which is testament to its enduring popularity.

The present climate for Lao writers living in Laos has been described as "tricky". Laos is still rather **restrictive** in what it will allow to be published, but a few Lao writers manage to make social commentary without the government's approval by publishing in Thailand in the Thai language.

Books

As Laos is one of the least-known countries in Southeast Asia, it should be no surprise to find that books about it are hard to come by, to say nothing of quality works on the country. You're likely to have more luck searching for many of the titles listed below at an online bookstore such as ⓦwww .amazon.com, ⓦwww.powells.com or Thailand's ⓦwww.asiabooks.com than you would wandering the aisles of your local bookshop. While some books need to be specially ordered, others are easier (and sometimes cheaper) to find at bookshops in Bangkok, Vientiane or Luang Prabang.

In the book reviews below, the abbreviation o/p means "out of print"; titles marked ★ are particularly recommended.

CULTURE, SOCIETY AND ENVIRONMENT

Sucheng Chan (ed) *Hmong Means Free*. Fascinating personal narratives by three generations of Hmong refugees from five different families, which describe their lives as farmers on the hilltops of Laos, as refugees in the camps of Thailand and as immigrants in the US.

Brett Dakin *Another Quiet American: Stories of Life in Laos*. A very personal account of modern Laos by an American who lived in Vientiane during the 1990s.

★**Natacha Du Pont De Bie** *Ant Egg Soup: the Adventures of a Food Tourist*. A wonderful foodie journey across the country, illustrated with excellent recipes that the author collected during her travels.

★**Anne Fadiman** *The Spirit Catches You and You Fall Down: a Hmong Child, Her American Doctors* and the *Collision of Two Cultures*. An excellent exploration of the sad, absorbing tale of Lia Lee, a severely epileptic child, born to a family of Hmong refugees living in California, who clash with their daughter's Western doctors over how to treat the child's condition.

Stephen Mansfield *Culture Shock! Laos*. A cultural starter kit detailing how to avoid such faux pas as touching your spouse in public, pointing your foot at someone and eating your sticky rice with chopsticks. Mainly aimed at soon-to-be expats in Laos, with details on working in the country. Its tone is at times a little patronizing.

Phia Sing et al. *Traditional Recipes of Laos*. Not only is this one of the rare books explaining how to prepare Lao cuisine, it's the only book containing the recipes of the former royal chef and master of ceremonies of Luang Prabang.

Liesbeth Sluiter *The Mekong Currency: Life and Times of a River*. An earthy account of green issues along the Mekong corridor, in Laos, Cambodia and Thailand, Sluiter's book does an excellent job of presenting environmental concerns from the perspective of the fishermen and farmers whose livelihoods are sustained by the Mekong and its tributaries, though it's now in need of some updating.

FICTION AND TRAVELLERS' ACCOUNTS

★**Marthe Bassenne** *In Laos and Siam*. The evocative account of a French expatriate woman's 1909 journey up the Mekong river to Luang Prabang.

Colin Cotterill *The Coroner's Lunch*. The first of an enjoyable series of crime novels about Doctor Siri, the reluctant chief coroner, set in Vientiane after the end of the Second Indochina War. An often farcical thriller, Siri is an engaging narrator as he tries to expose the secrets of a number of mysterious deaths.

Louis Delaporte *A Pictorial Journey on the Old*. Volume 3 of the Mekong Exploration Commission's report is devoted to the exquisite illustrations of the artist who accompanied French explorers Francis Garnier and Doudart de Lagrée during their 1866–68 expedition.

Francis Garnier *Travels in Cambodia and Part of Laos*. The English translation of the first volume of the report by France's Mekong Exploration Commission, which set out from Saigon to find a back-door route to China via the Mekong, details the group's travels from Cambodia to Luang Prabang.

Francis Garnier *Further Travels in Laos and in Yunnan*. Volume 2 of the Mekong Exploration Commission's report focuses on the weary explorers' travels in Upper Laos and Yunnan, with entries on a Muslim uprising in China and Garnier's explorations of alternative trade routes.

F.J. Harmand *Laos and the Hill Tribes of Indochina*. A cultural barbarian by today's standards, the French explorer nevertheless produced a valuable report on his late nineteenth-century journey through southern Laos, researching the region's natural history and searching for an overland route from Champasak to Hué. The account, which records funerary and religious customs of the highland tribal minorities of the Bolaven Plateau, also focuses on his encounters with the Phu Tai people of the Savannakhet region, and is liberally sprinkled with amusing and insightful anecdotes.

Henri Mouhot *Travels in Siam, Cambodia, and Laos*, The account of the final journey of the legendary "discoverer of Angkor Wat", filled with his characteristically blunt observations of the people of Laos, from the tobacco-hungry infants to the uncouth court officials whom he encountered on his journey to Upper Laos, which resulted in his death outside Luang Prabang.

HISTORY

★**Jane Hamilton-Merritt** *Tragic Mountains: the Hmong, the Americans, and the Secret Wars for Laos, 1942–1992*. This impressive account of the Hmong, written by a Pulitzer Prize-nominated correspondent during the Second Indochina War, ranges from the personal to the political as it follows the Hmong from the battlefields to life after the war.

Victor T. King *Explorers of Southeast Asia: Six Lives*. Six different authors examine the journeys of various nineteenth-century European explorers, including Frenchmen Henri Mouhot and Francis Garnier.

Christopher Kremmer *Bamboo Palace: Discovering the Lost Dynasty of Laos*. A continuation of the author's earlier *Stalking the Elephant Kings*, which tracked his journey into remote Laos in search of the monarch who disappeared shortly after the communists took over in 1975. By interviewing a former inmate of Laos' re-education camps, Kremmer is able to piece together the last days of the royal family, some of whom perished due to harsh living conditions in the caves of Hua Phan province.

★**Alfred W. McCoy** *The Politics of Heroin: CIA Complicity in the Global Drug Trade*. Laos, not surprisingly, figures prominently in this exhaustively researched, revised and expanded version of McCoy's landmark *The Politics of Heroin in Southeast Asia*.

Christopher Robbins *The Ravens: Pilots of the Secret War of Laos* (o/p). Although difficult to find, this book on America's secret war is well worth reading. Many of the details of America's secretive Laos operations during the Second Indochina War didn't come out until this gripping work by Robbins, a British journalist, was published in

1987. Based on interviews with American pilots who fought in Laos, this book is well worth tracking down.

★**Stan Sesser** *The Lands of Charm and Cruelty: Travels in Southeast Asia*. Among the five insightful essays in this superb book is a 53-page segment on Laos during the late 1980s and early 1990s. In presenting a well-observed account of the country as it struggles to rebuild itself after the war, Sesser mixes reflections on Laos's recent history with insights into the country's political leadership, culture and economic reforms. The book builds on articles Stesser originally wrote for *The New Yorker*.

★**Martin Stuart-Fox** *A History of Laos*. Written by an Australian scholar who covered the Second Indochina War as a foreign correspondent, this work is the best available overview of Laos's history, although it's extremely light on the country's early history.

Martin Stuart-Fox and Mary Kooyman *Historical Dictionary of Laos*. An encyclopedia of key people and events in the history of Laos which, though expensive and difficult to find, is worthwhile for the many insightful nuggets of information tracked down by the authors, and the extensive bibliography.

★**Roger Warner** *Shooting at the Moon: the Story of America's Clandestine War in Laos*. Winner of the Overseas Press Club's award for the best book on foreign affairs, Warner's thoroughly researched and crisply written account of American involvement reads like an adventure novel. Letting tragic events speak for themselves, Warner brings to life the key players and significant events as he follows the secret war from its origins at the end of World War II to the American withdrawal from Indochina.

Lao

Lao belongs to the Tai family of languages, which includes Thai; Shan (Tai Yai), spoken in Myanmar (Burma); Phuan, spoken in Laos and parts of Thailand; and Tai Leu, spoken by the Dai minority of southern China's Yunnan province. Besides Lao and its "cousin" languages, such as Tai Leu and Phuan, sundry other languages are spoken within the borders of Laos. These include tongues belonging to the Mon–Khmer and Tibeto–Burman families of languages, which are spoken by upland tribal peoples, as well as Vietnamese and Chinese, spoken by immigrants from Laos's neighbouring countries.

French was once the second language of the educated and elite classes, and fluent French-speakers can still be found among older Laotians, usually an indication that they were once functionaries of the old royal regime. In recent years French has fallen out of favour; since economic liberalization came into effect, **English** has become the preferred foreign tongue among the younger generation, who are convinced that learning English is the key to obtaining a high-paying job in the tourism sector. During the 1980s, Lao students were sent to study abroad in fellow Soviet-bloc countries such as Poland, East Germany and Cuba, and hence it is sometimes possible to find a rusty Polish-, German- or Spanish-speaking Lao.

Travellers will find that getting around in urban areas can be done using basic English. Once out in the countryside, however, the situation changes, and visitors will have to make an effort to learn some Lao phrases to get by. Don't feel too put out – urban Lao sometimes experience similar problems when travelling in rural areas.

One of the greatest obstacles to building a nation that successive Lao governments have had to deal with is language. While Lao as it is spoken in Vientiane has official language status, there are pockets of Laos where no dialect of Lao, much less the Vientiane version, will be heard. With little money or resources to post qualified teachers to isolated villages, **Vientiane Lao** is simply not being learned in these areas. The Lao government has experimented with the somewhat drastic step of relocating tribal children to lowland towns where they live in huts in the school grounds and where, theoretically, they are exposed to language and lifestyles that will help them assimilate and become more "Lao". In the meantime, many of the non-Lao-speaking ethnic groups in rural areas will continue to live as they always have done, speaking their own tongue among themselves while maintaining a handful of Lao phrases to conduct trade or other dealings with the lowland Lao.

To fully understand the contemporary state of the Lao language in urban areas, it is necessary to look at how it relates to Thai. The spoken Thai of Bangkok and the spoken Lao of Vientiane are similar, as akin as Spanish is to Portuguese. As vassals of the Thai, the Lao absorbed a fair amount of Thai vocabulary, mainly through the Buddhist monkhood and channels between the royal courts. This shared vocabulary was, for the most part, taken from **Pali**, in which the scriptures of Theravada Buddhism were written. During the Lao civil war, Thailand sided with the Lao royalists. The communist victory and death of the Lao monarchy saw the end of flowery court language, but although the communist government temporarily suppressed Lao Buddhism, no direct attacks on Pali-derived vocabulary were mounted. Some aspects of everyday spoken and written Lao were targeted, however. In an effort to erase class divisions, the communist government discouraged the use of personal pronouns that flaunted status or begged servitude. A typical banned pronoun was "*doi kha noi*", which translates into English as "I" but which literally means "I, small slave".

After the revolution the Lao government also made official changes to the **Lao alphabet** in order to simplify it, as well as purge it of aspects that the communists felt were too similar to Thai. The Lao government's policies had, for a time anyway, the desired effect of levelling class divisions, and the simplified alphabet has no doubt made teaching the illiterate to read an easier task. However, the changes and simplifications have had an unforeseen effect on the Lao language. What the government didn't anticipate was the growing sophistication of the **Thai media** and subsequent boom in popularity of Thai films, television and popular music in Laos. Every day, tens of thousands of Lao tune in to receive a dose of Thai, with its stratified personal pronouns and honorifics. Even broadcasts of the Thai royal language, almost identical to the extinct Lao royal language, can be heard daily on the Thai television news. These factors have conspired to give the Lao something of an inferiority complex about their own language, and they often compare it unfavourably to Thai by saying that Thai sounds more "beautiful" and "polite" than Lao.

Transliteration

Visitors who travel between Laos and Thailand may notice the similarity in the scripts of the two countries. This is because the Lao script was actually based on an early version of written Thai. During colonial times, the French considered replacing the **Lao script** with an alphabet similar to *quoc ngu*, the Romanized script now used to write Vietnamese. The project was never implemented, as French influence was waning at the time, but devising the system presented quite a challenge. The Lao language contains sounds that don't exist in French, or any other Western European language for that matter, making transliteration an inexact exercise at best.

Imperfect as it was, the fledgling **French transliteration system** has had some staying power. The Lao seem comfortable with the French system, and many educated Lao prefer to have their names transliterated in the French manner, which serves to differentiate them from the Thai, who use a different system. Official maps of Laos produced by the Lao government use a modified form of the old French system. This can create problems for English speakers who assume that the system was created for them. But if you keep in mind, for example, that the Lao "ou" rhymes with the French "vous", not the English "noun", reading Lao place names shouldn't be a problem. The transliteration of place names in this book follows the modified French system used by the Lao National Geographic Service. For the transliteration of Lao words in the following section, a simplified version of the same system is used. This is not to say that travellers will find exactly the system in use throughout Laos: the Lao are quite cavalier when it comes to **consistency** in transliteration. In Vientiane, for instance, it is possible to see the Arch of Victory monument transliterated as "Patouxai", "Patousai", "Patuxai" and "Patusai".

Consonants

b as in **b**ig

d as in **d**og

f as in **f**un

h as in **h**ello

j (or ch) as in **j**ar

k as in s**k**in (unaspirated)

kh as **k**iss

l as in **l**uck

m as in **m**ore

n as in **n**ow

ng as in si**ng**er (this combination sometimes appears at the beginning of a word)

ny as in the Russian **ny**et

p as in s**p**eak (unaspirated)

ph as in **p**ill

s (or x) as in **s**ame

t as in s**t**op (unaspirated)

th as in **t**in

w (or v) as in **w**ish

y as in **y**es

Vowels

a as in autobahn	i as in mimi
ae as in cat	ia as in India
ai as in Thai	o as in flow
aw as in jaw	oe as in Goethe
ao as in Lao	u (or ou) as in you
e as in pen	ua (or oua) as in truant
eu as in French fleur	

Lao is a **tonal language**, which means that the tone a speaker gives to a word will determine its meaning. While the tone system may make some visitors despair of ever learning any Lao, mastering a handful of simple phrases will greatly enhance your travels in Laos. The Lao are always delighted by foreigners who make the effort to converse with them in their own language and will reciprocate with more than the usual graciousness.

Lao words and phrases

As a stranger you should remember to utter a greeting first when you meet someone. Questions the Lao commonly ask in conversation may seem personal to Westerners ("Are you married?") but this is simply an indication of the importance of the family in Lao culture. Questions in Lao are not normally answered with a yes or no. Instead the verb used in the question is repeated for the answer; for example: "Do you have a room?" would be answered "Have" in the affirmative or "No have" in the negative.

GREETINGS AND SMALL TALK

Hello (said with a smile)	sabai di	How old are you?	jâo anyu ják pi
How are you?	sabai di baw	How many brothers	jâo mí âi nâwng ják khón
Thank you (very much)	kop chai (lai lai)	and sisters do you have?	
I'm fine	sabai di	Are you married yet?	jâo taeng ngan léu baw
Can you speak	jâo wâo phasâ angkit	Yes, I'm married	taeng ngan lâew
English?	dâi baw	No, I'm not married	yáng baw taeng ngan
No I can't	wâo baw dâi	How many kids	jâo mí lûk ják khón
I only speak a	khói wâo phasâ láo	do you have?	
little Lao	dâi nói neung	I've got two kids	mí lûk sâwng khón
Do you understand?	jâo khào jai baw	I don't have any	yáng baw mí lûk
I don't understand	khói baw khào jai	kids	
Where are you from?	jâo má tae sâi	Are you enjoying	thiàw méuang láo
I'm from England/	khói má tae angkit/	Laos?	muan baw
America/Australia	amelika/awsteli/	I'm enjoying it	muan lâi
New Zealand	/nyu silaen	very much	
What's your name?	jâo seu nyâng	Goodbye	lá kawn
My name is....	khói seu	Goodbye (in reply)	sok di

PLACES AND DIRECTIONS

Where are you going?	pai sâi	How much will you go for?	pai thao dai
(often used as a		One thousand kip	phù la phán kip
familiar greeting)		per person	
To the market	pai talat	Where is the...?	...yu sâi
To the guesthouse	pai bân phak	Where is the	bân phak yu sâi
To the ... Hotel	pai hong haem...	guesthouse?	
To the boat launch	pai thà heuá/**pier**	Where is the boat	thà heuá yu sâi
To the bus station	pai khiw lot	launch/pier?	
Will you go?	pai baw	Drugstore	hân kâi ya

Post office	paisani	Is the airport far away?	doen bin yu kai baw
Police station	sathani tamluat	It's far	kai
Museum	phiphithaphan	It's not far	baw kai
Thai embassy	sathanthut thai	Go straight	pai sêu sêu
Chinese embassy	sathanthut jin	Turn right	lîaw khwã
Vietnamese embassy	sathanthut wiatnam	Turn left	lîaw sâi
Is the ... far away?	... yu kai baw		

ACCOMMODATION

Do you have a room?	mí hàwng wàng baw	Where is the toilet?	hàwng suam yu sãi
Do you have a	mí hàwng sãwng tiang	How many nights	si phak ják khéun
double room?	baw	will you stay?	
Does the room have	hàwng mí phat lóm	I will stay two nights	si phak sãwng khéun
a fan?	baw	Sorry, no discounts	lút lakha baw dâi
Mosquito net	mûng	Can you clean the	het anamai hàwng
Bathroom	hàwng nâm	room?	dâi baw
Toilet	suam	Can I have the room	khãw kajae dae
Air conditioning	ae yen	key?	
Blankets	phà hom	Can I move to	yâi hàwng dâi baw
Hot water	nâm hâwn	another room?	
Can I see the room?	khãw beung hàwng	This room is full of	hàwng nî mí nyung lãi
	kawn dâi baw	mosquitoes	
How much per night?	khéun la thao dai	This room is too noisy	hàwng nî siäng dang
Seven thousand kip	khéun la jét phán kip	Do you have a	mí bawlikan sak
per night		laundry service?	phà baw
Can you discount the	lút lakha dâi baw	Do you have	mí lot thip hâi
price?		bicycles for rent?	sao baw

SHOPPING

Is this for sale?	an nî khãi baw	Washing powder	sabu fun
How much?	thao dai	Toilet paper	jîa hàwng nâm
How much is this?	an nî thao dai	Candles	thian
I'd like to buy...	khói yak sêu...	Mosquito coils	ya kan nyung baep jút
Cigarettes	ya sùp	Flip-flops	koep tae
Medicine	ya	How much is this?	an nî thao dai
Antiques	khãwng kao	How much is it in	ngóen dawn khit
Souvenirs	khãwng thilaleuk	dollars?	thao dai
Clothes	seuà phà	I only have kip	khói mí tae ngóen kip
Silk cloth	phà mãi	It's very expensive	phaeng lãi
Do you have...?	mí...baw	How much of a	lút lakha dâi thao dai
Do you have soap?	mí sabu baw	discount can you give?	
Toothpaste	yã si khâew		

ON THE ROAD

Does this vehicle go to...?	lot nî pai ... baw	It's taken	baw wàng
How much is it to go to...?	pai ... thao dai	Can I hire the vehicle	mão lot/heuá dâi baw/
How many hours	sai wela ják sua móng	boat outright?	
will it take?		How much to hire	mão lot/héua
What time will the	lot si awk ják móng	the vehicle/	thao dai
bus depart?		boat outright?	
What time will	si hâwt ják móng	Don't pick up any	baw tâwng hap phù
we arrive?		other passengers	doi sãn khon eun
Is this seat vacant?	bawn nang nî wàng baw	Do you agree to	tók lóng lakha baw
It's vacant	wàng	the price?	

I agree	tók lóng	What's wrong with	lot pen nyãng
I don't agree	baw tók lóng	the vehicle?	
Please stop here	jàwt nî dae	Will we be parked	jàwt yu nî don baw
Please stop so I	jàwt thai bao dae	here for long?	
can urinate			

EMERGENCIES AND HEALTH

Help!	suay dae	Please take me to	song khói pai hong
Can you help me?	jào suay khói dãi baw	the hospital	mãw dae
There's been an accident	mí ubatihet	I've been bitten by	khói theuk mã/ngu kát
I need a doctor	khói tâwng kan hã mãw	a dog/snake	
I'm not well	khói baw sabai	Where is the toilet?	hàwng suam yu sãi
I have a fever	khói pen khai	I lost my passport	pâm doen thang
I have diarrhoea	thâwng khói baw di		khãwng khói sĩã hãi
I'm in a lot of pain	khói jép nák	My pack is missing	kheuang khãwng khói
			sĩã hãi

COMMON ANSWERS TO QUESTIONS

I don't know	baw hû	It cannot be done	baw dâi
There isn't/aren't any	baw mí	It's uncertain	baw nàe

NUMBERS

0	sun	21	sao ét
1	neung	22	sao sãwng
2	sãwng	30	sãm síp
3	sãm	31	sãm síp ét
4	si	32	sãm síp sãwng
5	hà	40	si síp
6	hók	50	hà sip
7	jét	60	hók síp
8	pàet	70	jét síp
9	kâo	80	pàet síp
10	síp	90	kâo síp
11	síp ét	100	hôi
12	síp sãwng	200	sãwng hôi
13	síp sãm	1000	phán
14	síp si	2000	sãwng phán
15	síp hà	10,000	síp phán
16	síp hók	50,000	hà síp phán
17	síp jét	100,000	sãen
18	síp pàet	200,000	sãwng sãen
19	síp kâo	1,000,000	lân
20	sao	2,000,000	sãwng lân

DAYS OF THE WEEK AND TIME

Monday	wán jan	Tomorrow	mêu eun
Tuesday	wán angkhán	Morning	tawn são
Wednesday	wán phut	Noon	thiang wán
Thursday	wan phahát	Afternoon	tawn bai
Friday	wán súk	Early evening	tawn láeng
Saturday	wán são	Late evening	tawn khám
Sunday	wán thít	Midnight	thiang khéun
Today	mêu nî	Next week	athit nà
Yesterday	mêu wan nî	Last week	athit thi lâew

Next month	deuan nà	Now	tawn nî
Last month	deuan thi lâew	Later	theua nà
Next year	pi nà	Just now	ta kî
Last year	pi thi lâew		

A food and drink glossary

USEFUL PHRASES

Where can I buy...?	êu ... dâi bawn nǎi?	I'd like a plate of that	khǎw baep nân ján neung
Where can I buy food?	sêu ahǎn dâi bawn nǎi?	I can't eat meat	khói kin sîn baw dâi
Where is a restaurant?	hàwng ahǎn yu sǎi?	No sugar	baw sai nâm tan
Do you have a menu?	khǎw laikan ahǎn dae?	No ice	baw sai nâm kâwn
Do you have...?	mi...baw?	Bon appétit	soen sàep
Not spicy	baw phét	Bottle	kâew
I am vegetarian	khói kin te phák	Chopsticks	mâi thu
I would like...	khói ao...	Cup/glass	jawk
Can I have the bill?	khǎw sék dae?	Delicious	sàep
I didn't order this	khói baw dâi sang náew nî	Fork	sawm
What's this?	nî nyǎng?	Noodle shop	hǎn kǎi fõe
With/without	sai/baw sai	Spoon	buang
Without fish sauce	baw sai nâm pa	Restaurant	hân ahǎn

STAPLES

bai hóhlapha	basil	mu	pork
boe	butter	nâm kat	coconut milk
hét	mushroom	nâm pa	fish sauce
hua phák bua	onion	nâm tan	sugar
hua phák thiam	garlic	naw mâi	bamboo shoots
jaew	sauce	nok	bird
jeun khai	omelette	nóm sòm	yoghurt
kai	chicken	pa	fish
kha	galingale	pa dàek	fish paste
khai dao	egg, fried	pét	duck
khào jâo	rice, steamed	phák	vegetables
khào ji	bread	phák nâm	watercress
khào niaw	rice, sticky	phák salat	lettuce
khing	ginger	phõng sú lot	MSG
kûng	shrimp	pu	crab
màk kheua	aubergine	sìn ngúa	beef
màk len	tomato	tâo hû	bean curd
màk phét	chilli	tôm khai	egg, boiled

NOODLES

fõe	rice noodle soup	khào pûn	flour noodles with sauce
fõe hàeng	rice noodle soup without broth	mi hàeng	yellow wheat noodles without broth
fõe khùa	fried rice noodles		
khào piak sèn	rice noodle soup, served in chicken broth	mi nâm	yellow wheat noodles

EVERYDAY DISHES AND "DRINKING FOOD"

kaeng jèut	mild soup with pork and vegetables	mũ phát bai hólapha or lam	pork with basil over rice meat soup made with chilli wood, lemongrass, aubergine and dill
khào ji pateh	bread with Lao-style pâté and vegetables		
khào ji sai boe	bread with butter	pîng kai	grilled chicken
khào khùa or khào phát	fried rice	pîng pa or jeun pa	grilled fish
khào khùa sai kai	fried rice with chicken	tam màk hung	spicy papaya salad
khùa khing kai	chicken with ginger	tôm yam pa	spicy fish soup with
khùa phák baw sai sìn	stir-fried vegetables without meat		lemongrass
		yam sìn ngúa	spicy beef salad
larp mu	minced pork	yáw díp	spring rolls, fresh
man falang jeun	chips	yáw jeun	spring rolls, fried

FRUIT

lamut	sapodilla	màk muang	mango
màk hung	papaya	màk náo	lime/lemon
màk kîang	orange	màk nat	pineapple
màk kiang	rose apple	màk ngaw	rambutan
màk kûay	banana	màk nyám nyái	longan
màk lînji	lychee	màk phom	apple
màk mángkhut	mangosteen	màk sida	guava
màk mî	jackfruit	thulian	durian
màk mo	watermelon		

SWEETS

kalaem	ice cream	khào niaw màk muang	sticky rice with mango
khào lãm	sticky rice in coconut milk cooked in bamboo	nâm wãn	sweets in coconut milk
		nâm wãn màk kûay	banana in coconut milk

DRINKS

bia	beer	nâm deum	water
bia sót	beer, draught	nâm hâwn	water, hot
kafeh	coffee	nâm kâwn	ice
kafeh dam	black coffee	nâm màk phâo	coconut juice
kafeh hawn	hot coffee	nâm sá	tea
kafeh net	instant coffee	nâm soda	soda water
kafeh (nóm) hawn	hot Lao coffee (with sweetened condensed milk)	nâm tào hû	soy milk
		nâm yén	water, cold
		nóm	milk, usually sweetened condensed
kafeh (nóm) yén	iced coffee (with sweetened condensed milk)	owantin	Ovaltine (a chocolate drink)
lào-láo	rice whisky	sá jin	tea, Chinese
màk kuay pan	banana shake	sá yén	tea, iced
màk mai pan	fruit shake		

Glossary

Akha highland ethnic group

ARVN Army of Republic of Vietnam, the defunct South Vietnamese Army

baht Thai currency, also a unit for measuring gold

ban house or village

basi animist Lao ceremony

bia sot draught beer

bombi type of anti-personnel bomb which explodes when touched

Brahma Hindu god

bun (or boun) festival

dawk jampa plumeria (frangipani) blossom, the national flower of Laos

devaraja god-king a Khmer concept of divine kingship

devata female divinity

don (or dawn) island

dvarapala guardian divinities at doors and gateways of Khmer ruins

falang white person, person of European descent

fõe Vietnamese noodle dish ("pho" in Vietnamese) found throughout Laos

hân kin deum casual eating and drinking spot

HCMT Ho Chi Minh Trail, series of trails used by the NVA to infiltrate South Vietnam

heua sa slow boat

heua wai speedboat

Hmong highland ethnic group

Indra Hindu god

jataka mythological tales of the Buddha's previous lives

jumbo three-wheeled motorized taxi

kataw a game similar to volleyball, but played without the use of the arms; also played in Thailand and Malaysia, where it's called *takraw*

kha slave; formerly used as a pejorative for hill tribes

khào rice

khào ji French bread

khào niaw sticky rice

khiw lot bus stand

Khmer Cambodian

Khmu an upland ethnic group

khwaeng province

kip Lao currency

lak kilometre, often used in place names

lam wong traditional dance

Lane Xang ancient Lao kingdom

Lao Loum lowland Lao, mostly ethnic Lao

Lao Soum highland Lao; hill tribes

Lao Theung speakers of Mon–Khmer languages who live at higher altitudes than the Lao Loum

lào hái rice wine sipped from straws out of a large stoneware jar

lào-láo strong alcoholic drink made from sticky rice

larp minced meat dish

lintel horizontal beam or stone over a door or window

LNTA Lao National Tourism Administration

lustral water holy water used to bathe a Buddha image

makara mythical water monster

maw thiam spirit medium

Mien a highland ethnic group

muan fun, enjoyable

muang (or meuang) city or town

mudra hand and arm positions depicted in Buddhist and Hindu imagery

mukhalinga phallic-shaped stone symbolic of Shiva with an image of the god's face carved into it

naga benevolent mythical water serpent (pronounced "nak" in Lao)

nam river

nam phu (or nam phou) fountain

NBCA National Biodiversity Conservation Area

ngeuak malevolent mythical water serpent

NTAL National Tourism Authority of Laos

NVA North Vietnamese Army

pa dàek fermented fish paste, used as seasoning

pa kha Irrawaddy dolphin

pa pao blowfish with a vicious bite found in southern Laos

pak mouth of a river

Pathet Lao communist guerrilla movement which gained control of Laos in 1975

Patouxai monument in Vientiane

Pha Bang a Buddha image belived by many to be the talismanic protector of the Lao nation

Pha In Hindu god Indra

Pha Lak Pha Lam Lao version of the Ramayana

Pha Phut the Buddha

Pha Phutthahup Buddha image

phi spirit or ghost

phu (or phou) hill or mountain

Phuan lowland ethnic group

pirogue narrow dug-out canoe

Ramayana epic poem of Indian origin (Pha Lak Pha Lam in Lao)

rishi hermitic ascetic

Royal Lao Army (RLA) army of the defunct Kingdom of Laos

sala pavilion with a raised floor and roof but no walls

samana re-education camp, derived from the word "seminar"

sawngthaew pick-up truck used for public transport

Shiva Hindu god

Shivalinga phallic-shaped stone symbolic of Shiva

shop house Southeast Asian property, usually built in terraces and comprising a shop at ground level with residential areas above

sim building in a monastery housing the main Buddha image

sin women's wraparound skirt

Sipsong Chao Tai the Twelve Tai Principalities, a loose federation that once included parts of northwest Vietnam and northeast Laos

soi lane or alley

somasutra stone pipe for channelling lustral water

stupa Buddhist structure built to contain holy relics ("that" in Lao)

tad (or tat) waterfall

Tai ethnic Thai

Tai Dam lowland Lao ethnic group, found in Hua Phan and Xing Khuang provinces

Tai Leu lowland Lao ethnic group, found in northwest Laos

Tai Yuan northern Thai

talat market

Talat Sao Vientiane's morning market

thanon road or street

that Lao word for Buddhist stupa

tuk-tuk three-wheeled motorized taxi

ushnisha finial symbolizing enlightenment found on the crown of the head of Buddha images

UXO unexploded ordnance

Vishnu a Hindu god

wat Buddhist monastery

wiang (or vieng) town surrounded by wooden palisades

xe river (southern Laos only)

xieng town surrounded by brick or earthen ramparts

Small print and index

A ROUGH GUIDE TO ROUGH GUIDES

Published in 1982, the first Rough Guide – to Greece – was a student scheme that became a publishing phenomenon. Mark Ellingham, a recent graduate in English from Bristol University, had been travelling in Greece the previous summer and couldn't find the right guidebook. With a small group of friends he wrote his own guide, combining a highly contemporary, journalistic style with a thoroughly practical approach to travellers' needs.

The immediate success of the book spawned a series that rapidly covered dozens of destinations. And, in addition to impecunious backpackers, Rough Guides soon acquired a much broader readership that relished the guides' wit and inquisitiveness as much as their enthusiastic, critical approach and value-for-money ethos.

These days, Rough Guides include recommendations from budget to luxury and cover more than 120 destinations around the globe, as well as producing an ever-growing range of eBooks.

Visit **roughguides.com** to find all our latest books, read articles, get inspired and share travel tips with the Rough Guides community.

Rough Guide credits

Editor: Ruth Reisenberger
Layout: Pradeep Thapliyal
Cartography: Ashutosh Bharti
Picture editor: Yoshimi Kanazawa
Proofreader: Susannah Wight
Managing editor: Keith Drew
Assistant editor: Prema Dutta
Production: Charlotte Cade

Cover design: Nicole Newman, Chloe Stickland, Pradeep Thapliyal
Photographer: Tim Draper
Editorial assistant: Rebecca Hallett
Senior pre-press designer: Dan May
Programme manager: Helen Blount
Publisher: Joanna Kirby
Publishing director: Georgina Dee

Publishing information

This fifth edition published November 2014 by
Rough Guides Ltd,
80 Strand, London WC2R 0RL
11, Community Centre, Panchsheel Park,
New Delhi 110017, India
Distributed by Penguin Random House
Penguin Books Ltd,
80 Strand, London WC2R 0RL
Penguin Group (USA)
345 Hudson Street, NY 10014, USA
Penguin Group (Australia)
250 Camberwell Road, Camberwell,
Victoria 3124, Australia
Penguin Group (NZ)
67 Apollo Drive, Mairangi Bay, Auckland 1310,
New Zealand
Penguin Group (South Africa)
Block D, Rosebank Office Park, 181 Jan Smuts Avenue,
Parktown North, Gauteng, South Africa 2193
Rough Guides is represented in Canada by Tourmaline
Editions Inc. 662 King Street West, Suite 304, Toronto,
Ontario M5V 1M7
Printed in Singapore by Toppan Security Printing Pte. Ltd.

MIX
Paper from
responsible sources
FSC www.fsc.org FSC™ C018179

Help us update

We've gone to a lot of effort to ensure that the fifth edition of **The Rough Guide to Laos** is accurate and up-to-date. However, things change – places get "discovered", opening hours are notoriously fickle, restaurants and rooms raise prices or lower standards. If you feel we've got it wrong or left something out, we'd like to know, and if you can remember the address, the price, the hours, the phone number, so much the better.

Please send your comments with the subject line "**Rough Guide Laos Update**" to ✉ mail@uk.roughguides.com. We'll credit all contributions and send a copy of the next edition (or any other Rough Guide if you prefer) for the very best emails.

Find more travel information, connect with fellow travellers and plan your trip on ⓦ roughguides.com.

ABOUT THE AUTHORS

Edward Aves (@Ed_Aves) has had a soft spot for Laos ever since his first visit to the country in 1998. An in-house editor at Rough Guides' London HQ, he's periodically let out to get back on the road, and has contributed to numerous other guidebooks, including the Rough Guides to Sri Lanka and India.

Steve Vickers fell in love with Laos on his first-ever trip to Asia and has been returning ever since. Based partly in Sweden, he writes and reports for media outlets around the world, including *The Washington Post*, BBC Radio 4 and *The Independent*. He's also worked on around a dozen Rough Guides titles, including country guides to Thailand and Scotland. You can read his blog at ⓦstevevickers.co.uk or follow him on Twitter @StevenJVickers.

Acknowledgements

Edward Aves I owe a huge debt of gratitude to the Mr Fix-It of the north, the incomparable Mr Phong of Jungle Eco-Guide Services in Luang Namtha, without whom new sections of the north chapter of this guide could not have been written. Many thanks to James Mundy at Inside Vietnam in Bristol and James Pook et al at Exotissimo in Vientiane for making this happen. In Luang Prabang, thanks to Dan, Brendan and the staff at Ock Pop Tok for a lovely stay at the villa; and to Emily and Kathy at Orient Express and all at *La Résidence*. In Nong Khiaw, thanks to Nic, Kenny and Karen at the *Mandala Ou*, Harps at *Delilah's*/Tiger Trail and Home of NK Adventures – a fortuitous meeting on the boat to Hat Sa. Thanks too to the numerous travellers I met on the way, who gave me their thoughts, suggestions and reactions, especially Simone Georg for a boozy evening in Muang Khoua and her reflections on trekking around Phongsali. Back at HQ, thanks to Keith Drew for getting the ball rolling; Lao old hand Emma

Gibbs for contacts and brilliant pre-departure advice; and to Ruth Reisenberger, Pradeep Thapliyal and Ashutosh Bharti for pulling the book into shape.

Steve Vickers Thanks to Maeve Nolan and the team at Backyard Travel for some seriously helpful assistance out in the boondocks. Thanks also to Yea for his expert knowledge and local contacts in Sayaboury Province. In Vientiane, Ait Geurts, Aline van der Meulen and the team at Inthira deserve special thanks for their warm welcome and helpful tips, as does David Drabkin, who helped me out in Champasak. To Maggie and Lin in Vang Vieng, and Jozef in Sayaboury, thanks for the beers, laughs and horrible hangovers. At Rough Guides, big thanks to Ed and Keith, and to Ruth for her careful editing. A final *tack så mycket* goes to my beautiful Karin, who flew halfway around the world to meet me on Christmas Day.

Readers' updates

Thanks to all the readers who have taken the time to write in with comments and suggestions (and apologies if we've inadvertently omitted or misspelt anyone's name):

Ali Aspden, Sarah Ftaya, John Garratt, Liza Hawkins, Monica Mackaness, Sandie Schagen, Emily Trumbull, David Whiting and Yang Yang Chiu.

Index

Maps are marked in grey

Map symbols

The symbols below are used on maps throughout the book

✈ International airport	ⓘ Tourist office	▲ Mountain peak	⬦ Stupa/*that*
✗ Regional airport	✉ Post office	☀ Hill	⬛ Church/cathedral
★ Transport stop	🕐 Telephone office	🌊 Waterfall	▦ Building
🅿 Petrol station	✚ Hospital	⛳ Border crossing	☐ Market
🚣 Boat landing	♦ Museum	⌒ Cave	⬭ Stadium
)(Bridge	⊙ Statue/monument	♠ Temple/monastery	▦ Park/NBCA
13 Highway number	∴ Ruin	♜ Mosque	— — Ferry route
♦ Point of interest	🐘 Elephant camp	🏯 Chinese temple	▬▬ Wall
@ Internet access	⛰ Mountain range		

Listings key

■ Accommodation	
● Eating and drinking	
■ Drinking and nightlife	
● Shopping	

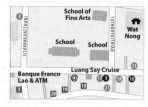

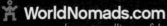